# COMPUTER NETWORKING

## CUSTOM EDITION

STANFORD H. ROWE     MARSHA L. SCHUH

Taken from:
*Computer Networking*
by Stanford H. Rowe and Marsha L. Schuh

**Custom Publishing**

New York   Boston   San Francisco
London   Toronto   Sydney   Tokyo   Singapore   Madrid
Mexico City   Munich   Paris   Cape Town   Hong Kong   Montreal

Cover Art: Courtesy of PhotoDisc and Glow Images/Getty Images, Inc.

Taken from:

*Computer Networking*
by Stanford H. Rowe and Marsha L. Schuh
Copyright © 2005 by Pearson Education, Inc.
Published by Prentice Hall
Upper Saddle River, New Jersey 07458

Printed in the United States of America

10  9  8  7  6  5

2008820059

KW

**Pearson**
**Custom Publishing**
is a division of

www.pearsonhighered.com

ISBN 10: 0-555-00968-8
ISBN 13: 978-0-555-00968-0

*Dedicated to our mothers, Katherine H. Rowe and Josephine A. Binnquist, who have loved and believed in us longer than anyone else.*

# PREFACE

*Computer Networking* is a comprehensive introduction to the rapidly changing world of wired and wireless computer interconnection. Designed as an introductory course in networking, the book is also an excellent reference source. It is easy to understand and contains an extensive glossary, acronym list, and index, which makes finding material on particular topics easy. The book is targeted for the individual who has little background in networking, other than what can be gained by reading business and popular press or by using a PC at home, school, or work. This text neither assumes nor expects that the reader has a background in programming or advanced computer technology.

## OBJECTIVES

The specific objectives of the text are:

- to provide comprehensive coverage for a first course in networking;
- to place emphasis on the basic principles and concepts of networking, those that don't change or change very little as technology advances and implementations become more sophisticated and specialized;
- to highlight networking standards that have become important in this field;
- to provide networking theory illustrated by real-world examples;
- to be appropriate for use at all levels, including community colleges, universities, and technical schools;
- to serve as a reference for people working in industry; and
- to be easy for the reader to understand.

# ORGANIZATION

*Computer Networking* is organized into five sections that group topics for ease of teaching and learning. Part One presents introductory material that lays the foundation and provides a framework for the more detailed material in subsequent chapters. Chapter 1 introduces the subject matter and provides an overview of networking concepts. Chapter 2 describes and illustrates several ways of classifying networks, many of which will already be familiar to readers. Chapter 3 introduces and explains the OSI model for networks and the TCP/IP architecture that is the foundation of the Internet and many contemporary networks. The importance of network standards is also explained, and the need for both network architectures and standards is discussed. Chapter 4 introduces protocols, the "rules of the road" for networks. The need for protocols is explained, and the basic components that make up a protocol are examined.

Part Two delves into the fundamental technology that underlies all telecommunications and networking, and provides the technical foundation for networks. Chapter 5 examines how data are coded for transmission on a network. Readers learn the requirements for a good coding system and the reasons certain codes are more appropriate than others for use on telecommunications networks. Chapter 6 describes analog and digital signals, transmission methods, and the way they are combined in various network systems. Four cases are studied: transmitting analog signals on analog circuits; analog signals on digital circuits, digital signals on analog circuits, and digital signals on digital circuits. The reasons why digital transmission is superior to analog transmission are explained. Chapter 7 describes the protocols that are used on data links. Several protocols are examined in detail, and many more are introduced. Both LAN and WAN protocols are emphasized. Chapter 8 examines the media used for circuits that make up a network. The attributes of each medium are studied and compared, and the advantages and disadvantages of selecting one medium over another for a particular application are studied and discussed. Chapter 9 describes communications circuits. Various types of analog and digital circuits are studied. Circuit switching, packet switching, and multiplexing are explained. The types of errors that can occur on a circuit and the way in which errors are detected and corrected are examined in detail.

Part Three examines networks in detail. LANs are studied first, followed by WANs. Chapter 10 examines the technology used for LANs. Various topologies, access control techniques, protocols, and routing techniques are explained. Chapter 11 looks at the way the technologies are combined to make LANs such as Ethernets and token rings. Wireless networks, in their many forms, are examined in detail. The intricacies and limitations of the technologies of real-world networks are covered. Chapter 12 examines the requirements for installing, operating, and managing a LAN. The need for LAN management and security is explained. The issues surrounding home networks are explored. Many of the principles in this chapter apply to WANs as well. Chapter 13 describes WANs and examines their topologies. Packet data networks and the way traffic is routed in a WAN are explained. Broadband networks are studied, and specific WAN systems, such as frame relay and ATM, are explained.

Part Four deals with the ways in which networks of all types are interconnected into internets. Chapter 14 looks at the technology required to interconnect networks that may be fundamentally different in design. TCP/IP, as well as domains and domain naming, are examined in detail. Tools that are useful in managing an internet are also introduced. Chapter 15 relates the history and technology of the Internet and the WWW, which have both become so pervasive throughout society in the past several years. Various ways to connect to the Internet are described. Chapter 16 presents various Internet applications such as e-mail and Internet telephony. Specifically, those of the WWW and the technologies that underlie its operation are explored. Browsers are introduced, and an explanation of how to create Web pages is given. Other Internet tools, such as FTP and Telnet, are also explained.

Part Five examines network security, network design, and network management. Chapter 17 covers the important topic of network security in detail. Network access control is described, and various techniques for implementing security are examined. Encryption is explained, and the importance of personnel and physical security is described. Security for home networks is also studied. Chapter 18 describes the process of designing and implementing new networks or changes to existing networks. Each phase of network design and implementation is discussed in detail. Chapter 19 examines techniques for operating and managing networks. The need for managing networks is first explained. Problem management, performance management, change management, and configuration control are described. Various types of management reporting of network operations are shown.

## PEDAGOGICAL FEATURES

*Computer Networking* contains many pedagogical features designed to assist both students and instructors.

- A set of Objectives appears at the beginning of each chapter, outlining what the student is expected to learn.
- Many WWW addresses (URLs) are given throughout the text, and are summarized in Appendix B, to direct the student to websites where they may find the most current information or conduct additional research.
- A list of Key Terms at the beginning of each chapter serves as a checklist of important terms, concepts, and ideas.
- A Case Study at the end of each chapter illustrates the way concepts and techniques are applied within real companies and networks.
- Extensive Review Questions for each chapter give readers an opportunity to test their knowledge of the material.
- A Problems and Projects section at the end of each chapter is designed to stimulate students' thinking. The problems are challenging questions that will lead the student beyond the text. In many cases, real-world situations are presented for the student's consideration. The projects are suitable for individual or team effort, and often take the student outside the classroom to talk to networking professionals or users or to research information on the Internet.
- A comprehensive Glossary and a separate list of Acronyms used in the book appear at the end of the text.

For instructors, there is a comprehensive Instructor's Manual that includes:

- suggestions for ways to organize the course, depending on the desired emphasis and focus;
- transparency masters of the chapter Outlines;
- a CD containing PowerPoint™ slides of all figures in the text;
- answers to the Review Questions in the text;
- suggested solutions to the Problems and Projects in the text;

- hints for the presentation of material in the classroom; and
- test bank questions for examinations.

## ACKNOWLEDGMENTS

Writing a textbook, like any major project, is rarely the work of a single individual. We especially want to thank the following people who contributed helpful information and suggestions: Greg Ford, who offered valuable insights into the security challenges and other important issues facing LAN managers; John C. Matter, III, who provided important advice during the writing of this book; Helen Rae Binnquist, who inspired and researched some of the case studies; Dr. Randall Guthrie, who ignited our initial interest in networks and challenged us to keep going; Rev. Curtis R. Zimmerman, who urged us to apply networking theory to the real world; and Laura Rowe and Theresa Srebinski, who kept us in touch with networking in an industrial setting.

In addition, we appreciate the contribution of the people who took the time to review the manuscript and made many excellent suggestions: George Barido, Rochester Institute of Technology, NY; Phillip Davis, Del Mar College, TX; Phil Nelson, Western Washington University; Lawrence Osborne, Lamar University, TX; Fred Seals, Blinn College, TX; Michael St. Clair, Texas State Technical College; and Reza Yazdi, DeVry University, CA.

The staff at Prentice Hall deserves special mention for their dedication to this book. Charles Stewart provided encouragement and insights about which material needed to be included. Alex Wolf provided excellent production coordination throughout the project. Others who made substantial contributions, for which we are grateful are Maria Rego, administrative assistant, Tricia Rawnsley, copy editor; and Norma Nelson, proofreader.

Finally, we can only give the highest level of thanks and praise to our families: Pam Rowe and Dave and Katie Schuh. They put up with our writing schedules and were extremely understanding when we disappeared into our offices for hours to research and write. Without their support and commitment, this project would not have been possible.

Stanford H. Rowe
Marsha Lee Schuh

# BRIEF CONTENTS

# CONTENTS

## Chapter 2    Network Classification    26

## Chapter 3    Network Architectures and Standards    48

## Chapter 4   Introduction to Protocols                                        72

## PART TWO   DATA COMMUNICATIONS                                        88

## Chapter 5   Data Coding                                                     90

## Chapter 6     Data Communication Fundamentals     108

## Chapter 7   Data Link Control Protocols                                        158

## Chapter 11  LAN Systems

**286**

## Chapter 15   The Internet                                                416

## Chapter 16    Internet Applications    450

## PART FIVE   NETWORK MANAGEMENT                                486

## Chapter 17   Network Security                                 488

# Appendixes

# Computer Networking

# INTRODUCTION

■ **OUTLINE**

Part One introduces you to networking terminology and concepts. You will learn background information about the uses of networks in businesses and other organizations, and the histories of telecommunications and networking.

Chapter 1 introduces the subject of computer networking, explains some simple vocabulary, and gives examples of networks in common use throughout the world, which you may already use.

Chapter 2 classifies networks in several ways and provides a framework that you will build upon as you gain additional knowledge while reading this book. You will see that network classifications overlap each other, and any real world network often fits into several categories.

Chapter 3 presents network architectures and standards that shape the way networks are designed and operated. The need for these architectures and standards is discussed, and their advantages and disadvantages are examined.

Chapter 4 provides an introduction to networking protocols—a network's "rules of the road"—and the reasons they are needed. A hypothetical protocol suite, which will serve as a model for later discussions of real protocols, is introduced and explained.

# INTRODUCTION
# AND OVERVIEW

## ◼ OUTLINE

## ◼ KEY TERMS

analog
Baudot code
central office (CO)
circuit
communications
communications line
communications network
digital

digital subscriber line
  (DSL)
digitized
line
medium
network
protocol
radio teletype (RTTY)

sink
source
telecommunications
Teletype
teletypewriter (TTY)
teletypewriter exchange
  service (TWX)
telex

# ■ OBJECTIVES

After you complete your study of this chapter, you should be able to:

- explain what a network is;
- understand the importance of networks in our society;
- explain the terms *communications, telecommunications,* and *network;*
- explain why someone would want to study networks;
- describe the history of networks; and
- give some examples of real networks that you have used.

## 1-1 INTRODUCTION

Most of us use computer-based networks every day. They are woven into the fabric of our everyday lives—at home, at school, and at work—making it almost impossible to function without them. Almost all of us grew up with a telephone network, and we use it automatically, without any special training. Networks of computers—data networks—have now moved into the same position in our society. In a remarkably short time, our lives have become virtually dependent upon them. The global Internet is ubiquitous, with the exception of some third world countries. Young people have grown up using the Internet, just as the previous two generations grew up using the telephone network. They sit down and use it without the assistance of manuals, help screens, or classes. They simply access the network through the computer and tap into a wealth of information, games, and other resources that were unavailable to their parents and grandparents when they were growing up.

In recent years, the distinction between computers and communication has blurred. Although the disciplines were quite separate in the past, today we cannot study one without the other. Most computers, large or small, are connected to a network in some way. The switching of data, voice, and other signals through a network is done by specialized computers rather than by the electromechanical equipment that was used in the past. Furthermore, there is no difference between the way data are stored in computers and the way they are transmitted on communications lines. Computer data have always been encoded in digital form, but today even most voice signals are digitized at some point on their way from sender to receiver. If we were to tap into a digital communications circuit, we would not be able to tell whether the signals were computer data, digitized voice signals, or digitized video.

Furthermore, small local networks that connected a few terminals to a computer within an office or building used to be different from the large multistate and international networks that only large organizations could afford. Even those distinctions are now blurred. The Internet is now pervasive, and the technology that ties networks of all sizes together enables people to communicate with whomever they need to contact, wherever they are. This fascinating technology allows us to transact business, request information, and communicate with friends or business associates around the world. Most of us simply assume that such communication will happen when we want it to and are completely unaware of what makes it possible.

What are some of these networks that we so easily and nonchalantly use today? The Internet, with its World Wide Web, is probably the first network that comes to mind. Many people could not do their jobs without it. The traditional wired telephone network is another network that we depend upon, and the importance of the wireless cellular telephone (cell phone) network has grown so much that we can no longer separate the two. Have you recently made a bank deposit using an automatic teller machine (ATM)? Or do you make withdrawals through one? ATMs are connected to a global banking network, which enables you to make deposits to or get cash from your bank account almost anywhere in the world. Debit cards work the same way, thanks to the global banking network. When you shop, the checkout terminal scans the bar code on your items with a laser beam that is connected to a network within the store or chain, thus tracking inventory levels and buyers' purchasing habits. The behind-the-scenes function of the network keeps the store from running out of your favorite products, because the terminal can issue automatic restocking orders. Replacement merchandise is automatically ordered and shipped within a few hours or days. When you hand over your credit card, it is checked through a network to be sure you haven't exceeded your limit or used someone else's card—all within seconds.

As you can see, networks have become so much a part of daily living that we are almost unaware that they exist. That is the way it ought to be. We should not need to worry about the details of their operation or whether they will function properly when we need them, just as we don't worry about whether water will flow when we turn on a spigot or whether lights will come on when we flip a switch. Water and electricity "networks" are elements of the utility infrastructure in most countries, but we don't even think about what it takes to deliver those services to our homes or offices. Data and computer networks are a much newer technology. Their communications capabilities are generally quite reliable, although they do not yet measure up to the fail-safe services of the older utilities. Computer networks, however, are as essential to our lifestyles today as the older networks.

## 1-2    WHY STUDY NETWORKS?

As a network user, why might you want to study networks, and the way they work, in greater detail than the average person? Probably the most common reason is that you hope to work in a communications field. You may have heard that there are good, high paying jobs in communications, and you want a part of the "action." It is true. Telecommunications and networking fields are expanding rapidly, and companies that provide the services, as well as organizations that use network services, need many skilled employees. Furthermore, it is an exciting field because it changes very rapidly. Networking technology advances continually, and the regulatory environment changes as governments gain new perspective on the potential uses and abuses of networking capabilities.

You might, however, have more of an academic interest in networking. Because you use networks every day, you may simply want to understand more about the way they work and you may not have any intention of working in the communications industry. You may want to learn more about some of the newer communications technologies, such as broadband or wireless communications. Studying networking will broaden your general knowledge, expand your vocabulary, and open your eyes to uses of communications that you may not have been aware of; which may be useful to you, regardless of which career you choose. This book addresses your interests because it can be read sequentially, or can be used as a reference to look up information about a specific topic. The case studies, review questions, and boxes will provide you with many examples of networks at work in the real world, which may be especially interesting to you.

In either case, this book is aimed at you, the readers, who are taking a required or elective course as part of your university or technical education. You'll find objectives at the beginning of each chapter that will tell you what to be looking for as you read, and questions at the ends of the chapters to check your understanding of the material. There are also problems and projects that will carry you into a more in depth study of the material (and out of the classroom) to investigate real networks. Sidebars (boxes) also give additional information about supporting topics and case studies that will get you thinking about real networking situations and problems. At the end of the book are appendices and glossaries of terms and acronyms, which provide additional resources.

## 1-3 THE SCOPE OF THIS BOOK

In this text, you'll learn about networking from start to finish. For our purposes, networking includes the transmission and reception of information using electrical or electromagnetic means from a transmitter (the source) to a receiver over a medium. Various types of transmitters, receivers, media, and the sets of rules or protocols that are used for those communications will be introduced and described in detail. We will begin with basic information that will lay a foundation for future study. You may be surprised at how much surface knowledge you already have about networking from your day-to-day living activities, such as using the Internet or the telephone. However, what happens behind the scenes in a network is probably a little murky to you. There are many terms that you may not be familiar with, and they will be introduced and defined for you as you learn how data are communicated from one place to another—whether across the room or around the world. In many cases, descriptions and discussions of actual networks will be used to illustrate the principles of networking and the way they work.

The primary focus of this book is networking as used in business, industry, education, and government. The types of communication that will be discussed involve the transmission and reception of voice, data, text, graphics, images, or combinations of these forms. You will see that once they are reduced to their most basic electrical form, all these types of communication look alike. There are no fundamental differences among text, voice, and image transmissions. This book does not specifically describe or analyze commercial radio or television; however, many of the principles and techniques described apply equally well in those settings.

It is important for you to realize that this is an introductory book. Most of the chapters in this book are the subjects of other books that delve into far more detail than is appropriate for an introductory course in networking. Furthermore, communications engineering is highly technical and mathematical, and is beyond the scope of this book. You'll find that *Computer Networking* gives you an excellent introduction to this complex field and

Students use terminals to do research and prepare homework assignments. (Source: Demetrio Carrasco / Dorling Kindersley Media Library. Reprinted with permission.)

provides a solid foundation for further study, if you decide to expand your knowledge of the subject.

## 1-4 INTRODUCTORY TERMINOLOGY

We have attempted to define and explain terms in this book before using them. However, even in the first few paragraphs, some key terms have already been used. Three terms you've already seen are: *communications, telecommunications,* and *network.* Because they are so fundamental, let us look at the detailed definitions of each.

### Definition of Communications

communications

**Communication** is defined as "a process that allows information to pass between a sender and one or more receivers," or "the transfer of meaningful information from one location to a second location." *Webster's New World Dictionary* adds, "the art of expressing ideas especially in speech and writing" and "the science of transmitting meaningful information, especially in symbols."[1] Each of these definitions has important elements. Communication is a process that is ongoing, and it obviously can occur between a sender and one or more receivers. The word "meaningful" in the second definition is significant. It is clear that communication is not effective if the information is not meaningful. One could also argue that if the information is not meaningful, no communication has occurred at all. There is a strong analogy here to a traditional question: If a tree falls in a forest and no one is within hearing distance, does the tree make a sound as it falls? One possible answer is that because sound requires a source and a receiver, without the receiver there is no sound.

The last definition relates most closely to the focus of this book. You will be studying the science of communication, using electrical or electromagnetic techniques. The information being communicated will be in coded form so that it is compatible with the transmitting and receiving technologies. For

[1] *Webster's New World Dictionary,* S.V. "Communication."

Satellite dishes are found everywhere and are frequently used for networking purposes as well as receiving television pictures. (Source: © K. Gillham, Robert Harding World Imagery. Reprinted with permission.)

our purposes, the practical application of communication in the business environment is essential to the definition and study of communication.

## Definition of Telecommunications

**telecommunications**

Webster's also tells us that the prefix, "tele," means far off, distant, or remote. Practically speaking, the word **telecommunications** means communication, by electrical or electromagnetic means, usually (but not necessarily) over a distance. Not long ago, telecommunication meant communication over a distance through a wire. Although this is still accurate in many situations, it is not completely accurate, because telecommunication frequently takes place through optical fiber or radio waves. In this book, the words "communication" and "telecommunication" will be used interchangeably.

## Definition of Network

**network**

A **network** can be many things, depending on the context. A network can be thought of as an interrelated group of objects connected together in some way; such as a network of hotels, an airline network, or a television network. The connection does not have to imply that wires or computers are used, though in many cases they are present. Computer networks connect many computers and computer-related pieces of hardware, such as printers and modems. A computer network may be as simple as two computers in an office, connected by a wire or cable, or it may be global in scope with hundreds of thousands of intercommunicating terminals. The Internet is an example of the latter.

## Acronyms

You'll find that the language of networking and communications is filled with acronyms. Acronyms are a convenient way for people who are familiar with a topic to communicate with each other, but they can be confusing for beginners. In this book, we will introduce acronyms with the full explanation of their meaning. Even when they are used later, we have sometimes given the full explanation again. You'll find an abundance of acronyms in the chapters on internetworking and the Internet. To help you, a complete alphabetical listing of all of the acronyms used in the book is provided, along with a reference to the chapter in which the acronym is first used (see the Acronyms section, which follows the appendixes).

## 1-5   BASIC ELEMENTS OF A NETWORK

source

medium

sink

In its simplest form, a network contains three basic elements: the **source**, the **medium**, and the **sink**. These are illustrated in Figure 1-1. More common terms would be *transmitter, medium,* and *receiver,* or *personal computer, cable,* and *personal computer.* Examples of each element in a network are abundant: voicebox, air, ear; terminal, data circuit, mainframe computer; telephone, telephone line, telephone. There are many possible combinations of the basic elements.

communication line

line

circuit

We will immediately begin by referring to the medium as the **communication line**, the **line**, or the **circuit**, and the terms will be used interchangeably. You can think of it as the cable that connects personal computers in your home or office or the telephone line that comes into your house. The line can be implemented in many physical forms, such as copper wire, optical fiber, or microwave radio, but visualizing it as a copper wire or a cable of wires is convenient and not inaccurate.

communications network

Communication lines connect computers, terminals, and other hardware to build **communication networks**. It is easy to visualize the cables that connect the personal computers at your school or business into a local area network (LAN). Similarly, businesses often lease communication lines from a communications company. They may, however, build their own network by installing cable to connect their locations so that employees at different locations can send e-mail to one another, share information stored in databases, or transact business in other ways.

FIGURE 1-1   Basic
elements of a
communication network.

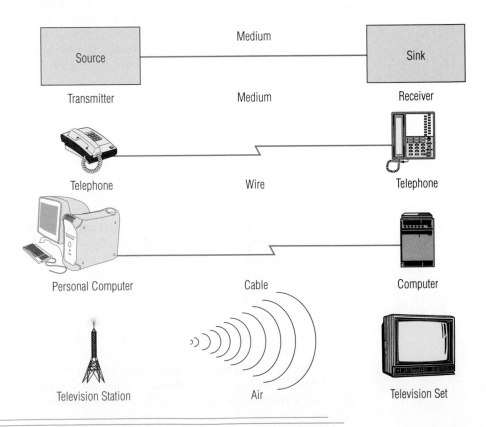

To ensure that messages sent on a network will be successfully received, rules must guide their progress. Although these rules are not technically basic elements of communications, they are absolutely necessary to prevent chaos. For two entities to communicate successfully, they must speak the same language. If you speak primarily Spanish and you try to communicate with someone who speaks primarily Japanese, you won't be successful. Perhaps through trial and error, you'll be able to negotiate a compromise, such as both of you speaking English. In that case, you'll be at least partially successful, depending on how well both of you speak English. You may find that by using gestures and hand signals, you can convey some simple ideas and thoughts to one another; but to communicate successfully, both of you must speak the same language.

At a different level, there are unwritten rules that guide our use of the telephone. Most of us learned them when we were very young. When an American receives a telephone call, the answering party traditionally initiates the conversation by saying "Hello." The caller and answerer then go through a brief dialogue to identify each other before they launch into the purpose of the call. This is illustrated in Figure 1-2. The process is often cut short by combining some of the exchanges or when one of the parties recognizes the other's voice. An example of this process is shown in Figure 1-3.

Similarly, when two pieces of equipment—such as two personal computers (PCs)—communicate, rules are needed to determine which device will

**FIGURE 1-2** Unwritten rules of telephone communication: the initiation of the conversation.

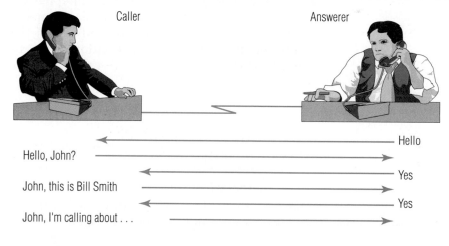

**FIGURE 1-3** Shortcutting the unwritten rules of telephone call initiation.

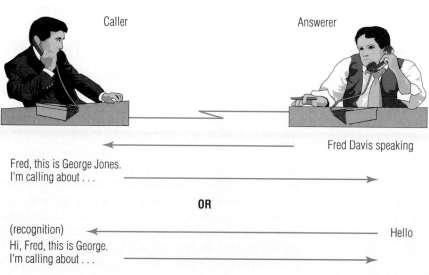

Cellular telephones are used more extensively in several other countries than they are in the United States.
(Source: Fritz Hoffmann/The Image Works. Reprinted with permission.)

transmit first, how they will be identified to each other, what happens if the communication gets cut off, and what happens if one device does not receive a transmission correctly. Unlike voice communication examples, when equipment is communicating automatically, all of the rules must be defined precisely and they must cover all situations—usual and unusual—that can occur. The rules of communication are called **protocols** and will be discussed in more detail in Chapter 4.

protocol

## 1-6  A BRIEF HISTORY OF TELECOMMUNICATIONS NETWORKS

### The Telegraph Network

The first true telecommunications network was established in the United States over 150 years ago. In 1844, Samuel F. B. Morse sat at a desk in the U.S. capitol building in Washington, D.C. and sent the first telegraph message ("What hath God wrought?") to a receiver thirty seven miles away in Baltimore, Maryland. The timing for Morse's invention couldn't have been better, because there was a need to improve communication capabilities between the business centers on the east coast of the U.S. and the new growth areas in the western part of the country. Morse assigned his patents to the Magnetic Telegraph Company, and the company signed up licensees to use the Morse patents. By 1851, there were fifty telegraph companies in the U.S. that operated telegraph offices, mainly at railroad stations. Also in 1851, twelve of the companies merged and formed the Western Union Company. By 1866, Western Union had more than 4,000 offices nationwide. By 1900, Western Union operated more than one million miles of telegraph lines and two transatlantic undersea cables. Operators at each location sent messages using telegraph keys and a series of long and short pulses, called the Morse code. They received messages by listening to the coded signals that came across the wires and interpreting the Morse code back into written letters. By today's standards, the telegraph network was incredibly primitive, but it established the foundation for many later communication network developments.

This equipment is typical of what was found in early telegraph and railroad offices.
(Source: www.faradic.net. Reprinted with permission.)

## Early Telephone Networks

While Western Union and other telegraph companies worked to establish the nationwide telegraph network, several inventors were already hard at work improving the telegraph system. Alexander Graham Bell of Boston and Elisha Gray of Chicago were both attempting to find a way to allow several telegraph signals to share one telegraph line. Neither man ever solved that problem, but almost simultaneously, both men jumped to the problem of sending voice signals by wire. By extreme coincidence, both men filed patent papers for a telephone system with the U.S. Patent Office on exactly the same day: February 14, 1876. However, Bell arrived a few hours before Gray, so he received the patent. Bell and his backers immediately turned all of their energy to perfecting and developing the telephone and to selling the invention to others.

The first year was so difficult for Bell that he became discouraged. In early 1877, he offered to sell the patent to Western Union for $100,000. Western Union was unimpressed with Bell's telephone and was so engaged in establishing the telegraph network that it declined Bell's offer, which may have been America's biggest business blunder up to that time. Some months later, however, it hired both Elisha Gray and Thomas Edison to develop a technically superior telephone, and the company began to establish its own telephone system to compete with Bell's. The Bell company filed suit, and after two years of legal wrangling, Western Union's lawyers recommended that the company reach a settlement with Bell because Bell had beaten Gray to the patent office and held the key patents for the telephone. Western Union settled with Bell and turned over its network of telephones to the Bell company. The legal victory gave Bell a monopoly in the telephone business in the U.S. The original Bell company spawned other companies, including the giant AT&T. Before its court-ordered breakup in 1984, AT&T was the largest company in the world, employing over one million people and operating over 100 million telephones.

## Early Teleprinting Services

Frequently, developments move in parallel, which was the case with the early communications networks. One might expect that voice communication was so far superior to the telegraph that voice networks would have

It didn't take long for great masses of telephone wires to appear in cities in the early part of the 20th century.
(Source: William Vanderson / Getty Images Inc.– Hutton Archive Photos. Reprinted with permission.)

completely and quickly replaced the former. There was, however, still a need for printed communication, which the voice network could not fulfill. The problem with the telegraph, however, was that trained and experienced operators who knew the Morse code were needed at both ends of the circuit to convert text and send it with the telegraph key and, at the receiving end, to interpret the Morse code and convert it back to printed characters.

What was needed was a system that would allow messages to be sent and received by less experienced operators, or no operators at all. In 1846, a man named Royal House invented a printing telegraph machine that

Two examples of early rotary dial telephones.
(Sources: Getty Images Inc.–Hutton Archive Photos; AT&T Archives. Reprinted with permission.)

could interpret code sent on the wires and print incoming messages. House's machine required *two* operators at each end of the circuit, so while it was claimed to be faster than standard Morse, it did not eliminate the need for operators. Other inventors worked on printing telegraph machines, but Frenchman Emile Baudot made more progress than the others. His printing telegraph used a typewriter-like keyboard and allowed up to eight machines to share a single wire. Baudot's machine did not use Morse code but a different code, **Baudot code,** that sent five pulses down the wire for each character transmitted. The code was such that the machines themselves could do the encoding and decoding, thereby eliminating the need for operators to become proficient at Morse code. An operator simply typed a message on the keyboard and the machine took care of converting each character to the five pulses that made up the Baudot code and sent the pulses on the wire. At the receiving end, no operator attention was required. The machine received the incoming pulses and converted them back to printed characters.

**Baudot code**

An English inventor, Donald Murray, improved on Baudot's work. Murray sold the American rights to his inventions to Western Union and Western Electric, a subsidiary of AT&T. The Murray patents became the basis for the machine known as the **teletypewriter (TTY),** also known by AT&T's brand name, **Teletype.** Both Western Union and AT&T used the technology to establish networks of teleprinters, which were the forerunner of today's e-mail systems. Western Union's service was called **telex** and AT&T's was called **teletypewriter exchange service (TWX).** Telex and TWX service peaked in the 1960s and 1970s, but in 1972, AT&T sold its TWX service to Western Union. Telex service is still in limited use around the world today, but primarily for communication within and among third world countries. It has largely been replaced by e-mail services on the Internet.

**teletypewriter (TTY)**

**Teletype**

**telex**

**teletypewriter exchange service (TWX)**

A model 32 ASR telex machine.
(Courtesy of Don House, North American Data Communications Museum. Reprinted with permission.)

## Radio Teleprinting

**radio teletype (RTTY)**

In the 1930s, several techniques were developed to allow the transmission of teleprinter signals by shortwave radio. This technique, called **radio teletype (RTTY),** was used by services such as embassies and consulates that needed to communicate where wires were not available; by news agencies such as the Associated Press (AP), United Press International (UPI), and Reuters; and for ship-to-shore communications. RTTY is still in limited use today, though it too has largely been supplanted by other more reliable and cost effective communication technologies. So, while you may have thought that wireless communication was a very new invention, it has really been around for a long time!

## The Telephone Network

**central office (CO)**

In the early days, the telephone network wasn't much of a network at all. Each telephone had to be connected, by wires, to every other telephone it was necessary to communicate with. Imagine what it would be like if you had to identify everyone you talked to on the telephone and have wires strung to each of their telephones! The concept of a **central office (CO)** quickly developed. Telephones were connected to a CO, most frequently by a pair of copper wires, and a temporary connection was made between two telephones. At the conclusion of the call, the telephones were disconnected from each other. This is exactly the way that telephone networks work today, but the connection process as been completely automated.

Telephone calls were originally connected by operators working at switchboards such as this one.
(Source: Archive Holdings, Inc., Archive Stillphotos 03RO / Getty Images Inc.– Image Bank. Reprinted with permission.)

**FIGURE 1-4** A simplified drawing of the telephone network.

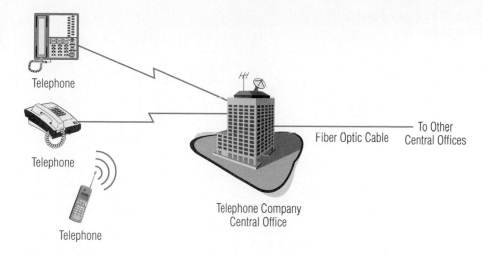

Telephone

Telephone

Telephone

Fiber Optic Cable — To Other Central Offices

Telephone Company Central Office

Originally, telephone operators performed the switching, but mechanical switches gradually replaced them. The early switches were noisy and prone to failure, but large computers that now make the connections quickly, quietly, and efficiently perform the switching. A simplified drawing of the telephone network is shown in Figure 1-4. Telephones are most commonly connected to the telephone company's CO by a pair of copper wires, although optical fiber cable is sometimes used. Calls between telephones connected to the same CO are connected by the computer in that office. Calls to telephones not connected to the same CO are forwarded to other COs in the telephone network until the office that handles the receiver's telephone is found. Complex tables stored in the computerized switches make the process very fast, as you know from your experience making long distance telephone calls. The average time to connect a call, and for you to hear the ringing begin at the other end, is under three seconds—even when you call someone who lives across the country.

Call switching is a major use of computers in the telephone network. However, computers are also used in many other ways, such as for keeping track of the length of calls, pricing them, creating telephone bills, and for troubleshooting and maintenance activities. It is almost ironic that the computer has become such a major factor in the modern telephone network, because technologically, the original telephone, telephone networks, and computers are quite different.

## Analog and Digital Telephone Service

**analog**

**digital**

Originally, the telephone and telephone network were entirely **analog,** whereas computers are **digital** devices. These two concepts will be discussed in detail in Chapter 6, but for now, consider an analog device to be one that is continuously variable (such as a speedometer or tachometer on most automobiles or a traditional wristwatch). By contrast, a digital device works in discreet steps, such as the dial that selects the channels on a television or the push buttons on a standard telephone. It is, for example, impossible to select channel 2.5 on the TV or to dial 8.6 on a telephone.

Analog and digital signals are depicted in Figure 1-5. There are several different ways that each signal type can be represented. Note that the digital signal has just two states or levels: "above the line" can represent a 1 bit and "below the line" can represent a 0 bit, with a sharp variation between them. By contrast, the analog signal has many levels and a gradual change between them.

Over time, and especially since 1950, the telephone network has become largely digital in operation. The only part of the network that often remains

**FIGURE 1-5**   Analog and digital signals.

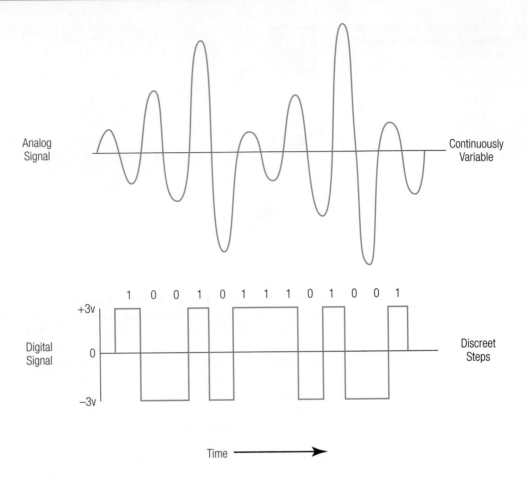

**FIGURE 1-6**   Analog and digital signals in the telephone network.

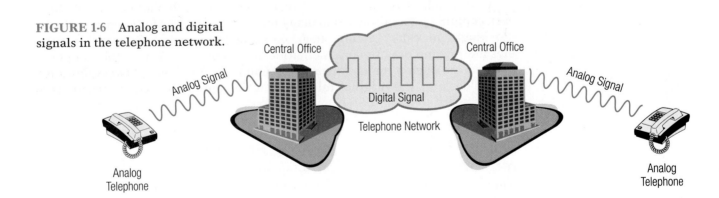

**digital subscriber line (DSL)**

**digitized**

analog is the telephone handset (although digital telephones are available) and the transmission of signals from it to the first telephone CO. At some point, the signal from your voice is converted from an analog signal to a digital signal, and it is transmitted through the network in digital form. Assuming that the receiver at the other end of the telephone call has an analog telephone, the digital voice signal is converted back to analog form shortly before being passed to the telephone, as illustrated in Figure 1-6. With new offerings, such as **digital subscriber line (DSL)**, available from many telephone companies, the analog voice signal may be **digitized**—converted to digital form by a digital telephone or another piece of equipment near the telephone handset—and transmitted digitally from the start of its journey.

Usually people aren't quite so happy to wait in line to use an ATM machine. (Source: Juan Silva Productions / Getty Images Inc.– Image Bank. Reprinted with permission.)

## 1-7 CONTEMPORARY EXAMPLES OF NETWORKS

Networks are in such widespread use today that finding examples to talk about is very easy. You have almost certainly used the Internet at home or in previous classes that you have taken. When you check a book out of a library, a network is most likely used to access a database of books that the library owns. If you can't find the book you want in your library, another network may be used to contact other libraries in your area to see if they have it available. When you order a product online, you are accessing a company's website through the Internet, and the company probably uses an internal network to check its inventory, to create shipping documents and a bill, and to schedule the product for shipment. When you shop at a supermarket, and a bar code reader scans your groceries, the checkout terminal accesses a database through a network and the inventory of available groceries is reduced. Also, your shopping preferences may be noted so that coupons can be printed. When you make a call on a cellular telephone, you are using a wireless network. If you connect to the Internet through your cable television system or a satellite, you are using still another form of networking. You can certainly think of many more examples where you use networking as a part of your daily routine.

A recent survey showed that school-age children who have a high speed (broadband) Internet connection at home say they're getting better grades and watching less TV. The survey of 2,200 children, ages 6 to 17, finds that 66 percent of those who have a home Internet connection say they spend more time online since getting a broadband connection. Also, 36 percent report that they watch less TV and 23 percent say they get better grades. The survey finds that in 2002, 37 percent of families who have home Internet access had a high speed connection, versus 10 percent in 2000. On average, school children spend 2.9 hours a day online, compared with 3.1 hours of TV time. Teens 13 to 17 spent 3.1 hours watching TV and 3.5 hours online.[2]

---

[2] From a survey: Connected to the Future, (©) Corporation for Public Broadcasting, 2002.

Supermarket scanners are usually connected to networks within the store. (Source: Ryan McVay / Getty Images Inc.– Photodisc. Reprinted with permission.)

## ■ SUMMARY

Communication networks are pervasive throughout our lives. We use them every day, sometimes almost without being aware that we are doing so. The Internet and the telephone network are the most common networks we use, but banking networks, credit card networks, and supermarket networks are used by most of us at least once a week. Studying networks and their underlying technology is of practical use to many people because they are interested in working in the communications industry, but everyone can benefit from understanding more about the way networks work in order to understand their capabilities and limitations.

The communications industry is less than 150 years old, and the developments and advancements from Samuel Morse's first message have been rapid and dramatic. One can only wonder what the next 150 years will bring.

In Chapter 2, you will study the ways that networks can be classified. Some of the ways may be familiar to you, and others will be new.

## ■ REVIEW QUESTIONS

1-1. Define *network*. What are some uses of a typical data network?

1-2. Distinguish among the terms *communications*, *telecommunications*, and *network*.

1-3. Why might a person want to study networks?

1-4. Explain the terms *source*, *medium*, *sink*, and *protocol*.

1-5. What is the importance of a communications protocol?

1-6. Describe the human protocol for making a telephone call.

1-7. What company passed up the opportunity to own the basic patents on the telephone?

1-8. What is the importance of a CO in a telephone network?

1-9. With your current level of understanding, explain the difference between an analog signal and a digital signal.

1-10. Give several examples of analog devices and digital devices that you use.

## TRUE OR FALSE

1-1. The telephone network totally and quickly eliminated the need for teleprinting networks and services.

1-2. Protocols are used in voice communication.

1-3. The switching of data, voice, and other signals through a network is done by specialized computers.

1-4. If you tapped into a digital communications circuit, you would not be able to tell whether the signals you saw were computer data, digitized voice signals, or digitized video.

1-5. Alexander Graham Bell was instantly successful with telephone technology after he received the patent for his device.

1-6. Analog communications devices handle continuously varying signals.

1-7. Switching must always be performed by computers.

1-8. The communications regulatory environment has stabilized and changes little.

1-9. There are fundamental differences among data, voice, and image transmissions.

1-10. A computer network may be as simple as two computers in an office connected by a wire or cable.

1-11. A communication circuit can be implemented in many physical forms, such as copper wire, optical fiber, or microwave radio.

1-12. Private companies can build their own communications networks.

1-13. Alexander Graham Bell offered to sell his patent for the telephone to Wal-Mart but the company declined his offer.

1-14. Teleprinter signals could never be transmitted by radio because of the speed at which humans type.

1-15. The average time to connect a telephone call is under three seconds.

1-16. Telephone handsets can be digital devices and can transmit digital signals.

1-17. When an analog voice signal is converted to digital form, it is said to be *digitized*.

1-18. When you make a call on your cell phone, you are using a wireless network.

## MULTIPLE CHOICE

1-1. Rules that guide the progress of messages through a network are called _____.

 a. media

 b. circuits

 c. switches

 d. protocols

 e. sinks

1-2. A teleprinter is a _____.

    a. talking typewriter

    b. device that switches analog signals

    c. successor to the telephone

    d. All of the above.

    e. None of the above.

1-3. In the telephone system, a computer in a CO _____.

    a. switches calls between telephones

    b. totally eliminates the need for telephone operators

    c. only exists to handle billing and administrative tasks

    d. is no longer required in modern telephone networks

1-4. Networks that connect computers _____.

    a. eliminate the need for wires between the computers

    b. are never used in banks for security reasons

    c. are found in most schools

    d. never have sources or sinks

    e. do not require protocols

    f. None of the above.

1-5. Telephone signals are _____.

    a. normally converted to digital form at some point during their transmission

    b. switched by computers

    c. transmitted through a communication company's CO

    d. All of the above.

    e. None of the above.

1-6. Basic elements of a network are called the _____.

    a. telephone, telegraph, and personal computer

    b. personal computer, modem, and Internet

    c. source, medium, and sink

    d. line, circuit, and cable

    e. hardware, software, and firmware

1-7. Two pioneers of the telephone industry were _____ and _____.

    a. Bell and Gray

    b. Morse and Code

    c. Baudot and Murray

    d. Rowe and Schuh

    e. Black and White

1-8. Digital signals, as shown in Figure 1-5 _____.

    a. have many levels and a gradual change between them

    b. represent the 1 bit and the 2 bit

    c. have just two states

    d. None of the above.

1-9. Networks you may have used include _____.

   a. the public switched telephone network (PSTN)

   b. the Internet

   c. a bank network

   d. a supermarket network

   e. a credit card network

   f. All of the above.

## ■ PROBLEMS AND PROJECTS

1-1. Talk with the IT or networking people and make a list of all of the networks at your school and the ways in which they are used.

1-2. Make a timeline showing the history of networks, beginning with the invention of the telegraph.

1-3. Data communication via a network is one way of making information available in the right place at the right time. Identify other ways that information can be transported rapidly, without using data communications. Also mention the tradeoffs in using these methods as compared to transporting the information on a network.

1-4. List several examples of ways that you use networks today that were not available to you 15 years ago, and describe how they have changed the way you work or live.

1-5. Describe how airline reservations must have been made before the advent of computers and networks.

1-6. Do you feel that the Internet will eliminate the need for printed reference books and library reference sections? Why or why not?

1-7. List all of the networks that you personally use on a regular basis. For each one, describe how you would cope if that network were not available to you.

## COMMUNICATING WITH EMPLOYEES

On the minds of company executives everywhere, especially since the terrorist acts of September 11, 2001, is the goal of maintaining communications with their employees. Many companies reduced the amount of air travel or let their employees decide whether they wanted to take a trip, which resulted in fewer visits by remote employees to home offices and, in some cases, a reduction in visits to customers. To help achieve the task of staying in touch with employees, managers are using communications services and networks in ever more impressive ways. Tools such as instant messaging, streaming media, voice over IP (VoIP), mobile phones, pagers, broadband and wireless technologies, and unified messaging are all being pressed into service.

One capability that is of interest to many companies allows the regular telephone system and the cellular system to be linked in a seamless way. An employee has a single telephone number, and when the company's PBX receives an incoming call for the employee, it immediately resolves the person's internal extension number and cell phone number and dials both devices. If either the desk phone or cell phone is answered, the unanswered device stops ringing and the call is connected to the user. If neither phone is answered within a specified number of rings, the call is sent to voice mail.

Other technology allows employees to take advantage of the corporate long distance plan from their cell phone. The system is able to detect dropped calls and automatically reconnect them. Voice recognition technology makes it possible for employees to speak another employee's name and have a call connected automatically. The idea is to give employees the power of their desk phones and PBX system with the mobility of their wireless phones.

New audio and video conferencing capabilities allow phone conferences to be set up without prior reservation. Employees are given a special telephone number and access code and can set up audio conferences with up to thirty people on the line at any given time. They can use it whenever they want—no advanced planning required.

Vendors are also beginning to offer text messaging and Internet browsing capabilities from cellular telephones. Another new capability, of interest in certain industries, is the ability to take photographs and upload them through the cell phone to a website. Realtors find this very useful when they are out taking photographs of newly listed properties.

### QUESTIONS

1. Do you think that the reduction in air travel and the resulting interest in improved communications technologies is a "passing fancy," or will the trend continue as we move farther away from September 11, 2001? Why?

2. Based on your home, school, or other experiences, identify some other communications capabilities that you would like to see vendors implement. Why do you suppose your ideas haven't been implemented so far?

# NETWORK CLASSIFICATION

## ■ OUTLINE

## ■ KEY TERMS

backbone network
bus network
dark fiber
distribution cable
drop wire
end office
feeder cable
hierarchical network
hybrid network
Institute of Electrical and Electronics Engineers Inc. (IEEE)

Internet
internet
internetwork
internetworking
local area network (LAN)
local loop
mesh network
metropolitan area network (MAN)
network
network topology

node
private branch exchange (PBX)
private network
private voice network
public network
public switched telephone network (PSTN)
public telephone network
ring network
root node

| serving central office (serving CO) | switching office | voice network |
| star network | toll office | wide area network (WAN) |
| subnetwork | trunk | wireless network |
| switch | value added network (VAN) | |

## ■ OBJECTIVES

After you complete your study of this chapter, you should be able to:

- ■ understand the many ways that networks can be classified;
- ■ explain the major types of communications networks as characterized by their geography, topology, and ownership;
- ■ distinguish among WANs, MANs, and LANs;
- ■ describe the characteristics of voice networks;
- ■ briefly explain the concept of internetworking;
- ■ explain why most networks fall into multiple classifications; and
- ■ explain why hybrid networks are so common.

## 2-1 INTRODUCTION

In this chapter, you will begin the study of networks by first looking at the many ways that networks can be classified and interconnected. In subsequent chapters, you will study the underlying technologies of networks and the elements, such as communications circuits, that are the components of networks. We'll begin by looking at a more formal definition of the term *network*.

## 2-2 DEFINITION OF NETWORK

network

node

A communications **network** is an interconnected system of computers, terminals, and other hardware established for the purpose of exchanging information or services between individuals, groups, or institutions. A **node** on a network is a point of connection into a network, such as a computer terminal, or a point, such as a router or a switch, at which one or more transmission lines (circuits) interconnect. Nodes are illustrated in Figure 2-1. Usually, when we think about a communications network in a business sense, we are referring to cables or communication circuits that connect personal computers and servers (the nodes) to one another, sometimes within the same room and sometimes over long distances. These networks can be classified in various ways, as you will see in the next sections.

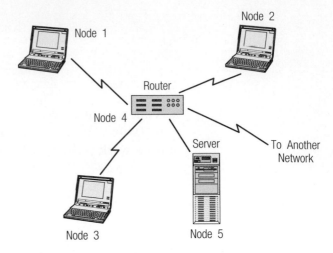

FIGURE 2-1 Nodes are points of entry into a network or interconnection within it.

## 2-3 NETWORKS CLASSIFIED BY GEOGRAPHY

**local area network (LAN)**

**wide area network (WAN)**

**metropolitan area network (MAN)**

One common way of classifying networks is by the geographic area they cover. The most common designations are the **local area network (LAN)** and the **wide area network (WAN)**. A third category, which is less well defined, is the **metropolitan area network (MAN).**

### Local Area Networks (LANs)

Perhaps the network you are most familiar with is the network that connects your personal computer at school to other personal computers in the building or around the campus. Because university campuses normally cover a rather small geographic area, the networks on them are considered to be local, and are called local area networks (LANs). We will define LANs more precisely later, but you can easily understand the difference between the locality of a campus network and the geographic diversity of the public telephone network that covers the entire world. There are also data networks that cover a wide geographical area, such as all of the U.S. or even the world, and these are called wide area networks (WANs). A WAN that you have undoubtedly used is the Internet, although the Internet is technically a collection of LANs and WANs that are connected together.

Coming back to the network on your campus, it probably has hundreds or even thousands of workstations and servers attached to it. Each of these devices is a node on the network. The key attribute of a LAN is its limited geographic scope, not the number of nodes that are attached to the network. Some LANs, such as one you may have established in your home, are very small and may have only a few nodes. A LAN is a geographically localized network consisting of both hardware and software that links personal computers, workstations, printers, servers, and other peripherals. Devices on the LAN typically communicate within buildings or between buildings located near each other.

LANs are almost certainly the most common type of network in existence today. Because of the capabilities they offer, they are widely installed in organizations of all sizes. The discussion of LANs is extensive and deals with many topics. For this reason, Chapters 10, 11, and 12 are dedicated to a coverage of LAN-related material.

## Wide Area Networks (WANs)

WANs may be made up of a combination of switched and leased, terrestrial and satellite, and private microwave circuits. Because communication carrier facilities are used, almost any circuit speed can be found in WANs.

The WAN for a large multinational company may be global, whereas the WAN for a small company may cover only several cities or counties. One large bank has built a private WAN to link its offices in Massachusetts, Hong Kong, London, Munich, and Sydney. It reports that international circuits operating at speeds of 256 Kbps or 1 Mbps provide a three-second response time to users at workstations anywhere in the world. Most international financial organizations have similar networks, because they must have them if they are to compete. Manufacturing companies that operate on a national or international scale have similar networks that link their offices and plants. Information about sales orders, sales forecasts, production, inventory, revenue, and expenses is routinely exchanged on a daily or more frequent basis. Every industry has numerous examples of WANs used to make organizations more productive. Chapter 13 provides an in-depth look at WANs.

## Metropolitan Area Networks (MANs)

By way of contrast, there are networks that cover a geographical territory larger than a building or campus, but smaller than a state or country. Networks that are between a WAN and LAN in size are sometimes referred to as metropolitan area networks (MANs).

Suppose your school has a primary campus but also conducts classes at other locations around the city. LANs would be used on the primary campus, and perhaps within other classroom buildings throughout the city. A MAN would be used to connect all of the LANs and tie all of the school's facilities into a single network. Students would have the same communication and computing capability regardless of where they attend class.

Figure 2-2 shows a typical MAN that connects several LANs in locations scattered around a city. Note that voice traffic is also carried on the MAN in the figure, a capability that is more common with MANs than with either WANs or LANs. High bandwidth (speed) between the locations on the MAN is usually a requirement, because MANs usually connect LANs, which always operate at high speed. The voice traffic would also demand high bandwidth, depending on how much it is carried. A MAN may be owned and operated by a single organization or it may be shared by several organizations.

In the past few years, a number of communications companies have begun business by installing optical fiber cable in metropolitan areas and then selling it to other companies that use it to establish MANs by interconnecting their locations within the city. Rights-of-way are obtained in many ways, such as on telephone poles, in subway tunnels, and under city streets. These companies primarily sell high-speed digital bandwidths and typically offer no value-added or other services. If the media used is optical fiber cable, the term frequently applied is **dark fiber,** because the fiber cable itself is supplied without the accompanying electronics and light source, such as an LED or a laser that puts light into the fiber to make it usable. When a customer leases dark fiber, he or she is responsible for providing all the equipment required to drive and operate the circuit.

The primary market for this service is the customer who needs a lot of high-speed communication service within a relatively small, often metropolitan, geographic area. These customers are often large companies with mul-

**dark fiber**

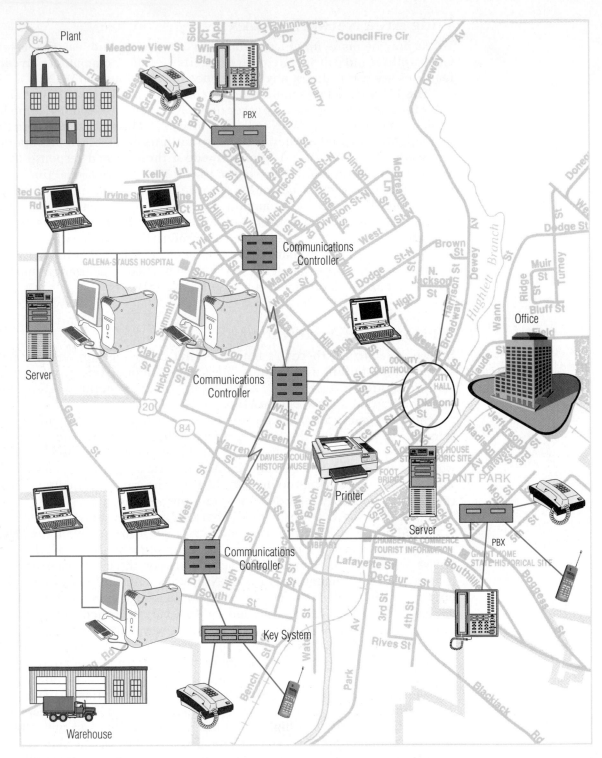

**FIGURE 2-2    A MAN.**

tiple offices or other locations within a city. The MAN providers typically of-fer lower prices than other communications carriers and diverse routing that provides backup in emergencies. They also claim to offer quicker installation and better service than the other carriers.

**Institute of Electrical and Electronics Engineers, Inc. (IEEE)**

MAN technology has been standardized by a committee of the **Institute of Electrical and Electronics Engineers, Inc. (IEEE)**, which developed the

MAN standard known as IEEE 802.6. The work was produced by the committees that defined LANs, and was a result of their unresolved concerns about how LANs could be connected across distances of a few kilometers or greater.

## 2-4   NETWORKS CLASSIFIED BY TOPOLOGY

network topology

The configuration of a communications network—the way the circuits are connected together—is called the **network topology**. If a map is drawn showing how all of the circuits and nodes are connected to one another, but without regard for the geography of where they are located, the topology of the network can be seen. Network topologies fall into six major categories.

### Star Networks

star network

A **star network** is illustrated in Figure 2-3. All circuits radiate from a central node, which is often a cluster of servers or a host computer. The star network puts the central point in contact with every other location, which makes it easier to manage and control the network than it is in some other configurations. There is no limit to the number of arms that can be added to the star or the length of each of the arms. Thus, it is relatively easy to expand a star network by adding more nodes. On the other hand, because the central node controls all transmissions, and all transmissions flow through it, the central node is a single point of failure. If it is down, the network is out of service. Another potential problem with star networks is that, in times of peak traffic, the central node may become overloaded and unable to keep up with all of the traffic that the outlying stations want to transmit.

Twenty years ago, when data networks were frequently controlled by a central host computer, star networks were very common. Where there was a central computer that supported many terminals, the star configuration was

FIGURE 2-3   A star network.

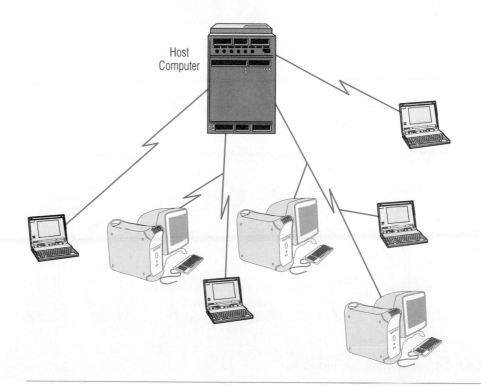

Host Computer

easy to implement. Because the central computer was the master node and controlled the network, the protocol for network operations was relatively simple. However, most networks now use a different topology, such as a mesh, ring, or bus topology, which provides more redundancy and eliminates the single point of failure. It is important to note, however, that the star topology is still often used for voice networks in which all of the telephones are connected to a CO switch. If the CO switch fails, the network goes down. However, CO switches are designed to be extremely reliable, so failure of the entire office is extremely rare.

## Hierarchical Networks

**hierarchical network**

**root node**

A **hierarchical network** is illustrated in Figure 2-4. This type of network has a tree structure, and the top node in the structure is called the **root node.** You may notice that the hierarchical structure mirrors a typical corporate organization chart, and in fact, it is in this setting that a hierarchical configuration is most likely to be found. Compare, if you will, the root node to the corporate headquarters on an imaginary organization chart and the nodes immediately below that to a divisional level. Under each division there are nodes corresponding to plants (in the case of a manufacturing division) and to district offices (in the case of sales and marketing divisions). Under the district offices, you might find nodes in local sales offices.

This type of network would most likely be implemented where the lower level nodes at the second or third level are themselves computers that have significant processing capability. You can envision a district office computer being connected to the local sales office computers and collecting data from them. The district data would be consolidated with similar data from other

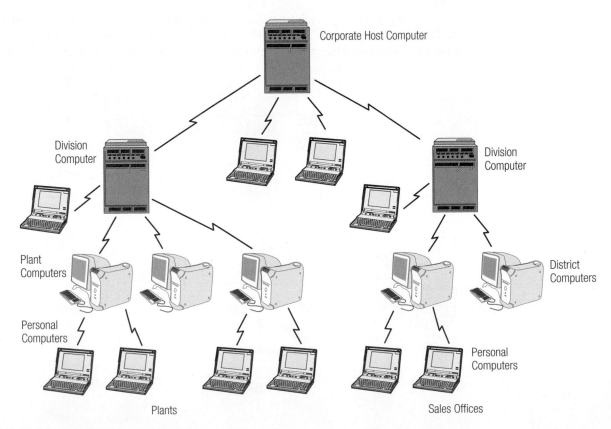

**FIGURE 2-4**   A hierarchical network.

districts at the divisional level. Finally, all of the divisional data would be consolidated at corporate headquarters. In this configuration, with proper planning and design, there is no single point of failure in the network. If one division's computer or network fails, the other divisions are not affected. Even if the root node at corporate headquarters fails, the divisions can go on doing their daily processing and can send and receive data from lower levels in the hierarchy. The results of divisional communications and processing can be transmitted to the higher level in the network when it is restored to service.

## Mesh Networks

mesh network

A **mesh network**, illustrated in Figure 2-5, is similar to a hierarchical network, except that there are more interconnections between nodes at different levels—or even at the same level. In fact, some levels may not exist at all. In a fully interconnected mesh network, each node is connected to every other node. However, for cost reasons, this is seldom implemented. The major nodes are usually connected, whereas minor nodes are connected to one or more locations, depending on their needs and criticality. The PSTN is an example of a mesh network that, because of good design and a high level of the connection, provides many alternate paths between nodes (COs). The heavy interconnection makes the telephone network virtually fail-safe.

WANs are usually configured in a star, hierarchical, or mesh topology that provides redundant connection and ensures that there is no single point of failure that can cause the entire network to fail.

## Bus Networks

bus network

A **bus network** is shown in Figure 2-6. Conceptually, a bus is a communication medium to which multiple nodes are attached, and each node normally receives any signals put on the bus. The term *bus* implies very high speed transmission, and bus networks are usually implemented in situations where the distance between all of the nodes is limited, such as a LAN within a department or building.

Devices are attached to the bus by a tap connection into the bus cable. Each tap causes a certain amount of signal loss on the cable, which is one reason bus networks have a limit as to the number of devices that can be attached to them. Another consideration with bus networks is that when problems do occur, faults can be difficult to locate. Because all of the devices

**FIGURE 2-5** A mesh network.

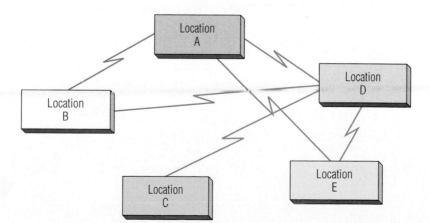

FIGURE 2-6   A bus
network.

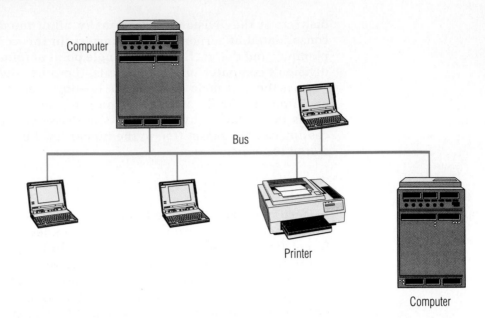

are connected serially on the bus, each device may have to be checked in sequence to locate the problem.

Although a bus network may look similar to star or hierarchical networks, the major difference is that, on a bus, all stations are independent of one another. There is no single point of control or failure—as there is in a star network. The loss of a single node on a bus has no impact on the other nodes, and unless the bus itself fails, the reliability of a bus network is excellent. However, because of their high-speed operation, bus networks usually are limited in the distance they can traverse, which is why the topology is normally found only in LANs.

## Ring Networks

ring network

A **ring network** is illustrated in Figure 2-7. Ring networks are also usually associated with networks on which the nodes are relatively close together, as they are in LANs. Each device is connected to the ring with a tap similar to the taps found on a bus network. As communications signals pass around the

FIGURE 2-7   A ring
network.

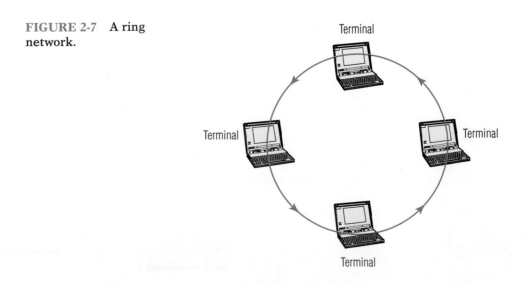

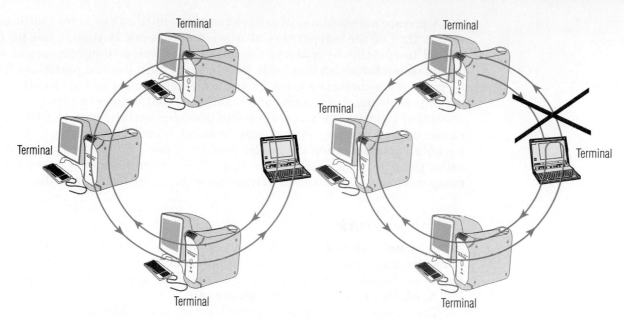

**FIGURE 2-8**   A ring network with two channels.

ring, a receiver/driver unit in each device checks the addresses of the in-coming signal and either routes it to the destination device or regenerates the signal and passes it on to the next device on the ring. This regeneration is an advantage over bus networks; the signal is less subject to attenuation. Furthermore, each device can check the signal for errors, which allows for more sophisticated error control and network management.

All of the stations on the ring are equal and must be active participants to make the ring work. If one of the nodes fails, the potential exists for the entire ring to be out of service because messages cannot be passed through the fail-ing node. Figure 2-8 illustrates a ring with two channels that transmit the data in opposite directions, which is the way rings are normally implemented. This allows transmission to continue, even if one of the links (nodes) fails. When that happens, the nodes on either side of the failure reconfigure themselves to be-gin using the second ring to transmit data in the opposite direction. All stations can be reached from either direction by transmitting on one ring or the other.

## 2-5   NETWORKS CLASSIFIED BY OWNERSHIP

private network

public network

Another way of classifying networks is by their ownership. Two broad cate-gories exist: **private networks** and **public networks.** We will look at each cat-egory and its variations.

### Private Networks

A private network is usually built by an organization for its exclusive use. The network is built from circuits available from a variety of sources and may in-clude a combination of privately installed and operated circuits and leased or switched facilities. While the network is considered private, the circuits making up the network may be obtained from a communications carrier— the circuits do not have to be privately installed and maintained. It is con-sidered private because a private network is built for the exclusive use of a company or other organization.

A private network may also have connections to one or more public networks. One of the advantages of a private network is that it can be designed to specifically address the data and/or voice requirements of the organization for which it is built. Because it is built around particular traffic patterns or communication flows, it can make better use of circuits than a public network could. Another advantage is that it gives the company full control of the network's operation and provides better security. Communication using a private network may, however, be more expensive than comparable communication on public networks. Because of the flexibility to tailor the private network to a company's exact requirements, many major companies have one or more private networks connecting their locations.

### Public Networks

A public network is a network built and owned by a communications company, a common carrier, or another organization for use by its customers. The two most familiar examples of public networks are the Internet and the PSTN, which we use to make telephone calls.

The advantage of a public network is that it provides services or access to locations that a company might not otherwise be able to afford. Companies frequently use public data networks to exchange messages with their small locations, such as a single-person sales office, where the installation of a private line cannot be justified. The communications company or a common carrier may have many similar customers in the area and can spread out the implementation and operational costs of providing service among all of its customers. The carrier can achieve good utilization of its network while providing high-quality service to infrequent users.

The Internet has changed our view of public networks because it has become so widely used. Before the Internet, public networks were available but were used by relatively few people and organizations. Now, everyone knows of the Internet and most network users also use it.

## 2-6   OTHER TYPES OF NETWORKS

Several other types of networks need to be mentioned, though they do not fit neatly into the previous classifications. They are, however, real networks that you may have heard about and used.

### Value Added Networks (VANs)

value added network
(VAN)

A **value added network (VAN)** is a particular type of public data network that, in addition to offering transmission facilities, contains intelligence that makes the basic facilities better suited for satisfying the communications needs of a particular type of user. The intelligence might provide code or speed translation, or the network might store messages and deliver them at a later time (store-and-forward). Computers located at network nodes provide the intelligence in a VAN. In addition to simple communications-related processing, they may also perform more sophisticated processing related to the business of the VAN's subscribers. This intelligence provides the "added value" from which the generic name for this type of network is derived.

Some examples of industry-oriented VANs include the SWIFT network, which connects international banks; the SITA network (http://www.sita.aero/), which connects airline and travel networks; the IVANS network (http://www.

ivans.com/), which connects many U.S. insurance companies; and, in the United Kingdom, the Tradanet service, which connects many retailers and their suppliers. Each of these networks contains the intelligence to perform certain types of processing for its users.

## Wireless Networks

wireless network

Any network, but especially a LAN, can be implemented either by using wires or cables to connect the nodes or by using radio technology in a configuration that does not require wires. A **wireless network** uses any unguided media, but typically uses a radio frequency technology as an extension of, or as an alternative to, a wired network. In a typical wireless network configuration, a transmitter/receiver (transceiver) called an access point connects to a wired network using standard cabling. Wireless networks are among the most rapidly growing segments of networking technology today. You'll learn more about wireless networks in Chapters 11 and 12.

## Backbone Networks

backbone network

Another concept for you to be familiar with is that of a **backbone network.** A backbone network is the main network in an organization or a location. It may be the network that carries the most traffic or is the most critical. It is likely to be a high speed network that connects other slower speed networks to one another.

What constitutes a backbone network is relative. Within a manufacturing building, it may be a LAN that connects all of the machines together. That network may, however, be connected to another plant-wide network that connects all of the buildings in the plant site. In turn, the plant-wide network may be connected to a company-wide network that connects all of the company's locations in the world. Depending on your perspective, any one of the networks might be a backbone. To the building manager, the LAN in his building would "break his back" if it were down for long. To the vice president of manufacturing who is responsible for many plants, the failure of a network in one plant might not be a "back breaker." In general, people think of a backbone network as the largest, most important network on which they regularly depend.

## 2-7  VOICE NETWORKS

voice network

public switched
telephone network
(PSTN)

public telephone
network

serving central office
(serving CO)

local loop

drop wire

distribution cable

feeder cable

The major focus of this book is data networking, however, **voice networks** constitute a major part of the networking scene and, in fact, voice networks existed long before data networks became a reality. It is important for you to understand at least the basics of voice networks.

### The Public Switched Telephone Network

The **public switched telephone network (PSTN),** sometimes just called the **public telephone network,** consists of many distinct pieces. Telephones in a home or business are most commonly connected to their **serving central office (serving CO)** by a pair of copper wires called the **local loop.** In a residential neighborhood, the wire coming from the house, called the **drop wire,** runs to a pole (or underground equivalent), where it joins other similar wires to form a **distribution cable.** Eventually, several distribution cables join together to form a **feeder cable,** which terminates at the CO, as shown

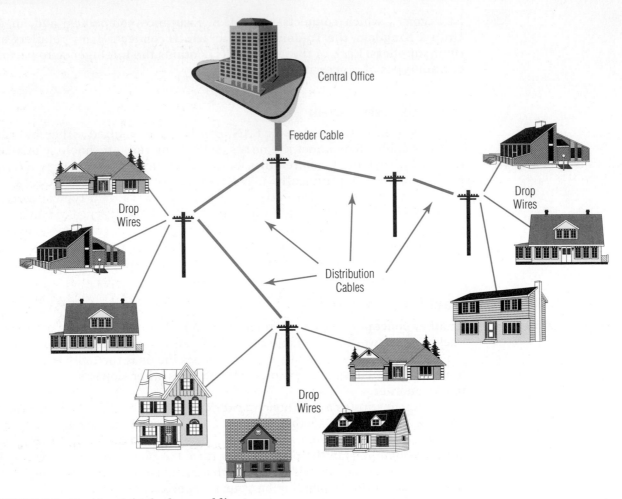

Central Office

Feeder Cable

Drop
Wires

Drop
Wires

Distribution
Cables

Drop
Wires

**FIGURE 2-9**   Residential telephone cabling.

trunk

in Figure 2-9. Clearly, the cable gets physically larger as it gets closer to the CO. Cables may run above ground (on poles) or under ground, but most new installations being made today are underground, where they are better protected and out of sight.

COs are connected to each other with multiple circuits called **trunks.** A trunk is defined as a circuit, connecting telephone switches or switching locations. Functionally, a trunk and a circuit do the same thing—carry communications—but a trunk connects switching equipment, whereas a circuit connects to a telephone, computer, or other device. Trunks may be implemented with regular copper wire but are more often implemented with coaxial cable, microwave radio, or fiber-optic cable.

The PSTN, with its millions of miles of circuits, handles virtually all of the voice and data communications in the world. It is diverse and highly redundant; therefore, it is impervious to massive outages. It is resilient when failures do occur. Most countries consider their public communications network to be a national asset and take steps, including regulation, to protect it.

In the U.S., the PSTN is facing a challenge. Local telephone networks have been engineered with the assumption that the average telephone call lasts about three minutes. However, when users of the Internet or other online services dial up from their computers, they stay on the line an average of twenty minutes, and sometimes for hours. With those local lines tied up, the network and switching equipment can become congested, making it impossible for other people to make calls. Telephone companies and others are studying alternative solutions to the problem, including charging data users on a per minute basis. One way or another, the problem will be solved.

**switch**

As has been previously described, COs contain computers, called **switches,** that route and connect telephone calls. CO switches are optimized to perform specific functions. Some are primarily designed to switch local telephone calls from and to businesses and residences. This type of CO is commonly known as an **end office.** The CO to which a specific telephone is connected is known as that telephone's *serving central office (serving CO)*. Each serving CO serves all of the telephones within a specific geographic area. The size of the area served depends upon the density of the telephones. In rural areas, the CO might serve many square miles, whereas in Los Angeles, Houston, or any major city, many COs are needed to handle all of the office buildings and residences because of the high density.

**end office**

**toll office**

**switching office**

Other central offices, called **toll offices** or **switching offices,** are designed primarily for forwarding long distance calls to other parts of the country. Offices are connected in a weblike pattern that provides a high level of redundancy and alternate routing, as shown in Figure 2-10. Any CO may be

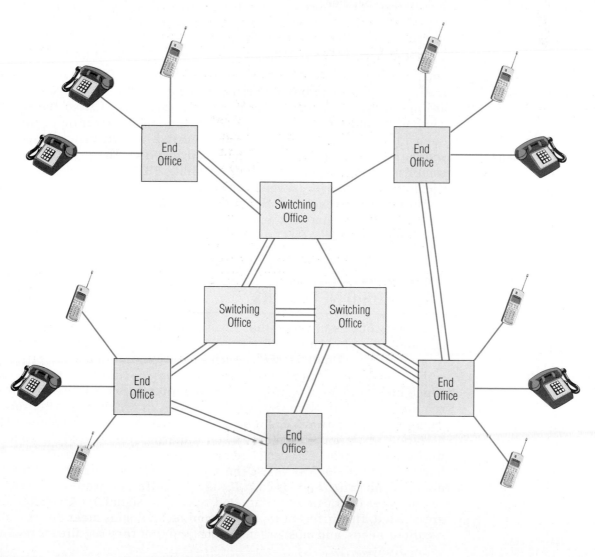

**FIGURE 2-10**   The connection of the COs in the nationwide telephone network.

connected to any other CO through direct trunks, but a major consideration, when deciding whether to connect two offices, is the amount of traffic (number of telephone calls) that flows between them. In some cases, several trunks are needed to carry the traffic; in other cases, a direct connection isn't needed and traffic is routed in a less direct fashion.

A telephone call is handled at the lowest level office that can complete it or provide the required service. The serving CO can often handle local calls by itself, because it handles the telephones of both the calling and receiving party. If the serving CO that first received it cannot handle a call, it is forwarded to the most appropriate CO. Tables stored in the memory of the central office switch determine the routing. For example, a call *from* a business in Dallas *to* New York City might be routed from the serving CO in Dallas to a switching office serving part of Dallas. The switching office's tables might tell it that calls for New York should be routed to a certain switching center in Atlanta or, if Atlanta is busy, to Saint Louis. The objective of the network is to route the calls to the destination CO via the shortest, fastest route possible. Think about how quickly your call gets routed the next time you make a long distance call. It is amazing when you consider that your call is passing through the switches in several COs on the way to the receiver.

## Private Voice Networks

**private voice network**

**private branch exchange**

Organizations that have several locations and a high volume of telephone traffic may choose to build a **private voice network.** Private voice networks are normally configured with circuits that are leased from the telephone companies under a variety of special rate plans. In addition to the private network, the organization may elect to install its own switch, a specialized computer called a **private branch exchange (PBX).** The primary reasons for establishing private networks and installing PBXs are to give the organization more control over its voice network, to save money, and to provide more features to telephone users than the PSTN offers. The other side of the coin is that the private network may require additional staff, and it must be managed like any other asset.

## 2-8   HYBRID NETWORKS

**hybrid network**

The reality of networking is that almost all networks are combinations of the geographies, topologies, and technologies described in the preceding sections. Only very small networks, such as those found in a small office, use a single topology or technology. Networks are generally **hybrid networks,** which blend the most appropriate combinations of capabilities to meet the requirements of an organization and the ways in which it uses networks. For example, a star network might have a ring on it, as shown in Figure 2-11, or a hierarchical network could have a star radiating from one of the nodes. Networks that are primarily designed for data may carry voice traffic as well. As long as all of the networks use the same protocol and basic operating technology, connecting them is easy. If they use different protocols, or carry different types of traffic (e.g. data and television signals), conversion devices are needed. The different topologies and technologies meet diverse communications needs, and most organizations find that they require a combination of capabilities.

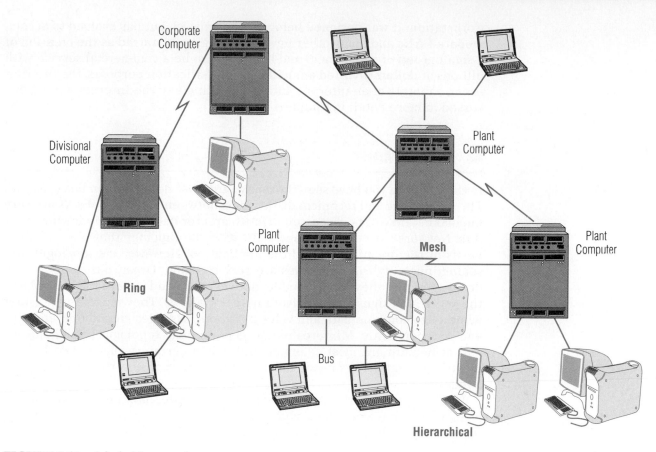

**FIGURE 2-11** A hybrid network.

## 2-9 INTERCONNECTING NETWORKS

**internetwork**

**internet**

**Internet**

When networks are connected so that data can be sent between them in a way that is transparent to the user, we refer to them as **internetworks**. Internetworks, or **internets**, are very common today, the most famous example being the **Internet**. (Note: In this text, the public, global interconnection of networks that is used by millions of people daily is referred to as the Internet—with a capital "I." When used with a small "i," the word *internet* refers simply to the interconnection of one or more distinct networks.) But within companies and other organizations, LANs and WANs are often highly interconnected, so that employees in any location can communicate with other employees wherever they are located. Additionally, organizations frequently need to connect their networks to the networks of other organizations. From the user's point of view, he or she wants to be able to communicate with other people, make inquiries, or process data on a wide variety of networks, both inside and outside of the organization, without worrying about how the networks are connected. In other words, users want transparency so that they can access all of the people and resources they need to do their jobs. WANs, LANs, and MANs all need to be interconnected, and as communications technology has advanced and made this capability available, the term **internetworking**, or internet, has been applied.

**internetworking**

**subnetwork**

An internet is an interconnected set of networks that may simply appear as a single, larger network. Because the interconnected networks maintain their own identity, they are usually referred to as **subnetworks**. The Internet was conceived in the era when timesharing was widely used on large mainframe computers, but has survived into the era of the personal computer and workstation. It was designed before LANs existed, but has evolved to accommodate LANs and many other new technologies. It started as the creation of a small group of researchers and has grown to be a commercial service with billions of dollars invested annually. For classification purposes, the Internet is one example of an internet. Internetworking and the Internet will be discussed in more detail in Chapters 14–16.

## ■ SUMMARY

In this chapter, you have seen the many ways that networks can be classified. The geographic and technical distinctions between LANs and WANs are very important and will be discussed in much greater detail in the following chapters. Networks are designed and built with the topology that best suits the needs of the organization and the application. However, the topologies are seldom pure. Hybrid topologies are very common. Organizations must also decide whether they can use public networks or need to have the control and the specific designs that a private network allows. They must also consider whether to combine data and voice networks, or to design and operate each one independently. Mixtures of the geographies, topologies, technologies, and ownership are most common, and it is a certainty that networks that meet an organization's needs today will have to evolve as the organization's needs change.

In Chapter 3, you will learn about network architectures and standards. Network architectures provide a model or framework for studying and implementing networks, while the standards specify how networks are implemented.

## ■ REVIEW QUESTIONS

2-1. Define the term *network*.

2-2. Explain what a node is.

2-3. Describe three ways that networks can be classified.

2-4. Distinguish between LANs, MANs, and WANs.

2-5. Which of the following is *not* a characteristic of a LAN?

  a. operates at high speed

  b. covers a large geographic area

  c. has multiple nodes

  d. interconnects devices that are located fairly close together

2-6. Why do WANs not operate at as high speeds as LANs typically do?

2-7. How can permission to cross a public right-of-way be obtained for a WAN when necessary?

2-8. Which of the following are characteristics of WANs?

  a. usually cross public rights of way

  b. use a bus topology

  c. usually use circuits provided by one or more communication carriers

  d. may operate at almost any speed

  e. could be installed in a home

2-9. Why are fully interconnected mesh networks rarely installed?

2-10. Why do ring networks often have two rings transmitting data in opposite directions?

2-11. What are the advantages and disadvantages to implementing a private network in an organization?

2-12. What kind of value is added in a typical value added network?

2-13. Explain what a backbone network is.

2-14. Explain the characteristics of star networks and ring networks.

2-15. Describe some situations in which public networks may be more appropriate than private networks.

2-16. Explain the term *dark fiber.*

2-17. Explain the concept of a hybrid network.

2-18. In the public voice network, what is the role of the CO?

2-19. Distinguish between an end office and a toll office in the PSTN.

2-20. What makes the PSTN so redundant and fail-safe?

2-21. What is the difference between a switch in a telephone company CO and a PBX?

2-22. Why do companies want to interconnect networks?

## TRUE OR FALSE

2-1. The primary purpose of the network topology is to indicate the technology used by the network.

2-2. Full mesh networks are rarely implemented.

2-3. A hierarchical network can be compared to a corporate organization chart.

2-4. LANs are rarely implemented because of high cost.

2-5. The key attribute of a LAN is its broad geographic scope.

2-6. Bus networks are only installed in moving airplanes and other vehicles.

2-7. Private networks are normally built for the exclusive use of an organization.

2-8. Wireless networks are rarely practical because of interference from commercial radio stations.

2-9. Subnetworks are components of internetworks.

2-10. A *node* on a network is a point of connection into a network, or a point at which one or more transmission lines (circuits) interconnect, such as where a router or a switch connects into the network.

2-11. WANs may be made up of a combination of switched, leased, terrestrial, satellite, and private microwave circuits.

2-12. MANs normally operate at high speed.

2-13. The term *dark fiber* refers to fiber that has been painted black to improve its reflectivity.

2-14. In our solar system, star networks are limited to five arms.

2-15. In a fully interconnected mesh network, each node is connected to every other node.

2-16. A potential problem with bus networks is that when problems do occur, faults can be difficult to locate.

2-17. Signals on a ring network are regenerated before being passed along to the next station on the ring.

2-18. A public network is a network built and owned by a communications company, a common carrier, or another organization for use by its customers or other constituency.

2-19. A wireless network uses radio frequency technology as an extension of, or as an alternative to, a wired network.

2-20. When looking at a network topology, it is always easy to pick out the backbone network.

2-21. A *trunk* is defined as a circuit that connects telephone switches or switching locations.

2-22. The PSTN is diverse and is highly redundant.

2-23. When people use the telephone to make a call to access the Internet, they stay online longer than if they were making a standard voice telephone call.

2-24. A serving CO is one that serves other local COs, which handle telephone customers.

2-25. Hybrid networks are rare because they are more difficult to maintain than pure networks.

2-26. When one or more distinct networks are interconnected, the result is called an *internet.*

## MULTIPLE CHOICE

2-1. Networks that cover a small geographic area are called _____.

    a. MANs

    b. LANs

    c. star networks

    d. hybrid networks

    e. mesh networks

2-2. Networks that cover a broad geographic area are called _____.

    a. hierarchical networks

    b. bus networks

    c. ring networks

    d. WANs

    e. universal networks

2-3. Networks in which all circuits radiate from a central node are called _____.

    a. radial arm networks

    b. pinwheel networks

    c. hierarchical networks

    d. star networks

    e. None of the above.

2-4. A network in which the top node in the structure is called the root node is called a(an) _____.

    a. tree network

    b. plant network

    c. hierarchical network

d. internetwork

e. star network

2-5. The stations on a ring network _____.

a. are equal

b. regenerate a signal before passing it on

c. check the address of all incoming signals

d. are connected to the ring with a tap

e. All of the above.

2-6. Private networks _____.

a. can be made from circuits acquired from a communications carrier

b. may be connected to a public network

c. allow the owners to have full control of the network's operation

d. may be more expensive on a per communication basis than public networks

e. All of the above.

2-7. Value added networks _____.

a. are a particular type of private network that offers translation capability as well as communication

b. contain intelligence

c. provide their value by discounting the message unit price

d. operate more swiftly than other types of networks

e. None of the above.

## ■ PROBLEMS AND PROJECTS

2-1. Visit a company in your area that has several locations within a thirty mile radius. Have they connected the locations together with a MAN? If not, find out why. If they have, find out how they are using the network, how reliable it is, and whether it is perceived to be meeting the company's communication needs.

2-2. How does one determine when a network ceases to be a MAN and becomes a WAN? Does it make any difference what you call it? Are different technologies used in MANs and WANs?

2-3. Visit a local hotel/motel and find out what type of telephone system it uses. Does the system have an automatic feature to handle wake-up calls? Are there any special features that seem to be unique for the hotel/motel industry? If the motel is part of a chain, is the telephone system networked to the chain's voice network?

2-4. Talk to the network administrator at your school and find out if the school has more than one LAN. If so, are they connected into an internet? Ask why the school doesn't just have a single large LAN instead of multiple smaller ones. If you can get the information, draw a picture of the school's network(s), showing the departments they serve and their interconnections.

## GROVE AND HOWE, CPA

Grove and Howe, CPA is a regional public accounting firm that has offices in Peoria, IL; Flint, MI; Milwaukee, WI; Davenport, IA; and Louisville, KY. The firm has been extremely diligent about ensuring that their accounting practices are up to date and ethical, and they have avoided any of the sense of scandal that has hit the public accounting industry in the years since the Enron case became public. However, until now, they have largely ignored the technology side of their business, particularly as it relates to networking. The firm uses PCs extensively in each of its offices, but has not connected any of them together. When data needs to be shared, it is written to either a diskette or a CD-ROM (depending on the size of the file) and hand carried, mailed, or shipped to the other offices in the firm. It has been estimated that approximately $200,000 per year is spent on transporting data in this manner.

The firm's partners have recently come to realize that networking their computers might provide a more effective way to transport data from computer to computer, and they have hired you to study, recommend, and implement a data network for them. What you know so far is:

- The firm's headquarters are in Peoria. All of the other offices have a partner in charge, who reports to the Peoria headquarters.

- The offices are all about the same size. Each has about thirty accountants and forty support staff.

- There is no IT department, and each of the offices has had free reign to implement whatever computers they felt were necessary.

- It is estimated that the amount of data exchange is quite uniform between all of the offices with slightly more shipments being sent from Peoria.

Based on your knowledge of networks and network topologies, your task is to recommend the type of network to install. However, because the partners have had so little exposure to computer networking, you know that you need to keep your first presentation to them very simple.

**QUESTIONS**

1. In your first presentation to the firm's partners, you plan to introduce them to a few network terms. Which ones would you select, and how would you explain the terms to them?

2. You will most likely need to recommend that the firm install a hybrid network that allows communication within each office and between offices. Draw a rough map showing what the network topology might look like.

3. Because the traffic between the firm's offices is quite uniform, you have been considering a full mesh network topology. Prepare a one or two paragraph summary of the advantages and disadvantages of implementing a full mesh network.

4. Would it be possible for Grove and Howe to install a MAN instead of a WAN to link its offices together? Explain your position.

5. Based on the limited information you now have, prepare a first draft of a written recommendation for the partners describing the best topology for the firm's network. Include the drawing or map from Question 2, showing your proposal in graphical form. Include a list of the benefits you think the firm will receive by implementing a network and any cost estimates or information you can provide.

CASE STUDY

# NETWORK ARCHITECTURES AND STANDARDS

## ◼ OUTLINE

## ◼ KEY TERMS

architecture

communication standards

diverse network technologies

encapsulation

Government Open Systems Interconnection Protocol (GOSIP)

International Organization for Standardization (ISO)

International Telecommunications Union (ITU)

ITU-T

layer

multiplexing

network architecture

Open Systems
   Interconnection (OSI)
   reference model

protocol stack

service generality

survivability

Systems Network
   Architecture (SNA)

Transmission Control
   Protocol/Internet
   Protocol (TCP/IP)

V. standards

X. standards

X.25

## ■ OBJECTIVES

After you complete your study of this chapter, you should be able to:

- explain the difference between communications architectures and communications standards;
- explain the need for network architecture;
- explain the need for network standards;
- identify a number of communications standards-making organizations;
- describe the seven layers of the ISO's OSI model architecture;
- describe the five-layer TCP/IP architecture;
- describe the architecture of the Internet; and
- discuss the advantages and disadvantages of layered architectures.

## 3-1  INTRODUCTION

This chapter examines network architectures and standards. The first network architectures, developed in the 1970s, tie many of the individual pieces of telecommunications into a unified whole. Standards in the communications industry are much older and have been developed by many national and international organizations. We will first look at the definitions of architectures and standards, the differences among them, and the need to have both. We will then look at some specific standards and architectures in more detail and examine their advantages and disadvantages.

## 3-2  DEFINITION OF ARCHITECTURES AND STANDARDS

architecture

In general terms, an **architecture** is a plan or direction that is oriented toward the needs of the user. It describes *what* will be built but does not tell *how*. A traditional architect must consult with the eventual occupants of a home to ensure that the new design will match the family's lifestyle or special requirements. If a family is musical, the house might have a music room that has additional soundproofing material and is used for practicing or teaching.

There might also be special cabinets to store music or to hold a collection of CDs, and a good audio system for listening to music. If a wheelchair-bound person will occupy the house, it will need to have ramps, extra wide doors, and perhaps lower counter tops in the kitchen and grab bars in the bathrooms. In the same way, a network architect must be aware of the needs of communications users in order to design a network to meet their needs. A network used for voice will be different from one used primarily for data. A data network used mainly to send e-mail messages will have different characteristics than one used in real time to track a rocket launch.

network architecture

A **network architecture** is a set of principles used as the basis for the design and implementation of a communications network. It provides a set of generic concepts that describe networks in a technology-independent way. It includes the organization of functions that must be performed by the network and the description of data formats and procedures. An architecture may or may not conform to standards. The architecture does not specify how the network will be implemented. Because most architectures (plans) are made for the long term, the architect must consider today's requirements and must ensure that the architecture is flexible enough to handle new capabilities that will arise in the future. This is particularly challenging in a field such as communications, where technology is advancing rapidly, and visions become reality in only a few years.

communications
standards

**Communications standards** are the rules that are established to ensure compatibility among similar communications products and services. Communications standards are the flesh on the architectural skeleton. They specify how a particular communications product, service, or interface will operate.

In the 1960s and 1970s, with the success of early data communications systems and with the reduction of communication costs because of improving technology, it was relatively easy to justify new online applications. However, because there had been neither an overall plan or architecture for the first networks and data communications applications, nor a vision for the future, the early networks were not flexible enough to support new requirements. As a result, separate networks were built for each application. This meant that one location of a company might have had multiple communications lines running to it, each one attached to a different set of workstations. Lines and workstations could not be shared between applications or networks because the rules (protocols) for using the lines were different and because the communications software was often unique for each application. Rather than keeping the communication software isolated in separate modules, early systems often had the communication and application software intermingled. Each application contained specialized (nonstandard) communications programming designed to meet the specific needs of that application. Little consideration was given by designers to sharing programs, workstations, or networks with other applications. As each new application was justified, its designers and programmers started over. They made design decisions to meet what they perceived to be the unique requirements of their application, with little regard for what had been done before or what might follow. It is hard to believe that back then each application had its own lines and terminals, but it really did happen!

## 3-3   WHY HAVE NETWORK ARCHITECTURES?

As communications systems and networks evolved, it became obvious to network designers and users that there had to be a better way. It didn't make good business sense to start over continually and build new, unique communications networks for each new application. There was a growing recognition of the need for an overall plan or architecture to guide network and application developments. What gave rise to this realization?

First, network developers and users recognized that communications systems were becoming too complex. Because of the lack of an overall plan and the desire to optimize communications systems to particular applications, a proliferation of transmission techniques, programs, and communications services evolved. Most of them were incompatible with one another. It became difficult for a company to manage the diversity of hardware and software. Making changes to a network was difficult and risky because of the complexity. There was always the possibility that the subtle implications of a hardware or software change would not be fully realized, and ensuing problems would crash the system.

Second, users wanted to be isolated from the complexities of the network. Communication networks do change, often more quickly than envisioned when they were originally designed. New lines or terminals may be required, and there is always a strong incentive to add new applications quickly as they are justified and developed. Workstation users should be isolated from these changes. They should not have to worry about modifications to the network infrastructure. A network user should not see changes in the way the network reacts from day to day. On the one hand, consistency, from the user's perspective, is a virtue! On the other hand, the network designer must be able to make changes in the topology of the network, the services it provides, and other characteristics—without affecting the current users. As user requirements change, traffic volume increases or decreases, or new networking products come to the market, the designer should be free to incorporate them into the network.

Third, network users wanted to connect different types of devices to the network. Networks must be able to service different types of personal computers, routers, switches, and other equipment. Most companies need various types of interactive devices. For example, a bank's network requires standard PCs and ATM machines. Furthermore, it is desirable for an organization to be able to acquire these terminals from different vendors and to take advantage of new technology improvements as they become available.

Fourth, distributed processing and client-server processing became practical. With the rapid increase in the number of personal computers, the ability to spread the computer processing among many computers became a reality and was often desirable. However, these distributed computers did not exist in a vacuum. Communication among them was necessary in order for them to share common data.

Finally, it became apparent that communication networks needed to be managed. Network managers and users wanted an integrated set of tools with which to track the status of the network and make operating changes when necessary. Diagnostic and performance measurement capability can help ensure that the network is operating efficiently and is effectively delivering the service for which it is designed.

Clearly, to be most effective and to meet modern user requirements for network capabilities, a communications architecture supported by appropriate standards is required to mask the physical configuration and capabilities of the network from the logical requirements of the user. Discipline is required to get the full benefits of networking and distributed processing. The chaos of multiple terminals, on multiple lines, using multiple transmission rules can be avoided only if an overall plan (architecture) supported by appropriate standards is in place.

International
Organization for
Standardization (ISO)

Fortunately, several vendors and the **International Organization for Standardization (ISO)** (http://www.iso.ch/), a group made up of representatives from the standards organization in each member country, recognized the need for communications architecture and for standards to support it.

## 3-4   TWO VIEWPOINTS ABOUT STANDARDS

Before you study standards and architectures in more detail, it is important to recognize that there are two prominent viewpoints regarding communication standards among people who design and implement networks. Probably because it is much older, the communications industry recognized long before the computer industry that standards were required so that communications equipment from different vendors could work together. Communications vendors realized that their equipment would have to connect to the equipment of other vendors. Hence, they developed open communications standards, and all vendors were encouraged to follow them.

By way of contrast, computer manufacturers were slower to recognize the need for national or international standards, and for a number of years they developed their own proprietary standards in order to force customers to use just one brand of equipment. As computers began to be interconnected through networks, customers were forced to stay with one equipment brand of computing and communications equipment in order for interconnections to work properly. Before long, however, customers insisted that they should be allowed to buy equipment from whichever manufacturer provided the best solution to their business problems. They demanded that computer vendors provide ways to connect their equipment to that of other vendors. The only solution was standardization, and the result is that communication standards are now followed throughout both the computer and communications industries.

Consequently, there are two different views of networks, depending on a person's network background and training. People who have a strong networking background see the computer as a tool to enhance a network's capability. To them, a modem is viewed as a signal converter that happens to have a computer chip inside. These people tend to wait for the standards and follow them closely, and by doing so they are likely to end up with solutions that are good for the long term but that may be implemented much later than those developed by people who have strong computer backgrounds.

Those who have a strong computer background tend to focus on what can be done with software or specially designed circuit chips for computers. To them, every piece of modern communications hardware is a computer—a modem is simply a special purpose computer used to convert signals. These people often forge ahead of the standards-making process, which is inherently slow, to develop solutions to networking and computing problems quickly in a customized way that may or may not be in line with standards if and when they are developed. While neither viewpoint is wrong, it sometimes leads to differing philosophies about the way networks should be implemented.

If an individual comes from the communications industry, his or her view of networks and computers tends toward viewing the collection of circuits that make up the network as the primary entity and viewing the computer as a piece of hardware that adds certain capability to enhance the network's features and usability. On the other hand, if an individual's early training was more computer-oriented, there is a tendency to look at the computer from an application viewpoint and see the network as an accessory that can enhance

**FIGURE** 3-1 Two different views of the relative roles of networks and computers.

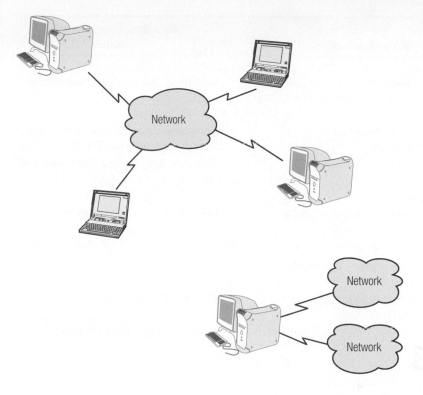

the reach of information gathering and distribution for whatever application is of interest, such as e-mail, data collection, reporting, or others. The former individual views the world as a network that has multiple computers attached; the latter individual views the computer at the center, with one or more circuits or networks attached. This difference in viewpoints is illustrated in Figure 3-1.

You may ask, "So what?" The point is simply that you must be aware of the differing viewpoints, both of which are legitimate and have their place. You may have leanings one way or the other, depending on your own background, but it is important that you recognize that the other viewpoint exists. Normally, everyone is after the same result: a good, reliable network. The differences arise only when deciding how to achieve that goal.

## 3-5 STANDARDS AND STANDARDS-MAKING ORGANIZATIONS

Before discussing specific architectures, we will look at the communication standards-making organizations and some of the standards they have developed.

A number of organizations in the world establish communication standards. Figure 3-2 lists many of these organizations and the main focuses of their standardization efforts. Because of the recognized need for common international standards, there has been a great deal of cooperation among these organizations, especially in recent years.

Normally, the way that a standard is developed is through consensus of the members of the standards organization. Remember that, depending on the standards organization, the members may be representatives from companies, other organizations, countries, or all three, so adoption of a new standard is usually very far reaching and a major event. While all of the

| Standards organization | Main telecommunications focus | Internet web address |
|---|---|---|
| **International:** | | |
| International Telecommunications Union—Telecommunications Standardization Section (ITU-T) | Telephone and data communications | http://www.itu.ch |
| International Organization for Standardization (ISO) | Communications standards of all types (coordinates with the ITU-T) | http://www.iso.ch |
| Internet Engineering Task Force (IETF) | Sets standards for how the Internet will operate | http://www.ietf.org |
| **United States:** | | |
| American National Standards Institute (ANSI) | Data communications in general | http://www.ansi.org |
| Electrical Industries Association (EIA) | Interfaces, connectors, media, facsimile | http://www.eia.org |
| Institute of Electrical and Electronics Engineers (IEEE) | 802 LAN standards | http://www.ieee.org |
| National Institute of Standards and Technology (NIST) | Standards of all types | http://www.nist.gov |
| National Exchange Carriers Association (NECA) | North American WAN standards | http://www.neca.org |
| **User/Vendor Forums:** (These groups feed information to the standards-setting bodies listed above.) | | |
| European Computer Manufacturers Association (ECMA) | Computer and data communication standards (feeds input to ISO) | http://www.ecma.ch |
| European Telecommunications Standards Institute (ETSI) | European telecommunications standards | http://www.etsi.org |
| Corporation for Open Systems (COS) | Promotes the use of equipment that meets ISO standards | |

**FIGURE 3-2**  Some of the organizations involved in setting telecommunications standards or in passing input to the standards-setting bodies.

standards organizations vary in their exact standards-making methods, they all have specific processes in place. Basically, a proposal for a standard is usually made by one of the members and is then assigned to a committee for study, investigation, and discussion. Eventually, the committee produces the first draft of the proposed standard, which is circulated to other members of the standards organization. Their comments, both technical and nontechnical, are invited. With that feedback, the standards committee revises the initial draft, sometimes in the form of another draft and sometimes as the final proposal. There may be several iterations of the process, but the final draft standard is eventually submitted to the members for voting. If the vote is positive, the standard becomes official and is adopted by the members. The process is not fast; it usually takes months or years for a standard to be adopted.

In many cases, the U.S. developed standards for domestic use ahead of the rest of the world. Later, when a similar need for a standard arose in other countries, they either used the U.S. standard or improved on it, and those improvements became the international standard. Sometimes, the process was reversed, and the U.S. standard was more advanced. It is not unusual to find one communication standard in use in the U.S. and another being used in the rest of the world. For example, the international telex system, an early form of electronic mail that is now used mainly in a few third-world countries, was an international standard. Telex uses the 5-bit Baudot code for individual characters, and the transmission speed is sixty-six words per minute. In the U.S., AT&T developed a similar system, the TWX, which used an 8-bit code and was transmitted at 100 words per minute. The two systems operated according to different sets of standards and were incompatible. It took the advent of computers to allow messages from one system to be translated and then exchanged with the other system.

In the telephone industry, there were similar problems. Early standards were mostly electrical in nature, such as the voltage required to cause the telephone bell to ring, the electrical resistance or impedance of telephone lines, and the drop in signal strength permitted over various distances. Not all countries adopted the same standards, which was fine as long as telephone calls stayed within national boundaries. When calls were made overseas, converters were inserted in the telephone lines to adjust to the standards of the called country so that the call could be completed. International standards organizations eventually got the differences ironed out and countries modified their telephone systems to meet the international standards. It is now easy to make calls virtually anywhere in the world.

It's one thing to make a connection, however, and still another to communicate. In the voice world, it is possible to make a connection between a telephone in the U.S. and a telephone in Japan, but if the American speaks only English and the Japanese person speaks only Japanese, communication will not occur.

In the data communications world, standards evolution has occurred more slowly, but many international standards are now in place. The situation is more complicated than with voice communication. In addition to electrical standards, protocols (the rules of data communications) must be standardized so that computers and other equipment on a network can understand each other. The issue is further complicated by the fact that the computer industry has been unregulated, and each company originally set its own communication standards. IBM's data transmission techniques were different from and incompatible with Hewlett-Packard's, which were different from those of other computer manufacturers. Although they all followed the same electrical standards for connecting their equipment, that was not enough to allow the equipment to communicate. Fortunately, the incompatibility problem has largely been resolved.

## 3-6  THE V. AND X. STANDARDS

International
Telecommunications
Union (ITU)

ITU-T

V. standards

X. standards

The **International Telecommunications Union (ITU)** (http://www.itu.int/home), an organization based in Geneva, Switzerland, is the most important telecommunications standards-setting body in the world. The ITU's work is broader than the aspects of telecommunications that you are studying in this book. The acronym **ITU-T** (http://www.itu.int/ITU-T/), which refers to the ITU's Telecommunication Standardization Sector, is used to distinguish the telecommunications work from its work related to radio and television activities. The ITU-T has created two sets of standards for the electrical connection of terminals to communications networks.

**V. standards** define the connection of digital equipment (terminals and computers) to the PSTN's analog lines. (Analog lines will be discussed in Chapter 9, but for now suffice it to say that they are the type of lines you use when you make a normal telephone call from home.) In other words, they deal with data transmission over the PSTN. **X. standards** define the connection of digital equipment to digital lines. (Digital lines will also be discussed in Chapter 9.) The wording of the standards themselves is highly technical, and even a brief summary uses many terms that you may not be familiar with yet. The names and meanings of the standards will become clearer as you get into the technical details of data communications in subsequent chapters.

*These are only electrical specifications for connection. Many other standards and rules are required before communication occurs.* Attention is drawn to the V. (pronounced V-dot) and X. (pronounced X-dot) standards here, because they will be referred to frequently throughout the book.

## 3-7  ADVANTAGES AND DISADVANTAGES OF STANDARDS

So far, the discussion of standards has probably left you with the impression that standards are entirely beneficial and yield positive results. While the advantages almost certainly outweigh the disadvantages, there are two sides of the coin.

On the positive side, standards allow products from multiple vendors to be connected to one another and to communicate. We all appreciate this flexibility when we are purchasing equipment. Furthermore, having one or only a few sets of standards allows vendors to concentrate on fewer products and sell more items of the same type, which leads to the economies of scale. For example, standard interfaces exist that allow us to purchase telephones from a wide variety of manufacturers and connect them to the jacks in our homes. We can choose among many styles, colors, and features. Imagine what it would be like if we could buy telephones from only one source. In another realm, standards exist for the connection of printers to personal computers. We can purchase our computer from Dell, Gateway, IBM, or even build one ourselves, and be assured that the printer we purchase from Hewlett Packard, Canon, or Epson will work with the computer.

On the negative side, the standards-setting process is slow. Writing and getting standards approved frequently takes years. In our fast-paced world, technology has sometimes moved on to better approaches before standards for the old approach get written. Standards can be obsolete before they are approved. Once they are approved, standards tend to freeze the technology, discouraging innovation, because the new way is "nonstandard." Furthermore, because there are a number of national and international standards-making organizations, there are sometimes multiple conflicting standards for the same thing. Fortunately, most of these organizations have been cooperating with each other in recent years, and the number of instances of multiple standards is getting smaller.

For internal use, it is very important that an organization adopt standards, not necessarily the international or national ones, but a set of standard products, protocols, and technologies for use within the organization. Without these internal standards—if every department can implement whatever communications technologies it wants—keeping the internal communication systems and network working together can become difficult or impossible. Furthermore, without standards, when changes are needed or when new capabilities must be added to meet changing business conditions, the effort and cost are multiplied several times. Communications management must insist on this set of internal standards.

## 3-8   COMMUNICATIONS ARCHITECTURES

**Open Systems Interconnection (OSI) reference model**

Working with the ITU-T, the ISO developed a communications architecture called the **Open Systems Interconnection (OSI) reference model** in 1978. When the model was developed, it was expected that it would be followed by the definition of a set of standards that would allow products to be developed to implement the model. However, the standards development process took so long that the OSI model never came into widespread use. It is, however, the standard reference point by which data communications networks are described and measured.

Understanding the OSI model will provide you with a framework into which you will be able to fit the technical information that is presented in subsequent chapters. With such a framework, you will be able to quickly apply the information on communications hardware, networks, and protocols, and make sense of what you learn.

## 3-9   THE ISO'S OSI REFERENCE MODEL

### Objectives

The architects of the OSI model had, as their primary objective, to provide a basis for interconnecting dissimilar systems for the purpose of information exchange. For their purposes, a system is viewed as consisting of one or more computers, associated software, and terminals capable of performing information processing. The intent was to define communications rules that, if followed, would allow otherwise incompatible systems, made by different manufacturers, to communicate with each other.

**layer**

The OSI model and most network architectures developed since use a layered approach in which each **layer** represents a component of the total process of communicating. A diagram of the seven OSI layers is shown in Figure 3-3. In reality, each end of the communication, for example a PC communicating with a server, must have an implementation of the seven-layer architecture, because each layer in one end system communicates with its peer layer on the other end system (shown in Figure 3-4). Layer 7 in the PC talks to layer 7 in the server, layer 6 talks to layer 6, and so forth.

Another way to visualize the layers is to picture an onion, and think of it as the way a computer system is layered. At the heart is the computer hard-

**FIGURE 3-3**   Layers of the ISO's OSI reference model.

| Layers | |
|---|---|
| 7 | Application/User |
| 6 | Presentation |
| 5 | Session |
| 4 | Transport |
| 3 | Network |
| 2 | Data Link |
| 1 | Physical Link |

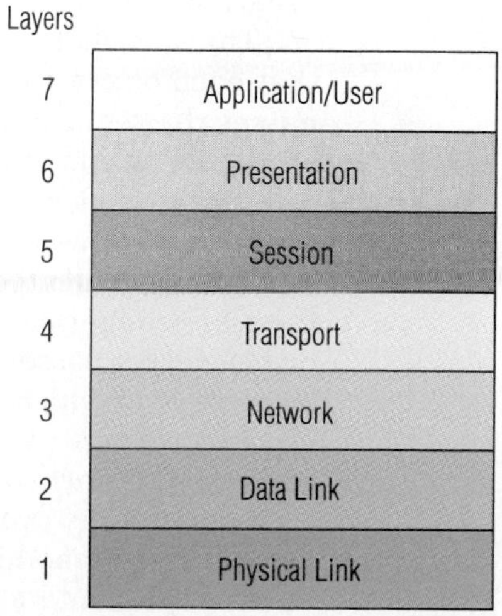

**FIGURE 3-4** The layers of the OSI model on each node communicate with each other.

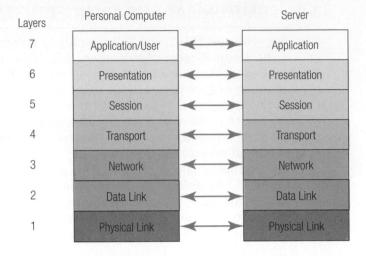

**FIGURE 3-5** Actual communication passes down through the layers on the sending node and then up through the layers on the receiving node.

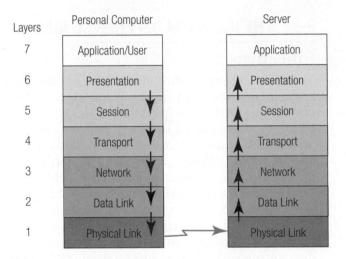

ware. The hardware is surrounded by operating system software. Outside the operating system is other specialized software, perhaps a communications program. Finally, the outermost layer is the application program. The application program is shielded from the complexities of the hardware by the operating system and other software. At the same time, the operating system and other specialized software provide useful services to the application program.

The way that the interaction between the layers actually takes place is that each one requests services from the layer below it. The next lower layer passes the request to the layer below it, as shown in Figure 3-5. When layer 6 on the PC wants to communicate with layer 6 on the server, it passes the request or data down to layer 5 on the PC. Layer 5 passes the request to layer 4, and so on down to level 1. The lowest layer, layer 1, is the only layer that actually communicates across the communication line to the other node, and so it passes the request or data across the line to layer 1 on the server. Layer 1 on the server passes the request up to layer 2, layer 2 to layer 3, and so on, up to layer 6; at which point the communication is complete, assuming that no errors have occurred along the way. Layer 6 on the server may respond to the request and start a communication back to layer 6 on the personal computer by reversing the process just described.

In the OSI model, the first three layers are well defined. Standards have been written and agreed upon, and these layers have become more widely

**X.25**

**Government Open Systems Interconnection Protocol (GOSIP)**

known and understood than the other layers. The combination of these three layers is the **X.25** standard for data transmission used in packet switching networks. X.25 will be discussed in detail in Chapter 13.

The United States government has defined a subset of the OSI model that vendors must support if they want to sell network services or equipment to the government. This subset is called the **Government Open Systems Interconnection Protocol (GOSIP)**. GOSIP is neither a new architecture nor a new standard. It is a more precise specification of what parts of the OSI model the government will use. Included in the GOSIP specifications are the standard LAN architectures and the internet protocol portion of TCP/IP (discussed in a later section). GOSIP is important because the government represents a huge customer for communications suppliers and, in order to do business with that customer, they need to ensure that their products fall within the GOSIP specification.

## The Seven Layers of the OSI Model

We will now look at the functions and responsibilities of the seven layers of the OSI model. We'll begin with layer 7, the application layer, because that is the layer you will be able to relate to most easily. Look again at Figure 3-5. The data or request from layer 7 is passed down through the layers, which are mostly implemented in software, to layer 1. Layer 1 is where the actual physical transmission across the communications line takes place. At the receiving end, the data passes upward through the layers, and each layer performs its specific role. This continues until it reaches layer 7, the application at the receiving end. In this way, a person or program at one end of a communication line communicates with a person or program at the other end.

**encapsulation**

In most cases, the layers at the sending end surround the original data or request with control characters or other information for message routing or error checking, a process called **encapsulation**. At the receiving end, these control characters are checked and removed by the corresponding layer. The analogy most frequently used is one of putting a letter (the original data) in an envelope and writing some addressing characters on the envelope. In big companies, the envelope is sent to the mailroom, where employees may insert the original envelope in a larger envelope that only contains mail (data) for a certain location. Other addressing characters are written on the second envelope. The large envelope is then sent through the postal system to the destination location (most of the time, we don't care exactly how it gets from one location to another). At the receiving location, the large envelope goes to the mailroom, where the address characters are checked to be sure the mail has arrived at the right place. Then the envelope is opened, the smaller envelopes inside are removed, and the large envelope is discarded. The addresses on the small envelopes inside are checked, and each envelope is sent to its addressee. Each recipient checks to be sure the mail has been delivered correctly, then opens the small envelope, discards it, and looks at the original message that was sent. In data communications, there are other steps, such as breaking the message into smaller pieces before it is sent. Extensive checking for errors also occurs during the transmission, but the process is very similar to the mail analogy.

The OSI model divides the tasks of moving information between networked computers into seven smaller task groups that correspond to each layer in the architecture. Each layer is reasonably self-contained. The tasks assigned to it can be implemented independently. This enables the implementation of one layer to be updated without affecting the other layers. Now we'll examine the layers in more detail.

**THE APPLICATION LAYER (LAYER 7)** The application layer is "where" the user works at a terminal with computer software. The application layer determines what data are to be sent through the network. At the receiving end, it processes data that is received. This is the start and end point for data transmission. Some examples are: 1) a user (the application layer at the sending end) sending a message to an application program in a server (the application layer at the receiving end) and 2) an application program in one PC transferring a file to an application program in another PC.

**THE PRESENTATION LAYER (LAYER 6)** The presentation layer handles the changes of data formats that are required between the user or application program and the network. For example, an application may be programmed to send data to terminals that have a certain screen size. If a user has a terminal that has a different screen size, the presentation layer is responsible for converting the data format to fit. This layer also handles the compression/expansion and encryption/decryption of data, if required.

**THE SESSION LAYER (LAYER 5)** The session layer is responsible for establishing the communications rules between specific machines or applications. If users of an application use video display terminals that have differing screen sizes, for example, the session layer ensures that the application program knows what size blocks of data it must send to each type of terminal to fill the screen. The session layer is also responsible for: 1) pacing the rate of transmission so data are not sent faster than the receiver can handle it, and 2) certain accounting functions.

**THE TRANSPORT LAYER (LAYER 4)** The transport layer identifies the actual address of the terminal or computer that will receive the message. The transport layer knows the final destination but does not know the detailed route that will actually be used when the message is sent. In large networks and internetworks, there may be more than one route between locations on the network, and parts of a message may be sent through the network on different routes. This layer also calculates a check sum for the entire message, which is recalculated by layer 4 at the receiving end and compared. Using this technique, layer 4 can determine if the entire message was received correctly. This layer also plays a role when messages are sent on an internet between two separate, but interconnected, networks.

**THE NETWORK LAYER (LAYER 3)** The network layer is responsible for routing a message all the way through the network, from the transmitter to the receiver. It normally maintains a routing table that tells how to send messages to different destinations. The network layer may break the message into pieces, called transmission units, and route each transmission unit through the network on a different route. When this happens, the network layer at the receiving end is responsible for assembling the entire message before delivering it to the transport layer.

**THE DATA LINK LAYER (LAYER 2)** The data link layer is responsible for establishing a link between two points on a network and ensuring that data are successfully transferred between the two points. The data link layer may further divide the data into smaller units for transmission. This layer must include means for detecting transmission errors and correcting errors when they do occur, so it adds header and trailer information to each unit of data it sends to assist with the error control. If several terminals are sharing a circuit, this layer also determines which terminal can use the circuit at any moment.

**THE PHYSICAL LINK LAYER (LAYER 1)** The physical link layer specifies the electrical characteristics between the communications line and the terminal or computer system. It specifies how the signals are carried on the wires, what types of connectors are used, their physical shape, and which pins in the connectors are used for which signals. It tells which way data are allowed to flow on the line. This is the only layer at which actual bits pass, and it is also the only layer that is implemented strictly in hardware. All other layers are implemented in software or a combination of hardware and software. All messages must be passed down to layer 1 to be communicated across the medium to layer 1 in the receiving system. However, layer 1 only knows about a stream of bits—it does not know about the meaning of the bits or how they might be grouped.

In the following chapters, references will be made to the layers of the OSI model, to help you fit that information into the OSI framework. *What you need to remember, however, is that as actual communications systems have been implemented over the years, most have not followed the OSI model exactly. Communication tasks have been grouped into layers differently, but the same tasks need to be done regardless of how they are grouped.* The OSI model remains a good basic reference, but you may be more aware of the TCP/IP architecture because, as the foundation for data transmission on the Internet, it has been so widely implemented.

## 3-10 TCP/IP ARCHITECTURE

When the OSI architecture model was developed in 1978, many felt that it would replace proprietary, vendor-specific architectures such as IBM's System Network Architecture (SNA), which was in widespread use in the late 1970s and 1980s. Also in the 1970s, the U.S. Department of Defense (DoD) wanted to interconnect computers and networks it had acquired from different vendors. Because progress on standards for the OSI model was slow, the government's Advanced Research Project Agency (ARPA) developed a set of protocols called the **Transmission Control Protocol/Internet Protocol (TCP/IP)** to enable the interconnection. The original use of these protocols was in the ARPANET, a network that connected various government and university research laboratories, which eventually evolved into the Internet. The DoD eventually mandated that TCP/IP be used in all of its computers and networks, which automatically provided a huge base of equipment with the protocols installed, and a large market opportunity for software and equipment vendors. Because of this and the slowness of OSI standards development on which products could be based, TCP/IP became the architecture and protocol on which the Internet was based. The rapid expansion of Internet usage in all facets of society has subsequently made TCP/IP the *de facto* standard architecture for a growing majority of public and private networks.

Although there is no official TCP/IP model like the OSI model, the TCP/IP structure is also a layered organization with four or five layers. Some people combine the bottom two layers, so as you look at other material such as the

**Transmission Control Protocol/Internet Protocol (TCP/IP)**

description provided by Cisco at http://www.cisco.com/univercd/cc/td/doc/product/iaabu/centri4/user/scf4ap1.htm or IBM at http://www.ibm.com/ (and then do a search for "tcp/ip tutorial"), you may find four-layer models that call the bottom layer either the link layer or the network access layer. For our purposes, we will use the five-layer model with the layers called:

- the application layer
- the transport layer
- the internet layer
- the network interface layer
- the physical layer

These layers can be roughly aligned with the OSI layers, as shown in Figure 3-6. The application layer contains the programming required to support the user's application. Different modules are required for each application, such as e-mail or file transfer.

The transport layer is responsible for providing reliable communication, including error checking procedures. This work is handled by the TCP protocol, which will be discussed in detail in Chapter 14.

In many situations today, the two parties of a communication, which could be two users at PCs or a user at a terminal communicating with a server at a remote location, are on different networks. The internet layer uses the IP protocol to route data between networks, when necessary.

The network interface layer handles the connection between the end system and the network to which it is attached. The specific implementation depends on the type of network because there are different standards and requirements for LANs and WANs. These will be discussed in more detail in Chapters 10 and 13.

The physical layer specifies the physical (connectors, plugs, adapters) and electrical (voltages and currents) interface between the data communication device and the network, and this varies by the type of network.

The details of TCP/IP will be discussed in greater detail in Chapter 14. TCP/IP can reliably send data across disparate networks with excellent assurance that transmission errors will be detected and the data will arrive at the receiving end error free. Its universality has propelled it into widespread use throughout the world.

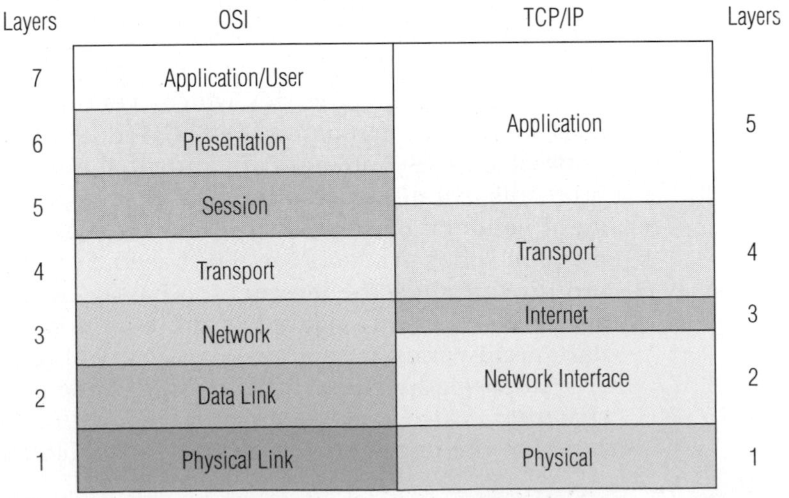

**FIGURE 3-6** A comparison of the layers of the OSI reference model and the implementation of TCP/IP.

| Layers | OSI | TCP/IP | Layers |
|---|---|---|---|
| 7 | Application/User | Application | 5 |
| 6 | Presentation | Application | 5 |
| 5 | Session | | |
| 4 | Transport | Transport | 4 |
| 3 | Network | Internet | 3 |
| 2 | Data Link | Network Interface | 2 |
| 1 | Physical Link | Physical | 1 |

## 3-11 THE ARCHITECTURE OF THE INTERNET

The Internet has become such an important part of the networking scene that it is worthwhile to spend a little time looking at the architectural principles under which it was developed and now operates. The architects of the Internet were very pragmatic people who were more interested in getting a network implemented than in spending a large amount of time documenting every detail before implementation began. As a result, informal architectural ideas guided the design of the Internet and its protocols, and the architecture was not formalized until later.

The primary initial requirements that the architects addressed were:

- multiplexing
- survivability
- service generality
- diverse network technologies

**multiplexing**

**survivability**

**service generality**

**diverse network technologies**

The basic issue of **multiplexing** was to determine how to send multiple independent data streams on one physical communications line, allowing the line to be shared by several people or computers. Because the original work was funded by the military, **survivability** meant that messages would be able to get through the network, no matter what happened—including war. This requirement also implied that the network could dynamically adapt itself when outages occurred. Ironically, survivability also turned out to be a high priority for many businesses that use networks. **Service generality** meant that the network should be usable for multiple purposes and should support the widest possible set of applications. Applications vary in their requirements for communications service. Some require the highest possible speed, while others require the highest possible reliability. Many require something between these two extremes, and the implication for the Internet was that all of these service requirements needed to be handled. **Diverse network technologies** meant that the Internet needed to be able to accommodate the technologies of several predecessor networks—such as the ARPANET, satellite-based networks, LANs, and others—and allow all of them to be interconnected into a single entity. In effect, the Internet had to be a network of networks.

To achieve these requirements, the architects focused on a few principles. They concerned themselves with:

- what entities, such as nodes and circuits, are named and how
- the ways in which naming and addressing network nodes, and the routing of messages, interrelate
- the ways in which functions are modularized
- how resources are allocated
- the ways in which security boundaries are drawn and enforced

These items require more knowledge of networking than you have now. However, by the time you finish studying the material presented in Chapters 4 through 15, you will understand them quite well.

The architects were successful, and implementation of the Internet architecture moved so quickly that on January 1, 1983, the Internet was born when the ARPANET switched to the TCP/IP protocol and TCP/IP became a military standard. At that time, the Internet didn't look like it does today because it was mainly a collection of military, university, and scientific networks—with relatively primitive tools, by today's standards, for accessing and displaying data. It wasn't until 1991 that the World Wide Web was introduced and the Internet began to move from being an academic and military tool to being the tool it now is for research, sales, and communication.

There is much more to tell about internetworking and the Internet, and you will find that coverage in Chapters 14 through 16.

## 3-12  MANUFACTURERS' ARCHITECTURES

Even before ISO began its work to develop the OSI model, the major computer manufacturers of the day, IBM, Digital Equipment Corporation, Burroughs, and Univac, were working to develop communication architectures on which to base their communications products. In the early 1970s, many of these companies found themselves supporting a wide variety of communications terminals and protocols. They felt that they could not afford to continue the proliferation of incompatible devices and software, so they began working to develop architectures on which to standardize future products. In 1974, IBM announced a proprietary architecture that all its future products would follow: the **Systems Network Architecture (SNA),** which became hugely successful and widely used. Soon after, Digital Equipment Corporation announced Digital Network Architecture (DNA) and Burroughs announced Burroughs Network Architecture (BNA).

**Systems Network Architecture (SNA)**

However, the original focus of the manufacturers was different from that of the ISO. The manufacturers were primarily interested in developing proprietary architectures on which to base their future products. They were not interested in having an open architecture that would allow easy interconnectivity of each other's equipment. The computer vendors' motivations were more along the lines of controlling their customers and locking them into one vendor's (their own) products. In most cases, their work was very practical, oriented toward solving immediate problems, and driven by economics. The ISO's primary goal, and later that of the DoD was to connect dissimilar networks and systems. The OSI and TCP/IP architectures were intended to establish a way to connect the proprietary architectures of the manufacturers and to connect the public packet switching networks, which were emerging at the time.

Because of customer and market pressures, the situation changed and computer manufacturers became fully supportive of the international communications standards. All of them now include TCP/IP software as a part of their communications product offerings. TCP/IP is supported on PCs servers, and even older mainframe computers, allowing all of them to be a part of TCP/IP networks and to connect to the Internet.

## 3-13  A CAVEAT ABOUT ARCHITECTURES AND STANDARDS

It is important to understand that writing the specifications for communications architectures and the related standards is difficult work. Precision is needed but is difficult to achieve. The architecture and standards are always subject to interpretation. Therefore, it is entirely possible for companies to implement networks that they believe correspond to a set of standards but then have the resulting networks unable to communicate with each other. True compatibility in communications must be confirmed by extensive testing of the components thought to be compatible.

In the last ten or fifteen years, the rise to prominence of the TCP/IP architecture has reduced this concern because it is so widely used and understood. The attitude of networking equipment and computer manufacturers has changed to fully embrace interoperability among their equipment, so any new hardware or software that is not fully TCP/IP compatible either gets rapidly corrected or does not survive in the marketplace.

## 3-14   ADVANTAGES AND DISADVANTAGES OF LAYERED ARCHITECTURES

Layering forces the modularization of function, which simplifies the structure of all of the aspects of data communications. The thinking process that is required to define the layers in the first place forces clarification of ideas and resolution of troublesome areas. The output of the layering definition process is standards that help ensure that implementers who subscribe to the standards will produce products that can communicate with one another. The combination of the layering and the standards helps technicians understand the entire communications process.

To the extent that the interfaces between layers are clearly defined, the implementation of one layer can be changed or modified without affecting the other layers, as long as the interface specifications are met. This means, for example, that certain layers of the architecture could be implemented in software or hardware, depending on the cost and the requirements for performance and flexibility. Furthermore, different implementations can be substituted relatively transparently. For example, by changing OSI layer 3, one type of communications line could be substituted for another type of line, and the rest of the communications process would not have to be changed or even be aware of it. This provides a way to meet changing communications requirements in a modular and nondisruptive manner.

On the other hand, the implementation of a layered architecture requires reasonably sophisticated software and hardware at each end of the connection. When layered architectures were originally conceived in the 1970s, in the days before PCs, providing powerful enough hardware at the terminal end of a connection was a problem because the necessary logic could not be put into each terminal or workstation at a reasonable cost. Initial implementations of layered architectures were frequently between mainframe computers that had dedicated front-end communications processors to provide the processing for the layers of the architecture. When terminals needed to communicate, the intelligence was most often provided by a hardware device, called a cluster control unit, that could support multiple terminals. In this way, the cost was shared.

Today, this obstacle is mitigated because any modern PC has enough power to perform the processing necessary to support a layered architecture such as TCP/IP. Frequently, part of the processing (especially at the lower layers) is implemented in hardware in the form of circuit cards that plug into a slot in a PC and provide an interface to the network, whereas the higher layers are implemented in software called a **protocol stack.**

protocol stack

For virtually all applications, the advantages of using a layered architecture greatly outweigh the disadvantages. Most modern communications applications are implemented by using a layered approach.

## ◼ SUMMARY

The data communications and networking world is dominated by network architectures and standards that enable products from different vendors to communicate with each other. The ISO's OSI model provides a generalized framework that is used as a basis for comparing network capabilities, but the TCP/IP model has become the practical model that is implemented on a vast majority of products and networks, including the Internet. Each layer of a communications model has a well-defined function to perform. The layers in one node of a network communicate with peer layers in other nodes by passing data or requests for service down through the layers at the transmitting end, across the network at the layer 1 level, and then up through the layers at the receiving end of the transmission. Each layer encapsulates the data and requests at the sending end, and the encapsulation is removed, layer by layer, at the receiving end.

Standards provide the rules by which an architecture can be implemented. The standards-making process is slow, however, and some vendors jump ahead of the process with proprietary products to solve specific communications problems long before the standards are in place. The V. and X. communications standards are the most generally used standards for networks, and have largely replaced proprietary and national standards that dominated in the past.

While there are some disadvantages, architectures and standards generally provide far more benefits and they truly enable the interoperability of equipment from multiple vendors and the interconnection of networks.

Chapter 4 provides an introduction to network protocols, the rules by which networks operate. The material is very important because networks use many protocols, and you will study them throughout the book.

## ◼ REVIEW QUESTIONS

3-1. Explain what network architecture is.

3-2. Why were communications architectures not in place when the first data communications systems were implemented?

3-3. What is the ISO's OSI reference model? Why is it important for you to learn about it?

3-4. What role does the OSI model perform for other communications architectures?

3-5. What are the functions of the OSI physical link, data link, and network layers?

3-6. Explain the difference between *connection* and *communication*.

3-7. When data are received, the OSI presentation layer is responsible for _____ before presenting it to the application layer for further processing.

3-8. Explain why TCP/IP has become the *de facto* standard for a growing majority of data communications networks.

3-9. What is the function of the internet layer in a TCP/IP-based network?

3-10. List the four initial requirements confronting the Internet's architects.

3-11. Discuss the relative advantages and disadvantages of layered architectures.

3-12. What are the advantages and disadvantages of standards and the standards-making process?

**TRUE OR FALSE**

3-1. A network architecture provides enough detail from which to implement a network.

3-2. Most architectures are designed for the needs of today and are only for short-term use.

3-3. Communications standards define *what* needs to be done but not *how* to do it.

3-4. All communications standards are developed by one organization, the ISO.

3-5. Computer vendors have been known to develop proprietary architectures to try to lock their customers into the vendor's product line.

3-6. Most business communication networks are quite static after their initial implementation, so companies can ignore architectures and standards.

3-7. Communication networks need to be managed.

3-8. To be most effective and to meet user requirements for modern network capabilities, a communications architecture supported by appropriate standards is required to mask the physical configuration and capabilities of the network from the logical requirements of the user.

3-9. Because of the recognized need for common international standards, there is a great deal of cooperation among communications standards-making organizations.

3-10. If you can connect with another person or machine, you can automatically communicate.

3-11. Data communication standards are more complicated than voice communication standards.

3-12. V. standards define the connection of voice equipment.

3-13. The standards-setting process is slow.

3-14. Writing standards is difficult work.

3-15. The OSI model has seven layers.

3-16. The OSI model was defined after the ISO people got it backwards the first time.

3-17. A layer in the OSI model represents a component of the total process of communicating.

3-18. The TCP/IP model has seven layers.

3-19. TCP/IP has become the *de facto* standard model for internets.

3-20. The official TCP/IP model is now maintained by the ISO.

3-21. The way that the interaction between the layers actually takes place is that each one requests services from the layer below it.

3-22. Layer 1 is the only layer that actually communicates across the transmission line to the other node.

3-23. The Internet is a network of networks.

3-24. The application layer (layer 7) in the OSI model is "where" the user works at a terminal with computer software.

3-25. In the OSI model, the data link layer is responsible for establishing a link between two points on a network and ensuring that data are successfully transferred between the two points.

3-26. The architects of the Internet insisted on documenting every detail of Internet operation before implementation work began.

3-27. As actual communications systems have been implemented over the years, most have not strictly followed the OSI model.

**MULTIPLE CHOICE**

3-1. The first three layers of the OSI model have been standardized, and together are called the _____.

a. V. standard

b. X.25 standard for data transmission

c. consolidated transmission standard

d. Consolidated Transmission Protocol

3-2. When data or a request from one layer is passed down to another layer, the data are surrounded by control characters or other information. This process is called _____.

a. enclosure

b. surrountion

c. encapsulation

d. isolation

e. permutation

3-3. A protocol stack is _____.

a. the way in which data are passed between layers in the TCP/IP architecture

b. a set of rules for making a club sandwich

c. never implemented because of the lack of OSI standards

d. software that implements the layers of a protocol

3-4. The Internet _____.

a. is implemented using the TCP/IP protocol

b. has the attribute of service generality

c. allows for diverse network technologies

d. allows multiplexing

e. all of the above

3-5. Manufacturers that developed network architectures _____.

a. were primarily interested in interconnecting their equipment with that of other manufacturers

b. were primarily interested in developing proprietary architectures on which to base their future products

c. were not successful with implementing their architectures

d. were primarily interested in the research value of the architecture rather than solving immediate problems

3-6. GOSIP is _____.

a. an international standard for communication

b. a subset of the OSI model that vendors must support if they want to sell network services or equipment to the U.S. government

c. a protocol for people who meet to talk and drink after work

d. All of the above.

e. None of the above.

3-7. A network architecture is _____.

    a. the plan for the Internet's evolution

    b. a description of how a network is to be implemented

    c. a set of design principles used as the basis for the design and implementation of a communications network

    d. None of the above.

3-8. The ITU-T has created two sets of standards for the electrical connection of terminals to communications networks. They are called _____.

    a. the ISO and OSI standards

    b. the TCP and IP standards

    c. the PC and modem standards

    d. the V. and X. standards

    e. the IEEE and EIA standards

3-9. The primary initial requirement that the architects of the Internet addressed were _____.

    a. multiplexing

    b. survivability

    c. service generality

    d. diverse network technologies

    e. All of the above.

3-10. IBM's SNA _____.

    a. was never widely implemented

    b. was a data link protocol

    c. was a proprietary architecture

    d. was an advanced mainframe computer for its time

    e. was a working version of the OSI model

## ■ PROBLEMS AND PROJECTS

3-1. The text used the mail system as an analogy for the seven layers of the OSI model. Make up another analogy to test your understanding of layered architecture concepts.

3-2. List some areas in your life where there are multiple conflicting standards.

3-3. Talk to the network administrator at your school or where you work and ask them whether their network uses TCP/IP protocols. See if they are familiar with the OSI model and whether knowledge of the model has made any difference in the way they implemented their network.

3-4. Do some research on the Internet and find examples of companies or authors who show the TCP/IP model as either four levels or five levels. Identify the differences in the approaches of those who favor one model over the other.

3-5. Do some research on the Internet and gather more information about the X.25 standard. Identify how the standard is being used in modern networks.

## STANDARDIZING THE NETWORK ARCHITECTURE

HTH Metals, Inc., a large supplier of a variety of metals for industrial uses headquartered in a suburb of Boston, found that it was facing a huge unnecessary expenditure for its corporate data communication network. The company, which has regional sales offices near major cities throughout the U.S., had a network that grew gradually, without an overall master plan, from the days when the company first bought computers in the mid-1960s. Originally, the network had been used only for exchanging messages between headquarters and the sales offices, but as the use of computers grew, so did the uses of the network. The crisis came to a head when George Simpson was brought in from outside the company to be the new director of Computing and Communications. After a preliminary study, Simpson told the company's executive committee that he thought HTH was spending at least a million dollars per year in "excessive communications charges," as he termed it, because the computer-based data network was obsolete. Naturally, the executive committee asked Simpson to recommend how the money could be saved.

Simpson gathered his IT staff together and presented the problem to them. He asked for their support and recommendations for a new network that would not only save the company money but would also provide better service to the employees of HTH as well. In a subsequent discussion, he learned that instead of a single data network, the company really had three networks, all based on the proprietary architectures of the vendors from which the company bought computers. The business network was based on IBM's SNA architecture. The technical network was based on Digital Equipment's DECNET and supported several older computers and their users. There was an entirely separate set of PCs in the company that were used exclusively for accessing the Internet, and that used the TCP/IP architecture and protocol. Essentially, each of these networks had its own set of terminals. In many departments, there were several different sets of terminals; for example, one set to access the business network and another set to access the Internet. Some departments even had three distinct sets of terminals.

The IT people said that it would be possible to consolidate the networks using the TCP/IP architecture and protocols, because both IBM and Digital Equipment (which had since been consolidated into Compaq Computer, which was then bought by HP) now fully supported TCP/IP as one of their standards. In fact, the technical staff was eager to begin making the change.

**QUESTIONS**

1. What are the likely changes that would have to be made to HTH's networks to consolidate their using TCP/IP?

2. What are the sources of cost savings that would be realized? What investments in new equipment might have to be made?

3. What benefits, other than cost savings, might HTH expect to gain from consolidating the networks?

4. Prepare an outline of a proposal for change that Mr. Simpson could take to the executive committee to get the funding to change the networks.

# INTRODUCTION TO PROTOCOLS

## ■ OUTLINE

## ■ KEY TERMS

application layer

check character

connectionless

connection-oriented

encapsulation

flow control

fragmentation

multiplexing

network access layer

protocol

protocol data unit (PDU)

reassembly

segmentation

transport layer

User Datagram Protocol (UDP)

virtual circuit

# ■ OBJECTIVES

After you complete your study of this chapter, you should be able to:

- explain why protocols are needed in communication systems;
- describe the basic layers of a protocol;
- describe the primary functions of the application, transport, and network access layers;
- describe the basic functions that any protocol must perform; and
- differentiate between connection-oriented and connectionless protocols.

## 4-1  INTRODUCTION

In Chapter 1, you were introduced to the concept of protocols, which are the rules of communication. In this chapter, you will learn more about the need for protocols, the principles that apply across protocol families, and the way protocols generally work. Subsequent chapters will look at data link control protocols in detail and at specific protocols that are commonly used in LANs, WANs, and internetworks. Because it is one of the most widely used protocols today, TCP/IP will frequently be used as an example in the material that follows.

## 4-2  A DEFINITION AND THE NEED FOR PROTOCOLS

protocol

In general terms, a **protocol** is a set of rules or guidelines that governs the interactions among people, between people and machines, or among machines. Protocols exist for all types of social situations. When two people meet on the street and one says, "Hello, Jim," to which Jim responds, "Hello, Bill, how are you?" they are following a simple protocol. This basic exchange gets the conversation going, and after the initial words of greeting, the two men launch into any of a variety of topics. Similarly, when the telephone rings, the convention or protocol is that the answering party says "Hello" and the calling party identifies herself by saying something like, "Hello, Mary? This is Jane Smith." How the conversation proceeds from that point depends upon the relationship between the individuals and the reason for the communication.

The important concept to understand is that all communicating parties understand and follow a common set of rules for the way the communication will begin, proceed, and end. When people communicate, the rules may be slightly different across languages and cultures, but the same basic set of rules applies. Therefore we can, for example, make telephone calls to people in other countries. Assuming we have a common language, we can initiate and carry on a conversation with relative ease.

Now suppose that, instead of people, we have two computers that need to communicate. The protocols for computer communication must be much more precisely defined than the protocols people use, because computers don't have the human ability to interpret subtleties in the tone of a voice or to apply judgment when unusual or unexpected events occur. In the previous chapter, two models for the overall architecture of computer-to-computer communications—the OSI model and the TCP/IP model—were introduced. Both of these models use a layered approach as a way of breaking the entire task of communicating into manageable pieces. You learned that in both architectures, messages are passed down through the layers on the transmitting end, sent across the communication media from layer 1 to layer 1 on the receiving end, and then up through the layers. In fact, this flow describes a protocol at a very high level. Higher-level layers at each end of the communication don't communicate across the medium to each other. They pass their message down to layer 1 and up from layer 1. To actually make this happen there are many more details that must be defined, but the overall flow gives the framework on which to define and build the detailed implementation.

Most protocols are primarily implemented in software. To make it easy to develop, test, and modify the protocol software, it is generally developed layer by layer. As was mentioned in Chapter 3, this collection of software modules is normally called a protocol stack.

## 4-3    A SIMPLE PROTOCOL SUITE

**application layer**

**transport layer**

**network access layer**

Let's look now at a hypothetical protocol suite that has some similarity to TCP/IP. This imaginary protocol has three layers: the **application layer,** the **transport layer,** and the **network access layer.** Figure 4-1 shows a simple case of two computers, each running an e-mail application and communicating through a network. The protocol is implemented with three software modules on each computer, one for the *e-mail application,* one for a collection of activities called *communication services,* and one for *network access.* The two e-mail modules on the two computers exchange e-mail messages and commands, but they don't deal directly with all the intricacies of the communication process. Rather, they rely on the communication services and network access modules to handle those details. The communication services modules are responsible for ensuring that the e-mail commands and data are exchanged reliably between systems. The network access module is responsible for interfacing with the network that interconnects the computers. Because many different types of networks could be used, it makes sense to keep

**FIGURE 4-1**   The layers of a hypothetical protocol.

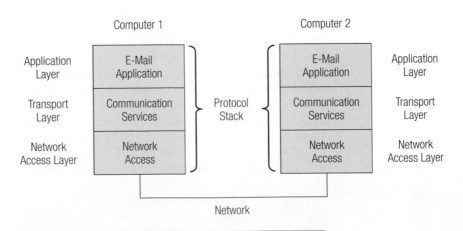

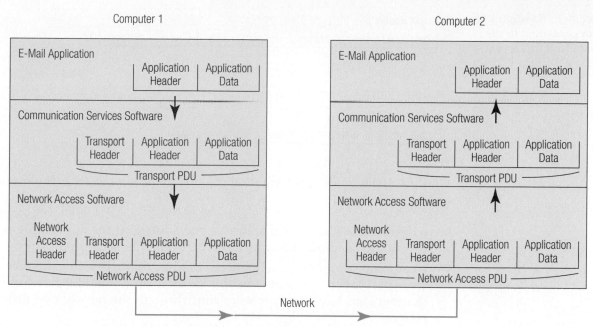

**FIGURE 4-2**  The flow of data and commands in the protocol stack.

the network access software separate from the other two modules, so that if the network is changed, only the network access software modules have to be replaced.

The way in which these modules work together is illustrated in Figure 4-2. If Computer 1 is sending an e-mail to Computer 2, its e-mail application passes its data, an e-mail message, and a header down to the communication services module, which views everything it receives from the e-mail application as data. The communication services module, in turn, adds its own header and passes the combined package down to the network access module. The network access module adds its header, then sends the entire package of data across the network to the receiving computer, Computer 2, where the network access module on that machine strips off the header related to network access, acts on the information in the header, and passes the remaining data package to the communication services module. The communication services module strips off the transport header intended for it, acts on it, and then passes the e-mail data and header up to the e-mail application for processing.

## 4-4  PROTOCOL LAYERS

To elaborate on the process: When the e-mail application in the application layer passes a block of data to the communication services software modules running in the transport layer, in the simplest case, the communication services software adds a transport header that contains transport control protocol information to the front of the data. In a more complicated case, the communication services module may break the e-mail data block into smaller pieces and add a transport header to each piece. This combination of data from the next higher layer and the header from the current layer is known as a **protocol data unit (PDU).**

protocol data unit (PDU)

The header in each transport PDU contains control information to be used by the peer transport layer in the receiving computer. As shown in

FIGURE 4-3 Examples of the data contained in the headers of the transport and network access PDUs.

**Transport Header**

| Destination application address | Sequence number | Error detection code |

**Network Access Header**

| Destination computer address | Special services requests |

Figure 4-3, the types of information that are typically stored in the transport header include:

- a destination application address—the address of the application on the destination computer to which the PDU must be delivered

- a sequence number—a sequential number that will allow the receiving transport layer to resequence the PDUs if they should arrive out of order, perhaps because they were sent through the network on different routes

- an error detection code—a code that is typically the result of a mathematical function performed on the contents of the remainder of the PDU that has been calculated by the sending transport layer. The receiving communications services module performs the same calculation and compares the results with the incoming code. A discrepancy indicates that there has been some error in transmission.

Finally, the transport layer hands the transport PDU to the network access layer for transmission to the destination computer. The network access software must also add control information, so it appends a network access header to the data it receives from the transport layer, creating a network access PDU. Examples of the data in the network access header include:

- a destination computer address—the address of the computer on the network to which the data are to be delivered

- special service requests—requests for special handling, such as giving it a high priority.

This technique, whereby each layer treats everything passed to it from above as data, is called encapsulation.

At the receiving end, the reverse process is carried out. The network access layer interprets the first bits of the network access PDU as the header, and acts on any commands it finds there. It may, for example, verify that the PDU has arrived at the correct computer by comparing the destination address in the PDU with its own address. It then strips the network access header and passes the remaining data—the transport PDU—up to the transport layer. The transport layer interprets the first bits of the data block as the transport header and performs any necessary calculations with the error detection code. Assuming the error check is okay, it looks at the application address to determine which application, of potentially many applications, running on the receiving computer is to receive this PDU. It removes the transport header and passes the remaining data up to the application level for processing.

## 4-5   PROTOCOL FUNCTIONS

We have looked at the basic capabilities of a simple protocol that typify the way protocols work. We can generalize on this model because there are a few basic functions that are at the heart of all protocols. Not all protocols have all these functions, and there are also many cases where the same function is performed at different levels in the protocol. The nine basic functions are as follows:

- encapsulation
- fragmentation and reassembly
- connection control
- ordered delivery
- flow control
- error control
- addressing
- multiplexing
- transmission services

### Encapsulation

**encapsulation**

As previously discussed, PDUs at lower layers in the protocol stack contain not only data from the layer above, but also a header that contains control information. The process of adding control information to data from a higher layer is called **encapsulation**. The control information falls into three general categories:

- address—address of the sender and/or receiver
- error detection code—typically a mathematically calculated check sum
- protocol control—additional information that is unique to the specific protocol

### Fragmentation and Reassembly

**fragmentation**

**segmentation**

Various levels of the protocol may require that the PDU be broken into smaller blocks. This process is called either **fragmentation** or **segmentation.** Fragmentation is sometimes required, because some networks will only accept blocks of data smaller than a certain size, for example, less than 4,096 bytes. Sometimes it is advantageous to break a long PDU to provide more equitable sharing of the transmission facilities with shorter delay. On the other hand, each time the PDU is fragmented, a header must be added to each fragment, which results in more overhead and less efficient transmission.

**reassembly**

The reverse of fragmentation is **reassembly**. At the receiving end, the fragmented data must be reassembled into messages corresponding to those that were originally sent by the application level.

Let's look at an example. In Figure 4-4, a 7,000-byte message, including an application header (AH1), is sent from the application layer in Computer 1 to the transport layer. The transport layer knows that this particular protocol does not allow PDUs of greater than 4,000 characters to be sent through the network, so it splits the message into fragment 1 of 4,000 characters and fragment 2 of 3,000 characters. It then adds transport headers, TH1 and TH2, to the beginning of each fragment.

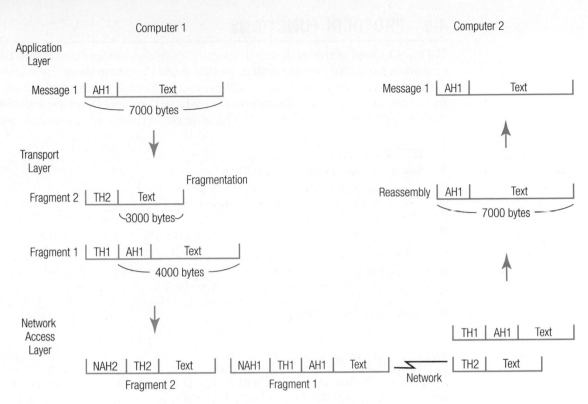

**FIGURE 4-4**   An illustration of message fragmentation and reassembly.

The fragments are sent to the network access layer, which adds its headers (NAH1 and NAH2) to the beginning of each fragment and sends them through the network. In this simple example, there is only one path through the network, so the fragments are sent in the sequence in which they were created, which simplifies the reassembly at the receiving end.

In the network access layer of Computer 2, the network access headers are removed (after error checking has occurred) and the two fragments are passed to the transport layer. The transport layer removes the transport headers and reassembles the fragments into the original 7,000-byte message before passing it to the application layer. When the application layer receives the message, it is in the form in which it was sent by Computer 1.

## Connection Control

From the standpoint of connection, there are two basic types of data transmission, **connection-oriented** and **connectionless.** Both will be explored

**connection-oriented**

**connectionless**

more fully later in this chapter. However, what you need to understand now is that when connection-oriented data transfer is used, a connection between the transmitting and receiving end must be established at the beginning of the transmission. This connection establishment phase entails the exchange of control information between the nodes and an agreement about the parameters of the transmission. Once the connection is established and the parameters are agreed to, the data transfer phase can begin. At the end of the transmission, there must be an orderly termination of the connection.

A key attribute of connection-oriented data transfer is that the transmitting node assigns sequence numbers to each PDU of the message before it is sent. These sequence numbers are stored in the header of the PDU. The receiving end checks the sequence number of each PDU it receives.

## Ordered Delivery

In many networks, and especially when several networks (an internetwork) are involved in the data transmission, it is possible for PDUs to arrive at the receiving end out of sequence. This can occur when the PDUs take different paths through the network (or networks). In connection-oriented protocols, the PDU order must be maintained. If each PDU is given a unique number, and numbers are assigned sequentially, the receiving end can reorder the PDUs it receives on the basis of the sequence number. The sequence number thus serves multiple purposes, because it allows the receiving end to check to ensure that all PDUs have been received, that they are in the right sequence, and that none has been duplicated.

## Flow Control

flow control

**Flow control** is the term used to describe the ability of the receiving end of the transmission to limit the amount or rate of data sent by the transmitting end. The most common way that flow control is achieved is for each PDU, or group of PDUs, to be acknowledged before further transmission can take place. If no acknowledgement is received, the transmitting end of the connection stops sending data. Acknowledgement is achieved by having the receiving node send an acknowledgement message back through the network to the message-transmitting node. This acknowledgement message is typically very short and simply identifies the sequence number of the next PDU that is expected. It may also contain a code that says, "stop sending PDUs for a while until I tell you to start again." In this way, the message receiving node can limit the traffic being sent to it.

## Error Control

There are two parts to error control: error detection and error correction. At the network access layer, error detection is usually accomplished by having the sender insert an error detecting code, sometimes called a **check character**, into the data before it is sent. The software applies a predetermined mathematical function to the bits in the message to calculate the check character. At the receiving end, the same calculation is performed. If the mathematical result is the same, the PDU is deemed to have arrived correctly. If the receiver's calculation yields a different result, an error is presumed to have occurred.

check character

When a transmission error is detected, there are several ways it can be corrected, but the most common is retransmission. The receiving end discards the PDU that contains the error and does not send an acknowledgement message to the sender. When the sender does not receive an acknowledgement for the PDU after a predetermined period of time, the PDU is retransmitted. Additional information about this type of error detection and correction will be presented in Chapter 9.

Error control must be performed at several layers of the protocol to ensure that a message from an application is correctly sent from the transmitting end to the receiving end. For example, while the network access layer may determine that all individual PDUs have been received correctly, one or more PDUs could have been lost—especially when PDUs take different paths through the network. As you have seen, sequence numbering is a technique that detects this type of error. The transport layer at the receiving end can then request retransmission of the missing PDU. On the other hand, if duplicate PDUs are somehow received, it is a simple matter for the receiving transport layer to discard one of the copies once the error is detected.

In summary, the network access layer is responsible for determining that each PDU is received correctly, while the transport layer is responsible for ensuring that all PDUs are received and that none are duplicated.

## Addressing

PDU headers often contain both the sender's and receiver's addresses, but different layers of the protocol contain different addresses that indicate where the message is to be delivered. In the e-mail application, for example, the application layer header probably contains the name of the PC of the individual who is to receive the e-mail. At the transport layer, the transport header contains the address of the e-mail application on the receiving computer that is to process the data. At the network access layer, the address in the network access header is that of the computer to which the message is to be sent. At all levels, there is an issue of ensuring that addresses are unique and not ambiguous.

## Multiplexing

*multiplexing*

Frequently, a computer uses a single communications circuit to establish multiple connections to different applications. For example, when a user dials into an Internet service provider (ISP), he or she may establish one connection for e-mail, another for browsing the Internet, and a third for transferring a file or program to a friend. **Multiplexing** provides the capability for all of these activities to occur simultaneously on a single circuit. It is closely related to the way the network and applications are addressed.

## Transmission Services

A protocol may provide additional services to a transmission, such as the ability to prioritize messages, the ability to specify the throughput that is required, or the ability to provide some type of security to restrict access to the messages. These services are optional and may or may not be provided. If they are provided, they may or may not be used by a particular communication connection.

The three-level architecture and resultant protocols described above are a simplified hypothetical model designed to help you learn the concepts of protocols. As the number of layers is expanded, as in the TCP/IP or OSI models, the principles remain the same and only the functions of each layer change.

## 4-6 TRANSPORT PROTOCOLS

The major function and responsibility of the transport layer and its protocols are to assure that messages are exchanged reliably between the sender and the receiver. The two primary elements that constitute reliability are 1) the arrival of all of the data at the destination and 2) their presentation to the receiving application in the same order the sending application intended. The transport protocols provide an end-to-end data transfer service while shielding the application layer from the details of the communication process, including the type of network that lies between the sender and the receiver.

Transport protocols provide the two types of services mentioned previously, connection-oriented and connectionless. In another context, a good example of a connection-oriented service is what you get when you make a telephone call. There is some setup timc at the beginning of the call, while a route is established through the network between the caller and receiver. This route, called a **virtual circuit**, remains in place for the duration of the call, and as soon as it is established, the telephone call can proceed.

**virtual circuit**

TCP and other protocols provide connection-oriented interfaces to data applications. Connection-oriented service can be accomplished on dial-up lines, as in the telephone call example, or on full-time circuits. The application must request that the protocol establish a connection before data can be sent; at the end of the communication, the application must ask the protocol to close the connection. This is similar to what happens when you hang up the telephone at the end of a phone call.

Connectionless transport allows an application to send a message to any destination, at any time. In the TCP/IP protocol suite, connectionless transport is provided by the **User Datagram Protocol (UDP)**. Each message the application sends must be accompanied by a destination address. However, an application could send a series of messages, each destined for a different receiver. The advantage of a connectionless protocol is that there is no setup time at the beginning of the communication. However, as you will see when you study TCP in more detail in Chapter 14, there is no guarantee that a message sent using a connectionless protocol will be delivered, and there are other overheads.

**User Datagram Protocol (UDP)**

## 4-7 DATA LINK PROTOCOLS

The major functions of the data link protocols in the network access layer are to deal with the specifics of the particular type of circuit that is used between the sender and receiver and to ensure that each PDU arrives accurately and with no errors. Data link protocols are *not* concerned with whether PDUs arrive in sequence or whether some are duplicated or missing. As you have seen, that is the responsibility of the transport layer protocols.

Data link protocols must have rules to address the following situations that occur during data communications.

- communication startup—There must be rules to specify the way the communication will be initiated: whether there is automatic startup, whether any station can initiate the communication, or whether only a station designated as the "master" station may initiate communication.

- character identification—There must be a way for the receiving terminal to separate the string of bits coming down the communication line into characters. Furthermore, there must be ways of distinguishing between control characters, which are a part of the protocol, and the data characters, which convey the message being communicated.

- PDU identification—The receiving terminal equipment must know how to separate the characters on the communication line into PDUs. In other words, it must know how to identify when one PDU ends and another begins.

- error control—Line control rules must exist to specify the way in which the receiving terminal signals the sending terminal whether it has received data correctly, how and under what circumstances the line will be turned around so that data can be sent in the other direction, and whether the receiving terminal is able to accept data as fast as the sending terminal is transmitting it. The protocol must contain rules that specify what happens when an error is detected, what to do if communication suddenly and inexplicably ceases, and the way communication is reestablished after it is broken.

- termination—Rules must exist for ending communications under both normal and abnormal circumstances.

In normal conversation between two people, there are rules or conventions that specify the way all situations are handled. Because of the human intelligence at both ends of the communication, the rules need not be precisely specified and there is room for considerable variation. Whether we end a telephone conversation by saying "Goodbye, Mr. Smith," "See ya later," or "Bye," matters little. The intention is clear and understood by both parties. Data communications between two pieces of equipment, however, must be more precise and rigid in the application of the rules because even the growing intelligence of workstations and computers is still no match for the human intellect. We will look at the specifics of several data link protocols in Chapter 7.

## ■ SUMMARY

This chapter has introduced information that gives you foundation information about the various protocols that are required to make a communication system work. There are layers of protocols in most networks, each corresponding to a layer in the network architecture, and each protocol has a specific function to perform. For each layer, many alternative protocols have been developed. In some cases, the network designer can select which protocol to use. In other cases, the communications company that offers a particular communication service selects the protocol. However, the TCP/IP protocol suite has become very widely used in many networks, so you will run into it frequently in networks you study.

All of the protocol concepts will be expanded in subsequent chapters when you study the way data communication takes place and how specific types of networks actually operate.

Chapter 5 provides information about the way data are coded for transmission through a network. You will examine various coding systems and look at the ways data can be compressed for more efficient transmission.

## ■ REVIEW QUESTIONS

4-1. Define the term *protocol*.

4-2. Why are protocols required in a communication system?

4-3. List the nine functions of a protocol.

4-4. Explain the term *encapsulation*.

4-5. Define the terms *segmentation* and *reassembly*.

4-6. Describe the major responsibilities of the transport layer.

4-7. How does the network access layer normally do error detection?

4-8. What is the role of the application layer?

4-9. Explain the concept of connection-oriented communication and give an example (other than the one listed in the text).

4-10. Why must protocols for computer-to-computer communication be more precisely defined than the protocols humans use when we communicate?

4-11. Explain the term *protocol stack*.

4-12. Why are messages sometimes fragmented, and what additional overhead does fragmenting entail?

4-13. Why is flow control required in a computer-based communication system?

4-14. Identify several types of addresses that are required as a message moves from the application layer on one computer to the application layer on another.

4-15. What is the main responsibility of the data link protocol in the network access layer?

4-16. In general terms, explain the concept of an error detecting code and the way it is calculated.

4-17. Why are sequence numbers sometimes assigned to PDUs before they are transmitted through the network?

4-18. How is it possible for PDUs to be rearranged during a transmission and to arrive out of order at the receiving location?

## TRUE OR FALSE

4-1. The combination of data from the next higher layer and the header from the current layer is called a *protocol data unit*.

4-2. An error detection code corrects all of the errors it finds during a transmission.

4-3. Error detection codes are typically the result of a mathematical function performed on the contents of a PDU.

4-4. A telephone call is an example of a connectionless service.

4-5. Connectionless protocols do not guarantee the delivery of a message.

4-6. Data link protocols are not concerned with whether PDUs arrive in sequence.

4-7. Flow control is a term used to describe the ability of the transmitting end of a transmission to limit the rate of data being sent.

4-8. Fragmentation is the error control process that is employed when only part of a message is delivered to the receiver.

4-9. Most protocols are primarily implemented in software.

4-10. When a PDU is broken into smaller blocks for transmission, the process is called PDU breakup.

4-11. When a PDU is fragmented, a header must be added to each fragment, which results in more overhead.

4-12. A key attribute of connection-oriented data transfer is that the transmitting node assigns sequence numbers to each PDU in the message before it is sent.

4-13. The sequence numbers in PDUs serve multiple purposes because they allow the receiving end to check to ensure that all PDUs have been received, that they are in the right sequence, and that none have been duplicated.

4-14. There are two parts to error control: error detection and error correction.

4-15. The network access layer is responsible for determining that each PDU is received correctly.

4-16. The transport layer is responsible for ensuring that all PDUs are received and that none are duplicated.

4-17. In the TCP/IP protocol suite, connectionless transport is provided by the UDP.

4-18. The advantage of a connection-oriented protocol is that there is no setup time at the beginning of the communication.

4-19. A major function of data link protocols is to ensure that each PDU arrives accurately and with no errors.

## MULTIPLE CHOICE

4-1. The process of reassembling a message that has been fragmented is called _____.

   a. segmentation

   b. reconstitution

   c. reassembly

   d. togetherness

   e. construction

4-2. A _____ is calculated mathematically as a part of the error checking process when transmitting and receiving a message.

   a. Greek character

   b. control character

   c. real character

   d. check character

   e. shady character

4-3. The _____ field in a header tells the destination of a message or PDU.

   a. destination

   b. block check

   c. ZIP code

   d. address

   e. None of the above.

4-4. When a computer uses a single communication circuit to establish multiple connections to different applications, it is called _____.

   a. multiplexing

   b. multiprogramming

   c. multitasking

    d. multicasting

    e. multicircuitousness

4-5. A set of rules or guidelines that govern interactions among people, between people and machines, and among machines is called _____.

    a. rules of the road

    b. conventions

    c. protocols

    d. customs

    e. etiquette

4-6. Protocols are most often implemented in _____.

    a. software

    b. layers

    c. hardware

    d. a and b

    e. a, b, and c

4-7. The header in a PDU contains information to be used by _____.

    a. the user at the receiving end

    b. the workstation at the transmitting end

    c. the owner of the communications circuit

    d. the peer layer in the receiving computer

4-8. From the standpoint of connection, there are two basic types of data transmission. They are _____.

    a. unconnected

    b. connectionless

    c. connection-oriented

    d. connected

    e. a and d

    f. b and c

    g. a and c

4-9. The term used to describe the ability of the receiving end of the transmission to limit the amount or rate of data sent by the transmitting end is _____.

    a. valve management

    b. check damming

    c. flow control

    d. transmit control

    e. flow limiting

4-10. PDU headers often contain _____.

    a. check control characters

    b. a bit to indicate whether the header is encrypted

    c. both the sender's and receiver's addresses

    d. end of message codes

    e. None of the above.

4-11. Frequently, a computer uses a single communication circuit to establish multiple connections to different applications. The term used to describe this is _____.

a. circuit sharing

b. multitasking

c. multithreading

d. multiprogramming

e. multiplexing

## ■ PROBLEMS AND PROJECTS

4-1. At your school or company, find out what protocols are used in the networks. Ask about the history of the networks and whether other protocols were used five or ten years ago.

4-2. Working alone or in a team, identify several uses for connectionless protocols. Consider that one of the attributes is that they do not guarantee that messages will be delivered.

## TELECOMMUNICATIONS WITHOUT LAYERS

In the early days of telecommunications, there were no architectural layers or elaborate protocols, and yet communications by wire still occurred. Can you imagine Samuel F. B. Morse trying to send "What hath God wrought?" but having to consult a reference card so that he could encapsulate the text with special protocol characters, and—oh yes—having an assistant with a calculator—no wait, they hadn't been invented yet—to calculate check characters? However, as was pointed out in the text, we routinely and without thinking use protocols in normal conversation. They don't seem to get in the way of communication. In fact, we often feel uncomfortable when a person we are speaking to, such as someone from another country or culture, uses an unfamiliar protocol.

Some things have changed which require modern electronic communications to have elaborate protocols and which make a layered architecture seem appropriate and simpler than not having one. What is different today compared to the early days of the telegraph?

**C A S E  S T U D Y**

# PART TWO

# DATA
# COMMUNICATIONS

■ OUTLINE

Part Two explains the principles of data communications that are the foundations of all networks. Building on the background and vocabulary from Part One, you will learn the underlying technical details of communications systems. These include the way data are coded for transmission, the characteristics of analog and digital signals, data link protocols for networks, and media for communication circuits.

Chapter 5 explains how data is coded and several data coding systems. You'll also see how data can be compressed for more efficient transmission.

Chapter 6 looks at the characteristics of analog and digital signals and the ways in which they are transmitted over analog and digital circuits. You'll study modems and the way they interface to PCs and communication circuits, and you will learn several ways to classify transmissions.

Chapter 7 digs into the details of data link protocols. You will examine the formats and data flows of several real world protocols, such as PPP, BSC, and HDLC. You will also study flow control and learn why such a mechanism is important.

Chapter 8 explores the various media used for communication circuits. You will learn to identify the characteristics of regular copper wire, coaxial cable, optical fiber, and other options such as satellite and wireless technology. You will consider the trade-offs between the various media, including the advantages and disadvantages of each.

Chapter 9 examines communication circuits. Circuits are classified several ways, and you will learn the differences and similarities among them. You will explore the subject of multiplexing and will learn several multiplexing techniques. You will also study circuit error conditions and ways to prevent, detect, and correct errors when they do occur.

# DATA CODING

## ■ OUTLINE

## ■ KEY TERMS

adaptive Huffman coding

algorithm

alphanumeric characters

American Standard
   Code for Information
   Interchange (ASCII)

binary

binary digit

bit

character assignment

character compression

character stripping

code

code efficiency

code point

compaction

control characters

data compression

device control characters

double byte character
   set (DBCS)

escape (ESC) character

escape mechanism

Extended ASCII

Extended Binary Coded
   Decimal Interchange
   Code (EBCDIC)

format effector characters

graphic characters

Huffman coding

information bits

International Telegraph
   Alphabet 5

MNP5

noninformation bits

parity bit

run length encoding

transmission control
   characters

Unicode

## ■ OBJECTIVES

After you complete your study of this chapter, you should be able to:

- define a code;
- describe several different coding systems;
- describe the three different types of characters that compose a code's character set;
- discuss typical functions of control characters;
- describe a method of error checking that can be built into a code; and
- explain the purpose of compression and describe ways in which data are compressed.

## 5-1  INTRODUCTION

In this chapter, you will study the ways in which data are coded when they are transmitted on a network or stored in computers. The characteristics of several coding systems commonly used in data communications and computing will be examined in detail. You'll also learn about data compression, which significantly improves the efficiency of communication by reducing the number of bits (characters) transmitted.

## 5-2  TWO-STATE PHENOMENA

In introductory computer or telecommunications classes, you learned that many natural and physical phenomena are two-state systems. A baseball runner is either out or safe; a basketball shot is either made or missed; a light bulb is either on or off; an electrical circuit is either opened or closed, resulting in a flow of electrical current or no flow. No ifs, ands, or maybes—it is one way or the other.

binary

binary digit

bit

We call two-state systems **binary** systems. They can be represented using the binary digits 1 and 0. The term **binary digit** is abbreviated as **bit.** When bits are used to represent the settings, we say that information has been coded. A 1 bit means the runner is safe, a 0 bit means the runner is out; a 1 could mean the basket is good or the current is flowing. Note that the 0 bit represents information just as the 1 bit does. It does not mean "nothing."

## 5-3  DATA CODING

code

A **code** is a predetermined set of symbols that have specific meanings. The key point is that the meanings are predefined; the sender and receiver must agree on the set of symbols and their meanings if the receiver is to make sense out of information that is sent. For data communications purposes,

FIGURE 5-1   Morse code.

| | | | |
|---|---|---|---|
| A | . — | T | — |
| B | — . . . | U | . . — |
| C | — . — . | V | . . . — |
| D | — . . | W | . — — |
| E | . | X | — . . — |
| F | . . — . | Y | — . — — |
| G | — — . | Z | — — . . |
| H | . . . . | , | — — . . — — |
| I | . . | . | . — . — . — |
| J | . — — — | 1 | . — — — — |
| K | — . — | 2 | . . — — — |
| L | . — . . | 3 | . . . — — |
| M | — — | 4 | . . . . — |
| N | — . | 5 | . . . . . |
| O | — — — | 6 | — . . . . |
| P | . — — . | 7 | — — . . . |
| Q | — — . — | 8 | — — — . . |
| R | . — . | 9 | — — — — . |
| S | . . . | 0 | — — — — — |

codes are assigned to individual characters. Characters are letters of the alphabet, digits, punctuation marks, and other special symbols such as the dollar sign, asterisk, or equals sign.

A character code you may have heard of is Morse code, which is shown in Figure 5-1. It is considered a binary code because it uses two code elements: a dot and a dash. Not all the characters, however, have the same number of code elements. The code was structured so that the most frequently used characters require the fewest number of dots and dashes. In contrast, less frequently used characters are represented by more dots and dashes. The pitch (frequency) and volume (amplitude) of the coded signal are irrelevant to the meaning of the Morse code.

Morse code was designed for human use, which is why the spaces between the letters and words have meaning. Translation of letters and numbers into Morse code is normally done by a human operator while sending a message. Decoding from Morse code into letters and numbers is done by the operator at the receiving end. With humans at both ends of the transmission, and spaces left between individual letters, it is not important that all characters consist of the same number of dots and dashes or that the dots and dashes be perfectly formed and exactly consistent. Officially, the ratio of length between a dot and a dash is 1:3. However, when a human is sending Morse code, using a telegraph key, this ratio varies widely. Expert telegraph operators can tell who is sending code just by listening to the way the characters sound.

## 5-4   MACHINE CODES

When two machines, such as a computer and a workstation, are used for communication, some of the attributes of Morse code (or any code systems designed for human use) are not desirable. It is much easier for a machine to process a code if the code has the following attributes:

- it is a true binary or two-state code
- all of the characters have the same number of bits
- all of the bits are perfectly formed
- all of the bits are of the same duration

A binary code works well for machines communicating by electrical means because the 0 bits and 1 bits can be represented by a current flow that is either on or off.

For transmission efficiency, it is ideal to have a coding system that uses a minimum number of bits to represent each character. How many bits are needed? With one bit we can have two states: 1 or 0. With two bits, there can be four combinations: 00, 01, 10, or 11. With three bits, there can be eight combinations: 000, 001, 010, 011, 100, 101, 110, or 111. Do you see a pattern? Each bit that is added doubles the number of combinations. If each combination of bits represents a character, then with three bits and eight combinations, eight characters can be represented. Mathematically, the number of unique combinations is expressed as $2^n$, where $n$ is the number of bits.

Figure 5-2 shows a table of the powers of 2. From it you can see that using 5 bits gives 32 combinations: and with 6 bits there are 64 possibilities. The number of possible combinations or characters in a coding system is called the **code points.**

**code points**

A code normally has unique groups of bits assigned to represent the various characters in a code. These unique sequences of bits are called **character assignment.** Different codes, even though they may have the same number of bits, use different character assignments. Character assignments must be made for three different types of characters: **alphanumeric characters, format effector characters,** and **control characters.** The alphanumeric characters are letters, numerals, or symbols such as punctuation marks and dollar signs. They are also referred to as **graphic characters** because they can be displayed on a workstation screen or printed on paper. Format effector characters control the positioning of information on a workstation screen or paper. Included in this group are tabs, backspaces, carriage returns, and line feeds. Control characters can be further divided into two subgroups: 1) **Device control characters** control hardware connected to a data processing or communications system. A device control character might instruct a printer to skip to the next sheet of paper, and another device control character might change the color on a display terminal. 2) **Transmission control characters** control the communications system and provide functions such as identifying the beginning and end of the transmission or acknowledging that data have been correctly received.

**character assignment**

**alphanumeric characters**

**format effector characters**

**control characters**

**graphic characters**

**device control characters**

**transmission control characters**

FIGURE 5-2   Powers of 2.

$$2^0 = 1$$
$$2^1 = 2$$
$$2^2 = 4$$
$$2^3 = 8$$
$$2^4 = 16$$
$$2^5 = 32$$
$$2^6 = 64$$
$$2^7 = 128$$
$$2^8 = 256$$
$$2^9 = 512$$
$$2^{10} = 1024$$

FIGURE 5-3   If *even* parity is being used, the parity bit is set to 1 when necessary to make the total number of 1 bits in the character an *even* number. If *odd* parity is used, the parity bit is set to 1 when necessary to make the total number of 1 bits an *odd* number.

| | |
|---|---|
| The 7-bit ASCII code for the letter *R* (no parity bit) | 1010010 |
| • with even parity | 10100101 |
| • with odd parity | 10100100 |
| The 7-bit ASCII code for the letter *S* (no parity bit) | 1010011 |
| • with even parity | 10100110 |
| • with odd parity | 10100111 |

## 5-5   PARITY CHECKING

parity bit

Many coding systems include an extra bit called a **parity bit.** The parity bit is added to each character representation for checking purposes, so that the total number of 1 bits in the characters will be an even (or in some cases, odd) number. From Figure 5-3, it can be seen that if the representation for the character *R* is 1010010, the number of 1 bits is 3, which is an odd number. If an even parity system is being used, which is the most common, a parity bit of 1 would be added to the character so that its complete representation would be 10100101. If odd parity were being used, a 0 bit would be added. Assume the representation for the letter *S* is 1010011. The number of 1 bits is already an even number. With an even parity system, a parity bit of zero would be added, giving a complete representation of 10100110. With odd parity, a 1 bit would be added.

When a character representation is transmitted on a communication line, and the transmitter and receiver have agreed to use even parity, the receiving machine checks to see whether there is an even number of 1 bits. If not, the machine detects the error and takes appropriate action. The types of actions that may be taken are discussed in detail in Chapter 9.

## 5-6   ESCAPE MECHANISMS

escape mechanism

escape (ESC) character

Most coding systems include a technique called an **escape mechanism.** One of the code points, often called the **escape (ESC) character,** is assigned a special meaning. When the ESC character is sent as part of the data, it means that the characters that follow are to be interpreted as having an alternate meaning. The concept is similar to the use of the SHIFT key on a PC. When pressed, SHIFT changes the meaning of the other keys on the keyboard. Lowercase letters become uppercase letters, numbers become punctuation marks, and so forth.

In some systems, the escape character changes the meaning of all characters that follow it until a second escape character is sent. In other codes, the escape character changes the meaning of only the single character that immediately follows it. Different systems use escape characters in different ways. It is also possible to have several escape characters in a code. ESC1 might cause one meaning to be assigned to all the following characters, whereas ESC2 might assign a different meaning.

The necessity to support escape characters complicates the design of equipment needed to code and decode the data. There is a trade-off between using escape codes to effectively obtain additional code points and adding another bit to the coding system to double the number of code points. If only a few more code points are needed, using escape codes may be an effective way to obtain them. Most coding systems in use today use seven or eight bits to represent each character, but still include an escape mechanism to provide alternate meanings, if required.

An ESC character in a coding system is normally not the same as the character that is generated when you press the ESC key on the keyboard of a PC. The ESC key generates a character that has a special meaning to the PC or its software, but it rarely has a special meaning to the code system being used by the computer.

## 5-7 SPECIFIC CODES

**American Standard Code for Information Interchange (ASCII)**

Many different codes are used in communications systems today, but the **American Standard Code for Information Interchange (ASCII)** code predominates.

### American National Standards Institute (ASCII)

ASCII grew out of work done by the American National Standards Institute (ANSI) and is the most widely used code in computers and communications networks today. ASCII is a 7-bit code and therefore has $2^7$ or 128 unique code points, as shown in Figure 5-4. The way to read the ASCII code chart is to use the bits over the column head (high order bits) followed by the bits on the

FIGURE 5-4    ASCII code.

| Last Four-Bit Positions (Bits 4, 3, 2, 1) | First Three-Bit Positions (Bits 7, 6, 5) | | | | | | | |
|---|---|---|---|---|---|---|---|---|
| | 000 | 001 | 010 | 011 | 100 | 101 | 110 | 111 |
| 0000 | NUL | DLE | SP | 0 | @ | P | ` | p |
| 0001 | SOH | DC1 | ! | 1 | A | Q | a | q |
| 0010 | STX | DC2 | " | 2 | B | R | b | r |
| 0011 | ETX | DC3 | # | 3 | C | S | c | s |
| 0100 | EOT | DC4 | $ | 4 | D | T | d | t |
| 0101 | ENQ | NAK | % | 5 | E | U | e | u |
| 0110 | ACK | SYN | & | 6 | F | V | f | v |
| 0111 | BEL | ETB | ' | 7 | G | W | g | w |
| 1000 | BS | CAN | ( | 8 | H | X | h | x |
| 1001 | HT | EM | ) | 9 | I | Y | i | y |
| 1010 | LF | SUB | * | : | J | Z | j | z |
| 1011 | VT | ESC | + | ; | K | [ | k | { |
| 1100 | FF | FS | , | < | L | \ | l | \| |
| 1101 | CR | GS | — | = | M | ] | m | } |
| 1110 | SO | RS | • | > | N | ∧ | n | ~ |
| 1111 | SI | US | / | ? | O | - | o | DEL |

International Telegraph
Alphabet 5

left side of the rows (low order bits). Thus, the ASCII code for the capital let-ter P is 1010000, and the code for the lower case letter s is 1110011. The ITU-T calls ASCII **International Telegraph Alphabet 5.**

Extended ASCII

Sometimes an eight bit is added to the ASCII code. It can have two pur-poses: In some cases it is used as a parity bit to provide additional error checking capabilities. In other cases, the eighth bit is used as an additional data bit, which increases the number of code points to $2^8$, or 256. In this case, the code is called **Extended ASCII.** In Extended ASCII, the characters above 127 are used to represent foreign language letters and other useful symbols, such as those needed to draw boxes. Characters below character 127 in ex-tended 8-bit ASCII are identical to standard 7-bit ASCII.

The standard 7-bit ASCII code has uppercase and lowercase letters, dig-its, punctuation, and a large set of control characters that will be discussed later in the chapter. There are 96 graphic (printable) characters and 32 non-printable control characters. Looking at Figure 5-4, notice that the difference between the codes for uppercase and lowercase letters is just one bit. Also, the last 4 bits of the code for the digits is their binary value. For example, the code for the digit 2 is 0110010. The last 4 bits, 0010, are the binary represen-tation of the digit 2. Similarly, the last 4 bits of the digit 9, 1001, are the bi-nary representation for the digit 9. These attributes are very useful when a computer manipulates data. The ASCII code is also designed for easy sorting by computer. Sorting by the binary value of the code yields a sequence that is meaningful to humans.

## Extended Binary Coded Decimal Interchange Code (EBCDIC)

Extended Binary Coded
Decimal Interchange
Code (EBCDIC)

The **Extended Binary Coded Decimal Interchange Code (EBCDIC)** was de-veloped by IBM. It is very widely used in IBM servers and mainframe com-puters, but not in IBM PCs, which use ASCII. EBCDIC is an 8-bit code that has the 256 code points shown in Figure 5-5. This chart is read like the ASCII chart described previously. The bits from the top of each column are com-bined with the bits at the left side of each row. Thus, the EBCDIC code for the capital letter P is 11010111, and the code for the lowercase letter s is 10100010.

Note the differences in the bit assignments between the ASCII and EBCDIC codes. The ASCII bits are numbered 7654321, whereas the EBCDIC bits are numbered 01234567. When data are translated from one coding sys-tem to the other, as is done frequently in data communications applications, it is important to be alert to these differing bit assignments to avoid incor-rect translation.

## Unicode

Whereas ASCII has 128 code points and EBCDIC has 256, neither of these cod-ing systems provides enough code points to handle all of the world's languages. A very simple example is that ASCII does not have unique codes for the British pound sign or the European Euro symbol. European languages have many unique characters, such as the accented characters of French and the umlauted characters of German. But the languages of the Middle East and Asia don't even use the Roman character set and have thousands of unique characters. Think of all the special Greeks symbols and the Russian language, which uses Cyrillic characters. Think about Japanese, Chinese, or Korean, which use "pic-ture" characters in addition to phonetic characters. Reading a Japanese news-paper requires a person to know about 2,000 Japanese kanji characters!

| Bits 4, 5, 6, 7 | 00 00 | 00 01 | 00 10 | 00 11 | 01 00 | 01 01 | 01 10 | 01 11 | 10 00 | 10 01 | 10 10 | 10 11 | 11 00 | 11 01 | 11 10 | 11 11 Bits 0,1,2,3 |
|---|---|---|---|---|---|---|---|---|---|---|---|---|---|---|---|---|
| 0000 | NUL | DLE | | | SP | & | - | | | | | | | | | 0 |
| 0001 | SOH | SBA | | | | | / | | a | j | | | A | J | | 1 |
| 0010 | STX | EUA | | SYN | | | | | b | k | s | | B | K | S | 2 |
| 0011 | ETX | IC | | | | | | | c | l | t | | C | L | T | 3 |
| 0100 | | | | | | | | | d | m | u | | D | M | U | 4 |
| 0101 | PT | NL | | | | | | | e | n | v | | E | N | V | 5 |
| 0110 | | | ETB | | | | | | f | o | w | | F | O | W | 6 |
| 0111 | | | ESC | EOT | | | | | g | p | x | | G | P | X | 7 |
| 1000 | | | | | | | | | h | q | y | | H | Q | Y | 8 |
| 1001 | | EM | | | | | | | i | r | z | | I | R | Z | 9 |
| 1010 | | | | | ¢ | ! | \| | : | | | | | | | | |
| 1011 | | | | | . | $ | , | # | | | | | | | | |
| 1100 | | DUP | | RA | ⟨ | . | % | @ | | | | | | | | |
| 1101 | | SF | ENQ | NAK | ( | ) | — | ' | | | | | | | | |
| 1110 | | FM | ACK | | + | ; | ⟩ | = | | | | | | | | |
| 1111 | | ITB | | SUB | \| | — | ? | " | | | | | | | | |

**FIGURE 5-5**   EBCDIC code.

**Unicode**

**Unicode** is a 16-bit character code designed to address these problems and to provide enough code points so that all the characters of all of the languages of the world have a unique 16-bit code point. Calculating $2^{16}$ yields 65,536 possibilities, but Unicode also provides an extension mechanism that allows for the encoding of 1 million additional characters without the use of any escape codes. This capacity is enough for all known character encoding requirements, including full coverage of all historic scripts of the world. Sixteen-bit characters are often called wide characters, although wide characters do not have to be Unicode characters. There are other 16-bit coding systems, such as IBM's **double byte character set (DBCS)** that provide some of the functions that Unicode offers, but all of the other solutions are partial and usually limited to a single vendor.

**double byte character set (DBCS)**

Unicode was developed by a group of companies called The Unicode Consortium. Members include IBM, Microsoft, Apple, Xerox, Sun, Compaq, Novell, Adobe, and WordPerfect—an influential group. With such backing, Unicode has been standardized and is gaining increasingly widespread use in new software and new versions of old software. Unicode must replace ASCII, EBCDIC, and all other data codes if we are to achieve truly international systems and applications. For further information, see Unicode's website at http://www.unicode.org.

## Other Coding Systems

Many other coding systems have been invented and used for communication and computing; however, most of them are not in widespread use today. Many were developed either to meet special purposes or by vendors who thought that having a proprietary code would give them a competitive advantage in the marketplace. However, in these days of wide and open exchange of information through internetworks that link the world together, the advantage is gained by using one of a few standardized open coding systems that allow the easy sharing and exchange without unnecessary overhead or processing.

## 5-8   CODE EFFICIENCY

code efficiency

**Code efficiency** is a measure of how few bits are used to accurately convey the meaning of a character. Efficiency of coding is important, because an efficient code minimizes the number a bits that are transmitted on expensive communication facilities. If only numeric data are to be transmitted, a 4-bit code would be significantly more efficient than a 7- or 8-bit code. All of the digits can be represented with 4 bits, and the total data transmission would occur twice as fast as if an 8-bit code were used. However, most data communications systems transmit alphanumeric data, and therefore require at least a 7-bit code to provide sufficient code points to encode all of the characters of a single language.

Another aspect of coding efficiency is the number of bits in a character that actually convey information. Bits that are used to determine the code points in a code are **information bits** and any other bits are called **noninformation bits.** Parity bits, for example, convey no additional information and are not part of the original data. They are, therefore, noninformation bits.

information bit

noninformation bit

Code efficiency is defined as the number of information bits divided by the total number of bits in the character. If an 8-bit code that includes one parity bit is being used, the code efficiency is calculated as 7/8 = .875 or 87.5 percent. Some codes use more than one parity bit or allow only certain combinations of bits to be valid, and those codes are less efficient. In addition, you have already seen that, as data are moved through communications lines for transmission, other bits and even whole "check" characters may be added for error detection purposes. Because of the checking that occurs during transmission (checking is discussed in Chapters 7 and 9), the commonly used 7-bit version of the ASCII code and the EBCDIC code were designed with no inherent checking. They are dependent on other means to ensure the data are received accurately. Hence, both coding schemes have 100 percent code efficiency.

## 5-9   CODE CONVERSION

In many data communication systems, code conversion occurs from one coding system to another. Even though ASCII is the most widely used code, it is not universal. Although nearly all communications networks and PCs use ASCII for both internal and external communication purposes, the use of Unicode is growing. In some environments that have large IBM mainframe computers, EBCDIC is still prevalent. As it passes through a network, it is possible that a particular message or data file will be translated at least once into a different code than the one it was originally created in.

FIGURE 5-6   A method for converting a 3-bit code to a 4-bit code.

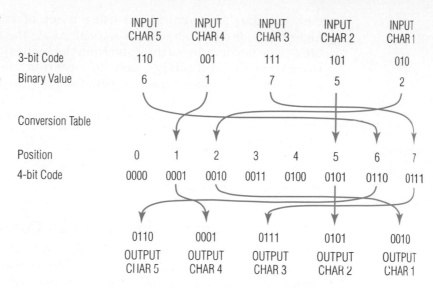

Code conversion is conceptually quite simple and is the type of task that a computer can perform quite readily. A table containing the target codes is usually stored in the memory of the computer. The binary value of the incoming character is used as an index for the table, and the target character is picked up as shown in Figure 5-6. The process gets more complicated when one code is converted to another code that uses a smaller number of bits. For example, when EBCDIC, which has 256 unique characters, is converted to ASCII, which has only 128 characters, many characters cannot be directly converted. The ESC character might have to be brought into play so that one EBCDIC character translates into two ASCII characters—ESC and another character.

## 5-10   DATA COMPRESSION/COMPACTION

**data compression**

**compaction**

**Data compression** or **compaction** is the process of reducing the number of bits used to represent a character, or reducing the number of characters before they are transmitted. The reasons for compressing data are to save storage space on the transmitting or receiving device or to save transmission time so that the message arrives faster and costs less to send. The results of successful compression are an increase in transmission throughput and a reduction of storage or transmission cost.

In a typical application, a data compression device is employed at both ends of a communications line, as shown in Figure 5-7. At the transmitting

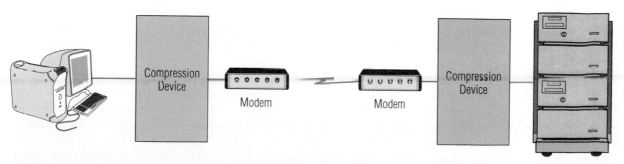

FIGURE 5-7   The locations of data compression devices on a telecommunications circuit. Some modems are able to compress data themselves.

algorithm

end, the data are compressed using a set of mathematical rules called **algorithms,** or a combination of algorithms. At the receiving end, a compatible device decompresses the data using the same algorithm(s) that were used to compress it. Most compression algorithms in use today are proprietary, so it is necessary to use the same manufacturer's equipment for compression and decompression.

Three major types of data compression can be employed:

character compression

run length encoding

character stripping

- **character compression**
- **run length encoding**
- **character stripping**

## Character Compression/Huffman Coding

Huffman coding

Character compression, also called **Huffman coding,** consists of an algorithm that determines which characters are being transmitted most frequently and assigns a shortened bit configuration, of perhaps two bits, to those characters. Characters that are used less frequently are assigned longer combinations of bits. If performed successfully, character compression can reduce the total number of bits transmitted by a factor of about 2. This allows twice as much of the user's data to be sent through the communications line in a given amount of time, doubling the throughput rate. A more sophisticated method, called **adaptive Huffman coding,** updates the algorithm as the data are being transmitted to ensure that the fewest bits are always being assigned to the most frequently transmitted characters during a given time period.

adaptive Huffman coding

## Run Length Encoding

Run length encoding is a technique in which the data stream is scanned by the compression hardware, looking for repetitive characters or repetitive groups of characters. The repetitive groups are replaced by a different, much shorter group of characters. For example, the sequence XXXXXXXXXX might become control character *10X.* This is a shorthand notation that says that the letter X is to be repeated ten times. The shorthand reduces the original ten characters to four, including the control character, which is only 40 percent of the original number of characters. If a file of names and addresses was being transmitted, and many of the addresses contained the same city name or zip code, many characters and measurable transmission time would be saved by substituting a one- or two-character sequence for the city name every time it appeared in the file. The shortened form would be transmitted and at the receiving end, the special character sequence would be replaced by the original word.

## Character Stripping

Character stripping removes the leading and trailing control characters from a message and adds them back at the receiving end. Although this technique may seem rudimentary, when combined with the other compression techniques, it becomes important. If the control characters were not removed from a message to be transmitted, they would be viewed by the character compression algorithm as being among the most frequently transmitted characters. This would reduce the effectiveness of character compression on the main body of the message.

The most effective data compression devices use all three of these compression techniques, and others, in combination. First, character stripping is performed, followed by character compression and run length encoding. To achieve maximum effectiveness, the compression algorithms must also be adaptive—that is, they must constantly analyze the data being transmitted and update their internal tables of the most frequently sent characters or groups in order to assign the fewest bits to them.

**MNP5**

One very popular compression algorithm, called **MNP5,** is a combination of Huffman coding and run length encoding. MNP5 is implemented in the hardware of many modems to effectively increase the transmission speed. It will be discussed again in Chapter 6.

Good data compression algorithms, such as the zip algorithm that is often used to compress data on PCs, are highly mathematical in nature but can reduce the data transmitted in many business applications by a ratio of 4 to 1. Even more remarkable results are being obtained when digitized voice and video signals are compressed. The resulting savings in the cost of storage or transmission time must be weighed against the cost of the data compression equipment. The economics almost always works out in favor of doing as much compression as possible, especially for voice and video signals. For some companies, the most important benefit of data compression is the higher throughput rate, which may translate into improved response time for the users of an interactive application.

## ■ SUMMARY

This chapter looked at various alternatives for coding information. For machine communications, a binary code in which each character contains the same number of elements is desirable. The most common code in use in the modern data communication world is the ASCII code, which contains 7 or 8 bits. EBCDIC's use is declining, while Unicode's use is growing. Code conversion is sometimes needed if nodes on the network use different coding systems. Data compression techniques reduce the number of bits that must be transmitted, thereby effectively increasing the throughput on a given communications circuit.

## ■ REVIEW QUESTIONS

5-1. Describe several attributes that are important in a code to be used for machine-to-machine data transmission.

5-2. What is a code point?

5-3. What are the advantages and disadvantages of an 8-bit code compared to a 5-bit code?

5-4. What is the minimum number of bits that would be required to encode only alphabetic data? How many bits would be needed if numeric data were to be included?

5-5. Explain why, if only numeric data are to be transmitted, the use of a 4-bit coding system would be significantly more efficient than using ASCII.

5-6. Name the three different groups of character assignments that are normally made in a coding system.

5-7. What is the problem that the adoption of Unicode solves?

5-8. Describe three different techniques of data compression.

5-9. What is the most important data coding scheme? Why?

5-10. What is the difference between even parity and odd parity?

5-11. Few words in any language have long strings of repetitive characters. That being true, in what circumstances is run length encoding most useful?

## TRUE OR FALSE

5-1. The term *binary digit* is abbreviated *bit*.

5-2. Machines cannot send Morse code because the coded characters have different numbers of code elements.

5-3. It is much easier for a machine to process a code if all of the bits are of the same duration.

5-4. When even parity is used, a 1 bit is added, if necessary, to make the total number of 1 bits in the character an even number.

5-5. The escape character in a coding system is the same character that is generated when you press the ESC key on the keyboard of a PC.

5-6. Extended ASCII is a 7-bit code.

5-7. Unicode provides enough code points so that all characters in all languages of the world have a unique 16-bit code point.

5-8. Code efficiency is a measure of how many bits are used to convey the meaning of a character.

5-9. Data compression is the process of reducing the number of bits used to represent a character, or reducing the number of characters before they are transmitted.

5-10. Character stripping is the process of removing redundant text characters from a message before it is transmitted.

5-11. The binary digits are *1* and *2*.

5-12. A *code* is a predetermined set of symbols that have specific meanings.

5-13. Morse code is considered a binary code, even though its two elements are of different length.

5-14. A binary code works well for machines communicating by electrical means because the 1 bits and 2 bits can be represented by a current flow that is either on or off.

5-15. For transmission efficiency, it is ideal to have a coding system that uses a minimum number of bits to represent each character.

5-16. Most coding systems include a technique called an escape hatch.

5-17. The necessity to support escape characters complicates the design of equipment that is to code and decode the data.

5-18. The ASCII code is the most widely used code in computers and communications networks today.

5-19. Unicode is a 32-bit character code.

## MULTIPLE CHOICE

5-1. Characters that control the positioning of information on a workstation screen or paper are called _____.

a. page control characters

b. screen control characters

c. device control characters

d. format effector characters

e. a and b

5-2. It is much easier for a machine to process a code if the code has the following attributes: _____.

    a. it is a true binary code

    b. all of the characters have the same number of bits

    c. all of the bits are perfectly formed

    d. all of the bits are the same duration

    e. All of the above.

5-3. The unique sequence of bits assigned to represent the various characters of a code are called _____.

    a. character assignments

    b. code points

    c. control characters

    d. character algorithms

    e. None of the above.

5-4. The purpose of escape characters is to _____.

    a. allow a program to abort a message prematurely

    b. implement a priority system by allowing one message to be prematurely ended so another can be sent on the circuit

    c. indicate that the characters that follow are to be interpreted as having an alternate meaning

    d. act as a null character in a transmission for timing purposes

    e. indicate that a PDU has been received correctly

5-5. The ASCII code is also known as the _____.

    a. EBCDIC code

    b. extended ASCII code

    c. 8-bit code

    d. PC code

    e. International Telegraph Alphabet 5

5-6. The EBCDIC code _____.

    a. was developed by IBM

    b. is an 8-bit code

    c. has 256 code points

    d. is used on IBM mainframe computers

    e. All of the above.

    f. None of the above.

5-7. Unicode _____.

    a. is a 16-bit code

    b. was developed by a group of companies

    c. supports the characters of all languages

    d. All of the above.

    e. None of the above.

5-8. Code efficiency is calculated _____.

    a. by dividing the information bits by the total number of bits in a character

    b. by dividing the total number of bits by the information bits in a character

    c. by measuring the error rate at the receiving end of a transmission

    d. by guess and by golly

5-9. Three major types of data compression are _____.

    a. character removal, run length encoding, and bit compression

    b. bit stripping, double clocking, and character stripping

    — c. character stripping, run length encoding, and character compression

    d. character compression, Huffman coding, and character stripping

    e. character squeezing, transmission hugging, and CPR

5-10. A 10-bit code could represent how many characters?

    a. 100

    b. $2^{10}$

    c. $2^9$

    d. 512

    e. None of the above.

5-11. The number of possible combinations or characters in a coding system is called the _____.

    a. character assignment

    b. binary code

    c. control character

    — d. code point

    e. code limit

5-12. Many coding systems include an extra bit, called a _____, for checking purposes.

    a. checking bit

    b. padding bit

    c. control bit

    — d. parity bit

    e. binary bit

5-13. When an ESC character is sent as a part of the data, it means that _____.

    a. the transmission is being aborted

    b. this is the end of the transmission

    c. the transmission should be ignored

    d. the characters that follow are encrypted

    — e. the characters that follow are to be interpreted as having an alternate meaning

## PROBLEMS AND PROJECTS

5-1. Amateur radio operators have written software for computers to send Morse code automatically when a key on the keyboard is pressed. Describe some of the difficulties that would be encountered by a computer at the receiving end when interpreting the transmission for display on the screen.

5-2. Using the ASCII table in the text, convert your name to bits (7 bits per character). Use upper- and lowercase characters, as you would to write your name. Now, assuming even parity, add the parity bit to each coded character in your name.

5-3. Using the 8-bit characters you generated in Problem 5-2, interpret those characters as EBCDIC to see what you get. The characters you look up, when combined, could be considered an encrypted form of your name.

5-4. A certain coding scheme contains 5 information bits and 2 noninformation bits for each character. Calculate the code efficiency of this code.

5-5. Do some research on the Internet to find out about the current status of Unicode implementation.

5-6. Do some research on the Internet to see what techniques are used for compressing digital voice and video signals.

5-7. Search on the Internet for information about JPEG compression and report the results of your investigation. If possible, find examples of photographs or artwork that has been compressed using JPEG, and show the class comparisons of the compressed and uncompressed images.

## COMPUTERS IN A UNIVERSITY LIBRARY

The University of LaBurge, a small school in a midwestern state, solved a networking and workstation problem in its library in a creative way. A year ago, the university was receiving many complaints from students who came to the library to use the PC workstations located there to do research on the Internet. The problem was that frequently the workstations were observed to be in use by students to do their personal e-mail rather than for research purposes, for which they were intended when they were installed. Herbert Gilson, the university's librarian, was under increasing pressure from the academic deans and the dean of student affairs, all of whom were hearing the increasing complaints from students that the library was useless as a research center because they could never get access to the Internet. After doing some investigation and observing many workstations tied up by students who were indeed using them for e-mail and other personal purposes (even playing games), Mr. Gilson agreed that action had to be taken.

He organized a small committee consisting of his assistant librarian, Miriam Johnston; two student representatives; and a representative from the academic council (made up of professors). As expected, at the first meeting there was some anger and many opinions were expressed. It seemed that each of the attendees had a slightly different idea about the true nature of the problem and what should be done. The professorial representative felt that a sign should simply be put up to inform the students that the terminals were for research use only. The students, however, felt that a sign would simply be ignored by many of their peers and that other action needed to be taken, although they didn't have a clear solution in mind. At the conclusion of the first meeting Ms. Johnston agreed to contact some of the other universities in the state to see if they had experienced a similar problem and found a suitable solution.

At the group's second meeting two weeks later, Ms. Johnston reported that several of the universities she contacted had indeed reported having similar problems with the computers in their libraries. She said that they had implemented a variety of solutions, ranging from actually removing the computers to forbidding access to e-mail from the library computers, and having

CASE STUDY

separate computers for research use and e-mail use located in different parts of the library. After listening to her report and then having considerable and sometimes heated discussion, the committee finally reached a consensus on a recommendation to take to Mr. Gilson.

The group felt that it was not practical to entirely forbid the use of the library's computers for e-mail, but felt that it would be possible to make it physically less comfortable to access e-mail by permitting its use only from computers that were located at stand-up workstations. That is, the computers designated for e-mail use would be placed on a surface that was approximately 45 inches high, so that students would have to stand while accessing these machines. A separate bank of computers designated for research use would be located elsewhere in the library, at workstations of normal height and that had chairs. Software on these machines would restrict access to common e-mail programs, such as Microsoft Outlook, Eudora, and America Online. Signs would be posted, stating that these computers were for research purposes only and not for e-mail. The recommendation also mentioned that the research computers should be located in an area that was not far from the reference desk, so that students doing research could easily consult the reference librarians. It was also pointed out that the e-mail computers should be located in an area that was quite visible, so that their use could be monitored. The recommendation was presented to Mr. Gilson in written and oral form at a meeting a few weeks later.

Gilson was pleased with the group's work and had only a few questions, but he was concerned about the cost to implement the recommendation. While the committee felt that no additional computers would be required, there would be cost to construct or purchase the new "stand up" e-mail workstations, to purchase and implement the software for the research computers to restrict access to the e-mail systems, and to reconfigure the university's computer network to support the new arrangement. As is typical in a university environment, budgets were tight and the library's funds for that academic year were already committed to other projects. Gilson stated, however, that he would carry the recommendation to the academic council and see if there was any way it could be funded in the short term.

A few weeks later, Gilson was able to get the academic deans to help fund the project, and the library was able to implement the committee's recommendation within three months. As with any change, some of the students initially resisted the new procedures. However, within a few weeks, it appeared that computer usage was settling into a new pattern. Complaints dropped dramatically, and casual observation of the computers by the library staff indicated that, for the most part, the people were using the machines as intended.

Three months later, Mr. Gilson called for an informal audit of the computer usage by the university's information technology (IT) staff. Using monitoring software and taking samples at random times throughout the library's operating hours, IT was able to show that over 95% of the computer usage conformed to the new procedures that had been established. That is, the e-mail computers were being used for e-mail and the research computers were not. Furthermore, detailed monitoring of the availability of the research computers showed that there was only one time during the monitoring period when all of the computers were in use, and other students were waiting to use them. This was judged to be acceptable. However, when he reported the results of the audit to the academic council, one of the deans pointed out that the usage should be closely monitored again in the last 2 to 3 weeks of the semester, when students were rushing to complete term papers and other assignments and the research load might be higher. Mr. Gilson agreed and immediately made plans for further monitoring, because the end of the semester was only six weeks away.

QUESTIONS

1. Instead of forming a committee to study the situation, should Mr. Gilson simply have taken a stronger stand and banned e-mail access from the library's computers?

2. Would a similar procedure for computer usage in the library be necessary in your school? Would it work?

3. What impact would the reconfiguration of the library workstations likely have had on the university's network usage and response time?

4. About how much work did the IT department need to do to reconfigure the network to support the new configuration of PCs?

CASE STUDY

# C H A P T E R   6

# DATA COMMUNICATION FUNDAMENTALS

## ■ OUTLINE

## ■ KEY TERMS

adaptive differential pulse code modulation (ADPCM)

adaptive equalizer

amplitude

amplitude modulation (AM)

analog

analog data

analog signal

analog-to-digital (A/D) converter

analog transmission

asynchronous transmission (asynch)

attenuation

bandwidth

baseband transmission

baud

biphase coding

bipolar, nonreturn-to-zero (NRZ)

bipolar, return-to-zero

bit synchronization

bits per second (bps)

block

broadband transmission

cable modem

carrier wave
character synchronization
circuit speed
coder/decoder (codec)
crosstalk
current loop
cycle
data circuit-terminating
    equipment (DCE)
data service
    unit/channel service
    unit (DSU/CSU)
data terminal
    equipment (DTE)
decibel (dB)
delta modulation
demodulation
detector
dibits
differential Manchester
    coding
differential phase shift
    keying (DPSK)
digital
digital data
digital signal
digital-to-analog (D/A)
    converter
digital transmission
digital
    transmitter/receiver
digitizing distortion
direct sequence
duplex
equalizer circuitry
exponential
fixed equalizer
frequency
frequency division
    multiplexing (FDM)
frequency hopping

frequency modulation
    (FM)
frequency shift keying
    (FSK)
full-duplex (FDX)
    transmission
gigahertz (GHz)
guard band
guard channel
half duplex (HDX)
    transmission
handshaking
Hertz (Hz)
kilohertz (KHz)
level
line turnaround
Manchester coding
mark
megahertz (MHz)
modem
modem eliminator
modulation
modulator
network interface card
    (NIC)
null modem
parallel mode
parallel transmission
phase
phase amplitude
    modulation (PAM)
phase modulation (PM)
phase shift
phase shift keying (PSK)
pulse code modulation
    (PCM)
quadbits
quadrature amplitude
    modulation (QAM)
quantization

quantizing noise
RS-232-C
RS-232-D
RS-336
RS-449
serial mode
serial transmission
signal processors
signaling
signaling rate
signals
simplex transmission
sine wave
space
spread spectrum
    transmission
start bit
start/stop transmission
stop bit
synchronization
    character (SYN)
synchronous transmission
transmission efficiency
trellis code modulation
    (TCM)
tribits
unipolar
V.32
V.32bis
V.33
V.34
V.34bis
V.42
V.42bis
V.44
V.90
V.92
X.21
X.21bis

## ■ OBJECTIVES

After you complete your study of this chapter, you should be able to:

- describe the characteristics of analog and digital signals;
- describe what is meant by the signaling rate of a circuit;
- describe four modes of data transmission;
- distinguish between asynchronous and synchronous transmission;
- explain how a modem works;
- discuss the various modem standards that are in use today;
- explain why digital transmission is generally superior to analog transmission; and
- distinguish between simplex, half duplex, and full duplex transmission.

## 6-1    INTRODUCTION

In this chapter, you will study the characteristics of analog and digital signals and the ways in which they are transmitted on a communications line. You will first look at definitions of the two different types of communications signals, and then at the way in which they are converted to be sent on communications circuits. Then you will examine four transmission cases:

- transmitting analog signals on an analog circuit
- transmitting analog signals on a digital circuit
- transmitting digital signals on a digital circuit
- transmitting digital signals on an analog circuit

With the understanding you will gain, you will be well prepared for information about data link control protocols, data circuits, and networks in the chapters that follow.

## 6-2    DEFINITIONS OF ANALOG AND DIGITAL

analog

digital

analog data

digital data

signals

signaling

The terms **analog** and **digital** are so freely used that it is easy to assume that everyone understands their meanings. The word "analog" comes from the word "analogous," which means "similar to." A good approximation of the meaning is "continuous." Thus, **analog data** are continuous data, such as the speed of an automobile, and an analog signal is a continuous signal that represents the data. By contrast, **digital data** are discrete, such as text or integers. A digital signal is made up of discrete elements, such as voltages, that represent those discrete points. **Signals** are electromagnetic representations of the data, and **signaling** is the propagation of the signal on a medium such as a wire or an optical fiber.

## 6-3    ANALOG SIGNALS

analog signal

A voice signal is a continuously varying pattern of pitch and intensity. When a voice signal is converted to an electrical signal through a microphone, it provides a continuously varying electrical wave like the one shown in Figure 6-1. This electrical wave matches the pressure pattern of the sound that created it. The wave is an **analog signal** because it is analogous to the continually varying sound waves created when sound is generated by speech or other means. Voice signals make excellent examples for studying analog signals; therefore, they will be used for reference throughout this chapter.

**FIGURE 6-1** Analog wave of a typical voice signal.

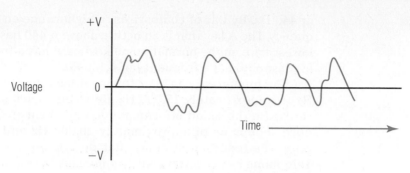

**FIGURE 6-2** Sine waves of differing frequencies.

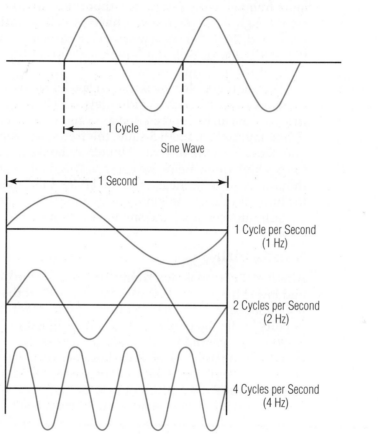

## Signal Frequency

frequency

sine wave

cycle

Hertz (Hz)

The sound waves generated when we speak and the electrical waves that result after the sound has been converted for transmission have many common characteristics. One attribute of both waves is their **frequency,** which (for sound waves) is the number of vibrations per second that cause the particular sound. If you press the A key above middle C on a perfectly tuned piano keyboard, you generate a very pure tone that is created by the A string on the piano vibrating back and forth 440 times per second. If you were to hold your telephone up to the piano and strike the A key, the microphone in the telephone handset would convert the 440 vibrations per second to an electrical signal on the telephone line that also changes 440 times per second. This pure, simple signal is commonly diagrammed as a **sine wave,** as shown in Figure 6-2. Each complete wave is called a **cycle,** and the frequency of the signal is the number of cycles that occur in one second. The unit of measure for frequency is the **Hertz (Hz).** We say that the A key we struck on the piano generated a tone with a frequency of 440 Hz. The corresponding (analogous) electrical signal also has a frequency of 440 Hz. By way of comparison, a higher tone on the piano has a higher frequency. The A key that is an octave above A 440 has a frequency of 880 Hz. The lowest note on the normal piano keyboard has a frequency of 27.5 Hz and the highest note has a frequency of 4,186 Hz.

The human ear can hear sound with a range of frequencies from about 20 Hz to approximately 15,000 Hz. Between 15,000 and 20,000 Hz, most people can sense the sound but can not actually hear it. Good stereo systems reproduce sounds up to approximately 20,000 Hz and have better fidelity (they sound better) than systems that do not reproduce frequencies that high. Telephone systems transmit frequencies between 300 and 3,000 Hz because most human voices fall within that range. If you have ever tried to play music through a telephone, you have probably noticed that the fidelity is not very good. That's because most music has a much wider frequency range than the 300–3,000 Hz that the telephone system transmits. Figure 6-3 illustrates some of these frequency ranges.

Sound waves, electrical waves traveling in wire, and electromagnetic waves traveling to space, such as radio waves, all have essentially the same characteristics. Each can be represented as a sine wave whose frequency is measured in Hertz. Figures 6-4 and 6-5 show the frequency spectrum, the full range of frequencies from 0 Hz to several hundred thousand million Hertz. When referring to very high frequencies, we commonly use the designations **kilohertz (KHz)** for thousands of Hertz, **megahertz (MHz)** for millions of Hertz, and **gigahertz (GHz)** for billions of hertz, to more easily describe the frequencies. Figure 6-6 shows the full range of large and small units of measure in the scientific world.

**kilohertz (KHz)**

**megahertz (MHz)**

**gigahertz (GHz)**

## Bandwidth

Another way to look at a frequency range is the difference between the upper and lower frequency. This difference is called the **bandwidth.** In the case of a telephone signal, the bandwidth is 300 to 3,000 Hz, or 2,700 Hz. Analog voice circuits in the telephone system are designed to handle frequencies from 0 to 4,000 Hz, as shown in Figure 6-7, but special circuitry limits the voice frequencies that can pass through it to those between 300 and 3,000 Hz. The additional space between 0 and 300 Hz and between 3,000 and 4,000 Hz is called the **guard channel** or **guard band,** and it provides a buffer area so that telephone conversations or data signals on adjacent circuits don't interfere with each other.

**bandwidth**

**guard channel**

**guard band**

## Signal Amplitude

Another characteristic of analog signals is their loudness, or **amplitude.** As you speak more loudly or softly into the telephone, the sound waves create larger and smaller electrical waves that are represented by the higher peaks and valleys of the signal's voltage (shown in Figure 6-8). The amplitude of the signal is also called its **level.** With sound, the amplitude relates to loudness;

**amplitude**

**level**

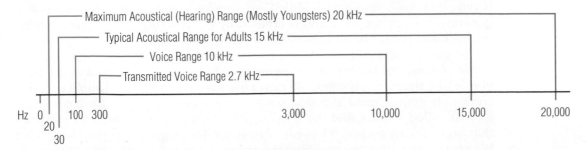

FIGURE 6-3  The frequency ranges of some common sounds.

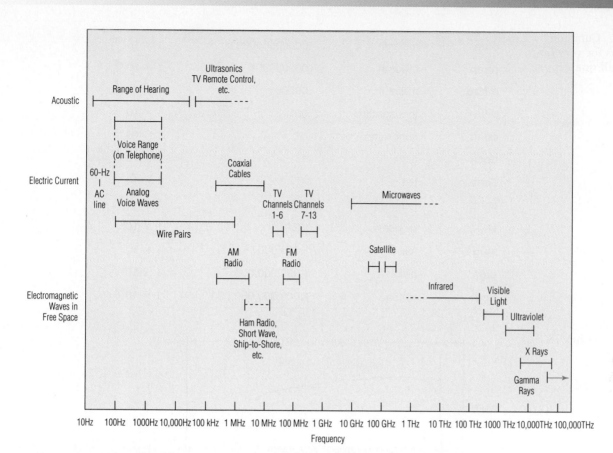

**FIGURE 6-4**   The frequency spectrum showing the common names applied to certain frequency ranges.

**FIGURE 6-5**   A more detailed view of the frequency spectrum relevant to telecommunications.

| | |
|---|---|
| AM radio | .535–1.7 MHz |
| Shortwave | 1.7–30 MHz |
| Cordless phones | 43–49 MHz |
| TV channels 2–4 | 54–72 MHz |
| FM radio | 88–108 MHz |
| Police, weather | 150.8–174 MHz |
| TV channels 7–13 | 174–216 MHz |
| Military, space | 225–400 MHz |
| TV channels 14–69 | 470–824 MHz |
| Cellular phones | 824–849 MHz |
| Cellular phone towers | 869–894 MHz |
| Airplane phones | 894–896 MHz |
| Pagers | 928–932 MHz |
| Radio astronomy | 1,400–1,427 MHz |

FIGURE 6-6 Common abbreviations for very large and very small quantities.

| pico | trillionth | .000000000001 | $1 \times 10^{-12}$ |
|------|-----------|---------------|---------------------|
| nano | billionth | .000000001 | $1 \times 10^{-9}$ |
| micro | millionth | .000001 | $1 \times 10^{-6}$ |
| milli | thousandth | .001 | $1 \times 10^{-3}$ |
| centi | hundredth | .01 | $1 \times 10^{-2}$ |
| deci | tenth | .1 | $1 \times 10^{-1}$ |
| deca | ten | 10 | $1 \times 10^{1}$ |
| centa | hundred | 100 | $1 \times 10^{2}$ |
| kilo | thousand | 1000 | $1 \times 10^{3}$ |
| mega | million | 1,000,000 | $1 \times 10^{6}$ |
| giga | billion | 1,000,000,000 | $1 \times 10^{9}$ |
| tera | trillion | 1,000,000,000,000 | $1 \times 10^{12}$ |

FIGURE 6-7 Bandwidth of a voice channel.

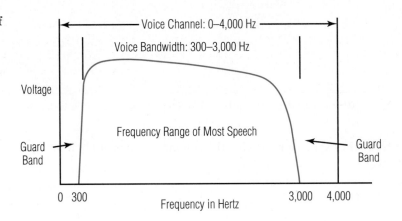

FIGURE 6-8 Analog wave with constant frequency and varying amplitude.

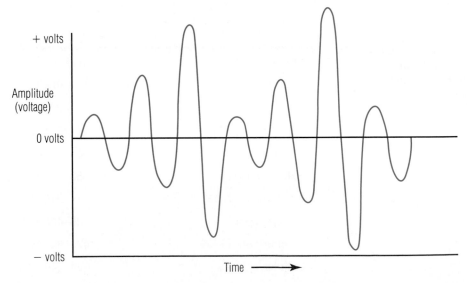

in an electrical signal, the amplitude is the difference between its most negative voltage (the lowest point in the sine wave) and its most positive voltage (the highest point in the sound wave).

    Analog signal level is measured in **decibels (dB),** which is a logarithmic ratio of signal input and output power. Because the dB is a logarithmic meas-

**decibel (dB)**

**FIGURE 6-9** The relative power of a signal measured in decibels.

| Decibels | Relative power |
|----------|----------------|
| +30 dB | 1000 |
| +20 | 100 |
| +10 | 10 |
| +3 | 2 |
| 0 dB | 1 |
| −3 dB | 1/2 |
| −10 | 1/10 |
| −20 | 1/100 |
| −30 | 1/1000 |

ure, doubling the strength of the signal increases its level by 3 dB. This is true, regardless of the signal's original strength. If we say that this signal increased by 3 dB, we mean it doubled in strength, without knowing what the original or new signal strengths are. In the same way, increasing its strength by a factor of 10 raises its level by 10 dB; by a factor of 100, 20 dB; and so on. Working in the other direction, we find that reducing the signal to one-half of its former level causes the strength to be measured as –3 dB; one-tenth of the power is –10 dB; one one-hundredth of the power is –20 dB, and so on. Figure 6-9 shows these values.

For electrical communication signals, 0 dB is defined as 1 milliwatt of power. An increase of the power to 2 milliwatts is a doubling of the power. Therefore, the signal would have a relative strength of +3 dB. Doubling the power again to 4 milliwatts would yield a signal that has a strength of +6 dB. The mathematical formula for the relationship between power and signal strength is

$$dB = 10 \log \left( \frac{\text{power out}}{\text{power in}} \right)$$

The quotient of power out to power in is a mathematical way to show the number of times the power was increased. If the power out is 30 watts and the power in was 10 watts, then the power was increased three times and the multiplier used in the formula would be 3. So, the formula may be expressed in words as: decibels equals ten times the logarithm of the power increase. By the way, the formula also works if the power is decreased. If the power is reduced from 5 milliwatts to 2 milliwatts, then the multiplier used in the formula would 0.4. We need to use logarithms in this equation because the speed at which signals traveling through a medium weaken is **exponential**. Logarithms relate to exponents, therefore they accurately reflect the signal's behavior through a transmission medium.

**exponential**

Decibels and the strength of a signal are of considerable interest in telecommunications. If too much power is put on a communications circuit, a particular type of interference, called **crosstalk** (which will be discussed in Chapter 9), can occur. The loss of signal strength is also of interest because if a signal does not have enough strength at the receiving end of a communication path, it will be unusable. This loss, which is called **attenuation**, is measured between two points on a line, as shown in Figure 6-10. At the point where the signal is injected on the line, it has a certain strength. As the signal moves

**crosstalk**

**attenuation**

**FIGURE 6-10**  A signal loses strength as the distance it travels increases. This loss of strength is called *attenuation.*

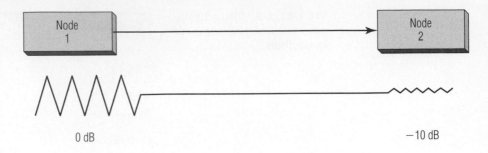

0 dB                                    −10 dB

**FIGURE 6-11**  Example of a phase shift.

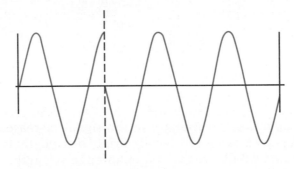

phase

away, its strength is reduced due to the attenuation of the line. The reduction is measured in decibels.

## Signal Phase

A third attribute of an analog signal is its **phase.** In contrast with frequency and amplitude, phase is harder to relate to the physical world and is therefore somewhat harder to understand. Sine waves can be measured in degrees, where 360 degrees is one complete cycle of the wave. A signal's phase is the relative position of the sine wave measured in degrees. Figure 6-11 shows a sine wave that appears to break and start again, skipping a portion of the wave. This is a phase shift. Because one quarter of the wave has been skipped, it is called a 90 degree phase shift. Phase shifts are created and detected by electronic circuitry.

While amplitude and frequency changes can be detected by the human ear, phase changes cannot. Therefore, they are of less importance in voice transmission. They are very important in data transmission, however, and we will study phase shifting in more detail.

## 6-4    ATTRIBUTES OF VOICE SIGNALS

Whereas single tones produce clean sine waves of a specific frequency and amplitude, the human voice, music, noise, and most other sounds are made up of a large range of frequencies and amplitudes. As a result, the wave pattern is far more complex than the simple sine waves we have looked at thus far (as you saw in Figure 6-1). Normal speech is made up of sounds that have frequencies in the range of 100 to 6,000 Hz, but most of the speech energy falls in the 300 to 3,000 Hz range. Although some people who have high-pitched voices emit occasional sounds above 6,000 Hz, the majority of the sound still falls in the range of 300 to 3,000 Hz. That is why the PSTN is designed so that all of the lines, handsets, and other components will pass voice frequencies in that range. Frequencies outside that range are filtered out by electronic circuitry and are not allowed to pass.

## 6-5  FREQUENCY DIVISION MULTIPLEXING (FDM)

frequency division
multiplexing (FDM)

While the individual telephone circuit has a bandwidth of 4,000 Hz, the pair of wires or other media carrying it have a much higher bandwidth capacity. Twisted pair wires have a bandwidth of approximately 1 million Hz. Dividing 4,000 Hz into 1 million Hz shows us that, at least theoretically, a standard pair of telephone wires should be able to carry approximately 250 telephone conversations. This is a very theoretical number; however, 12 or 24 analog voice signals are normally carried.

This technique of packing several analog signals onto a single wire (or other media) is called **frequency division multiplexing (FDM)**. It is accomplished by translating each voice channel to a different part of the frequency spectrum that the media can carry. Using the telephone wire pair as an example, if a second voice signal could be relocated from its natural frequency of 0–4,000 Hz to 4,000–8,000 Hz, and a third signal could be relocated to 8,000–12,000 Hz, as shown in Figure 6-12, many telephone conversations could be packed onto one pair of wires. When FDM is employed, the signal's frequency is shifted by equipment at the transmitting end and restored to its original frequency by similar equipment at the receiving end.

## 6-6  MODULATION

carrier wave

modulation

modulator

frequency modulation
(FM)

amplitude modulation
(AM)

Frequency division multiplexing is accomplished by transmitting a sine wave signal in the new frequency range in which the original signal is to be relocated. The new sine wave is called a **carrier wave.** The carrier wave contains no information, but its attributes are changed corresponding to the information in the original signal. This change to the carrier wave is called **modulation,** and the machine that changes the signal is called a **modulator.** Modulation converts a communication signal from one form to another form that is more appropriate for transmission over a particular medium between two locations.

You have learned that three attributes of sine waves can be changed. If the frequency is changed, it is called **frequency modulation (FM);** changing the amplitude is called **amplitude modulation (AM)** and changing the phase

FIGURE 6-12  Frequency multiplexed voice signals.

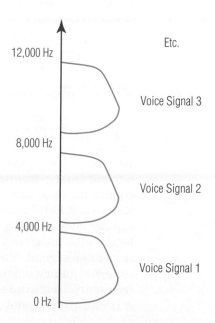

12,000 Hz

Etc.

Voice Signal 3

8,000 Hz

Voice Signal 2

4,000 Hz

Voice Signal 1

0 Hz

**FIGURE** 6-13 Amplitude and frequency modulation.

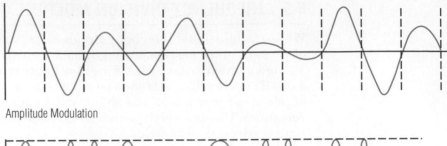

Amplitude Modulation

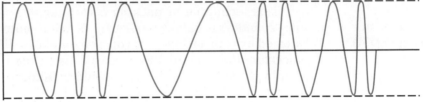

Frequency Modulation

phase modulation (PM)

phase amplitude modulation (PAM)

detector

demodulation

is called **phase modulation (PM).** Amplitude and frequency modulation are shown in Figure 6-13; phase modulation will be discussed later. Combinations of these modulation techniques are also possible, for example, **phase amplitude modulation (PAM).**

Shifting the frequency of the signal to a different frequency range is one important use of modulation (we will look at the other use later in this chapter), and the result is that the original signal is relocated to a different set of frequencies. At the receiving end, an electronic circuit called a **detector** must be able to unscramble the modulated signal and relocate it back to the original frequencies, which is a process called **demodulation.** In the telephone world, the modulation of the original 0 to 4,000 Hz voice signal occurs at the telephony company's CO near the person who is speaking, and demodulation occurs at the CO near the listener.

Although the preceding discussion shows the way telephone companies can achieve efficiency through FDM techniques, they have now changed virtually all of their high-speed circuits and interoffice communications to digital transmission, which yields even higher efficiencies. Digital techniques are applicable to data transmission as well, and will be covered shortly. Suffice it to say that when a voice signal is digitized, it becomes a stream of bits that is indistinguishable from digitized data. As a result, digital voice and data signals can be multiplexing together on the same line, and the efficiencies are higher than with the analog techniques that have been discussed so far.

## 6-7   CIRCUIT SIGNALING RATE

signaling rate

baud

We saw that an analog circuit's bandwidth is the difference between the highest and lowest frequencies that the circuit can carry. We also saw that the standard telephone circuit has a bandwidth of 4,000 Hz. In 1928, Harry Nyquist of Bell Laboratories showed that the maximum signaling rate that can be achieved on a noiseless communication channel is $2B$, where $B$ is the bandwidth measured in Hz. The **signaling rate** is defined as the number of times per second that the signal on the circuit changes, whether in amplitude, frequency, or phase. The signaling rate is measured in **baud.** Thus, if the frequency, amplitude, or phase of a signal is changed 600 times per second, it is said to be signaling at 600 baud.

Nyquist's work suggests that on a circuit with a 4,000 Hz bandwidth, the maximum theoretical achievable signaling rate is 2 × 4,000 Hz, or 8,000 baud. The signaling rate that can actually be achieved is often significantly less than the theoretical maximum because in the real world, noise and other transmission impairments occur on every circuit. Furthermore, the time available for a modem or other device to detect the signal changes at the receiving end becomes very small as the speed increases. At 2,400 baud, for example, the signal changes 2,400 times per second. Therefore, the receiver must detect the signal change within 1/2,400 of a second, or 416.5 microseconds.

The more time the electronic circuitry at the receiving end has to detect the signal change, the more accurate the detection will be. Modem designers would like to keep the baud rate low to provide as much time as possible for the signal change to be detected. However, to achieve the highest possible throughput rates, a signaling rate of 8,000 baud, or as close to it as possible, must be used.

## 6-8 CIRCUIT SPEED

circuit speed

bits per second (bps)

**Circuit speed** is defined as the number of bits that a circuit can carry in 1 second. It is measured in **bits per second (bps)**. The abbreviation "bps" is often incorrectly used interchangeably with the term "baud." If only one bit is sent with each signal change on the circuit, the baud rate and the bps rate are the same, assuming all of the bits are of the same length. Today, sophisticated techniques allow more information to be encoded in each signal change. Therefore, the baud rate and bps rate of most data transmissions are normally quite different.

Suppose there were four unique signal changes on a circuit—that is, four unique changes of amplitude, frequency, or phase. With four possibilities, each of the four signal changes could represent 2 bits of information. For example, if the circuit transmitted four unique frequencies, one frequency could represent the bit combination 00, a second could represent 01, the third could represent 10, and the fourth frequency could represent the bit combination 11. This is shown in Figure 6-14. When 2 bits of information are coded into one signal change, they are called **dibits**.

dibits

tribits

quadbits

What if eight different frequencies were used? Then each frequency could represent 3 bits, called **tribits,** also shown in Figure 6-14. Using such techniques, dibits, tribits, and even **quadbits** can be encoded in each signaling change. Thus, circuit speeds can be achieved, as measured in bps, that are

**FIGURE 6-14** If four different frequencies are used, each can represent 2 bits ($2^2 = 4$). If eight frequencies are used, each can represent 3 bits ($2^3 = 8$).

| Frequency | Dibit | Frequency | Tribit |
|-----------|-------|-----------|--------|
| f1 | 00 | f1 | 000 |
| f2 | 01 | f2 | 001 |
| f3 | 10 | f3 | 010 |
| f4 | 11 | f4 | 011 |
| | | f5 | 100 |
| | | f6 | 101 |
| | | f7 | 110 |
| | | f8 | 111 |

several times greater than the circuit's signaling rate as measured in bauds. When the signaling rate is 2,400 baud, it is possible to send 2,400, 4,800, 7,200, or even 9,600 bps, depending upon how many bits are coded in one baud.

**data terminal equipment (DTE)**

On a data communications circuit, the **data terminal equipment (DTE)** (the computer, terminal, or other device that is sending or receiving the signal) at both ends of the circuit must send and receive bits at the same rate. Therefore, the bit rate of the circuit is the maximum bit rate that can be sent between the equipment. Of course, if the sending DTE is not generating data at the speed the circuit can handle, the actual bit rate sent will be less.

We have seen that bauds and bps are units of measure for different characteristics of a communications circuit. It is surprising that many people who work in the communications industry do not understand the difference between these two concepts and think that the terms are interchangeable. In fact, the only time that the baud rate and bps rate of the circuit are the same is when each signal change on the circuit indicates 1 bit. Although this would be the case with slow-speed transmissions of up to 1,200 bps, it is still incorrect to use the terms interchangeably.

## 6-9    DIGITAL SIGNALS

A typical analog signal generated by the human voice has a very complex wave form, as was shown in Figure 6-1. In contrast, the signal generated by a terminal, computer, or other DTE is very simple because it is made up of discreet, discontinuous voltage pulses. In simplest terms, each pulse represents one of the binary digits, either 1 or 0, which represent the coded data to be transmitted. This type of signal is called a **digital signal.**

**digital signal**

**unipolar**

**bipolar, nonreturn-to-zero (NRZ)**

**bipolar, return-to-zero**

There are several forms of digital signals, a shown in Figure 6-15. **Unipolar** signals are those in which a 1 bit is represented by a positive voltage pulse and a 0 bit is represented by no voltage. **Bipolar, nonreturn-to-zero (NRZ)** signals have the 1 bits represented by a positive voltage and the 0 bits represented by a negative voltage. **Bipolar, return-to-zero** signals are similar to NRZ signals, but the pulses are shorter and the voltage always returns to zero between pulses. Unipolar signals are rarely used today. Bipolar signaling has the clear advantage of making the distinction between the 0 bit and a no-signal condition, a distinction useful in troubleshooting when problems occur.

The challenge at the receiving end of a transmission is for the receiving equipment to know exactly when to look at the communication line to check for bit pulses. While both the transmitting and receiving equipment contain extremely accurate clocks, there is still the issue of ensuring that the clocks are synchronized. Because the devices may be many miles apart, the synchronization has to be accomplished through interpretation of the pulses on the communications circuit—the same pulses that represent the bits of data that are being transmitted.

**Manchester coding**

**differential Manchester coding**

**biphase coding**

NRZ coding techniques have certain inherent limitations that have to do with synchronization and that become apparent at high speeds. To overcome these limitations, other coding techniques have been developed. Two in particular—**Manchester coding** and **differential Manchester coding,** also known as **biphase coding**—have become very widely used in digital transmission systems, including LANs. Data coded with the Manchester code have a transition in the middle of each bit period. A low-to-high tran-

**FIGURE 6-15** Digital signals.

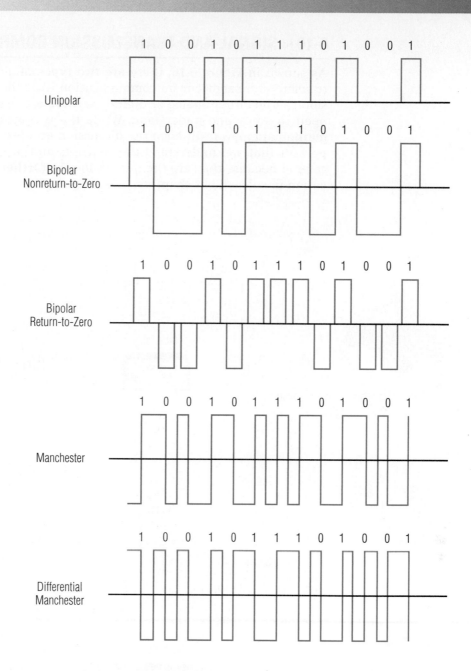

sition represents a 1 bit and a high-to-low transition represents a 0 bit. In differential Manchester coding, the transition in the middle of the bit period is still there, but a 0 is represented by a second transition at the beginning of the bit period and a 1 is represented by no transition at the beginning of the bit period.

The benefits of biphase coding techniques are as follows: 1) Because there is a predictable transition during each bit time, the receiver can synchronize on that transition, making the coding self-clocking; and 2) the absence of the expected transition can be used as an error detection mechanism. Manchester coding has been specified for the IEEE 802.3 standard for data transmission and differential Manchester coding has been specified for the IEEE 802.5 standard. Both of these standards will be studied in Chapter 10.

## 6-10  SIGNAL AND TRANSMISSION COMBINATIONS

As shown in Figure 6-16, there are two types of signals and two ways that transmission can occur on communication lines. Both signals and transmission can be either analog or digital, so there are four combinations that you need to study and understand. While the technical details can get highly mathematical, we will keep the discussion at a less technical level. It is important that you understand the concepts and principles presented in this section because they are the foundation for further study of data communication in subsequent chapters.

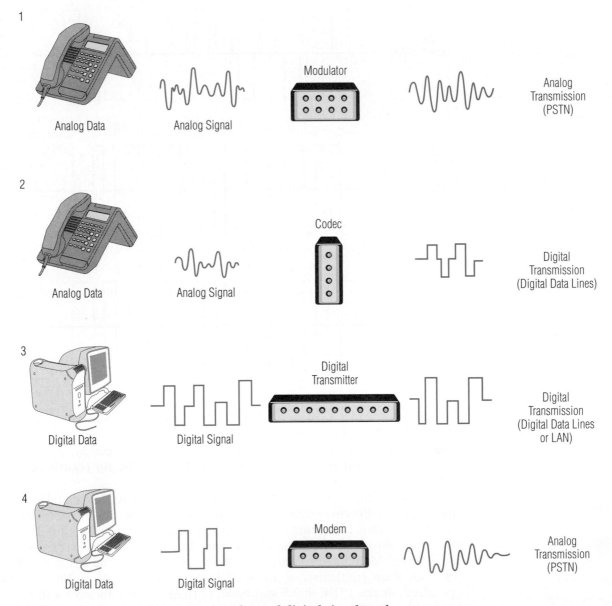

**FIGURE 6-16**  The four combinations of analog and digital signals and transmission techniques.

## Analog Transmission of Analog Signals

The standard telephone is a device that converts analog data (sound) to an analog electrical signal that can be transmitted. At the other end of the connection, another telephone performs the reverse conversion, taking the incoming electrical analog signal and converting it to a sound (also analog) that the listener can hear. You have been introduced to the analog signal's characteristics, its bandwidth, and the meanings and purposes of FDM and modulation. You have also learned how analog signals can be transmitted over the PSTN which, at least as most users see it in their homes or businesses, is an **analog transmission** analog network. So the way we view the PSTN and the way it carries telephone calls is a good example of the **analog transmission** of analog signals.

## Digital Transmission of Analog Signals

In reality, however, most of the PSTN operates digitally. Analog signals from telephones are converted to digital signals, sometimes by a digital telephone but usually at the first telephone company CO they enter. The digital signals are carried through the network to the last CO, where they are converted back to analog signals for delivery to the receiving telephone. We'll look now at how the analog signal is converted to digital form.

You have seen that when a user speaks into the microphone of the telephone handset, the resulting signal takes the shape of a continuously varying wave—an analog signal. If we look at the wave electronically and measure its height (voltage) at specific points in time, we obtain a series of voltages that have values. These values can be represented in binary form and can be transmitted as a series of bits. This is the way analog signals are digitized.

Figure 6-17 shows that at every unit of time, the height of the curve can **analog-to-digital (A/D)** be measured by a special instrument called an **analog-to-digital (A/D) con-** **converter** **verter.** An A/D converter is essentially a digital voltmeter that can take many

**FIGURE 6-17**
Quantization of an analog voice signal.

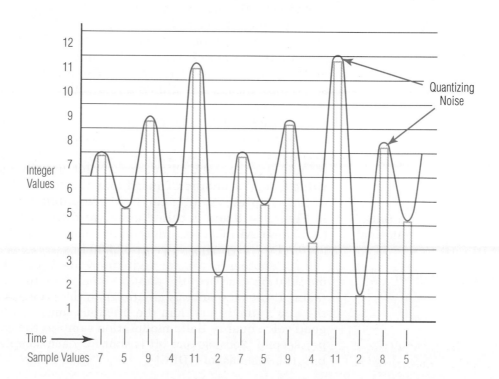

readings per second. Instead of reading actual voltages, however, the A/D converter measures a series of integer values. In effect, the scale of integers is superimposed over the voltages so that the different heights of the curves (voltages) can be represented as integers. This is important because integers can be converted accurately to binary numbers, whereas fractional numbers cannot. The process of approximating the actual analog signal voltage to the predetermined integer steps is called **quantization**. It is similar to rounding. The difference between the exact height of the curve when the sample is taken and the nearest integer value is called **quantizing noise** or **digitizing distortion.**

**quantization**

**quantizing noise**

**digitizing distortion**

Although the diagram in Figure 6-17 shows only twelve values, there are typically 256 different integer values that can be obtained each time a sample is taken. Conveniently, these 256 values can be represented by an 8-bit binary number ($2^8 = 256$). The eight bits are transmitted over the communications line and during the next unit of time, another sample is taken and the process is repeated.

At the receiving end, the process is reversed. The bit stream is divided into 8-bit groups. The groups are interpreted as 8-bit binary numbers and are converted to voltages by a **digital-to-analog (D/A) converter.** The original waveform is reproduced with only minor error caused by the quantizing noise. The more frequently samples are taken, the more accurately the original waveform can be reproduced. The name that is commonly applied to A/D and D/A converters in the communications world is a **coder/decoder (codec).**

**digital-to-analog (D/A) converter**

**coder/decoder (codec)**

**pulse code modulation (PCM)**

One relatively old technique for digitizing voice signals is called **pulse code modulation (PCM).** PCM uses 256 integer values and samples the signal 8,000 times per second. Because 8 bits are used for each sample, the effective data rate is $8,000 \times 8$, or 64,000 bps. The telephone companies used this technique for digitizing voice internally in the 1960s and 1970s, especially on long distance communications lines.

Later developments showed that the original signal could be reproduced quite accurately and good voice quality could be maintained at a lower sample rate of 4,000 samples per second. This means that the effective data rate was lowered to $4,000 \times 8$ bits, or 32,000 bps. As the sample rate is slowed, the effect is similar to compressing the bandwidth of an analog signal. If the sample rate is slowed to 2,000 or 1,000 samples per second, voice quality is lost and the reconstructed voice at the receiving end loses its distinguishing characteristics, though it is still understandable. At even lower sample rates, the reconstructed voice is unintelligible.

**adaptive differential pulse code modulation (ADPCM)**

Another technique for reducing the number of bits that must be transmitted is to keep the sample rate at 8,000 bps but reduce the number of bits transmitted for each sample. Because voice signals do not change amplitude very rapidly, adjacent samples usually are not very different in value from one another. Thus, if only the "difference" in the integer values of the samples is sent, it can be represented with 4 bits. This is illustrated in Figure 6-18 and is called **adaptive differential pulse code modulation (ADPCM).** ADPCM was adopted by the ITU-T in 1985 as the recommended method for digitizing voice at 32,000 bps.

**delta modulation**

Yet another method of digitizing voice is called **delta modulation.** Delta modulation compares the analog signal level to the level of the last sample taken. If the new value is greater than the previous sample, a 1 bit is sent; if the new value is less than the previous sample, a 0 bit is sent. To maintain good voice quality, delta modulation samples the analog signal 32,000 times per second. Because one bit is sent for each sample, the data rate is 32,000 bps, the same as for ADPCM.

**FIGURE 6-18** ADPCM codes the difference in signal strength in bits each time a sample is taken.

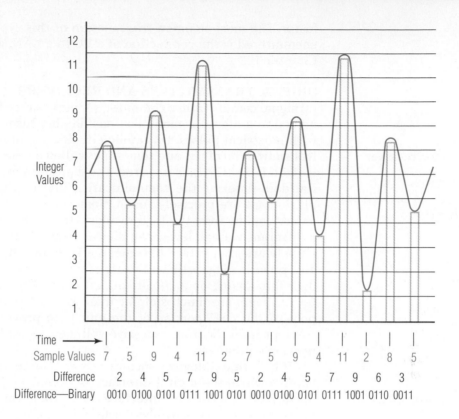

Research is continuing into methods of reducing the data transmission rate required to send digitized voice signals while maintaining acceptable quality.

Analog-to-digital converters that are small and cheap enough to fit into a telephone handset are available and are the tools that some telephones use to transmit digitized voice. This capability is frequently found in telephones for PBX-based telephone systems.

When analog voice data are digitized, the resulting bit stream is the same as the bit stream of coded data. If someone were monitoring a digital communications line and knew nothing about what was being transmitted, it would be impossible to tell whether the bits on the line represented digitized voice, coded data, or an image from a digital facsimile (fax) machine. Another by-product is that the same mathematical techniques for compression and encryption can be applied to digitized voice, data, or images because they all look the same in digital form. Digital multiplexing equipment can also be employed to mix the bits into a consolidated bit stream. Therefore, the recipient of a transmission must know how to interpret the bits of data received.

## Digital Transmission of Digital Signals

**digital transmission**

**baseband transmission**

If we already have data in one of the digital forms shown in Figure 6-15 and want to transmit it digitally, the situation is relatively easy. **Digital transmission,** also called **baseband transmission,** is simply the transmission of the pulses of the digital signal in the form of electrical pulses. The pulses above the line in Figure 6-15 might be represented by a voltage of +3 volts and the pulses below the line by a voltage of −3 volts. This pulsing typically occurs at speeds of at least 1 million pulses per second, but it often occurs much faster. The most common transmission of this type that you have probably encountered is the connection of a PC to a LAN, which will be discussed in Chapter 10.

**DIGITAL TRANSMITTERS AND RECEIVERS**   It may seem that the digital signal coming from a computer, server, or other DTE could be directly connected to a digital communications line because both operate digitally and with electrical pulses. On public circuits, an interface unit called a **digital transmitter/receiver,** and sometimes called a **data service unit/channel service unit (DSU/CSU),** is required. The digital transmitter ensures that the digital data entering the communication line is properly shaped into square pulses that are precisely timed. Sometimes it needs to convert the digital pulses coming from the DTE to a form that is suitable for the line, such as to a different voltage level. The digital transmitter also provides the physical and electrical interface between the DTE and the line. The transmitter may also provide diagnostic and testing facilities. Because they do not perform a digital-to-analog or analog-to-digital conversion, however, digital transmitter/receivers are much simpler than traditional modems. The primary purpose of the CSU portion of the unit is to provide circuitry to protect the carrier's network from excessive voltage coming from the customer's transmission equipment.

When digital devices such as PCs are connected to LANs, which are privately owned, the digital interface between the PC and the LAN circuit is performed by a **network interface card (NIC),** which is a simple digital transmitter/receiver. NICs will be discussed again in Chapter 10.

### Analog Transmission of Digital Signals

The world's telephone system, and therefore most of its network, was originally designed to carry analog voice signals. As was mentioned earlier, this network has largely been converted to digital operation, but in most cases the local loop connection between a business or home and the telephone company's or other communication carrier's CO, the so-called "last mile," still operates in analog mode. Hence, when the PSTN or other analog circuits are used for data transmission, the digital signal from PCs or other devices must usually be converted to analog form to get onto the public network, even though the signal is likely to be converted back to digital form for transmission within the network. Converting a signal from digital to analog or from analog to digital is the function of a modem.

Modems and DSU/CSUs are sometimes called **data circuit-terminating equipment (DCE).** DCE provides the interface between DTE and the communications line.

### 6-11   MODEMS

A **modem** (from *mo*dulation and *dem*odulation) is a specialized digital-to-analog and analog-to-digital signal converter that works by modulating a signal onto a carrier wave and demodulating it at the other end. A modem is connected in the communications network between the digital data terminal equipment and the analog transmission network, as shown in Figure 6-19.

Figure 6-20 shows a general block diagram of a modem with its major components. The power supply takes 110 volt AC power (standard in the U.S.) and converts it to lower voltages, which is necessary for internal operation. In the transmitter, a modulator and digital-to-analog converter changes the

*(margin terms)*
digital
transmitter/receiver

data service
unit/channel service unit
(DSU/CSU)

network interface card
(NIC)

data circuit-terminating
equipment (DCE)

modem

**FIGURE 6-19** Location of modems in a communications system.

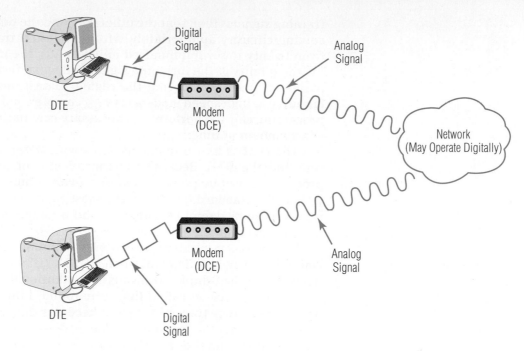

**FIGURE 6-20** Block diagram representation of a modem.

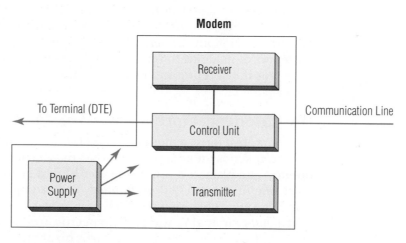

digital bits (pulses) from the DTE to a modulated analog signal appropriate to the type of modulation being used. The output is a sine wave of the proper amplitude, frequency, and phase to represent the digital input signal.

**equalizer circuitry**

    **Equalizer circuitry** compensates for variability in the actual transmission line used. Although analog telephone circuits have standard parameters and specifications, there is a range of acceptable characteristics. As a modem's speed increases, it becomes critical for the modem to detect and compensate for the exact parameters of the particular circuit being used. **Fixed**

**fixed equalizers**

**equalizers** assume that a certain average set of parameters exists, and they shape the transmitted wave accordingly. Fixed equalizers were adequate when transmission speeds were relatively slow, such as 1,200, 2,400, or 4,800

**adaptive equalizers**

bps; however, with higher transmission speeds, more sophisticated **adaptive equalizers** are used to adjust the transmission speed and other attributes to the actual parameters of the line being used.

    To equalize a circuit, a standard training signal of known characteristics is sent from one modem to the other. The received signal is examined and, based on its shape and any errors that have occurred, the receiver's circuitry adjusts itself to the exact characteristics of the incoming waveform. The training signal is then sent the other way, and the other modem adjusts its receiving circuitry appropriately. After the initial training time, which takes from twenty to several hundred milliseconds, the modems constantly monitor the quality of the incoming signal and make further equalization adjustments, as necessary, during the regular data transmission. The equalizing circuitry in high-speed modems is very complex and requires powerful signal processing chips to perform the necessary calculations and adjustments in a short amount of time.

The control unit of modems deals with the interfaces to the telephone line and the DTE. Because the control unit of most modems is a microprocessor, it can be programmed to provide a number of special features as well as the standard functions. The most common features, provided even in inexpensive modems, are auto dial and auto answer capabilities, discussed later in this chapter.

**half-duplex (HDX) transmission**

**line turnaround**

Transmission in either direction on a circuit, but not in both directions simultaneously, is called **half-duplex (HDX) transmission.** When a modem is designed for half-duplex transmission, additional control circuitry is added to perform a process called **line turnaround.** Line turnaround occurs when one modem stops transmitting and becomes the receiver, and the receiving modem becomes the transmitter. The modems exchange synchronization signals to ensure that they are ready to operate in the new mode, and then transmission begins again in the opposite direction. Line turnaround can occur very frequently, and the speed of this process is an important factor in overall line throughput. Commonly, it takes between fifty and 200 milliseconds for a pair of modems to turn the line around. This may not seem like a lot of time, but it can represent a significant portion of total transmission time.

## How Modems Work

In its simplest form, a modem senses the signal from the DTE. When it senses a 0 bit, it sends an analog signal that has certain attributes (amplitude, frequency, and phase). When it senses a 1 bit, it sends a different signal, with at least one of the attributes changed. For example, when frequency modulation is used, a 0 bit from the DTE causes the modem to turn on an oscillator that sends an analog wave of a specific frequency on the telephone line. When a 1 bit is sent, the modem turns on another oscillator, which generates

A typical industrial modem.
(Courtesy of 3Com Corporation. Reprinted with permission.)

a wave that has a different frequency. At the receiving end, the process is reversed. The waves are converted to a digital signal (electrical pulses) representing the original 0 and 1 bits. This specific type of frequency modulation is called **frequency shift keying (FSK)**.

We will look at the operational details of a very simple modem that uses FSK. This type of modem was designed for very slow transmission, so it is not used any more. However, it serves as an excellent learning tool for basic modem operation. When two modems of this type communicate, one is designated as the "originate" modem and the other is designated as the "answer" modem. The originate modem transmits the 0 bits at 1,070 Hz and the 1 bits at 1,270 Hz. The answer modem uses 2,025 Hz for 0 bits and 2,225 Hz for 1 bits. These frequencies are well within the range of human hearing, and each signal sounds like a musical tone. The tones change so fast that if you listen to a telephone line when this type of modem is transmitting, the signals produce a warbling sound.

Looking at the signal diagrammatically in Figure 6-21, we can see where all of the frequencies fit within the bandwidth of a standard telephone line. This allows the transmissions from both modems to occur simultaneously, so full duplex transmission can occur. Figure 6-22 shows how the wave form of the originate modem looks as it shifts back and forth from one frequency to another.

One practical difficulty with this type of modem is that as the speed increases, the frequency changes occur so fast that it becomes difficult for the

**frequency shift keying (FSK)**

**FIGURE 6-21** Frequencies used by a slow-speed FSK modem.

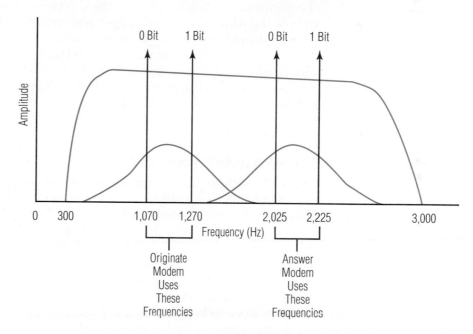

**FIGURE 6-22** Frequency modulation in a slow-speed FSK modem.

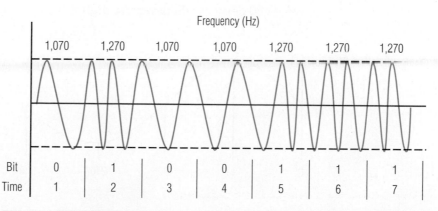

A U.S. Robotics 56Kbps
V.92 modem.
(Courtesy of U.S. Robotics.
Reprinted with permission.)

receiver to detect them. At the very slow speed of 1,200 baud, each tone is transmitted for only 1/1,200 of a second, or .0833 second. At higher speeds, the duration is shorter. Widening the difference between the frequencies can reduce the difficulty, but the upper transmission speed is still quite slow.

Amplitude modulation is an alternative, but in reality it is never used by itself in modems because noise on the transmission line makes it relatively unreliable. As you have learned, the third attribute of an analog signal that can be changed is the phase of the signal. Rapid phase changes of the signal can be electronically detected more easily than rapid frequency changes, which makes phase modulation best suited for use in high-speed modems.

### Phase Modulation (PM)

PM is the technique of changing an analog signal's phase in order to modulate it. An analog signal's wave is called a sine wave because it is the shape generated by the geometric sine function. Figure 6-23 shows how it can be labeled with degree markings at any point on the X axis. An analog signal's phase can be thought of as the timing offset, as shown in Figure 6-24. If two waves are offset from one another, they are **phase shifted** a certain number of degrees. Figure 6-24 shows waves that are offset by 90, 180, and 270 degrees from one another. The phase shift could be any number of degrees; it does not need to be a multiple of 90 degrees.

In the simplest case, phase modulation is performed by shifting a sine wave 180 degrees whenever the digital bit stream changes from 0 to 1. It would

*phase shift*

**FIGURE 6-23** Angles of a sine wave.

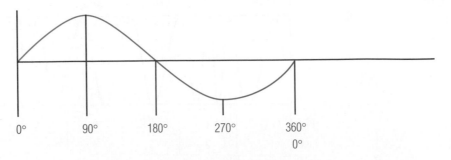

FIGURE 6-24 Phase shifts.

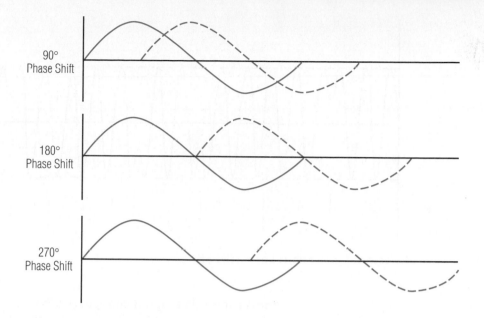

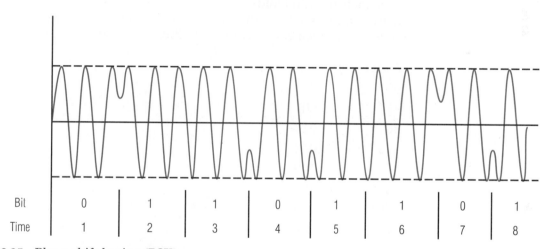

FIGURE 6-25 Phase shift keying (PSK).

**phase shift keying (PSK)**

**differential phase shift keying (DPSK)**

shift 180 degrees again when the signal changed from 1 to 0. The wave would look like Figure 6-25. This type of modulation is called **phase shift keying (PSK)**. The more usual type of phase shift modulation of this type is a **differential phase shift keying (DPSK)**. In DPSK, the phase is shifted each time a 1 bit is transmitted; otherwise the phase remains the same. This is illustrated in Figure 6-26. Notice that the waveform is the same in Figures 6-25 and 6-26, but the bits are different.

Suppose that instead of 180 degrees, the phase were shifted only 90 degrees. Now there are four possible shifts: 0, 90, 180, or 270 degrees. With a binary signal, each shift could represent a dibit. For example,

| Phase shift | Dibits |
| --- | --- |
| 0° | 00 |
| 90° | 01 |
| 180° | 10 |
| 270° | 11 |

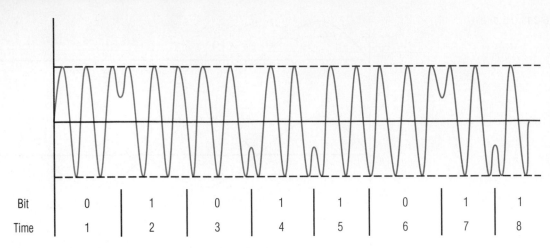

| Bit | 0 | 1 | 0 | 1 | 1 | 0 | 1 | 1 |
|-----|---|---|---|---|---|---|---|---|
| Time | 1 | 2 | 3 | 4 | 5 | 6 | 7 | 8 |

**FIGURE 6-26** Differential phase shift keying (DPSK).

Whenever there is a signal change, two bits of information are transmitted. The data rate, measured in bits per second, will be two times the signaling rate, measured in bauds.

If the phase is shifted in 45 degree increments, there are eight possible shifts, each of which can represent a tribit.

| Phase shift | Tribits |
|-------------|---------|
| 0° | 000 |
| 45° | 001 |
| 90° | 010 |
| 135° | 011 |
| 180° | 100 |
| 225° | 101 |
| 270° | 110 |
| 315° | 111 |

For each signal change, three information bits are transmitted. The bit rate of the circuit will be three times the baud rate.

## Quadrature Amplitude Modulation (QAM)

quadrature amplitude modulation (QAM)

If the phase is shifted less than 45 degrees, the receiver has a very difficult time detecting it. To get to higher speeds, modem designers have developed modulation techniques that use a combination of phase and amplitude modulation. The objective is to get 16 distinct combinations of phase and amplitude. This allows 4 bits, a quadbit, to be represented by each combination. There are several techniques through which this has been achieved, but all are called **quadrature amplitude modulation (QAM)**. The most common technique is shown in Figure 6-27. Note that there are 8 phase changes and 4 amplitudes in use, representing 32 possibilities—but not all combinations are valid. Also note that the quadbits are not assigned in a neat, logical sequence. The reasons are very technical, but have to do with ensuring that the receiver detects as many transmission errors as possible.

FIGURE 6-27 An example of the phase changes and amplitudes used in one type of modem that uses QAM.

| Phase Change (degrees) | Relative Amplitude | Quadbit |
|---|---|---|
| 0 | 3 | 0001 |
| 0 | 5 | 1001 |
| 45 | $\sqrt{2}$ | 0000 |
| 45 | $3\sqrt{2}$ | 1000 |
| 90 | 3 | 0010 |
| 90 | 5 | 1010 |
| 135 | $\sqrt{2}$ | 0011 |
| 135 | $3\sqrt{2}$ | 1011 |
| 180 | 3 | 0111 |
| 180 | 5 | 1111 |
| 225 | $\sqrt{2}$ | 0110 |
| 225 | $3\sqrt{2}$ | 1110 |
| 270 | 3 | 0100 |
| 270 | 5 | 1100 |
| 315 | $\sqrt{2}$ | 0101 |
| 315 | $3\sqrt{2}$ | 1101 |

## Trellis Code Modulation (TCM)

As the speed of a transmission is pushed above 9,600 bps, the techniques used to achieve error-free transmission become very sophisticated. As the bit rate increases, noise and other impairments of the communications line have a more significant effect. The following table shows the number of bits and characters that are affected by a noise pulse on the communications line that lasts just one-tenth of a second.

| Speed (bps) | Bits affected | 8-bit characters affected |
|---|---|---|
| 300 | 30 | 3+ |
| 1,200 | 120 | 15 |
| 2,400 | 240 | 30 |
| 4,800 | 480 | 60 |
| 9,600 | 960 | 120 |
| 19,200 | 1,920 | 240 |
| 28,800 | 2,880 | 360 |
| 33,600 | 3,360 | 420 |
| 56,000 | 5,600 | 700 |

You can see from this table how important it is to have quiet, error-free communications lines and sophisticated means to detect transmission errors when they do occur. At the speeds commonly used today, even on the relatively slow dial-up lines we use from home, a 0.1 second noise pulse can easily wipe out a transmission from our PC to the Internet, such as a request to move to a new Web site.

**trellis code modulation (TCM)**

**Trellis code modulation (TCM)** is a specialized form of a QAM that codes the data so that many bit combinations are invalid. If the receiver detects an invalid bit combination, it can determine what the valid combinations should have been. Trellis coding allows the transmission of 6, 7, or 8 bits per baud. A 2,400-baud signaling rate yields speeds of 14,400 bps, 16,800 bps, and 19,200 bps.

**signal processors**

As modulation techniques get more sophisticated, the amount of signal processing that the modem must do increases significantly. Indeed, today's more sophisticated modems depend on powerful circuit chips, called **signal processors,** to code the data for the transmission and decode it at the receiving end.

The following paragraphs describe some of the current international standards for modems that are used on dial-up connections.

## V.32 and V.32bis Modem Standards

**V.32**

A significant use of TCM has been to provide 9,600 bps transmission on dial-up or leased telephone lines. The ITU-T has published standard **V.32,** which specifies 9,600 bps, full-duplex operation using TCM with an echo cancellation technique. Echo cancellation permits high-speed signals traveling in opposite directions to exist on the same dial-up circuit, at the same time, in the same frequency band.

**V.32bis**

A further improvement was made in the way a modem encodes data for transmission and an improved standard, **V.32bis,** was written. A modem following the standard can transmit data on a dial-up or leased circuit at 14,400 bps.

A U.S. Robotics 56Kbps V.92 modem designed to be mounted in an ISA slot inside a PC. This modem also handles fax transmission.
(Courtesy of U.S. Robotics. Reprinted with permission.)

## V.33 Modem Standard

V.33

The **V.33** standard defines modem transmission at up to 14,400 bps on 4-wire leased circuits. A V.33 modem uses the same modulation techniques as one that is V.32 compliant.

## V.34 and V.34bis Modem Standards

V.34

V.34bis

**V.34** is the ITU-T standard for modems that operate at 28.8 Kbps through a standard telephone line. In 1996, the ITU-T revised and upgraded the standard to allow a higher data rate of 33.6 Kbps. The upgraded standard, **V.34bis**, is sometimes known as V.34+.

V.34 and V.34bis assume that most of the data transmission occurs on digital lines and that analog lines are used only in the first and last parts of the connection—the local loops. Because digital circuits are electrically cleaner and experience fewer errors, V.34 uses a baud rate up to 3,429 in combination with TCM. When V.34 modems first connect, they send signals to each other to test the characteristics of the circuit and determine its quality. This exchange of signals is called **handshaking.** Based on the results of the handshaking, the modems decide the best combination of baud rate and modulation technique from among fifty-nine predefined possibilities to produce the fastest throughput. If the modems detect more errors than expected during the transmission, they can change the combination dynamically. However, this may result in a slower transmission speed.

handshaking

V.34bis continues to use the same baud rate (3,429) as V.34, but uses an upgraded form of TCM, which averages 9.8 bits per baud to achieve a throughput rate of 33.6 Kbps. Experience has shown, however, that many telephone lines are not of sufficient quality to support the higher transmission speed, so many people using V.34bis modems do not actually get the 33.6 Kbps data rate.

## The V.90 Modem Standard

V.90

In February of 1998, the ITU-T adopted the **V.90** standard for 56 Kbps modems. V.90 technology assumes that at least one end of the communication line has a pure digital connection to the telephone network. In fact, the normal configuration that V.90 expects is shown in Figure 6-28, an example that shows a typical home connection to the Internet.

V.90 transmission is asymmetric, in that the 56 Kbps data rate is only achieved on the half of the transmission that comes from the all-digital end of the connections (the Internet in this example). Transmissions from the analog end follow the V.34bis standard and occur at a maximum rate of 33.6 Kbps. In most applications, this difference in transmission speeds makes little difference because the amount of data flowing from the workstation to the Internet—keystrokes and mouse commands—is normally much less than the amount of data flowing from the Internet to the workstation as it downloads websites or files. In this application, the higher speed is needed for data coming from the Internet more than for the data flowing to it.

V.90 uses PCM for the digital half of the transmission. You may wonder why V.90 achieves only 56 Kbps, because PCM is capable of 64 Kbps. There are several reasons, including noise on the analog portion of the circuit and the fact that some telephone companies use one of the bits in PCM for control signaling, which leaves only 7 bits available for data (7 bits × 8,000 samples per second = 56,000 bps). Another reason is that the FCC and other regulatory agencies have established signal power level requirements. To meet agency

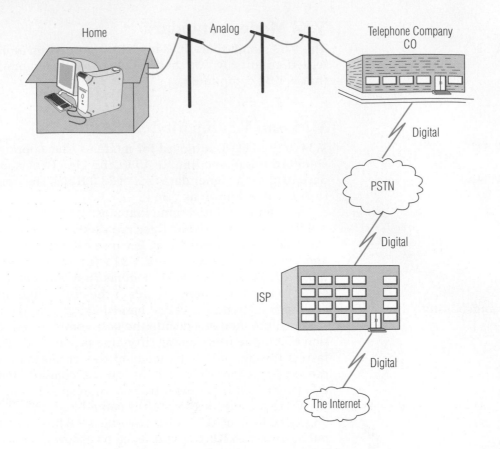

requirements for maximum signal strength, the telephone companies must reduce the power of the data signal, and this reduction further reduces the maximum theoretical data rate to 54 Kbps.

In reality, if you have a reasonably good telephone line and are within three
and one-half miles from your telephone company CO, you should get transmission speeds between 40 Kbps and 53 Kbps. Some lines are electrically noisy or
have other impairments that cause the actual transmission speed to be lower.

## V.92 Modem Standard

V.92

In November of 2000, the ITU-T approved the **V.92** modem standard. Although
the top speed for downloads is still 56 K, V.92 has a number of enhancements:

- Startup time: the time needed to establish a connection has been reduced by about half. Known as Quick Connect, this feature makes hopping on and off the Internet or other applications much faster and easier.

- The maximum upload speed has been increased from 33.6 Kbps to 48
  Kbps. This improves general uploading speed for applications such as
  videoconferencing or e-mails that have large attachments.

- V.92 has a standard method of disconnecting the modem long enough to
  let you know that someone is trying to call you on the telephone without
  losing the data connection, a feature referred to as "Internet call waiting." Many households use the same phone line for both voice calls and
  data (Internet), so when the user is browsing the Internet, an incoming
  call cannot get through. Modem-on-hold allows you to receive an incoming call and stay connected to the Internet (call-waiting service from your

FIGURE 6-29 Modem standards.

| Name of Standard | Provisions of Standard | Comment |
|---|---|---|
| V.21 | Transmission at 300 bps, full-duplex. Primarily used outside the U.S. | An old standard. Bell 103 is the comparable standard used in the U.S. |
| V.22 | Transmission at up to 1200 bps. Full duplex. Primarily used outside the U.S. | An old standard. Bell 212A is the comparable standard used in the U.S. |
| V.22bis | Standard for transmission at up to 2400 bps, full-duplex. Used globally. | |
| V.23 | Transmission at up to 1200 bps in one direction and 75 bps in the other direction (pseudo full-duplex). | Developed in the early 1980s as way to reduce modem costs. Used primarily in Europe. |
| V.32 | Transmission at up to 9600 bps, full-duplex. Includes error correction and negotiation standards. | |
| V.32bis | Transmission at up to 14,400 bps, full-duplex. | |
| V.34 | Transmission at up to 28,800 bps, full-duplex. | Assumes that most of the transmission is digital. |
| V.34bis | Transmission at up to 33,600 bps, full-duplex. | Assumes that most of the transmission is digital. |
| V.90 | Transmission at up to 56,000 bps in one direction and 33,600 bps in the other. | One of the local loops must be digital. |
| V.92 | Transmission at up to 56,000 bps in one direction and 48,000 bps in the other. | Other features differentiate V.92 modems from V.90. |

phone company is all that is required). It also works in reverse; you can initiate a voice call while keeping the modem's data connection active.

Go to http://www.v92.com/ on the Internet to read the latest information about this standard.

A summary of the modem standards for dial-up lines is shown in Figure 6-29.

## Modem Data Compression

V.42bis

V.42

The effective throughput of a data transmission using dial-up modems can be improved by compressing the data before it is transmitted. The ITU-T **V.42bis** standard is a data compression standard used on dial-up modems in combination with standard **V.42**, an error-correction standard. V.42bis specifies the way modems will compress data, typically by stripping off unnecessary bits, before it is transmitted. Used together, the two can achieve a compression ratio of up to 2:1, thereby doubling the throughput on a line. A newer, and as

**V.44**

yet not widely utilized standard, **V.44,** is approximately 25 percent more effective than V.42bis in compressing data.

By using the V.42bis compression technique, the effective throughput on a line can normally be increased by a factor of between 3.5:1 and 4:1, assuming that the data has not already been compressed by data compression software. Thus, a V.34 modem that has a data rate of 33.6 Kbps could provide an effective data rate of up to 134.4 Kbps when V.42bis is used, and a V.32 modem could provide an effective data rate of up to 38.4 Kbps when upgraded to use V.42bis.

A company called Microcom, Inc. developed its own error-correction and compression algorithms. Microcom Networking Protocols, called MNP5, uses a combination of run length and Huffman coding compression algorithms that were discussed in Chapter 5. These protocols have become very popular, despite the fact that they are not quite as efficient as the V.44 or V.42/V.42bis combination. Microcom has enhanced its protocols with MNP7 and MNP10, which yield higher compression in particular circumstances.

## Higher Speeds

You can see the evolution of modems from those that assume a purely analog circuit to those that assume a partially digital circuit, to the assumption that one end of the circuit is a direct digital connection. The next step is the case in which both ends are connected directly to a digital circuit. When that occurs, transmission speed into millions of bits per second becomes possible.

## Modems for Fiber-Optic Circuits

When the medium carrying the communications circuit is an optical fiber, a special optical modem is used to convert the electrical signals coming from the DTE to light pulses. Because light waves have the same characteristics as electromagnetic waves—albeit at a much higher frequency—the same con-

This cabinet full of modems might be found in a large facility that handles thousands of users who dial in to a network.
(Courtesy of the Department of Aerospace Engineering, Penn State University. Reprinted with permission.)

cepts of bandwidth and modulation apply but the transmission is entirely digital. The conversion that takes places is not from digital to analog, but from digital-electrical to digital-optical.

## Cable Modems

cable modem

A **cable modem** links a DTE to a cable television (CATV) system cable. Until recently, different cable systems required different cable modems, but now there is a standard cable modem for all systems. CableLabs, an industry technology organization, developed the standard, called DOCSIS, which stands for Data Over Cable Service Interface Specification. The standard was developed to ensure that cable modem equipment built by a variety of manufacturers is compatible. Whereas traditional dial-up modems provide speeds of up to 56 Kbps, a cable modem operates at speeds of more than 1 Mbps, about twenty times faster. Speeds greater than 1 Mbps in a WAN application

broadband transmission

are classified as **broadband transmissions** and represent one of the fastest growing segments of the WAN market today. Broadband WANs will be discussed again in Chapter 13.

When a cable modem is installed, a splitter is installed on the main television cable and a separate cable is run from the splitter to the cable modem, which is located near the customer's computer. The modem is typically connected to the computer through CAT-5 cable (discussed in Chapter 8) and an Ethernet card (discussed in Chapter 10) in the computer. Sometimes a connection is made through a computer's Universal Serial Bus (USB) port instead.

The benefits of the higher speed afforded by cable modems are especially apparent when large files, such as pictures, graphics, audio, or video are downloaded from the Internet. Another attribute of cable modems is that they are always on, so that whenever the customer's computer is running it is connected to the Internet—there is no connection or logon procedure. You simply click on your browser and you are on the Internet and are ready to go. Many cable modem users tout the convenience of this capability as being as important as the increased speed.

Cable modem service is still relatively limited. In mid-2000, about 30 million homes in the U.S. and Canada were eligible to receive the service, but that was less than one third of all households in those two countries. Market demand is motivating cable companies to upgrade their facilities and broaden availability as quickly as possible. For more information and an up-to-date picture of cable modem technology and availability, consult the Cable Modem Information Network on the Internet at http://www.cablemodem.net or the Cable Modem University at http://www.catv.org/ or http://www.cablemodemhelp.com/.

## Null Modems

If distances are very short, such as when two pieces of equipment are in the same room but are not on a LAN, and the DTEs can be connected by a cable, modems may not be needed at all. Simply plugging a cable between two DTEs won't work, however, because both devices deliver data to be transmitted on the same pin of the standard connector used for this situation. Conceptually, what is needed is a device with a cable that cross-connects the transmit and receive pins of the connectors so that the transmit pin on one device is connected to the receive pin on the other, and vice versa. A

null modem

modem eliminator

schematic of this type of device, called a **null modem** or **modem eliminator** is shown in Figure 6-30.

FIGURE 6-30 Modem
eliminator (simplified).

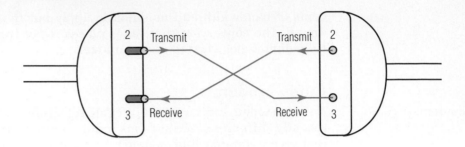

## 6-12    DTE-DCE INTERFACE STANDARDS

Standards have been developed that specify the way DTE, such as PCs, and DCE, such as modems, will be connected. The standards include three elements:

1. mechanical characteristics: such as what type of connectors will be used and the number of pin connections
2. signaling characteristics: such as how many signals there will be and what each signal will mean
3. electrical characteristics: such as what voltages and current levels will be on each pin of the connector

Several standards have been developed for the interface, but none is universally used. The most popular standard interfaces are discussed here, although many others exist.

### RS-232-C

RS-232-C

Virtually all computer and terminal equipment that communicates conforms to an interface standard, **RS-232-C,** which was developed by the Electrical Industries Association (EIA) in the early 1960s and has been revised several times since. Some years ago, the EIA decided to rename the standard to EIA-232, which is now its proper name. Because nearly everyone still refers to the standard as RS-232-C, we will use that name here. The C version of the standard is still the most commonly used, although a later D version exists and will be described later. RS-232-C has been adapted for international use by the ITU-T under the name V.24 and, while the two standards are not identical, they are functionally equivalent for most applications.

The actual hardware used to connect a DTE with a DCE using the RS-232-C standard is a cable with 25 wires and a 25-pin connector at either end, as shown in Figure 6-31. The use of each of these wires or pins, as well as the lev-

FIGURE 6-31   A RS-232-C
cable with male and female
25-pin connectors.

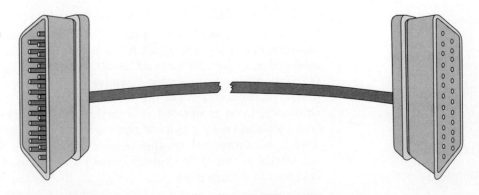

els (voltages) of the signals, is specified in the RS-232-C standard document. The signals sent across the connection are, in all cases, digital and serial. The standard also specifies the mechanical attributes of the interface, specifically that the DCE will have a female connector and the DTE will have a male connector. Another specification is a 50-foot maximum length for a cable connecting a DTE and DCE.

The RS-232-C standard has some limitations that are inconvenient and are unacceptable in some applications.

- The cable length of 50 feet. At 50 feet, transmission speeds of 20,000 bps can be handled but the distance limitation is a real problem in many situations. In actual practice, cable lengths of up to 100 feet at speeds of 9,600 bps are common, but the operability and speed is neither guaranteed nor supported by equipment manufacturers.

- A technical problem with the way electrical grounding is handled that can lead to difficulties in detecting the difference between a 0 and 1 bit if the speed is high and the cable is long.

If you look at actual RS-232-C cables and connectors, you may notice that many of them do not have 25 pins. Many PC-to-modem connections use a cable with a 25-pin connector at one end and a 9-pin connector on the other. This occurs because many vendors choose not to comply with the complete RS-232-C standard in order to keep costs down. Furthermore, some of the functions of RS-232-C are rarely used, and the elimination of the capability causes few problems in most situations. So, in this configuration, the extra wires on the 25-pin end of the cable are simply not connected on the 9-pin end. Nine pin connectors are shown below.

Male and female RS-232-C 9-pin connectors.
(Courtesy of Startech.com Ltd. Reprinted with permission.)

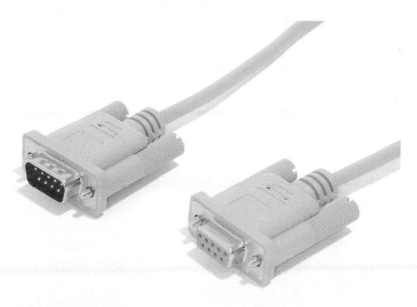

A list of the 25 signals and their functions is shown in Figure 6-32. Not all of the pins have been assigned a use. This is to provide for future expansion of the standard. Pins 2 and 3 are the ones on which the actual data are passed. All of the other pins are used for signaling between the DTE and the DCE.

**FIGURE** 6-32   RS-232-C connector pin assignments.

| Pin | Description |
| --- | --- |
| 1 | Protective ground |
| 2 | Transmitted data |
| 3 | Received data |
| 4 | Request to send |
| 5 | Clear to send |
| 6 | Data set (modem) ready |
| 7 | Electrical ground |
| 8 | Received line signal detector |
| 9 | (reserved for modem testing) |
| 10 | (reserved for modem testing) |
| 11 | unassigned |
| 12 | Secondary receive line signal detector |
| 13 | Secondary clear to send |
| 14 | Secondary transmitted data |
| 15 | Transmission signal element timing |
| 16 | Secondary received data |
| 17 | Receiver signal element timing |
| 18 | unassigned |
| 19 | Secondary request to send |
| 20 | Data terminal ready |
| 21 | Signal quality detector |
| 22 | Ring indicator |
| 23 | Data signal rate selector |
| 24 | Transmit signal element timing |
| 25 | unassigned |

## RS-232-D

**RS-232-D**

In 1987, the RS-232-C interface standard was revised and renamed **RS-232-D**. RS-232-D made the following changes to the standard:

■ addition of a shield on the cable
■ redefinition of the protective ground
■ definition of pin 18 (local loopback), pin 25 (test mode interchange circuit), and redefinition of pin 21 from signal quality detector to remote loopback
■ upgraded specifications for the 25-pin connector

Although these changes solved the grounding problem of the RS-232-C standard and made RS-232-D equivalent to the ITU-T V.24 standard, the RS-232-D interface has not seen widespread usage.

### RS-449

RS-449

Another interface standard that overcomes some of the problems of RS-232-C is the **RS-449** standard. RS-449 uses 37 signal wires, as opposed to 25 for RS-232-C. The extra ones were added for automatic modem testing. The RS-449 standard also overcomes the RS-232-C's bandwidth (speed) and length limitations. An RS-449 connection can transmit data at 100 Kbps for 4,000 feet or 10 Mbps for about 40 feet.

One of the weaknesses of the RS-449 standard is that it makes no provision for automatic dialing between modems. Although the RS-449 standard was the intended successor to RS-232-C, it has been neither well accepted in the marketplace nor widely implemented.

### RS-336

RS-336

**RS-336** is an interface standard that does allow for automatic dialing of calls under modem control. However, it does not adequately provide for high-speed data transmission or the use of private circuits. Its primary use has been for applications in which the computer automatically calls numerous remote data terminals for data collection.

### X.21 and X.21bis

X.21

The **X.21** interface was developed by the ITU-T and is widely accepted as an international standard. X.21 uses a 15-pin connector and is designed for a digital connection to a digital PSTN. When the X.21 standard is used, data signals are encoded in serial form and kept that way throughout the transmission. All other signaling is also in digital form. For example, a digital dial tone is a series of + (plus) signs. The basic rate of a digital channel is 64,000 bps, which not only exceeds most dialup data transmission speeds today but can also handle digitized voice.

X.21bis

Until digital networks that run all the way to the home or desktop are fully in place, the ITU-T has defined a temporary standard called **X.21bis**, which (electrically) is virtually identical to RS-232-C and V.24. Its application, however, is for connecting a terminal to a packet-switched network via analog lines.

This DB37 connector is used for the RS-449 interface.
(Courtesy of Nationwide Electronics. Reprinted with permission.)

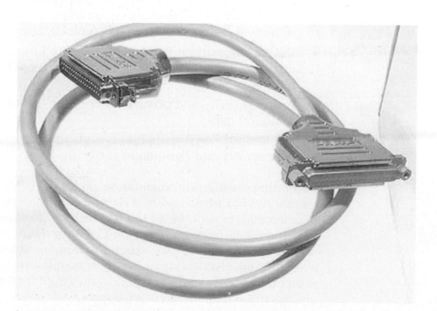

### Current Loop

The **current loop** interface, although outdated, is mentioned because it is still in use today. Originally designed for use by teletypewriters, the current loop indicates 0 and 1 bits by the presence or absence of an electrical current on the circuit. A 1 bit is defined as the flow of either 20 milliamps or 60 milliamps of current, depending on the type of equipment. Cables connecting current loop devices can be up to 1,500 feet long and can pass data at up to 9,600 bps. Although the current loop is very popular because it is simple and inexpensive to produce, it is totally nonstandard, which means that one manufacturer's equipment may not be able to connect to another manufacturer's equipment, even though both are using a current loop interface.

## 6-13　WHY DIGITAL TRANSMISSION IS SUPERIOR

You learned earlier that the PSTN is primarily an analog network, at least as far as the general public sees it. It was designed to do analog transmission because its original function was to transfer voice signals. Today, however, virtually all new telephone line and cable installations are being designed for digital transmission. One reason is that data transmission is growing more rapidly than voice, but a more significant reason is that digital transmission has many advantages compared to analog transmission. The benefits are so significant that it is worthwhile to convert analog signals to digital signals for transmission when digital transmission lines can be used. As you have learned, most transmissions between telephone company COs are already made in digital mode, and many private networks installed in companies and other organizations use digital transmission as well.

The reasons that digital transmission is superior to analog transmission are the following:

- **Better data integrity:** Digital transmission has fewer errors than analog transmission. Because the data are binary, the errors that do occur are easier to detect and correct.

- **Higher capacity:** It has become possible to build very high capacity digital circuits, including those that use fiber-optic cable. Multiplexing techniques used with digital transmission are more efficient than the frequency division multiplexing (FDM) that is typically used with analog circuits.

- **Easier integration:** It is much easier to integrate voice, data, video, and other signals using digital transmission techniques than it is with analog transmission.

- **Better security and privacy:** Encryption techniques can easily be applied to digital data.

- **Lower cost:** Large-scale integrated circuitry has reduced the cost of digital circuitry and equipment faster than the cost of analog equipment.

Extending the digital transmission capability to the millions of homes, apartments, and businesses around the world presents a major challenge that will take decades to achieve. In the U.S. and some other countries, rapid progress is being made by using existing CATV systems, which can be upgraded to carry digital signals. Also, existing telephone lines can carry digital signals over limited distances using new transmission technologies such as DSL, even though they weren't originally designed for digital transmission. We will discuss these technologies in Chapter 9.

An application of high-speed digital transmission that is envisioned is for movie studios to transmit movies directly to theaters rather than shipping cans of film. This would allow new films to be distributed very quickly, and proponents claim the digital images projected at the theater would be far superior to those we see today from film. Film wears with every run through a projector, so all showings after the first one are somewhat degraded. Digital projection, on the other hand, would always be the same and would be of a better quality than even the first running of a film. Transmitting a movie requires very high speed transmission lines, and digital receiving and projection equipment in theaters would be necessary. The capital cost for new equipment is high, so it will take several years before the capability becomes widely available.

A summary of four of the transmission cases you studied is illustrated in Figure 6-33.

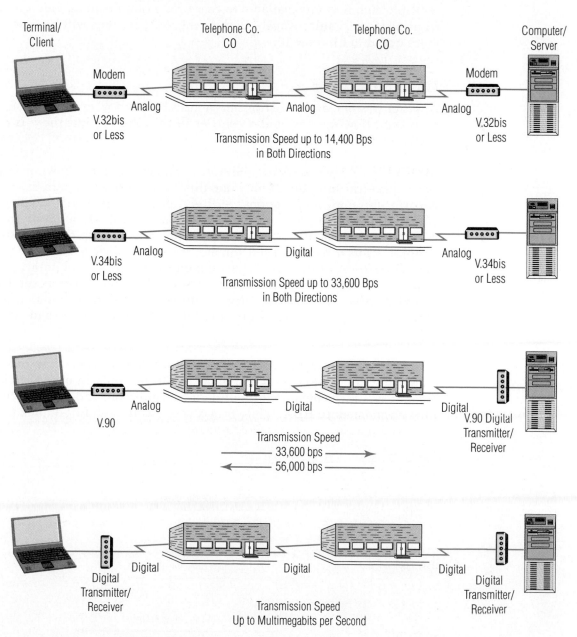

**FIGURE 6-33** The ways in which increasingly higher data transmission rates have been achieved on dial-up communication lines.

## 6-14   OTHER WAYS OF CLASSIFYING TRANSMISSION

Data transmission can be classified in many ways. Four important ways are according to the type of signal transmitted, the data flow, the type of physical connection, and the timing. We'll look at each of these in detail and introduce you to some additional terms that are frequently used when data communications and networking are being discussed.

### Type of Signal Transmitted: Baseband and Broadband

As was mentioned earlier in the chapter, baseband transmission is essentially another name for digital transmission. When broadband transmission is used in a LAN application, the signal is transmitted in analog form and multiple channels are available to carry, for example, data, video, and voice transmissions simultaneously. Both of these techniques will be described in more detail in Chapter 10.

### Data Flow

Another way of classifying transmissions is by the flow of the data on the circuit. Data flow was touched on earlier in this chapter but there is more to the story.

**simplex transmission**

SIMPLEX TRANSMISSION   **Simplex transmission,** as shown in Figure 6-34, is data transmission in only one direction on the communications line. No transmission in the opposite direction is possible. Although simplex transmission is not what we usually think of first when we discuss data transmission, it is more common than you might imagine. In businesses, simplex transmission is used for monitors and alarms, where a signal is sent from a sensor back to a central monitoring or control point. A similar application occurs in hospitals, where sensors on the patients send signals to the nurses' stations. Security monitoring cameras at banks and other stores use simplex transmission, and television and radio broadcasting are other examples.

**half-duplex (HDX) transmission**

HALF-DUPLEX TRANSMISSION   **Half-duplex (HDX) transmission** is transmission in either direction on a circuit, but only in one direction at a time. It is a very common form of data transmission, and many circuits will only accommodate HDX. While it may seem as though full-duplex transmission would always be desirable, in many cases HDX is perfectly acceptable.

FIGURE 6-34   Simplex, half-duplex, and full-duplex transmission.

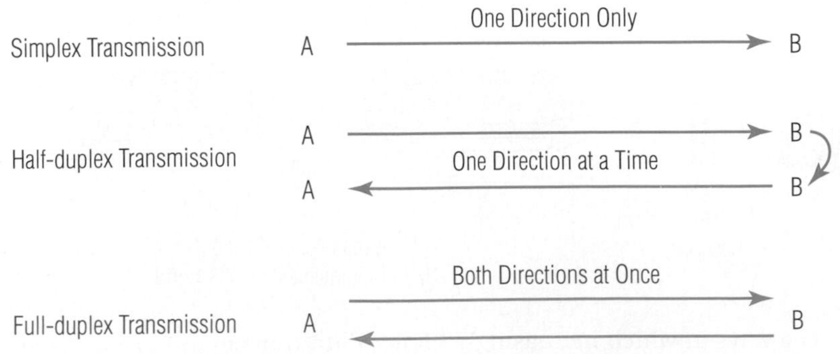

In a computer-based application where an inquiry is sent to the computer and then a response is sent back on the same circuit to the terminal, HDX is really all that is required. Citizens band and amateur radio are other examples of half-duplex transmission.

**full-duplex (FDX) transmission**

**FULL-DUPLEX TRANSMISSION**  **Full-duplex (FDX) transmission** is data transmission going in both directions on a circuit simultaneously. It requires more intelligence at both ends of the circuit to keep track of the two data streams. One place where FDX transmission is frequently used is between computers. Computers have the intelligence and the speed to perform the necessary line control functions to take advantage of the speed that FDX transmission offers. Whereas the computer power necessary to handle the complexities of FDX transmission once resided only in mainframes, now any PC can take advantage of FDX transmission if the underlying transmission circuit supports it. As a result, FDX transmissions are used more frequently than they were a few years ago, and the throughput benefits are realized more often.

**duplex**

The definitions given in this section are those used in the U.S. In Europe, the word *simplex* is applied to the definition of half-duplex, and full-duplex is simply called **duplex.**

## Type of Physical Connection

Yet another way of classifying transmissions is according to the way in which the hardware is connected.

**parallel transmission**

**parallel mode**

**PARALLEL MODE**  When digital devices are in close proximity to one another, as in the case of a PC and a printer, a cable that has one wire for each bit in the character of the data code being used often connects them. That is, if a 7-bit coding scheme, such as ASCII, is being used, the cable would have seven wires for the data bits, as shown in Figure 6-35. There would also be several additional wires for control, timing, and checking. With multiple wires, all the bits of a character can be transferred between the devices at once. This is called **parallel transmission** or **parallel mode.** It is extremely fast, but

**FIGURE 6-35**   Parallel and serial transmission.

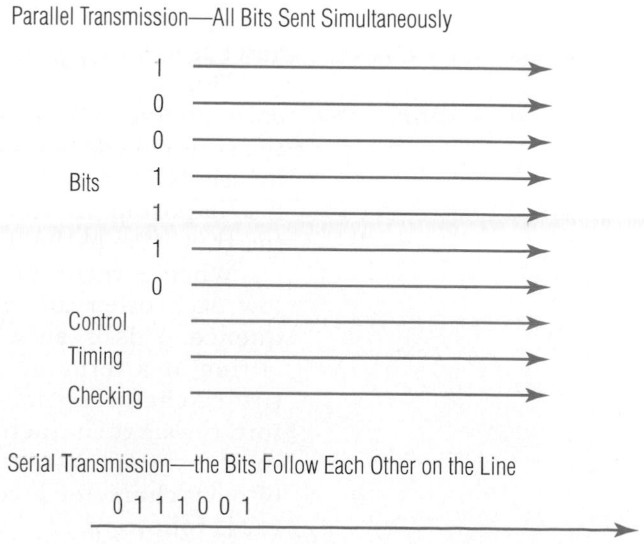

Parallel Transmission—All Bits Sent Simultaneously

```
          1  ──────────────────────────────►
          0  ──────────────────────────────►
          0  ──────────────────────────────►
Bits      1  ──────────────────────────────►
          1  ──────────────────────────────►
          1  ──────────────────────────────►
          0  ──────────────────────────────►
Control      ──────────────────────────────►
Timing       ──────────────────────────────►
Checking     ──────────────────────────────►
```

Serial Transmission—the Bits Follow Each Other on the Line

```
     0 1 1 1 0 0 1
─────────────────────────────────────────────►
```

because of the number of wires involved, it is expensive and is not practical for long distances.

serial transmission

serial mode

**SERIAL MODE**    As distance increases, **serial transmission** or **serial mode** is used. Each bit of each character is sent down a cable or communications line one after another, or serially. This type of transfer is also illustrated in Figure 6-32 and is used for all communications applications we will study. There is a trade-off, however. With serial transfer, the transmitter and receiver are more complicated because they have to decompose the character, serialize the bits for transmission, and reconstruct the bits into a character at the receiving end. With parallel transfer, the entire character is sent and received at one time.

## Timing

The final transmission classification system we will look at is the timing of the transmissions.

asynchronous transmission (asynch)

start bit

stop bit

start/stop transmission

mark

space

bit synchronization

**ASYNCHRONOUS TRANSMISSION**    **Asynchronous transmission,** sometimes abbreviated **asynch,** is a transmission technique in which each character sent on a communication line is preceded by an extra bit called a **start bit** and is followed by one or more extra bits called **stop bits.** It is sometimes called **start/stop transmission.**

Asynchronous transmission originated with the early mechanical teletypewriter terminals. For those teletypewriters, the start bit gave the mechanism in the receiving terminal time to start rotating, get up to speed, and get ready to receive the rest of the bits that made up the character. The stop bit gave the rotating mechanism time to get back to a known position and get ready to receive the next character. Long ago, the convention was established that an idle line is one on which the signal for a 1 bit, also called the **mark** signal, is being sent. The opposite condition, the signal for a 0 bit, is called the **space.**

To start the mechanism of the receiver, the line is brought from the idle or mark state to the 0—the space state—for one bit time, thus creating the start bit. For the next 7 bit times (when a 7-bit code is being used), the signal is changed between the 0 and 1 bits to represent the character being transmitted. Then the stop bit(s), a 1 bit, is sent. After the stop bit is sent, the line remains in idle mode (mark [1-bit] condition) until the next character is sent.

The mark and space signals, coupled with the mechanical design of the early teletypewriters, allowed **bit synchronization** to be maintained. That is, the receiving device was able to determine just when to sample the communications line to detect a pulse or no-pulse condition. For maximum accuracy, it is important that the line be sampled at the center of the bit, not during the transition period between bits.

When asynchronous transmission is used, characters do not have to follow each other along the communications line in a precisely timed sequence. This is easy to visualize if you think about an amateur typist sitting at a terminal and typing characters somewhat erratically. Ten or twelve characters may come rather quickly, followed by a long pause before the next character or group is sent. Erratic pulses are not a problem in asynchronous transmission because the start bit appended to the front of each character gives the receiving terminal some notice that a character is following.

transmission efficiency

Asynchronous transmission is relatively simple and inexpensive to implement. It is used widely by PCs, inexpensive terminals, and commercial communications services. A penalty in terms of **transmission efficiency** is paid, however, because at least two extra bits are added to each character being transmitted. The exact penalty depends on the number of bits that make up the character. The following table below shows the transmission efficiency calculations when the Baudot, ASCII, and EBCDIC codes are used.

| Code | Number of bits in code | Start/stop bits | Total bits | Transmission efficiency |
|------|------------------------|-----------------|------------|-------------------------|
| Baudot | 5 | 2 | 7 | 5/7 or 71% |
| ASCII | 7 | 2 | 9 | 7/9 or 77.7% |
| EBCDIC | 8 | 2 | 10 | 8/10 or 80% |

When the ASCII code is transmitted with an extra parity bit added for checking purposes, its transmission efficiency is 8/10, or 80 percent, like that of EBCDIC.

character synchronization

Asynchronous transmission does not require maintenance of precise synchronization between the transmitter and receiver for an extended period of time. When a start bit is sensed, the receiver knows that the next $n$ bits (where $n$ depends on the code being used) on the line make up a character. This is called **character synchronization**. After receiving a stop bit, the receiver simply waits for the next start bit. The only synchronization that has to occur is during the transmission of the 5 to 8 bits that make up a character, so that the receiver looks at or samples the line at the right time. The sampling rate depends on the line speed, a rate that is predetermined and known by both the transmitting and receiving terminals. Without some form of character synchronization, a receiver might not know which was the first bit of a character, and the character could be misinterpreted.

Asynchronous transmission is used where equipment cost must be kept low. The transmission inefficiencies of asynchronous transmission were a big disadvantage when line speeds were primarily 1,200 bits per second or less. Now, with higher speed circuits, concern about the inefficiency is heard less frequently.

synchronous transmission

**SYNCHRONOUS TRANSMISSION** Asynchronous transmission is relatively inefficient because of the extra start and stop bits transmitted with each character; **synchronous transmission** is a more efficient transmission technique. When synchronous transmission is used, bit synchronization is maintained by clock circuitry in the transmitter and in the receiver. The timing generated by the transmitter's clock is sent along with the data so that the receiver can keep its clock synchronized with that of the transmitter throughout a long transmission. The clock circuitry, of course, adds to the cost of the hardware at both ends of the circuit, so the trade-off is equipment cost versus transmission efficiency.

block

synchronization character (SYN)

With synchronous transmission, data characters usually are sent in large groups called **blocks.** The blocks contain special synchronization characters that have a unique bit pattern inserted at the beginning and sometimes in the middle of each block. These **synchronization characters (SYN)** perform a function similar to that of the start bits in asynchronous transmission. When the receiver sees the synchronization character, it knows that the next bit will be the first bit of a character, thus maintaining character synchronization.

Synchronous communication has between one and four synchronizing characters for each block of data. Asynchronous communication has two synchronizing bits for each character. If the ASCII code is used and 250 characters are to be sent, the number of bits sent by each transmission method is:

**Asynchronous**
250 characters × (7 data + 2 start/stop bits per character) = 2,250 bits

**Synchronous**
(250 data characters + 4 synchronizing characters) × 7 bits per character = 1,778 bits

In this example, the synchronous transmission technique sends 21 percent fewer bits. It is, therefore, 21 percent more efficient than asynchronous communication in this example. The efficiency advantage of synchronous transmission improves as longer blocks of data are transmitted.

Because it has a higher transmission efficiency, especially when large blocks of data are being transmitted, synchronous transmission is preferred over asynchronous transmission when large amounts of data must be transmitted—especially when it can be done on dedicated communication lines. Sending data between servers in the same room that are connected by cable is one case where synchronous transmission is useful to take advantage of its efficiencies. It is not as effective, however, when the public communication networks, such as the Internet or the telephone system, are used because these networks break the data into blocks according to their own needs and the efficiencies of large block sizes are lost.

On the other hand, transmissions between two PCs, or between a PC and a server in dial-up mode, are almost always asynchronous. The driving forces to use asynchronous instead of synchronous transmission are lower equipment cost and the fact that the amount of data to be transmitted is frequently relatively small.

## 6-15  SPREAD SPECTRUM TRANSMISSION

**spread spectrum transmission**

**frequency hopping**

**direct sequence**

A form of communication that does not easily fit into the other categories discussed in this chapter is **spread spectrum transmission**. Spread spectrum is a form of radio communication that uses an analog signal to transmit either analog or digital data. The concept is that the signal is spread over a wider-than-usual bandwidth to make interception more difficult. Two techniques are used: **frequency hopping** and **direct sequence**. Most spread spectrum uses the frequency hopping technique, in which the signal is broadcast over a seemingly random series of radio frequencies, hopping from frequency to frequency at split-second intervals.

A conventional radio signal has a frequency that does not change with time. Think about listening to your FM radio: The station's signal does not vary in frequency. You know that you can always listen to the same station if you tune to the same frequency. A station at 98.5 Mhz, for example, is always at 98.5 Mhz. It does not broadcast at 101.5 on some days and 97.8 on others. The digits on the radio's frequency dial stay the same at all times. The frequency of a conventional radio station's signal is kept as constant as possible, so that someone who wants to retrieve the information can locate the signal easily.

## SIDEBAR 6-1

Actress Hedy Lamarr (1913–2000) was a glamorous actress and, surprisingly, the inventor of the frequency hopping spread spectrum transmission technique. In 1942, U.S. patent #2,297,387 was awarded to her for a "Secret Communications System" that laid the groundwork for frequency hopping spread spectrum communications. Her invention was for a radio guidance system for torpedoes, which was used in World War II. It was the forerunner of key developments in spread spectrum communications that are the heart of modern cell phone technology.

(Courtesy of Getty Images Inc. Reprinted with permission.)

There are at least two problems with conventional radio communications that can occur under certain circumstances. First, a signal that has a constant frequency is subject to interference. This occurs when another signal is transmitted on or very near the frequency of the desired signal. This interference can be accidental, as often occurs in amateur radio communications, or it can be deliberate, as in jamming. Second, a constant frequency signal is easy to intercept and is therefore not well suited to applications in which information must be kept confidential between the source (transmitting party) and destination (receiving party).

To minimize these problems, spread spectrum equipment deliberately varies the frequency of the transmitted signal. This variation is done according to a specific, but complicated, mathematical function that usually employs a psuedorandom number generator. To receive the signal, a receiver must be tuned to frequencies that vary precisely according to this function and must employ the same random number sequence to determine which frequency to listen to at a given point in time. The receiver must also know at what time the psuedorandom number sequence was started in order to synchronize the frequency hopping with the transmitter. Eavesdroppers who don't know the mathematical function hear only short sections of the transmission because they don't know the frequency hopping sequence.

If someone wants to jam a spread spectrum signal, that person must have a transmitter that uses the same mathematical function and knows its starting-time point. Obviously, the spread spectrum function must be kept out of the hands of unauthorized people.

The direct sequence technique combines bits from the original signal with bits generated by a psuedorandom bit stream generator using Boolean math. The receiver, using the same psuedorandom bit stream, can reverse the Boolean math process and recover the original bits.

## ■ SUMMARY

In this chapter, you have learned many important facts about communication signals and transmission that are a foundation for further study. Analog and digital signals were explained and the attributes of both were illustrated. Analog and digital transmission were also covered, and you learned how the two types of signals can be transmitted either digitally or by analog means. Modem operation and modem standards were discussed, and you learned why digital transmission is superior to analog transmission. Finally, several other ways that data transmissions can be classified and the terminology associated with them were introduced.

In Chapter 7, you will study the protocols of layer 2 of the OSI model, the data link layer. These protocols are the foundations of every network transmission.

## ■ REVIEW QUESTIONS

6-1. What are the three attributes of a sine wave?

6-2. What is the bandwidth of the AM radio broadcasting band of frequencies in the U.S.? The FM radio band? (If necessary, do some research on the Internet.)

6-3. An analog signal is fed into one end of a twisted pair of wires. At the other end, the relative strength of the signal is measured as $-10$ dB. How much has the power of the signal dropped as it traveled through the wire?

6-4. List an example of an electrical wave that has a frequency of 60 Hz, a radio wave that has a frequency of 640 kHz, a radio wave that has a frequency of 102 MHz, and a sound wave that has a frequency of 880 Hz.

6-5. In normal speech, some sounds above 3,000 Hz are generated. What happens to these frequencies when they are sent through the PSTN?

6-6. Explain the term *modulation.* For what is it used?

6-7. Compare and contrast the meanings of the terms *baud* and *bits per second.*

6-8. How many unique signal changes do dibits, tribits, and quadbits require to be transmitted?

6-9. Compare and contrast *simplex, half-duplex,* and *full-duplex* transmissions.

6-10. Distinguish between *parallel* and *serial* transmission.

6-11. Describe the purpose of the start and stop bits in asynchronous transmission.

6-12. Explain the terms *bit synchronization* and *character synchronization.*

6-13. Explain why synchronous transmission is more efficient than asynchronous transmission when long blocks of data are to be transmitted.

6-14. Using the ASCII code, a block of 1,000 characters of data is to be sent on a communications line. Calculate the relative efficiency of synchronous and asynchronous transmission methods. Calculate the efficiency again for a block containing 50 characters.

6-15. Why is synchronous communication more expensive to implement than asynchronous transmission?

6-16. Explain the terms *mark* and *space*.

6-17. The purpose of the clock in synchronous transmission is _____.

6-18. Why is phase modulation better suited for high speed transmission than frequency or amplitude modulation?

6-19. What are the differences between fixed equalization and adaptive equalization in a modem?

6-20. Describe how high-speed transmission has been achieved in modems that use the V.34 standard.

6-21. What are the upper limits to data transmission speed on analog lines?

6-22. How do high-speed modems achieve their high throughput rates?

6-23. Explain the functions of DSU/CSU when lines designed for digital transmission are used.

6-24. Explain the concept of line turnaround in half-duplex transmission.

6-25. List five advantages of digital transmission over analog transmission.

6-26. Explain why, using PCM, it takes 64,000 bps to transmit a voice signal. How does ADPCM cut the data rate in half?

6-27. Describe the functions of an A/D converter.

6-28. Explain *quantization*.

6-29. Why is there interest in transmitting digital voice signals at slower data rates?

6-30. How does asynchronous transmission work?

6-31. Describe *transmission efficiency*.

6-32. V.34 and V.34bis assume that most data transmission takes place on _____ lines.

6-33. Explain the unique characteristics of data transmission that follows the V.90 standard.

6-34. Explain the purpose of V.42bis and MNP 5.

## TRUE OR FALSE

6-1. Signaling is the propagation of a signal on a medium.

6-2. Playing the A key above middle C on a piano results in a digital signal that has 440 pulses per second.

6-3. Sound waves, electrical waves, and electromagnetic waves have essentially the same characteristics.

6-4. An analog signal level is measured in decibels.

6-5. The loss of signal strength between two points on a communication circuit is called *distortion*.

6-6. The amplitude of a voice signal remains constant while its frequency and phase change.

6-7. FDM is accomplished by shifting each channel to a different part of the frequency spectrum.

6-8. The signaling rate on a circuit is measured in baud.

6-9. A 2,400 baud signal can carry data at a maximum rate of 2,400 bps.

6-10. When 3 bits of information are coded into one signal change, they are called tribits.

6-11. The most common digital signals are unipolar.

6-12. When transmitting analog signals on an analog circuit, a modem is used.

6-13. An analog signal that has been digitized can be exactly restored to its original analog shape by a D/A converter.

6-14. ADPCM is the ITU-T's recommended method for digitizing voice at 32 Kbps.

6-15. In a modem, equalizer circuitry compensates for the variability of the actual transmission line used.

6-16. Line turnaround time in a modem is an insignificant part of the total transmission time.

6-17. Modems can never handle full-duplex transmission.

6-18. Phase modulation is the technique of changing an analog signal's phase in order to modulate it.

6-19. V.34 modems assume that most data transmission occurs on digital lines.

6-20. The transmission speed between a pair of V.90 modems is asymmetric.

6-21. Cable modems for each CATV system are unique.

6-22. Modem eliminators are a low-cost alternative to modems on WAN circuits.

6-23. There are many practical uses for simplex transmission.

6-24. Parallel mode transmission is practical on WANs.

6-25. Asynchronous transmission is widely used today.

6-26. Start bits precede every data block in synchronous transmission.

6-27. To jam a spread spectrum signal, one simply broadcasts a jamming signal on the spread spectrum signal's carrier frequency.

**MULTIPLE CHOICE**

6-1. The reasons that digital transmission is superior to analog transmission are _____.

   a. better data integrity

   b. higher capacity

   c. easier integration

   d. better security and privacy

   e. lower cost

   f. All of the above.

   g. only a, b, c, and d

6-2. A modem is a form of a _____.

   a. codec

   b. DTE

   c. A/D converter

   d. D/A converter

   e. c and d

   f. None of the above.

6-3. The three attributes of an analog signal discussed in the chapter are _____.

   a. frequency, decibels, and modulation

   b. amplitude, carrier, and sine

   c. bit rate, speed, and error rate

    d. phase, frequency, and amplitude

    e. unipolarity, quantization, and equilibrium

6-4. Parallel transmission occurs _____.

    a. during spread spectrum transmission

    b. when a PC sends data to a printer using a serial cable

    c. on most WAN circuits

    d. All of the above.

    e. None of the above.

6-5. Differential Manchester coding _____.

    a. is more reliable than unipolar

    b. is almost never used

    c. is subservient to Manchester coding

    d. requires an analog circuit to work properly

    e. None of the above.

6-6. The most widely used interface standard between PCs and modems is _____.

    a. point-to-point

    b. USB

    c. RS-232-C

    d. RS-232-D

    e. X.25

6-7. The X.21 interface standard _____.

    a. is a replacement for RS-232-C

    b. uses a PL-259 connector

    c. interfaces to a digital circuit

    d. All of the above.

    e. None of the above.

## ■ PROBLEMS AND PROJECTS

6-1. A PC sends blocks of ASCII data that are, on average, 30 characters long to a server. The server returns data blocks that average 500 characters in length. Calculate the transmission efficiency if asynchronous transmission is used, assuming 1 start bit and 1 stop bit per character. Calculate the efficiency for synchronous transmission, assuming three synchronizing characters per block. Ignore the effects of line turn around, and assume that no transmission errors occur.

6-2. How long will it take to transmit a file of 22 megabytes, using a 7-bit code and a transmission speed of 28,800 bps? If the speed of the circuit is increased to 10 Mbps, how long will the transmission take? What factors would account for variations in the transmission time on successive transmissions?

6-3. You may have both analog and digital wristwatches. List four or five other devices in your home that could have analog or digital versions.

6-4. An ASCII file of 1 megabyte is to be sent between two locations at a speed of 256 Kbps. The file will be sent in 100 Kbyte blocks. After each block is sent, the receiving node must turn the line around and ac-knowledge receipt to the transmitting node by sending a 1 byte ac-knowledgement character. Line turnaround takes 100 milliseconds. Assume that no transmission errors, which require a block of data to be resent, occur. After initial modem handshaking, how long will it take to send the file? Recalculate, assuming the file is sent in 10 Kbyte blocks instead. What conclusion do you reach about the impacts of block size and line turnaround time?

6-5. Talk to the network administrator at your school or company. Find out if digital or analog lines are being used for the network. At what speeds do they operate? If there are WAN circuits, are they reliable? If specifications are available for any modems that are used on the network, find out how fast the modem can turn the line around.

6-6. Do some research on the Internet to see if modems that have capabil-ities beyond those of the V.92 standard are in development and ex-pected on the market soon. Report your findings.

## ECKLES, FEINMAN, AND MACKENZIE—PART 1

Eckles, Feinman, and MacKenzie (EF&M) is a large law firm based in At-lanta, Georgia. In addition to its headquarters office in Atlanta, the firm has offices in Augusta, Memphis, Little Rock, Jacksonville, and Charlotte. Each office currently has a LAN that links the PC workstations in the office. How-ever, the offices are not connected to each other by a data network. Eldon Block, the firm's partner in charge of technology initiatives, is studying the possibility of establishing a WAN network to link the offices. The primary uses of the network would be to exchange e-mail between employees and to transfer documents between offices.

While they are gross averages, each EF&M office sends approximately 75 e-mails and 30 documents to each of the other offices during every workday. Sur-prisingly, the volume of traffic between offices is quite uniform. Because there are six offices, each one sends about 375 e-mails and 150 documents per day, and each one receives about the same number. On days when volume is heavy, the number of messages and documents can be 20 percent higher. An e-mail av-erages 1,500 characters in length, and a document averages 72,000 characters.

**QUESTIONS**

1. If all of the message and document traffic for an office came in and went out on one line, how many data characters would be transmitted on the line on a busy day?

2. Assuming the ASCII code is used, how many bits would be transmitted?

3. If a line were installed with modems that could transmit data at 56 Kbps, how long would it take to transmit and receive the data? If a dig-ital line that could transmit data at 1 Mbps were used, how long would it take to send the data?

4. What simplifying assumptions have been made in the preceding three questions?

5. Based on this preliminary information, what speed range do you think would be justifiable for circuits in the EF&M network? Explain your answer.

# DATA LINK CONTROL PROTOCOLS

## ■ OUTLINE

## ■ KEY TERMS

acknowledgement (ACK) character

asynchronous balanced mode (ABM)

asynchronous response mode (ARM)

Asynchronous Transfer Mode (ATM)

Binary Synchronous Communications (BSC) Protocol (BISYNC)

bit-oriented protocol

bit stuffing

block check character (BCC)

broadcast address

byte-count–oriented protocol

character-oriented protocol

collision

contention

cyclic redundancy check (CRC)

data circuit

data link

data link control protocol

data link protocol

Digital Data Communications Message Protocol (DDCMP)

end of text (ETX) character

fast select polling

flag character

frame

go-back-n

group address

header

High-Level Data Link Control (HDLC) Protocol

hub polling

information frame

KERMIT

Link Access Procedure, Balanced (LAPB) Protocol

Link Access Procedure, D-Channel (LAPD) Protocol

Link Access Procedure for Frame-Mode Bearer Services (LAPF) Protocol

multipoint operation

non-acknowledgement (NAK) character

normal response mode (NRM)

point-to-point operation

Point-to-Point Protocol (PPP)

polling

polling list

protocol converter

roll-call polling

selective repeat

Serial Line Internet Protocol (SLIP)

sliding window flow control

start of header (SOH) character

start of text (STX) character

stop-and-wait flow control

supervisory frame

synchronization (SYN) character

Synchronous Data Link Control (SDLC)

text

token

token passing

trailer

transparent mode

unnumbered frame

XMODEM-1K

XMODEM-CRC

XMODEM Protocol

YMODEM

YMODEM-G

ZMODEM

## ■  OBJECTIVES

After you complete your study of this chapter, you should be able to:

- ■ explain what a data link protocol is and describe the function it performs;
- ■ describe desirable attributes of protocols;
- ■ distinguish between contention and polling protocols;
- ■ explain the distinguishing characteristics of bit-oriented, character-oriented, and byte-count–oriented protocols;
- ■ explain, in general terms, the ways in which several protocols work; and
- ■ explain protocol conversion and situations in which it is likely to be useful.

## 7-1 INTRODUCTION

Chapter 6 dealt with the general subject of sending signals through a transmission circuit. In this chapter, we will look at the more specific case of sending data through a data circuit. To send data, additional rules or protocol are required. When used for data, the transmission medium is frequently referred to as either a **data circuit** or a **data link.**

Communication networks are made up of circuits that are like roads and highways in the national highway system; they provide a mechanism over which communications can travel. However, circuits have no "rules of the road." Just as there must be rules for the use of highways to ensure efficient and safe transportation, there must be rules for the use of circuits that make up a network to ensure that data are transported efficiently and accurately. Like the national highway systems, where different roads may have different rules, different circuits in a communications network may have different protocols that govern their operation.

**Data link control protocols,** often called simply **data link protocols,** are concerned with the transmission of data on a single circuit. Data link protocols are not sufficient to allow transmission of a message through a network of circuits; additional protocols are needed to enable that. However, data link protocols are fundamental to data transmission because the journey of a message through a network begins with its transmission through the first circuit. Depending on the complexity of the network, different data link protocols may be used for various links in the network, so the message may be *encapsulated,* a term you learned in Chapter 4, in various data link and other protocols during its journey. Data link protocols are the protocols of the data link control layer, layer 2 of the OSI reference model.

## 7-2 DATA LINK PROTOCOL FUNCTIONS

Data link protocols must address the following situations as they occur during data communication.

- **Communication startup:** There must be rules to specify the way communications will be initiated: whether there is automatic startup, whether any station can initiate communications, or whether only a station designated as the "master" station may initiate communications.

- **Character identification and framing:** There must be a way for the data terminal equipment to separate the string of bits coming down the communications line into characters. Furthermore, there must be ways of distinguishing between control characters, which are part of the protocol, and data characters, which convey the message being communicated.

- **Message identification:** The DTE must separate the characters on the communications line into messages.

- **Line control:** Rules must exist to specify the way the receiving terminal signals the sending terminal if it has received data correctly, how and under what circumstances the line will be turned around, and whether the receiving terminal can accept more data.

- **Error control:** The protocol must contain rules that specify what happens when an error is detected, what to do if communications suddenly and

*Margin terms:* data circuit · data link · data link control protocol · data link protocol

unexplainably cease, and the way communications are reestablished after they are broken.

- **Termination:** Rules must exist for ending the communications under normal and abnormal circumstances.

## 7-3   DESIRABLE ATTRIBUTES OF DATA LINK PROTOCOLS

In addition to the functional requirements specified above, there are several other desirable attributes for a data link protocol.

- **Transparency:** It is desirable for DTE to be able to transmit and receive any bit pattern as data. The complication occurs because certain bit patterns are assigned to represent control characters that have a specific meaning within the protocol.
- **Code independence:** It is desirable for the protocol to allow the transmission of data from any data coding system, such as ASCII, EBCDIC, Baudot, or any other. (Some protocols require a certain data code to be used.)
- **Efficiency:** The protocol should use as few characters as possible to control the data transmission so that most of the line capacity can be used for actual data transmission.

## 7-4   PROTOCOL IMPLEMENTATION

A data link protocol is implemented by transmitting certain bit patterns or characters on the communications circuit. The specific characters are determined by the code and protocol being used. If you look at the table of ASCII characters shown in Figure 5-4 on page 95, you will see that there is a set of characters on the left side of the table that begin with the bits 000 and 001. These are control characters in the ASCII code. Some of them are used to implement the data link protocol.

By way of contrast to the other characters in the table, which are sometimes called graphic characters, control characters usually are not printable or displayable by a printer or terminal. Not all of these characters are used in the data link protocol. Some of them are used for other control purposes, such as skipping to a new line on a terminal, tabbing, and printer control.

## 7-5   PREDETERMINED COMMUNICATIONS PARAMETERS

Many communication parameters used to establish compatibility between terminals or between a terminal and a computer are set manually by switches or are specified as parameters in software. The code used for the data, such as ASCII, EBCDIC, or some other code, is usually predetermined. The code determines how many bits make up a character, such as seven in the case of ASCII. Whether parity bits will be used and the choice of odd or even parity is often determined by a switch setting in the DTE. The modems, especially on dial-up lines, usually determine the transmission speed automatically through their handshaking routines, which determine what data rate can be sustained given the specifics of the line quality.

Establishing these parameters is necessary so that the control characters of the protocol may be correctly received and interpreted, allowing communication to be established and maintained.

## 7-6　PROTOCOL CONCEPTS: A GENERAL MODEL

This section explores protocols in a generic sense. The elements that make up a protocol will be introduced, and they will serve as a general model that can be used for comparison when specific protocols are examined later in the chapter.

## 7-7　LINE ACCESS

Before a DTE can begin communicating, it must gain control of (access to) the circuit. Without control, several devices could try to use the circuit, and if two or more sent data at the same time, the result would be a **collision**. Collisions invariably cause messages to be both garbled and unintelligible at the receiving end. When a collision is detected, the characters must be retransmitted.

There are three primary ways that circuit access can be obtained: contention, polling, and token passing.

### Contention

**Contention** systems are quite simple. A DTE that has a message to send listens to the circuit. If the circuit is not busy, the DTE begins sending its message. If the circuit is busy, the DTE waits and keeps checking periodically until the line is free. Once the DTE gains access to the circuit, it can use the circuit for as long as necessary. In simple contention systems, there are no rules to limit how long the DTE may tie up the circuit once it acquires it.

The contention approach works best in the following situations:

- on circuits that have only two DTEs
- on circuits that have multiple DTEs, when message traffic is not too heavy
- when the speed of the circuit is relatively fast, so the traffic can be sent and the circuit can be cleared quickly

The third point suggests that contention systems work well on LANs, because LANs generally operate at much higher speeds than WANs. Indeed, that is where contention systems are most often found. This will be discussed more fully later in the chapter.

### Polling

**Polling** is a technique in which one station on the line is designated as the master and the others are slaves. The master, also known as the control station, asks each slave terminal if it has a message to send. When the control terminal polls other terminals on the line, it ensures that two terminals do not try to transmit a message at the same time. The primary disadvantage of a polling system is the addition of characters (polling characters) that must be transmitted on the line. Another disadvantage is that the slave terminals must wait until they are polled before they send data. If there is a large number of terminals on the line, the delay can be long.

*collision*

*contention*

*polling*

roll call polling

**ROLL CALL POLLING**  **Roll call polling** is the most common implementation of a polling system. The master station sends out special polling characters that ask each slave station if it has a message to send. If the slave has no messages, it sends a control character indicating so. If the slave does have a message, it sends the message. Each station on the line responds only to its unique polling characters, which usually correspond to its address. In most systems, there is a list called a **polling list** that specifies the sequence in which terminals are polled. Terminals that normally have more data to send may have multiple entries in the list and they may be polled—and given the opportunity to use the circuit—more frequently than terminals that have less traffic.

polling list

fast select polling

**FAST SELECT POLLING**  **Fast select polling** speeds up the polling process because a slave station that doesn't have traffic isn't required to return a character to the master station. The master station polls several terminals on the circuit and then waits long enough for any of the slave terminals to respond. If a message is not received, the master station continues polling the other stations on the circuit. Using the fast select technique can significantly reduce the time it takes to poll stations.

hub polling

**HUB POLLING**  Another type of polling is called **hub polling.** It is most easily visualized if one thinks of a circuit that is connected to several DTEs. One station begins by polling the next station on the line. That station responds with a message if it has one. If it does not have a message, it passes the polling message on to the next station on the line, and so on. It requires more complicated circuitry in each terminal because each is performing a part of the overall line control, a function that is concentrated in the master terminal when the roll call polling technique is used.

Polling is a suitable technique if there is a master station on a network; however, many of today's networks don't have a master station—all the stations (terminals, clients, and servers) are peers. In that case, another way to gain control of the line must be used.

## Token Passing

token passing

token

**Token passing** is similar in concept to hub polling, but the access technique is more complicated. A particular sequence of bits, called a **token,** is passed from node to node. The node that has the token at any point in time is allowed to transmit, and a node that has a message to send waits until a free token comes to it. The node changes a bit in the token, thereby changing the token's status from "free" to "busy," and attaches its message to the "busy" token.

All of the stations on a token passing system are equal, but at least one of the stations must have logic to ensure that there is always one, but only one, token circulating on the circuit. The advantage of the token passing technique is that the response time of the network is deterministic or predictable.

## 7-8  MESSAGE FORMAT

Communication begins once the line has been seized, whether by contention, polling, or token passing, and the DTEs have both indicated they are ready.

header

text

trailer

A data message normally consists of three parts: the **header,** the **text** of the message, and the **trailer** (as shown in Figure 7-1), but the exact format depends on the data link protocol being used. The header contains information

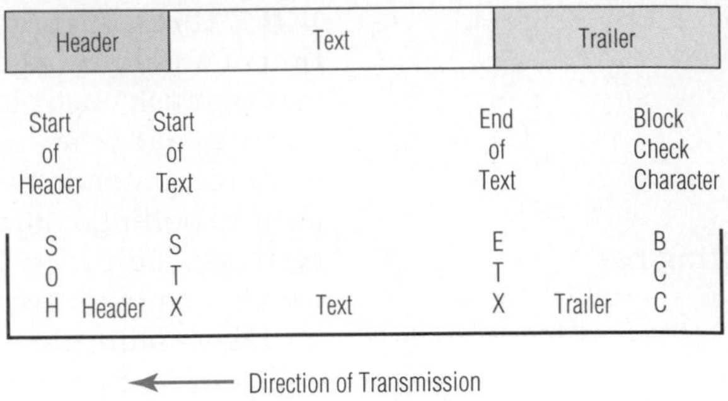

FIGURE 7-1 Message
format showing examples of
the kinds of control
characters the protocol
might employ.

| Header | Text | Trailer |
|---|---|---|

| Start of Header | Start of Text | | End of Text | Block Check Character |
|---|---|---|---|---|

| S O H | Header | S T X | Text | E T X | Trailer | B C C |

← Direction of Transmission

about the message, such as the destination node's address, a sequence number, and perhaps a date and time. The text is the main part of the message; it's what the communication is about. In most protocols, the trailer is quite short and contains only checking characters.

    In some protocols, each part of the message begins and ends with special control characters, such as the **start of header (SOH)** and **start of text (STX)** (which also marks the end of the header) characters. In other protocols the header may be of a fixed length, and a special end of header character is unnecessary. The end of the text is marked either by a special control character, such as the **end of text (ETX) character,** or its location can be calculated from a "text length" field in the header. In many protocols, the trailer consists of only a **block check character (BCC),** which is generated by the error checking circuitry or software. Obviously, it is better if the protocol does not require special characters to mark the beginning and end of the parts of the message because, without them, fewer "overhead" characters are required to be sent on the line.

    During the transmission of a message or a group of messages, error checking and synchronization occur at points in time determined by the specific protocol in use. Error checking may occur at the end of each block or message, at which time the line is usually turned around and the receiving terminal sends an **acknowledgement (ACK)** or **non-acknowledgement (NAK)** character to the sending terminal, indicating whether the data block that was just received was correct. In some protocols, blocks of data can be sent continuously until an error occurs, which minimizes the number of line turnarounds required.

    **Synchronization characters (SYN)** may be inserted in the data stream from time to time by the transmitting station to ensure that the receiver is maintaining character synchronization and properly grouping the bits into characters. The synchronization characters are removed by the receiver and do not end up in the received message.

**start of header (SOH)
character**

**start of text (STX)
character**

**end of text (ETX)
character**

**block check character
(BCC)**

**acknowledgement (ACK)
character**

**non-acknowledgement
(NAK) character**

**synchronization (SYN)
character**

## 7-9  FLOW CONTROL

Flow control is a technique used to ensure that a fast transmitting node does not send data faster than the receiving node can receive and process it. Flow control mechanisms give control to the receiver and allow it to tell the sender when it is okay to send another block or other blocks of data. The reason this is desirable is that the receiver has a certain amount of processing to do for each block of data it receives, such as recalculating check digits and passing the data to higher layers of software. If the communications line is fast and the processor in the receiver is slow, it is possible that data could come

FIGURE 7-2 The data flow of stop-and-wait flow control.

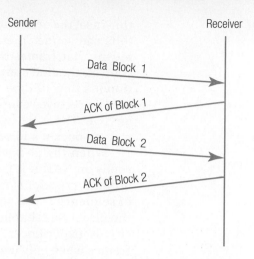

through the line faster than the receiver can handle it. In that case, some of the data would probably be lost.

## Stop-and-Wait Flow Control

**stop-and-wait flow control**

The simplest form of flow control is called **stop-and-wait flow control**. The sender transmits a frame of data. When the frame is received, and assuming it is received correctly, the receiver gives the "go ahead" by sending an ACK frame back to the sender. The sender must wait until it receives the ACK frame before sending any additional data frames, as shown in Figure 7-2. As you might guess, the stop-and-wait technique is relatively inefficient because there are pauses on the line after every frame of data is sent. The line must be turned around twice and only one (or, in some protocols, a few) frame at a time can be in transit.

## Sliding Window Flow Control

**sliding window flow control**

The efficiency can be greatly improved by allowing multiple frames to be in transit on the line at one time. This can be accomplished by allowing the sender to transmit several frames of data before it receives an ACK from the receiver, as shown in Figure 7-3. This is called **sliding window flow control**. In

FIGURE 7-3 The data flow in a simple sliding window flow control.

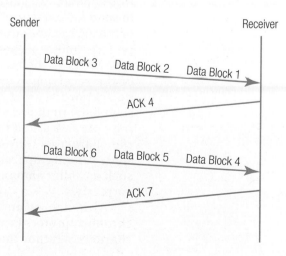

this case, the acknowledgement message includes a sequence number, $n$, that tells the sender the sequence number of the next frame expected. It also means that frames through $n-1$ have been received. With this type of flow control, the line starts to behave more like a pipeline, with a relatively continuous flow of data interrupted only occasionally by the ACK frames, and yet the receiver can still control the flow of data by delaying or not sending an ACK. There are two common implementations of sliding window flow control: **go-back-n** and **selective repeat.**

When the go-back-n flow control protocol is used, the receiving station sends an NAK if it receives a damaged frame or if it receives a frame out of order. On receipt of the NAK, the sending station resends the damaged or out of sequence frame along with all frames after it. This technique works well if the circuit is reliable and frames are rarely lost, damaged, or delayed. If the circuit experiences problems, however, the overhead of resending many frames when only one is lost or damaged becomes excessive, especially if the particular protocol allows many frames to be on the line at the same time. In that case, many frames have to be resent, which adds to the traffic load on the circuit.

The selective repeat flow control protocol requires that both the sending and receiving stations buffer the frames. When a frame arrives damaged, the receiving station sends an NAK and the sending station resends only that frame. The receiving station must buffer frames until it has all of the frames in a group. It then forwards the group to the next layer in the protocol so that the message can be presented to the application or user completely and in the proper sequence.

Both the go-back-n and selective repeat implementations have additional logic to handle situations, such as the case when the NAK message is damaged or is not received by the sending station, but the preceding descriptions give you a good picture of the way they function. Now we will look at a number of specific protocols.

## 7-10   ASYNCHRONOUS DATA LINK PROTOCOLS

Asynchronous data transmission is the oldest form of data communication. It evolved from the early days of teletypewriter operation, when operators sat at teletypewriter terminals at both ends of a circuit. With operators at both ends and with most transmissions occurring manually, few protocols were needed. Usually, it was very simple. The operator who had a message to send looked to see if his teletypewriter was printing a message. If it wasn't printing, the operator could assume that the circuit was free. He would then type the message, and the message was printed simultaneously on the teletypewriter at the receiving end of the connection. Error checking consisted of the receiving operator's reading the message. If it was understandable, he acknowledged it, perhaps by sending the sequence number of the message back to the sender. If some of the characters were garbled, the receiving operator asked for a repeat of all of the message or portions of it until the characters were correct. Frequently, when the message was originally sent, sending operators automatically repeated the words or numbers—such as dollar amounts or addresses—to ensure that they would be received correctly.

Although communication has become more automated, many asynchronous protocols have remained quite simple. They deal with individual characters rather than blocks of data. Typically, the only protocols used are the start and stop bits surrounding each character and the parity checking performed if certain data codes are used. Although the ASCII code defines special control characters, they are used only when more elaborate protocols are employed. Typical, modern, asynchronous transmission is still character-oriented.

As terminals began to have more intelligence and communication between terminals and computers rose in popularity during the 1960s and early 1970s, synchronous transmission grew at a faster rate than asynchronous transmission because it was a more efficient way to transmit data. With the development of the PC and its communications capability, asynchronous communications began to regain favor. Asynchronous communications now provides adequate capability for most PC communication and requires less sophisticated—therefore less expensive—equipment.

As the desire for more automatic verification of messages and file transfers between PCs occurred, it became necessary to define and implement more elaborate protocols. More elaborate asynchronous protocols allow the transmission of data in blocks. They perform additional checks on the blocks of data to ensure that the transmission is correct.

## Point-to-Point Protocol (PPP)

**Point-to-Point Protocol (PPP)**

The **Point-to-Point Protocol (PPP)** is primarily used by PC workstations to send IP over dial-up lines, typically when dialing in to an ISP for connection to the Internet. PPP supports many operating modes and types of transmission. The only absolute requirement imposed by PPP is the provision of a full-duplex circuit, whether dedicated or switched, that can operate in either an asynchronous or a synchronous mode. PPP can operate at any transmission speed that the DTE and DCE can handle. PPP performs authentication, data compression, error detection and correction, and packet sequencing.

**Serial Line Internet Protocol (SLIP)**

PPP has largely replaced an older protocol called **Serial Line Internet Protocol (SLIP)**. SLIP had no error detection or correction and was designed as a temporary protocol for use between a workstation and an ISP. These limitations are the main reasons it has been replaced.

PPP uses the principles, terminology, and frame structure of HDLC (discussed later in this chapter). PPP's frame structure is shown in Figure 7-4. The fields are as follows:

- Flag: A single byte that indicates the beginning or end of a frame. The flag field consists of the bit sequence 01111110.

- Address: A single byte that contains the bit sequence 11111111, which is the address for a broadcast message used by HDLC. PPP does not use individual station addresses.

- Control: A single byte that contains the bit sequence 00000011, which calls for the transmission of user data in an unsequenced frame (datagram).

- Protocol: Two bytes that identify the protocol encapsulated in the data field of the frame.

- Data: A variable length field normally containing between 0 and 1,500 bytes. By prior agreement, consenting PPP implementations can use

**FIGURE 7-4** PPP's frame format.

| Flag | Address | Control | Protocol | Data | FCS |
|------|---------|---------|----------|------|-----|
| 1 | 1 | 1 | 2 | Variable | 2 or 4 |

Field length in bytes

other values for the maximum field length. The end of the field is found by locating the closing flag and allowing two bytes for the FCS field.

■ Frame check sequence (FCS): Normally contains a CRC-16 (2 byte) check "character," but by prior agreement a 4-byte (CRC-32) check may be used.

PPP has been carefully designed to retain compatibility with most commonly used hardware. In addition, an escape mechanism is specified to allow control data to be transmitted transparently over the link. The PPP encapsulation also provides for multiplexing different network layer protocols simultaneously over the same link. PPP was designed to provide a common solution for easy connection of a wide variety of devices.

## The XMODEM Protocol

**XMODEM Protocol**

The **XMODEM Protocol** was developed for use between PCs, especially for transfers of data files between them. Using this protocol, one PC is designated as the sender and the other is designated as the receiver. The receiver indicates that it is ready to receive by sending an ASCII NAK character every ten seconds. When the transmitting system receives a NAK, it begins sending blocks of 128 data characters surrounded by a header and trailer. The header consists of a start of header character, followed by a block number character, followed by the same block number with each bit inverted. The trailer is a checksum character, which is the sum of the ASCII values of all of the 128 data characters divided by 255.

At the receiving end, the message is checked (usually by software) to ensure that the first character is an SOH, that the block number is exactly one more than the last block received, that exactly 128 characters of data are received, and that the check sum computed at the receiving end is identical to the last character received in the block. If all these conditions are true, the receiver sends an ACK back to the transmitter, and the transmitter sends the next block. If the data are not received correctly, a NAK is sent and the transmitter resends the block of data that was in error.

The entire message or data file is sent in this way, block by block. At the end, the transmitter sends an end of text character that is acknowledged by the receiver with an ACK, and the transmission is complete.

Because the XMODEM protocol is quite simple, its error checking is not very sophisticated. Therefore, the reliability of the received data is not as good as with other protocols. XMODEM is considered to be a half-duplex protocol because the sender waits for an ACK (it stops and waits) of each block of data before sending the next block. Thus, if a full-duplex transmission facility is used, XMODEM is inefficient.

## Other Asynchronous Protocols

There are many other asynchronous protocols in use today. They have been developed by a variety of sources and are available from the developers and on the Internet, and sometimes they are included in other software packages. One of the improvements that most of these protocols have made over XMODEM is in the error checking procedures. Most of them use a sophisticated

**cyclic redundancy check (CRC)**

check character, called a **cyclic redundancy check (CRC)** at the end of each block. CRCs are discussed completely in Chapter 9, but for now you just need to know that CRCs are calculated with a sophisticated mathematical algorithm that virtually guarantees error detection.

Some of the more popular asynchronous protocols and their distinguishing features are as follows:

XMODEM-CRC

- **XMODEM-CRC:** This was the first evolution of XMODEM and is assumed by most programs when XMODEM is specified. It improves the error handling of the XMODEM protocol by replacing the check sum with a one-byte CRC character (CRC-8). As a result, it is much more robust in detecting transmission errors.

XMODEM-1K

- **XMODEM-1K:** The next step up in sophistication, XMODEM-1K increases the efficiency of XMODEM-CRC by transmitting 1,024-character blocks instead of 128-character blocks.

YMODEM

- **YMODEM:** YMODEM is essentially XMODEM-1K with a 2-byte CRC (CRC-16). It allows multiple files to be transferred with a single command.

YMODEM-G

- **YMODEM-G:** YMODEM-G is a variant of YMODEM. It expects the modem to provide software error correction and recovery. Therefore, this protocol should be used only with modems that support hardware error correction such as V.42 or MNP. Because it does not have error correction and recovery, YMODEM-G is very fast.

ZMODEM

- **ZMODEM:** ZMODEM is a different protocol, not an upgrade from XMODEM. ZMODEM uses a 4-byte CRC (CRC-32) and adjusts its block size depending on line conditions. ZMODEM is also very fast and provides good failure recovery. If the transmission is canceled or interrupted, it can be restarted later and the previously transferred information does not have to be resent.

KERMIT

- **KERMIT:** Developed and copyrighted by Columbia University, KERMIT is a very popular protocol, especially in the university setting. Normally it uses 1,000-byte blocks and a 3-byte CRC (CRC-24), but the block size can be adjusted dynamically during the transmission based on line conditions. Whereas most other asynchronous protocols handle only 8-bit data codes, KERMIT can also handle 7-bit codes. The protocol is error checked and very fast, and it works equally well in PC-to-PC and PC-to-server connections.

For more information on any of these protocols, you can search the Internet with a tool such as Google, using the protocol name as the keyword.

## 7-11 SYNCHRONOUS DATA LINK PROTOCOLS

Synchronous data link protocols typically deal with blocks of data, not individual characters. Synchronous protocols may be divided into three types, according to the way the start and end of message are determined. The three types are character-oriented protocols, byte-count–oriented protocols, and bit-oriented protocols.

### Character-Oriented Protocols

character-oriented protocol

A **character-oriented protocol** uses special characters to indicate the beginnings and ends of messages. For example, the SOH character is used to indicate the beginning of a message and the ETX character indicates the end. The best known character-oriented protocol is the **Binary Synchronous Communications (BSC) Protocol (BISYNC)**, also known as **BISYNC**.

Binary Synchronous Communications (BSC) Protocol (BISYNC)

### Byte-Count–Oriented Protocols

byte-count–oriented protocol

**Byte-count–oriented protocols** have a special character to mark the beginning of the header, followed by a count field that indicates how many characters

Digital Data
Communications
Message Protocol
(DDCMP)

are in the data portion of the message. The header may contain other information as well. It is followed by the data portion of the message, followed by a block check character or characters. The best known byte-count–oriented protocol is the **Digital Data Communications Message Protocol (DDCMP).** DDCMP was developed by Digital Equipment Corporation, which is now a part of Hewlett Packard. DDCMP has largely been supplanted by TCP/IP.

## Bit-Oriented Protocols

bit-oriented protocol

flag character

A **bit-oriented protocol** uses only one special character, called the **flag character,** which marks the beginning and end of the message. "Bit oriented" means that the protocol looks at frames as bit streams and does not look at bytes as units—as the byte-count–oriented protocols do. Within the message, the header and the fields within it are of a predefined length, and the header is followed by the data field with no intervening control character. No special control character is used to mark the beginning of the trailer segment of the message, if one exists. The flag character also marks the end of the message. The receiving terminal knows that the bits preceding the flag are the check characters for the message.

High-Level Data Link
Control (HDLC) Protocol

Synchronous Data Link
Control (SDLC) Protocol

The best known bit-oriented protocols are the ISO's **High-Level Data Link Control (HDLC) Protocol** and IBM's **Synchronous Data Link Control (SDLC) Protocol,** which is a proper subset of HDLC. Other bit-oriented protocols include CSMA/CD (discussed in Chapter 10) and token protocols used on LANs.

We will now look more closely at three synchronous data link protocols, proceeding from simplest to most complex: BSC, DDCMP, and HDLC. Each of these protocols also adds greater capability to the one before.

## The Binary Synchronous Communications (BSC) Protocol (BISYNC)

BISYNC was introduced by IBM in 1967. While it is a very old protocol, it was implemented by many companies for a wide variety of equipment and applications. Despite its age, BISYNC is worth studying because it is still in use and it serves as an excellent example of a character-oriented protocol. Also, it is relatively straightforward and easy to understand and it is a useful illustration of many concepts that apply to all protocols.

BISYNC supports only three data codes: the 6-bit transcode (SBT) which is now rarely used, ASCII, and EBCDIC. Certain bit patterns in each code have been set aside for the required control characters: SOH, STX, ETB, ITB, ETX, EOT, NAK, DLE, and ENQ. Some additional control characters are really two-character sequences: ACK0, ACK1, WACK, RVI, and TTD. All of these control characters and sequences are defined in Figure 7-5.

transparent mode

BISYNC operates in either nontransparent or transparent mode. **Transparent mode** means that any bit sequence is permissible in the data field, even if it is the same as a character used for control. Transparency is needed when transmitting binary data such as computer programs and some data files. In transparent mode, the data link escape (DLE) character is inserted before any control characters. DLE STX initiates transparent mode and DLE ETX or DLE ETB terminates the block. Because the combination DLE ETX could also occur in the middle of the data portion of the message and could inadvertently terminate the transmission, the transmitter scans the text portion of the message. Whenever it finds a DLE character, it inserts

FIGURE 7-5  Binary Synchronous Communications control characters.

| Symbol | Description | Purpose |
|--------|-------------|---------|
| **SOH** | Start of header | Marks the beginning of the header of a transmission. |
| **STX** | Start of text | Marks the end of the header and the beginning of the data portion of the message. |
| **ITB** | End of intermediate | Marks the end of a data block, but does not reverse the line or require the receiver to acknowledge receipt. A block check character follows the ITB for checking purposes. |
| **ETB** | End of text block | Marks the end of a data block. Requires the receiver to acknowledge receipt. |
| **ETX** | End of text | End of data block and no more data blocks to be sent. |
| **EOT** | End of transmission | Marks the end of transmission that may have contained several blocks or messages. |
| **ACK0** **ACK1** | Positive acknowledgment | Previous block was received correctly. ACK0 is used for even-numbered blocks, ACK1 for odd-numbered ones. |
| **NAK** | Negative acknowledgment | Previous block was received in error. Usually requires a retransmission. |
| **WACK** | Wait before transmit | Same as ACK, but receiver is not ready to receive another block. |
| **SYN** | Synchronization | Sent at beginning of transmission to ensure characters will be received correctly. |
| **ENQ** | Enquiry | Requests use of the line in point-to-point communication. |
| **DLE** | Data link escape | In transparent communication, creates two-character versions of ACK, WACK, and RVI. |
| **RVI** | Reverse interrupt | Positive acknowledgment and asks transmitter to stop as soon as possible because receiver has a high-priority message to send. |
| **TTD** | Temporary text delay | Transmitter uses this to retain control of the line when it is not ready to send data. |

an additional DLE. On the receiving side, the data stream is also scanned. Whenever two DLEs are found together, one is discarded. The receiver also knows that when it sees the sequence DLE DLE ETX in the data portion of the message, the sequence is not to be interpreted as a set of control characters indicating message termination, but only as data.

**SYNCHRONIZATION OF CHARACTERS AND MESSAGES**  Character synchronization is accomplished in BISYNC by sending SYN characters at the beginning and periodically in the middle of each transmission. The exact number of SYN characters is somewhat dependent on the hardware, but at least two are usually transmitted. The hardware scans the line searching for the SYN character (e.g., 00010110 in ASCII). Once the SYN character is found, character synchronization is established, and the following characters can be interpreted correctly.

Message synchronization in BISYNC is accomplished with the SOH, STX, ETB, and E0T characters. These control characters mark the beginning and end of each message being sent.

**BLOCK CHECKING**   BISYNC uses various techniques for error detection and requests that blocks be repeated until the transmission is received correctly. When ASCII code is being used, a parity check is performed on each character, and a horizontal parity check is performed on the whole message. When EBCDIC or a 6-bit transcode is being used, no parity check is made, but a CRC is calculated for the entire message.

In all cases, if the block check character or characters transmitted with the data do not agree with the characters calculated by the receiver, a NAK is sent back to the transmitter, which is then responsible for resending the block in error. When the block check characters agree, a positive acknowledgement is sent: ACK0 for an even-numbered block and ACK1 for an odd-numbered block. Alternating between ACK0 and ACK1 provides an additional check against totally missing or duplicated blocks of data. If two ACK0 acknowledgements are received in succession, the transmitting station knows that a block of data has been lost.

**TRANSMISSION SEQUENCES**   BISYNC has well-defined rules that govern the sequence of transmission, acknowledgement, and placement of control characters in various situations. Two common sequences are described here.

**point-to-point operation**

- **Point-to-Point Operation:** In point-to-point operation, a station that has a message to send first requests permission to use the line from the other station. Once permission is granted, the transmission proceeds as shown in Figure 7-6. After the positive ACK of the last block the data, the line is again available and either station may request use with the SYN SYN ENQ sequence.

**multipoint operation**

- **Multipoint Operation:** In multipoint operation (more than two stations on a circuit), a control station uses a polling technique to solicit input from the stations on the circuit. This is illustrated in Figure 7-7. When the

**FIGURE 7-6**   The operation of a point-to-point circuit using the BISYNC protocol.

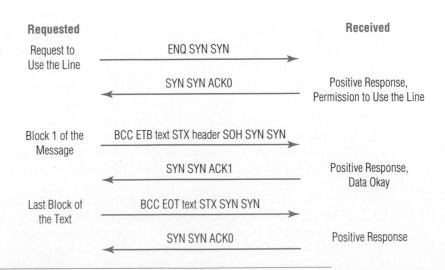

| Requested | | Received |
|---|---|---|
| Request to Use the Line | ENQ SYN SYN → | |
| | ← SYN SYN ACK0 | Positive Response, Permission to Use the Line |
| Block 1 of the Message | BCC ETB text STX header SOH SYN SYN → | |
| | ← SYN SYN ACK1 | Positive Response, Data Okay |
| Last Block of the Text | BCC EOT text STX SYN SYN → | |
| | ← SYN SYN ACK0 | Positive Response |

**FIGURE 7-7** The polling operation on a multipoint circuit using the BISYNC protocol.

**FIGURE 7-8** The addressing operation on a multipoint circuit using the BISYNC protocol.

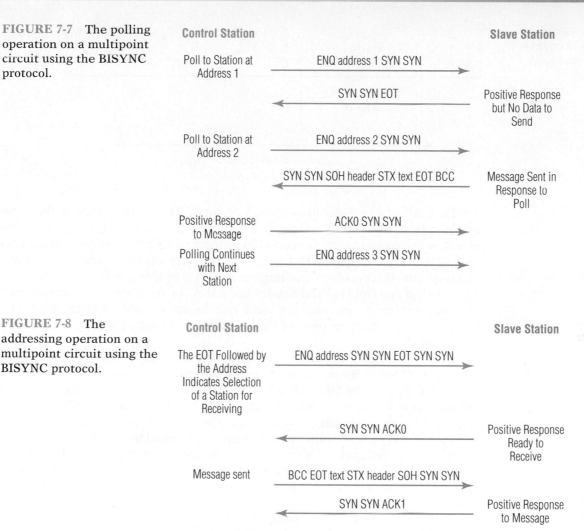

control station has a message to send, it uses the addressing sequence shown in Figure 7-8. After the last ACK, the line is again free.

Overall, BISYNC is a relatively efficient protocol that is easy to understand and implement. This led to its wide popularity among computer and terminal vendors. Its primary drawbacks are as follows:

- it is not code independent
- it is a half-duplex protocol, which cannot take advantage of full-duplex circuits
- its implementation of transparency is cumbersome

## The Digital Data Communications Message Protocol (DDCMP)

DDCMP was developed by Digital Equipment Corporation (now a part of Hewlett Packard Corporation) as the data link protocol for its DNA. Over the years, the protocol was enhanced several times to make better use of high-bandwidth and high-latency (satellite) links, but the basic principles of the protocol remained the same. The protocol is rarely used anymore, because TCP/IP has largely replaced it.

FIGURE 7-9 General
format of a byte-count–
oriented protocol data
message.

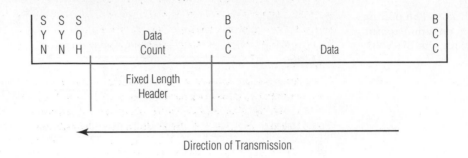

DDCMP is a byte-count–oriented protocol. The general format for byte-count–oriented protocol messages is shown in Figure 7-9. The header of the message is a fixed length, preceded by at least two SYN characters and a special SOH character. The SOH character is the only unique character required in the protocol. Therefore, the implementation of transparency is relatively easy. One of the fields in the header indicates the number of characters that the message contains, and the data can be of variable length. Both the header and the data portions of the message are checked with a block check character.

DDCMP has two message types. The data message is similar in format to the general format for byte-count–oriented protocols shown in Figure 7-9. Additional fields in the DDCMP header, shown in Figure 7-10, allow the data message sent in one direction to also acknowledge the receipt of a data message sent in the other direction. (More on this later in this chapter.) The other DDCMP message type is the control message. Control messages are of a fixed length, the same length as the header of the data message. Control messages are used to initiate communications between two stations, to send an ACK or NAK about a previously received message, and to request an ACK for previously sent messages.

DDCMP operates in point-to-point or multipoint configurations on either half-duplex or full-duplex lines. In full-duplex operation, both stations can transmit simultaneously. As previously mentioned, the data message from one station can contain an ACK or NAK for a message received from the other station. A station can send several messages in sequence without receiving an ACK, but if the receiver cannot handle them, they may have to be retransmitted. There can never be more than 255 outstanding messages before an ACK is sent.

FIGURE 7-10 The fields
in the header of a DDCMP
data message.

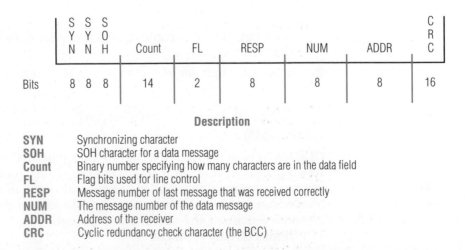

| | Description |
|---|---|
| **SYN** | Synchronizing character |
| **SOH** | SOH character for a data message |
| **Count** | Binary number specifying how many characters are in the data field |
| **FL** | Flag bits used for line control |
| **RESP** | Message number of last message that was received correctly |
| **NUM** | The message number of the data message |
| **ADDR** | Address of the receiver |
| **CRC** | Cyclic redundancy check character (the BCC) |

FIGURE 7-11 DDCMP protocol: half-duplex, point-to-point.

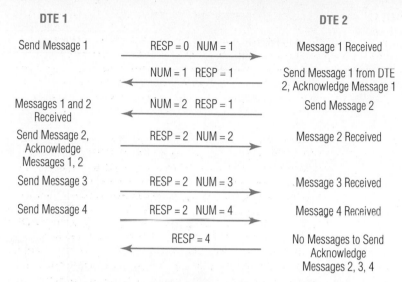

**MESSAGE SEQUENCE NUMBERS** One significant difference between DDCMP and BISYNC is the implementation of a message sequence number. With DDCMP, each transmitted message is assigned a unique and increasing sequence number. When the receiver provides an acknowledgement, it only needs to indicate the sequence number of the last message received correctly. This tells the sender that all messages, up through that message, have been received and checked. The implication is that not all messages need to be specifically acknowledged. This adds to the efficiency of the DDCMP protocol.

Compared to BISYNC, DDCMP and other byte-count protocols implement transparency in a much more efficient manner. Furthermore, with message sequencing, full-duplex operation is easily implemented. An example of the DDCMP protocol in a half-duplex, point-to-point environment is shown in Figure 7-11.

## The High-Level Data Link Control (HDLC) Protocol

HDLC is one of the most important data link protocols. Not only is it widely used, but it is also the basis for several other important protocols that use the same, or similar, formats. HDLC is based on IBM's SDLC, which was developed first and which is widely used in IBM mainframe-based network environments. SDLC was developed to be the data link protocol in IBM's SNA, the company's proprietary architecture for networking. After developing SDLC, IBM submitted the protocol to various standards organizations and ISO modified it to create HDLC. Later, the ITU-T modified HDLC to create the LAP and LAPB protocols, and the IEEE modified HDLC to create the IEEE 802.2 protocol. (Are you suffering from acronym overload yet? If so, consult the Acronyms section at the back of the book.) All of these protocols will be discussed later in the text.

HDLC is a bit-oriented protocol that supports both half-duplex and full-duplex operation. As shown in Figure 7-12, HDLC defines three types of stations.

- **Primary stations** issue commands to other stations and act according to their responses. Primary stations also establish and manage connections with other stations.

**FIGURE 7-12** HDLC
station configurations.

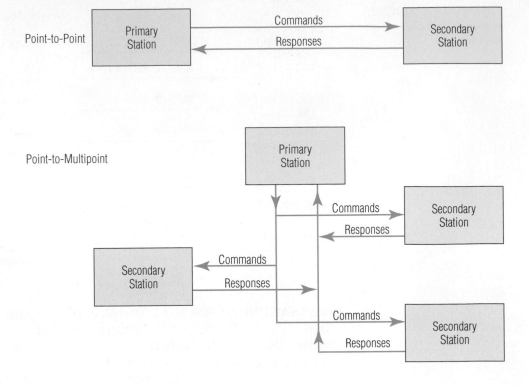

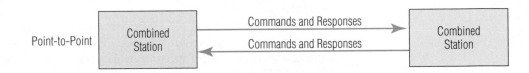

- **Secondary stations** respond to commands issued by primary stations. A secondary station has a connection with just one primary station at a time. It can send data but does not issue commands to other stations.

- **Combined stations** act as both primary and secondary stations. They can issue commands to, and respond to commands from, other combined stations.

**OPERATING MODES**    HDLC operates in one of three modes:

normal response mode
(NRM)

- **Normal response mode (NRM):** NRM is used when there is a primary station and one or more secondary stations on a circuit. The primary station polls the secondary stations, which may only send data in response to a poll. Normal response mode can be used on either multipoint or point-to-point links. SDLC operates only in normal response mode.

asynchronous balanced
mode (ABM)

- **Asynchronous balanced mode (ABM):** ABM is used with combined stations; that is, either node may initiate a transmission on the circuit without receiving permission from the other, a typical situation when two computers communicate. ABM is the most widely used of the three modes because it makes the most efficient use of full-duplex lines on which there is no polling overhead.

FIGURE 7-13   HDLC
frame format.

| Fields | Beginning Flag 01111110 | Address | Control | Data | Frame Check Character | Ending Flag 01111110 |
|---|---|---|---|---|---|---|
| Bits | 8 | 8 or 16 | 8 or 16 | 8 × n Any multiple of 8 bits | 16 or 32 | 8 |

asynchronous response mode (ARM)

- **Asynchronous response mode (ARM):** ARM is used when there is a primary station and one or more secondary stations. In this mode, the secondary stations may initiate the transmission of data or control without permission from the primary station, but it cannot send commands. The primary station retains responsibility for the circuit, including initialization, error recovery, and disconnection. ARM mode is most common on point-to-point circuits that have primary and secondary stations.

frame

**FRAMES**   The basic operational unit for HDLC is a **frame**, as shown in Figure 7-13. Frames are sent across a network to a destination node that verifies their successful arrival. HDLC defines three types of frames:

- the supervisory (S) frame
- the information (I) frame
- the unnumbered (U) frame

Frames can be in one of two formats: normal or extended. We'll first look at the fields in the frame and then look at the different frame formats.

**Flag Field**   HDLC and all bit-oriented protocols use a special grouping of bits to mark the beginning and ending of frames. This special character is the flag character, and its unique bit pattern is 01111110. When a node receives a flag character, it knows a frame follows. Because the number of bits in a frame can vary, the node looks for the next flag to mark the end of the frame. Because of the number of consecutive 1 bits in the flag character, it also serves as a SYN character, so no special SYNs are required.

To ensure a flag's uniqueness, no other sequence of six consecutive 1 bits can be allowed in the data stream. To accomplish this, the bit stream of all transmissions is scanned by the hardware. Using a technique called **bit stuffing**, a 0 bit is inserted after all strings of five consecutive 1 bits in the header and data portions of the frame. At the receiving end, the extra 0 bit is removed by the hardware. Bit stuffing is illustrated in Figure 7-14.

bit stuffing

FIGURE 7-14   Bit stuffing.

Message Being Sent:                                    Direction of Transmission⟶
0011111110000111110101000111111111111111111000011111

Zero Bits Will Be Inserted

Transmitted Bit Stream Will Be:

0011011111000011111010100011101111101111101111000011111

Receiver Will Remove the Underlined 0s That Have Been Inserted

**Address Field**  The address field identifies the destination node for a frame. It is normally 8 bits long, but in the extended frame format, it may be 16 bits when a larger address is needed to identify more stations. If a primary station sends the frame, the address field contains the address of the secondary station to which the frame is being sent. This is necessary on multipoint circuits, where there may be several secondary stations. If a secondary station sends the frame, the address field contains its own address because there is only one primary station. Secondary stations do not communicate with one another. With the address, the primary station can determine which secondary station the frame came from.

broadcast address

group address

Sometimes the address field may contain a **broadcast address** or **group address.** Frames that have broadcast addresses are accepted by all secondary stations with which the primary station has established communication. Frames that have group addresses are accepted by stations that are members of a predefined group.

**Control Field**  The format of the control field depends on whether it is in an information, supervisory, or unnumbered frame, as shown in Figure 7-15. Information frames begin with a 0 bit, supervisory frames with a 10, and unnumbered frames with a 11. The sent number, often abbreviated N(S), is the number of the frame being sent. If the poll/final bit is set to 1 and is sent by a primary station, it is a poll requesting a secondary station to respond. When sent by a secondary station and set to 1, it indicates that this is the final frame in a group. The received number field, often abbreviated N(R) indicates that all frames up to N(R) – 1 have been received correctly. The S and M fields will be described in a moment.

The control field identifies the type of frame as either supervisory, information, or unnumbered. The sent and received sequence numbers may be 3 or 7 bits long, depending on whether the regular or extended frame format is being used. Transmitting nodes increment the sent sequence number, and receiving stations increment the received sequence number. These sequence numbers provide an additional check to ensure that no frames are missing or duplicated.

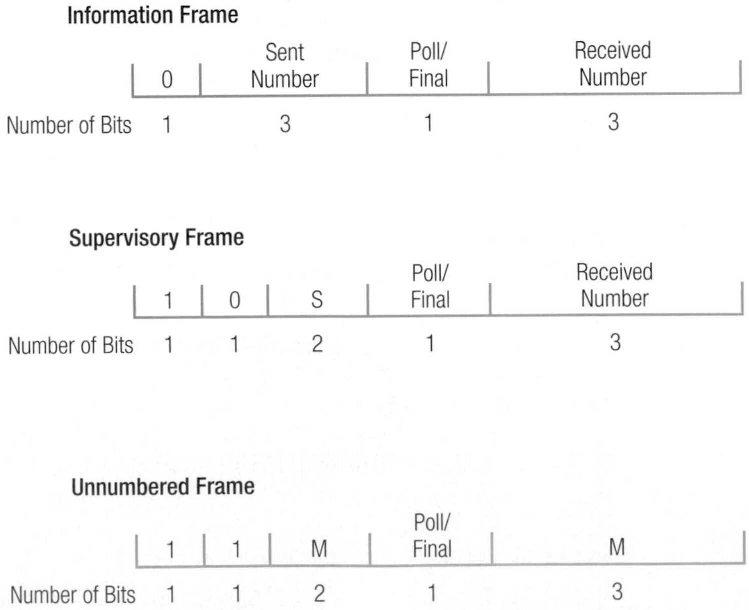

FIGURE 7-15   The formats of the control field in a HDLC frame.

**Information Frame**

| 0 | Sent Number | Poll/Final | Received Number |
|---|---|---|---|
| Number of Bits   1 | 3 | 1 | 3 |

**Supervisory Frame**

| 1 | 0 | S | Poll/Final | Received Number |
|---|---|---|---|---|
| Number of Bits   1 | 1 | 2 | 1 | 3 |

**Unnumbered Frame**

| 1 | 1 | M | Poll/Final | M |
|---|---|---|---|---|
| Number of Bits   1 | 1 | 2 | 1 | 3 |

**Data Field** The data field is present in I frames and some U frames only, and its length is variable. It is always a multiple of 8 bits in length, up to a network-defined maximum. This does not imply, however, that an 8-bit coding scheme must be used. If seven 7-bit characters are sent, the 49 data bits are padded with an additional 7 bits to bring the total number of bits to 56 (a multiple of 8).

**Frame Check Sequence (FCS) Field** The FCS field is the error-detecting field that contains a CRC-16 or CRC-32 character, depending on whether the standard or extended frame format is being used.

Now we'll look at the three frame formats.

**information frame**

**INFORMATION FRAMES** **Information frames** contain the data field that holds the information being transmitted across the network. The received number field effectively implements the sliding window protocol for either acknowledging frames received correctly or requesting repeats when needed.

**supervisory frame**

**SUPERVISORY FRAMES** **Supervisory frames** are used to send a NAK when a frame is received incorrectly or when it indicates status. The 2-bit S (status) field has the following meanings:

- RR—Receive Ready (00): Indicates that the station is ready and able to receive data. This status is also sent to acknowledge received frames when the receiving station has no outgoing data of its own to send.
- REJ—Reject (01): HDLC's NAK, it requests that the other station resend all outstanding frames beginning with the one whose number is in the received number field.
- RNR—Receive Not Ready (10): Used for flow control purposes when the receiving station's buffers are filling or when it detects an error. RNR tells the sender to stop sending frames.
- SREJ—Selective Reject (11): Similar to a NAK, it requests that the other station resend frames beginning with the one whose number is in the received number field.

**unnumbered frame**

**UNNUMBERED FRAMES** **Unnumbered frames** establish the way the protocol will proceed. The two M fields together have five bits that allow communication between the sender and receiver of messages, such as whether the normal or extended frame format will be used, whether selective repeat or go-back-n sliding windows will be used, requesting a test response from the other station, and initializing and disconnecting communication.

**FRAME FLOW** The flow of frames in HDLC depends on which mode (NRM, ABM, or ARM) is used, but in all cases there is an initialization phase, a data transfer phase, and a disconnect phase. The flows can become quite complicated, especially on full-duplex circuits when both nodes may be sending and receiving data simultaneously.

Figure 7-16 shows the flow of information frames between nodes A and B in ABM mode and shows the use of the go-back-n sliding windows after a communication has been established. Each transmission is shown as an arrow. The letters and numbers on the arrow indicate the frame type (I=Information frame), followed by the sent number and the received number. The numbered steps below describe the actions in the figure.

FIGURE 7-16 An example
of information frame flow
in HDLC.

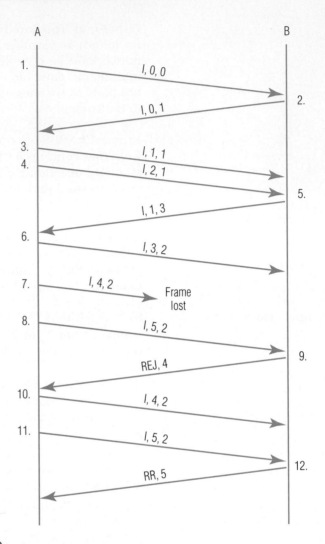

1. Node A sends frame 0

2. Node B sends its frame 0 and acknowledges correct receipt of A's frame 0 by setting its N(R) to 1

3. Node A sends frame 1 and acknowledges B's frame 0

4. Node A sends frame 2 and leaves its N(R) at 1 because it has not received another frame from B

5. Node B sends its frame 1 and acknowledges A's frame 2

6. Node A sends frame 3 and acknowledges B's frame 1

7. Node A sends frame 4 but it is lost or discarded somewhere between A and B so B never receives it

8. Node A, not knowing that frame 4 hasn't been received, sends its frame 5

9. Node B receives frame 5, but has not received frame 4 so it sends a REJ frame for 4 indicating that A should repeat all frames beginning with 4

10. Node A resends frame 4

11. Node A resends frame 5

12. Node B, having no data of its own to send, sends an RR frame acknowledging all frames through 5 and indicating that it is expecting frame 6

While this is only an example of HDLC's frame flow, it should give you an idea of the way the protocol operates.

## 7-12 OTHER DATA LINK PROTOCOLS

There are several other important data link protocols with which you need to be familiar. All of them are unique variants of HDLC, and they are mainly used in WANs.

### Link Access Procedure, Balanced (LAPB)

Link Access Procedure, Balanced (LAPB) Protocol

The **Link Access Procedure, Balanced (LAPB) Protocol,** a subset of HDLC, provides only the ABM mode of operation. LAPB operates in full-duplex, point-to-point mode. It is most commonly used between an X.25 DTE and a packet switching network.

### Link Access Procedure, D-Channel (LAPD)

Link Access Procedure, D-Channel (LAPD) Protocol

The **Link Access Procedure, D-Channel (LAPD) Protocol** standard was issued by the ITU-T as a part of its recommendations for ISDN WANs, which you will study in Chapter 13. LAPD is a subset of HDLC that provides data link control on an ISDN D channel in AMB mode. LAPD always uses a 16-bit address, 7-bit sequence numbers, and a 16-bit CRC.

### Link Access Procedure for Frame-Mode Bearer Services (LAPF)

Link Access Procedure for Frame-Mode Bearer Services (LAPF) Protocol

The **Link Access Procedure for Frame-Mode Bearer Services (LAPF) Protocol** is a data link protocol for frame relay networks, another type of WAN, which you will study later. Frame relay technology is designed to provide streamlined capability for high-speed packet switching networks operating on digital circuits that have very low error rates. LAPF is actually made up of a control protocol, which is similar to HDLC, and a core protocol, which is a subset of the control protocol. The control protocol uses 16- to 32-bit addresses, 7-bit sequence numbers, and a 16-bit CRC. The core protocol has no control field, which means that there is no mechanism for error control, thus streamlining the network's operation.

### Asynchronous Transfer Mode (ATM)

Asynchronous Transfer Mode (ATM)

**Asynchronous Transfer Mode (ATM)** is also designed to provide streamlined data transfer across a high-speed, digital, error-free network. Unlike frame relay, ATM uses a completely new protocol based on a cell rather than a frame.

Figure 7-17 shows a comparison between the various HDLC-based synchronous data link protocols.

## 7-13 PROTOCOL CONVERSION

protocol converter

With the advent and widespread use of the TCP/IP protocol, especially in situations where many otherwise incompatible networks are linked, the need for protocol conversion is not as great as it was a few years ago. However, it is still sometimes necessary or desirable to convert a data transmission from one protocol to another. This is the function of the **protocol converter;** which can be implemented using hardware, software, or a combination of both. This equipment or software takes a transmission in one protocol and changes it, as required, to a different protocol. The most common protocol

FIGURE 7-17  A comparison of HDLC-based synchronous data link control protocols.

| Protocol | HDLC Subset | HDLC Mode | International Standard | Uses |
|---|---|---|---|---|
| **HDLC** | | NRM, ABM, ARM | Yes | Many types of networks when subsets are included. |
| **SDLC** | Yes | NRM | No | IBM mainframe-based networks |
| **LAPB** | Yes | ABM | Yes | Workstations connecting to a packet network |
| **LAPD** | Yes | ABM | Yes | ISDN circuits |
| **LLC** | Partial | | Yes | Local Area Networks |
| **LAPF** | Partial | ABM | No | Frame relay high-speed networks operating on essentially error-free digital lines |
| **ATM—cell based** | No | | No | ATM high-speed networks operating on essentially error-free digital lines |

conversion being performed today is from the protocol of one LAN to the protocol of another, as a transmission passes through several networks. That conversion is typically done by one of the servers on a LAN. Another popular conversion is from an asynchronous protocol to a synchronous protocol, such as one of the variations of HDLC. This particular conversion occurs when a PC that uses an asynchronous protocol needs to log onto a network that uses HDLC.

Protocol conversion involves, at a minimum, changing the control bits or characters that encapsulate the data. Because there is not always a one-for-one correspondence of control characters in different protocols, the process is more complex than simple character translation. Sometimes blocks of data must be reformatted or changed to a different length. The protocol converter may have to receive an entire message, made up of several blocks, before it can do the reformatting. Protocol converters also frequently perform error checking on the incoming data stream and request a retransmission if an error is detected.

## ■ SUMMARY

This chapter looked at the rules, or data link protocols, under which data communications circuits operate. The need for circuit control was discussed and circuit access control techniques were examined. The details of specific protocols that are in widespread use on networks were explored. Data link protocol standardization is paving the way toward greater interconnection of terminals and computers from all manufacturers into complex, global networks.

In Chapter 8, you will study the various media used to build networks: copper wire, coaxial cable, satellites, and optical fiber. Wireless transmission is also covered.

## ■ REVIEW QUESTIONS

7-1. Define the term *protocol*.

7-2. Why are data link protocols required?

7-3. Identify the six functions of a data link protocol.

7-4. Explain the term *transparency* as it relates to data link protocols.

7-5. What is meant by the phrase *predetermined communications parameters*?

7-6. Compare and contrast polling techniques for accessing a circuit with contention techniques.

7-7. In a list of terminals to be polled, why might a terminal's address be listed more than once?

7-8. What is the function of the header of a message?

7-9. Why is XMODEM not a particularly reliable means of transmitting large blocks of data?

7-10. What advantages does ZMODEM have over XMODEM?

7-11. Can BISYNC transmit Baudot code? Why or why not?

7-12. How is character synchronization established in BISYNC?

7-13. Describe BISYNC's approach to error correction.

7-14. Give some reasons why DDCMP is more efficient than BISYNC.

7-15. What is the purpose of a flag in HDLC?

7-16. What is *bit stuffing*?

7-17. Describe the characteristics of the PPP protocol.

7-18. Is SDLC an offshoot of HDLC? Explain your answer.

7-19. What is the purpose of a protocol converter? Why do protocols need to be converted?

### TRUE OR FALSE

7-1. Data link protocols are concerned with the transmission of data on a single circuit.

7-2. Data link protocols are sufficient to allow the transmission of messages through a network of circuits.

7-3. Data transparency allows a protocol to be able to transmit and receive any bit patterns as data.

7-4. A protocol is implemented by transmitting certain bit patterns or characters on the communication circuit.

7-5. All protocols can transmit and receive all data codes because the codes are independent of the protocol.

7-6. Because of collisions, contention systems are rarely used for line access.

7-7. Polling systems require one station on the circuit to be the master station.

7-8. Roll-call polling is the most common implementation of a polling system.

7-9. Polling systems are functional in election years only.

7-10. Token passing systems require one station on the circuit to take responsibility to ensure that there is always one, but only one, token circulating on the circuit.

7-11. Data messages normally consist of three parts: the header, text, and footer.

**7-12.** The ACK character normally acknowledges the receipt of a block of data.

**7-13.** Stop-and-wait flow control is inherently efficient because of its simplicity.

**7-14.** Sliding window flow control allows multiple blocks of data to be in transit on the line at one time.

**7-15.** SLIP has largely replaced the PPP protocol because it has better error detection.

**7-16.** KERMIT is error checked and is a very fast protocol.

**7-17.** A bit-oriented protocol uses only one special character, the flag character.

**7-18.** HDLC is a bit-oriented protocol.

**7-19.** The best known character-oriented protocol is BISYNC.

**7-20.** SDLC was an outgrowth of the original work on HDLC.

**7-21.** HDLC operates in one of three modes; however, one mode is rarely used.

**7-22.** The basic operational unit for HDLC is a frame.

**7-23.** HDLC uses a flag character to mark the beginnings and ends of frames.

**7-24.** BISYNC supports all data codes.

**7-25.** BISYNC supports transparency.

**7-26.** DDCMP has largely been replaced by TCP/IP.

## MULTIPLE CHOICE

**7-1.** In HDLC, when a 0 bit is inserted after all strings of five consecutive 1 bits, the term applied is _____.

   a. zeroing

   b. synchronizing

   c. oneing

   d. bit stuffing

   e. string breaking

**7-2.** When two stations on a circuit transmit at the same time, a(n) _____ occurs.

   a. altercation

   b. division

   c. collision

   d. polling

   e. bit stuffing

**7-3.** In order to know what stations to poll and in what sequence, the master station uses a _____.

   a. message header

   b. start of header character

   c. polling list

   d. polling PDA

   e. cyclic redundancy check

**7-4.** When a receiver must acknowledge every block of data before the next block is sent, the _____ type of flow control is being used.

   a. sliding window

   b. stop-and-go

    c. stop-and-shop

    d. stop-and-flop

    e. stop-and-wait

7-5. The name of the flow control protocol in which the sending station, on receipt of a NAK, resends the damaged or out of sequence frame and all frames after it is _____.

    a. selective reject

    b. selective repeat

    c. go-back-n

    d. send them again

    e. HDLC

7-6. HDLC is an example of _____.

    a. sliding window flow control

    b. a serial line interface protocol

    c. an asynchronous protocol

    d. All of the above.

    e. None of the above.

7-7. When an HDLC node receives a flag character, it knows that _____.

    a. an error has occurred

    b. a frame is beginning or ending

    c. it should signal the sender to stop sending traffic

    d. it should switch to transparent mode

    e. None of the above.

7-8. HDLC's information frames _____.

    a. are used to send an NAK when a frame is received incorrectly

    b. are used to establish the way the protocol will proceed

    c. contain the data field that holds the information being transmitted

    d. are used to send information from one node to a router for flow control

    e. are not used in ABM mode

7-9. The part of a message that contains the destination address is called the _____.

    a. zip

    b. text

    c. trailer

    d. header

    e. flag

7-10. Software or hardware that changes one protocol to another is called a _____.

    a. CODEC

    b. modem

    c. router

    d. encryptor

    e. protocol converter

7-11. Contention systems work best _____.

    a. on circuits that have only two DTEs

    b. on circuits that have light message traffic

    c. when the speed of the circuit is relatively fast

    d. All of the above.

    e. None of the above.

7-12. Desirable attributes for a data link protocol to have are _____.

    a. transparency

    b. code dependency

    c. efficiency

    d. a and c

    e. a, b, and c

7-13. Techniques to ensure that a fast transmitting node does not send data faster than the receiving node can receive and process it are called _____.

    a. token passing

    b. parity checking

    c. cyclic redundancy checking

    d. flow control

    e. error control

## ■ PROBLEMS AND PROJECTS

7-1. In what situations or application is a predictable rate of access to a network, as provided by token passing access techniques, more important than having the fastest access?

7-2. Do some research on the Internet and write a one- or two-page paper about KERMIT, including its history, strengths, and weaknesses.

7-3. Do some research on the Internet about the Ethernet system. What kind of line control does it use? What protocols can be used with Ethernet? At what speeds can Ethernet handle data on a circuit?

7-4. Do some research and draw flow diagrams similar to Figure 7-8 for HDLC link setup and disconnect and reject recovery.

## ECKLES, FEINMAN, AND MACKENZIE—PART 2

Mr. Block, EF&M's partner for technology, continued his analysis of the firm's needs for a network to link its offices. He realized that it was not enough to do a simple analysis of the traffic that would be sent on the network because, in addition to the data characters sent on the network, the protocol characters represent a type of overhead that must be taken into account.

He knew that, during transmission, the text portion of the e-mail messages and documents would be surrounded by protocol characters that would be added at the transmitting end and stripped off at the receiving end. To try and make his estimates more accurate, he decided to estimate the additional load that the protocol characters would add.

Using the traffic volumes given in Part 1 of this case (see chapter 6), assume that whatever protocol is chosen allows a maximum of 1,000 data characters in a transmission block. That is, e-mail messages or documents that are longer than 1,000 characters are first segmented into 1,000-character (or less) blocks. Each block is then surrounded by 50 protocol characters that are transmitted with the data.

**QUESTIONS**

1. Including the protocol characters, how many total characters and bits would be sent on EF&M's circuit(s) on busy days?

2. What would be the transmission time on 56 Kbps and 1 Mbps lines?

3. What percentage increase in time was caused by the addition of the protocol?

**CASE STUDY**

# TRANSMISSION MEDIA

## ■ OUTLINE

## ■ KEY TERMS

British Naval Connector (BNC)

category 1 (CAT 1) cable

category 2 (CAT 2) cable

category 3 (CAT 3) cable

category 4 (CAT 4) cable

category 5 (CAT 5) cable

category 5E (CAT5E) cable

category 6 (CAT 6) cable

category 7 (CAT 7) cable

cladding

coaxial cable (coax)

conducted media

core

crosstalk

direct broadcast satellites (DBS)

dispersion

downlink

free space optics (FSO)

geosynchronous orbit

guided media

infrared

laser

light emitting diode (LED)

low Earth orbit (LEO) satellite

medium Earth orbit (MEO) satellite

microwave radio

multimode fiber

optical fiber

propagation delay

punchdown block

radiated media

registered jack 11 (RJ-11)

registered jack 45 (RJ-45)

SC connector

shielded twisted pair (STP)

single mode fiber

ST connector

terminating block

twisted pair

unguided media

unshielded twisted pair (UTP)

uplink

very small aperture terminals (VSAT)

wavelength division multiplexing (WDM)

wireless

## ■ OBJECTIVES

After you complete your study of this chapter, you should be able to:

- describe the characteristics of the various types of media used to carry communications circuits;
- describe the pros and cons of the various media;
- explain the benefits and costs of using optical fiber as a media;
- explain why satellites are not often used as a media for transmissions that need realtime response; and
- explain concerns about security when wireless media are employed.

## 8-1 INTRODUCTION

conducted media

guided media

radiated media

unguided media

wireless

This chapter discusses the various media used for communications circuits. In general, media can be divided into two categories: **Conducted** or **guided media** provide some type of physical path, such as wire, cable, or optical fiber, along which the signal moves from end to end. **Radiated** or **unguided media,** most commonly known today as **wireless,** employ an antenna and the transmission of waves, such as radio waves, microwaves, or infrared waves, through air, water, or a vacuum. Although there is a wide overlap in their characteristics and capabilities, each medium has found a particular niche in which it is most commonly used.

## 8-2 CONDUCTED MEDIA

Conducted media, such as the wires and cables that connect our stereo components and PC equipment, are what most people think of when the term "medium" is used in a communications context. Indeed, wire and cable are still the most common media used today. While there are many different types, the number of different connectors at the ends of those wires and cables is even larger and often confusing, as anyone who has ever hooked up a PC or home theater system will attest. The information that follows will help sort out the various types of wire and cable that are used in communications systems and networks.

Telephone wires can be an eyesore on the urban landscape.
(Courtesy of Nick Gunderson / Getty Images Inc.–Stone All Stock. Reprinted with permission.)

**FIGURE 8-1** Twisted pair wires are the most commonly used medium for communications transmission.

## Unshielded Twisted Pair Wire

The most common medium used for communications circuits is ordinary wire, usually made of copper. Over the years, telephone companies and other carriers have laid millions of miles of wire into virtually every home and business in the country, so wire is used for virtually all local loops. Originally, open pairs or wires were used. However, they were affected by weather and were very susceptible to electrical noise and other interference. Today, the pairs of wires are almost always insulated with a plastic coating and are twisted together. This type of wire is called either **twisted pair** or **unshielded twisted pair (UTP),** and it is illustrated in Figure 8-1.

twisted pair

unshielded twisted pair

Wire emits an electromagnetic field when carrying communications signals, but twisting the pair together electrically cancels the signals radiating from each wire. This almost completely prevents the signals on one pair of wires from interfering with the signals on an adjacent pair. This type of interference is called **crosstalk.** UTP cable relies on the cancellation effect produced by the twisted pairs to limit signal degradation caused by electromagnetic interference (EMI) and radio frequency interference (RFI). To further reduce crosstalk, the number of twists in the wire pairs varies, but there are precise specifications for the number of twists required per foot (or meter) of cable. The wire used for inside applications and local loops normally is either 24 or 22 gauge. The smaller the gauge numbers, the larger the wire.

crosstalk

The Electrical Industries Association (EIA) has defined six categories of UTP for telephone and data transmission use. These categories are defined in the following list. With the exception of CAT 1, all wire is typically 24-gauge solid copper. CAT 1 wire is normally 26 gauge.

category 1 (CAT 1) cable

■ **Category 1 (CAT 1):** Basic twisted pair wire for telephone (analog voice) use. Not recommended for data.

category 2 (CAT 2) cable

- **Category 2 (CAT 2):** Four unshielded, solid twisted pairs. Supports data transmission to 4 Mbps.

category 3 (CAT 3) cable

- **Category 3 (CAT 3):** Wire containing at least three twists per foot. About the same as normal telephone cable installed in most office buildings. Supports data transmission to 10 Mbps, but with proper design and over limited distances it may support up to 16 Mbps. If there is more than one pair in the same jacket, it must not have the same number of twists per foot in order to minimize interpair crosstalk. CAT 3 cable normally has four pairs of wires.

category 4 (CAT 4) cable

- **Category 4 (CAT 4):** Similar to CAT 3, but CAT 4 has more twists per foot. Supports data transmission to 20 Mbps.

category 5 (CAT 5) cable

- **Category 5 (CAT 5):** Three to four twists per inch. Data grade cable certified for data transmission to 100 Mbps. CAT 5 cable normally contains four pairs of wires and is the type that is most commonly being installed in new homes and businesses, particularly when a computer network will be used.

category 5E (CAT 5E) cable

- **Category 5E (CAT 5E):** A developing nonstandard cabling system intended primarily to support Gigabit Ethernet (1,000 Mbps). It is similar to CAT 5 but is manufactured to tighter specifications.

category 6 (CAT 6) cable

- **Category 6 (CAT 6):** Four twisted pairs separately wrapped in foil shields and twisted around one another. CAT 6 cable is designed to yield the highest performance possible from UTP cable. While CAT 5E cable will work at 1 Gbps, CAT 6 cable will yield high speed performance that is more reliable over longer distances.

The two most popular specifications are CAT 3 and CAT 5, because CAT 3 wire is the type that is installed in most existing office buildings and CAT 5 is the type that most companies are choosing for new installations. While the two cables look identical, CAT 3 is tested to a lower set of specifications and can cause transmission errors if pushed to faster speeds.

category 7 (CAT 7) cable

shielded twisted pair (STP)

In addition to the six existing standards for UTP cable, there is another developing standard that you may hear about. **Category 7 (CAT 7) cable** is a developing standard for **shielded twisted pair (STP)** wiring. CAT 7 cable will have individually shielded twisted pairs and an overall shield on the outside. It will be heavier and bulkier than CAT 6 cable and will have a larger outside diameter. Some people believe that because if its larger size, relative inflexibility, and higher cost, CAT 7 cable will never become widely utilized because prospective users will choose optical fiber cable instead.

UTP cable offers many advantages. It is easy to install and is less expensive than other types of networking media. Because it is small, it can be fed through small holes. The ability to do this is important when an older building is being rewired. Furthermore, it does not fill up wiring ducts as rapidly as other types of cable. However, UTP is more prone to electrical noise and electrical interference than other media, and the distance it can carry signals without an amplifier or repeater is less than that of optical fiber or coaxial cables.

Wire, whether it is twisted pair or not, can be bundled into cables when more than a two-wire connection is needed. This is exactly how some LANs are wired: A cable consisting of multiple wires is run between workstations and a server or a hub. These cables are normally terminated with one of several standard connectors, depending on the requirements of the LAN or other hardware. For telephones, the **registered jack 11 (RJ-11)** is normally used. For networking applications, the **registered jack 45 (RJ-45)** is very common, especially in LANs. The RJ-45 connector can connect up to eight wires

registered jack 11 (RJ-11)

registered jack 45 (RJ-45)

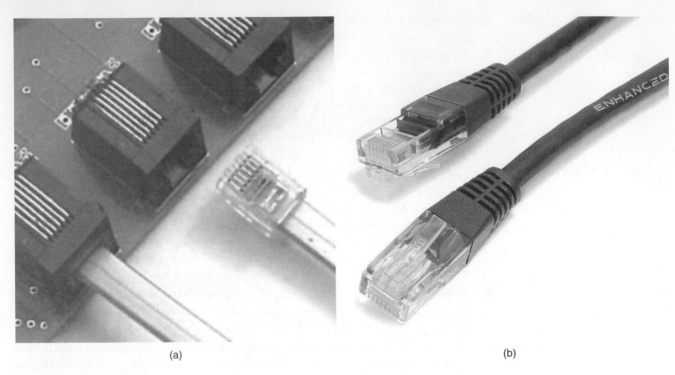

(a)

(b)

(a) RJ-11 and (b) RJ-45 connectors.

[Courtesy of (a) Artisan Instruments and (b) starTech.com Ltd. Reprinted with permission.]

FIGURE 8-2   Wires installed outside may be buried or hung from poles above ground.

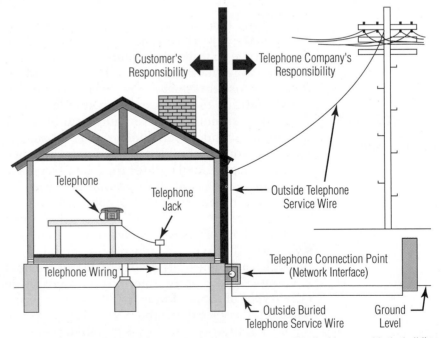

The telephone connection point (network interface) may be located either inside or outside the building.

(four pairs). Only four wires are used for slower speed LANs (10baseT), but all eight are used when the speed is increased (100baseT). Because there is always a reason to increase the speed of a network, it is a good idea to install cabling and connectors for higher speeds when a LAN is first installed. LAN networks will be discussed in Chapters 10, 11, and 12.

When wiring is installed outside, it is either buried in the ground or suspended from overhead poles, as shown in Figure 8-2. As it approaches the

A punchdown block provides a convenient connection point for two sets of wires.
(Courtesy of Autodesk, Inc. Reprinted with permission.)

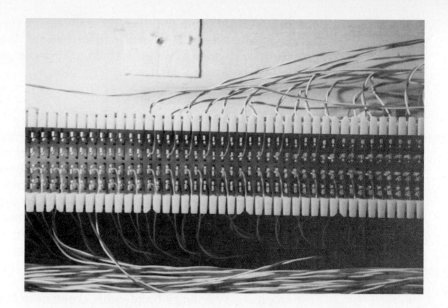

communication carrier's office, it is grouped together in cables that get larger as they get closer to the office. Up to several thousand pairs are grouped together into the largest cables. They are sometimes surrounded by either a wire shielding to provide protection from electrical interference or heavy metal armor for physical protection. On local loops, one pair of wires usually is dedicated to one telephone or data circuit.

**terminating block**

**punchdown block**

Where UTP wire enters a building, it is often connected to a **terminating block,** sometimes called a **punchdown block,** with lugs or clips. This terminating block marks the demarcation point between the common carrier and the building owner, who is responsible for providing and maintaining all wiring within the building.

## Shielded Twisted Pair Wire

**shielded twisted pair**

**Shielded twisted pair (STP)** is a variation of twisted pair wiring. Twisted pair wire is placed inside a thin metallic shielding, similar to aluminum foil and then enclosed in an outer plastic casing. When several shielded twisted pairs are wrapped together in a cable, the entire bundle is wrapped in a metallic braid or foil. The shielding provides further electrical isolation of the signal-carrying pair of wires, both from other pairs and from interference from outside the cable. STP wires are less susceptible to electrical interference caused by nearby equipment or wires and are less likely to cause interference themselves. STP cable is usually installed with special STP data connectors, although RJ connectors can also be used.

Because they are electrically "cleaner," STP wires can carry data at a faster speed than UTP wires. The disadvantages of STP are that it is physically larger and more expensive than UTP, and it is more difficult to work

This shielded twisted pair cable has several pairs inside the shield.
(Courtesy of IBM Corporation. Reprinted with permission.)

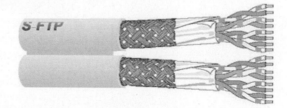

with and to install connectors on or connect to a terminating block. Because it is physically larger, more difficult to handle, less flexible, and more expensive than regular unshielded wire, most companies try to avoid using shielded twisted pair wire if at all possible.

## Coaxial Cable

**coaxial cable (coax)**

**Coaxial cable (coax)** is cable made of several layers of material around a central core, as illustrated in Figure 8-3. The central conductor is most often a copper wire, although aluminum is occasionally used. It is surrounded by insulation, most typically made of plastic. Spacers are sometimes put in the cable to keep the center conductor separate from the shielding. In that case, the insulation material is air or an inert gas. Outside of the insulation is the shielding, also a conductor, which is typically fine, braided copper wire but is sometimes foil. The shielding is surrounded by the cable jacket, which is almost always a form of plastic that provides insulation and physical protection for the cable.

Coax has a very large bandwidth, commonly 400 to 600 MHz, and therefore has a very high data carrying capacity. The telephone industry uses pairs of coaxial cable in areas where the population density is high. One coaxial cable can carry up to 10,800 voice conversations when amplifiers, spaced about a mile apart, are used to boost the signal. The cable television industry uses coaxial cable extensively for carrying television signals from a central transmitter to individual homes or other subscribers. Well over 100 television channels and simultaneous high-speed data transmissions can be carried on a single coaxial cable.

Coax is easy to tap. This is advantageous when it is used around an office or factory where many taps are needed, but is a disadvantage if one is concerned about security and illegal taps. The cable can be bulky and, therefore, difficult to install. Some cable has a rather large bending radius, which must be considered when planning the installation. Because of its shielding, coaxial cable is quite immune to external electrical interference, which makes it a good candidate for use in electrically noisy environments.

**FIGURE 8-3** Parts of coaxial cable.

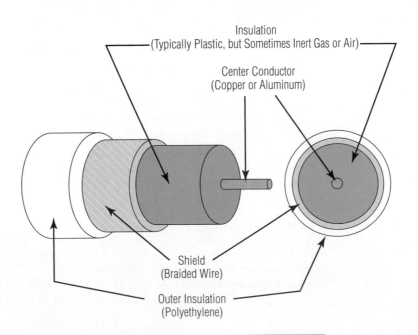

Insulation
(Typically Plastic, but Sometimes Inert Gas or Air)

Center Conductor
(Copper or Aluminum)

Shield
(Braided Wire)

Outer Insulation
(Polyethylene)

A BNC connector.
(Courtesy of Stella Doradus.
Reprinted with permission.)

There are many different types of coax, which has varying electrical characteristics and is available in many different physical sizes (diameters). Depending on the application and the size of the cable, different types of connectors are used. The most common connector used in networking applications is the **British Naval Connector (BNC),** which has a twist lock mechanism that holds the male connector onto the female jack.

British Naval Connector
(BNC)

## SIDEBAR 8-1   PLENUM CABLE

Network cable is often installed in the plenum (the air return duct for heating and air conditioning systems) of buildings. In some modern buildings, the plenum is not a true duct, it includes the entire space between the drop ceiling and the floor above. In the event of fire, ordinary cable presents a risk because its jacket is made of polyvinyl chloride (PVC), which emits a toxic smoke when it burns. Plenum cable, though much more expensive than normal cabling, is often jacketed with polyvinylidene diflouride (PVDF), which has low flame spread and smoke producing properties. Thus, it does not circulate toxic smoke, which may suffocate the building's occupants through the ventilation system. Most cities now have codes that require you to run special plenum-grade cable specifically designed to be run in plenum areas if cable is to be installed there.

## 8-3   OPTICAL FIBER

optical fiber

**Optical fiber** technology is one of the most rapidly advancing segments of communications technology. The worldwide use of optical fibers grew at a compounded growth rate of 20 percent per year from 1998 to 2001. One of the byproducts of this rapid installation of optical fiber in the U.S. is that by 2001, the U.S. telephone infrastructure had more than 80 times the capacity it had five years before. This fantastic buildup in capacity is a boon for consumers and businesses alike, and at least one industry executive predicts that, in the not-too-distant future, long distance calls may be offered free to consumers who buy a bundle of services that includes high-speed Internet access and wireless telephony. The latest developments frequently have to do with the bandwidth or speed that a single fiber can carry and the rapid conversion of networks to be optical fiber based.

core

The optical fiber itself, illustrated in Figure 8-4, is a very thin glass fiber of high purity. The glass **core** at the center provides the transmission-carrying capabilities. It looks like a very fine fishing line but is a very pure, clear strand

**FIGURE 8-4** Parts of optical fiber cable.

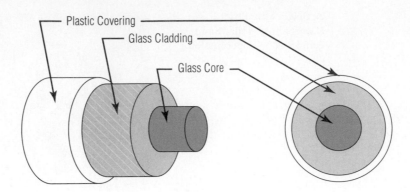

cladding

of silica glass that has a high index of refraction, meaning that it conducts light well. The core is surrounded by another type of glass called **cladding,** which has a low index of refraction (is reflective) and acts like a mirror to the core. The cladding has a protective covering, usually plastic. The total diameter of the fiber is less than that of a human hair. Individual fibers are often bundled together in groups around a central metallic wire that provides strength for pulling the fiber cable through conduit when it is laid.

light emitting diode (LED)

laser

Data are placed on the cable with a light source, either a **light emitting diode (LED)** or a **laser.** The laser is more powerful and is used when the distance between the transmitter and receiver is greater than 5 to 10 miles. For shorter runs, the less expensive LED can be used. The light stays in the core because the cladding has a low refractive index. When the light beam hits the edge of the core, it is reflected toward the center by the cladding's mirror-like surface. The light output of the LED or laser is modulated to provide the variations in the signal that can be interpreted at the receiving end. Without special techniques, a fiber carries a signal in one direction only, so fibers are normally used in pairs.

single mode fiber

Two primary types of fiber are used in data networking. **Single mode fiber** uses a fiber that has a glass core of approximately 9 microns (.009 mm) in diameter. With this very small core size, the light beam travels down the center of the core with little reflection from the cladding. Because the core is so small, however, it requires a very concentrated light source to get the signal into the fiber with adequate strength for long distances. Single mode fiber has almost unlimited bandwidth, due to the small core that supports only one light mode, but this requires very high precision alignment in both joints and connectors. These factors combine to make a single mode installation approximately four times more expensive than a multimode installation.

multimode fiber

The other type of fiber is called **multimode fiber.** The usual core size is either 62.5 microns (.0625 mm) or 50 microns (.0500 mm) in diameter. Both single mode and multimode fibers have the same outer diameter of 125 microns (.125 mm), so the mechanical properties of the fibers are identical though the optical properties vary significantly. With a larger core size it is easier to get the light into the multimode fiber, so the lower cost LEDs can be used as a light source. However, there is more reflection from side to side off the cladding. Some of the light rays travel straight down the center of the fiber, but others reflect at various angles, a phenomenon called **dispersion.** Those that travel straight through the fiber arrive at the destination faster. Dispersion causes the square pulses of a digital signal to become rounded, which limits the signaling rate that can be achieved. The trade-off, then, is that implementing a multimode fiber system costs less than a comparable system built with a single mode fiber. The cable and light source cost less, but the signal-carrying capacity is also less than that of a single mode fiber system.

dispersion

A cable of optical fibers.
(Courtesy of Corbis Digital
Stock. Reprinted with
permission.)

One of optical fiber's most notable characteristics is its high bandwidth. A pair of fibers can carry 160 channels, each running 10 Gbps, for a total capacity of 1.6 terabits per second (Tbps) over long distances. A quick comparison: The total bandwidth of radio is 25 GHz, whereas an optical fiber has a bandwidth of 25,000 GHz. Signals do not travel faster in fiber than in copper, but the density or data capacity of fiber is much greater. Light has higher frequencies, hence shorter wavelengths, so more bits of information can be packed into the same space. Furthermore, photons (the base element of

Optical fiber cables are much smaller than coaxial cables and have a far greater capacity.
(Courtesy of AT&T Bell Laboratories. Reprinted with permission.)

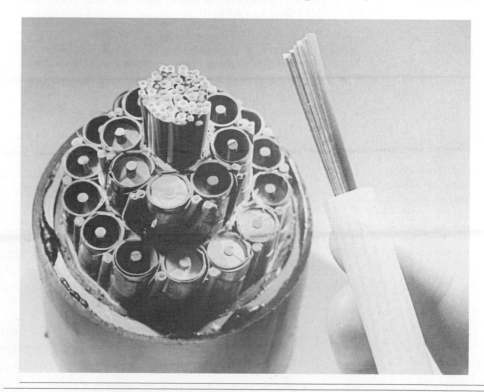

light) can occupy the same space. To visualize this concept, think of two flashlight beams that cross each other. The light from one passes through the other, and both are unaffected. Utilizing this principle, and a technique called **wavelength division multiplexing (WDM),** many light beams of different wavelengths can travel along a single fiber simultaneously without interfering with one another. Each light beam can carry many individually modulated data streams, hence the high data rates that optical fibers can achieve.

**wavelength division multiplexing (WDM)**

Optical fiber cables are very difficult to splice, which requires specialized tools and skills. They are best suited for long point-to-point runs for which few or no splices are required. Splices can be detected using a reflectometer, an instrument that sends a light wave down the fiber and measures the reflection that comes back. From a security standpoint, this difficulty in splicing optical fiber cables and the ability to detect unwanted taps is an advantage. In addition, because the transmission is optical rather than electrical, the cables do not radiate signals as all electrical devices do. Given these attributes, optical fiber cables are excellent in situations that require very high security.

Another advantage of optical fiber cables over wire or coaxial cables is that the fibers are so thin that an optical fiber cable has a very small diameter and is lightweight. This makes the cables easier to install, because they can be pulled through smaller conduits and bent around corners much more easily than coaxial cable. They can even be installed under carpeting or floor tiles, providing additional flexibility when laying out an office.

**SC connector**

**ST connector**

While there are many types of optical fiber connectors in use in the communications industry, two of the more common are the **SC connector** and the **ST connector.** The male SC connector simply pushes into the female receptacle, similar to the audio connectors on a stereo system. The ST connector provides a more secure connection, because after the male connector is inserted into the socket, it is twisted in a clockwise direction and locks into place.

An interesting phenomenon has occurred as fiber cables have been laid across the U.S. Because the cost of the fiber is low and the cost of cable installation is high, it is always more economical to lay cables that have extra capacity than to have to go back and lay additional cable later. As a result, considerable extra fiber capacity has been installed, and it is estimated that only 2% to 5% of the fibers in the USA are lit, hooked up, and carrying traffic. The rest are dark, lying in the ground in anticipation

An SC type optical fiber connector is shown on the left and an ST type connector on the right. (Courtesy of Corning Cable Systems. Reprinted with permission.)

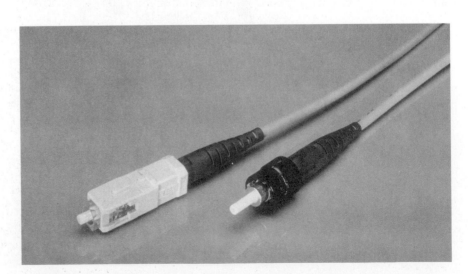

of future demand. Even though the fiber is in the ground, it is far from being usable. For every $1 spent to put an optical fiber in the ground, a company has to spend $20 for electronics, attachment, and configuration to make it usable.

## SIDEBAR 8-2

In mid-2003, the biggest telecommunications companies in the U.S. took a major step toward building superfast optical fiber lines directly to homes. SBC Communications, Verizon Communications, and BellSouth announced that they had agreed on standards for so-called "fiber-to-the-premises" equipment, and they sent a letter to equipment makers asking for bids. By acting in concert, the phone companies can place massive orders and can demand lower prices. Because the three companies have so much clout, the rest of the industry will probably adopt the same standards, creating even greater economies of scale. Trials of the equipment may begin in 2004, but replacing existing copper lines with fiber will take longer because it involves digging up streets. While the impact won't be seen for several years, the momentum for running fiber to homes has been given a kickstart by this agreement.

The first undersea wire-based telephone cable between the U.S. and Europe was installed in 1956 and could handle 36 simultaneous telephone calls. In late 1988, the first optical fiber undersea cable, TAT-8, was completed on approximately the same route and could handle 40,000 simultaneous calls, using two pairs of fibers. That capacity was subsequently upgraded with advances in shore-based electronics. One of the newest trans-Atlantic cables, called "Atlantic Crossing," can handle 2.4 million voice conversations at one time. In 1998, Lucent Technologies unveiled the capability to transmit as many as 10 million calls over a single fiber by dividing the strand into 80 separate wavelengths.

In summary, the characteristics of optical fiber are as follows:

- high bandwidth: very high data carrying capacity
- little loss of signal strength: depends on the details of the cable construction, but the overall characteristics are excellent
- immunity to electrical interference: because it operates in the optical part of the spectrum, electrical noise is not an issue
- excellent isolation between parallel fibers: crosstalk between fibers does not exist
- small physical size; lightweight
- very secure: difficult to tap and splice and does not radiate electrical signals

One large company in New York installed several fiber optic cables to connect several locations in its community. In one case, the fiber cable was run along railroad track, and in another situation, the fiber was run through some abandoned underground conduit formerly used for electrical wires. The fibers carry voice traffic and allow a single telephone system to serve the company's multiple locations around the city, and also carry high-speed data traffic between LANs.

## 8-4　WIRELESS MEDIA

Wireless networking is one of the hottest topics in communications. Users want the convenience of not being tethered to a telephone jack or other communications port, especially if they are using a laptop computer. Network managers like the flexibility that wireless technology gives them. For example, when offices are moved or rearranged, it isn't necessary to rewire the office and pull new cables to the new office locations. However, security is a significant concern with wireless communication because it is accomplished using radio transmissions that are susceptible to being intercepted. However, security problems are being solved and wireless usage is growing by leaps and bounds.

### Microwave Radio

**microwave radio**

**Microwave radio** was one of the first forms of wireless communication and was the medium most used by common carriers for transmitting long distance communications before optical fibers became so prevalent. Microwave radio transmissions occur in the 4 to 28 GHz frequency range. Specific frequency bands are set aside and channels are allocated within the bands. Up to 6,000 voice circuits are carried in a 30 MHz radio channel.

At the frequency range in which they operate, microwave radio signals travel in a straight line. Therefore, the transmitting and receiving antennas must be in a direct line of sight (LOS) with each other. Because of the curvature of the Earth, microwave antennas are usually placed on high towers or building roofs to extend the LOS to the greatest distance possible before another antenna is required. Practically speaking, a range of 20 to 30 miles between towers is common if the terrain is not too hilly. Where the distance to be covered is short, microwave antennas can be placed on the sides of buildings or even in office windows.

A tower with several microwave antennas. (Courtesy of Bryce Flynn / Index Stock Imagery, Inc. Reprinted with permission.)

Microwave signals may carry data in either analog or digital form. Voice, data, and television signals are carried, but each is given its own channel. Depending on the frequency used, some microwave signals are subject to interference by fog, snow, or heavy rain. When this occurs, the channel is unusable until the weather changes. Therefore, when a microwave system is designed, provisions must be made for this possibility. Temporarily stopping the transmission, sending it on an alternate path, and transmitting via a different medium are alternatives to be considered.

To operate a microwave link, a radio license must be obtained from the Federal Communications Commission (FCC), but no right-of-way permits are necessary. Microwave links are sometimes installed privately by companies to connect locations that are near but not adjacent to one another. Several companies in New York City have private microwave links that connect offices in different parts of Manhattan, and similar private microwave installations can be found in most major cities.

Microwave systems should be considered when wired high-speed circuits are not available, when there is a financial advantage or other requirement to have a privately owned transmission system, or when alternative routing is required for critical communications links. Sales engineers from microwave equipment vendors help to obtain the required transmission license and configure the equipment for the specific terrain, transmission speed, and reliability requirements.

## Satellite

Transmission using an Earth satellite is a particular type of radio transmission, and microwave transmission is frequently used. In a typical satellite system, a radio signal is transmitted from an antenna on the ground to a satellite in orbit 22,300 miles above the Earth. At that distance, the circular speed of the satellite exactly matches the speed of rotation of the Earth, and the satellite appears to be stationary overhead. This is called a **geosynchronous orbit**. An antenna on the Earth can be aimed at the satellite and because the satellite appears stationary, the aim doesn't have to be changed. Although the distance is great, the antennas are definitely in sight of each other. The radio signal is beamed to the satellite on a specific frequency called the **uplink**, where it is received, amplified, and then rebroadcast on a different frequency, called the **downlink**. This is illustrated in Figure 8-5.

Because of its distance from Earth, a geosynchronous satellite can see and can be seen from approximately one-third of the Earth. Any antenna and receiver in that area can, at least theoretically, pick up the signals broadcast from the satellite. This broadcast attribute is an advantage in some applications and a disadvantage in others. It is advantageous for organizations that want to use satellites to reach a mass market. Home Box Office (HBO) uses the broadcast capability to distribute movies to CATV companies. Financial companies use satellite transmission to distribute stock market information to brokers all over the country.

For companies that want to use the satellite for point-to-point transmission, the broadcast capability presents a security concern. Anyone who has the proper equipment can receive the broadcast as it is transmitted from the satellite. When this concern is serious, the data can be encrypted before it is transmitted to the satellite, which makes it difficult to interpret the broadcast on the downlink.

Another characteristic of satellite transmission is that, because of the great distance involved—22,300 miles up to the satellite and 22,300 miles back—there is a noticeable delay from the time the signal is sent until it is

**geosynchronous orbit**

**uplink**

**downlink**

**FIGURE 8-5** Satellite transmission.

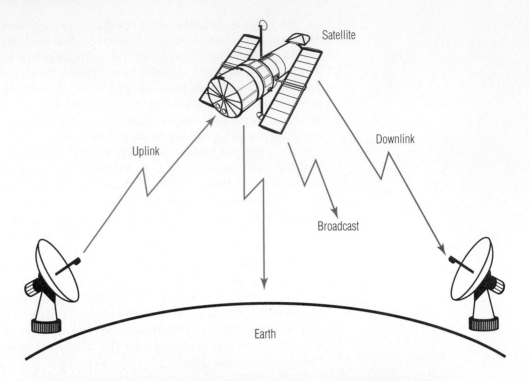

An array of satellite dishes such as this might be found at the head-end of a cable television system. (Courtesy of Kim Mould / Omni-Photo Communications, Inc. Reprinted with permission.)

**propagation delay**

received. This delay, called **propagation delay,** exists for all communications circuits and radio broadcasts. It is a function of the fact that light signals or radio waves travel at a maximum speed of 186,000 miles per second in a vacuum. A signal traveling 4,000 miles across the U.S. on a terrestrial circuit will travel somewhat slower than 186,000 miles per second, but an approximation of the propagation delay can be calculated as follows:

4,000 miles/186,000 miles per second = .0215 second (21.5 milliseconds)

When the signal goes via a synchronous satellite, the propagation delay is:

(22,300 + 22,300 miles)/186,000 miles per second = .2398 seconds
(239.8 milliseconds)

A satellite dish attached to a tower.
(Courtesy of Geostock / Getty Images, Inc.–Photodisc. Reprinted with permission.)

The satellite signal takes eleven times longer to reach its destination! If a return signal is required, the same amount of delay would be encountered a second time. You may have noticed this satellite delay on some domestic long distance telephone calls a few years ago, and it still can be heard on some international telephone calls today. Most people find the delay annoying and the common carriers in the U.S. have switched voice transmission back to terrestrial media. You also see it on news broadcasts when the news anchor in the U.S. switches to a reporter in a remote location. There is often a noticeable pause before the reporter continues the story.

The propagation delay when using a satellite can be extremely significant when data are being sent. Thinking about the protocols you studied in Chapter 7, you realize that there are many interactions between the two ends of a transmission. If almost a quarter of a second is added to each transmission in either direction, the response time would be noticeably longer on a satellite compared to a terrestrial transmission time and would adversely affect the total response time in an interactive application.

Satellites use varying frequencies for transmitting and receiving, which is one reason why satellite dish antennas vary greatly in size. The other main reason has to do with the power output of the satellite transmitter. Those with high-powered transmitters put out a stronger signal, and the receiving antenna on the ground can be smaller. Satellites that transmit in the Ku band of microwave frequencies have such a short wavelength that the Earth station antennas, called **very small aperture terminals (VSAT),** can be as small as eighteen inches in diameter. That's the type typically used by the reporters in the field on news broadcasts. A different application is the **direct broadcast satellite (DBS)** systems commonly used to send television programming via satellite directly to homes. DBS antennas are available in the U.S. for as little as $100 when purchased with one year of television programming. DBS systems will be discussed in more detail in Chapter 9.

In addition to geosynchronous satellites, there are other types of satellite systems in use. **Medium Earth orbit (MEO) satellites** circulate at about 6,000

very small aperture terminals (VSAT)

direct broadcast satellite (DBS)

medium Earth orbit (MEO) satellite

A communications satellite in space orbiting the earth. (Courtesy of Photo Researchers, Inc. Reprinted with permission.)

**low Earth orbit (LEO) satellite**

miles above the Earth, while **low Earth orbit (LEO) satellites** orbit at between 300 and 1,000 miles high. Because of their lower orbits, both of these types of satellites are in motion relative to the rotation of the Earth. Nine to twelve MEO satellites, or about seventy LEO satellites must be in orbit to ensure that at least one can be seen from anywhere on Earth at all times. Users of MEO or LEO satellites need to have omni-directional antennas to receive the signal from the satellite as it passes overhead in its orbit.

## SIDEBAR 8-3    IRIDIUM PHONE SYSTEM

The Iraq war in 2003 gave a boost to LEO-based telephone systems. Thousands of U.S. soldiers and international media correspondents made calls on LEO-based phones from the Iraqi desert where there were no landlines or cell towers.

Iridium was an LEO-based phone system set up by Motorola as a separate company in the late 1990s. Iridium's costs were high because it required sixty-six satellites and eight spares to provide global coverage. Iridium charged $7 a minute for calls on handsets that cost $3,000. There were few buyers.

In the spring of 2000, Iridium filed for Chapter 11 bankruptcy protection. Nobody was interested in buying the company, so it decided to let the satellites fall from orbit and burn up. When the bankruptcy judge offered one last chance for a buyer to step in, Dan Colussy and a group of investors offered $25 million for the system that cost Motorola and its partners $5 billion to build. That's one-half cent on the dollar! It's like getting a $150,000 Rolls Royce for $750.

The new Iridium, now operating at one-tenth the cost of the old Iridium, could turn a profit with calls costing $1.50 a minute. Handsets still run around $1,500. The old Iridium needed 1 million users to break even. The new Iridium needs tens of thousands. The U.S. military signed a deal for unlimited use for up to 20,000 soldiers and the British army signed up for service, too. The media in Iraq also used hundreds of phones.

While it's too early to tell whether the new Iridium will be a financial success, it certainly has a better chance with its new cost structure than it did when it was originally launched.

## Infrared

infrared

**Infrared** transmission uses light waves below the visible spectrum. Generally speaking, the transmitter and receiver must be in direct LOS, although infrared waves can reflect off light-colored surfaces, such as the wall of a room. The signals can also be blocked by fog, smoke, or even heavy rain. Companies sometimes use infrared transmission between nearby buildings. Other applications are to provide wireless communication between PCs and printers, between personal digital assistants (PDAs) such as the Palm Pilot, and between remote control units and television sets.

## Free Space Optics (FSO)

free space optics (FSO)

**Free space optics (FSO)** is the use of laser beams to send data between locations that are within each other's LOS. The technology is emerging as one way to avoid the bottleneck that occurs when fiber optic lines don't extend the "last mile" to offices. Instead of spending time and money to extend or tap into those lines, companies can use laser beams to relay massive amounts of data from one building to another where the data can be shifted more easily to a fiber optical line for transmission over greater distances.

First developed by the military in the 1960s, FSO works by modulating the laser light beam. The laser can be placed on the roof of a building or even behind a window and, because FSO beams work in a spectrum that is unregulated by federal law, no license is required. FSO systems can often be installed in days, and for a fraction of the cost of a fiber optic link when lines have to be laid or even if the fiber is in place but not hooked up.

Because the laser beam has to be precisely aimed at the receiver, one interesting complication is dealing with the normal expansion, contraction, and swaying of buildings that can cause the laser beam to miss its target. Systems have been developed that can track these movements and re-aim the laser beam up to 300 times per second to keep it pointed at the receiving antenna.

## 8-5 WIRELESS COMMUNICATIONS FOR LANS

Wireless communication is used extensively in LANs, where it allows people to move around in the workplace and stay connected to the network. This topic will be covered in detail in Chapter 11, but the main point to emphasize is the concern for security on any type of wireless network. A wireless network can broadcast far outside its intended reception area. With a good antenna and some widely available hacking software, anyone sitting within several hundred yards of the transmitter, or even just driving by, can passively (without alerting the target) scan all data flowing in the network.

There are many preventative steps that can be taken, and they will be covered later. Suffice it to say, it is important for you to consider the security implications of any media you select—especially wireless media.

## 8-6 SUMMARY OF MEDIA CHARACTERISTICS

The chart in Figure 8-6 summarizes the characteristics of the main media used for communications transmission. You can see that each medium has its strong and weak points; there are always trade-offs to be made when deciding which medium to select for a particular network and application combination.

| | UTP (CAT-5) | Coaxial cable | Microwave radio | Satellite | Optical fiber | Free Space Optics |
|---|---|---|---|---|---|---|
| **Transmission speed** | 10 Mbps to 1,000 Mbps | 500 Mbps | 275 Mbps | 90 Mbps | 100 Mbps to 100 Gbps | Varies |
| **Ease of installation** | Easy | Moderate | Difficult | Difficult | Difficult | Moderate |
| **Cost** | Least | Moderate | Moderate | Moderate (not including the cost of the satellite) | High | Moderate |
| **Maintenance difficulty** | Low | Moderate | Low | Low | Low | Low |
| **Skill required to install** | Low | Moderate | High | High | High | Moderate |
| **Most common uses** | Within buildings for LANs | Campus multidrop | Point-to-point, short distance | Point-to-point, long distance | Point-to-point | Between buildings, short distance |
| **Advantages** | Inexpensive, familiar, easy to install, widely available | Less susceptible to interference than other copper media, speed | Speed | Speed, availability | Security, capacity, speed, not susceptible to EMI | Price/ performance |
| **Disadvantages** | Susceptible to interference, limited distance without repeaters or amplifiers | Bulky, difficult to work with | Can be intercepted | Propagation delay, can be intercepted | Difficult to splice and terminate | Can be intercepted |
| **Security** | Good | Good | Poor | Poor | Excellent | Fair |
| **Notes** | Shielded twisted pair allows higher speed but is more difficult to work with | Broadband use is more maintenance intensive | Requires radio license from FCC | Private systems not common | Higher speeds always on the horizon | New technology |

**FIGURE 8-6**    A comparison of the attributes of the media most commonly used for networks.

# SUMMARY

In this chapter, you have learned about the various media on which circuits can be implemented. The choice of media is frequently not really a choice for the network designer at all but is dictated by other technology or by the vendor providing a communication service. For example, LANs are most commonly implemented using twisted pair or wireless media. WANs frequently use optical fiber for the long haul links, but use preinstalled copper wire for connections into buildings where the network has nodes. In any case, preestablished conditions (e.g. cable that is already installed) or the communications carrier frequently determine the medium that is used.

When wireless media of any type are employed, special attention must be given to network security. Wireless transmissions are relatively easy to intercept and it is easy to modify or monitor the contents, especially if the data are not encrypted.

In Chapter 9, you will learn about many types of communications circuits, and the ways in which they are implemented. You will also study the error conditions that can arise, especially on WANs, and you will learn about ways in which the errors can be prevented, detected, and corrected.

# REVIEW QUESTIONS

8-1. What is the difference between unguided and guided media? Give two examples of each.

8-2. Identify five different media used for carrying communications signals and discuss under what circumstances each is most appropriately used.

8-3. Describe the characteristics of CAT 3 and CAT 5 wire.

8-4. What are the advantages of STP wire as compared with UTP?

8-5. Under what circumstances would it be most appropriate to use broadband coaxial cable instead of fiber optic cable?

8-6. List the characteristics of optical fiber.

8-7. What are some potential disadvantages of using microwave radio for data transmission?

8-8. Explain the term *propagation delay* and discuss why it is important for satellite transmission.

8-9. Explain the differences among synchronous, MEO, and LEO satellites.

8-10. Under what circumstances would a company consider installing a private fiber-optic link that connects two of its locations?

8-11. Identify several reasons why a business may or may not select satellite service for high-speed access to the Internet.

8-12. How does FSO differ from microwave radio? How is it similar?

## TRUE OR FALSE

8-1. Optical fiber is an example of a guided medium.

8-2. Unguided media are also known as wireless media.

8-3. Wireless media are the most common media used today.

8-4. Wire emits an electromagnetic field when carrying communications signals.

8-5. CAT 2 cable is most frequently used for telephone transmission in older buildings.

8-6. CAT 5 cable is commonly being installed in new homes and businesses.

8-7. A disadvantage of UTP wire is its high cost.

8-8. Coaxial cable can be tapped easily.

8-9. Optical fiber can be tapped easily.

8-10. Coaxial cable comes in many types and sizes.

8-11. Cladding reflects an optical signal back to the transmitting end so there is no line turnaround.

8-12. Lasers can be used to inject a signal into an optical fiber.

8-13. Single mode optical fiber is more expensive than multimode fiber.

8-14. Signals travel noticeably faster through optical fibers than through coaxial cable.

8-15. Microwave radio signals travel in a straight line and therefore the transmitting and receiving antennas must be in a direct LOS.

8-16. The operation of a microwave radio transmitter requires a license from the FCC.

8-17. Satellites in geosynchronous orbit circle the Earth at the same speed the Earth rotates.

8-18. An antenna aimed at a geosynchronous satellite must be adjusted as the Earth rotates.

8-19. Propagation delay on a circuit through a geosynchronous satellite is about the same as the delay on an optical fiber circuit.

8-20. Large satellite antennas are sometimes required because of sunspots.

8-21. The orbits of LEO satellites are higher than those of geosynchronous satellites.

8-22. Security is always a concern with wireless media.

## MULTIPLE CHOICE

8-1. The shielding on STP wire is typically made from _____.

    a. Kevlar

    b. Teflon

    c. foil

    d. PCBs

    e. plastic

8-2. The most popular cable for networking being installed in new office buildings is _____.

    a. CAT 1

    b. CAT 3

    c. CAT 5

    d. optical fiber

    e. STP

8-3. Multiplexing on optical fibers is performed by using _____.

a. WDM

b. PAM

c. multimode fibers

d. FSK

e. color shifting

8-4. The time it takes a LEO satellite to make one orbit of the Earth is _____.

a. 24 hours

b. less than that of a geosynchronous satellite

c. exactly 1 month

d. None of the above.

8-5. Infrared transmissions can be intercepted _____.

a. by anyone who has a shortwave receiver

b. by putting a receiving device in the neighborhood of the transmitter

c. through fog and smoke

d. All of the above.

e. None of the above.

8-6. The type of media that provides some type of physical path is called _____.

a. physical media

b. conducted media

c. wireless media

d. unguided media

e. news media

8-7. The most common medium used for communication circuits is _____.

a. optical fiber

b. STP wire

c. coaxial cable

d. ordinary copper wire

e. microwave radio

8-8. Twisting a pair of wires together has the effect of _____.

a. shielding the wire from outside interference

b. electrically canceling the signals radiating from each wire

c. strengthening the pair against breakage

d. amplifying the signal flowing through the wire

e. None of the above.

8-9. The purpose of a terminating block or a punchdown block is to _____.

a. mark the end of a cable run

b. signal the end of a block of messages in a transmission

c. block a jab that might knock a boxer off his feet

d. serve as the demarcation point between a wired circuit and a wireless circuit

e. None of the above.

8-10. The core of an optical fiber is surrounded by another type of glass called the _____.

a. shield

b. plenum

c. protective covering

d. padding

e. cladding

8-11. Data are placed on an optical fiber cable with a(n) _____.

a. infrared flashlight

b. LED

c. laser

d. candle

e. photocell

f. b or e

g. b or c

8-12. Some of the light rays travel straight down the center of the fiber, whereas others reflect at various angles. Those that travel straight through the fiber arrive at the destination faster, a phenomenon called _____.

a. dispersion

b. dispensation

c. dyslexia

d. reflective retardation

e. core circuitousness

8-13. An example of wireless media is _____.

a. microwave radio

b. satellite

c. infrared

d. All of the above.

e. None of the above.

8-14. The radio signal beamed from the Earth at a satellite is called the _____.

a. aperture

b. geosynchronous orbit

c. uplink

d. propagation delay

e. downlink

8-15. Infrared transmissions _____.

a. require the sender and receiver to be in direct line of sight

b. can be blocked by fog

c. are sometimes used between PCs and printers

d. All of the above. —

e. None of the above.

8-16. The use of modulated laser beams to send data between locations that are within LOS of each other is called _____.

a. laser optic transmission

b. fiber optic transmission

c. infrared transmission

d. free space optics —

e. free laser optics

8-17. Which of the following statements is true?

a. There are always trade-offs to be considered when deciding which medium to select for a particular network.

b. Each network situation has one and only one proper medium that should be selected.

c. The network designer always has a free choice in selecting media. -

d. Vendors are never involved in selecting the media for a network.

## ■ PROBLEMS AND PROJECTS

8-1. Visit a company that has installed fiber optic links. Why did they install optical fiber? What difficulties did they have when installing the fiber? What error rate are they experiencing for data transmission on the fiber? How often has the fiber link failed, and why? Overall, how has the fiber operated compared to the previous communications technology that was installed?

8-2. What type of wiring would you recommend for a small service business that has just moved into a building formerly occupied by a supermarket? The business does no manufacturing, so employees will be sitting in an office environment. The company expects to install a LAN with a data rate of 100 Mbps, and will have a private PBX system for voice communications.

8-3. Investigate the alternatives for getting high-speed access to the Internet in your home. What services are available today where you live? If you have several alternatives to choose from, which would you select, or which have you selected? Why?

8-4. Calculate and compare the time needed to send a 5-megabyte file from New York to Los Angeles by coaxial cable and by geosynchronous satellite, assuming that the file is sent in 100,000 byte blocks, that line speed is 56 Kbps, that line turnaround for the coax cable takes 50 milliseconds, that there are no errors in transmission, and that each block must be acknowledged with a one-byte ACK character before the next block can be sent.

## BURKHARDT VACUUM AND SEWING MACHINE

Marsha Burkhardt, proprietor of Burkhardt Vacuum and Sewing Machine located in Ukiah, California, faced a difficult decision. She had recently purchased a stand-alone building from a small accounting firm that was closing its doors, and she was about to move her company from the space it rented in a strip mall. The new building was about twenty years old and had been wired for telephones and computer terminals with cabling that was modern for its time, approximating what is today called CAT 3 cable. The decision Marsha faced was whether she should spend the money to rewire the building with CAT 5 cable before she moved the company into the building. Her concerns were whether she could afford to make the change now and whether she would ever recoup her investment.

Burkhardt Vacuum and Sewing Machine had been founded by her father in the 1950s. The company was a sole proprietorship that operated the single store and specialized in the sale and repair of vacuum cleaners and sewing machines for home use. The company had built an outstanding reputation for handling quality products such as Royal vacuum cleaners and Bernina sewing machines. They were also known for conducting excellent training classes for customers who bought the sewing products, and for a repair center that was second-to-none in the area when comparing speed of repair, quality, and price. Steve Burkhardt, Marsha's brother, was the driving force behind the service center and deserved full credit for its outstanding reputation. He had superb technical knowledge of all the machines the store sold, and could resolve virtually any problem himself.

As the senior Mr. Burkhardt got up in years, he gradually turned the overall responsibility for the business over to Marsha, because she had the best business sense in the family and had spent many years working with the customers in both sales and training roles. On her own initiative, she had earned an MBA with a specialty in Information Science at a local university, so she had a solid business foundation. In addition, she loved computers and had looked for every opportunity to automate the store's operation with PCs and even a LAN. She faced the latest decision—not the biggest one she had ever made, but significant, especially in an environment where vacuums and sewing machines were increasingly sold by large chains and home improvement stores at deeply discounted prices—with some confusion.

In its current location, PCs had been installed in the office, the service and repair center, and in two locations on the main display floor. In addition, there were several specialized terminals in the service center that were used to contact the sewing machine and vacuum manufacturer's computers when technical support was required for particularly difficult problems. All were connected to a small server through a LAN. The company also had a small telephone system that had four telephones in the store and a connection to Steve's home, so that he could answer calls from there when necessary. All of the computer and telephone equipment would need to be moved and reinstalled in the new building.

The new building needed some renovation to make it suitable as a retail store. Some office walls had to be removed to create a display space for the vacuums and sewing machines, and a workshop area needed to be constructed for the service center. The big question was whether the old CAT 3-like wiring for the telephones and PCs should be removed and replaced with modern CAT 5 wiring. Marsha had received an estimate of $9,000 to redo the wiring. She knew that it would be less expensive to do the work while the building was undergoing other renovation, but she was also concerned about the additional expense on top of the other renovation costs.

**QUESTIONS**

1. What immediate benefits would the Burkhardt company receive if the wiring were upgraded now?

2. What would be the advantages and disadvantages of leaving the old wiring in place and continuing to use it?

3. If you had been hired as a consultant to Ms. Burkhardt, and based only on what you know now, would you recommend that she replace the existing wiring?

4. What additional information would you want to obtain so that you could give her a recommendation you felt completely comfortable with?

**C A S E   S T U D Y**

# CHAPTER 9

# COMMUNICATIONS CIRCUITS

## ■ OUTLINE

## ■ KEY TERMS

analog circuit

asymmetric digital subscriber line (ADSL)

attenuation

attenuation distortion

automatic repeat request (ARQ)

background noise

block check character (BCC)

broadband

cable TV (CATV) circuits

callback unit

call setup time

channel

circuit

circuit switching

concentrator

conditioned line

continuous ARQ

crosstalk

cyclic redundancy checking (CRC)

datagram

data link

data service unit/channel service unit (DSU/CSU)

dialback unit

digital circuit

digital satellite service (DSS)

digital subscriber line (DSL)

digital transmitter/receiver

direct broadcast satellite (DBS)

dropouts

E-1 circuit

echo

echo checking

echo suppressors

envelope delay distortion

error correction

error detection

forward channel

forward error correction (FEC)

four-wire circuit

fractional T-1

Gaussian noise

head end

impulse noise

inverse concentrator

leased circuit

line

link

longitudinal redundancy checking (LRC)

low-speed circuit

multidrop circuit

multipoint circuit

node

packet

packet assembly/disassembly (PAD)

packet data network (PDN)

packetizing

packet switching

parity checking

permanent virtual circuit (PVC)

phase jitter

point-to-point circuit

polynomial error checking

private circuit

reverse channel

shielding

signal-to-noise ratio (SNR)

statistical time division multiplexing (STDM)

stop and wait ARQ

subvoice-grade circuit

switched virtual circuit (SVC)

symmetric digital subscriber line (SDSL)

T-1 circuit

T-2 circuit

T-3 circuit

T-4 circuit

T-carrier system

time division multiplexing (TDM)

two-wire circuit

vertical redundancy checking (VRC)

very-high–rate digital subscriber line (VDSL)

voice grade circuit

white noise

wide band circuit

## ■ OBJECTIVES

After you complete your study of this chapter, you should be able to:

- distinguish among communications lines, circuits, channels, and links;
- explain the term *node* in a data communication context;
- discuss the differences between analog and digital circuits;
- describe two-wire and four-wire circuits;
- differentiate between point-to-point and multipoint circuits;
- discuss circuit switching concepts;
- explain the advantage of packet switching over circuit switching when data is being transmitted;

- describe several types of multiplexing;
- describe various T-carrier service offerings; and
- describe conditions that cause errors on circuits, and discuss error prevention, detection, and correction.

## 9-1   INTRODUCTION

Previous chapters discussed communications lines or circuits without defining them. In this chapter, circuits are defined more precisely and the characteristics of many types of circuits are explained. Communications circuits provide the physical path on which the communications signals flow, and you must understand the characteristics of circuits to learn how they can be combined to form networks. Information about the ways in which circuits can be configured and used is presented. As signals travel on a circuit, they may be processed, enhanced, and combined for various purposes, and you will study how this is accomplished. Signals may also be subjected to conditions that cause errors. You will look at the types of errors that can occur and will learn about ways in which they can be prevented, detected, and corrected.

## 9-2   COMMUNICATIONS CIRCUITS

Any of the media described in Chapter 8 can be used to establish a communications circuit. Authorities differ somewhat in the details of the definition of the word **circuit**; however, a commonly accepted definition is *the path over which two-way communications take place.* The word **line** is often used interchangeably with the word circuit, although the former gives a stronger implication of a physical wire connection. In fact, many modern circuits do not run on wires at all, as you have learned. The longer the distance, the higher the probability that the circuit runs on at least one medium other than wire, such as optical fiber or microwave radio.

circuit

line

link

data link

A **link** is a segment of the circuit between two points. As shown in Figure 9-1, a data circuit might have a link between the user's PC and a nearby hub or router. Another link would run from the hub to the local server and there could be other links to other servers, depending on the exact nature of the data transaction. When the term **data link** is used, it almost always includes the DTE, modems, and all other equipment necessary to make the complete data connection—software as well as hardware. For a telephone circuit, links exist between the residences or businesses of the parties making the phone

FIGURE 9-1   Links are segments of a circuit. Nodes connect links or lines or may be an end point on a link.

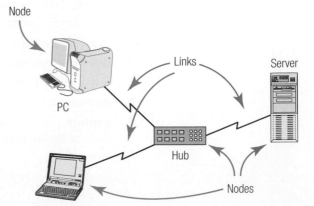

call and their local telephone company COs. Other links exist between the COs along the path between the parties.

node

A **node** is a functional unit that connects two transmission links or lines, as shown in Figure 9-1. It also can be an end point on a circuit or a junction point of two or more circuits. The term "node" is derived from graph theory, in which a node is a junction point of links, areas, or edges. Typical nodes on data circuits are PCs, routers, and servers.

channel

Circuits are often subdivided into **channels,** which are one-way paths for communications. Channels may be derived from a circuit by multiplexing or they may be independent entities, such as television channels. A data circuit is sometimes divided into two channels, one of which operates at high speed for data transmission and the other operates at low speed for control infor-

forward channel

mation. The data channel is called the **forward channel,** and the control

reverse channel

channel is the **reverse channel**. As the name implies, the reverse channel carries information in the opposite direction from the data channel. The type of information carried on a reverse channel depends on the rules of communication or the protocol that is used

broadband

The term **broadband** deserves special attention because it is so widely used. There are two distinct meanings for the term. As it relates to a LAN, "broadband" refers to a multichannel, analog circuit that uses coaxial cable as the medium. You will hear people refer to a broadband cable system which, because of its multichannel capability, might be carrying a LAN on one channel, a television signal on another channel, and voice signals on a third channel. By way of contrast, when "broadband" is used in relation to a WAN, it means a high-speed circuit that has a transmission speed of 256 Kbps or greater, though the exact speed isn't precise. The term is most often used for circuits carried on high speed facilities; such as T-1, DSL, CATV, or satellite, which you will learn about in this chapter.

## 9-3 THE ENVIRONMENT IN WHICH CIRCUITS OPERATE

There is a wide difference in the environments where circuits are installed. Circuits that are a part of a LAN are installed within buildings and around campuses, but the distances are limited and the environment is relatively clean, electrically speaking. On the other hand, circuits that make up WANs are implemented over long distances, sometime covering thousands of miles. The circuit media of a WAN often exists in a relatively hostile environment, which can be caused by weather, thunderstorms, other electrical interference, or even squirrels and other rodents chewing on the cables! As a result, WAN circuits are much more prone to transmission errors than LAN circuits, and error detection and correction are vital for successful WAN operation. This topic will be explored in detail later in the chapter.

## 9-4 TYPES OF CIRCUITS

Circuits can be categorized in many different ways, and the following breakdown is useful for discussion purposes.

### Point-to-Point Circuits

point-to-point circuit

A **point-to-point circuit,** illustrated in Figure 9-2, connects two—and only two—nodes. A typical circuit of this type might connect a PC to a server located some distance away, or may connect two locations of a small company.

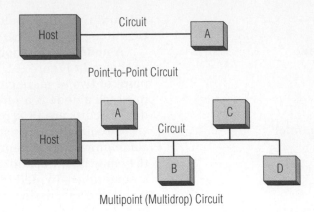

**FIGURE 9-2** Types of circuits with nodes A, B, C, D, and the host computer.

A standard telephone call between two locations is another example of a point-to-point circuit.

## Multipoint Circuits

**multipoint circuit**

**multidrop circuit**

If there are several nodes connected to the same circuit, also shown in Figure 9-2, it is called a **multipoint circuit** or a **multidrop circuit.** With multipoint circuits, there is a clear distinction between the circuit and the links. The connections from the host to A, from A to B, from B to C, and from C to D are links. The overall connection from the host to D is the circuit. In most cases, a multipoint circuit is less expensive to rent from a communications carrier than four point-to-point circuits, each connecting the host to one of the nodes (A, B, C, and D), especially if the nodes are widely separated. Multipoint circuits are often used to connect locations that 1) have a relatively low volume of traffic, 2) can share the line without interfering with one another, and 3) can perform adequately while sharing the line.

While the terms "point-to-point" and "multipoint" are applicable to any type of circuit, you'll hear them used more often to describe WAN circuits than LAN circuits.

## Two-Wire and Four-Wire Circuits

**two-wire circuit**

**four-wire circuit**

Point-to-point and multipoint WAN data circuits are normally implemented with either two wires or four wires connecting the nodes. Normally, two wires are required to carry a communication in one direction. Therefore, a **two-wire circuit** is called a simplex (or half-duplex) circuit and a **four-wire circuit** is a full-duplex circuit. Some modems, however, are capable of splitting a circuit into two channels through FDM or other techniques. In that case, it is possible to obtain full-duplex operation on a two-wire circuit. In most cases, however, four-wire circuits are preferable for data communications. With four-wire circuits, two wires provide the forward channel in one direction while the other two wires provide the forward channel in the other direction.

Standard dial-up telephone circuits are two-wire circuits. Four-wire circuits must be ordered from a communications carrier and are normally installed on a leased basis. The advantage is that the circuit is then available for full-time use. The disadvantage is that a leased circuit may cost more than a dial-up connection, and it may not be economical if relatively little data will be transmitted.

## Analog Circuits

analog circuit

Because the PSTN was originally designed to carry voice transmissions in analog form, most of the circuits that run to individual businesses or homes were designed for analog use. As we saw in Chapter 6, using **analog circuits** to carry data requires the use of a modem to convert the digital signal from a PC or other DTE to analog form before it is transmitted. Then, you must use another modem to convert the signal back to digital form at the receiving end before the data can be presented to another PC or DTE. Analog circuits are limited by the speed at which they can carry data and are also more prone to noise and errors than digital circuits. Hence, communications carriers of all types are installing digital circuits as quickly as they can to take advantage of the benefits that digital transmission offers.

low-speed circuit

subvoice-grade circuit

voice grade circuit

wide band circuit

Whereas the modem usually determines the actual speed at which analog circuits transmit data, carriers offer analog circuits that are capable of certain speed ranges. Traditionally these have been known as **low-speed circuits** or **subvoice-grade circuits, voice grade circuits,** and **wide band circuits.** Subvoice-grade circuits are designed for telegraph and teletypewriter usage but may also be used for low-speed signaling applications such as fire alarms, burglar alarms, door opening indicators, or process monitoring systems where the data rate is low and/or infrequent. These circuits operate at speeds of 45 to 200 bps. They cannot handle either voice transmission or data at higher speeds. In fact, subvoice-grade circuits are normally derived from a voice grade circuit by dividing it into twelve or twenty-four low-speed circuits.

Voice grade circuits are designed for voice transmission, but they can also be used to transmit data at up to 56,000 bps when sophisticated modems are used. This is the type of circuit that is most commonly described throughout this book.

Wideband circuits are high-speed analog circuits designed to carry multiple voice or data signals. They are delivered to customers in a bandwidth of 48,000 Hz, which, with the use of appropriate multiplexing equipment, will carry twelve 4,000 Hz voice channels. However, these circuits are rarely sold because digital circuits have largely superseded them.

## Digital Circuits

digital circuit

A **digital circuit** is one that has been designed and engineered expressly to carry digital signals. The direct digital transmission of data is simple and eliminates the signal conversions at each end. Digital transmission capability became available to end users in the late 1970s, although the common carriers had been using digital transmission techniques and circuits for many years before that. Most new circuits being installed now are designed especially for digital transmission.

One of the main advantages of digital transmission is that the distortion of pulses that inevitably occurs along the transmission path is easier to correct than the distortion of an analog transmission. Analog signals are periodically amplified to increase their signal strength, and the distortions in the waveform are amplified along with the original signal, as shown in Figure 9-3. Digital signals are made up of simple pulses, as shown in Figure 9-4. They are never amplified, but are regenerated by a repeater. The regeneration eliminates any distortion that has occurred. Thus, the signal that arrives at the receiver is cleaner. The result is that digital transmissions have a lower error rate than their analog counterparts do.

Another advantage of using digital transmission is that no analog-to-digital conversion is required. Assuming digital links exist from one end of

**FIGURE 9-3**
Amplification of an analog signal.

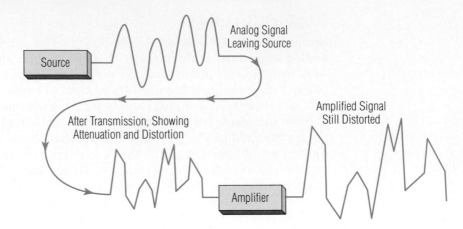

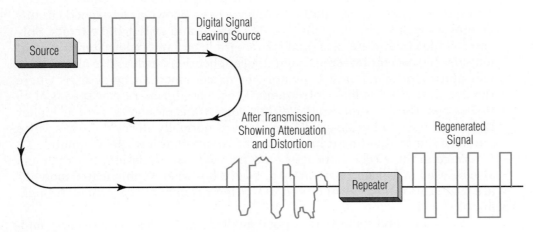

**FIGURE 9-4**    Regeneration of a digital signal.

the circuit to the other, the digital output from the DTE can be simply shaped and timed to conform to the requirements of the digital network and can be transmitted directly. The device that performs the shaping and timing is called a **digital transmitter/receiver** or **data service unit/channel service unit (DSU/CSU),** which was discussed in Chapter 6. DSU/CSUs are much less complicated and considerably less expensive than modems.

**digital transmitter/receiver**

**data service unit/channel service unit (DSU/CSU)**

## T-Carrier Systems

**T-carrier systems**

A family of high-speed digital transmission systems, known as **T-carrier systems,** has evolved within the communications carrier companies over the past forty years. T-carrier systems are designated according to their transmission capacity, as shown in the table below.

| Designation | Bit Capacity |
| --- | --- |
| T-1 | 1.544 Mbps |
| T-2 | 6.312 Mbps |
| T-3 | 44.736 Mbps |
| T-4 | 274.176 Mbps |

**T-1 circuit**

**T-3 circuit**

**T-2 circuit**

**T-4 circuit**

**T-1 circuits** and **T-3 circuits** are used by both carriers and their customers. **T-2 circuits** and **T-4 circuits** are primarily used by the carriers for communication between their offices.

A T-1 system normally uses a standard pair of copper wires for transmission. Repeaters are spaced about every mile to regenerate the signal and transmit it over the next length of the circuit. A T-1 system can carry twenty-four circuits of 64,000 bps each ($24 \times 64,000 = 1.536$ Mbps; the extra 8,000 bps are used for signaling). Multiplexing equipment is used to combine the signals for transmission over the T-1 system and to separate them at the receiving end. A 64,000 bps channel normally carries two digitized voice signals, assuming ADPCM is used to modulate the signal.

**E-1 circuit**

It should be noted that in Europe, T-carrier systems are also in use. They are defined slightly differently, however. A European **E-1 circuit** is made up of thirty-two 64 Kbps channels, for a total capacity of 2.048 Mbps. Other E circuits are multiples of the E-1 capacity

Companies should acquire T-1 or T-3 facilities when they have a high volume of voice, data, or video transmissions between two locations. Either the carrier or the customer may provide multiplexing equipment to divide the capacity of the T-1 into usable circuits. Some carriers offer full T-1 packages that include the equipment at both ends of the circuit, configured to the customer's specification, while other carriers offer the bare T-1 circuit without the multiplexers.

The major reasons for using T-1 circuits are that they can save large amounts of money, they give flexibility in reconfiguring the T-1 capacity to meet different needs at different times of the day, and they improve the quality of voice and data transmission because the information being transmitted is in digital form. One company found it economical to install a T-1 circuit to carry just three 56 Kbps data circuits and five voice lines. Even though the capacity of the T-1 circuit was not fully used, it was less expensive than if the individual slower speed voice and data circuits were leased separately.

## Fractional T-1

**fractional T-1**

In the past, companies that required digital transmission service had no choice of speed between 56 Kbps and T-1's 1.544 Mbps. **Fractional T-1** service provides companies with other transmission speed choices by subdividing a T-1 circuit into multiples of 64 Kbps. Thus, carriers now offer leased digital circuits that operate in any multiple of 64 Kbps, although speeds of 64, 128, 256, 512, and 768 Kbps are most common. A company can select and pay for only the capacity it needs instead of leasing a full T-1 circuit. This capability is particularly interesting to organizations that have smaller networks and therefore cannot justify the cost of a full T-1 circuit. Most carriers provide fractional T-1 service, but potential customers must check to make sure it is available in their area.

## Digital Subscriber Line (DSL)

**asymmetric digital subscriber line (ADSL)**

**digital subscriber line (DSL)**

In 1987, in anticipation of competition with cable companies for delivering video signals to homes, the telecommunications research and development company, Bellcore, developed a technology called **asymmetric digital subscriber line (ADSL)**. ADSL was originally designed to enable telephone companies to deliver digitized signals to subscribers at about 1.5 Mbps over existing twisted pair copper telephone wire—wire that had originally been installed to provide standard telephone service. The general name for the service is **digital subscriber line (DSL),** and it has spawned many variants that, collectively, are also referred to as xDSL. While originally developed as a competitor for cable television, xDSL has turned out to be a boon for home and business users who want higher data communication speeds, especially for accessing the Internet.

U.S. Robotics®
*SureConnect*™ ADSL
Ethernet modem.
(Courtesy of U.S. Robotics.
Reprinted with permission.)

xDSL services provide dedicated, point-to-point, public network access over twisted pair copper wire on the local loop between a network service provider's CO (typically the telephone company) and the customer's site. ADSL technology is asymmetric, as the name implies. It allows more bandwidth downstream from the CO to the customer site than upstream from the customer to the CO. This asymmetry makes it ideal for Internet surfing. Therefore, ADSL is viewed as more of a consumer-oriented product than a business-oriented product.

DSL technology is very sensitive to distance and is not available to customers who are located more than a few miles from the service provider's CO. The speed of the service depends on the distance, but for ADSL, it is in the range of 64 Kbps to 1.54 Mbps upstream and 256 Kbps to 9 Mbps downstream. The actual speed that can be obtained depends on a number of factors, including the distance from the CO, the wire size that is used, and the quality of the circuit.

ADSL circuits have a multiplexer at each end, which divides the circuit into the high-speed downstream channel, the medium-speed upstream channel, and a standard telephone channel (as shown in Figure 9-5). Customers can, therefore, obtain telephone service from the same wires that supply the ADSL service. The DSL provider almost always supplies the modems and includes a fee for the multiplexer rental in the total price for the ADSL service.

There are other offerings that use DSL technology, including G.Lite ADSL, SDSL, and VDSL. G.Lite ADSL is a newer ADSL service that offers a

**FIGURE 9-5** An ADSL circuit is divided into several channels, and uses a much wider frequency range than a standard telephone circuit.

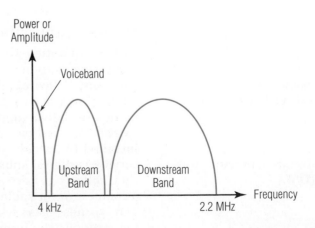

maximum speed of 1.5 Mbps downstream and 384 Kbps upstream, and some carriers will allow the customer to order lower bandwidths for lower cost. Because the speed is limited, the specifications for the wire are not as severe, and G.Lite is easier to install and maintain.

**symmetric digital subscriber line (SDSL)**

Another offering is **symmetric digital subscriber line (SDSL).** SDSL provides equal speed channels in both directions and may not include a telephone channel. SDSL is capable of speeds up to 2.3 Mbps in each direction, and is targeted at business customers. It technically is easier for the network service provider to implement SDSL than ADSL because simpler, less expensive equipment is required at both the head end and the customer end of the circuit.

**very-high-rate digital subscriber line (VDSL)**

The newest development is **very-high-rate digital subscriber line (VDSL).** VDSL transmits data at top speeds of 51 to 55 Mbps over short twisted pair telephone lines of up to 1,000 feet and at a lower speed of 13 Mbps at 4,000 feet. Early versions of this technology are asymmetric, like ADSL, and have an upstream channel of 1.6 to 2.3 Mbps.

While DSL is a very interesting capability for many businesses and consumers at home, it is important to remember the distance limitation: the customer must be located within a few miles of the communication carrier's CO. This means that DSL service will not be available to at least 30 percent of the potential users in the U.S. Hence, there will still be plenty of need for other high-speed access services, such as CATV and direct satellites. On the other hand, DSL is evolving and new versions are becoming available, such as DSL Lite, which gives slower access speeds at a lower monthly cost than the other products. For more information about the status of DSL development and implementation, check the websites at http://www.2wire.com/ and http://www.dslforum.com/.

## Cable TV (CATV) Circuits

CATV systems are being used increasingly as a media for data transmission. The use of CATV systems is a rapidly evolving technology that has made great strides in just the last few years. Many CATV systems were neither designed nor engineered to carry data at the same time as television signals. Furthermore, CATV was primarily designed to carry signals one way—from the cable company's site, called the **head end,** to the home. Carrying data the other direction is outside the design limits of many CATV systems, so they need to be upgraded to handle 2-way traffic.

**head end**

Using a CATV system for data transmission requires a modem to be installed on the cable at the user's home or office. When a cable modem (discussed in Chapter 6) is to be installed, a splitter is first installed on the main television cable. Following the splitter, one cable is run to the customer's television set and a separate cable is run to the cable modem, which is located near the customer's computer.

Using a television cable as a high-speed circuit is an option that is widely available to Americans today, especially in metropolitan areas. The service has proven to be quite reliable from the user's perspective, and it provides an additional source of revenue for CATV companies.

## Satellite Circuits

**direct broadcast satellite (DBS)**

**digital satellite service (DSS)**

**Direct broadcast satellites (DBS),** sometimes known as **digital satellite service (DSS),** is also a competitor to cable television and DSL for high speed communications circuits. DSS is the most widely available of the three technologies and has been in use by millions of Americans since 1997. As long as you have a clear line of sight toward the sky above the equator, you are a potential DSS customer.

DSS service is most frequently used to provide high-speed access to the Internet. DSS is a receive-only service, meaning that the customer must also use a telephone line and modem to send data to the Internet. When you click a link to pull up a Website, your signal travels via the phone line to your ISP and then to the Internet. The information you requested is sent 22,300 miles up to the satellite, and back down 22,300 more miles to your DSS dish. There is a noticeable delay in response, which is okay for file downloads but is probably not acceptable to most people if they are trying to chat interactively with another person. So, while the download speeds from the satellite are in the range of 350 Kbps, the overall service is much slower. As usual, the suitability of this technology depends on the application for which it will be used.

## 9-5    CIRCUIT ACQUISITION AND OWNERSHIP

While we generally think of WAN communications circuits being owned by a communications carrier, it is possible for private companies, or even individuals, to own their own circuits. In this section we'll look at various ownership alternatives.

### Private Circuits

private circuit

**Private circuits** are those installed and maintained by a company other than a common carrier. For example, a company may run coaxial cable between buildings on a campus and wire within the buildings to form a data communications network. Private circuits are typically installed either for LANs, where the reach of the network is within a building, or in a campus environment, where all property is owned. It becomes more complicated if the circuit must cross property owned by others, because permission to cross the property must be obtained. It is even more complicated when public roads or highways must be crossed, but it is possible to obtain permission to cross or bury cable under them. Permission must be obtained from the agency in control of the road; it may be the city, county, state, or the federal government.

In some states, it is possible for private companies to get permission to run wire or cable on public utility poles. Usually, the utility company charges a small fee for the use of the pole. Private circuits also have been installed on the shoulders of public roadways, alongside railroad tracks, and on pipeline routes.

When a company installs a private circuit, that company is totally responsible for its design, engineering, installation, operation, and maintenance. The upside, however, is that the circuit is available for the company's full-time exclusive use, and once the circuit is installed it is inexpensive to operate. One company that had many locations in a city received permission to run a private cable for its MAN on the poles of the local electrical utility company. The rental charge was $6 per year per pole, an amount the company considered very reasonable. Using the private cable, the company was able to connect all of its locations in the city into a common data network.

### Leased Circuits

leased circuit

**Leased circuits** are circuits owned by a common carrier but leased from them by another organization for full-time exclusive use. Leased facilities are attractive when some or all of the following conditions are present:

- It is impossible or undesirable to install a private circuit.
- The cost of the leased circuit is less than the cost of a dial-up connection for the amount of time required.
- Four-wire service is required (four-wire service cannot be obtained on dial-up connections).
- High-speed transmission is required.

The primary advantage of a leased circuit is that it is engineered by the carrier, installed, and left in place so that the same facilities are always used. This means that once the circuit is adjusted and operating correctly, it will normally continue to operate the same way for long periods of time. For most business data transmission, this consistency and reliability are significant benefits because they help to ensure that the communications service is reliable and trouble-free.

When a leased circuit does fail, the carrier that provides the circuit performs the diagnostic and maintenance work required to restore it to service. Carriers have special testing equipment, located at their COs, with which they can examine all the parameters of the circuit to determine the cause of failure. Furthermore, technicians at all of the COs through which the circuit passes can communicate with each other to determine which link in the circuit is experiencing a problem. In most instances, failures are isolated and corrected and the circuit is restored to normal operation within hours. Often, service is restored in minutes.

The price of leased circuits is based on the capacity (speed) and the distance it travels. There is a charge for the local channel from the customer premises to the carrier's serving CO, and there are interoffice channel charges for circuits connecting the carrier's offices. For point-to-point circuits, the carrier computes the shortest airline mileage between the customer's two offices and bases the monthly charge on that distance. For multipoint circuits, the carrier normally computes the shortest airline mileage between all the points on the circuit.

One final note: Leased circuits are often called "private" circuits in common use. People in the communications industry frequently do not distinguish between the two types, which has been done in this book. It is common to hear someone talk about "our private line" when they really mean "our leased line." For many purposes, the distinction makes no difference, but if the distinction makes a difference and you are in doubt, it is best to request a clarification.

## 9-6   CIRCUIT SWITCHING

The transmission of signals (including voice, image, and video) in WANs normally occurs on a series of communications links that connect nodes in the network. Some of the nodes have user stations connected to them, represented by the small dark circles in the cities in Figure 9–6. Other nodes, represented by the open circles, are internal to the network and do not serve user stations directly. Communications by **circuit switching** means that there is a dedicated communication line between the two stations, but perhaps only for short time. This is the way the PSTN works. When you make a call, there is a period of time, called the **call setup time**, after you dial the number. During this time period, the switches in the network determine how to route your call and then they make the connections to establish a temporary dedicated path for your call to use. This is represented by the connection between telephone A and telephone B in Figure 9-6.

circuit switching

call setup time

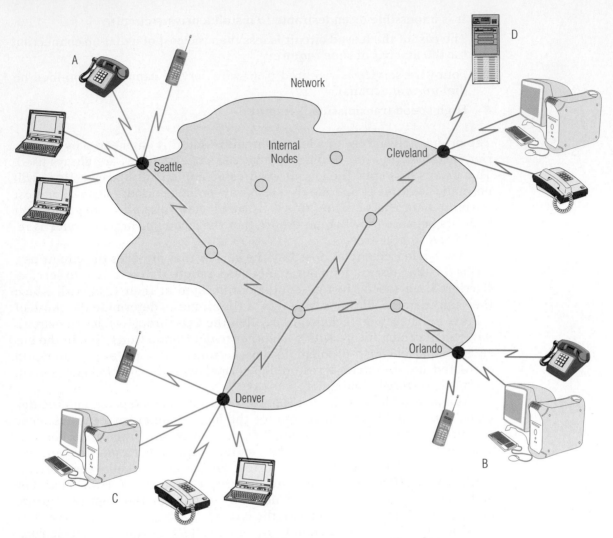

**FIGURE 9-6**   Circuit switching networks build temporary connections between devices that wish to communicate.

Similarly, switched circuits can be established for data transmission, as shown by the connection between terminal C and computer D. At the beginning of the call, the circuit is "set up" and at the end of the call, the connection path is "torn down" and the links that made up the switched circuit become available for other calls. Data transmission speeds of up to 56 Kbps can normally be obtained on switched circuits. Charges for switched circuits used for data transmission are based on both the duration and the distance of the call, just like a standard telephone call.

One factor that must be dealt with when using switched circuits is that when a dial-up connection is made, the actual carrier facilities used in routing the call depend on the facilities that are available at the moment. For this reason, switched circuits vary in quality and may be very good on one connection but marginal on another. We have all experienced this phenomenon on long distance telephone calls. Sometimes, it seems as if the person we are talking to is just next door. At other times, the volume of the person's voice is low or crosstalk can be heard. For the same reasons, on a dial-up data connection, you may find that one time the modems are able to transmit at 33.6 Kbps while the next time they will only transmit at 26.2 Kbps.

When an organization uses switched circuits, it exposes itself to certain security risks. If the organization has dial-in capability that allows employees (or others) to call a computer, it faces the possibility that unauthorized people may dial in and access the computer—either accidentally or maliciously. There are standard security precautions, such as user IDs and passwords, that can be implemented, but a clever hacker can often bypass these measures fairly quickly. One method that has been used is to dial in with a computer that is programmed to try all possible combinations of letters and numbers for the user ID or password in order to find a combination that works.

**callback unit**

**dialback unit**

One technique to combat unauthorized dial-in is to use a **callback unit** or **dialback unit.** The authorized user dials in and identifies himself or herself to the callback unit. The connection is immediately broken, and the callback unit looks up the user's ID in an internally stored table and calls the user back at a prestored telephone number. Of course, this means that the user always has to call in from the same place. The technique does not work well for travelers. Another problem is that the cost of the telephone call now falls on the central location that is being called.

Circuit switching is reasonably efficient for voice calls, because conversation occurs almost constantly during most calls—although voice conversation does not use the entire capacity of the circuit by any means. For data calls, the circuit is used less efficiently, which you can picture in a simplistic way if you think about a terminal-to-computer connection. Even if the typist at a terminal is reasonably fast, and the computer's response time is good, the circuit is still idle a lot of the time. From the standpoint of circuit utilization, there are more efficient ways to transmit data.

## 9-7 PACKET SWITCHING

The nationwide circuit switching telephone network was originally designed to handle voice traffic, and the majority of traffic on that network still is voice. A key characteristic of circuit-switching networks is that resources within the network are dedicated to a particular call. For voice connections, the resulting circuit enjoys a high percentage of utilization because most of the time either one party or the other is talking. As the telephone network began to be used for data connections, it became apparent that circuit switching was not the optimum way to handle data transmission. In a typical user/host data connection, much of the time the line is idle while the user thinks about what he is going to type next or waits for a response from the computer. Therefore, circuit switching is inefficient for data transmission. Packet switching was originally designed as a way to use communication lines more efficiently and to share them between several users simultaneously.

**packet switching**

**packet**

When **packet switching** technology is used, messages are broken down into fixed length pieces called **packets,** which are sent through a network individually as illustrated in Figure 9-7. Packets are typically 1,000 bytes in length, or less. Each packet contains a portion of the user's data, as well as some control information. The control information includes the information that the network requires to be able to route the packet through the network and deliver it to its destination. At each node, the routing information is examined and the packet is passed on to the next node. For data transmission, this approach has a number of advantages over circuit switching, among which is that the line efficiency is greater because many packets from different users can share the line at the same time.

**packetizing**

The process of segmenting messages into packets is called **packetizing.** Packetizing is performed by hardware or software called the *PAD,* which

FIGURE 9-7   Packets from the three PCs are interspersed on the circuit.

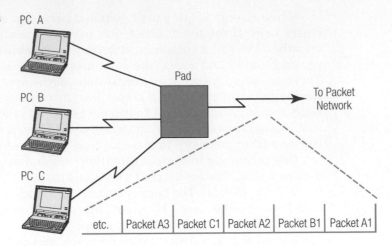

| etc. | Packet A3 | Packet C1 | Packet A2 | Packet B1 | Packet A1 |

packet assembly/disassembly (PAD)

stands for **packet assembly/disassembly.** The pad may exist in the user's DTE or in the packet data network's node. At the receiving end, another PAD assembles the message from the packets, which may arrive out of sequence. Other checking and control characters or fields are usually added to the packet to ensure data integrity, depending on the protocol being used.

## Connection Types

Packetized messages can be sent through the network in one of three ways. Most commonly, the user or terminal equipment establishes a dial-in (switched) connection with the nearest node of a **packet data network (PDN).** The destination node is identified, and the PDN establishes a **switched virtual circuit (SVC)** between the sending and destination nodes. This SVC circuit exists only for the duration of the session, which may be for one message or for a long exchange between the user and a host computer. When the session is finished, the SVC is dissolved

packet data network (PDN)

switched virtual circuit (SVC)

permanent virtual circuit (PVC)

If two packet nodes communicate frequently, a **permanent virtual circuit (PVC),** similar to a leased line, may be established. PVCs save the time it takes to establish a connection between two nodes, a useful attribute if communication traffic is heavy and frequent. Many companies have PVCs between their private host computers and one or more packet data networks.

datagram

A third type of connection, called **datagram** service, is available in PDNs. Datagrams are short messages of one packet, which can potentially traverse the network at high speeds. However, according to international standards, neither the delivery nor the arrival order of datagram packets is guaranteed. The user is responsible for detecting missing packets and initiating a retransmission, if necessary. Because of these characteristics, datagram service is not widely used outside of a few specialized applications.

Packet switching technology will be discussed again in Chapter 13, when you study how packet switching technology is used to form packet data networks.

## 9-8   MULTIPLEXING

Packet switching is one technique for simultaneously sharing a circuit between multiple users in order to improve the circuit's utilization efficiency. There are other techniques, however, and the generic name for all of them is

**FIGURE 9-8** FDM channels have full time use of a limited range of frequencies. TDM channels can use the full range of frequencies, but only during predetermined time slots.

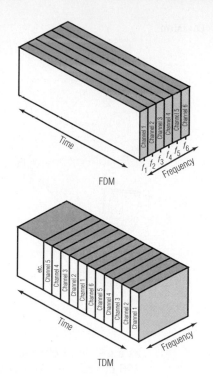

"multiplexing." Chapter 6 discussed FDM, whereby analog signals from different sources are shifted to different parts of the frequency spectrum so that a single circuit can carry more than one transmission.

## Time Division Multiplexing (TDM)

**time division multiplexing (TDM)**

When signals are in digital form, some form of **time division multiplexing (TDM)** is normally used. TDM is a technique that divides a circuit's capacity into time slots. Each time slot is used by a different data signal. With TDM, a channel can use the entire frequency range the circuit allows, but only for specified periods of time. Other channels use the other time slots. Figure 9-8 illustrates this concept.

If, for example, the circuit is capable of a speed of 28,800 bps, four terminals each transmitting at 7,200 bps could simultaneously use its capacity. TDM takes one character from each terminal and groups the four characters together into a frame that is transmitted on the circuit. This process is shown in Figure 9-9. At the receiving end, another TDM breaks the frame apart and presents data to the computer on four separate circuits

TDM is totally transparent to the terminal, the computer, and the user. If a terminal has nothing to send at any point in time, its time slot in the frame is transmitted empty. A typical application for TDM is having multiple terminals at one location communicating to a computer at another location. Although four terminals are shown in Figure 9-9, more than four could be multiplexed (however, multiples of four are most common). Eight terminals transmitting at 3,600 bps would work just as well on a 28.8 Kbps line with the proper TDM equipment.

Another form of TDM takes 1 bit from each terminal, instead of one character, and transmits a frame of bits. The bits are assembled into characters at the receiving end. A third technique, frequently used when the transmission is synchronous, is to multiplex entire messages. In this case, a message is defined

FIGURE 9-9   Time Division
Multiplexing (TDM).

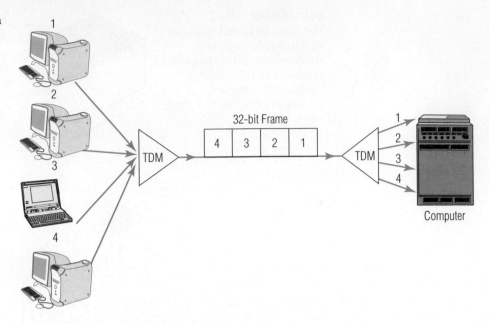

as a group of characters not exceeding some predetermined length, say 128 or 256 characters. When message multiplexing is used, the frame of data that is transmitted is much longer than when character or bit multiplexing is used.

## Statistical Time Division Multiplexing (STDM)

If you think about the way terminals are really operated, it is obvious that no terminal with a human operator is transmitting data continuously. The wait or "think" time between transmissions may be much longer than the actual transmission time. With a time division multiplexer, this means that many of the time slots are transmitted empty and the capacity of the circuit is not fully used.

**statistical time division multiplexing (STDM)**

**Statistical time division multiplexing (STDM)** uses a multiplexer that does not assign specific time slots to each terminal. Instead, STDM transmits the terminal's address along with each character or message of data, as illustrated in Figure 9-10.

If the address field in a STDM frame is 4 bits long, there are $2^4$ combinations and 16 terminals can be handled. With a 5-bit address, 32 terminals can be multiplexed. In any case, extra bits are required for the addresses when STDM is used. For most applications, this additional overhead is a good tradeoff. Most of the time, the user will not notice any difference in performance or response time, and the line will be better used.

There are times when most or all the terminals want to send data simultaneously. During these times, the aggregate data rate may be higher than the circuit can handle. For these situations, STDM contains a storage area, or buffer, in which data can be saved until the line can accept it. The user may experience a slight delay when buffering occurs.

STDM takes advantage of the fact that individual terminals frequently are idle and allows more terminals to share a line of a given capacity. Students who are writing or debugging programs on a university computer system normally fit this model nicely. They spend some time typing the program into the computer and a great deal of time interpreting error messages and determining how to correct their program's problems. Using an STDM, 12 terminals running at 9,600 bits per second could be handled by a 56,000 bps line in most cases.

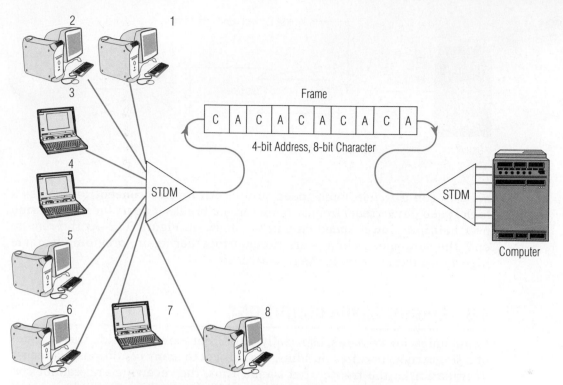

**FIGURE 9-10**  STDM tries to avoid having empty slots in a frame, thereby improving the line use. If a terminal has no data to send in a particular time period, STDM will see if the next terminal has data that can be included in the time slot. When STDM at the receiving end breaks the frame apart, it uses the terminal address to route the data to the proper device.

**FIGURE 9-11**  Line concentration.

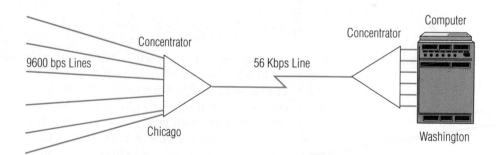

## Concentration

concentrator

**Concentrators** combine several low speed circuits into one higher speed circuit. A concentrator can be thought of as a circuit multiplexer. For example, six 9,600 bps circuits might be concentrated onto one circuit that has a 56 Kbps capacity, as shown in Figure 9-11. The intelligence and buffering in the concentrator take care of the fact that 6 × 9,600 bps = 57,600 bps, which is greater than the 56,000 bps capacity of the circuit. A primary reason for performing line concentration is economics. In most cases, it is less expensive to lease a 56 Kbps circuit between two points than six 9,600 bps circuits.

## Inverse Concentration

In some cases, high speed circuits are not available between two points, but it is desirable to provide high speed service. An example is when there is a

**FIGURE 9-12**   Inverse
concentration.

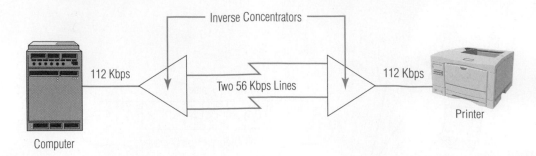

inverse concentrator

need to run a remote high speed printer. An **inverse concentrator** takes a high speed data stream from a computer and breaks it apart for transmission over multiple slower speed circuits, as shown in Figure 9-12. At the remote end, the slow-speed circuits are brought together again, providing a single high-speed data stream to the remote device.

## 9-9   CIRCUIT ERROR CONDITIONS

Communications circuits, especially those that extend outside the confines of a single room or office building, are subject to many conditions that cause degradation of the transmitted signal. Thus, the receiving end cannot correctly determine what was sent. Some of these conditions arise because of normal characteristics of signal propagation, others are due to faulty circuit design, and still others are due to natural physical phenomena, such as electrical storms. The following section describes many conditions that can cause errors on a communication line. Of these, the most common are the various forms of noise, distortion, and attenuation.

### Background Noise

background noise

white noise

Gaussian noise

**Background noise,** also known as **white noise** or **Gaussian noise,** is a normal phenomenon in all electrical circuitry. It results from the movement of electrons. It is present, to some extent, on every communications circuit. If the noise is at a high enough level, it can be heard as a hissing sound, similar to what you may here from your stereo system speakers if you turn up the volume when no source, such as a DVD player or tape, is active. It rarely represents a problem for data transmission because it is a known, predictable phenomenon and the modem manufacturers and communications carriers have designed their circuitry and equipment to deal with it.

### Impulse Noise

impulse noise

**Impulse noise** is a sudden spike on the communications circuit when the received amplitude exceeds a certain level. It is caused by transient electrical impulses, such as lightning, switching equipment, or a motor starting. You may have heard it as annoying static crashes or clicking during a voice conversation. If the noise occurs during a data transmission, the impulse may cause one or more bits to be changed, invalidating the transmission.

### Attenuation

attenuation

**Attenuation** is the weakening of the signal over a distance, which occurs normally in all communications. Attenuation is illustrated in Figure 9-13.

**FIGURE 9-13** A signal loses strength as the distance it travels increases. This loss of strength is called *attenuation*.

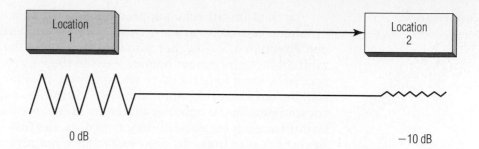

Just as your voice sounds weak at the back of an auditorium, or a radio signal fades as you get further from the transmitter, communications signals traveling through wires fade as the distance increases because of resistance in the medium. When the signal strength gets too low, it is impossible for the receiver to pick out the individual signal changes accurately. Amplifiers or repeaters are inserted in communications circuits often enough so that in normal operation, the signal's strength is boosted before attenuation causes a problem.

## Attenuation Distortion

**attenuation distortion**

**Attenuation distortion** occurs because the signal does not attenuate evenly across its frequency range. Without special compensating equipment, some frequencies on a circuit naturally attenuate faster than others. Communications circuits are designed, and special equipment is inserted on the circuit so the signal attenuates evenly across the frequency spectrum. However, attenuation distortion can still occur if equipment is improperly adjusted or if there is other maintenance activity.

## Envelope Delay Distortion

**envelope delay distortion**

**Envelope delay distortion** is an electrical phenomenon that occurs when not all frequencies propagate down a communications circuit at exactly the same speed. The absolute propagation delay is not relevant—only the difference between the delays at different frequencies is relevant. Envelope delay distortion can be made worse when the signal passes through filters that are inserted in the circuit to filter out noise. Noise filters tend to delay certain frequencies more than others.

## Phase Jitter

**phase jitter**

**Phase jitter** is a change in the phase of the signal induced by the carrier signal. It is especially problematic when phase modulation is used, because the sudden shift in the phase of the received signal makes it difficult for the receiving modem to sense legitimate phase changes that the transmitting modem sent.

## Echo

**echo**

**Echo** is the reversal of the signal, bouncing it back to the sender. Echo occurs on a communications circuit because of the electrical waves bouncing back from an intermediate point or the distant end of the circuit. Echoes are sometimes heard on long distance voice circuits, and you notice them as your own voice coming back a fraction of a second after speaking. On a data circuit, echoes cause bit errors.

echo supressors

Carriers install **echo suppressors** on switched circuits to eliminate the problems caused by echoes. Echo suppressors permit transmission in only one direction at a time. Because transmission in the reverse direction is prohibited, the echo cannot bounce back to the source. Although echo suppressors are a great help for voice transmission, they are a problem when data is sent because they take approximately 150 milliseconds to reverse and permit transmission in the opposite direction. Many modems turn signals around in 50 milliseconds or less, so if they send data, the first several hundred bits may be lost because the echo suppressors have not reversed.

The solution to this problem is to have the modem disable the echo suppressors at the beginning of a data transmission. When a connection is made, the modems send a tone that disables the echo suppressors and they stay deactivated as long as the modem sends the carrier signal on the circuit. When the communication ends and the carrier signal is no longer sent, the echo suppressors automatically reactivate. Leased data circuits do not have echo suppressors.

## Crosstalk

crosstalk

As mentioned earlier, **crosstalk** is interference that occurs when the signals from one communications channel interfere with those on another channel. In a voice conversation, you may occasionally hear crosstalk as another conversation that is lower in amplitude than your own. Crosstalk can be caused by one signal overpowering another, by two pairs of wires that are in close proximity and are improperly shielded, or because the frequencies of two or more multiplexed channels are too close together.

## Dropouts

dropouts

**Dropouts** occur when a circuit suddenly goes dead for a period of time, similar to an electrical power outage. Dropouts last from a fraction of a second to a few seconds, and then normal operation resumes. They can be caused by brief transmission problems, switching equipment, and even natural phenomena.

## 9-10    THE IMPACT OF ERRORS

Many of these errors, especially those caused by noise, occur in short bursts that last anywhere from a few milliseconds to a few seconds. Often a short pause in the transmission or a retransmission of a block of data that is affected will circumvent the problem. An error of a given duration will affect more bits during higher speed transmission than at lower speeds, as was shown in Chapter 6. One alternative for some types of data transmission problems is to reduce the speed at which the data are being transmitted.

The effect of transmission errors is more significant in data transmission than in voice or television. In voice conversations, a crackle of static on the line does not usually cause a big problem. Human speech is predictable, and the people at both ends of the circuit can interpolate and fill in a missing syllable or word. On television sets, transmission errors often are seen as white flecks or "snow" on the screen, but a limited amount does not impair our ability to comprehend or enjoy the picture.

In data transmission, on the other hand, an incorrect or missing bit can change the meaning of a message entirely. Given the speed at which circuits now operate, when an error occurs it is very likely to affect more than a single bit. That is why it is particularly important to use sophisticated techniques that can identify data transmission errors of more than one bit and to take the necessary steps to correct them.

## 9-11    ERROR PREVENTION

Given that errors do occur in data transmissions, it is necessary to take steps to prevent, detect, and correct them. Economics must be considered because most error prevention techniques cost money to implement. A manager must judge whether the increased reliability is worth the cost. Certain standard techniques are in common use, however, and they are discussed here.

### Line Conditioning

conditioned line

When a leased circuit is acquired from a common carrier, it is possible to request that it be conditioned. A **conditioned line** is one that meets tighter specifications for amplitude and distortion. Signals traveling on a conditioned circuit are less likely to encounter errors than when the circuit is unconditioned. The higher the level of conditioning, the fewer errors that will occur on the circuit. With fewer errors and faster signaling rates, faster transmission speeds can be achieved.

Conditioning is accomplished by testing each link of the circuit to ensure that it meets the tighter parameters that conditioning implies. If necessary, special compensating or amplifying equipment is inserted in the circuit at the carrier's COs to bring the circuit up to conditioned specifications.

Communications carriers can provide several levels of conditioning for an additional charge. Two commonly used levels are known as class C and class D. Class C conditioning adjusts a line's characteristics so that attenuation distortion and envelope delay distortion lie within certain limits. Class D conditioning deals with the ratio of signal strength to noise strength, called **signal-to-noise ratio (SNR),** and distortion.

signal-to-noise ratio (SNR)

With the improved sophistication of many newer modems, circuit conditioning is sometimes not required at all. Some modems have enough signal processing capability that they can tolerate the higher error rate of an unconditioned circuit. Modem manufacturers generally specify the type of conditioning that their modems require. In comparison to the total cost of the line, conditioning is relatively inexpensive. Therefore, it is usually prudent to request it, especially if the modem manufacturer recommends it.

Conditioning cannot be obtained on switched circuits, because the physical facilities used to make the connections vary from one call to the next. The variance is wide enough that conditioning facilities cannot realistically or cost effectively be provided.

### Shielding

shielding

**Shielding** of a communications circuit is best understood by looking back at Figure 8-3, which shows a coaxial cable. A metallic sheath surrounds the center conductor. Frequently, this shielding is electrically grounded at one and. Shielding prevents stray electrical signals from reaching the primary conductor. In certain situations, shielding on critical parts of the communications circuit may reduce noise or crosstalk. Electrically noisy environments, such as in factories or where circuits run near fluorescent light fixtures or elevator motors, are situations in which communications circuits can benefit from shielding.

## Improving Connections

One rule of thumb for communications wiring is "always check the cables and connections first." More problems seem to be caused by poor quality cables and loose, dirty, or otherwise poor connections than anything else. Checking to ensure that all cables and connectors are clean and properly seated, with retaining screws tightened (where they exist), is an excellent error prevention technique, simple as it may seem. Avoiding cable splices is another good practice. Splices in fiber cables can cause echoes, which are a source of interference and slow the throughput. Splices in wire cables can become defective with age, due to mechanical movement or corrosion causing noise or spikes on the circuit.

## 9-12    ERROR DETECTION

*error detection*

Even when circuits are well designed and good preventive measures such as circuit conditioning are implemented, errors will still occur. Therefore, it is necessary to have methods in place to detect these errors so that something can be done to correct them and data integrity can be maintained. **Error detection** normally involves some type of transmission redundancy. In the simplest case, all data could be transmitted two or more times and then compared at the receiving end. This would be fairly expensive in terms of the time consumed for the duplicate transmission. With the error rates experienced today, especially on digital circuits, a full duplication of each transmission is not necessary in most situations.

## Echo Checking

*echo checking*

One of the simplest ways to check for transmission errors is called **echo checking,** in which each character is echoed from the receiver back to the transmitter. Of course, the original data transmission could be correct, and an error might occur on the transmission of the echo message back to the sender. In either case, the operator can rekey the character or the sending node can automatically retransmit it. Echo checking is rarely used because more sophisticated and automatic methods are available.

A more sophisticated type of checking is to calculate some kind of a check digit or check character and transmit it with the data. At the receiving end, the calculation is made again and the result is compared to the check character that was calculated before transmission. If the two check characters agree, the data have been received correctly.

## Vertical Redundancy Checking (VRC) or Parity Checking

*vertical redundancy check (VRC)*

*parity checking*

The next most sophisticated error detection technique is called **vertical redundancy checking (VRC)** or **parity checking.** This technique was introduced in Chapter 6 and is illustrated in Figure 9-14. When parity checking is used, an error that changes one bit in a character can be detected because the parity bit will be incorrect. Unfortunately, noise on the communication line frequently changes more than one bit. If two 0 bits are changed to 1s, the VRC will not detect the error because the number of 1 bits will still be an even

FIGURE 9-14 If *even* parity is being used, the parity bit is set to 1 when necessary to make the total number of 1 bits in the character an *even* number. If *odd* parity is used, the parity bit is set to 1 when necessary to make the total number of 1 bits an *odd* number.

| | |
|---|---|
| The 7-bit ASCII code for the letter *R* (no parity bit) | 1010010 |
| • with even parity | 10100101 |
| • with odd parity | 10100100 |
| The 7-bit ASCII code for the letter *S* (no parity bit) | 1010011 |
| • with even parity | 10100110 |
| • with odd parity | 10100111 |

number. So an odd number of bit errors can be detected, but an even number cannot. Therefore, more sophisticated checking techniques are employed in most data transmission systems.

## Longitudinal Redundancy Checking (LRC)

**longitudinal redundancy checking (LRC)**

**block check character (BCC)**

Horizontal parity checking is called **longitudinal redundancy checking (LRC)**. When LRC is employed, a parity character is added to the end of each block of data by the DTE before the block is transmitted. This character, also called a **block check character (BCC),** is made up of parity bits. Bit 1 in the BCC is the parity bit for all the 1 bits in the block, bit 2 is the parity bit for all of the 2 bits, and so on. For example, assuming even parity and the use of the ASCII code, the BCC for the word "parity" is shown below.

| | *p* | *a* | *r* | *i* | *t* | *y* | *BCC* |
|---|---|---|---|---|---|---|---|
| **Bit 1** | 1 | 1 | 1 | 1 | 1 | 1 | 0 |
| **Bit 2** | 0 | 0 | 0 | 0 | 0 | 0 | 0 |
| **Bit 3** | 1 | 0 | 1 | 0 | 1 | 1 | 0 |
| **Bit 4** | 0 | 0 | 0 | 1 | 0 | 1 | 0 |
| **Bit 5** | 0 | 0 | 0 | 0 | 1 | 0 | 1 |
| **Bit 6** | 0 | 0 | 1 | 0 | 0 | 0 | 1 |
| **Bit 7** | 0 | 1 | 0 | 1 | 0 | 1 | 1 |
| **VRC** | 0 | 0 | 1 | 1 | 1 | 0 | 1 |

A VRC check will catch errors in which 1, 3, or 5 bits in a character have been changed, but if 2, 4, or 6 bits are changed, they will go undetected. Thus, VRC will catch about half of the transmission errors that occur. When combined with LRC, the probability of detecting an error is increased. The exact probability depends on the length of the data block for which the BCC is calculated, but even when used together, VRC and LRC will not catch all errors.

## Cyclic Redundancy Checking (CRC)

**cyclic redundancy checking (CRC)**

**polynomial error checking**

**Cyclic redundancy checking (CRC)** is a particular implementation of a more general class of error detection techniques called **polynomial error checking.** The polynomial techniques are more sophisticated ways for calculating a BCC than an LRC provides. All of the bits of a block of data are processed through a mathematical algorithm by the DTE at the transmitting end. One or more BCCs are generated and transmitted with the data. At the receiving end, the DTE performs the calculation again and the BCCs are compared. If differences are found, an error has occurred. If the BCCs are the same, the probability is very high that the data is error free. With the proper selection of polynomials used in the calculation of the BCC, the number of undetected errors may be as low as 1 in $10^9$ characters. To put this in more familiar terms: On a 28,800 bps circuit transmitting 8-bit characters 24 hours per day, one would expect no more than 1 undetected error every 77+ hours (3.2 days).

Several standard CRC calculations exist; they are known as CRC-12, CRC-16, and and CRC-CCITT. The standard specifies the degree of the generating polynomial. CRC-12 specifies a polynomial of degree 12, CRC-16 and CRC-CCITT specify polynomial of degrees of 16. For example, the polynomial for CRC-CC ITT is $x^{16} + x^{12} + x^5 + 1$, where $x$ is the bit being processed. CRC-16 and CRC-CCITT generate a 16-bit BCC that can

- detect all single bit and double bit errors
- detect all errors in cases where an odd number of bits is incorrect
- detect two pairs of adjacent errors
- detect all burst errors of 16 bits or fewer
- detect over 99.998 percent of all burst errors greater than 16 bits

Cyclic redundancy checking has become the standard method of error detection for block data transmission because of its high reliability in detecting transmission errors.

## 9-13   ERROR CORRECTION

In most applications, data validity and integrity are of prime importance, so once an error is detected, some technique must be employed to correct the data.

### Retransmission

**error correction**

**automatic repeat request (ARQ)**

The most frequently used and usually the most economical technique for **error correction** is the retransmission of the data in error. Although there are many variations, the basic technique used is when the receiving DTE detects an error, it signals the transmitting DTE to resend the data. This is called an **automatic repeat request (ARQ)** technique and it is part of the line protocol. For ARQ to work, the transmitting station must hold the data in a buffer until an acknowledgement comes from the receiver that the block of data was received correctly. Another requirement is that there must be a timely way for the receiver to signal the transmitter, such as by using a reverse channel.

### Stop and Wait ARQ

**stop and wait ARQ**

In the **stop and wait ARQ** technique, a block of data is sent and the receiver sends either an ACK if the data were received correctly or an NAK if an error was detected. If an ACK is received, the transmitter sends the next block of data. If an NAK is received, the data block that was received in error and is still stored in the transmitter's buffer is retransmitted. No data is transmitted while the receiver decodes the incoming data and checks it for errors. If a reverse channel is not available, the line must be turned around for the transmission of the ACK or NAK and then turned around again for the transmission (or retransmission) of the next (or previous) data block. Stop and wait ARQ is most effective where the data blocks are long, error rates are low, and a reverse channel is available.

## Continuous ARQ

continuous ARQ

Using the **continuous ARQ** technique, data blocks are continuously sent over the forward channel while ACKs and NAKs are sent over the reverse channel. When a NAK arrives at the transmitter, the usual strategy is to retransmit, beginning with the data block the receiver indicated was in error. The transmitting station's buffer must be large enough to hold several data blocks. The receiver throws away all data received after the block in error for which the NAK was sent because it will receive that data again.

An alternate strategy is for the transmitter to retransmit only the block in error. In this case, the receiver must be more sophisticated because it must insert the retransmitted data block into the correct sequence among all of the data received. Of the two approaches for continuous ARQ, the first strategy, sometimes called "go back N blocks," is more commonly used.

If a reverse channel is not available, the line must be turned around whenever ACKs or NAKs are sent from the receiving to the transmitting node, and then turned around again to resume normal data transmission. Continuous ARQ is far more an efficient than stop and wait ARQ when the propagation times are long because they are in satellite transmission.

## Forward Error Correction (FEC)

VRC, LRC, and CRC checking methods are effective in detecting errors in data transmission. However, they contain no method for automatically correcting the data at the receiving end. By using special transmission codes and adding additional redundant bits, it is possible to include enough redundancy in the transmission to allow the receiving station to automatically correct a large portion of any data received in error, thus avoiding retransmission. This technique is called **forward error correction (FEC).**

forward error correction (FEC)

Research into FEC techniques has been conducted by organizations including Bellcore and the military. The military's interest lies in being able to make one-way transmissions to submarines or aircraft, knowing that messages will arrive with a predetermined but very low probability of error. Three well-known error correcting codes are the Bose-Chaudhuri code, the Hagelbarger code, and the Hamming code. The Bose-Chaudhuri code, in its original version, uses 10 check bits for every 21 data bits and allows the receiving node to detect up to 4 consecutive bit errors and correct all double bit errors. The Hagelbarger code allows the receiving node to correct up to 6 consecutive bit errors if the group of bits in error is followed by at least 19 good data bits.

The Hamming code, in its 7-bit form, contains four information bits and three check bits per character and allows single bit errors in each character to be corrected. However, with only four information bits, only 16 unique characters are allowed in the character set. Other modifications to the Hamming code, that allow a larger character set and have a corresponding increase in the number of checking bits, exist.

FEC codes have a high cost in terms of the number of redundant bits required to allow error correction at the receiving end. In some cases, the number of checking bits exceeds the number of data bits. However, in certain applications—particularly where only one-way simplex transmission is allowed or possible—the cost is well justified. Because the FEC techniques are sophisticated, a specially programmed computer in the DTE or DCE is normally used to calculate the FEC codes and perform the error correction.

## ■ SUMMARY

Communication circuits can take on many forms and in this chapter you have studied their attributes and characteristics. More often than not, an organization's communications needs dictate that several types of circuits are required. Because LANs and WANs are both used in many organizations, there may be a combination of high- and low-speed circuits, private and leased, and frequently some use of switched circuits as well. Only by understanding the characteristics and trade-offs between the many types of circuits and the requirements of the organization's communications applications can the network designer make the choices that yield a successful and economical network.

Errors occur on even the best engineered communications circuits, and it is important to have measures in place to detect and correct them so that the recipient of messages can be highly assured that it contains information identical to what the sender transmitted. You studied the many causes of errors and several ways they can be detected and corrected.

In Chapter 10, you will learn about the technology of LANs. LAN topologies and the way that LANs are configured, built, and accessed will be examined. LAN software is also covered.

## ■ REVIEW QUESTIONS

9-1. Explain how a line, a circuit, a link, and a channel differ.

9-2. Describe a multipoint circuit.

9-3. Why is a four-wire circuit preferable to a two-wire circuit for data transmission?

9-4. Compare and contrast the functions of a modem and a DSU/CSU.

9-5. What is the data-carrying capacity of a T-1 circuit? Can a T-1 circuit be used to carry analog voice signals?

9-6. What is the normal maximum data transmission speed of an analog voice-grade circuit?

9-7. Distinguish among T-1, T-2, T-3, T-4, and E-1 circuits.

9-8. Explain the term *circuit switching.*

9-9. Under what circumstances would a company consider installing a private circuit as opposed to leasing a circuit from a communications carrier?

9-10. Explain the purpose of multiplexing.

9-11. What are the advantages of STDM over TDM?

9-12. Explain the circuit attributes of attenuation, envelope delay distortion, phase jitter, and crosstalk.

9-13. Why are communications line errors more significant when data is being transmitted than when a voice conversation is being transmitted?

9-14. What is the purpose of communications line conditioning?

9-15. What is the difference between LRC and CRC checking?

9-16. Compare and contrast the stop and wait ARQ and continuous ARQ techniques.

9-17. What is the difference between an amplifier and a repeater on a communications circuit?

9-18. What is noise on a circuit? What causes noise?

9-19. Explain the difference between a private circuit and a leased circuit.

9-20. Distinguish between the capabilities of ADSL and SDSL.

9-21. Describe several ways to get high-speed access to the Internet. Are all of those methods available everywhere today? Why or why not?

9-22. What is a CRC? How does it work?

9-23. Why isn't FEC routinely employed on all circuits?

## TRUE OR FALSE

9-1. Links and circuits are different words for the same thing.

9-2. A link is a segment of a circuit.

9-3. A node is a functional unit that connects two transmission links or lines or it can be an endpoint on a circuit.

9-4. Circuits that make up LANs are more prone to errors than circuits that make up WANs because they are frequently installed by amateurs rather than professionals.

9-5. A point-to-point circuit connects two, and only two, nodes.

9-6. When several nodes are connected to the same circuit, it is called a *multiplexed circuit.*

9-7. Standard dial-up telephone circuits are four-wire circuits.

9-8. To carry data, analog circuits require the use of a modem to convert the digital signal from DTEs.

9-9. Digital circuits have just become available to end-users in the last 10 years.

9-10. Signals on digital circuits are regenerated when needed rather than being amplified.

9-11. T-carrier systems are a family of high-speed digital transmission systems.

9-12. T-1 circuits operate at 1.544 Kbps.

9-13. Fractional T-1 service provides companies with full speed T-1 service at a fraction of the cost of normal T-1 service.

9-14. DSLs can operate over very long distances without amplification.

9-15. Some DSL offerings are asymmetric, yielding a lower speed from the user to the communications carrier than the reverse.

9-16. CATV systems often have to be reengineered before they can carry signals in both directions.

9-17. Satellite circuits require that the user have a clear line of sight toward the North or South Pole in order to aim the antenna at satellites in polar orbits.

9-18. DSS is frequently used to provide high-speed access to the Internet.

9-19. Private circuits are normally installed and maintained by a company other than a common carrier.

9-20. Leased circuits are circuits owned by a common carrier, but leased from them by another organization for full-time exclusive use.

9-21. When a leased circuit does fail, the carrier that provides the circuit performs the diagnostic and maintenance work required to restore it to service.

9-22. Communications by circuit switching means that there is a dedicated communication line between the two stations, but perhaps only for short time.

9-23. Switched circuits vary in quality and may be very good on one connection but marginal on another.

9-24. Organizations that use switched circuits do not need to worry about security risks because the switched circuit is "torn down" at the end of the call.

9-25. From the standpoint of circuit utilization, standard circuit switching is one of the most efficient ways to transmit data.

9-26. When packet switching technology is used, messages are broken down into fixed length pieces called packets, which are sent through a network individually.

9-27. The process of segmenting messages into packets is called packeteering.

9-28. If two packet nodes communicate frequently, a PVC, similar to a leased line, may be established.

9-29. TDM is a technique that divides a circuit's capacity into slots that are only available during a certain time of the day for which the user has paid.

9-30. One form of TDM takes 1 bit from each terminal instead of one character, and transmits a frame of bits.

9-31. When STDM is used, the error rate on the circuit is statistically determined before the message is transmitted.

9-32. WAN circuits are more likely to see errors than LAN circuits.

## MULTIPLE CHOICE

9-1. Background noise (white noise) on a circuit _____.
   a. is one of the most difficult problems to work around
   b. is rarely a problem because it is a known, predictable phenomenon
   c. occurs in spikes
   d. delays some frequencies more than others

9-2. *Attenuation* is _____.
   a. the increase of signal strength by a factor of ten
   b. seldom a problem on very long communication circuits
   c. only an issue on circuits provided by ATT
   d. the weakening of a signal over a distance
   e. None of the above.

9-3. *Echo* is _____.
   a. an electrical phenomenon that occurs when not all frequencies propagate down a communications line at the same speed
   b. a change in the phase of a signal induced by the carrier signal

    c. the reversal of a signal, bouncing it back to the sender

    d. interference that occurs when signals from one communications channel interfere with those on another channel

    e. a condition that occurs when a circuit goes dead for a period of time

9-4. *Crosstalk* is _____.

    a. an electrical phenomenon that occurs when not all frequencies propagate down a communications line at the same speed

    b. a change in the phase of a signal induced by the carrier signal

    c. the reversal of a signal, bouncing it back to the sender

    d. interference that occurs when signals from one communications channel interfere with those on another channel

    e. a condition that occurs when a circuit goes dead for a period of time

9-5. Parity checking _____.

    a. can detect an even number of bit errors

    b. adds an odd bit, even if no errors occurred, for safety

    c. is not used if the circuits are at parity with one another

    d. can detect a single bit error in a transmission

9-6. CRC _____.

    a. is a particular implementation of a more general class of error detection techniques called polynomial error checking

    b. provides additional bits so errors can be corrected at the receiving end

    c. requires a math coprocessor in the node's CPU to calculate its value

    d. is not sophisticated enough for most data transmission applications

    e. uses Hamming codes to improve the accuracy of the received data

9-7. FEC _____.

    a. adds redundant bits to a transmission so that errors may be corrected at the receiving end

    b. requires the receiver to send an ACK or an NAK at the end of each block

    c. uses a reverse channel so that ACKs and NAKs can be sent while data blocks are continuously sent on the forward channel

    d. is not needed if CRCs are used

    e. is impractical to implement because of the cost and the time it takes to send redundant bits

## ■ PROBLEMS AND PROJECTS

9-1. Identify the trade-offs a company would have to consider when deciding whether to implement switched or leased communications circuits for a WAN. The company has locations throughout the U.S. The applications are primarily business transactions, such as customer order entry, shipping, purchasing, accounts receivable, and accounts payable.

9-2. Using the VRC and LRC parity checking techniques and the ASCII code, calculate the parity bit and BCC for your last name.

9-3. Recalculate the time needed to send the 5 megabyte file described in Problem 8-4. Use the same assumptions, except that a T-1 line is used.

Calculate the time once more, assuming a fractional T-1 line running at 256 Kbps is used.

9-4. Visit a company in your area that has a WAN. Find out what type of circuits they use, who provides the circuit, and their characteristics (e.g. leased or private, speed at which they operate, who provided the modems, experience with errors, if known, etc.). Based on what you have learned so far, does it seem as though the network is optimized from a topology standpoint? Would you consider any alternate network configurations or combinations of equipment if you were running the network in the company?

## CASE STUDY

## ECKLES, FEINMAN, AND MACKENZIE—PART 3

After gathering additional information, Mr. Block determined that EF&M would install terrestrial leased lines, which they would obtain from a communications carrier for the firm's exclusive use. He could see that the overall volume of traffic wasn't very large and he felt that some type of shared circuits—or even sending traffic through the Internet—might be a less expensive alternative, but some of the senior partners in the firm were very concerned about the security of the e-mail messages and files of information that would be sent on the network. They were very protective of their attorney-client privileged relationships and they wanted to be absolutely certain that information would never be compromised. It was felt that leased lines provided better data security than the other alternatives. Use the traffic data from Parts 1 and 2 of this case to answer the following questions.

### QUESTIONS

1. Would you recommend that Mr. Block order two-wire or four-wire leased circuits? Why?

2. The senior partners committee has been asking Mr. Block about the use of satellite circuits to link the offices. Prepare a memo for Mr. Block, explaining the pros and cons of satellite circuits for the firm's e-mail and document exchange applications.

3. While the decision to use leased circuits may have "almost" been made, what arguments would you use to try to persuade the firm to consider other alternatives, such as sending the traffic through the Internet?

# PART THREE

# COMMUNICATIONS NETWORKS

## ■ OUTLINE

Part Three delves into the types of networks that are found in businesses and other organizations. Both LANs and WANs are extensively discussed. MANs are also covered.

Chapter 10 discusses the technology on which LANs are based. You will study the architecture and standards of LANs, the way access is controlled, various LAN topologies, and LAN applications.

Chapter 11 explores real world LAN systems such as Ethernet, Token Ring, FDDI, and various wireless LANs such as 802.11, Bluetooth, and Hiper-LAN2. You will also look at the increasingly important topic of network storage.

Chapter 12 examines the considerations for installing and operating a LAN. You will learn about the criteria that need to be considered before selecting which type of LAN should be installed, as well as the steps required to install a LAN and the considerations for operating it after the LAN is up and running.

Chapter 13 wades into WANs. You will learn about the topologies of WANs, packet networks, and the ways that traffic can be routed through a WAN from source to destination. You will also study several specific WAN systems.

# LOCAL AREA NETWORKS (LANS)

## ■ OUTLINE

## ■ KEY TERMS

access point

active hub

American National Standards Institute (ANSI)

applications server

balun

baseband transmission

bridge

broadband transmission

broadcast routing

bridge router (brouter)

cabling plan

carrier sense multiple access with collision avoidance (CSMA/CA)

carrier sense multiple access with collision detection (CSMA/CD)

client

client/server network

communications server

cut-through switch

database server

deterministic

disk server

electromagnetic interference (EMI)

fat client

file server

fragment free switching

gateway

home page

hub

hypertext markup language (HTML)

Hypertext Transfer
Protocol (HTTP)

infrared (IR)

Institute of Electrical
and Electronics
Engineers (IEEE)

intelligent hub

International
Organization for
Standardization (ISO)

local area network (LAN)

logical link control (LLC)

logical topology

MAC frame

multistation access unit
(MAU), multiplexer,
concentrator

network interface card
(NIC)

nodes

nondeterministic

passive hub

peer-to-peer network

physical topology

print server

protocol data unit (PDU)

radio frequency (RF)

repeater

roaming

router

routing algorithm

segment

server

site licenses

software metering

spooling (background
printing)

store and forward switch

switch

switching hub

thin client

token

token-passing protocol

topology

universal resource
locator (URL)

Web browser

Web server

workgroup

## ■ OBJECTIVES

After you complete your study of this chapter, you should be able to:

- describe the key characteristics of a LAN;
- explain the differences between a peer-to-peer network and a client server network;
- describe the different types of servers that are shared by clients on a LAN;
- describe the roles and functions of LAN servers;
- discuss the reasons why organizations install LANs;
- describe the IEEE standards that apply to LANs;
- describe the different physical LAN topologies;
- explain how CSMA/CA differs from CSMA/CD;
- describe the types of media and transmission techniques used to connect LANs;
- differentiate between baseband and broadband transmission techniques;
- explain the purpose of a NIC; and
- describe the various types of hardware used to expand LANs.

## 10-1   INTRODUCTION

local area network
(LAN)

As you learned in Chapter 2, there are three types of networks, based on their geographical range: LANs typically range from 1 meter to 2,000 meters; MANs range from approximately 2,000 meters to 50,000 meters; and WANs range beyond LANs and MANs to global coverage. **Local area networks (LANs)** are one of the fastest-growing and most exciting components of the telecommunications and networking scene.

The technology that makes LANs possible and practical is relatively new compared to many WAN technologies. Sophisticated network control and application software are making LANs productive for millions of workers in small offices and large organizations alike. Most people feel a strong ownership in a LAN because of its "local" nature and because of the way it helps them do their jobs better. As a student, you are more likely to have used a LAN than any other type of data network, except perhaps the Internet. LANs have been installed in thousands of schools to enable computer use in the classroom and to aid faculty and administration. Although you may have used a WAN also—for example, to dial into a service such as America Online or CompuServe—you probably didn't feel as strong a sense of the network involved in making such a connection. If you've used a LAN at school or work, however, you most likely have a much greater awareness of the network itself. You probably know the basics of how it works and have an awareness of its advantages and its problems.

There are several reasons for the popularity and widespread use of LANs today, and they all relate to sharing. As in every sharing activity, from car pools to time-share condos, there are rules. In networking, we call these rules standards and protocols. Several major components of LANs make this sharing possible. They include:

- network operating system
- networked peripherals (printers and modems)
- network interface card (NIC)
- connectivity devices (hubs, repeaters, bridges, routers, switches, and gateways)
- transmission media (coaxial cable, twisted pair wiring, fiber optic cable, and radio waves)

This chapter introduces the characteristics and applications of a LAN, the various standards and protocols that have been established for LANs, and the key elements of LAN technology. Chapter 11 discusses LAN systems in greater detail, and Chapter 12 examines the installation and operation of a LAN.

## 10-2   CHARACTERISTICS OF LANS

A LAN is a high-speed data network that covers a relatively small geographic area. It often fits in a small building or even a single room. Typically, a LAN connects personal computers and other types of workstations, printers, and servers. More specialized LANs may also connect telephones, facsimile machines, a group of automation devices in a manufacturing plant, or any combination of these types of terminals. A key characteristic of LANs is the limited distance they cover. We generally think of a LAN as

With a few components such as the ones shown here, a NOS, printer, and some PCs, one can construct a LAN suitable for use in a small business.
(Courtesy of Linksys.com. Reprinted with permission.)

serving a single department, building, or plant, or several buildings in close proximity to one another on a campus. LANs may even extend a few miles, but special equipment, called **repeaters,** is usually required to regenerate the signals. Different types of networking cable have maximum distances over which they can move data signals. A repeater can extend the normal run for a particular type of cable, although it can neither direct traffic nor decide routing issues.

**repeater**

Another characteristic of LANs is that they ordinarily operate at high data rates: from 2 Mbps to 1 Gbps. Applications that require the transfer of large amounts of data, such as graphics, audio, or video, are now common. This, along with the general increase in LAN use, has made higher speeds more and more necessary. Higher data transfer rates are possible because of the relatively short distances that the data travel and the resulting low error rates in their transmission. These characteristics mean that users of LANs normally have very good response times, as compared to users of WANs. Response time on a LAN is less likely to be limited by the speed of the transmission facility than it is on a WAN. Other factors, however, such as the speed of the serving computer or the number of users sharing the LAN, limit the response time.

LANs are almost always privately owned and installed; therefore, a regulatory agency is not involved. As long as the LAN does not cross a public right-of-way, such as a highway, no governmental agency is involved with the LAN's establishment or operation. Some LANs connect to WANs, which are subject to regulation, but the LANs are generally exempt. Good candidates for a LAN installation are a typical university campus, a hospital, a corporate headquarters, a manufacturing site, or a research center. Some LANs are installed within departments, so PC users can share expensive hardware such as laser printers or large disk storage units. Other LANs are installed simply to provide a fast data path and good response time from terminals or PCs to a large central computer. Home networks, which are discussed in Chapter 12, are also classified as LANs.

## 10-3   ARCHITECTURE

peer-to-peer network

client/server network

There are two types of networks for homes and local areas: **peer-to-peer networks** and **client/server networks.** Each has advantages and disadvantages. The approach chosen depends on the number of users and the types of services that are needed.

### Peer-to-Peer Networks

In small office or home situations, where only a few files and perhaps a printer need to be shared, peer-to-peer networks work particularly well. Setting up a peer-to-peer network in a home also makes it easy to share a single connection to the Internet. In a peer-to-peer situation, the peer computers can operate, even when other computers are not available, because they don't depend on a central server machine to log in or access resources. A client/server network is better in cases where many users want to share files or other network resources. A server-based network also makes resources more secure and centrally controlled.

workgroup

In a peer-to-peer network, also often referred to as a **workgroup,** the computers on the network function as peers—each acting as both a client and a server. Peer computers can access resources on the network, but they can also supply resources to other peer computers in the same way a server does on a server-based network. Although a maximum of ten computers can share a peer-to-peer network, many experts recommend no more than five computers. This is because performance is lowered for those supplying the resources when too many peers request information at once. Figure 10-18 (see page 281) shows a wireless peer-to-peer group.

Peer-to-peer networking has been around since the early days of personal computing. The Macintosh OS offered peer-to-peer networking capabilities from the beginning, and Macintosh computers were built with a hardware interface that allowed two computers and a printer to be connected. With the addition of a couple of special cables, the network was in operation. Apple's newest PCs, such as the iMac, come with a built-in Ethernet interface—although the operating system (OS) still offers built-in workgroup capabilities.

The DOS operating system on early IBM clone PCs did not provide for peer-to-peer networking. During the late 1980s and early 1990s, resources could be shared over a small network through add-on products like Artisoft's LANtastic and Novell's NetWare Lite. Since 1992, when Windows for Workgroups 3.11 (which ran on top of DOS) was launched, Microsoft has provided for workgroup networking in Windows.

Because Microsoft Windows and Mac OS dominate today's PC market, peer-to-peer networking is an economical, easily configured way to share files and printers at home or in a small business. For those who wish to work only slightly harder, Linux (in any of its many "flavors" such as Redhat, SuSE, and Caldera) can also be used as the OS on PCs configured for peer-to-peer networking. They can share resources with each other as well as with Windows-based computers.

The only real requirements for building a peer-to-peer network include installing an OS on computers that support peer-to-peer networking and physically connecting the PCs. See Chapter 12 for more details on setting up a home or small office peer-to-peer network.

## Client/Server Networks

server

The client/server network, the most common LAN, allows for larger networks than peer-to-peer and offers a greater range of resources to users because of the variety of specialized computers called **servers** that can be included on the network. Many types of terminals or workstations can be connected to a LAN, including those normally found in an office, a laboratory, or a factory. The most common types in an office setting are PCs, because they have the intelligence to take advantage of a LAN's capabilities in a client/server environment.

Most LANs have one or more attached servers. Servers provide unique capabilities that can be shared by all other devices on the LAN. The most typical types of servers include:

file server

- **file servers,** which allow all users to share one or more large capacity disk drives

print server

- **print servers,** which provide access to one or more printers

communications server

- **communications servers,** which provide access to other LANs, host computers, or dial-up lines

applications server

- **applications servers,** which provide processing capacity for applications that are shared by many people

Web server

- **Web servers,** which allow the creation of a website that employees can access internally, or one that gives access to the World Wide Web

The server function can be performed by a computer that is also used as a normal workstation, or by a dedicated computer that has the sole purpose of providing server capabilities to other users on the LAN. Dedicated servers, the norm in most LAN configurations, are able to provide better performance because there is no interference from a user trying to use the same computer for other purposes. Server computers have special software that will be discussed later in the section on LAN software.

## Client/Server Computing

client

When a network includes computers that have the sole or primary function of acting as a server, the other workstations on the network are called **clients.** The outgrowth is the concept called "client/server computing," which has gained broad recognition and enormous popularity in recent years because of the availability of powerful, low-cost computers that can act as servers and sophisticated software that can manage the client/server environment. The basic concept is that a client's processing or data may come from a number of different machines located in widely scattered locations. The objective is to have software manage the environment in such a way that the user neither knows nor cares where the data being used is located or where the processing is performed. True client/server applications may have some of the processing performed on the client computer and some on the server. If little or no application processing is done on the client computer, it is called a **thin client** approach. If all or almost all of the

thin client
fat client

processing is done on the client computer, it is termed a **fat client** approach. The terms "thin" and "fat" refer to the size of the client processor

Servers come in a wide range of speeds and capacities, from those that serve a single application to large server complexes that serve an entire corporation. (Courtesy of Cisco Systems. Reprinted with permission.)

that is required to do the work. In either case, the implementation of client/server computing requires a fast communications network and applications that are designed to work in the client/server environment.

## File Servers

File servers allow a large-capacity disk to be shared by the users of a LAN. Users may have multiple files, limited only by the overall capacity of the disk. File server software provides the capability for users at workstations to use the server's hard drive as if it were their own. That is, a user may have a hard disk of 10 gigabytes on his PC, but when that computer is attached to a LAN that has a file server, he may have access to a 500-gigabyte server disk. The user can store programs or files on the server disk and can access them as easily as if they were on the PC's disk.

Because file servers are shared among many users, they need to be fast, powerful machines that have fast, reliable hard disk drives. PCs based on fast or multiple Pentium processors are excellent candidates to be used as servers because they can provide good service to LAN users.

With easy access to the server's disk, new possibilities emerge. The user can access the program on the server's disk and run it. Files stored on the server's disk can be designated as shareable, thereby allowing other users to look at the data or, if authorized, to change it. Files can easily be transferred to other individuals, either by giving them access to a copy of the server's disk or by allowing them to transfer a copy of the file from the server's disk to their own PC's disk.

File serving leads to some new data integrity problems, however. Because two or more users could be given access to a data file on the server's disk, some form of protection must be instituted to ensure that users don't update the same data at the same time. If user A and user B access the same record in a file simultaneously and make changes to it, the last person to update the record will wipe out the changes made by the first person to do so. Good file server software provides a mechanism that prevents two or more users with update authority from accessing the same record in the file at the same time. If one user has the record and a second user tries to access it, the second user receives a message that the record is unavailable.

disk server

A variation on the file server idea is a **disk server.** Disk servers divide the capacity of their large disk into smaller disk volumes. Workstation users have their own private disk volumes on the disk server. The administration of disk servers can be complex, however, and there are security and data integrity considerations that are more difficult to manage than on file servers.

## Print Servers

Print servers are microcomputers that allow one or more printers to be shared by users on the LAN. Printers managed by the print server may have unique capabilities, such as high speed for printing large reports, high quality, or color. These types of printers are often too expensive to attach to each workstation, and the print server allows its capability and cost to be shared.

spooling (background printing)

Because more than one user may try to use a printer at the same time, some type of queuing capability must be provided by the print server software. This queuing capability is called **spooling (background printing).** If the printer is busy printing another user's output, it allows data from a second user to be stored temporarily on the print server's disk. When the printer finishes printing the first user's output, the spooling software takes the second user's output from the disk's queue and prints it.

Spooling software is transparent to the user or application program that requests the print operation. The print server accepts data, whether or not the printer is busy. Good spooling software provides data integrity by taking care of operational problems, such as the printer's running out of paper. The software ensures that all data are printed properly.

## Communications Servers

Communications servers provide the capability to communicate with other networks or with other computers that are not connected to the LAN. Communications software on the server provides the interface with other networks or computers and surrounds the data with the appropriate protocol for transmission. Communications server software most often works in conjunction with network interface hardware such as routers, bridges, and gateways.

## Applications Servers

Applications servers are computers dedicated to application processing. They may be large mainframe machines or PCs. Organizations typically require a mix of applications servers, because some applications may be used enterprise-wide, while others are used by only a few people or departments. Also, some applications require different operating systems, such as Unix or Sun's Solaris, and each of these environments would require a different computer. Applications servers may have **database servers** attached to them if the database is large or complex. The need for dedicated database servers is dictated by the application design and the amount of data to be stored and processed. A diagram of a typical LAN with servers is shown in Figure 10-1.

database server

**FIGURE 10-1** A ring LAN with servers attached.

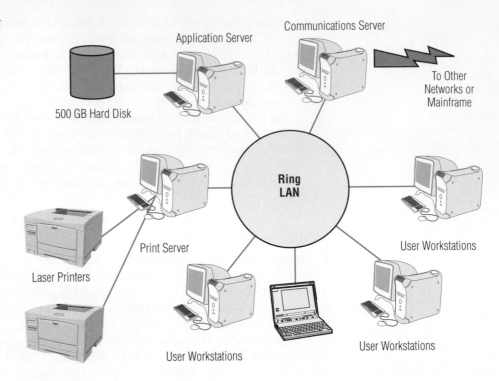

## Web Servers

Hypertext Markup
Language (HTML)

universal resource
locator (URL)

Hypertext Transfer
Protocol (HTTP)

Web browser

home page

Web servers are computers that, among other things, store data in pages that are formatted with a tool called **Hypertext Markup Language (HTML).** HTML is a very flexible tool that allows the author to format a Web page and define links to other pages, then store the information on the same server or anywhere on the World Wide Web. Web pages are addressed with a **universal resource locator (URL),** an address that specifies the location and format of the page. A Web server uses the **Hypertext Transfer Protocol (HTTP)** to send information to the client software, typically a browser. **Web browsers** are programs that can read and display HTML formatted pages. The user enters a website at the top page in a hierarchy called the **home page.** The home page indicates what information is available. Then, by using HTML links, the user can jump to other pages at the site or to other sites that have information of interest. These concepts are described in more detail in the chapters that describe the Internet: Chapters 15 and 16.

## 10-4   LAN APPLICATIONS

Organizations install LANs for many purposes; such as data processing, office or factory automation, energy management, process control, and fire and security control.

### Information Sharing

The primary reason for the installation of many LANs is the ability to share information within workgroups or departments. Studies have shown that a very high percentage of information generated within an organization is distributed and used close to home. Whether it is e-mail or analytical reports, approximately 50 percent of all information is used only within the originating department, 25 percent is distributed and used within nearby departments, and 15 percent is sent to other people in the organization. Only about 10 percent of all information is sent outside the company. Financial people process and use financial information; marketing and sales people use customer, market, and order information; and other departments use their own specific types of information. Normally, only summarized information is sent to other departments. This distribution pattern suggests the need for a high-speed, efficient, local information distribution system—a role that a LAN fills effectively.

## Hardware Sharing

LANs provide an opportunity to share relatively expensive pieces of equipment, such as laser printers, document scanners, or large hard disks. Sharing resources holds down the cost of supplying a department with a full range of computer equipment. Indeed, lowering costs is a key requirement for PC networks. Sharing usually works well because most PC users do not need a laser printer often enough to keep it busy and/or to justify its cost for one person. If the device is shared by a group of people, however, the cost may be justified more easily. Of course, there are other ways to share printers (such as with switches), but they usually impose more stringent distance limitations because users must be located within 50 or 100 feet of each other. LANs do not have such stringent limitations.

Large hard disks can also be shared. Again, economies of scale play a significant role: It is almost always less expensive to buy one large disk than multiple medium-sized disks. Furthermore, with a large shared disk, it may be possible to buy only one copy of certain software and allow it to be shared, or to store all of a department's data files on a common disk that can be backed up regularly and can remain accessible to all department members. Other devices may be shared as well, and the savings can help to compensate for the cost of installing and operating a LAN.

## Software Sharing

Frequently, organizations install LANs for the purpose of using new applications or using existing applications in a new way. Data on a computer that is attached to a LAN may be shared more easily between users of PCs without the necessity of copying the data to a diskette and carrying it from one office to another. For example, the tax department of a company, aided by the information technology department, can set up a LAN that enables several tax accountants to use an application package to help prepare the company's tax returns. Each accountant can work on different tax schedules at the same time, while sharing a common data file that contains basic corporate financial data on which the return must be based.

When software is available for a LAN, it is tempting to purchase one copy, install it on the LAN, and let everyone use it simultaneously. If this could be done, the software cost savings would be significant. This is illegal, and naturally, most companies have policies that prohibit the practice. Most software contracts require the customer to purchase one license for each workstation where people will be using the software. Because this is difficult to keep track of, some programs have a **software metering** routine that keeps track of the number of simultaneous users and doesn't allow more users than the number of licenses that have been purchased. Other software companies sell **site licenses** that allow an unlimited number of people to use the software for a single flat fee.

**software metering**

**site licenses**

Application software packages, such as word processing, spreadsheet, and graphics programs, must be written so that they can take advantage of the features that a LAN offers. If the application has been programmed in such a way that it cannot use the LAN's disk or printers, the LAN is of little use. The biggest problem that most applications have is the data integrity of shared files. Many applications were not originally written with the idea that multiple people might be accessing or updating the data at the same time. The applications must be modified to provide a new level of access control that allows several people to access the same files at the same time. For these reasons, many application software packages have separate versions that are designed for LAN use.

## Service

LANs may provide better service in the form of response time or availability to users than mainframe-based networks. Although careful design and control are required, it is inherently easier to provide consistent service to a small group of users than to a large group. Because the transmission rates are high, most users should be able to get low-second or sub-second response time unless they request excessive processing, extensive image handling, or voluminous output.

## Local Control

LANs provide the ability for the local department to operate and make decisions about the network. This may be more effective than working through a centralized network management group that is located miles away and is not familiar with local needs and problems. With this decision-making authority, however, comes a certain responsibility for proper LAN management (see Chapter 12), which the local department may or may not want to assume.

## 10-5  LAN STANDARDS

**Institute of Electrical and Electronics Engineers (IEEE)**

The **Institute of Electrical and Electronics Engineers (IEEE)** has done a great deal of work to set standards that define LANs and how they operate. Each standard designates a MAC method, data rate options, and various transmission media. In February of 1980, a committee known as the IEEE 802 committee—named for the month and year of its inception—was created to develop LAN standards. They issued a set of standards, originally known as the American National Standards, which were adopted by the **American National Standards Institute (ANSI).** Later revised and reissued as international standards, they were subsequently adopted by the **International Organization for Standardization (ISO).** The committee recognized that different LAN applications might have different technical requirements and therefore established several standards for LANs that have different characteristics. The IEEE 802 committee has published a number of LAN standards, and their work continues as the technology evolves. A list of the IEEE 802 subcommittees is shown in Figure 10-2.

**American National Standards Institute (ANSI)**

**International Organization for Standardization (ISO)**

Four standards in particular, 802.2, 802.3, 802.4, and 802.5, form the heart of LAN network standardization. The LAN systems defined in them are explained in Chapter 11. They define the **logical link control (LLC) protocol** and the contention and token-passing methods of accessing a

**logical link control (LLC) protocol**

FIGURE 10-2  IEEE 802
standards subcommittees.

| Standard number | Committee's purpose |
|---|---|
| 802.1 | Higher layer LAN protocols |
| 802.2 | Logical Link Control |
| 802.3 | Ethernet |
| 802.4 | Token Bus |
| 802.5 | Token Ring |
| 802.6 | MAN |
| 802.7 | Broadband |
| 802.8 | Fiber optics |
| 802.9 | Isochronous LAN |
| 802.10 | Security |
| 802.11 | Wireless LAN |
| 802.12 | Demand priority |
| 802.13 | Not used |
| 802.14 | Cable modem |
| 802.15 | Wireless personal area networks |
| 802.16 | Broadband wireless |

LAN. Standard subcommittee 802.11 has been especially active in the past few years developing standards for wireless LANs, which are also covered in Chapter 11. Manufacturers design hardware and software to conform to these standards, providing interoperability by enabling equipment from a variety of manufacturers to communicate with each other.

## 10-6  LAN ACCESS CONTROL

In Chapter 3, you studied the ISO's OSI model for data communications networks. LAN architectures follow the OSI model but require a modified view of the lower two layers because they have different configuration requirements. The IEEE 802 committee developed a slightly modified version of the OSI reference model, which is shown in Figure 10-3.

Notice the underlying reference to the medium in the IEEE 802 model. It is there because the transmission medium and its topology have a major impact on LAN design. Thus, they are specified in the IEEE standards. The LAN model includes the physical, MAC, and LLC layers.

- Layer 1 specifies the physical connections to the medium environment that are specific to the LAN, as well as its topology.
- Layer 2 is split into the MAC and LLC sublayers. The MAC layer contains the logic for access to a shared medium, typically CSMA/CD or token access, which is not contained in OSI layer 2. Therefore, for the same LLC, two MAC standards (CSMA/CD or token access) can exist.

### Logical Link Control (LLC)

The LLC sublayer performs the function of interfacing to higher level layers and providing flow and error control, functions that are normally associated

**FIGURE 10-3** A Comparison of the OSI and IEEE 802 models.

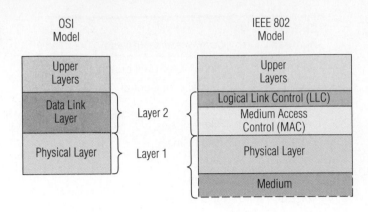

**FIGURE 10-4** The LLC PDU format.

| | Header | Destination Address | Source Address | Control Field | Data | Trailer |
|---|---|---|---|---|---|---|
| Bits | * | 8 | 8 | 8 or 16 | 8 × n | * |

*The format and length of the header and trailer depend on the media being used.

with layer 2 of the OSI model. LLC, or IEEE 802.2 as it is better known, is a bit-oriented data link protocol that is similar but not identical to HDLC (discussed in Chapter 7). The LLC frame is called a **protocol data unit (PDU),** and its format is shown in Figure 10-4.

**protocol data unit (PDU)**

The destination address identifies the node to which the information field is to be delivered, and the source address identifies the node that sent the message. The control field contains the commands, responses, and sequence numbers necessary to control the data link. The information (data) field can contain any multiple of 8 bits, and any combination of the bits (transparency) is acceptable.

## Medium Access Control (MAC)

The medium access control (MAC) layer regulates access to the shared transmission medium by the devices attached to a LAN so that its capacity is used in an orderly, efficient way. It also establishes the basis by which congestion control is exercised. The medium access control frame is called a **MAC frame,** and its general format is shown in Figure 10-5. The exact format depends on which MAC method is used, generally either CSMA/CD or token passing. Notice that the LLC data from the next higher level is included in the frame.

**MAC frame**

## 10-7 MAC PROTOCOLS

### Carrier Sense Multiple Access with Collision Detection (CSMA/CD)

**carrier sense multiple access with collision detection (CSMA/CD)**

**Carrier sense multiple access with collision detection (CSMA/CD)** is also known as IEEE 802.3. CSMA/CD is the primary form of contention access to

FIGURE 10-5  General
MAC frame format.

| | MAC Control | Destination MAC address | Source MAC address | LLC PDU | CRC |
|---|---|---|---|---|---|
| Bits | * | 48 | 48 | varies | 32-bit check sum |

**MAC Control**—Contains all appropriate information regarding flow control, connection establishment and teardown, and error control as designated by the protocol of the network interface type. *Number of bits depends on the type of network interface (Ethernet, Token Ring, FDDI, etc.)

**Destination MAC Address**—MAC address of the transmitting device

**Source MAC Address**—MAC address of the receiving device

**LLC PDU**—Logical Link Packet Data Unit from the upper LLC sublayer

**CRC**—Mathematical algorithm run to verify the integrity of the frame

circuits used in LANs. It was originally developed by the Xerox Corp. and was redefined by Digital Equipment Corporation (now part of Hewlett Packard) and Intel. It is the contention scheme used on Ethernet LANs, which are described in Chapter 11.

CSMA/CD is a broadcast protocol. There is no master station on a network that uses CSMA/CD; all stations are equal. When a terminal has a message to send, it examines the carrier signal on the network to determine whether a message is already being transferred. If the network is free, the station begins to transmit, using an address to indicate the destination terminal that is to receive the message. All connected terminals monitor the network at all times and act on messages only if they see their own address characters in the message. Figure 10-6 shows the frame format for the CSMA/CD protocol.

At times, two stations on the network may examine the network, see that it is free, and begin transmitting simultaneously, causing a data collision that garbles the transmission. When the collision is detected, the stations that caused the collision wait a random period of time that is determined by circuitry in their communications interface, and attempt to retransmit the message. If a collision is detected again, the stations wait twice as long to attempt retransmission. This is known as exponential back off. The length of the random delay is critical because if it is too short, repeated collisions usually will occur. However, if the delay interval is too long, the circuit remains idle. Random delay makes it unlikely that two stations will try to transmit and collide too many times in a row.

CSMA/CD works quite well when the traffic is light. Its biggest weakness is the **nondeterministic** nature of its performance when the network

nondeterministic

| | Preamble | Start Frame Delimiter | Destination Address | Source Address | Length | Data | Pad | CRC |
|---|---|---|---|---|---|---|---|---|
| Bits | 56 | 8 | 16 or 48 | 16 or 48 | 16 | ≥ 0 | ≥ 0 | 32 |

FIGURE 10-6  The frame format for the CSMA/CD (802.3) protocol.

is heavily loaded. That is, the network delays become unpredictable as the number of terminals or the amount of traffic grows. There is a theoretical network limit of 60 percent utilization due to collisions. Thus, CSMA/CD is not a good protocol to use when response time must be consistent, as in a manufacturing plant where control signals need to be sent to a machine. CSMA/CD can work well, however, in an office application where inconsistencies in response time (as long as they aren't too great) can be tolerated.

**broadcast routing**

**Broadcast routing** is a very simple technique used by the CSMA/CD protocol to broadcast all packets to all stations on the network. When it is used, all stations on the network see the packet. Only the station for which the packet is intended copies it, and all other stations ignore it. Although broadcast routing is practical on a small network with few nodes, it is impractical on a large one because it would quickly saturate the network with traffic.

## Carrier Sense Multiple Access with Collision Avoidance (CSMA/CA)

Wireless LANs (WLANs) must use a modified form of CSMA. Because all the computers participating in a WLAN are configured to the same radio frequency, they must "share the air," just as other LANs share cabling and take turns sending packets. Even though electromagnetic energy radiates in all directions, the range of WLANs is much shorter than that of conventional LANs. The signal can also be blocked, especially by metal objects. Therefore, devices that are too far apart or are blocked in some way cannot receive transmissions from each other. To overcome the problem of collisions that would inevitably occur, wireless LANs use a transmission scheme known as **carrier sense multiple access with collision avoidance (CSMA/CA)** rather than the CSMA/CD used by Ethernet networks.

**carrier sense multiple access with collision avoidance (CSMA/CA)**

Two computers on a network may be too distant from one another and unable to "see" each other, and one computer may not sense that the other computer has begun to transmit. To remedy this situation and avoid multiple collisions, the computer that needs to send a frame first transmits a brief control message telling the other computers of its intention to transmit data. When the computer for which the message is intended receives the control message, it sends its own control message indicating that it is ready to receive the transmission. The original computer begins to transmit a frame after it receives the response from the second computer. Once a computer sends its response, all computers wait for the packet to be transmitted. Collisions of control messages can occur. If they do, both senders back off and wait a random amount of time before resending the control message. Because control messages are much shorter than data frames, a second collision is much less likely than on a conventional Ethernet.

## Token Passing Protocol

**token passing protocol**

**token**

According to the **token passing protocol,** a small frame called a **token** circulates on the network until a station with a message to send acquires it, changes the token's status from "free" to "busy," and attaches a message. The token and the message move from station to station, and each one examines the address to determine whether it is the intended receiver of the message.

| | Starting Delimiter | Access Control | Frame Control | Destination Address | Source Address | Data | CRC | End Delimiter | Frame Status |
|---|---|---|---|---|---|---|---|---|---|
| Bits | 8 | 8 | 8 | 16 or 48 | 16 or 48 | $\geq 0$ | 32 | 8 | 8 |

General Frame Format

| | |
|---|---|
| Starting Delimiter | Indicates start of frame. The actual format depends on the type of signal encoding on the medium |
| Access Control | Variable format depending on type of frame |
| Frame Control | Indicates whether this is an LLC data frame. If not, bits in this field control operation of the token ring MAC protocol |
| Destination Address | Specifies the station for which the frame is intended: 16 or 48 bits is an implementation decision |
| Source Address | The address of the station that sent the frame |
| Data | The data being transmitted |
| CRC | A 32-bit cyclic redundancy check |
| End Delimiter | Contains an error-detection bit, which is set on if any repeater detects an error |
| Frame Status | Contains certain redundant error-checking bits |

**FIGURE 10-7**    The frame format for the token passing (802.5) protocol.

When the message arrives at the intended destination, that station copies it. If the CRC check is okay, the receiving station sends an acknowledgment to the sender. The token and acknowledgment return to the originating station. That station removes the acknowledgment from the circuit and changes the token's status from "busy" to "free." The token then continues to circulate, giving other stations an opportunity to use the circuit. Figure 10-7 shows the frame format for the token passing protocol.

deterministic

The performance of the circuit using the token passing protocol is predictable, or **deterministic,** meaning that it is possible to calculate the maximum amount of time it takes for any end station to be able to transmit. This feature and certain fault management mechanisms employed by token ring networks make the protocol ideal for systems such as factory automation environments that need to be predictable and robust. However, if the number of stations on the circuit is large, it may take a long time for the token to get around to a station that has a message to send. Therefore, although response time is predictable, it may be longer than on a CSMA/CD circuit.

## 10-8   LAN TOPOLOGIES

topology

**Topology** is a term used to describe the ways in which networks are physically connected. Because of the speeds at which LANs operate, there are distance limitations that must be observed. Equipment manufacturers specify the distances over which their equipment will operate, but the limitations have a physical basis related to the propagation delay of the signal on the circuit and the distance the signal can travel without being amplified or regenerated. A LAN topology influences certain factors important to network selection and management, including the complexity and cost of network cable installation,

**FIGURE 10-8**   LAN topologies.

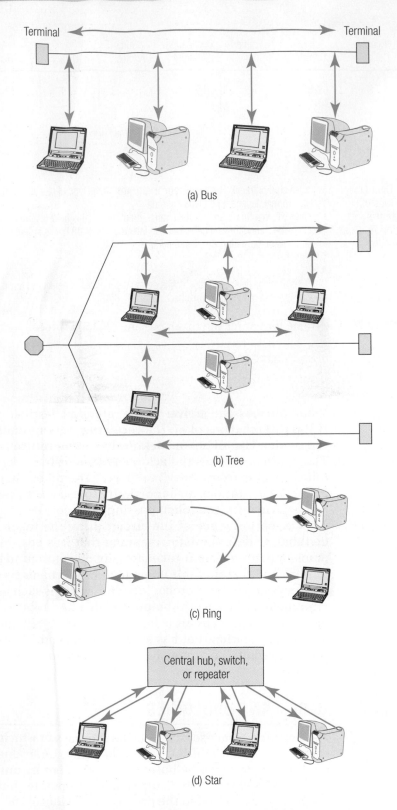

(a) Bus

(b) Tree

(c) Ring

Central hub, switch, or repeater

(d) Star

redundant or fail-safe designs, fault isolation, and the strategy for physically expanding and reconfiguring a network. The four basic topologies used in a LAN are once again illustrated in Figure 10-8; however, LANs are almost always implemented using either a bus or a ring topology. Chapter 11 discusses the individual topologies in conjunction with the LAN systems that most often implement them.

**FIGURE 10-9** A ring LAN installed as a physical star.

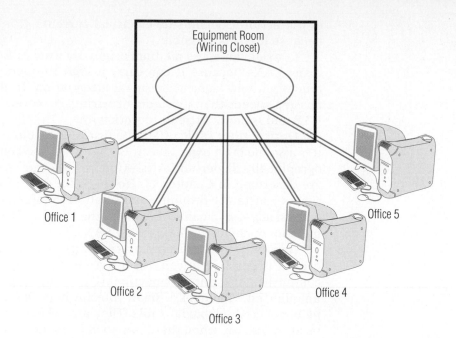

physical topology

logical topology

It is important to differentiate between a physical and a logical topology. A **physical topology** is the way in which the wires actually connect computers; the **logical topology** is the flow of data from workstation to workstation. For example, in the case of a token ring, the physical topology of the wiring is a star, but the communication path—or logical structure—is actually a ring. LANs that have a ring topology are most frequently installed as a physical star connected into a logical ring, as shown in Figure 10-9.

Most office buildings have an equipment room on each floor where the telephone and other network wiring and equipment are located. Wire is run from the equipment room to each office in a star configuration. In the equipment room, the wire is connected to form a ring. The advantage of this type of installation becomes evident when problems occur. Rather than having to trace a ring all over the floor of the building, the technician can work with the ring in the equipment room. Once the technician determines which part of the ring is causing the problem, that leg running to an office can be followed or traced. This same type of installation has similar advantages in a factory, hospital, or almost any other setting.

## 10-9 LAN MEDIA AND CABLING

Manufacturers design their LAN equipment and software to use specific media, according to the IEEE 802 standards discussed earlier in this chapter. When a LAN technology is selected, the choice of media is immediately predetermined by the requirements of the particular LAN type.

The characteristics of UTP, STP, and coaxial cable were discussed in Chapter 8. For LAN installations, UTP wire is very popular and is probably the most frequently used. UTP is the least expensive option. In most cases, wiring that was originally installed for telephones can be used for a LAN. To maintain signal strength at acceptable levels, cable runs are generally about 100 meters or less. Because it is an unshielded medium, UTP has greater susceptibility to **electromagnetic interference (EMI).** To reduce EMI, STP wire is used in some applications. It is more expensive, but provides a high degree

electromagnetic interference (EMI)

of protection from outside electrical currents. It is also harder to work with because it is a thick cable.

Coaxial cable, the medium originally used in Ethernet, is now used with many LANs because it can carry a high frequency signal over longer distances without significant signal attenuation. It also provides faster transmission speeds than twisted pair wiring. However, it is more expensive than UTP and is more difficult to work with.

Optical fiber cable offers the fastest possible speed and throughput, but it is also the most expensive. It is, therefore, used only in the largest, most geographically dispersed LANs—Gigabit Ethernet, ARCnet, and FDDI—which are described in Chapter 11. However, the cost of the fiber and its installation is constantly dropping and in all probability, optical fiber will be used extensively for smaller LANs in the future. It has already become the medium of choice for high speed LANs.

**balun**

Normally, the same type of wire or cable is used throughout a LAN; however, it is possible to connect different types together. One device that accomplishes this interconnection is a **balun,** which stands for "balanced unbalanced." Baluns are small transformers that allow twisted pair wire to be connected to coaxial cable. They are relatively inexpensive and also are used frequently when there is a need to connect one type of wire to a device such as a terminal that was designed to connect to a different type of cable.

**radio frequency (RF)**

**infrared (IR)**

WLANs ordinarily use **radio frequency (RF)** or **infrared (IR)** waves, though RF is more prevalent because IR requires LOS. Wireless media impose distance limitations, and physical obstructions can cause signal attenuation; however, WLANs are becoming more popular because they offer the advantage of portability and do not require cabling.

## Wiring Cost

The cost of installing the wire and cable for a LAN can be a significant portion of its overall cost. The least expensive alternative is to use previously installed UTP telephone wire if it is of adequate quality and if the LAN type permits its use. If new wiring must be installed, it is important to remember that the major portion of the cost of installing new wiring is generally not the cost of the wire or cable, but the cost of the labor to install it. Therefore, remembering the steadily increasing demand for bandwidth, it is far better to install higher quality cable or more pairs of wires than seems to be necessary at the time the wiring is designed. Many companies today install four pairs of CAT 5 wiring to each desktop when they are doing new wiring installations. One pair is designated for the telephone, one pair for data (the LAN), and two pairs as spares. Perhaps in the future, the extra spare could be used for a FDX LAN, for desktop video conferencing, or even for some other unimagined application.

## Wiring Documentation

**cabling plan**

The LAN wiring should be documented with a diagram that shows where each pair of wires or cable runs and to which piece of equipment it connects. A **cabling plan** specifies all this information before the wire is installed, but inevitably, changes are made during the course of installing the wire. It is very important to go back and update the cable plan to show what was actually installed. Engineers sometimes called this the "as built" drawing.

The wire and cable should be physically labeled with tags at each end that relate to the wiring diagram. Because LANs are prone to frequent change, reconfiguration, and expansion, it is easy to let this documentation get out of date. Only strong commitment on the part of the LAN owner/administrator, with management insistence and support, will ensure that the wiring documentation is kept up-to-date.

## 10-10   LAN TRANSMISSION TECHNIQUES

baseband transmission

There are two transmission techniques used for LANs. One technique, called **baseband transmission,** uses a digital signal. When baseband transmission is used, the medium is directly pulsed, and the entire bandwidth is used for a single signal. Baseband transmission typically occurs at speeds of 1 Mbps and higher. Baseband transmission is used when data are being transmitted, but it is only suitable for voice or television if the signals are digitized.

broadband transmission

The other transmission technique is called **broadband transmission,** and the signal is transmitted in analog form. The capacity of the cable is subdivided, using FDM, into whatever circuits or channels are required for the particular applications. The difference between broadband and baseband transmission is the way the bandwidth of the circuit is used, not necessarily in the capacity or the medium. A chief advantage of broadband transmission is that many different kinds of communications can occur simultaneously. The broadband system can be used for multiple purposes—such as data, voice, and television—without necessitating the installation of separate lines for each type of traffic.

The majority of today's LANs use baseband transmission: Ethernet, token ring, and FDDI are all baseband technologies. LANs often are used to connect PCs so they can communicate with one another or share a large disk or printer. Because only one transmission can be carried on at a time, baseband techniques rely on handling each transmission very quickly, using the high speed at which baseband operates. A transmitting node gets control of the medium and transmits its message. The transmission speed is high, so the transmission is completed quickly and the medium becomes free for another node to use.

Broadband transmission is typically found in an environment where there are diverse requirements for many types of transmissions. The only IEEE standard for broadband LANs is 10Broad36 (10Mbps; broadband; 3,600 meters maximum distance). The broadband system can be divided as if it had several baseband channels inside it. In addition, broadband systems typically carry transmissions that do not meet the technical qualifications of a LAN. In a manufacturing plant, for example, a broadband system might be used to connect the following:

- robots to a minicomputer serving a production line
- VDT terminals to a host computer
- laboratory instruments to a central computer used for quality testing
- a series of PCs that are connected to each other in LAN fashion (on one channel of the broadband system)
- a plant television studio, to television sets located around the plant, for broadcasting organization news, notice of job opportunities, and other information of interest to employees

All of these transmissions could occur simultaneously on a broadband system, and each would operate at a speed appropriate for the type of transmission. Thus, a broadband system has a greater ability to handle a wider range of signals than a baseband system does.

Broadband and baseband systems should be seen as complementary, not competitive. Both have distinct advantages. Baseband systems are simpler; new terminals can be attached by simply tapping into the cable. Broadband systems require modems to modulate the signal to the proper frequency range. Thus, they are more expensive to implement. Broadband cable is normally much larger than baseband cable. Therefore, they are more expensive and difficult to install. However, broadband systems can handle more diverse communications requirements. DSL and TV cable, which are discussed as types of Internet access in Chapter 15, are generally referred to as broadband services in the downstream direction.

## 10-11    LAN HARDWARE

### The Network Interface Card (NIC)

**network interface card (NIC)**

Several different kinds of hardware are involved in networking, no matter what type of topology is used. One of the most important of these is the **network interface card (NIC).** This circuit card provides the electrical interface between the workstation and the network and connects to the physical medium. Each PC or peripheral device requires that a NIC be added to it, unless the network clients and servers come with NICs as part of their standard hardware configuration. Although newer machines such as iMacs have built-in Ethernet NICs, most older Apple computers need them to be added. The NIC not only provides a connection to the network, but also handles data conversion. On the computer's bus system, data travels in a parallel stream (several bits transmitted at the same time); but on the network medium, it is transmitted in a serial stream (one bit after

These network interface cards (NICs) plug into a slot in a personal computer. (Courtesy of Intel Corporation. Reprinted with permission.)

another). On the NIC card, a transceiver (transmitter and receiver) converts the data from parallel to serial and vice versa. The MAC address is burned into a chip on the NIC, and this supplies the basic addressing system that enables network data to get from one computer to another. The first 24 bits of the 48-bit address identify the vendor, and the last 24 bits identify the card itself. The logical Internet Protocol address (discussed in Chapter 14), which identifies each host on the network and the Internet, must be resolved to this hardware (MAC) address before any data can be received.

## Hubs

**segment**

**nodes**

**hub**

The single shared medium of an Ethernet is called a **segment;** it is one continuous electronic portion of the network. The devices (computers and peripherals such as printers) that attach to that segment are referred to as stations or **nodes.** At the place where all the wires and cables from individual workstations come together, typically in the wiring closet, a device called a **hub** is normally installed. A hub is the simplest connectivity device used to connect computers. Hubs operate at the physical layer, Layer 1 of the OSI model. Hubs provide an easy way to connect all the wires and cables, and most of them allow different types to be interconnected.

**passive hub**

There are different kinds of hubs. A **passive hub** acts as a pathway, allowing data to flow from one device on a segment to another. It simply resends a signal without regenerating it. Hubs can also serve as repeaters to boost the signal strength, thereby allowing longer cable runs out to individual workstations or servers. These are considered **active hubs** because they regenerate and process signals. An **intelligent hub** can detect errors and can provide assistance to a technician when attempting to locate a failing component, such as a cable with a high error rate, a cut cable, or a failing workstation. Most simple hubs rebroadcast every packet to every port, though one special type of hub, called a **switching hub,** reads the address of the destination for each packet and forwards it to the proper port. Hubs are sometimes called **multistation access units (MAU), multiplexers,** or **concentrators.** Other LAN hardware is usually required to expand the LAN beyond a few connected computers.

**active hub**
**intelligent hub**

**switching hub**

**multistation access unit (MAU), multiplexer, concentrator**

A Netgear 4 port 10Base-T Ethernet hub.
(Courtesy of Netgear. Reprinted with permission.)

## 10-12   EXPANDING THE LAN

Only the smallest organizations find that one LAN meets all of their requirements. An organization may have offices several miles apart in the same town, or even in different towns. A token ring LAN may be installed in a company's office, but an Ethernet LAN may be required in their factory. A large organization may have a LAN in each department. In most cases, organizations find that it is beneficial to connect the LANs to allow people who use one LAN to communicate with people on any other LAN.

If the networks are a long distance apart, the network designer must carefully consider the speed of the communications circuit connecting the LANs. Because LANs operate at speeds measured in millions of bits per second, a MAN made up of one or more high-speed communication lines, such as T-1 or T-3 circuits, is desirable to maintain high throughput. However, the cost of high speed circuits may be prohibitive for all but the largest organizations. In that case, a lower speed circuit with the resulting performance compromise would have to be tolerated.

LAN interconnection can be done in several ways, depending on considerations such as the LAN technologies, the distance between the LANs, and the volume of communication that flows between the LANs. As you might guess, connecting two LANs that use the same data and network protocols—for example, from one Ethernet LAN to another—is easier than connecting LANs that have dissimilar technologies. Depending on the factors, LANs may be directly connected to each other using one of several devices. They may also be connected to a high-speed backbone LAN, which might, for example, use optical fibers and the FDDI protocol to transport data among the lower speed LANs. These connectivity devices may simply regenerate signals from one LAN to another, boost the data signal traveling on the network medium, or actually be involved in determining how the network data traffic should flow. Let us examine each of the various options in detail. Each operates at a different layer of the OSI model, as shown in Figure 10-10.

### Repeaters

As they travel through physical media over distances, signals lose strength because of resistance, signal radiation, and other factors. Repeaters are simple network devices that connect two similar LAN networks and extend the reach of electrical signals over wire. Fundamentally, they repeat signals while connecting two or more network segments that use the same protocol. For example, the maximum distance that a signal can travel on an Ethernet cable segment is 500 meters, but one repeater can double the effective length of an Ethernet to 1,000 meters.

Repeaters are not capable of connecting two dissimilar network technologies. They operate at the physical layer and are used to regenerate or replicate signals. They do nothing to change the data. Repeaters can only send an exact copy of what they receive from one LAN to the other: receiving, amplifying, and resending data one bit at a time. They allow workstations on each network to communicate as though a single network existed. They cannot do the intelligent routing performed by other LAN-extending devices.

### Bridges

bridge

**Bridges** increase efficiency and security beyond what repeaters are able to do. They operate at layer 2—the data link layer—of the OSI model and perform error detection, frame formatting, and frame routing. They have a variety of

**FIGURE 10-10**  Network interconnection hardware operates at various layers of the OSI model.

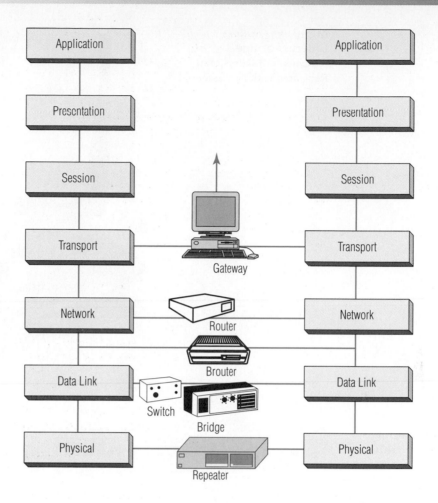

applications, such as extending a LAN to longer distances and to a greater numbers of ports. They also divide a busy LAN into two smaller ones to improve throughput and reduce congestion.

Bridges "listen" to all traffic on one segment and pass on data intended for other segments. Most bridges have filtering logic and software to allow them to "learn" the data link addresses of the devices on the network. A Spanning Tree Protocol (STP) bridge, specified in IEEE 802.1, is an example of the type of bridge that can reconfigure itself automatically and send data over an alternate path in case of segment failure.

When a bridge receives data, it looks at the MAC address of the device that sent it and compares the address to those already stored in an internal table. If the device is not already in the address table, the bridge adds it, along with the network segment on which it resides. In this way, the table gradually increases in size and reflects the addresses and locations of all the devices on the network. Using this table, the bridge can determine more quickly where to send future data.

When a bridge receives data with a destination address that is not in its table, it sends the data out on all network segments except the one on which it came. If the destination address is on the same network segment on which the data came in, the bridge can discard the data because the device to which it is addressed would have received it already.

Bridges isolate high traffic areas. By locating stations that communicate frequently with one another on the same LAN, a network designer can avoid unnecessary traffic. As illustrated in Figure 10-11, all computers in

A Linksys wireless
Ethernet bridge.
(Courtesy of Linksys.com.
Reprinted with permission.)

**FIGURE 10-11** Bridges connecting LANs with frequent traffic.

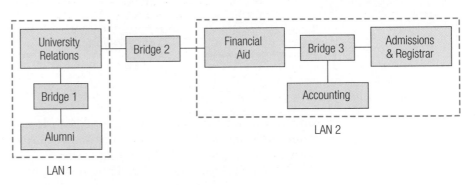

the university relations department communicate most frequently within the department and secondarily over bridge 1 with the alumni department and over bridge 2 with the financial aid office. The admissions office and other departments like the accounting department do not receive frequent communication from university relations, although they do communicate with each other. The bridges allow interdepartmental traffic when necessary, but forward only frames between the bridged networks, thus eliminating excess traffic. The bridges can also prevent certain frames from being sent throughout the entire network, thus providing greater protection for the alumni database maintained by the alumni department because only the university relations and alumni departments view the transmissions between them.

## Switches

switch

A **switch** provides the answer to scalability and latency problems encountered in networks connected to a hub, by accommodating growth without

A network switch such as this one can significantly increase a network's traffic speed.
(Courtesy of Linksys.com. Reprinted with permission)

sacrificing performance. A switch is a device that connects two or more network segments and allows different nodes to communicate smoothly with each other as if they are the only two connecting at the time. Unlike a hub, which rebroadcasts from all ports to all devices on a network, a switch makes a direct connection between the transmitting device and the receiving device.

Switches are implemented in hardware as well as software and allow all the connections to operate at the same time, making them very fast. Computers connected to a switch don't have to compete for bandwidth as do computers on a network connected by a hub. Collisions and network failure are also less frequent because devices connected to a switch port are able to use full bandwidth while those connected to a hub must share bandwidth with every other device on that hub. They have FDX access to networking media and can send and receive data simultaneously.

If, for example, a switch connects four LAN segments (A, B, C, and D, as shown in Figure 10-12), segments A and B can be communicating while segments C and D are communicating. The switch interconnects the segments, as needed, on a packet-by-packet basis. This fast switching and simultaneous connection ability gives the overall throughput a significant boost compared to other configuration options. In a recent article, the author compares a hub to a four-way intersection, where everyone has to stop, slowing traffic significantly and even adding to the possibility of collisions. A switch, however, is likened to a cloverleaf intersection, where cars flow on an exit ramp to their destination without having to stop for other traffic.[1]

A switch normally operates at layer 2, the data link layer, and uses the destination and source MAC addresses contained in a frame's header to connect devices. It learns the location of different nodes on the network and stores their MAC addresses in a lookup table. When a switch detects a packet, the switch routes it to an address listed in the table.

**cut-through switch**

There are two main types of switches with which to be familiar. A **cut-through switch** looks at an incoming packet's address and immediately sends it out to the destination LAN segment. However, if that segment is in use, a collision will occur and error recovery must be invoked. A cut-through switch is inexpensive and fast. A **store-and-forward switch** brings

**store-and-forward switch**

[1] Tyson, Jeff. "How LAN Switches Work." http://www.howstuffworks.com/lan.switch.htm.

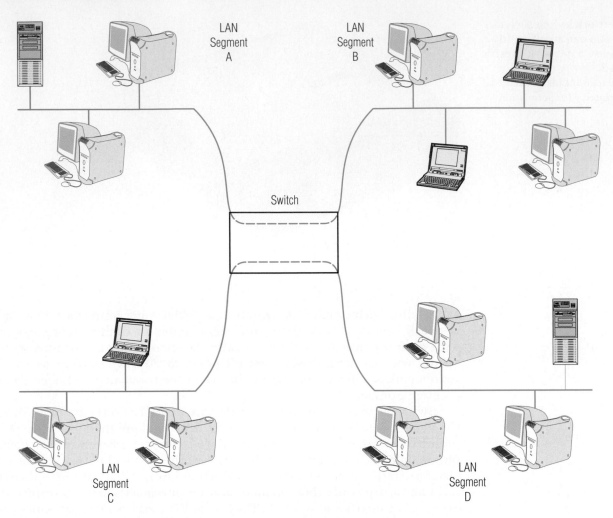

**FIGURE 10-12**   A switch allows simultaneous connection of LAN segments.

**fragment free switching**

each incoming packet into memory. The switch examines the destination segment and if it is busy, the switch holds the packet until the segment is free and then sends it out. Store-and-forward switches are, in general, slower and more expensive because of their memory, but buffering results in fewer errors on the LAN. As in all things, one must take the bitter with the better. A third, less common method of switching is called **fragment free switching.** It sends the packet out to the destination determined by the MAC address after storing only the first 64 bytes because that is where most errors and collisions occur.

In an ideal world, each node would have a dedicated segment connected to a switch, but realistically this is too expensive for most companies to consider. Organizations often use a combination of hubs and switches. For example, on a college campus, the university relations computers might be connected to a central hub and then interconnected by switches to other hubs in the admissions office and the alumni department.

Although the majority of switches operate at the data link layer, some operate in a similar manner to routers at layer 3, the network layer. They look at layer 3 addresses (IP) and decide how to send packets like a router does, but they are faster because they are built on switching hardware that can be reprogrammed dynamically with current routing information.

A router such as this one is a mainstay of all contemporary networks. (Courtesy of Juniper Networks Inc. Reprinted with permission.)

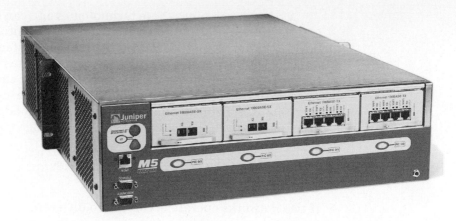

## Routers

**router**

**Routers** perform the function of passing messages from one network to another and translating the destination address to the format required by the network receiving the message. Routers operate at layer 3 of the OSI model, and the networks they connect may or may not be similar at that layer. They use a combination of software and hardware to route data. The router divides large networks into logical pieces called subnetworks.

A router performs two basic activities: determining the optimal routing paths and transporting data through the network. The optimal path may be measured several different ways, such as the fewest number of links to the destination, the least cost, or the optimum speed of the circuits along the way. The router uses a packet's destination address and a routing table stored in its memory to determine how to forward the packet. Routers can keep track of several possible routes to a destination and can then forward the packet along an alternate path if the primary route is busy or is out of service.

Routers communicate with one another and maintain their routing tables with the latest information about the status of the network. By analyzing updates from other routers, a router can maintain an up-to-date picture of the network topology.

**routing algorithm**

The logic that routers use to determine how to forward data is called a **routing algorithm.** Routing algorithms have been proposed and described in computer science literature for many years. They are designed to be simple, yet robust, stable, and flexible. They need to be capable of selecting the best route for a packet, which depends on the metrics, such as cost, number of links, bandwidth, delay, and traffic load. As you can gather, routers perform a very critical function. Routing of messages in a large network is a very complex topic, and Chapter 13 discusses WANs and routing in greater detail. For an excellent, animated explanation of the way that routers work, see the 13-minute movie at http://www.warriorsofthe.net/.

## Brouters

**bridge router (brouter)**

A **bridge router (brouter)** performs both the functions of a bridge (OSI layer 2) and a router (OSI layer 3) in a single device. A bridge connects LANs that use the same protocol and ordinarily offers only one path to an interconnected LAN. A router connects one network to any number of others and is usually part of a WAN. It can offer different routes to a destination, and therefore it needs more information about destinations on the networks.

A brouter combines these technologies and can bridge multiple protocols and provide routing over a limited number of protocols. A brouter is a single device that examines all data units and understands how to route specific types of packets, such as TCP/IP packets. It routes and bridges where possible, and any other protocols (i.e., packets) that it cannot route are simply forwarded to other connected networks. The main problem with a brouter is that the useful ability of a router to isolate broadcasts and multicasts from other networks is defeated because the bridge part of the brouter passes them on.

## Gateways

gateway

If two networks operate according to different network protocols, a **gateway** is used to connect them. Gateways usually operate at OSI layer 4 or higher, and basically translate the protocols to allow terminals on two dissimilar networks to communicate. Some gateways also translate data codes, for example, from ASCII to EBCDIC code. This capability would be useful on a LAN when a communication server routes traffic from a PC-based network using ASCII to an IBM mainframe that uses the EBCDIC code.

Gateways can be either/or combinations of hardware and software. They may be implemented on a specially designed circuit card or by using specialized software in a standard PC. An Internet service provider (ISP), which connects users in a home to the Internet, is a gateway. The computer routing traffic in an organization from individual workstations to an outside network's Web server is a gateway.

Gateways can suffer from slow performance because of protocol translation, so their performance must be considered and tested when a gateway installation is contemplated. A dedicated computer acting as a gateway, if it is of reasonable speed, usually eliminates any performance problems.

Gateways perform an important role in allowing an organization to interconnect different types of LANs so that, to the user, the network appears as a single entity. Figure 10-13 illustrates the difference between gateways and bridges.

Gateways are a mainstay of most networks.

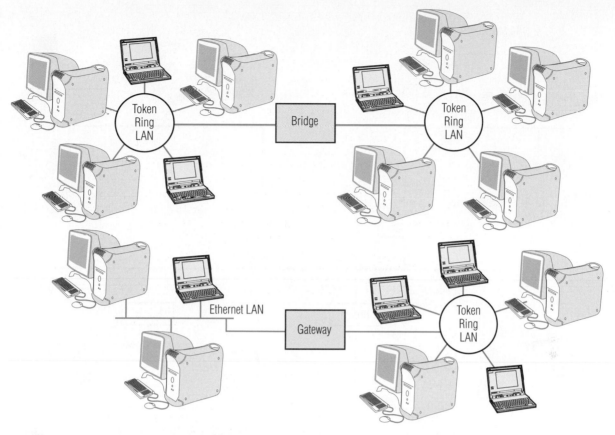

**FIGURE 10-13**   Bridges connect networks that use the same protocols. Gateways connect networks that use dissimilar protocols.

As the number of LANs or LAN segments that need to be interconnected increases, the design approach often taken is to connect the LANs to a high-speed backbone LAN, as shown in Figure 10-14. The backbone may use any one of several media and protocols, but the use of optical fibers and the FDDI protocol is common. The backbone design works well, but is subject to the limitation that the backbone is still a LAN and its capacity must be shared by all of the LANs connected to it.

A different approach is to connect all of the LANs to a switch instead of a backbone LAN, as shown in Figure 10-15. The switch has intelligence and multiple paths through it, so if LAN A wants to send a message to LAN B, the switch can make the connection. If, at the same time, LAN C wants to send a message to the server on LAN D, the switch can also make that connection simultaneously. Now, instead of all the LANs sharing the 100 Mbps speed of the backbone LAN (if it is an Ethernet), they all essentially have their own, dedicated link. Throughput goes up dramatically, in practice by as much as 200 percent. Token ring LANs can be switched in a similar way.

Taking the concept one step further, if additional intelligence is added to the switch, it can forward messages to a MAN or onto a WAN. This will give the benefits of fast switching to users who need to make Internet connections outside of their immediate LAN network.

This may sound good, but there are down sides. If the switch fails, the entire ability to interconnect the LANs goes down. Switches are pretty reliable pieces of hardware, but backup plans must be made for the eventuality that the switch may fail. Also, in most real-world implementations,

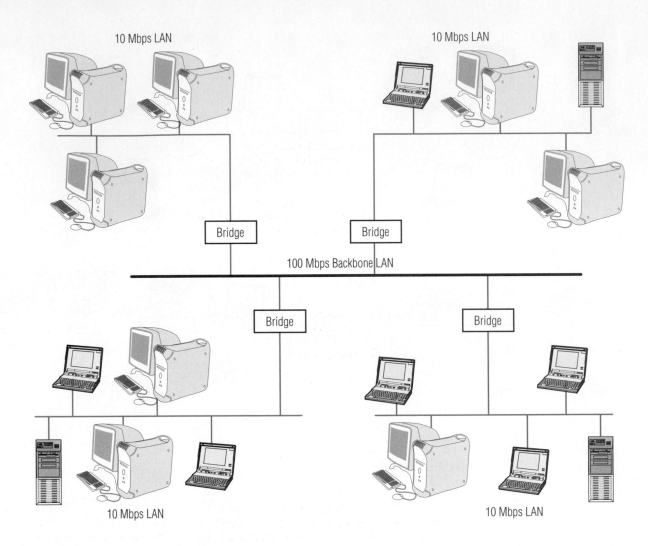

**FIGURE 10-14** LANs interconnected with a backbone LAN.

it requires more wire or cable to connect all the LANs to the switch. Considering that the installation cost for cable is high, the economics must be compared to the cost and benefits of the switch. Suffice it to say that many companies have done the economic evaluation and have concluded that the benefits of the faster throughput by using a switch far outweigh the cost.

One caution is that terminology and technology used by vendors is not always as consistent and as distinct as the examples in this book. The distinction between hubs, bridges, switches, routers, and gateways is blurred. For example, you might encounter terms such as "intelligent bridge" used to describe a device that combines the features of a bridge and a router, or "intelligent router" used to describe a device that combines the functions of a router and a gateway. Your defense against these vagaries of the marketplace is to understand clearly and define what networking problem you are trying to solve and ask a lot of questions to determine if a vendor's proposed solution will meet your requirements. Figure 10-16 compares the hardware (devices or interfaces) used to connect LANs.

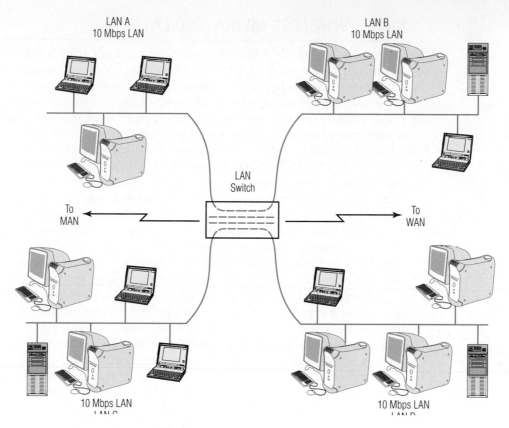

**FIGURE 10-15** A LAN switch can be used to connect several LANs together and to connect LANs to a WAN or a MAN.

|  | Repeater | Bridge | Switch | Router | Brouter | Gateway |
|---|---|---|---|---|---|---|
| **OSI layer** | 1 (physical) | 2 (data link) | 2 (data link) or 3 (network) | 3 (network) | 2/3 (data link/network) | 4 (transport) |
| **Relative throughput** | Lowest | Moderate | Fastest | Fast | Fast | Fast, but can be slowed by protocol translation |
| **Complexity** | Simplest | Simple | Complex | Most complex | Medium | Medium |
| **Capability** | Regenerates signals between two segments | Connects two network segments | Connects two nodes on separate segments | Connects two dissimilar networks, routing data | Fulfills functions of both switches and routers | Connects two types of networks with different protocols |
| **Cost (scale of 1 being most costly)** | 4 | 5 | Layer 2: 2 Layer 3: 1 | 2 | 3 | Depends on whether it is implemented in hardware or software |

**FIGURE 10-16** A comparison of network hardware.

## 10-12   WIRELESS MEDIA AND LAYOUT

**access point**

Ordinarily, if you are a mobile person, you cannot simply roam around your campus or office with a laptop computer and continue to use the LAN. The adapters and wires keep you tethered fairly close to your desk or workspace. In certain situations, wireless technology can be a solution for this problem.

A WLAN uses radio frequency technology as an extension of, or as an alternative to, a wired LAN. In a typical wireless LAN configuration, a transmitter/receiver (transceiver), called an **access point,** connects to a wired LAN using standard cabling, as shown in Figure 10-17. An antenna is usually mounted high enough to give radio coverage in the desired area. The access point acts like a hub—receiving, buffering, and transmitting data among the wireless workstations on a wired network. A single access point can support a small group of users within a range of up to several hundred feet. Many real-world applications exist in which a single access point services 15 to 50 user devices at a range of about 500 feet indoors and 1,000 feet outdoors. Technology changes constantly, however, and these distances continue to be pushed to new levels.

Users access the WLAN through WLAN adapters, which are implemented as PC cards in their computers. The WLAN adapter provides the interface between the computer and the radio signal via an antenna. The computer and its software are unaware of the fact that the connection to the LAN is wireless rather than through a standard cable.

In another configuration, a number of computers, each equipped with a WLAN adapter card, may communicate with each other without going

**FIGURE 10-17**   A WLAN with two access points.

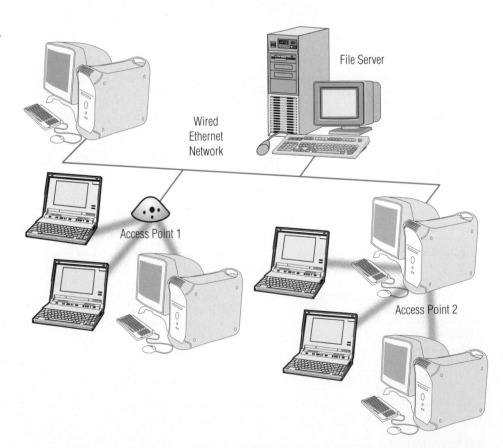

**FIGURE 10-18** A peer-to-peer WLAN network.

through an access point, as shown in Figure 10-18. This is called a peer-to-peer wireless network, and the users can share files and printers but are not able to access wired LAN resources.

In a large facility or in a campus setting, multiple access points can be installed to provide wide coverage. Access point positioning is determined by means of a site survey. The goal is to blanket the coverage area with overlapping coverage cells, as illustrated in Figure 10-19, so that users can move freely without disruption to their LAN communication. This capability, called **roaming,** operates transparently for users, much like a cellular telephone system. The wireless networking hardware automatically shifts to the access point that has the best signal.

Most manufacturers have adopted the IEEE 802.11 standard for transmission, allowing different brands of equipment to work together. The IEEE 802.11 standard is discussed in Chapter 11.

**FIGURE 10-19** Multiple access points with overlapping coverage.

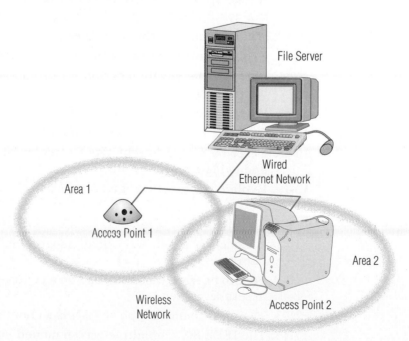

roaming

## ■ SUMMARY

This chapter has examined the infrastructure of LANs, the physical "highways" that data travel, and the rules for those highways. We have discussed the key elements of LAN technology: the MAC technique, the topology and layout, the transmission media, and the basic standards and protocols that govern them.

In Chapter 11, we will explore the most widely used LAN systems outlined in the IEEE 802 standards.

## ■ REVIEW QUESTIONS

10-1. What are the major components that make it possible to share resources on a LAN?

10-2. Describe the characteristics that distinguish a LAN from other types of networks, such as a WAN or a MAN.

10-3. Why do LANs have distance limitations?

10-4. Explain the differences between peer-to-peer and client/server networking.

10-5. Describe the purpose of a server and the various types that are available.

10-6. Discuss some of the reasons why organizations install a LAN.

10-7. Distinguish between the IEEE 802.2, 802.3, and 802.5 standards.

10-8. What is the function of LLC?

10-9. Explain what is meant by CSMA/CD.

10-10. How does CSMA/CA differ from CSMA/CD?

10-11. How do token ring and CSMA/CD differ when there is heavy traffic or a large number of stations on a network?

10-12. A token passing access technique is said to be deterministic. Explain this concept and describe why a CSMA technique is nondeterministic.

10-13. What is meant by the term *topology*?

10-14. Explain the differences between *physical topology* and a *logical topology*.

10-15. Describe the advantages and disadvantages of broadband and baseband transmission.

10-16. What is the importance of a NIC?

10-17. Compare and contrast a hub and a switch.

10-18. Describe four different types of network interconnection hardware and explain how they differ.

10-19. Explain the function of an access point.

### TRUE OR FALSE

10-1. LANs cover a relatively small geographical area and operate at high data rates.

10-2. Peer-to-peer networks depend on a central server machine to log in or access resources.

10-3. The most common type of LAN is a client/server network.

10-4. The IEEE 802 committee was so named because it was started in August of 2002.

10-5. The LLC frame is called a PDU.

10-6. 802.2 defines CSMA/CD.

10-7. The greatest weakness of CSMA/CD is the nondeterministic nature of its performance when the network is busy.

10-8. One of the positive aspects of the token passing protocol is that its performance is predictable.

10-9. A logical topology is the way in which wires actually connect computers.

10-10. The problem with IR is that it requires LOS.

10-11. Each PC or peripheral device must have a NIC to connect to the network.

10-12. A passive hub resends a signal without regenerating it.

10-13. Some hubs are also called MAUs, which means Many Accessible Utilities.

10-14. Switches operate at either layer 2 or layer 3 of the OSI model.

## MULTIPLE CHOICE

10-1. A device that performs some of the functions of both a bridge and a router is called a _____.

a. gateway

b. repeater

c. switch

d. routing bridge

e. brouter

10-2. A device that operates at the physical layer and is used to regenerate signals is called a _____.

a. gateway

b. repeater

c. bridge

d. brouter

e. switch

10-3. A device that operates at either the data link layer or the network layer and connects two nodes on separate segments by making a direct connection is called a _____.

a. bridge

b. router

c. brouter

d. switch

e. gateway

10-4. A device that operates at the network layer and can select the best route for a packet to travel over dissimilar networks is called a _____.

a. router

b. brouter

c. switch

d. bridge

e. repeater

10-5. Wireless LANs use a transmission scheme known as _____.

a. WSMA/CA

b. ATM

c. Token Passing Protocol

d. CSMA/CA

e. CSMA/CD

■ ## PROBLEMS AND PROJECTS

10-1. You are the owner of a small, but growing business and have decided to configure a LAN to make it possible for your twelve employees to share files on a server and your three network printers. They will not have Internet access—yet. You have a single-story structure with a reception area, six small offices, and three shared workspaces. Choose a LAN topology and explain (and diagram) how you will lay out the physical components of your system.

10-2. Do some research on the Linux operating system and explain, in detail, how it differs from other vendor software.

10-3. The University of Hawaii developed one of the earliest examples of a LAN, the ALOHAnet, in the 1970s. Research this network on the Internet or in written literature and discuss the details of its architecture and the impact it had on later developments in LAN technology.

## CASE STUDY

## PICTURE ARCHIVING COMMUNICATIONS SYSTEMS

Perhaps you've seen movies in which a patient anxiously waits for the results of his X-rays and the diagnosis, or a doctor must send X-rays to another physician for consultation or analysis. Perhaps you have experienced the wait yourself. Because of current dramatic advances in imaging technology, radiology images can now be created digitally and filed on a computer system. Doctors are then able to share images across a network.

Consider the case of an elderly woman, Mrs. Martha Snyder, who lives on a small island in the far Northeast. She lives in a rural area and has fallen and injured herself seriously, but the injuries are undetermined. Her local doctor is treating her in a small local hospital, but feels that it is important to consult with an orthopedic specialist. The only way for her to travel to the mainland is by ferry, and because it is late fall, the weather is unpredictable. To travel to the mainland in the patient's condition is inadvisable, and the injuries should be treated as soon as possible. The hospital has implemented a picture archiving and communications system (PACS), which allows computerized communication of images among hospitals and replaces the light boxes that were used to view X-rays and other diagnostic images. Dr. Barnes takes X-rays of Mrs. Snyder. They are converted to digital images and are sent electronically to the large mainland hospital. There, they are read by an orthopedic surgeon and a radiologist, who determine that she has broken her hip. She is quickly transported by helicopter to the mainland and is treated.

This may be an extreme case, but such technology is being implemented all over the world. Digital radiology is beginning to replace film X-rays that were projected on the wall and viewed by using light boxes, carried by hand, and stored in file cabinets. Broadband networking, powered by Gigabit

Ethernet and Layer 3 switches, allows hospitals to implement such band-width-intensive applications. Gigabit Ethernet is usually used for the hospital backbone and also within radiology departments. Images are captured and stored in a server farm dedicated solely to PACS archives.

It is important that such networks are able to transport very large files without delays and without degradation to the images. It is also necessary that the network never fail, because medical personnel rely on the PACS to make lifesaving decisions. Because nothing created by humans is that perfect, however, the network needs to be self-healing in the event of failure. The network also must be very stable and reliable. Automatic backups are extremely important because these digital files completely replace physical film copies.

As with all cutting edge technology, the rewards are great but the full and successful implementation of PACS requires manpower, financial backing, and extensive training.

**QUESTIONS**

1. Are you prepared to trust your health to a network that is prone to failure? Though most advocates claim 99.999% reliability, are there risks? Can you see any drawbacks to this type of technology?

2. Can you think of any other requirements of a network system that would be needed to support PACS?

3. What other advantages do you see to PACS?

4. A PACS system implements very expensive networks and very expensive equipment. Do the advantages, like convenience and efficiency and the lowering of operational costs, outweigh the expense of building and maintaining networks to support them?

**CASE STUDY**

# CHAPTER 11

# LAN SYSTEMS

## ■ OUTLINE

## ■ KEY TERMS

ad hoc mode

Advanced Encryption Standard (AES)

Asynchronous Transfer Mode (ATM)

Attached Resource Computer Network (ARCNET)

Bluetooth

bus

carrier extension bits

cells

centralized mode

copper distributed data interface (CDDI)

direct mode

fiber distributed data interface (FDDI)

fibre channel

fibre channel switch

frame bursting

HiperLAN2

infrastructure mode

Internet Small Computer System Interface (iSCSI)

isochronous communication

LAN Emulation (LANE)

LocalTalk

mobile terminal

multistation access unit (MAU)

network attached storage (NAS)

open nodes

orthogonal frequency division multiplexing (OFDM)

piconet

quality of service (QoS)

radiated (unguided) media

redundant array of inexpensive (or independent) disks (RAID)

scatternet

shared medium hub

slot time

storage area network (SAN)

switching hub

Temporal Key Integrity Protocol (TKIP)

third party copying

time division duplex (TDD)

virtual channel identifier (VCI)

virtual path identifier (VPI)

war chalking

war driving

Wi-Fi protected access (WPA)

Wired Equivalent Privacy (WEP)

## ■ OBJECTIVES

After you complete your study of this chapter, you should be able to:

■ describe Ethernet and token ring LANs and their methods of operation;

■ differentiate among the various Ethernet alternatives;

■ describe the FDDI standard network and its method of operation;

■ describe the characteristics of other common LAN systems;

■ describe the various wireless technologies used in LANs and explain their differences; and

■ identify distinguishing attributes of NAS as compared to SANs.

## 11-1   INTRODUCTION

In Chapter 10, you studied the basic characteristics of a LAN and the hardware components that make LANs possible. These include the NIC, other connectivity hardware such as switches and routers, and the various types of transmission media used to connect workstations and peripheral devices to the network. You also looked at the key elements of LAN technology, including topology, layout, and MAC. This chapter examines the different LAN systems described in the IEEE 802 standards and the protocols that were introduced in Chapter 10.

Ethernet LANs, token ring LANs, and the others described in this section collectively make up the vast majority of LANs installed in organizations throughout the world. We will examine them in greater detail in this chapter. We will also discuss the newest addition to the LAN scene, the WLAN, the specifics of which are outlined in the IEEE 802.11 standard.

## 11-2  ETHERNET

The original work on LANs was done at the Xerox Corporation Palo Alto Research Center (PARC) in the early 1970s. Xerox originally introduced the Ethernet LAN technology, which was based on a 1973 Ph.D. dissertation by Bob Metcalfe. It was further developed by Xerox, Digital Equipment Corporation, and Intel, and was jointly announced publicly in 1980. Ethernet is the oldest of the LAN technologies and remains popular today because of its high-speed, low cost, and the multitude of vendors that support its technology. Ethernet is based on the IEEE 802.3 standard. In its basic form, it operates on a bus topology at 10 Mbps using baseband transmission with Manchester data coding, which was explained in Chapter 6. The term **bus** implies a high-speed circuit of limited distance, and the bus is generally implemented within a single building. Although the layout of an Ethernet LAN is normally shaped like a physical star, it is wired internally to adhere to a bus topology. Figure 11-1 shows the way an Ethernet LAN is usually drawn.

**bus**

**FIGURE 11-1**  An Ethernet LAN—a conceptual view.

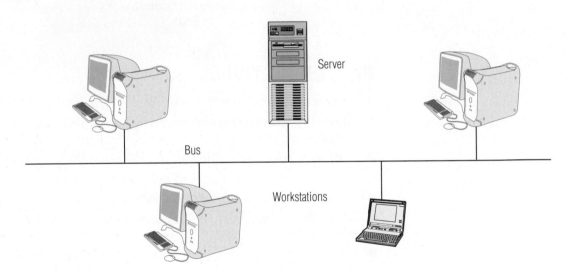

**FIGURE 11-2**  An Ethernet LAN as typically installed.

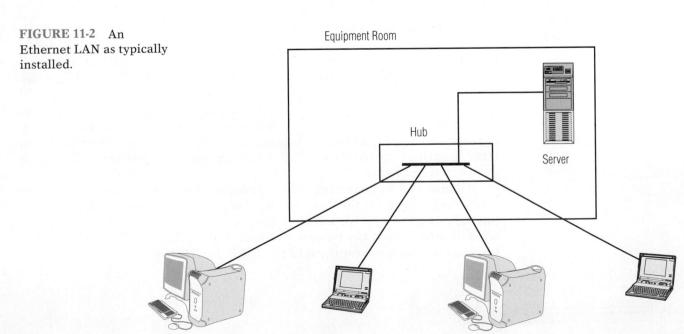

To simplify testing and debugging, as well as to improve security, it is desirable to confine as much critical cabling and hardware as possible to an equipment room, connecting wires or cables to a central hub. In actual practice, therefore, Ethernet networks are more generally implemented as shown in Figure 11-2.

One of the most important decisions that can be made when constructing a network is the type of medium that is used to connect the nodes. Media choice can affect not only the speed of the network but also the type of NICs that are installed and the ability of the network to meet the needs of an organization in the future. Wrong decisions can be very costly. Figure 11-3 compares the various types of media that are commonly used in all types of Ethernet LANs. Coaxial cable or CAT 5 wire, both of which were discussed in Chapter 8, are typically used in Ethernet LANs to connect devices in close proximity to one another.

Because electrical signals weaken as they travel and interference from devices that are nearby can scramble a signal, network cables must be short enough so devices at opposite ends of the bus can receive each other's signals clearly and in good time. Many network devices, such as repeaters (see Chapter 10), help to extend the distance that signals are able

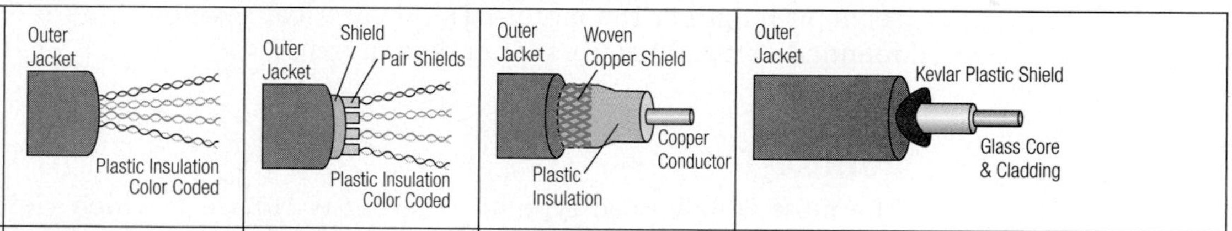

| | Unshielded Twisted Pair | Shielded Twisted Pair | Coaxial Cable | Multimode Fiber-optic Cable | Single-mode Fiber-optic Cable |
|---|---|---|---|---|---|
| Segment Length (Max) | 100 Meters | 100 Meters | 185 Meters (Thinnet) 500 Meters (Thicknet) | 2 km + | 10 km + |
| Speed | 10–1000 Mbps | 10–100 Mbps | 10–100 Mbps | 100 Mbps–9.92 Gbps | 100 Mbps–100 Gbps |
| Cost | Least | Higher than UTP | Higher than UTP, but Less Cable Often Needed | Highest | Highest |
| Pros | Installs Easily, Inexpensive, Widely Used, Widely Available | More Resistant to EMI, Crosstalk Reduced | Usable Over Greater Distances Than UTP or STP, Relatively Inexpensive | Not Susceptible to EMI, Better Security (Cannot be Tapped), Usable Over Greatest Distances, Highest Data Rate | Not Susceptible to EMI, Better Security (Cannot be Tapped), Usable Over Greatest Distances, Highest Data Rate |
| Cons | Limited Distance, Susceptible to Interference | Limited Distance, Difficult to Work With | Thicknet Difficult to Work With, Thinnet Difficult to Ground Properly | Difficult to Terminate, Expensive | Difficult to Terminate, Expensive |

FIGURE 11-3  Media commonly used in networks.

to travel. Others, like switches, help to alleviate problems of congestion. The Ethernet alternatives used originally and those now used most commonly include the following:

### 10Base-5: Thick Ethernet

Ethernet was originally implemented using standard coaxial cable, which is 0.4 in. in diameter. The LANs were given the name 10Base-5 Ethernet, which means a speed of 10 Mbps using baseband transmission for a maximum distance of 500 meters. The 500 meter distance limitation constitutes a segment of the 10Base5 Ethernet LAN. If the distance needs to be exceeded, a second segment must be installed and the two segments must be connected with a bridge or switch. Now, Ethernets implemented with 0.4 in. diameter cable are frequently called "thick Ethernets."

### 10Base-2: Thin Ethernet

More flexible coaxial cable, only 0.25 in. in diameter, is often used for PC LANs because it is cheaper and easier to install than the alternatives. The specification is 10Base-2, meaning 10 Mbps over 200 meters. The common names are "thin Ethernet" or "cheapernet." Because 10Base-2 uses thinner cable, which supports fewer taps and shorter distance, its actual maximum segment length is 185 meters. The theoretical segment length distance was rounded up to 200 meters for ease in naming.

### 10Base-T

The most widely used type of Ethernet is 10Base-T, which yields 10 Mbps over UTP wire, normally for a distance of only 100 meters per segment because of the relatively poor transmission qualities of UTP. Because excess UTP is often found in buildings prewired for telephones, it is an economical and easily implemented alternative.

### 10Base-F

As an alternative to UTP, optical fiber may be used, thereby increasing the maximum segment length to 500 meters and enhancing transmission characteristics. The standard contains three specifications, but all three use a pair of optical fibers for each transmission link (one for each direction). The signaling uses Manchester encoding, and each signal element is converted to an optical signal element. The absence of light corresponds to low, and the presence of light corresponds to high.

### 100Base-T: Fast Ethernet

The never-ending demand for more bandwidth and higher transmission speed has pushed vendors to develop higher speed Ethernets. The most common higher speed Ethernet in use is 100Base-T. This 100 Mbps Ethernet operates over two pairs of UTP cable, known as 100Base-TX; two optical fibers, known as 100Base-FX; or four pairs of Category 3 UTP, known as 100Base-T4. Fast Ethernet retains the IEEE 802.3 frame format, size, and error detection mechanisms. It supports all applications and networking software running on 802.3 Ethernet networks. Therefore, it is relatively easy for network managers to upgrade to a higher speed, especially if they have Category 5 cabling installed. Fast Ethernet has become a very popular technology because it is relatively inexpensive.

## Gigabit Ethernet

Gigabit Ethernet, also known as 1,000Base-X, is an extension of the IEEE 802.3 standard. The IEEE 802.3 committee formed a study group in 1995 to investigate high-speed Ethernet, and the committee approved the standards in mid-1998. Gigabit Ethernet is usually carried on optical fiber, though it can run on copper over shorter distances. In that case, it uses four pairs of CAT 5 cable and is used for applications that have very high bandwidth requirements. Versions of Gigabit Ethernet include:

- 1,000Base-CX, a system that uses specialized STP copper cable intended for use as short jumpers between devices in a common equipment room or rack. The transmission range is no more than 25 meters in distance. With a single repeater, however, 50 meters is possible.
- 1,000Base-SX, a short-wavelength laser system that can transmit reliably no farther than 550 meters through multimode fiber.
- 1,000Base-LX, a long-wavelength laser system that can transmit reliably over approximately 3 kilometers through single mode fiber (SMF).
- 1,000Base-T, which uses four pairs of CAT 5 UTP to support transmission of data over distances of up to 100 meters.

An important feature of Gigabit Ethernet is that existing Ethernet LANs with 10 Mbps and 100 Mbps can feed into it. It was originally used as backbone technology for server connections and is being used now as the backbone in many enterprise networks. Figure 11-4 illustrates a typical application of Gigabit Ethernet.

Gigabit Ethernet is ten times faster than 100Base-T Fast Ethernet. When the speed of an Ethernet is increased so dramatically, certain technical complications occur that must be overcome. Gigabit Ethernet can use

**FIGURE 11-4** A typical gigabit Ethernet configuration.

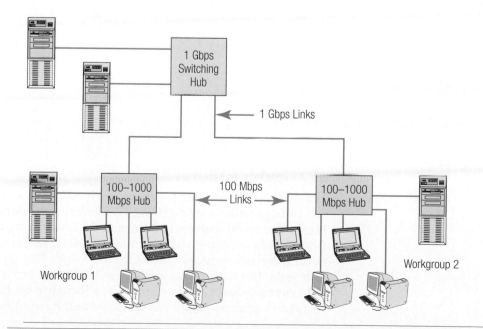

**switching hub**

**shared medium hub**

**slot time**

**carrier extension bits**

**frame bursting**

either a shared medium hub or a **switching hub.** A switching hub reads the destination address of the packet and sends it to the proper port. A **shared medium hub** simply acts like a pipe through which data can flow, allowing packets to go from one segment of the network to another or from one device to another.

In the case of a shared medium hub, if frames are too small, collisions could go undetected by other NICs on a large-sized network when the speed of transmission is increased so greatly. According to the 802.3 standards, **slot time** is the minimum amount of time an NIC has to transmit a frame. A minimum Ethernet frame is 64 bytes, or 512 bits. That means a minimum Ethernet slot-time is 512 bit-times. Although CSMA/CD protocol is still used with Gigabit Ethernet, a couple of changes have been made to the basic format. First, extra **carrier extension bits** are added to the end of small MAC frames so the resulting slot time is increased from 512 to 4,096 bit-times. This makes the transmission longer by a factor of 8. The transmitting node has longer to receive a notice of collision when the network is congested, and collisions are easier to detect. Another development, **frame bursting,** allows a node to transmit several small frames consecutively without relinquishing control between frames for collision detection, thus eliminating the need for the overhead that carrier extension bits add. In the case of a switching hub, which affords dedicated medium access, these two provisions are not needed. Because Ethernet technology is progressing so rapidly, you may find the most up-to-date information about gigabit Ethernet at the following websites: http://www.cisco.com/warp/public/cc/techno/media/lan/gig/tech/gigbt_tc.htm and http://www.nwfusion.com/research/ge.html. An excellent white paper is also available at http://www.10gea.org/GEA1000BASET1197_rev-wp.pdf. The characteristics of the current forms of Ethernet are summarized in Figure 11-5.

| Characteristic | 10Base-5 | 10Base-2 | 10Base-T | 10Broad-36 | 100Base-TX | 100Base-FX | 100Base-T4 | 1,000Base-T |
|---|---|---|---|---|---|---|---|---|
| **Medium** | Coaxial Cable | Coaxial Cable | Two Pairs of Cat 5 UTP | Coaxial Cable | Two Pairs of Cat 5 UTP | Two Optical Fibers | Four Pairs of Cat 3 UTP | Four Pairs of Cat 5 UTP |
| **Topology** | Bus | Bus | Star | Bus | Bus | Bus | Bus | Bus |
| **Signaling** | Baseband | Baseband | Baseband | Broadband | 4B/5B NRZI | 4B/5B NRZI | 8B/6T NRZI | NA |
| **Transmission speed (Mbps)** | 10 | 10 | 10 | 10 | 100 | 100 | 100 | 1,000 |
| **Maximum segment length (meters)** | 500 | 185 | 100 | 1,800 | 100 | 400 | 100 | 100 |

**FIGURE 11-5**   Characteristics of Ethernets.

## 10-Gigabit Ethernet

The 802.3 IEEE Committee is currently working on standardizing technology for 10-Gigabit Ethernet (10GigE), which offers data speeds up to 10 billion bits per second! Currently known as 802.3ae, it prescribes the use of optical fiber and is expected to interconnect LANs, WANs, and MANs. Smaller 1 Gigabit Ethernet networks feed into the larger 10 Gigabit Ethernet backbones. The high cost of such technology inhibits the rapid transition to 10 Gigabit Ethernet products. Most vendors are focusing on LAN rather than WAN interfaces, which are more complicated and have to interoperate with SONET, a WAN technology (see Chapter 13) with a different transmission rate. 10GigE uses the same Ethernet MAC protocol as other 802.3 networks. Its FDX transmission supports distances up to 300 meters on multimode fiber (MMF) and 40 kilometers on single mode fiber. The technology is to be used primarily in campus and metropolitan networks. The highest priority specification is one that supports a distance of 10 kilometers on SMF. For up-to-date information on 10GigE, go to http://www.10gea.org/.

## 11-3 TOKEN RING

Token Ring technology was originally developed by IBM and has been standardized as IEEE 802.5. According to accepted convention, the term "Token Ring" is capitalized only when it refers to the IBM technology but appears with lower case letters otherwise. The IEEE 802.5 standard is completely compatible with IBM Token Ring and almost (with slight variations) exactly the same. Developed in the 1970s, it is second only to Ethernet in general popularity. A token ring network is almost collision free, because the waiting time before the next token can be transmitted is calculable. It is beneficial, therefore, in applications such as factory automation environments where delays must be predictable. Banks often rely on token ring's equal access for sending data to guarantee real-time delivery of important information.

As the name implies, token ring LANs use a token passing access technique and protocol on a ring topology, as described in Chapter 10. Data are encoded in IBM Token Ring or 802.5 networks using the differential Manchester technique, which was described in Chapter 6.

IBM Token Ring specifies that networks must be set up in a star topology, though the frames move in a circle from node to node. Individual computers attach to a **multistation access unit (MAU),** which is similar to, though more sophisticated than a hub in an Ethernet network. The logical ring exists within the MAU, and data travels in one direction. To form a single large ring, the MAUs can be wired together with patch cables to interconnect workstations. For convenience, they are usually grouped together in a wiring closet. As a result, a major advantage of token ring LANs is fast media fault correction. Bypass relays included in the MAU also allow stations to be removed from the ring if problems occur. Figure 11-6 shows the logical ring established within a MAU.

**multistation access unit (MAU)**

FIGURE 11-6    A MAU.

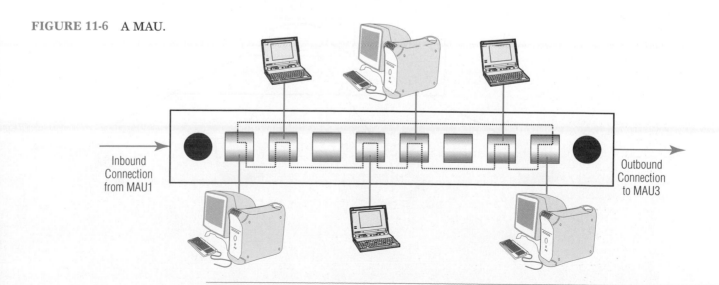

Inbound Connection from MAU1

Outbound Connection to MAU3

**FIGURE 11-7**   A token ring LAN: a conceptual view.

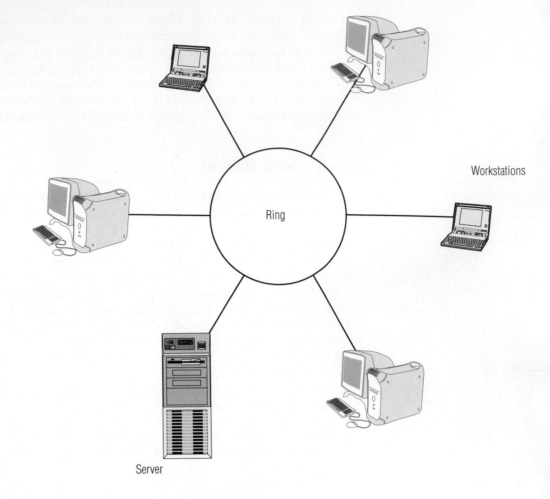

Workstations

Ring

Server

**FIGURE 11-8**   A token ring LAN as typically installed.

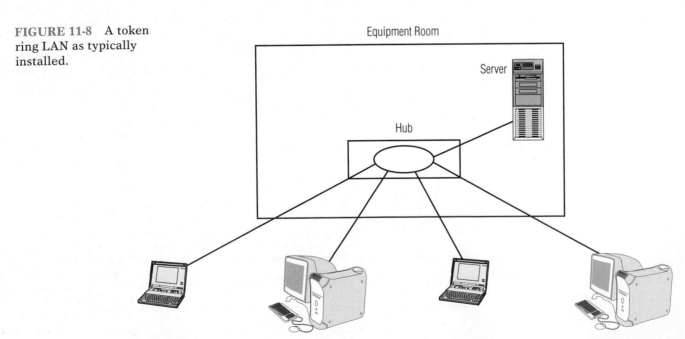

Equipment Room

Server

Hub

Most IEEE 802.5 networks are also based on a star and use twisted pair wiring, although the standard does not specifically designate the topology or the media type. Figure 11-7 shows the conceptual view of the way token rings are usually pictured, and Figure 11-8 shows the way they are normally installed.

Token ring LANs normally operate at 4 Mbps on UTP wire or at 16 Mbps on STP or CAT 5 UTP. The system for numbering and categorizing cables is different from that used for Ethernet. STP is referred to as type 1 and UTP is called type 3, which is less expensive. Generally, UTP wiring allows the connection of up to 72 workstations per ring, while STP allows up to 260 connections. The typical token ring installation is usually less than 100 connections. Devices must be within 100 feet of a MAU, although the MAUs can be thousands of feet apart. The fiber optic cable used to connect MAUs is known as Type 5 cable.

Faster versions of token ring LANs and new switching technologies continue to be developed. Several hardware companies, especially IBM, are currently making 100 Mbps NICs for high-speed token rings (HSTR). Without changing LAN cabling, they can be used on existing infrastructures. The 100 Mbps 802.5 token ring uses the physical layer specifications of 100 Mbps Ethernet. Also, for high-speed backbones to connect token ring LANs using fiber optic cabling, the IEEE is standardizing Gigabit Token Ring (1,000 Mbps).

## 11-4   THE FIBER DISTRIBUTED DATA INTERFACE (FDDI) STANDARD

**fiber distributed data interface (FDDI)**

The **fiber distributed data interface (FDDI)** standard for a 100 Mbps fiber optic LAN was developed during the mid-1980s by a subcommittee of ANSI and was completed in 1990. As LANs based on the IEEE 802 standards reached capacity, optical fiber LANs based on the FDDI standard became an alternative growth path. In their first implementations, FDDI LANs were used to provide high-speed backbone connections between distributed LANs. Now, however, FDDI is used for normal LANs that have a large number of users or need to operate at very high speed.

The primary transmission medium used for FDDI is optical fiber, and the standard defines two types: SMF and MMF. SMF can deliver connectivity over longer distances, with higher performance than MMF. It is used, consequently, for connections between buildings or over greater geographical areas. MMF is usually used to connect devices within a building or a small geographically contained area.

**copper distributed data interface (CDDI)**

It is interesting that FDDI has also been implemented over twisted pair copper wire. The **copper distributed data interface (CDDI),** as it is now called, uses only STP or UTP CAT 5 cabling, but supports distances of 100 meters and data rates of 100 Mbps. Other than the media, the implementation of FDDI and CDDI is the same.

Because optical fiber conducts signals as pulses of light over threads of glass, it offers greater security, performance, and reliability than copper cabling, although it is more expensive. Copper media, which emits electrical signals, can be secretly tapped, allowing unauthorized data access. Optical fiber cannot be tapped without the owner knowing that something is amiss. Though recent advances in technology have enabled greater data rates with copper, fiber has always supported higher bandwidth and greater distances between stations. Theoretically, the limit of Ethernet, measured in 64-byte packets, is 14,800 packets per second. In contrast,

**FIGURE 11-9** An FDDI network with primary and secondary token rings. During normal conditions, only one of the rings is used and data travels in one direction. When a station or a cable segment fails, the traffic loops to form a closed ring, moving data in the opposite direction.

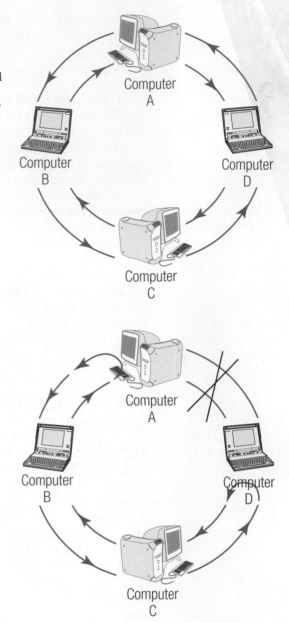

token ring is 30,000 and FDDI is 170,000 packets per second. Finally, an important advantage of fiber is that it is not susceptible to EMI and radio frequency interference (RFI).

The FDDI standard defines a LAN based on two 100 Mbps token rings that flow in opposite directions; that is, they are counter rotating rings. One of the rings is designated as the primary ring and the other as the secondary ring. All stations on the LAN are connected to both rings. Data are passed on the primary ring during regular operation while the secondary ring is idle. Should the primary ring fail, the stations on each side of the failure point reconfigure themselves, as shown in Figure 11-9, so that data flow continues using a combination of the primary and secondary rings. The token passing technique defined by FDDI is similar to the one defined by IEEE 802.5, but with significant enhancements in the areas of fault tolerance and topology.

The FDDI standard allows up to 1,000 stations to be connected to the ring in a priority system. High-priority stations can access the ring for longer pe-

**FIGURE 11-10  FDDI LAN message passing.**

1. A seizes the token and transmits frame 1 (F1) addressed to C. Token is appended to F1.

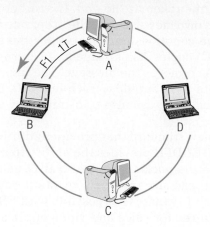

4. D copies F2.

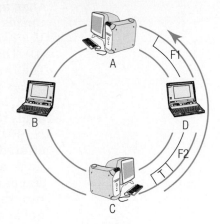

2. C copies frame F1 as it goes by.

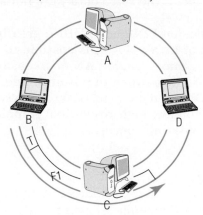

5. A absorbs F1 and lets F2 token pass.

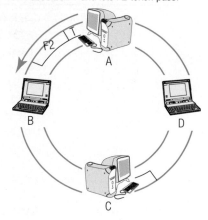

3. B seizes token and transmits frame (F2), addressed to D. Token is appended to F2.

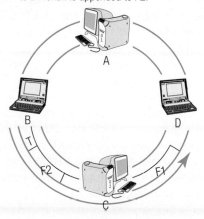

6. B absorbs F2 and lets token pass.

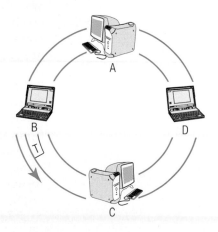

riods of time. Stations must be located no more than 2 kilometers apart, but the maximum length of the ring can be up to 200 kilometers when 100 segments are connected. Because it would be inefficient for only one message to be on the ring at a time when the LAN is so spread out, the FDDI standard allows multiple messages to circulate simultaneously. Figure 11-10 illustrates message passing in a FDDI LAN. Only one token circulates, but when a station (A) receives the token, it can remove it from the ring and transmit a message, appending the token at the end. If another node (B) sees the token, it can piggyback its own message onto the other one and then append the token. The first message continues until it reaches the original intended recipient (D). That node (C) copies A's message and returns it as an acknowledgment. The first node (A) removes the message. The piggybacked message (B's) continues to circulate to its intended recipient (D). During an established time limit, an individual node can also transmit many messages consecutively if it holds the token.

FDDI-II is a new standard that provides additional capability beyond that offered by FDDI. FDDI-II provides the ability to handle circuit switched traffic in addition to the packet switched traffic handled by the original FDDI standard. FDDI-II can also provide a constant data rate connection between two stations, an ability that is not possible with FDDI. Constant data rate connections are required for voice and video applications. FDDI-II uses TDM to allow **isochronous communication.** "Iso-" (equal) "-chronous" (time) communication means "at the same time, without delay." Imagine what a telephone call might sound like if the voice data were not able to get through the network at a constant rate!

**isochronous communication**

It is easy to see that FDDI and FDDI-II greatly expand the speed and operating distances of LANs. Now it is possible to connect a large campus or corporate complex into a single LAN or to easily connect smaller LANs in buildings or departments when that is desirable. Eventually, there will be a need to have FDDI speed on many desktops to support applications such as full motion, color video, high resolution graphics and photographs, traditional data, and voice—all concurrently!

## 11-5  ARCNET

**Attached Resource Computer Network (ARCNET)**

**Attached Resource Computer Network (ARCNET)** is a LAN architecture that was developed by Datapoint Corporation in the 1970s. It became popular because of its low cost, ease of installation, and early availability compared to other LANs. ARCNET was one of the four major LAN technologies, but because it does not follow any of the IEEE 802 LAN standards, it has lost popularity in recent years to Ethernet, token ring, and FDDI. It is an example of a baseband token-bus scheme.

ARCNET networks are established with either a bus or star topology using UTP, coaxial cable, or optical fiber media. Transmission speeds are 2.5 Mbps or, using a newer Arcnet Plus architecture, 20 Mbps on a coaxial cable.

Repeaters, called active hubs, allow the connection of multiple workstations and perform signal amplification. Passive hubs allow the connection of multiple workstations without the signal amplification function. Using combinations of active and passive hubs, ARCNETS were arranged in many different configurations with varying distance limitations. A typical ARCNET configuration is shown in Figure 11-11.

## 11-6  LOCALTALK

AppleTalk LANs have gained wide popularity among the users of Apple Macintosh computers because they are inexpensive and easy to install. AppleTalk networks are usually used with small groups of workstations that are in close proximity to one another and wish to share network printers and

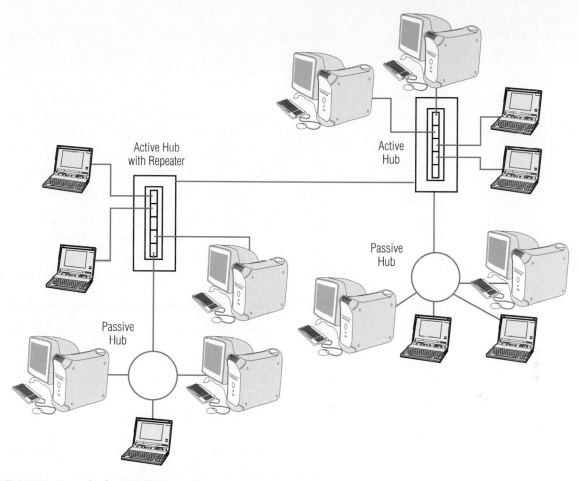

**FIGURE 11-11** A typical ARCNET configuration.

other resources. Most of the required hardware, which is also available for other brands, is included with Macintosh computers.

AppleTalk is a suite of protocols that provides all necessary features for network communication. Figure 11-12 shows some of the members of the AppleTalk Protocol stack and the way they relate to the OSI model. AppleTalk uses the IEEE 802.2 LLC Protocol at the Data Link Layer.

According to the routable AppleTalk protocol, larger networks can be logically divided into zones. The zones are similar to workgroups in Microsoft's peer-to-peer networking, in which computers configured with the same workgroup name are divided into logical groups to share files, printers, and other resources.

The AppleTalk MAC protocol is a modified form of CSMA/CD called CSMA/CA, which was discussed in Chapter 10 in relation to wireless networks. Rather than waiting for collision detection to occur, an AppleTalk workstation sends a small 3-byte packet on the network, signaling its intent to transmit data. When other terminals on the network see this packet, they stand by until the data from the first terminal have been sent. This method greatly decreases the number of collisions, but the added packets do tend to slow the network somewhat. Transmission speed is 230.4 Kbps, which is quite slow compared to other LANs, especially Ethernet.

**LocalTalk**   AppleTalk networks may be configured in a bus or star topology using Apple's **LocalTalk** cabling system. The medium can be twisted pair, coaxial cable, or fiber optic cable, but STP wiring is most commonly used because of

**FIGURE 11-12** AppleTalk protocol stack and the OSI model.

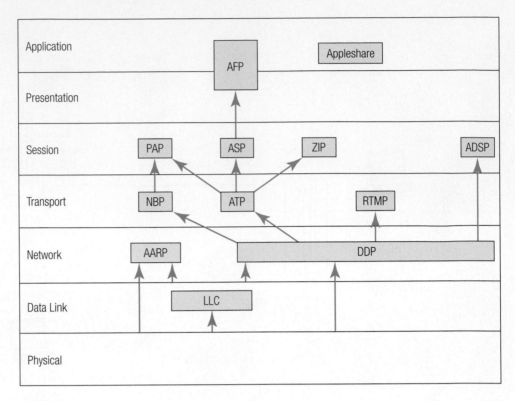

**Data/Link**
- *LCC* — corresponds to the IEEE 802.2 standard, and provides connectivity

**Network**
- *AARP (AppleTalk Address Resolution Protocol)*—maps logical network layer addresses to data link hardware addresses, and makes it possible for AppleTalk to run on any data link
- *DDP (Datagram Delivery Protocol)*—provides datagram delivery and routing to higher layer protocols

**Transport**
- *ATP (AppleTalk Transaction Protocol)*—manages connection between computers
- *NBP (Name Binding Protocol)*—maps computer host names to network layer addresses
- *RTMP (Routing Table Maintenance Protocol)*—manages routing information for networks

**Session**
- *PAP (Printer Access Protocol)*—manages virtual connection to printers and servers, coordinates data transfer
- *ZIP (Zone Information Protocol)*—controls AppleTalk zones, maps zone names to network addresses
- *ADSP (AppleTalk Data Stream Protocol)*—provides data channel for hosts, guaranteeing data are delivered in sequence and with flow control

**Presentation/Application**
- *AFP (AppleTalk Filing Protocol)*—provides and handles file sharing
- *Appleshare* provides services at the application layer

its low cost and availability. Up to 32 workstations can be connected to any AppleTalk LAN, with a maximum total distance of about 1,000 feet. Multiple AppleTalk networks can be connected using routers or other intermediate devices.

The major problems with AppleTalk are its low transmission speed, by today's standards, and its use of nonstandard protocols. Most networked Apple computers, especially the newer iMacs, include an Ethernet NIC. AppleTalk can still be used on networks that don't connect to the Internet; however, almost everyone is interested in connecting today, so most Macintosh computers use the TCP/IP protocol suite and Ethernet instead.

## 11-7   ASYNCHRONOUS TRANSFER MODE (ATM) LANS

**asynchronous transfer mode (ATM)**

**Asynchronous transfer mode (ATM)** is primarily a backbone technology for WANs and MANs, but it was conceived as a universal technology. That is, ATM was meant to be both a WAN and a LAN technology used to carry digitized voice and video as well as data traffic. ATM switches utilize a rather complicated technology called **LAN Emulation (LANE)** to imitate token ring and Ethernet LANs on an ATM backbone, usually over high-speed fiber optic cable. Because this is an introductory book on networking, only the basic concept of ATM technology is presented in this chapter. Chapter 13 discusses ATM technology in relation to WAN systems.

**LAN Emulation (LANE)**

**cells**

The ATM protocol stack is made up of protocols at layers 1, 2, and 3 of the OSI model. Data are broken into small packets called **cells** that are always exactly 53 octets (bytes) long. That cell size is a compromise between the best size for voice (where delays and echo are intolerable) and data (where loss of packets is intolerable). The cell contains 48 octets of data and 5 octets of header. The format of the cell can be one of two types, which differ in the size of the **virtual path identifier (VPI)** field. The format illustrated in Figure 11-13 is the user network interface (UNI). The other format is known as the network-to-network interface (NNI), and it has a 12-bit VPI field, created by appropriating the 4 bits of the GFC field. It will be illustrated in Chapter 13.

**virtual path identifier (VPI)**

**virtual channel identifier (VCI)**

Virtual circuit identifiers called the virtual path identifier (VPI) and the **virtual channel identifier (VCI)** include information about the cell's destination on the network in the header. ATM, unlike the other LAN systems, is a connection-oriented interface. The virtual channel (VC) is the circuit, or the connection, between sender and receiver. A virtual path (VP) is a group of channels for an organization that needs to have redundant connection channels. The identifiers change as the cell passes through the ATM network, and forwarding tables in the switches must be coordinated to create effective VPs.

ATM technology is expensive compared to other types of LANs. Other drawbacks exist as well. The time required to create VCs for distant communication is long, and the headers add extra overhead for such small amounts of data contained in an individual cell. Additionally, broadcast and multicast are not as efficient as on other types of LANs. For these reasons, ATM LANs have not been as widely accepted as was first anticipated.

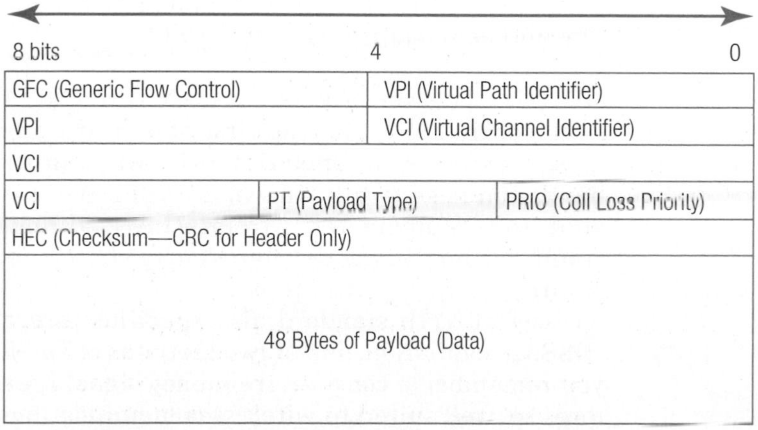

**FIGURE 11-13**   An ATM cell (UNI).

| 8 bits | 4 | 0 |
|---|---|---|
| GFC (Generic Flow Control) | VPI (Virtual Path Identifier) | |
| VPI | VCI (Virtual Channel Identifier) | |
| VCI | | |
| VCI | PT (Payload Type) | PRIO (Cell Loss Priority) |
| HEC (Checksum—CRC for Header Only) | | |
| 48 Bytes of Payload (Data) | | |

## 11-8    WIRELESS LANS

If you pick up any computer or networking magazine, you will find references to wireless LANs. In fact, your daily newspaper or general interest magazines are full of the latest scoop on wireless technology. Wireless LAN technology has been successfully implemented in a variety of situations. Doctors and nurses in hospitals can update patients' data from their terminals while visiting with patients in their rooms. Students have established study groups to share data as they work together. Warehouse workers use wireless LANs to exchange information with central databases, updating inventory counts as they ship or store merchandise. Wireless LANs are becoming more widely recognized as a general-purpose connectivity alternative for a broad range of situations.

**radiated (unguided) media**

**Radiated (unguided) media** (wireless) connections employ an antenna and the transmission of waves. Wireless communications can also take place through cellular telephone technology for longer distances, as in the case of Web-ready cellular phones, and through microwave or satellite transmission, both of which are used for WANs. The two types of connectivity used most often for WLANs, however, are radio and IR technology.

IR systems carry data using very high frequencies just below visible light in the electromagnetic spectrum. Opaque objects can block signals, however, so this technology is not suitable unless there is clear LOS. Distances between two devices are also very limited. IR is used to provide local area connections between buildings and in some wireless LANs, but the most common use for IR wireless is to connect a printer or wireless mouse to a laptop computer, or to "hot sync" personal data assistants.

### IEEE 802.11

**infrastructure mode**

**ad hoc mode**

Most modern WLANs today use radio technology based on IEEE 802.11 standards. The 802.11 system works in two modes: **infrastructure mode** and **ad hoc mode.** In infrastructure mode, communication to a wired LAN takes place through access points or base stations. Each access point and its wireless devices make up a basic service set (BSS). Two or more BSSs in the same subnet make up an extended service set (ESS). The farther away from an access point that the wireless device is located, the lower the speed of the transmission. Ad hoc (peer-to-peer) mode means that the wireless devices, usually laptop computers, can communicate directly with each other without the use of an access point. Wireless LANs use the CSMA/CA MAC protocol described in Chapter 10 and in the section on LocalTalk earlier in this chapter.

Three 802.11 standards are currently being implemented; the list reads like alphabet soup. Each standard defines a different physical layer.

**802.11b**    This set of wireless LAN IEEE 802.11 technologies was first introduced in 1997, and the first standard to be implemented was 801.11b (yes, *b* before *a*). It specifies 1–11 Mbps in the unlicensed 2.4 GHz radio band, and is generally known as Wi-Fi. Wi-Fi is still the most widely available and implemented wireless LAN, although newer technologies and standards now being developed may challenge that distinction in the near future.

The 802.11b standard also specifies direct sequence spread spectrum (DSSS) modulation, one of two methods of spread-spectrum transmission. As you remember, a constant frequency signal is easy to intercept, and is therefore not well suited to wireless communications because of its lack of security. It is also susceptible to interference. To increase signal reliability, DSSS sends data over several different frequencies at the same time, dividing the data stream into small pieces, each allocated to a frequency channel across the spectrum. Special pseudo noise codes (called chipping codes) are modulated with the data stream, and the signal is spread over a wide range of the 2.4 GHz frequency band. Receivers recognize a spread signal and return the message to its original form. This method resists the effect of narrowband interference, noise jamming, and unauthorized detection.

While 802.11b is used in home networks, it also offers a cost effective solution for large facilities like department stores and warehouses, where a wider range is important because fewer access points are needed than for other wireless systems. Many organizations are beginning to invest in WLANs, despite the security issues that must be dealt with to make Wi-Fi as secure as traditional corporate networks. UPS, expecting a 35 percent gain in productivity, is spending $120 million to equip its worldwide distribution centers with wireless networks. Boeing Co. is now equipping many of its jets with wireless technology so flyers can log onto the Internet for around $25 per use. The company expects to have almost 4,000 planes prepared with "flying cybercafes" by 2010. Of course, Wi-Fi is rapidly becoming the first choice for most home network users because it is less costly than other solutions.

orthogonal frequency
division multiplexing
(OFDM)

**802.11a** A newer standard named 802.11a transmits in the 5GHz band and is much faster, at 6 to 54 Mbps, though its range of 60 feet is shorter. For this reason, a larger number of access points are required to cover a large facility. 802.11a has also been called Wi-Fi5 because of its use of the 5 Ghz band. However, confusion among consumers has caused the Wireless Ethernet Compatibility Alliance (WECA), a leading standards body for wireless networking, to back off on adoption of the name. 802.11a uses **orthogonal frequency division multiplexing (OFDM)**, a next-generation modulation technique that handles the higher data rates that are required for multimedia applications. OFDM splits the data stream into multiple lower-speed subsignals that the system transmits in parallel, at different frequencies, and at the same time. The subcarriers are just far enough apart to avoid interference with one another (theoretically).

802.11a offers higher performance, supporting higher-end applications like video and voice, as well as the transmission of large data files and images. It also provides better security features, allows a higher concentration of end users, and can transmit data five times faster than Wi-Fi. Because it operates in the 5 GHz band, it avoids interference from the growing number of Bluetooth devices, 2.4 GHz wireless phones, and 80211b users. Greater total throughput makes it ideal for environments like airports, hotels, convention centers, and computer labs that need to support a higher population of users.

The main disadvantage to 802.11a is that it is not backward compatible with existing 802.11b systems, which number several million, because the two use different modulation types and radio frequencies. There is no provision for interoperability between the physical layers of the two standards. The future looks brighter for the creation of combination Ethernet cards, however. For the next generation of Microsoft Windows, only Ethernet cards that support both networks will be approved. An engineering company in London has developed a dual 802.11a/b chipset. Several other vendors—including Atheros Communications, Agere Systems, and Texas Instruments—are producing chipsets that support both systems. Future wireless radio LANs, therefore, should be able to "speak" both 802.11b and 802.11a, allowing devices to sense which standard an access point uses and to communicate accordingly.

**802.11g**    The newest version of the standard, 802.11g, was ratified by the IEEE on June 12, 2003. It combines the best qualities of 802.11a and 802.11b. It has two main attributes to commend it: a faster data rate than 802.11b and backward compatibility with 802.11b, which the 802.11a standard does not offer. The range of 802.11g is also wider than that of 802.11a. It is no wonder that several vendors were eager to release networking products before the new standard was ratified, even though their products conformed only to the 802.11g draft specification. In 2003, the chair of the IEEE 802.11 working group said that although "the IEEE is pleased to see early development of products based on our work, it is quite speculative to release products at this time." During the first quarter of 2003, according to a study by the Dell'Oro Group, products based on 802.11g accounted for 16% of the wireless networking market's revenue—before ratification!

802.11g works in the same range (2.4 GHz) as 802.11b, but at a faster data rate of up to 54 Mbps. In the 2.4 GHz band, it is susceptible to the same RF interference as Wi-Fi devices. Like 802.11a, it uses OFDM technology, enabling higher-end applications like video and voice. Unlike 802.11a, however, it is backward compatible with the older Wi-Fi standard and its access point will interface directly with an 802.11b card at 1–11 Mbps. Thus, existing systems will be able to be upgrade fairly easily.

In the 2.4 GHz band, 802.11g uses about one third of the bandwidth (30 MHz) for the transmitted signal, thus limiting the number of overlapping access points to three, the same as Wi-Fi. In contrast, the 802.11a standard, which operates at 5GHz with twelve separate nonoverlapping channels, allows 12 access points to be set at different channels and not interfere with one another.

## 802.11 Wireless Security Issues

Many organizations are not yet convinced that security problems have been dealt with adequately and hesitate to adopt WLANs. Although you will study network security in Chapter 17, it is important to consider this vital issue in relationship to wireless networks. Currently, wireless networks are fundamentally insecure, and updates to the 802.11 standards need to be implemented. WLAN security is a work in progress. Experts recommend that network administrators treat wireless stations as they would unknown users requesting access to network resources over an untrusted network.

**Wired Equivalent Privacy (WEP)**

Two reports from the University of California, Berkeley and the University of Maryland revealed the inadequacy of the original encryption technology, **Wired Equivalent Privacy (WEP)**. Flaws exist in any version of WEP, whether based on 40-bit or 128-bit encryption. The main problem is that it uses static keys. Shareware software, such as AirSnort, can break them after listening to only 100 to 1,000 MB of data. Most vendors even ship their products without having WEP enabled, and many users neglect to "turn it on."

**Wi-Fi protected access (WEP)**

In May of 2003, the Wi-Fi Alliance announced the certification of products using the latest security specification, **Wi-Fi protected access (WPA)**. Certification means that approved products should work with each other no matter which company manufactured the product. WPA replaces the existing security protocol, WEP, and is a subset of what will become the 802.11i standard. It offers better security than WEP, it is stable, and it can be achieved via software upgrades. In many cases, those who already have Wi-Fi networks will be able to upgrade via firmware supplied by vendors of their equipment.

With WPA, in contrast to WEP, the password entered only initializes the encryption process. The actual key changes constantly, because a new key is used every time a data packet is sent over the air. WPA works equally well with 802.11b, 802.11a, and the new 802.11g standard. The improved encryption technology is much more difficult to break than WEP.

**FIGURE 11-14** The 802.1X/EAP authentication process.

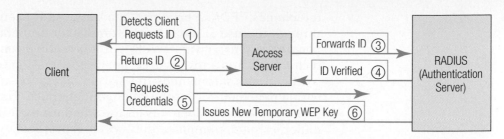

In corporate settings where WPA will work with authentication servers, IT personnel will be able to manage network security. In small offices or homes that don't have authentication servers, it will work in a preshared key-mode in which users merely enter the network key to gain access. WPA does not work in ad hoc mode where there is no access point or gateway and, by default, WPA will not be enabled after a user upgrades. As with WEP, those who desire the increased security it provides must remember to "turn it on." Additionally, each of the devices on a wireless network must be upgraded to WPA for the new standard to work. If any are still using WEP, the entire network will use the older, weaker security algorithm.

802.1X, the basic building block of Ethernet security, was ratified in June of 2001. It was originally designed for wired networks only. It requires user authentication before granting network access and, combined with the Extensible Authentication Protocol (EAP) standard, it handles authentication and key management. 802.1X defines the roles of the client, the access point, and the authentication server. EAP is the method used to exchange information among the client (supplicant), the access point or gateway (authenticator), and the network user system (authentication server). Figure 11-14 illustrates the process.

When a router or wireless access point (network access server) detects a new client, it sends a message requesting the client's ID. The client returns the ID and the access server passes it to the remote authentication dial-in user service (RADIUS) for approval. If the ID is valid, the client requests credentials from the authenticator using 802.1X and EAP. The authentication server issues a new temporary WEP key, and the access server allows the WEP session to proceed for the client. Thus, one of the key shortcomings of WEP is solved because keys can be unique for individual users and sessions.

The newer IEEE 802.11i standard incorporates 802.1X/EAP into wireless networking. It also has other, stronger encryption processes, such as **Temporal Key Integrity Protocol (TKIP),** which includes frequent updating of the encryption key. Also included in 802.11i is Counter with Cipher Block Chaining Message Authentication Code Protocol (CCMP), which is designed for future WLANs. It uses the current government approved encryption method, **Advanced Encryption Standard (AES).** AES replaces WEP and RC4 (the algorithm upon which WEP is based) and is more robust. The only problem is that older 802.11 hardware cannot be upgraded.

One other solution to the wireless security issue is the Virtual Private Network (VPN), discussed further in Chapters 12 and 17, which uses a public network—usually the Internet—to connect remote sites and users via a private "tunnel." Connection and data are kept secure through firewalls, strong encryption systems, Internet security protocols (IPsec), and AAA (authentication, authorization, and accounting) servers.

**Temporal Key Integrity Protocol (TKIP)**

**Advanced Encryption Standard (AES)**

## Bluetooth

**Bluetooth**

**Bluetooth** is a wireless standard that is used to emit signals over a relatively short range. It was originally built to connect devices such as PCs, cordless telephones, PDAs, printers, headsets, and eventually home appliances through the use of a microchip transceiver embedded in each device. Some people see it as a rival to Wi-Fi, but it is really intended as a different type of technology. It is a royalty free, open-specification technology.

Bluetooth was named after Harold Blaatand—a 10th century Danish King with a penchant for teeth-staining blueberries (can that be true?), who unified Denmark. The idea was for the standard to unify many different devices under a single, common digital wireless protocol to create a portable, ad hoc network. Some have called it a "cable replacement technology." Bluetooth is backed by a long list of influential supporters like Microsoft, Motorola, Nokia, Lucent, IBM, Intel, and Toshiba.

**piconet**

Bluetooth uses radio technology at a much lower power level than the 802.11 standards, and normally operates at about 720 Kbps with a range of about 30 feet. Bluetooth has a maximum capacity of 1 Mbps. A connection of from two to eight devices is called a **piconet.** Pico means $10^{-12}$, or one trillionth. Each device has a microchip embedded in it to receive and transmit radio signals in the 2.45 GHz range. The devices constantly send out messages looking for other devices and when they identify one another, they send signals to establish whether they will communicate or not, depending on the profiles coded into their hardware.

Bluetooth devices use spread-spectrum frequency hopping, changing their frequencies 1,600 times per second to prevent radio signals from interfering with other devices. A Bluetooth radio module hops to a new frequency as soon as it transmits or receives a packet. All devices on a piconet are peers. During a shared connection, however, to determine frequencies among which to switch, one device acts as master and the rest act as slaves. Piconets can link to one another, and Bluetooth devices can be part of several piconets. When a device from one piconet is also a member of another piconet, a

**scatternet**

**scatternet** is created. Figure 11-15 illustrates two piconets that have formed a scatternet.

Bluetooth is not designed to connect an entire network, but to connect devices point-to-point when speed is not an issue. It is well suited to applications such as using a mobile phone as a modem, "synchronizing" PDAs, or sharing printers and connecting other peripherals. Some useful applications for PDAs include chatting in real-time, using virtual whiteboards, and printing from Bluetooth enabled printers. Its proponents predict that Bluetooth will one day connect all home appliances within a 30–60 foot area.

**FIGURE 11-15** Two Bluetooth piconets create a scatternet.

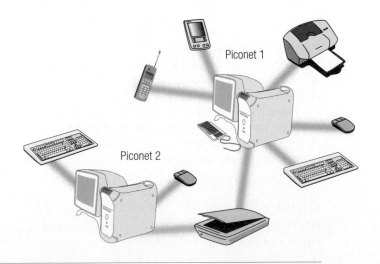

# HiperLAN2

Developed by the European Telecommunications Standards Institute (ETSI), *HiperLAN2* is one of a new generation of standards and competes with 802.11a and 801.11g. It operates in the 5 GHz frequency band, has a transmission rate of 54 Mbps, and uses OFDM to achieve its data rates. Developers boast that HiperLAN2 is as "future proof as possible," meaning that it not only satisfies today's needs, but it also envisions interoperability with future technologies and applications.

Although the physical layer of HiperLAN2 is almost identical to that of IEEE 802.11a, the two standards differ in their MAC layer, and in the way they form data packets and address devices. In many ways, HiperLAN2 is more like wireless ATM than 802.11a. Its data packets are equally sized and are formed with a payload of 48 octets. A convergence layer is needed to convert between it and other LAN formats. Several types of convergence layers, such as Ethernet, ATM, and 3G (proposed), have been defined and others can be added. The Ethernet convergence layer is supposed to make HiperLAN2 operate as a wireless Ethernet extension. It can be used as the "last hop" of a switched Ethernet. A HiperLAN2 network can run all applications that today run over a fixed infrastructure.

**mobile terminal (MT)**

In its network topology, HiperLAN2 looks like any other WLAN. A user's **mobile terminal (MT)** connects to the access point (AP) with the best radio signal (measured by the SNR), allowing the user to move around in the geographical area controlled by that access point. The MT requests "handover" if an AP with a better signal strength is available. This allows the MT to continue communication; however, some packet loss may occur during the handover.

**centralized mode**

**direct mode**

**Centralized mode** (infrastructure or network mode) refers to communication between an AP and the MT. **Direct mode** refers to communication between two or more MTs (peer-to-peer) for ad hoc networking. Figure 11-16 illustrates a HiperLAN2 network in centralized mode.

Unlike other WLAN standards, HiperLAN2 is a connection-oriented technology like ATM. Data are sent on connections that have been established prior to transmission. Connections can be either point-to-point (bidirectional) or point-to-multipoint (one way toward the MT). There is also a dedicated broadcast channel that can transmit from one access point to all its mobile terminals.

**time division duplex (TDD).**

The access point schedules traffic to optimize the use of radio resources. This is especially important when the number of users increases. Traffic is transmitted in a 2 ms. MAC frame that contains user data for both uplink and downlink directions, in addition to the protocol control information. HiperLAN2 refers to this slotted structure as **time division duplex (TDD)**.

**FIGURE 11-16** A HiperLAN2 network in centralized mode.

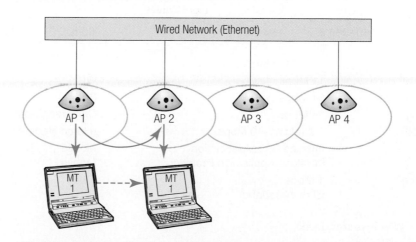

quality of service (QoS)

For the uplink, the AP assigns a descriptor in the MAC frame for each mobile terminal specifying when and how long an MT is allowed to transmit. For each MT, traffic resources for both uplink and downlink directions can be dynamically allocated. Data are carried over multiple connections and a user can have several connections established, each assigned a specific **Quality of Service (QoS)** to prioritize traffic for different types of applications and levels of users. Thus, bandwidth can be managed with a predictable performance for each user and application.

This ability to guarantee specific bandwidth to specific users is one of the features that appeals to those interested in new WLAN technologies. Another important feature of HiperLAN2 is its automatic frequency allocation, whereby an AP can listen to other APs as well as all radio sources in its area, then select an appropriate radio channel to minimize interference with its environment. Finally, at a time when security is one of the major concerns for those considering a WLAN, HiperLAN2 networks purport to have a high level of security, including authentication. To learn more about HiperLAN2, visit the Global Forum at http://www.hiperlan2.com.

## Wireless Summary

Wireless networks are the hot topic in LAN technology today. An excellent website, http://www.80211planet.com, contains news from around the globe as well as tutorials, product reviews, and lively forums. Each month, new articles come out in magazines, newspapers, and on the Internet. Wireless networking equipment sales jumped 80 percent in the year from 2000 to 2001, and the number of wireless users grows every year. Even in an economy where other computer and network technologies are struggling, the number of WLANs continues to grow. One market research firm, IDC, predicts that by 2005, the wireless networking market will reach $3.2 billion. The market will continue to grow as commercial networks develop, technology advances, and grassroots groups proliferate. While removing physical constraints frees people to use networks in ways they never thought possible, it also creates WLAN users' most pressing concern—security. Figure 11-17 summarizes the most common wireless standards and their characteristics.

| Standard | 802.11b | HomeRF | IrDA | 802.11a | 802.11g | Bluetooth |
|---|---|---|---|---|---|---|
| Application | WLAN | WLAN | Device Beaming | WLAN | WLAN | Personal Area Network |
| Maximum speed | 11 Mbps | 10 Mbps | 4 Mbps | 54 Mbps | 54 Mbps | 1 Mbps |
| Frequency | 2.4 GHz | 2.4 GHz | Light Waves | 5 GHz | 2.4 GHz | 2.4 GHz |
| Indoor range | 150–300 ft. | 150 ft. | 1 m | 60 ft. | 150–300 ft. | 30 ft. |

| | | | |
|---|---|---|---|
| 1997 | 802.11 | 1 Mbps–2 Mbps | |
| 1999 | 802.11b | 11 Mbps max | Wi-Fi |
| 2002 | 802.11a | 54 Mbps | (Wi-Fi5) |
| 2003 | 802.11g | 54 Mbps | Combines Best Aspects of a and b |
| 1998 | HomeRF | 1.6 (older)–10 Mbps | (Home Radio Frequency) |
| 1993 | IrDA | Infrared Data Association | Mobile |
| | WAP | Wireless Application Protocol | Mobile |
| 1995 | Bluetooth | 1 Mbps | PANs |
| | UWB | Ultra Wideband | |

FIGURE 11-17   Wireless standards.

Corporations and organizations that want to save money on cabling and technology infrastructure, as well as avoid the hassle of transporting equipment or ripping out wires when moves are made, account for a large part of the growth of wireless networking. Part of the popularity of Wi-Fi, however, is due to the way it has expanded the boundaries of the Internet. Wireless nets are popping up in airports, cafes, and other new "hotspots," where broadband Internet access is available to anyone who has an antenna. Several companies, such as Boingo (http://www.boingo.com) offer access to Wi-Fi networks for a small fee. The number of "hot spots" nationwide quadrupled in 2002 to almost 4,000. For an ever-expanding list of wireless access points (many of them free) around the world, go to http://www.80211hotspots.com.

**open nodes**

**war driving**

**war chalking**

Wireless networks have even spawned several new terms. Some grass roots, public-minded groups offer free public access and peer-to-peer networking, although ISPs (and others) complain they use up bandwidth without paying for it, and allow others to freeload. One listing of such **open nodes** can be found at http://opennodes.org. A new pastime around the globe, which has gained momentum among security analysts, hobbyists, and hackers alike, is called **war driving**. It involves roaming with a laptop computer, a wireless NIC, and appropriate software (and sometimes a high gain antenna) to search for wireless networks. War driving has become so popular that an information architect in the United Kingdom named Matt Jones developed a way to alert others to the location of free wireless Internet access. His symbols, which he calls **war chalking**, are based on the chalk drawings that hobos used during the Great Depression in the 1930s to mark the location of free food or lodging. He posted his original symbols, illustrated in Figure 11-18, on his website, http://www.warchalking.org, in June of 2002 and invited others to help him develop the new language.

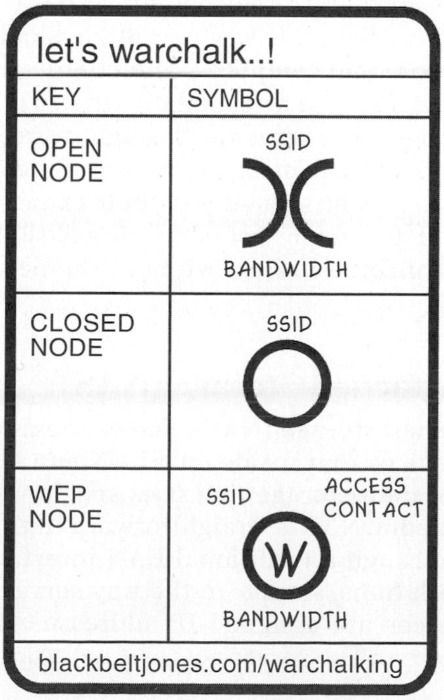

**FIGURE 11-18** Original war chalking symbols. (Courtesy of Matt Jones, www.warchalking.com).

These warchalking symbols were written on a sidewalk to provide information about a nearby wireless network.

## 11-9    NETWORK STORAGE

The topic of LAN technology would not be complete without a discussion of storage for the ever-increasing mass of data with which organizations have been overwhelmed in recent years. As companies use online transaction processing and databases more frequently, and as more and more industries become dependent on bandwidth-hungry multimedia technologies, the amount of information that needs to be managed and stored can become intimidating even to the most experienced network administrators. The need for centralized data management, company growth through mergers or acquisitions, and government regulations that require longer periods for data storage also contribute to the need for faster, more efficient solutions.

Basically, network storage is simply about using a method that makes data accessible to users on the network. It is also about taking some of the pressure off LANs. Data storage has evolved through various phases because of the change in the way we use technology, the volume of data that needs to be stored, and the new developments that make the effective storage and management of that data possible.

In the days of mainframe computers, data was accessible only through processing units, though it was stored physically separate from the actual computer. As personal computers and client/server networks became popular, storage devices were attached directly to a host system, as either an internal hard drive in the server or through storage devices in an external box. Although this is still the most common method of data storage for computer systems and servers do a good job, their capacity is limited. There can be a "bottleneck" if too many users try to access the same information. New technologies continue to improve both the accessibility and speed of data retrieval.

### Network Attached Storage (NAS)

**network attached storage (NAS)**

**Network attached storage (NAS),** one of the newer technologies, is a device or group of devices that reside on a LAN and are dedicated to storage. NAS is a method of data storage that uses special devices connected directly to the network media. NAS is straightforward in that storage devices connect to the network through a traditional LAN interface, such as Ethernet, and attach to network hubs, similar to the way servers and other network devices do. These devices are assigned IP addresses and can then be accessed by clients via a server. The server acts as a gateway to the data or, in some cases,

**FIGURE 11-19** NAS.

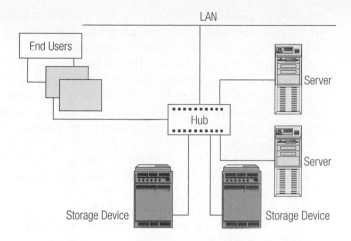

allows the device to be accessed directly by the clients without an intermediary. Figure 11-19 shows an example of NAS.

The advantages of the NAS structure are that storage, security, management, and backup of the data can be centralized. NAS can also expand easily when the LAN needs more storage space by simply adding another NAS device. When storage is directly attached to the host system and a server goes down, the data on the server are no longer available. With NAS, the data are still accessible by clients on the network.

## Storage Area Networks (SAN)

storage area network (SAN)

redundant array of independent (or inexpensive) disks (RAID)

**Storage area networks (SANs)** actually constitute a second network and offer even greater levels of speed, accessibility, and reliability. No, a SAN is not simply NAS spelled backwards. It is a dedicated network of storage-related devices such as tape backups, hard drives, and disk arrays—**redundant arrays of independent (or inexpensive) disks (RAID),** as illustrated in Figure 11-20. The devices are connected to each other and to a server, or a cluster of servers, and communicate directly with each other over very fast media. A SAN is a separate network physically removed from, but still connected to, the main network. Users gain access to the storage devices through server systems connected to both the LAN and the SAN. Data are kept on the SAN, but are immediately accessible to users. For

**FIGURE 11-20** Storage Area Network (SAN).

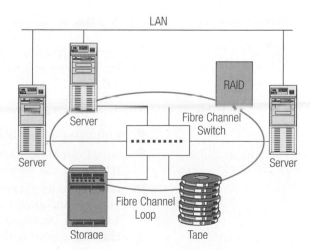

large organizations that have a need to centralize or streamline data storage, they provide a perfect solution, although their price tag is high for small or even medium-sized companies.

**third party copying**

A SAN provides the ability to back up all data on a LAN without having to burden the network infrastructure with gigabytes of data. Serverless backup, often referred to as **third party copying,** allows a disk storage device to copy data directly to a backup device across the high-speed links of the SAN without any intervention from a server. Though they can be as far as 10 kilometers (6 miles) away, devices on a SAN write to the network storage resources directly, as if they were internal drives. This is just one of the advantages of a SAN that now makes it a popular choice with companies. It has also prompted some people to forecast that it will become the favorite data storage technology of the future. SANs will account for 70 percent of all network storage by 2004, according to research company IDC (http://www.idc.com).

There are several other advantages to SANs. When more storage is needed, additional drives can be added to the storage network and can be accessed from any point, rather than connected to a specific server. Additionally, SANs can:

- provide alternative paths from server to storage device. That is, if a particular server is unavailable or is just slow, another can provide access to the storage device
- provide for making multiple copies available, mirroring data
- allow for the addition of bandwidth without polluting the main LAN
- make it easier to conduct online backups without creating bandwidth pinch
- allow all the devices to be centrally managed as a single entity

## Fibre Channel

**fibre channel**

In a SAN environment, storage devices are connected via a high-speed interconnection such as **fibre channel,** a set of communication standards developed by ANSI. Just as the Small Computer System Interface (SCSI) allows data to move quickly in and out of a computer microprocessor and its peripherals, fibre channel allows information to move quickly in and out of a LAN and its SAN. Fibre channel can move data at speeds up to 1 gigabit per second, and 10 Gbps speeds will be implemented in the future. It also allows for devices to be connected over much greater distances than other technologies—up to 10 kilometers—and allows devices to be placed in the most appropriate physical location. This distance capability allows storage devices to be placed offsite, making fibre channel a good choice for disaster recovery as well.

Fibre channel can be used in a:

- point-to-point configuration between two devices.
- ring-type model known as a fibre channel arbitrated loop (FC-AL), arbitrated on the basis of level of privilege.
- fabric model (star topology) of one or more fibre channel switches in a single configuration that can connect up to $2^{24}$ devices in a cross-point switched configuration, which allows many devices to communicate at the same time without having to share media.

**FIGURE 11-21** A SAN with a fibre channel interface.

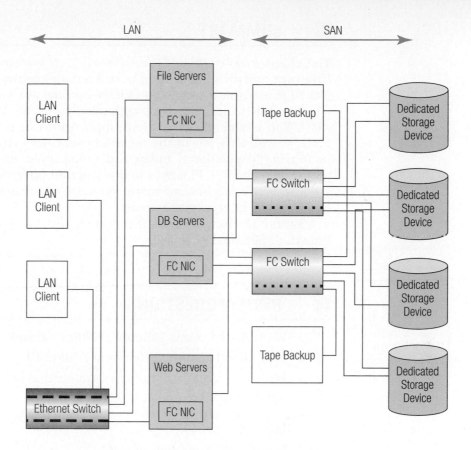

fibre channel switch

Devices on the SAN are normally connected through a special **fibre channel switch,** which performs basically the same function as a switch on an Ethernet network. Because fibre channel is a switched technology, it can provide a dedicated path between devices in the fabric so they can use the entire bandwidth for the duration of the connection. The storage devices connect to the fibre channel switch using either MMF (up to 2 kilometers) or SMF (up to 10 kilometers) cable. Special fibre channel interfaces in the storage devices provide connection. They can be built-in adapters in storage subsystems designed for SANs, or interface cards installed in server systems like NICs. Figure 11-21 shows a SAN with a fibre channel interface.

In addition to its role in SANs, fibre channel is also used in applications that require high bandwidth, such as real time audio and video file transfer, and in video playback applications for post-production digital video and movie studios, as well as in the broadcast backbone.

The trend is toward converging SAN and NAS technologies to take advantage of the strong points of both. For further reading, the Fibre Channel Industry Association (FCIA) at http://www.fibrechannel.com provides excellent information on fibre channel SANs. It also explains new advances in the technology, like **Internet Small Computer System Interface (iSCSI),** a technology that allows data to travel to and from storage devices over an IP network like the Internet. iSCSI is used to bridge SANs together and uses a combination NIC and SCSI controller that is a PCI-based interface card. Another new technology, Storage Wide Area Networking (SWAN), expands the scope of the SAN and allows fast backup of data to a remote location (fibre channel nodes can be no more than about 10 km apart).

Internet Small Computer System Interface (iSCSI)

## ■ SUMMARY

This chapter has examined the different LAN systems that are now available. Ethernet, and all of its variations, still remains the most popular type of LAN, although many new technologies have become available in the last few years. Gigabit and 10GigE backbone technologies enable faster and faster connections. You examined the various applications of token ring and the FDDI LAN, as well as a few of the lesser-known LAN systems. Wireless LANs are increasing in popularity today, and you studied several different technologies in this chapter. Finally, you investigated different solutions for network storage, which has become more and more necessary to handle the data deluge faced by many organizations.

Chapter 12 discusses LAN installation and operation and the recent rapid growth of personal networking.

## ■ REVIEW QUESTIONS

11-1. What do the terms 10Base-T, 100Base-T, and 1,000Base-T mean?

11-2. How does 10Base-T differ from 10Base-F?

11-3. Which Ethernet technologies are commonly used as the backbone in many networks?

11-4. Explain the difference between a shared medium hub and a switching hub.

11-5. Explain the functions of a MAU.

11-6. How does FDDI differ from IEEE 802.5?

11-7. What are the main characteristics of the FDDI and FDDI-II standards?

11-8. How does FDDI differ from the CDDI?

11-9. Compare and contrast Ethernet with a token ring LAN.

11-10. Compare ARCnet and Ethernet. Why has ARCnet lost in popularity to other technologies, such as Ethernet, token ring, and FDDI?

11-11. What are the services provided by IEEE 802.11?

11-12. Compare and contrast infrastructure and ad hoc modes.

11-13. Explain the major differences among 802.11b, 802.11a, and 802.11g.

11-14. What is the function of OFDM and why is it used?

11-15. How does Bluetooth differ from other wireless standards?

11-16. Explain the differences between a piconet and a scatternet.

11-17. Compare and contrast HiperLAN2 with 802.11a.

11-18. Discuss the advantages and disadvantages of WLANs.

11-19. Compare and contrast NAS with SANs.

### TRUE OR FALSE

11-1. Ethernet is the most widely used LAN technology today.

11-2. A single shared medium of an Ethernet is called a segment.

11-3. The most commonly used medium in Ethernet is coaxial cable.

11-4. Gigabit Ethernet is usually carried on optical fiber.

11-5. A shared medium hub reads the destination address of the packet and sends it to the proper port.

11-6. 10 Gigabit Ethernet transmits data at 10 million bits per second.

11-7. Token ring is the oldest of the LAN technologies.

11-8. Token ring LANs have more collisions than Ethernet LANs.

11-9. Token ring LANs are normally installed in a star topology.

11-10. FDDI usually uses optical fiber as its transmission medium.

11-11. MMF can deliver connectivity over longer distances than SMF.

11-12. 802.11b transmits in the 5 GHz band.

11-13. 802.11g has a faster data rate than 802.11b, and its range is wider than that of 802.11a.

## MULTIPLE CHOICE

11-1. A separate network that is physically removed from, but is connected to a LAN and that houses data immediately accessible to users is called a _____.

a. NAS

b. DNA

c. SAN

d. VPN

11-2. A wireless standard used to connect short range devices is called _____.

a. Wi-Fi

b. Bluetooth

c. Blaatand

d. Shortrun

11-3. 802.11a uses a modulation technique that handles higher data rates. It is called _____

a. DSSS

b. QAM

c. FHSS

d. OFDM

11-4. 802.11b is a wireless technology with devices using radio technology known as _____.

a. FHSS

b. DSSS

c. OFDM

d. RUSS

11-5. The main disadvantage to 802.11a is that _____.

a. it is slower than other technologies

b. it shares the same band with cordless phones and microwaves

c. it is not backward compatible with 802.11b products

d. it is less secure than other wireless standards

## ■ PROBLEMS AND PROJECTS

**11-1.** Draw diagrams and describe the operation of LANs implemented using the 802.3, 802.4, and 802.5 standards.

**11-2.** Do some research to find out how the disks on LAN servers are most commonly backed up.

**11-3.** Talk to a network administrator at your school or organization. What are his or her responsibilities? What is the LAN's architecture? If there is more than one LAN, are they interconnected? How? What is the greatest challenge facing the LAN administrator?

**11-4.** What type of wiring is used in your school's network? Are different types used in different locations? Find out why such choices were made.

**11-5.** More and more universities, colleges, and other organizations are using wireless LANs rather than, or in addition to, wired networks. Find out if your school has wireless LANs, how widespread their use is, and why they were implemented where they are used.

**11-6.** If you had to choose between NAS and a storage area network for your corporation, which would you choose? Discuss the pros and cons of each choice. What would the deciding factors for your decision be?

## LORDSBURG UNIVERSITY UNPLUGS ITS DORMS

Information technology (IT) budgets are always too low, and there are never enough personnel to handle the steady stream of problems that pour into a network administrator's office. "I know I've had a good day when no one calls to complain," says Craig Packard. Craig, who works at a small liberal arts college in the southwest, actually wears three hats: network administrator/engineer, network analyst, and network and node security administrator. He is an hourly employee and he puts in long days, often twelve hours or longer. It is as a security administrator that Craig has been especially challenged during the last year or two.

Security looms as the greatest challenge and the greatest budget concern for network administrators everywhere. While over $300 billion was spent worldwide on Y2K remedies, only 1/12 of that amount is being spent on security. Security threats are not predictable or finite, as was the threat of Y2K problems, but it is sometimes difficult to convince management of the fact that they can be not just inconvenient, but catastrophic to any network, including a college campus.

"There is always a security concern or equipment concern on a network," Craig says. "These threats will exist as long as a network exists." Invasions from other nodes, viruses, worms, stealth trojans, and attacks through many ports are becoming more and more common today. Breaches in security and an increase in the number of attacks through messaging technologies are on the rise.

For Lordsburg University, the main sources of concern were the dormitory LANs, which were part of the campus-wide system and shared Internet connection and bandwidth with all departments. Security for the campus network was threatened by students who could deliberately launch an attack on the Lordsburg University system, particularly between 7 p.m. and 7 a.m. when administrators were not on campus. They could also unwittingly infect the main system through worms or viruses they received by e-mail, messaging, or Internet chats. Much of Craig's time, and that of the assistant administrator, was taken up in troubleshooting and monitoring dorm network activity.

Another problem posed by the dorm LANs was the draining of valuable bandwidth resources. Students running peer-to-peer applications and downloading bandwidth-hungry video and audio files caused administrators to realize that bandwidth reallocation to more important academic and administrative systems for business and instructional needs was imperative.

The need was to implement greater safeguards to the main network system and reallocate bandwidth before the beginning of the fall semester. The challenge was to do so without taxing an overworked IT budget and without disallowing student access to the Internet. Craig and the assistant administrator needed to spend their time more productively than in watching the dormitories constantly and troubleshooting the additional security breaches and server downtime resulting from denial of service attacks primarily caused by student use or misuse.

Information Technology Director, C. H. Brown, scheduled a special network support team meeting to address the problems. After a spirited discussion of all aspects of the problem, the committee decided to move the dorms off the main network, outside the campus firewall, and provide them with separate internal wireless 802.11b networks with DSL Internet connection.

## QUESTIONS

1. Do you think the decision to create WLANs for the dormitories was a wise decision? What concerns did the solution resolve?

2. What additional future problems could the decision cause? What are some precautions that need to be considered because of them?

3. What additional costs did the move incur? Do you think that the benefits outweigh the new concerns and the additional costs? Why or why not?

# LAN INSTALLATION AND OPERATION

## ■ OUTLINE

## ■ KEY TERMS

application program interface (API)

crossover cable

industry standard architecture (ISA)

internet connection sharing (ICS)

Internetwork Packet Exchange (IPX)

Linux

Network Basic Input-Output System (NetBIOS)

network operating system (NOS)

patch cable

peripheral component interconnect (PCI)

personal computer memory card interface adaptor (PCMCIA)

phone line network

power line networks

proxy server

Sequenced Packet Exchange (SPX)

tunneling

UNIX

uplink port

virtual private network (VPN)

# ■ OBJECTIVES

After you complete your study of this chapter, you should be able to:

- discuss the criteria for selecting an LAN technology;
- describe the factors that affect LAN performance;
- describe the tasks involved in a typical LAN installation;
- explain the necessity for LAN management and the types of problems that may be encountered;
- discuss the necessity for maintaining LAN security measures;
- describe and explain the purpose of a VPN;
- explain the reasons for installing a home network;
- describe what choices are available for home networks; and
- discuss the process of setting up a home network.

## 12-1   INTRODUCTION

LANs are an important, fast-growing subset of the total network environment. You have studied the various elements of a LAN in the last two chapters, but the technology is developing rapidly. As quickly as new standards are finalized, others are under development. A LAN designer is faced with a wide variety of choices for building a network. Only by understanding the characteristics and tradeoffs among various types of LANs can the designer reach a reasonable solution for a particular organization or application.

After the LAN is installed, it must be managed. Security implications must be considered, and LAN performance must be monitored and tuned. A recognized network administrator who has the backing of management is a necessity for ensuring that the LAN is well controlled and operates effectively to meet the changing needs of its users. This chapter discusses the selection, implementation, and management of a LAN, first in the context of business organizations, and then in the rapidly growing area of home networking.

## 12-2   LAN SELECTION CRITERIA

Choosing a LAN from the many alternatives available is not an easy decision for several reasons. First of all, LAN technology continues to evolve at a brisk pace, and a system that is fully featured today may be only an average system or even an outdated one in a couple of years. More important than the technology change, however, are the needs of the users or potential users of the LAN. Their needs also continue to evolve. It is important to do some long-range thinking, planning, and forecasting for the ways a LAN might evolve before any decisions are made about the original implementation.

Whereas an initial sponsor may champion the installation of a LAN, participation and buy-in from a variety of people is desirable. Forming a committee or "LAN selection team" to study and recommend a specific LAN may be the best way to ensure participation and understanding of the LAN's implications. Participants should include prospective users of the LAN, technical and managerial representatives from the information technology department, and one or more representatives from general management. A broad view of the organization's business requirements, along with the specific needs of one or more user departments, brings a balance to the group.

It is very useful—and highly recommended—for people to make a management-oriented checklist of the criteria to be considered when choosing a LAN. A simple checklist is shown in Figure 12–1. This sample list serves as a good starting point, although it is neither complete nor in priority sequence; each organization may have very different considerations. Large organizations may need to ensure that a new LAN can be connected to other existing LANs or WANs. This obviously would not be a factor for a smaller company installing its first network. Each organization or department needs to make its own list, customized to specific circumstances.

The most important considerations, however, relate to the entire organization. Its requirements need to be defined, understood, and agreed upon first. Once they are understood, the choices for meeting these requirements (for example, what type of LAN, what type of cabling, and which network operating system) can be determined. Motives need to be tested against real business requirements because installing a LAN is potentially expensive and can certainly require a lot of time and effort. The decision should not be taken lightly.

Another point that should be considered carefully is who will be responsible for the LAN after it is installed. LANs constantly grow and change. A

**FIGURE 12-1** LAN selection criteria for managers.

☐ Objectives of the LAN: Why is it being proposed and what problems is it expected to solve?

☐ Number of users and their geographic spread

☐ Applications to be used

☐ Performance required

☐ Cost constraints

☐ Security requirements

☐ Availability of wiring that can be used, or must new wiring be installed?

☐ Availability and sophistication of technically trained people to install and maintain the LAN

☐ Vendor support and training provided

☐ Expected expansion of the LAN in the future
    in this department
    in other departments

☐ Workstations to be used: Readily available or need to be purchased?

☐ Other LANs in the organization

☐ Required interfaces to other networks

LAN administrator needs to be a person who can act as a "clearing house" for changes and day-to-day problems that arise. The identification of a LAN administrator and his responsibilities should be done before the LAN is installed, ideally while the evaluation and selection is being made.

One additional point that deserves mention is the economics involved with setting up a LAN. Costs of new workstations, servers, and software are always on people's minds when expenses are considered. Two costs that are often underestimated—or not even considered—are the cost of installing the wiring or cabling and that of upgrading existing workstations to operate on a LAN. An organization is fortunate if it can use existing telephone wiring for the LAN it plans to install. In many cases, however, new wiring must be installed, and the cost of doing so in existing offices can be high. The cost and nuisance of cable installation is one of the reasons so many organizations are beginning to install wireless LANs, although they too have their own set of drawbacks.

Some LAN planners also forget to include the expense of the NICs that have to be added to existing workstations to connect them to the LAN. While newer PCs may come with NICs already installed, older workstations may need to have cards added. Although the prices of these cards vary and continue to come down, the cost must be included. Cabling and the NICs can be a significant portion of the LAN's total cost. Some of the costs that need to be considered are shown in Figure 12–2.

It is very important to think about future growth requirements when planning the LAN. Saving money in the short term but inhibiting the ability to expand the LAN may be short sighted and costly. One of the worst scenarios is the case of installing a LAN and then having to tear it out a few months later to start over with new cabling, NICs, and software because the original LAN could not be expanded.

After all LAN selection criteria are identified and prioritized, they should be weighted. Some needs are more important than others. It is important to gain an understanding of which criteria the organization feels should carry the most weight in making the final decision about a LAN. Using the weights, points can be assigned to the LAN choices that are being considered as a way of quantifying what can be a fairly emotional decision.

**FIGURE 12-2** LAN cost considerations.

☐ Workstations: New or upgrade existing ones?

☐ Servers: Large personal computers, usually dedicated to performing the server function

☐ Printers: Upgrades to existing equipment or additional printers may be required

☐ Cabling: Cost of the cable itself and its installation

☐ Bridges, routers, brouters, gateways: Interface to other networks

☐ Software: NOS; updated, LAN-ready versions of applications; LAN management

☐ Training users and the LAN administrator

☐ Consultant, if one is used

☐ LAN administrator: Perhaps a new person or a new job for an existing person

☐ Maintenance: A contract with an outside company may be needed

☐ Space: Server and other network hardware should be in a secure location, preferably a locked room

After considering all the factors, the LAN selection team should make its recommendation, including cost and benefit estimates, to management. The final decision will be made by a manager who has sufficient authority and who is aware of the overall impact the LAN will have on the organization.

## 12-3   LAN PERFORMANCE

The performance of a LAN is based on several factors, including the protocol that is used, the speed of the transmissions, the amount of traffic, the error rate, the efficiency of the LAN software, and the speed of server computers and disks.

### Protocol

The CSMA/CD protocol provides quite good throughput, as long as the overall traffic load on the network doesn't exceed a certain threshold. When the load gets too high, more collisions occur, which means that a higher percentage of the traffic must wait before it can be sent. When traffic is below the critical point, however, messages can be sent almost immediately, so response time can be very fast.

Token passing protocols have the advantage of giving a guaranteed, calculable response time. This is possible because the time it takes a token to circulate on the ring or bus and the amount of time a workstation is allowed to keep the token or send data are known and controlled. However, because there is an inherent delay while the token circulates the best response time on a token-passing network may not be as fast as on the CSMA/CD network. Thus, token passing protocols have an inherent delay as a trade-off for their predictability.

### Speed of Transmission

Obviously, a LAN that transmits data at 100 Mbps can deliver a given message faster than a LAN that sends the data at 10 Mbps. In practice, however, the throughput of the former LAN is not ten times faster than the latter, because many other factors are involved in the overall LAN performance. One company reported that in its office environment, the installation of a 16 Mbps LAN to replace a 4 Mbps LAN was scarcely noticeable to most users who were doing transaction processing. The higher speed LAN did, however, make a difference during file transfers and situations in which it was used as a backbone, connecting several other LANs.

The widespread use of high-speed backbone LANs and LAN switches helps to improve the performance of the network component of LANs. Perhaps, however, it is better viewed as allowing the performance to keep up with the increasing demands of a larger number of users!

### Amount of Traffic

If a LAN is extremely busy, delays will invariably be introduced into some or all of the transmissions. Workstations may have to wait until collisions are resolved or the token is passed to get control of the LAN so their data can be sent. Some of the traffic may tie up the LAN for relatively long periods of time, causing still further delays. Generally speaking, a LAN that has a light load will deliver better performance than one that is heavily loaded. Splitting a LAN into segments, each with fewer users, and connecting the segments with a switch is one way that may help performance and throughput.

The ever-increasing demand for bandwidth, fueled by intranets and the Internet, continues to push network designers and vendors to find innovative and creative ways to obtain more capacity from existing network facilities and to install new, higher-speed facilities at accelerating rates.

### Error Rates

When errors occur, data must normally be retransmitted. For the user whose data were in error, there must be a delay. If the error rate and the number of retransmissions is high, all users may be affected—even those whose data are sent correctly—because the apparent traffic load on the LAN would be higher. In most LANs, however, because distances are relatively short, high error rates are not as big a problem as they can be with analog lines in a WAN.

### Efficiency of LAN Software

As with any software, some LAN software operates more efficiently than others and can deliver better throughput with a given set of hardware and LAN protocols. Reviews in PC or network magazines often measure the throughput and efficiency of various LAN software packages. Vendors are continually improving their products with new versions of the software, however, so the inefficiencies of a given piece of software may be corrected within a few months, when the next version of the software is released.

### Speed of the Server Computers and Disks

A server using a 2 GHz Intel Pentium microprocessor operates faster and generally delivers better performance than a server using a 500 MHz Pentium microprocessor. Similarly, disks that have faster access times provide faster delivery of data in response to a user's query than slower disks. The speed and efficiency of the server hardware/software combination have a significant impact on the overall speed and response time of a LAN.

## 12-4   INSTALLING A LAN

Once the LAN has been selected, it must be installed. This work usually falls upon people within the organization, although consultants can be hired to do all or most of the work or to oversee the portions, such as installing wire or cable, that employees may not be able to do themselves. Several suppliers of LAN hardware and software may have been contacted in the course of evaluating and selecting the LAN, and these companies may offer installation and maintenance services. Negotiating the installation should have been considered part of the LAN's total cost calculation.

Even if the basic work is to be done by an outside company, it is a good idea for the organization's LAN administrator to be involved in the installation process. By being involved, she can gain detailed knowledge of the LAN and its components, and will be better able to handle problems and make changes after it is operational.

**FIGURE 12-3** The tasks of installing a LAN.

☐ Install: New workstations
  NICs on existing workstations
  Wiring or cabling
  Server hardware
  Bridges, routers, brouters, or gateways
  LAN software

☐ Determine the access and capability required by each user

☐ Document the LAN's hardware and software configuration

☐ Train the users

☐ Begin using the LAN and its new capabilities

☐ Troubleshoot any startup problems

A list of typical LAN installation tasks is shown in Figure 12–3. As with any project, it is beneficial to have a project plan that identifies the tasks (in detail), the person or group responsible for performing the task, the date for starting the task, and the target date for completing the task. The sophistication of the project management process should, of course, be geared to the size of the project. Sufficient planning and control should be in place without burdening the project team with unnecessary overhead.

After the LAN software (discussed later in this chapter) is installed, it needs to be configured. Configuration entails telling the software, through parameters or tables, what resources are available and what capabilities each user should have. The hard disks on PCs other than the server are frequently considered "LAN resources," and are available for access and sharing. The LAN software needs to be told exactly what hardware is available. An important part of a network administrator's job is establishing and maintaining these resource tables.

Finally, at some point after the installation is complete and the users have been trained, the LAN is ready to be used. Despite the careful planning and testing that took place during installation, some problems will be apparent only after the LAN begins to be used. Some users may not be able to access data they need. The connection to another network may not work properly. There may be problems sharing server hardware or software. Performance for a certain user or group of users may be poor or worse than expected. The LAN administrator, the installation company, and the consultant need to be available to solve problems as soon as possible after they arise. Unless the LAN is very small, having a central place or telephone number for users to call to report problems—a help desk—is advantageous. It may also be desirable to keep a list of all outstanding problems and to update it daily (or as often as required) as problems are solved and new problems are identified. Gradually—and hopefully, quickly—the problems can be solved, the LAN operation will smooth out, and the benefits of the network will be realized.

## 12-5  MANAGING THE LAN

When companies or departments consider installing and operating a LAN, one of the most underestimated functions is ongoing LAN management. LANs are often proposed and installed by people who have very good technical skills but who lack an understanding of the necessity of managing the LAN on an ongoing basis and providing appropriate policies and procedures.

LAN cabling can quickly become like this if it is not managed. Using cable ties to group the cables and labeling them goes a long way toward improving the appearance, thereby making it easier to troubleshoot and maintain the network.

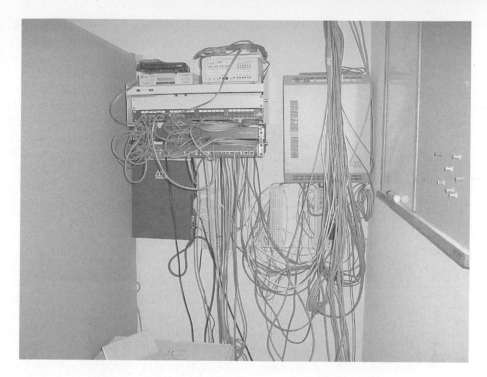

Many times, the need to physically protect the LAN hardware, to provide backup for the data stored on the file servers, and to establish procedures for authorizing access to the data are ignored. The need may only become apparent after a problem has occurred. LANs have a way of growing and changing, which mandates that some controls be in place.

Whenever a LAN is established, the following management items should be considered:

- **Organization and management**—A LAN administrator or manager should be formally designated. Policies and procedures should be established and communicated to all LAN users.

- **Physical safeguards**—LAN hardware, such as the cables and servers, should be physically protected from unauthorized tampering. Keeping servers in a locked room is the preferred technique.

- **Documentation**—The LAN must be documented. Documentation should include the network topology, types and locations of attached workstations, names and version numbers of installed software, and authorized users and their capabilities.

- **Change control**—Procedures should be established for making changes to the network or its software. These procedures should include notification to users, testing, and fallback plans.

- **Hardware and software backup**—Effective backup provisions and contingency plans for both the hardware and software must be made. Users will depend on the LAN to help them do their jobs.

- **Access to network facilities**—Adequate security mechanisms should be provided to protect access to network hardware, software, and data from unauthorized people.

- **Network application standards**—There should be adequate controls and training regarding applications to ensure compatibility, integrity, and effective application usage.

■ **Network performance monitoring**—Network performance monitoring mechanisms should be established to ensure effective network throughput, load leveling, and overall performance reporting.

From the preceding list, it is evident that establishing and operating a LAN is a task that needs good planning and control. In many ways, operating a LAN is like operating a small computer center. The LAN manager must consider and develop plans for most of the same items that a company's IT organization considers for a mainframe computer or collection of servers. For that reason, a central network group is responsible for the installation and control of the LAN in many organizations. Although this would seem to take away some of the departmental or workgroup autonomy often associated with LANs, it ensures that the network is managed properly and is protected from unforeseen problems.

## 12-6    LAN SOFTWARE

Simply connecting several microcomputers according to the rules of one of the architectures described in Chapter 10 or Chapter 11 is not sufficient to have a functioning LAN. Like the WANs you will study in Chapter 13, LANs must have software to control their operation. In fact, it is software that provides most of the capabilities that we associate with the LAN.

At the heart of any LAN is a variety of software, which provides much of the intelligence that tells the hardware how to operate. Each workstation connected to the LAN must have software that tells it how to communicate with the servers. Servers require software to perform their functions. Application software for a LAN may be different from software for a single PC because the probability exists that the software, and perhaps data files, will be accessed by more than one user at a time. Finally, there is a need for management software to provide commands for controlling the LAN and status information to the person who manages it. Each of these types of software is discussed in more detail in the following sections.

### Software for the Client Workstation

For PCs, the basic communications software for a LAN can be viewed as an extension of the operating system—an extension that provides the data link and network layer capability. Application programs communicate with the LAN through software called the **application program interface (API)**. In the IBM DOS "world," the operating extension, or API, is called **Network Basic Input-Output System (NetBIOS)**. NetBIOS operates at OSI layers 2 and 5 (the data link control layer and the session control layer). At the data link layer, it provides for applications programs to send and receive short messages, but without an acknowledgment. At the session layer, it supports two-way, reliable communications between applications programs, with acknowledgments that the messages have been received. At the higher level, a LAN workstation program uses NetBIOS and provides the capability for application programs in the PC to use servers and share network resources.

Microsoft Windows 98 and later versions include software modules to interface with a variety of LANs and server software. Normally, a user selects the one module that is appropriate for the network he or she will be using. Including basic networking capability with the general purpose operating system began with an earlier version of Windows, called Windows for Workgroups (also known as Windows 3.11). Versions before Windows 3.11 did not

*Marginal terms:*

**application program interface (API)**

**Network Basic Input-Output System (NetBIOS)**

include networking; therefore, the user was required to purchase additional software, such as Microsoft's LAN Manager, to add to the operating system. The inclusion of networking software is now standard.

One of the most notable developments that affects networking software for the workstation is the rise of TCP/IP to widespread use. If the TCP/IP protocol is included in the workstation software suite, it provides connectivity to almost any network that is also using TCP/IP software. In the past, it was almost mandatory to acquire all of the LAN software from one vendor in order to ensure compatibility. Novell's workstation software could only communicate with Novell's server software; Microsoft's workstation software with Microsoft's server software, and so forth. Because TCP/IP is now so widely used, it is much easier to build networks that use heterogeneous software, rather than the homogeneous networks of the past.

Dumb terminals need only basic communications software that allows them to interface with the LAN. Because these terminals cannot run programs, they need not share files on file servers or use other functions that PCs must. Thus, their software is much simpler and it is usually provided by a cluster control unit to which the dumb terminal is attached.

## Software for the Server

**network operating system**

Software for the server, often called the **network operating system (NOS)**, can be viewed as providing the overall control for a specific LAN. There is no standard configuration for a NOS, and different vendors implement NOS capability in different ways. Adding the LAN capability on top of an existing OS was the approach used by several vendors a few years ago, including IBM and Microsoft. Developing a separate OS specifically designed to support LANs, networking, and client-server configurations is the approach that both Novell and, more recently, Microsoft have used.

The implication is that you do not simply select a LAN architecture; the software must be selected at the same time. In fact, it may be argued that the software should be selected first; the hardware architecture is not really selected but depends on what the selected software will support. More and more network operating systems, however, are developed to interoperate with hardware from other vendors. Most users don't care whether their data are being transmitted using a token ring or an Ethernet. They are much more interested in such QoS parameters as ease of use, reliability, and speed.

LAN software must provide commands and information that assist in daily operation of the LAN. This capability is usually provided by the network operating system (NOS). Users may not be in close proximity to the LAN's servers, or the servers may be located in a locked room for security reasons. Therefore, it is helpful if the users can inquire as to the status of the servers. Knowing how many jobs are in the print queue may give some indication of when one's output will be printed. Knowing how many users are logged on to the LAN may give an indication of the response time and other performance levels that can be expected. Having the ability to send a message to all users on the LAN is useful so the LAN manager can inform people when the LAN will be taken down for maintenance. In addition to these daily operational types of commands, the LAN software should also collect statistics that show network usage over periods of time, such as a day, a week, or a month. This helps the LAN manager monitor growth and anticipate the need for additional disks, faster printers, or even a faster LAN.

Major suppliers of NOS software for LANs include Novell (http://www. novell.com/products/netware/), Microsoft (http://www.microsoft.com/windows/ default.mspx), Hewlett Packard (http://www.hp.com/country/us/eng/prodserv/

software.html), and Sun Microsystems (http://www.sun.com/learnabout/ solaris/). There are others, of course, but the products of these companies supply a very high percentage of the NOS market. The following paragraphs simply introduce the major NOS products, their capabilities and vendor-specific terminology, and provide references where you can find more complete information about each of them.

## Novell NetWare

NetWare is a NOS originally developed by Novell, Inc. in 1983 to run on a Novell proprietary PC, but it was later developed into a multiplatform NOS. There are several versions of the operating system, from those written to run on 286 machines (NetWare 286 version 2.x) to newer versions that run on virtually any size computer system—from PCs to mainframes. NetWare specifies the upper five layers of the OSI reference model and, as such, runs on virtually any data link protocol. NetWare has its own layer 3 and layer 4 protocols, called **Internetwork Packet Exchange (IPX)** and **Sequenced Packet Exchange (SPX)**, and provides full-function interfaces to networks using other protocols. Because of the need for Internet connectivity, however, it uses TCP/IP as the default protocol stack.

NetWare provides a complete set of LAN capabilities, including software for the management and operational monitoring of the LAN. The NOS provides a full range of distributed network services, including printer sharing, remote file access, and application support. Newer versions have also strengthened support for open source programs.

*To communicate with the NetWare server, a client must be configured with NetWare client software.* This was true on older versions of NetWare, but since the advent of NetWare 6.0, a workstation is not required to have a client loaded in order to access its resources. Novell has provided open Internet standards and Web browser access. NetWare 6.5, introduced in 2003, is based around standard protocols like HTTP, XML, WAP, and Java and will connect to just about anything. Users are able to print to a printer, access data, and run applications from anywhere, regardless of location or platform. If a user can log onto the Internet, he can use a Web browser to access the server remotely.

For example, suppose you are in a hotel that is 3,000 miles away from the office. You log onto the Web from your laptop, go to your company's URL, and gain access to whatever files or applications you request. The same is true whether you use your laptop, a Web enabled cell phone, or a Linux-based computer. NetWare 6.5 allows you to connect to your company's network from any nodes that uses standard protocols.

NetWare provides premium connection services for computers, peripheral devices, LANs, and WANs. Services include printing, storage, management, directory, Web, and security solutions.

- **Printing**—Netware 6.5 not only allows users to print to networked devices in a LAN, it also allows them to locate and print to printers anywhere in the world through the Internet. It enables users to locate printers on a map through the Web browser, then download and install drivers automatically using iPrint, one of the services included with NetWare 6.5.

- **Storage**—Both SAN capabilities for huge quantities of data (including backup restore and failover) and NAS support are included with Netware 6.5. NetWare allows network clients and application servers of all types to access and share stored files.

**Internetwork Packet Exchange (IPX)**

**Sequenced Packet Exchange (SPX)**

- **Management**—Included in the NOS is iManager, which allows Web-based management of resources and applications and the ability to manage eDirectory, DNS Server, FTP Server, iPrint, iSCSI, and other services.

- **Directory**—NetWare 6.5 includes the Novell eDirectory as well as DirXML, which has drivers for eDirectory, Windows NT, and Microsoft Active Directory. It synchronizes user data, passwords, and account information between dissimilar systems and applications.

- **Open source enablement**—NetWare 6.5 includes open source development resources including Apache Web server, MySQL relational database, Perl, and PHP (among others) to allow organizations to develop and host Web-based applications.

- **Security**—NetWare's security is based on some of the industry's strongest security mechanisms like RSA security technology and Secure Sockets Layer (SSL)—the leading security protocol on the Internet.

- **Web-based access**—With Virtual Office, iFolder, iPrint and other tools, users can access not only websites and e-mail from any Internet location, but can also access files, applications, printers, and collaboration tools—securely.

When installing previous versions of NetWare on a server, a volume called SYS was created. A volume is a partition on a NetWare server, and each partition has a name. You can create and name other volumes beyond the SYS volume to create areas on the disk drive for file storage and sharing. Since version 4.0, a hierarchical database called the Novell Directory Services (NDS) provides a tree structure, which has a root that you must name. You also create a context (usually the name of a company) that describes the position of all the network users, resources, and objects that are within the tree structure.

In NetWare 6.5, a DOS boot partition is required (as on older versions), but the bootable CD installation software creates it automatically, then starts the NetWare kernel and installs the Apache administration server and Tomcat application server. Other services can also be installed later. The OS configuration options allow you to choose manual or default settings. You can create a basic NetWare file server, a customized server, or any of several preconfigured types, like DNS/DCHP, LDAP, Backup, Web Search, Novell iFolder, iSCSI, Virtual Office, or any combination of these and other servers and services. Next, you specify a server name and IP settings, DNS Name and Name Servers, specify the eDirectory, and restart your computer. This description of the setup is simplified, but the actual installation is not complicated. Online help is available from http://www.novell.com.

## Microsoft Windows Servers

**WINDOWS NT SERVER (NTS)** Microsoft's NOS product for LANs has long been the OS called Windows NT Server. Like NetWare, it is a complete operating system that was designed to support LANs. NTS is a 32-bit operating system that provides a full set of server functions, including disk mirroring whereby two copies of data are written to two different disk drives. If one disk fails, the other copy of the data is still available. NTS also provides comprehensive security features. One of Windows NT Server's strengths is its support of applications, and it has become one of the leading pieces of software for applications servers. NTS supports TCP/IP, NetBIOS, Appletalk, and IPX/SPX protocols, so it can work with most networks and workstations, regardless of what protocols and software they use.

**WINDOWS 2000 SERVER**   This software allows file and printer sharing and allows the administrator to build Web applications and connect to the Internet, as well as run thousands of compatible business applications. This upgrade improves on NT's performance in many ways—by reducing the number of maintenance tasks that require rebooting; by providing resource partitioning, which prevents application failures from forcing reboots; and by enabling an administrator to completely shut down an application that is not functioning properly—all of which greatly decrease downtime. New boot options also let administrators restart the system quickly. Clustering technologies allow one server to assume the load if another fails, so the application keeps running. Load-balancing technology allows network traffic to be distributed across as many as thirty-two servers for increased performance and availability.

**WINDOWS SERVER 2003**   This software, launched in April of 2003, is a replacement for Windows NT and is a multipurpose OS. It can handle various server roles, either centralized or distributed, depending on your needs. These include file and print server, mail, remote access and virtual private network (VPN) server, Web and Web application services, directory services, Domain Name System (DNS), Dynamic Host Configuration Protocol (DHCP), Windows Internet Naming Service (WINS), and streaming media server.

Windows Server 2003 is intended to be a hub for Microsoft's new .NET products, such as e-mail, Web server, database, and software management programs that enable companies to make better use of their networks. There are basically four different products:

- The standard edition for departmental use and small organizations, which builds on Windows 2000 Server technology, but promises to be easier to deploy, use, and manage with greater security, reliability, and scalability.

- The enterprise edition, intended for medium to large businesses, provides support for high performance servers and differs in that it is able to cluster servers for greater load handling to keep systems available, even in the face of problems in a network. It is available in both 32-bit and 64-bit versions through original equipment manufacturer (OEM) partners.

- The datacenter edition, Microsoft's most powerful and functional server operating system ever, is also available in both 32-bit and 64-bit versions. It is meant to deliver mission-critical solutions for databases, enterprise resource planning software, high-volume, real-time transaction processing, and server consolidation.

- The Web edition is intended for easily deployed and managed Web serving and hosting. It is intended for building and hosting Web applications, Web pages, and XML Web services.

Enhanced technologies include network load balancing, server clusters, and ActiveDirectory service to provide a dependable server operating system—one that is faster and more robust over unreliable WAN connections. Common language runtime technology safeguards networks from malicious or poorly written code.

Security improvements include Internet Information Services (IIS) to provide reliable, secure, and manageable Web server capabilities over the Internet, intranets, and extranets; Public Key Infrastructure (PKI), which is overseen by the National Institute of Standards and Technology (NIST) and supports digital signatures and other public key-enabled security services;

and Kerberos, a powerful network authentication protocol originally developed by MIT as a solution to many network security problems.

Network management is carried out in Windows Server 2003 by the Microsoft Management Console (MMC) and Active Directory in a new task-based design. Administrators can perform most tasks from the command console with command line tools. Automated management tools include Microsoft Software Update Services (SUS) and server configuration and management wizards. Remote server administration allows administrators to manage a computer from any other computer on the network, and remote assistance allows them to control a remote desktop computer if a user needs assistance.

Microsoft has built several important networking enhancements in Windows Server 2003. These include Internet Protocol version 6 (IPv6), Point-to-Point Protocol over Ethernet (PPPoE), and Internet Protocol Security (IPsec) over network address translation (NAT), all of which will be discussed in the chapters dealing with internetworking and the Internet. Because more and more companies now communicate with customers and partners over the Internet, the importance of these improvements and others like IIS, XML Web Services, and the .NET Framework is that they make it possible for users to stay connected—from anywhere and on any device—over the Internet.

The enterprise and the datacenter editions also provide additional features such as cluster services which, according to Microsoft, "provide high availability and disaster tolerance for mission-critical database management, file sharing, intranet data sharing, messaging, and general business applications." Server clusters can be configured to handle NAS, SANs, and geographically dispersed clusters of servers.

The down side to this new Windows NOS is that Microsoft no longer intends to support Windows NT after 2004, and Microsoft products developed in the future will no longer run on NT. For this reason, many technology buyers are looking at less restrictive alternatives based on open source OSs.

## UNIX

UNIX

**UNIX,** a complex operating system that was written in the high level C programming language in the early 1970s, was initially designed for medium-sized minicomputers, then moved to more powerful mainframe computers, and finally to PCs. It provides multitasking, multiuser capabilities so that many people can use a single computer, and multiple programs can be run simultaneously. Unix was designed to let a number of programmers access the computer at the same time and share its resources. Legend has it that Unix was developed when the original programmers (including Kenneth Thompson and Dennis M. Ritchie who are credited for having developed the system) wanted to play an early computer game called Space Travel. The game, developed by Thomson in his spare time in 1969, is explained in an interesting article about the history of UNIX (http://www.bell-labs.com/history/unix/). It "simulated the motion of the planets in the solar system. A player could cruise between the planets, enjoy the scenery, and even land the ship on the planets and moons."

At a time when different brands of computers and even different computer lines from the same vendor couldn't talk to each other, the major contribution of the UNIX system was its portability. It permitted a move from one brand of computer to another, with a minimum of code changes. New versions of UNIX were backward compatible with older versions, making the task of upgrading easy. (What a concept!) Because the Internet ran on UNIX from its early beginnings, it was spurred on in its own development by the operating system.

UNIX, one of the most popular operating systems in the world, comes with hundreds of programs—some that are necessary for operation of the computer and some that provide additional capabilities. E-mail was first used on UNIX machines so users could communicate on the same mainframe computer via their terminals. Although it uses a command-line interface (CLI), graphical user interfaces (GUIs) have been designed to help users navigate. UNIX is often used in universities because it was originally distributed to them for free. When it moved into universities, programmers everywhere began to develop programs for UNIX, and hundreds of applications can be purchased today from third-party vendors. It provides a high performance network for database, application, and Web servers.

The UNIX system is functionally organized at three levels: the kernel, the shell, and the tools and applications grouped into categories like programming, word processing, or business applications. The tools add additional capabilities to the OS, and many have been developed by third-party vendors. The kernel schedules tasks and manages storage. It is the heart of the OS and controls the hardware and tells the computer what to do at the programmer's command. For instance, if one asks the computer to list all the files in a directory, it is the kernel that tells the computer to read all the directory files from the disk and display them on the screen. The shell acts as an interpreter between user and computer, then calls programs from memory and executes them.

A number of companies sell UNIX-based systems, such as Solaris from Sun Microsystems, HP-UX from Hewlett-Packard, AIX from IBM, and Tru64 UNIX from Compaq. The UNIX system has greatly influenced the entire computer industry for more than twenty-five years. Its visionary ideas of deliberate generality and openness have influenced a wide variety of later operating systems. The following two network operating systems are examples of UNIX-based systems.

**SUN SOLARIS**    The UNIX-based Solaris Operating Environment supports 32-bit applications and their data. Furthermore, its 64-bit technology is beneficial for high resolution graphics, computer-aided design, simulation, scientific data analysis, multimedia Web servers, and data warehousing applications. Resource manager software incorporated into the environment helps administrators manage system resources such as CPU, physical memory, and network bandwidth. Other features include disk and storage management, naming and directory services, and security features such as enhanced encryption algorithms and an enterprise firewall for network protection. Solaris IP multipathing enables a server to have multiple network ports connected to the same subnet. Mobile IP allows a mobile computer to communicate as if it were located on its home network, even if it changes its location to a foreign network. Solaris has built-in Linux compatibility.

**HP-UX 11.X**    Hewlett Packard's HP-UX 11.i is their newest UNIX OS, and it offers a choice of four different operating environments: Internet, enterprise, mission critical, and technical. The basic Internet HP-UX 11.i is designed for Web servers, content servers, and front-end servers and features manageability and interoperability as well as open-source development and deployment tools for Java and Linux APIs. The enterprise environment also includes tools to improve availability and response time under the heavy loads of database application servers and logic servers. The mission critical environment provides tools for the best possible availability, reliability, and performance of large, powerful, back-end application and database servers. The technical operating environment provides tools for high performance and stability in computation-intensive workstation and server applications. HP-UX 11.i allows system administrators to manage a multiplatform environment for Windows and Linux, as well as HP-UX.

## Linux

Linux

**Linux** (http://www.linux.com/) is a UNIX-like operating system that is different from all other operating systems in that it is free (like free speech) and its source code is available to anyone (it is open source software). Anyone can copy the source code, share it with friends, and make changes—as long as the modified source code is provided to everyone else. Linux was originally intended for use on home PCs, but it now runs on a wide variety of platforms.

Linux was originally developed in 1991 by Linus Thorvalds, a Finnish university student, at the University of Helsinki. It has evolved from the contributions of thousands of developers around the globe. There is no single owner of Linux. It is customizable, meaning that a user can pick and choose what features she needs. Support comes from the global, informal Linux user groups, which were presented with the *Infoworld* magazine Best Support award in 2001. There are millions of users around the world.

Among the strengths of Linux, other than the fact that it is open source software, are its stability and its speed. Linux machines have been known to run for years at a time without crashing, and they are efficient at handling resources like memory, CPU power, and disk space. Linux is made for networking, and most networking protocols in use on the Internet are native to Linux or UNIX, from which it is derived. After Linux is given the correct addresses, it handles most of the work necessary to set up a network just as other operating systems can. Linux is considered an excellent platform for developers because C, C++, and an assembler come by default on all Linux distributions, and a wide variety of other languages are also available. New varieties of software are constantly being developed because of the concept of open source, which keeps programmers around the world busy creating everything from household appliance control and World Wide Web tools to audio, video, and ham radio applications.

There are a number of different versions of Linux, including Red Hat (http://www.redhat.com), the best-known Linux distribution in the U.S. and the choice for companies using it for servers in a corporate setting. You can get it free on the Internet or you can buy it in a box from Red Hat or several retailers. Another version, SuSE, offers support for large-scale servers but is oriented toward home users and small offices. Linux-Mandrake (http://www.linux-mandrake.com) is downloadable free or for sale in boxed sets with support and manuals. Many people believe it is the easiest version for new users to install and learn. There are many other distributions available, and http://www.Dmoz.org has a long list of them.

For technical support and encouragement, Linux Users Groups (LUG) outshines the largest operating systems vendors in the world—and they are free! There are LUGs all over the world, and they hold local meetings and even "installfests" to help new users install Linux on their computers. Two lists of such groups can be found at http://lugww.counter.li.org/ and http://www.ssc.com/8080/glue/groups/.

## 12-7　LAN SECURITY

Providing appropriate security for the LAN, its data, and its users is the combined responsibility of management, the network administrator, and the LAN software. Management must set the environment by providing security policies and by communicating the message to all employees that security is important. They may also insist that regular audits of the LAN be performed to ensure that internal control requirements are being met.

LAN hardware, such as servers, hubs, and routers, should be kept in a locked room where unauthorized people cannot access them. The LAN administrator is normally responsible for this hardware, and it is her responsibility to ensure that the equipment is physically protected and secure.

**proxy server**

If the LAN is connected to the Internet, the installation of a **proxy server** should be strongly considered. A proxy server acts as an intermediary between the Internet and net-equipped computers. Whenever a net-equipped computer seeks to access a page on the Internet, it contacts the proxy server. The proxy server stands in for the PC and communicates with the Web directly, so others on the Internet do not know the actual terminal address of the workstation. Conversely, outsiders cannot get into the company's network without going through the proxy server. Another benefit of a proxy server is that it can give network administrators a level of control over the Internet habits of users on the network by filtering certain sites or restricting employees' access to nonbusiness-oriented websites. For further detail about how proxy servers work, see Chapter 17.

The network administrator is also the person responsible for maintaining the security and access control tables that are part of the LAN software. However, the administrator should establish and change those tables only with appropriate authority from management. A form should be used that shows the level of access for each user, and the user's manager should approve it. Subsequent changes should also be approved, and a LAN administrator should not make changes without proper endorsement.

These servers are mounted in racks for convenience. Large server installations are sometimes called server farms.
(Courtesy of University Corporation for Atmospheric Research. Photo by Lynda Lester. Reprinted with permission.)

Other policies and procedures, depending on the needs of the organization, may be required to ensure the right level of security and LAN management. Items to be considered include:

- Password policies regarding the use and frequent changing of passwords to be used when logging onto the LAN.

- A sign-off policy, requiring users to sign off the LAN when they leave their workstations.

- The encryption of data sent on a LAN or stored on servers.

- Regular backups of the server disks, usually a responsibility of the LAN administrator.

- Policies for downloading data from other computers or networks to the LAN disks.

- Policies regarding the scanning of disks for viruses.

- Policies regarding dial-up access to the LAN.

- Policies stating that only legal, licensed software may be used on the LAN.

By now it should be clear that operating a LAN in a safe and secure manner is a major responsibility that requires careful attention at both the managerial and technical levels of the organization. Another type of network also needs to be examined as we consider the importance of maintaining fast, secure, and reliable communications among members of business networks.

## 12-8   VIRTUAL PRIVATE NETWORKS (VPNS)

virtual private networks (VPNs)

As businesses have found that they must consider global markets to a greater extent than ever before, the Internet has also grown in its popularity. The use of **virtual private networks (VPNs)** has become important to many organizations that find themselves spread out around the world. Security is not the only reason that organizations implement a VPN. Companies are finding that they can expand networking capabilities and geographical boundaries, as well as reduce costs, by choosing VPNs over leased lines. Because a VPN often covers great distances, it is often used in WANs.

A VPN is a private network that uses public networks like the Internet as the medium to transport data and connect remote sites or users. It uses virtual connections that are routed through the Internet from the company's private network to remote users rather than using a dedicated leased line. A typical VPN might have a main LAN at the company headquarters, LANs at remote offices or facilities, and LANs for business partners and remote telecommuters or field workers. Figure 12–4 illustrates a typical VPN.

To protect sensitive data and communications from outsiders, a VPN takes advantage of several types of security provided by the real network on which it is riding. These include firewalls, encryption systems, IPsec, and authentication, authorization, and accounting servers. These technologies are discussed in Chapter 17. Many believe that VPNs are an ideal solution to wireless networking security needs because they provide encapsulation, authentication, and full encryption over WLANs.

Remote access, or user-to-LAN connections are intended for remote employees who need to connect to the private company intranet. Telecommuters, who have client software installed on their desktops, connect by dialing up the network access server that is set up by a third party enterprise

**FIGURE 12-4** A VPN creates a private connection of remote users over the Internet.

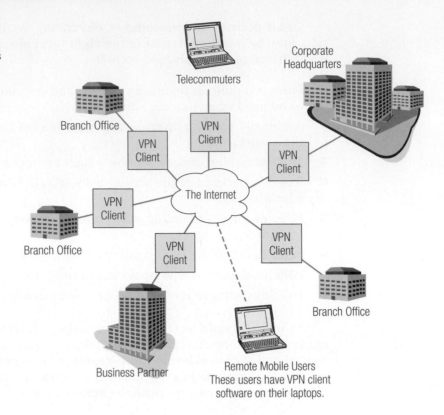

service provider. This type of VPN provides secure, encrypted connections between the employee and the company network through the service provider.

A site-to-site or LAN-to-LAN connection joins two networks to form an extension of a company's intranet or extranet. An intranet-based VPN allows remote offices to join in a single virtual private network over the Internet. An extranet-based VPN connects the LANs of various closely related companies, allowing them to work together in a shared environment.

**tunneling**

To reach through the very public Internet to form a secure private network, VPN technology uses a process called **tunneling,** which places one packet inside another to send it over the network. It requires three different protocols: carrier, encapsulating, and passenger. The passenger protocol is the original data being carried. The encapsulating protocol can be one of several and is wrapped around the original data. The following, which are not compatible with each other, are the most popular tunneling protocols:

- Point-to-Point Tunneling protocol (PPTP), which packages data in PPP packets to be carried by IP packets through the Internet. It supports 40-bit and 128-bit encryption and any PPP authentication scheme. It is used most frequently in Windows, which includes built-in client support for PPTP.

- Layer 2 Tunneling Protocol (L2TP), which combines features of a protocol developed by Cisco called Layer 2 Forwarding (L2F) with those of PPTP. It is primarily used in Cisco products.

- IPsec, a collection of many related protocols, can be used as an encryption scheme within the other two protocols or as a complete protocol on its own for VPNs.

The carrier protocol is the one used by the network over which the data travel. The protocol of this outside packet is understood both at the point

FIGURE 12-5  A corporate VPN using the Internet.

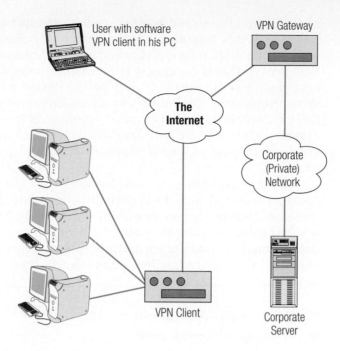

where the packet enters and where it exits the network. For example, packets in one of the VPN protocols are encapsulated within IP packets for Internet-based VPNs.

A company that wishes to build a VPN must acquire the requisite hardware and software for each of its sites and install it between its internal private network and the public network, as illustrated in Figure 12–5.

Each VPN system is then configured with the addresses of the VPN equipment at the company's other locations. Once the configuration is complete, packets are restricted from traveling outside the VPN. Furthermore, the system restricts outside packets on the public network from entering the VPN. When a user or computer at one site wishes to communicate to a person or computer at another site, the packets are routed to the local VPN node. The VPN node looks at the destination address, determines that it is valid, and then routes the packet across the public network to the destination site. When the packet arrives, the VPN node at the destination verifies that it came from a valid site on the VPN network, and then forwards the packet to the destination computer or user.

An excellent source for more information on VPNs can be found at http://www.vpnlabs.com, an open community for research, reviews, and discussion.

## 12-9   HOME NETWORKING

Home networking has become one of the hottest topics in networking. New technologies that make home networks easier to install and maintain are also more affordable. Although the U.S. still lags behind countries like South Korea and Taiwan, which boast almost 40 percent of users with broadband links, high-speed Internet connections to the home have become increasingly available, cost effective, and popular. Ten percent of all Internet users in the U.S. had broadband connections as of June, 2002. Broadband Internet access is one of the major stimuli to growth in the home networking industry. During the year 2002, broadband Internet usage soared 59 percent because Web users desired faster and faster speeds to conduct their online tasks. People have found that broadband access is actually cheaper in the long run than paying for a dial-up connection and a second phone line used exclusively for Web access. This is especially true if more than one user wants Internet access in a home. Interestingly, it is people between the ages of 55 and 64 who show the greatest inclination to adapt broadband services like cable and DSL, according to a Nielson study conducted from December, 2001 to December, 2002. The war with Iraq in 2003 also spurred the demand, as more and more consumers sought to acquire the most up-to-the-minute coverage of events.

The growth of wireless home networks has also added to the impetus, although the stimulus works in both directions—desire for broadband has also increased demand for home wireless networking. The prospect of connecting without cables is a definite plus for home users. Public awareness of these new technologies has propelled the sale of networking products to private users. More and more families are networking two or more computers in their homes to:

- share a high-speed Internet connection
- exchange files more easily
- share peripherals like printers
- play networked games

The requirements for home users differ in several ways from those demanded by businesses. Home users require ease of installation, reliability, scalability, and standards compliance. The ability to choose wireless networking is appealing to people who have been reluctant to string new wires throughout their homes. Many look forward to having the ability some day to control all home entertainment, household appliances, and data devices from a central location. Some users simply want the feeling of ownership that comes with having a home network.

One of the most important prerequisites for home networks is ease of installation. Most users just want to hook a few computers together to share resources and access the Internet without paying for multiple connections. They don't want to worry about the considerations that keep network administrators up at night. They simply want to connect, log on, and have fun or get something done. Home networks must be easy to install and simple to use with little maintenance. While new hardware and automated software installation have enhanced the ability to provide ease of use, nothing is ever as easy as it sounds. With some perseverance, however (and occasional visits from expert networking friends), home networking can be fairly simple—and very satisfying when it all works. Plug and play capabilities and home networking wizards in newer versions of Windows OSs have encouraged more people to get started. Increased reliability, the scalability of products to allow future growth and control of the network, and the adherence to IEEE, ANSI, and other standards by manufacturers have also spurred the growth of home data and entertainment networks.

Home networks can be configured as either client/server, in which all client computers connect to one that functions as the server, or as peer-to-peer, in which all computers share resources with one another. They can also be combination networks—connected to a server for accessing certain applications, yet retaining the ability (because peer-to-peer networking is built into the OS) to transfer files and access printers connected to other clients.

Before the actual setup, it is important to plan a home network. As in businesses, such planning helps home users to avoid unnecessary expenditures, hardware conflicts, and the need to replace current equipment after a short time. It is important to choose the type of network that is best for the situation and compare the advantages and disadvantages because each involves trade-offs. Hybrid networks that use both wired and unwired products are available for those who find it difficult to settle on one type. The most common network choices are Ethernet, wireless, phone-line, and power-line.

## Ethernet

Ethernet is the most popular, reliable type of network with the widest distance range available today. For high speed, scalability, and economy, it is still the best—although other types have gained momentum in the last couple of years. For wired networks, token ring and other technologies discussed in Chapter 11 are not recommended because they are unnecessary for home use. Another advantage is that because Ethernet is one of the oldest technologies, technical support is widely available.

## Wireless Networks

Among the wireless networking alternatives, 802.11b is currently the most popular though other standards like 802.11a, 802.11g, and HiperLAN2, which were discussed in Chapter 11, are being refined and may someday overtake it. Wi-Fi is reasonably priced—and getting more so—and quick to set up. Many hardware options are available, and though it doesn't always live up to its 11 Mbps promise, it is still fast enough for shared Internet access and file sharing.

## Phone Line Networks

**phone line network**

In a **phone line network,** computers plug into a nearby phone jack and use existing phone lines—without interfering with telephone use. Interference can occur because of the presence of other devices like fax machines and cordless phones, but inserting a low pass filter between them and their phone jacks should solve the problem. Products such as HomePNA are available in a kit that was developed by the Home Phone Networking Association (HPNA). Two PCs plug into the phone jacks, and Window's **internet connection sharing (ICS)** allows them to share one Internet connection. You need a HomePNA card or external adapter and the software for each computer. A hub is not necessary, and it is possible to connect up to twenty-five devices on a phone line network if that many phone jacks are available! Phone line networks are easy to install at low cost. However, because it acts like a hub, the PC connected to the Internet must remain on continuously. If it isn't on, no other PCs can access the Internet.

**internet connection sharing (ICS)**

## Power Line Networks

**power line network**

**Power line networks** allow computers to plug into existing electrical outlets in a home and into the parallel port of the computers to be connected. Home-Plug is one such product. One obvious advantage to power line networks is that every room in a home usually has at least one electrical outlet. Power line networking is theoretically the least expensive way to connect computers in a home, although prices for Wi-Fi have decreased enough that that may no longer be true. Power line networking is slower than other technologies

These Phonex Neverwire 14 adapters allow electrical power lines to be used as the media connecting devices on a network.
(Courtesy of Phonex Broadband. Reprinted with permission.)

and must plug into the wall, not a power strip. Because neighbors also share the same electrical transformer, data encryption is probably a wise course of action. Air conditioners, refrigerator compressors, and other high-power surge devices can cause power fluctuations that affect signals.

Manufacturers are beginning to create standardized technologies, and products like the Phonex Broadband NeverWire 14 offer several advantages. The Phonex does not require software and is supposed to work right out of the box. It consists of at least two "nodes." One node connects directly to the cable/DSL modem or router and plugs into any electrical outlet. The second node connects to the computer and plugs into a separate outlet. A Phonex network can handle up to 16 nodes and a range of about 1,000 feet. Though speeds of 14Mbps are promised, the network usually runs at more like 8 Mbps, and can be slowed by appliances such as halogen lamps.

## 12-10   COMPONENTS OF A HOME NETWORK

Because we have discussed phone-line and power-line networks in greater detail, we will now turn to installing the two most common networks: wired (Ethernet) and wireless (Wi-Fi). Setting up a home network involves three components: hardware, connections (cables or wireless), and software. There are several different arrangements for home networks, but we will discuss the most common ones that involve either a hub with a star topology or a wireless network with an access point.

### Hardware

**peripheral component interconnect (PCI)**

**industry standard architecture (ISA)**

Hardware for the PC consists of a NIC, which typically costs from $5 to $25, for each computer on the network. Although most current computers have a **peripheral component interconnect (PCI)** bus, which comes as either 32-bit or 64-bit, some older computers may use an **industry standard architecture**

The Linksys HPRO200 device allows standard telephone lines to be used as the medium for an in-home LAN.
(Courtesy of linksys.com. Reprinted with permission.)

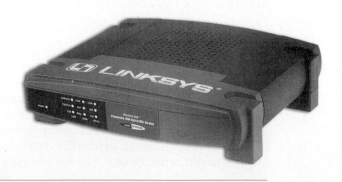

PCMCIA cards like this one fits into slots in laptop computers and provide various functions.
(Courtesy of D.C. Robotics. Reprinted with permission.)

**(ISA)** bus, which sends 16 bits of data at a time. It is important to know which type of bus a computer has before purchase. Some NICs plug into a USB port (if one is available) instead and don't require opening the computer. To install the card on a desktop computer:

■ turn off and disconnect the computer, place it on a worktable, and remove the outside case

■ make certain that you safeguard against static damage by touching a metal object to discharge your body of any static electricity

■ find an empty PCI expansion slot and remove the metal backplate (which is connected with a machine screw that loosens with a Phillips screwdriver) from its end at the back edge of the computer

■ carefully insert the network card into the PCI slot and secure it with the metal screw

**personal computer memory card interface adapter (PCMCIA)**

That is all that is required for the network adapter. On a laptop computer, the adapter is called a **personal computer memory card interface adapter (PCMCIA),** but most people refer to them as PC cards. The side of the card that fits into the PCMCIA slot has a row of sixty-eight holes that fit the sixty-eight pins inside the slot. The only installation that is required is to firmly push it into the slot. Some computers, both desktop and laptop, come equipped with built-in NICs.

## Connections

**patch cable**

The next step is to run cable (standard 10Base-T cable, usually UTP). The **patch cable,** which comes in several different fixed lengths and has RJ-45 connectors at each end, attaches to the NIC in the computer and on the other end to the hub or router. Figure 12–6 illustrates a typical home network that is set up with a central hub and connected computers, either desktop or laptop.

**uplink port**

The hub has several ports for patch cables and an **uplink port** that connects, via **crossover cable,** two hubs. This might be needed as a home network

**crossover cable**

**FIGURE 12-6** A single hub with several computers connected by patch cable.

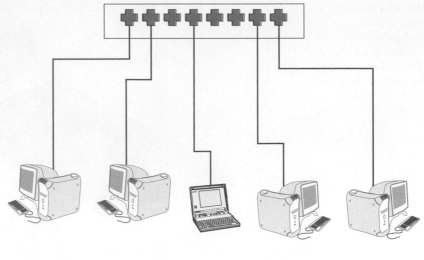

**FIGURE 12-7** Two hubs connected with crossover cable, each connected to separate computers.

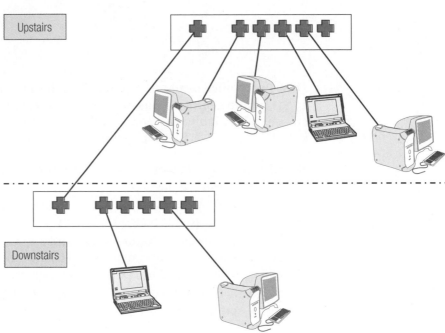

grows, or for computers that are on opposite ends of a house, widely separated from each other. More than one hub allows the creation of different zones for different areas of the house. Because each computer does not have to connect to the same hub, a network requires less cable when multiple zones are created. Zoning also provides for network growth, without the need for additional equipment. Figure 12–7 illustrates two hubs connected with a crossover cable, creating two zones in a home.

As you read in Chapters 10 and 11, a wireless network using radio frequency technology connects via a central access point (infrastructure mode) or from one NIC-equipped computer to another in a peer-to-peer (ad hoc) wireless network. The two types of wireless networks are illustrated in Figure 12–8.

A relatively new type of hardware product allows home networkers to set up a combination Ethernet and wireless network. Products such as the Linksys BEFW11S4, for example, combine four Ethernet ports for wired PCs, a wireless access point for laptops or other wireless devices, and a port

**FIGURE 12-8** The two types of wireless networks. a) infrastructure; b) peer-to-peer.

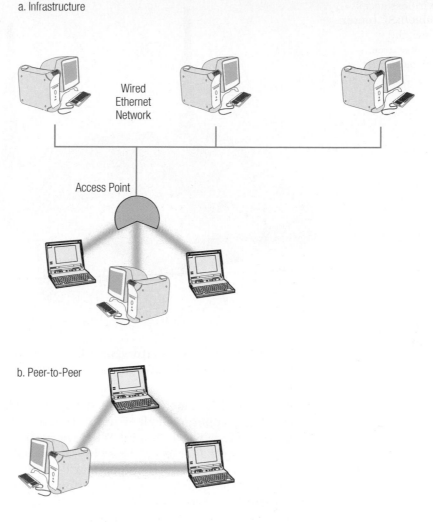

for a cable/DSL modem, creating the best of all choices—so far. (See the case study at the end of this chapter for further discussion of this choice.)

## Software

When the computer is turned on, the newer versions of Windows recognize the new hardware and install the proper drivers. The only remaining task is the hardest one—configuring the network. Though many home-networking kits and the Windows operating system include wizards and automatic configuration programs, they are all a little different. There are many books on home networking such as *The Essential Guide to Home Networking Technologies* by Gerard O'Driscoll. Because technology is moving so rapidly, it is even more helpful to find websites like http://www.homenethelp.com, which not only has installation tips and helpful tutorials, but also has an excellent forum dedicated solely to home networking.

If you have problems, it is good to know what steps to take to configure the network manually. You will need to know:

■ how to name the computer (each computer must have a unique name, but must belong to the same named network)

A Linksys wireless access point and cable/DSL router with 4-port switch. (Courtesy of linksys.com. Reprinted with permission.)

- how to share files, printers, and Internet connections (usually enabled through the configuration tab in Windows Network Neighborhood/ Properties)

- how to enable some kind of security (through a firewall installed on individual computers or the firewall that a router provides). Wireless standards include 64- or 128-bit WEP encryption, but though it can make a message unreadable—at least by the casual observer—it does not prevent hackers from getting into your computer. A firewall is a must to provide greater security in a wireless network. Chapter 17 discusses network security in greater detail.

## ■ SUMMARY

LANs have become an increasingly pervasive presence in today's business world, and even within many homes. The reasons for having a LAN are as varied as the applications and the individuals who use them. The processes of selecting, installing and managing a LAN, however, are similar no matter how large or how small it is, and regardless of the situation or application that causes its implementation. This chapter has laid the foundation for that implementation, either in your business or home environment.

In Chapter 13, you will learn about WANs, including packet switching networks. Several specific WAN systems will also be described.

## ■ REVIEW QUESTIONS

**12-1.** What are the criteria for selecting a LAN technology? Can you think of other considerations that were not discussed in this chapter that you would add to the list?

**12-2.** Discuss some of the key elements that must be considered when designing a LAN. What are some ways that LAN costs can be reduced?

12-3. Discuss the factors that can affect a LAN's performance. How can LAN performance be improved?

12-4. Why do LANs have distance limitations?

12-5. What are the responsibilities of a LAN administrator?

12-6. Why is it important for an organization to emphasize LAN management?

12-7. Describe the functions of a NOS.

12-8. What are some of the security issues that must be considered by network administrators? Why is management's support essential?

12-9. Explain the function of a proxy server.

12-10. What is a VPN?

12-11. Discuss the major reasons for installing a home network.

12-12. When choosing a home network, what are some of the major elements that must be considered?

12-13. Compare and contrast phone line and power line networks.

12-14. Discuss the major components of a home network.

12-15. Explain the process of installing a NIC on a desktop computer.

12-16. What is a patch cable and how does it differ from a crossover cable?

12-17. Is it possible to combine wired and wireless devices on the same home network? If so, how is it done?

12-18. Discuss some of the considerations that are especially important for a wireless network. What precautions should be taken when installing a wireless network in the home?

## TRUE OR FALSE

12-1. The most important criteria to consider when selecting a LAN are the needs of users and potential users rather than the needs of the entire organization.

12-2. Two costs that are often not considered when setting up a LAN are the cost of wiring and cabling and the cost of upgrading existing workstations.

12-3. Throughput is usually faster on a CSMA/CD protocol, but a token passing protocol is more predictable.

12-4. The speed and efficiency of the server hardware/software combination have a negligible effect on the overall speed and response time of a LAN.

12-5. LANs are often installed by people who have good technical skills, but who lack knowledge of LAN management.

12-6. A NOS is a Network Operations Service, the third-party vendor that manages a network for a large corporation.

12-7. The client software called NetBIOS, which stands for Network Basic Input-Output Systems, operates at both layer 2 (the datalink layer) and layer 5 the (session control layer) of the OSI model.

12-8. IPX/SPX is the proprietary layer 3 and layer 4 protocol of Microsoft Windows Server 2003.

12-9. The kernel is the heart of the UNIX system and tells the computer what to do at the programmer's command.

12-10. Solaris, from Sun Microsystems, is based on the Linux operating system.

**12-11.** A proxy server acts as an intermediary between the Internet and network-equipped computers.

**12-12.** A VPN uses tunneling technology to create a VPN through the Internet for businesses that want to extend a secure connection to remote users.

**MULTIPLE CHOICE**

**12-1.** More and more families are creating home networks to _____.

a. avoid the high cost of ISPs

b. share a high-speed Internet connection

c. practice their networking skills

d. tap into a neighbor's connection

e. ensure greater network security

**12-2.** One of the most important prerequisites for home networking is _____.

a. thorough knowledge of networking

b. an MSCE certification

c. ease of installation

d. broadband cable access

e. all wired media

**12-3.** The most popular and reliable type of home network is _____.

a. Ethernet

b. token ring

c. Wi-Fi

d. Bluetooth

e. power line networks

**12-4.** Among wireless alternatives, the most popular for home networks is _____.

a. 802.11b

b. HiperLAN2

c. 802.11g

d. 802.11a

e. Bluetooth

**12-5.** Power line networks are desirable because _____.

a. they cost less than other alternatives

b. they have better security than other technologies

c. they are faster than other types of network

d. they allow you to plug into existing, readily available electrical outlets

e. they don't suffer from interference like other technologies do

## ■ PROBLEMS AND PROJECTS

**12-1.** Using the sample LAN selection criteria checklist shown in Figure 12–1, develop a complete list for a LAN at your organization or school. Prioritize your items and explain the reasons for ranking them as you did.

12-2. Visit an organization that has a LAN and study the LAN management techniques that are in place. Prepare a written report of your findings, including a critique of the company's management techniques.

12-3. Investigate several NOSs and present your findings in the form of a recommendation to management of which system best fits the requirements of your own organization's LAN.

12-4. Maintaining network security has become one of the most important—and time consuming—tasks of a network administrator. Why has this aspect of LAN management become so important? List the security controls that are in place for the LAN you use. Comment on their effectiveness. Does the organization have a disaster recovery plan for its network?

12-5. Do some research to find out if there are developments in network security that could be implemented at your school or organization. What steps do you think could or should be taken to make the network a safer place?

12-6. Plan and diagram your own home network. Do some research to find out the costs for implementing your plan. Do not forget the cost of cables and all the necessary hardware and software, as well as the cost of Internet access.

12-7. Prepare a 5 to 10 page proposal to install a LAN for a small insurance company in your town that has twenty employees who have little or no technical expertise. Your proposal should briefly explain what hardware, software, cabling, and services you recommend to meet their basic needs. The business will need connectivity to a company intranet, the Internet, and e-mail. Consider that some of the employees will be working "in the field" and will need notebook computers and wireless connectivity. Do not forget security considerations.

## HOME, HOME ON THE NETWORK, WHERE SELDOM IS HEARD . . .

Home networking is becoming so popular that many computer stores cannot keep networking hardware and software on their shelves. The problem is that much of the equipment that goes home with customers also comes back. Often, the only packages on the shelf are ones that have been returned, repackaged, reshrinkwrapped, and then sit waiting for the next do-it-yourself home network administrator to begin the cycle all over again.

You may think, "This is my network and I can order it the way I like; I can set up my own rules for accessing data, sharing resources, and providing security. I am in charge." People assume they don't need a "tech" to lord it over them. An article in *PCWorld* warns, "The usefulness of a network equals zero if you can't get the net to work at all."[1]

Some people do enjoy the challenge of learning something new, however, and agree with Thomas Edison who said, "I have not failed; I have simply learned 10,000 ways not to do a thing." Being that kind of person and possessing the determination of a badger to hang on and not let go of a project until it was completed, Kathleen Ahsram decided that it was time to set up her own home network. Her husband, Lloyd, knew nothing about computers, except how to use a word processing program as a glorified

CASE STUDY

[1] Manes, Stephen. "Networking: You Still Need a Geek." *PCWorld*, July, 2002.

typewriter. Kathleen, who knew a little bit about networking, did a lot of reading and talked to her techie friends and several vendors. Finally, Kathleen and Lloyd decided to take a Saturday and set up their network.

The family had just consolidated two households, and now owned two desktop computers running Windows ME and a new laptop equipped with Windows XP. One desktop was connected to a 56K modem in the den. The laptop connected to the den modem with a 50 ft. phone wire. The other desktop connected to a 56K modem in the kitchen, about 45 feet away as the crow flies, but much farther away as cable is laid. The den computer, Kathleen's, received Internet access through an ISP that charged $9.95 per month for unlimited access. The kitchen computer, Lloyd's, connected through a different ISP at $14.95 a month, also unlimited. They paid for two different phone lines and really wished for three. The laptop came with free Compuserve access for a year, after which regular charges would apply.

Lloyd and Kathleen decided they could save money by connecting via a high speed cable modem and sharing Internet access. The cable company installed the necessary equipment and provided the modem free of charge. The charges were $19.95 a month for the first six months, $39.95 thereafter. Because her computer was connected to an HP LaserJet 4P printer and his was connected to a color printer, they thought sharing printers would be an added benefit. Additionally, being able to share files would allow Kathleen to help Lloyd with the financial and word processing needs of his home-based business.

They decided to connect the two desktops by running a 100 ft. CAT 5 cable from the den, under the house, to the kitchen, but they really wanted to be able to use the laptop computer anywhere in the house or on the front porch. Most stores told them that mixing wireless and wired was impossible. After talking to several vendors, however, they found a Wireless Access Point and Cable/DSL router with a 4-port Ethernet switch. They also purchased a NIC for Lloyd's machine (Kathleen's computer already had one) and one for the laptop. All the new hardware was from the same manufacturer.

The Ahsrams set up the physical equipment, installed the drivers, and by using the networking wizards in Windows, configured their computers to talk to one another and access the Internet. It all seemed very simple. The problem was that it didn't work. The computers were able to share files and printers, but only Kathleen's could access the Internet. Then none of them could. Then the computers could not see each other on the network, but the den computer could access the Internet.

Kathleen pinged the router; she pinged the other computers. She rebooted. She called the cable company, thinking there was something wrong with the connection. They told her to reboot everything, and then said it was probably the router. She called the router company and was told to reboot everything. Kathleen spent half a day talking to a technician who finally said he'd never had such a problem, but they would send a new NIC for the laptop and one the for PC. She called her brother, a computer technician and programmer. He spent a day with her, valiantly trying to solve the problem. Nothing worked, although they did manage to enable intranetworking of all three computers and Internet access for Kathleen's computer.

The next day, in desperation, Kathleen searched the Internet and found www.homenetworking.com. There she posted a message on one of the forums (out of many) dedicated to high-speed cable modem access. The next day, when she checked the forum, there was her answer! The kitchen computer had a software firewall that wasn't allowing Internet access. After reconfiguring the firewall, everyone connected! To date, the Ahsram network is doing well with sharing and Internet access for all.

1. Do you think networking your computers at home would simplify or complicate your life? Can you think of ways that setting up a home network could benefit you? How would it make your life more complicated?

2. What would you do if you ran into problems with your network? Who would you contact first? How would you research the answer to your dilemma? Where would you turn?

3. The high demand for home networking technology has brought about the need for people trained in special skills that the average homeowner does not possess. Do you think knowledge is keeping pace with developments in technology? What do you think should be done to help consumers cope with the daunting task of staying current with the skills they need to use the technology available to them?

# CHAPTER 13

# WIDE AREA NETWORKS (WANS)

## ■ OUTLINE

## ■ KEY TERMS

adaptive routing

asynchronous transfer mode (ATM)

available bit rate (ABR) service

basic rate interface (BRI)

broadband ISDN (BISDN)

broadcast routing

call accept packet

call request packet

cell

cell relay

centralized routing

choke packet

clear request packet

committed information rate (CIR)

common channel interoffice signaling (CCIS) system

congestion

congestion control

connectionless routing

connection-oriented routing

constant bit rate (CBR) service

control plane

datagram

distributed routing

dynamic routing

frame relay

integrated services digital network (ISDN)

IP security (IPsec)

## ■ OBJECTIVES

After you complete your study of this chapter, you should be able to:

■ identify distinguishing attributes of WANs as compared to LANs;

■ discuss alternative methods of routing traffic in a network;

■ discuss the impact that queuing can have on network performance;

■ describe how packet data networks work;

■ explain frame relay and why it is more efficient than packet switching;

■ describe ATM and the various transmission services it provides; and

■ explain the advantages and disadvantages of using VPNs for constructing a WAN.

## 13-1  INTRODUCTION

As was discussed in Chapter 2, **wide area networks (WANs)** are those that cover a large geographic area, require the crossing of public rights-of-way, and usually use circuits provided by one or more communication carriers. The communication circuits that make up a WAN exist in a much harsher environment than those of a LAN and are therefore more likely to experience errors, making the need for error detection and efficient error correction very important. Also, WANS need to be able to scale up to serve hundreds, if not thousands of locations spread over a broad geographic area such as might exist in a large company that has offices and plants across the country or around the world.

In this chapter, you will look at the characteristics of WANs and some specific WAN capabilities that the communications carriers offer.

## 13-2  WIDE AREA NETWORK TOPOLOGY

Wide area networks are generally designed as hybrids of star, hierarchical, and mesh topologies. National and global organizations often implement WANs to connect their many locations. While an organization's overall network probably includes bus and ring topologies as well, they are normally used for LANs and not for WAN implementations.

Organizations generally do not literally build their own WAN by laying cable or installing microwave towers. Rather, they lease circuits from communications carriers and use the services of the carriers to build the network. The carriers provide plain circuits that operate at a variety of speeds, as you saw in Chapter 9, and also offer circuits with enhanced capabilities such as packet switching, frame relay, ATM, and ISDN, which you will study later in this chapter. While some of these services are offered by most carriers, others are offered only by a few of the carriers or on a regional basis. This diversity makes the job of the network designer more difficult.

Companies are increasingly looking for the convenience that wireless network implementations offer. While only satellite circuits can provide long distance wireless links, it is possible to provide wireless connections into a wired WAN by establishing wireless connectivity in the company's offices and other locations. Assuming an organization's network operates as an integrated, seamless whole, once an employee connects into the network via wireless technology, she would be able to access the entire network—regardless of whether it is entirely implemented with wireless technology or not.

## 13-3  NETWORK SIGNALING

In wide area, circuit switched networks, control signaling is required to manage the network and perform certain operations. Network management and call management require that signals be sent between callers and switches, between switches, and between switches and the receiver. Control signaling is the way that calls are established and terminated, accounting records are kept, and troubleshooting is performed. On data networks, the control signals are sent as a part of the protocol, but on voice networks, the control is handled with special signals sent on the circuits.

There are several ways that signaling is accomplished on voice networks. The one you are probably most familiar with is **tone signaling,** which is what occurs when you press the buttons on the touchpad of a telephone to dial a number. The touch pad generates tones or combinations of tones that tell the CO switch what number you are dialing. Other tone signals are the dial tone, busy signal, and fast busy signal.

**Signaling System No. 7 (SS7)**

The most widely used signaling system on the telephone network operates between CO switches and is called **Signaling System No. 7 (SS7).** SS7 was first proposed by the ITU-T in 1980 and is fully implemented in most countries. SS7 signals are carried over circuits that are completely independent of the voice channels. In fact, there is an entire separate network of circuits reserved exclusively for signaling information, called the **common channel interoffice signaling (CCIS) system,** and one control signal path can carry the signals for a number of voice circuits.

**common channel interoffice signaling (CCIS) system**

SS7 is optimized for use in digital networks in conjunction with intelligent, computerized switches in the COs. It allows for database access as a part of the call setup, which allows the telephone companies to provide enhanced telephone services such as automatic callback and calling number identification. With SS7, control messages (short blocks or packets) are routed through the network to perform their control functions. What exists, therefore, is a packet-switched network overlaid on a circuit-switched network to control and operate the circuit-switched network.

## 13-4  PACKET DATA NETWORKS (PDNS)

**packet data network**

**packet switching network**

**packet network**

One type of WAN is called a **packet data network,** also called a **packet switching network,** or simply a **packet network.** Packet networks have been operational since 1969 when the Advanced Research Projects Agency (ARPA) of the U.S. DoD first developed the technology. The first packet network was known as ARPANET, and was used to connect ARPA research centers. Later, the ARPANET evolved to become the Internet. The first commercial packet switching network, known as Telenet, became available in the U.S. in 1975.

Rather than dedicating a circuit between points in a network, packet networks take a different approach. As you saw in Chapter 9, when packet switching technology is employed, transmissions are broken into small pieces called packets. Each packet is passed through the packet network from node to node.

### Packet Transmission through the PDN

Packets are sent through the network autonomously along a path leading from the source to the destination. Computers at each network node route the packet through the network toward the destination node, but packets from the same message may take different routes through the network and may arrive at the receiving node out of sequence. The packet assembly/disassembly (PAD) hardware or software at the receiving node, which can be owned by the customer or the communications carrier, is responsible for reassembling the packets into the correct sequence before passing them on to the user. Packet switched services allow multiple connections to exist simultaneously between nodes in the network; therefore, packets from the same message may take different routes to reach their destination. Packets from different terminals or computers are interspersed on the network at any point in time, as shown in Figure 13-1. In other words, packet switching is another form of multiplexing that allows better utilization of circuits when digital data are being transmitted.

A packet switching network does not establish an actual physical link between two nodes that wish to communicate. As shown in Figure 13-2, the only

FIGURE 13-1 Packets from the three PCs are interspersed on the circuit.

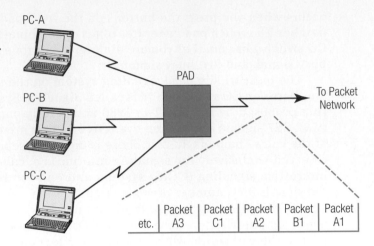

FIGURE 13-2 The blue dots are the nodes that provide an entry/exit point to the packet network. The nodes are actually computers that may also perform the PAD.

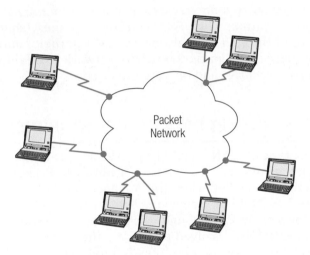

direct connection is between the user's terminal and the nearest node of the packet network at each end of the connection. Because a direct connection is not established between the sender and the receiver, there can be delays in communications. Therefore, the use of packet switching networks for interactive access to computers or in applications that require extremely fast or extremely consistent response time must be studied carefully to be sure that the response time that the packet network can deliver will be adequate. If, for example, the primary application is e-mail, which are messages that do not normally require instantaneous delivery, the use of a packet switching network may be ideal. On the other hand, if consistent, rapid response time is required—such as in a chemical plant's process control application where computers control the opening and closing of valves based on changes in temperature and pressure, and where delays of a few seconds may make a difference in the manufacturing process—a packet network may not be the best alternative.

Packet switching networks are designed so that there are at least two, but usually several, alternative high-speed paths from one node to another, as shown in Figure 13-3. A message from Detroit to San Francisco might normally be routed through Chicago. However, if the Chicago node or the link from Detroit to Chicago is down or extremely busy, the node in Detroit would use internally stored tables to determine that it could route the messages via St. Louis instead. This provides a redundant, fail-safe capability and implies

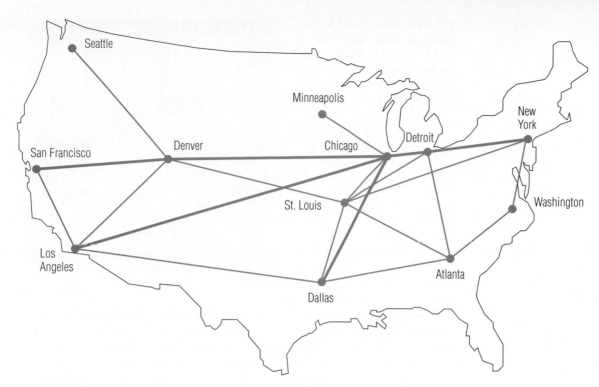

**FIGURE 13-3**   A hypothetical packet switching network (heavier lines indicate multiple or higher speed circuits).

that the route a specific message takes is, in part, a function of the traffic load and other conditions on the network when the message is sent.

## Packet Switching Techniques

**datagram**

**virtual circuit (VC)**

There are two methods that packet data networks use to handle the stream of packets that flow from a computer or terminal that has a message to send. The first method, called **datagrams,** is a connectionless service. The second method, **virtual circuits (VC),** is a connection-oriented approach. When the datagram approach is used, each packet or datagram contains a destination address and is handled independently by the network. Packets may arrive out of sequence because they take different routes through the network, or may be lost or destroyed if, for example, an intermediate node along the path crashes at an inopportune time. Datagram service does not guarantee that packets will be delivered.

**call request packet**

**call accept packet**

When the virtual circuit approach is used, a route through the network is established before any data packets are sent. The sending node first sends a special control packet, called a **call request packet** through the network, and each intermediate node decides how it will route the data packets for that message when they come through. After the route is established, a VC number is assigned and the receiving node sends a **call accept packet** back to the sender, which completes the call setup phase. This process has some similarities to the setup phase of a telephone call when the route through the voice network is being established.

Looking at Figure 13-4, when a message is to be sent from San Diego to San Francisco, a VC might be established through San Bernardino, Bakersfield, and Fresno. Later, because of different traffic or other conditions on

FIGURE 13-4    A VC for a message being sent from San Diego to San Francisco might be set up to pass through San Bernardino, Bakersfield, and Fresno.

the network, a virtual circuit for another message that has the same source and destination might pass through Los Angeles and San Luis Obispo. If the packet network was highly interconnected in a mesh-like configuration, VCs might be established through almost any combination of cities, though the computers that establish the circuits always try to establish links in the direction of the final destination.

When the call setup phase is complete and the VC is established, the transmission of data packets can begin. The transmitting node puts the VC number (instead of a destination address) in the header of each packet, appends the data and passes the packet to the next node on the virtual circuit. All data packets follow the VC. Each intermediate node on the VC knows where to forward packets with the specific VC number. Eventually, either the sending or receiving node terminates the connection with a **clear request packet** and the VC connection is ended.

**clear request packet**

The fact that a VC is established does not mean that the physical circuit it uses is dedicated to the particular message being sent. As was illustrated in Figure 13-1, other packets on other VCs may share the same physical circuit at the same time. Some networks provide additional services, such as packet sequencing and error checking, to VCs.

As you can see, there is a trade-off between the datagram and virtual circuit approaches. An advantage of the datagram approach is that the call setup phase is avoided, so if a computer wishes to send only a few packets, datagram delivery will be quicker. For longer messages, or for continual communication between two nodes over an extended period of time, the virtual circuit approach may provide faster service, because individual decisions do not have to be made about the way to route each packet. The routing for all packets sent on the virtual circuit is preestablished at call setup time.

Many contemporary packet switching networks use VCs for internal operation, primarily because of the packet sequencing and error checking procedures that can be provided. However, internetworks and connections to the Internet commonly use datagram services because the connections are frequently not of long duration, the messages are often short, and the fastest possible packet delivery time is desired. If, for example, you send a request to a website on the Internet and get no response (because, unbeknownst to you, your datagram was lost and never delivered), you simply repeat your request after a few seconds.

## 13-5 ROUTING TRAFFIC IN A NETWORK

Most WANs have several paths that a packet could take from its source to its destination, as was illustrated in Figure 13-4. Routing packets through the network is one of the important responsibilities of the network layer (layer 3) of the OSI model. There are many ways to route packets, ranging from fairly simple techniques suitable for small networks to elaborate, adaptive techniques that only large networks need and can afford.

### Connection-Oriented and Connectionless Routing

**connection-oriented routing**

**connectionless routing**

**routing**

Some messages sent through a network can be sent as a single unit because they will fit in a single packet or frame, but most messages are longer and must be broken into pieces to fit the parameters of the transmission method. The application doesn't care how the transmission layer handles the messages, but the application at the receiving end does expect to receive an entire message, regardless of how it might have been divided for transmission. In some networks, as you have seen, a VC is built between the sending and receiving nodes and then the entire message, or all of its packets if it has been divided, can be sent at one time on the VC. This is called **connection-oriented routing.** In other networks, each packet is sent independently, and all may travel to the destination on different routes. This is called **connectionless routing,** and when it is used, the network layer at the receiving end must reassemble the message as the packets arrive, including handling those that arrive out of sequence.

In either case, the network hardware and software must decide how to build a VC circuit or how to route the individual packets—the process called **routing.** Figure 13-5 shows the attributes of the major routing techniques.

### Centralized Routing

**centralized routing**

When **centralized routing** is employed, a central or control computer keeps a table of all the terminals on the network and the paths or routes to each. All packets flow to the central computer, which then uses the table to determine the best route to use to send the packet to its destination.

Centralized routing is sometimes used in star or hierarchical networks, where a central computer controls all communications flows. Centralized routing is relatively simple, but it is normally static. That is, a routing table is created in software that shows the primary and backup routes to each location. These routes are established when the software routing table is created, and they do not normally change based on network traffic loads or

**FIGURE 13-5** Advantages and disadvantages of various network routing techniques.

|  | Static | Dynamic |
|---|---|---|
| **Centralized** | Relatively simple<br>Least flexible<br>Single point of failure<br>Potential performance bottleneck | More flexible<br>Reacts to changing traffic conditions |
| **Distributed** | No single point of failure<br>Routing table updates may be a burden on the network | Most flexible<br>Most complicated to implement |
| **Broadcast (LAN only)** | Simplest<br>Adequate with small network | Ineffective with moderate to heavy traffic loads |

communication line failures. Therefore, if a communication line fails, traffic will be sent on the alternate route (if one has been established in the table), but if a backup route does not exist or if it is also out of service, traffic will be held. There will be no searching to see if any other routes are available. Furthermore, the central computer can become a performance bottleneck if it gets overloaded, or worse, a point of failure if it crashes.

Despite these disadvantages, centralized routing is used because it is simple and it can be very successful. Planning is required, however, to ensure that the proper routes are built into the software tables.

## Distributed Routing

**distributed routing**

**Distributed routing** places the responsibility for building and maintaining routing tables on at least some of the nodes in the network. Each node that performs routing is responsible for knowing which paths or links are attached to it and their status. Each node also must advise other nodes in the network when the status of paths changes, so that they can update their tables. This transmission of path status information puts a communications load on the network itself, and if the path status messages are voluminous, the load can become a burden that affects performance. Distributed routing avoids the single point of failure problem associated with centralized routing. However, it is more complicated to implement, especially when the practical problems of updating routing software and routing tables in each of the nodes are considered.

## Static and Dynamic Routing

**static routing**

**Static routing** means that the route or routes between two nodes on the network are fixed and can be changed only when the network is taken down and software tables are modified. Messages must always be sent on the predefined route(s). If the route or its backup(s) are down, messages must be held. Some static routing schemes allow alternate paths to be statically defined so that a limited backup routing capability exists. Static routing is most often used when the routing is also centralized, and mainly in older networks.

**dynamic routing**

**adaptive routing**

**Dynamic routing,** sometimes called **adaptive routing,** is considerably more flexible in that each node chooses the best path for routing a packet to its destination. Consecutive packets to the same destination can be routed by different paths, if necessary, and the node can adapt to changing network traffic volumes, error rates, circuit outages, or other conditions. As would be expected, dynamic routing is more difficult to implement, particularly when it is combined with distributed routing, but the benefits may make the implementation cost worthwhile.

## Broadcast Routing

**broadcast routing**

A very simple technique, **broadcast routing,** used by the CSMA/CD protocol, is to broadcast all packets to all stations on the network. It is used only on LANs, so it is not really relevant to our discussion of WANs in this chapter, but it is mentioned here for completeness. When broadcast routing is used, all stations on the network see the packet, but only the station for which the packet is intended copies it. All other stations ignore it. Broadcast routing is practical on a small network with few nodes, but is impractical on a large network because it would quickly be saturated with traffic.

A Cisco router.
(Courtesy of Cisco Systems.
Reprinted with permission.)

## Routers

router

Today, specialized computers called (appropriately) **routers** are most often used to perform routing in networks. Routers are available with a wide variety of capacities and capabilities and can be used in even the smallest networks. Router technology has advanced dramatically in the past several years, to the point where router hardware and software are very capable of coping with the complexities that dynamic routing entails. If several routers are placed at different points in the network, distributed routing can be employed.

Routing techniques have been the subject of considerable research for many years, and many trade-offs must be considered when trying to design an appropriate routing strategy. Performance is always a consideration because it is usually desirable to get packets to their destination by the shortest or quickest path. Other situations that must be handled are circuit failure and alternate routing when primary circuits are out of operation. Yet another factor that routing algorithms must deal with is congestion on one or more of the circuits due to heavy traffic. Additionally, any routing technique requires some processing at each node in the network. More elaborate routing algorithms require more processing, and the designer must be sure that the sophistication of the algorithm and resultant processing does not impair the efficiency of the transmission by delaying it unnecessarily. With the speed of today's routers, this is rarely a major factor, but the penalty of such overhead needs to be less than the benefit accrued.

## 13-6 CONGESTION CONTROL

congestion

**Congestion** in a network occurs when traffic arrives at a node or for transmission on a circuit faster than the node or circuit can handle it. A circuit's ability to handle traffic may be slowed because of errors, because the circuit fails by being cut or damaged, or because it does not have the inherent capacity to carry the traffic load presented to it. Nodes such as routers may not be able to process peak traffic volumes fast enough because they are too slow, or because they partially or totally stop working due to hardware or software failure.

When network congestion occurs, the transmission delay for packets increases so that the time it takes individual packets to move from the source to the destination increases beyond normal propagation delay. If congestion persists, nodes may run out of buffer space and may begin discarding packets.

Although retransmission can ensure that the discarded packets ultimately get through, retransmission takes time and adds to the traffic load on the network. At its worst, an entire network can be bogged down by congestion, which makes it unusable. Protocols and hardware, such as routers, attempt to avoid such a severe situation by monitoring the network and reacting quickly when congestion starts to occur.

**congestion control**

**Congestion control** is the attempt to manage the congestion by reducing the flow of new packets into the network or by routing packets around the congested circuits or nodes. (Think of congestion on the highway system as a good analogy.) One technique is to notify sending terminals to slow down or stop sending new traffic. Routers or destination terminals can send a special control packet, sometimes called a **choke packet,** to the sources of traffic requesting that they slow the rate at which they are sending packets to the network or to stop sending altogether.

**choke packet**

When circuits are of high quality and are error free, a source can assume that most requests it receives for the retransmission of packets are caused because packets have been discarded during transmission, not because errors occurred on the line. If a source notices a higher-than-usual number of requests for retransmission, it follows that the increased requests are most likely coming because packets have been discarded because of network congestion. With those assumptions, the source can automatically reduce the rate at which it is sending packets into the network, even if it hasn't received a choke packet requesting the reduction.

There are several issues related to congestion management that complicate the matter. Simply discarding the last packets to arrive at a point of congestion may not be the best strategy. Applications have differing needs for network service, and it may be desirable to discard packets based on the type or **quality of service (QoS)** that is required. For example, voice and video transmissions are very sensitive to delays in transmission but are not as sensitive to losses. If you are talking on the telephone, delays might make the other person sound like they are stuttering or may cause irritating, unnaturally long pauses in response. The loss of a packet or two of speech might sound like a clipped syllable, which you would hardly miss, if you noticed it at all. Other applications, such as e-mail or file transfer are not very sensitive to delays but are very sensitive to losses of data. Whether an e-mail arrives in 10 seconds or 1 minute usually makes little difference, but a missing packet might mean that some numerical data in the e-mail—an address, a flight number, or a sales forecast—is incorrect. Still other applications, such as interactive computing applications, are both delay and loss sensitive.

**quality of service (QoS)**

During periods of network congestion, it is desirable to treat the packets from each of these types of applications differently to try to maintain a QoS that is appropriate for the application. For example, packets from telephone conversations should get through quickly; those from e-mail applications can be delayed. To accomplish this, nodes may keep separate queues of packets for different application types, and transmit packets from some queues ahead of others in order to maintain the desired and expected service. Other techniques may also be employed.

## 13-7    DELAYS IN NETWORKS AND QUEUING

Traffic in all networks experiences various delays that keep it from getting to its destination in the shortest possible time. Ordinary delay in a network can be measured by how long it takes a bit of data to travel across the network from the sender to the receiver, as measured in seconds or fractions of

propagation delay

switching delay

queuing delay

queue

a second. Some delay is normal because of the **propagation delay** for a signal to get from one point to another. On a typical LAN within a building, the propagation delay is normally about 1 millisecond but on a WAN, the delay is much longer because the distances are greater. Networks that use satellites have the longest propagation delays, as you saw in Chapter 8.

Each device on the network—switches, routers, and bridges, for example—adds additional delay, commonly known as **switching delay**. Each device waits for the bits of a packet to arrive and then processes the packet according to the device's purpose. A router, for example, takes time to decide how to route the packet and send it on its way. Because of the speed of processors, switching delay is normally one of the smallest of the delays in a network.

A third type of delay seen in networks is **queuing delay**. A **queue** is a waiting line, and queues occur frequently in communications systems. Queues form when transactions (packets in the case of a packet network) arrive faster than a server can handle them. Think about the waiting lines at airports, especially before flights are about to depart. Passengers arrive faster than the clerks can handle them, and a waiting line (queue) develops. There are three ways to eliminate queues or avoid having them form in the first place:

1. transactions (passengers) arrive more slowly
2. servers (clerks) process transactions more quickly
3. more servers are made available to process transactions

At the airport, item 1 is hard to control; however, an airline can choose to do something about item 3 in the short term. Item 2 can possibly be accomplished over the long term through training.

Queuing can be the largest and most variable source of delay in a network because of the number of places where queues can occur. The total time it takes a packet to transit the network from source to destination can vary dramatically, depending on the number and length of queues it encounters along the way. Packets may have to wait for another packet, or group of packets, to finish using a circuit. Packets may have to wait for a router to finish processing (routing) the previous packet. When packets begin to arrive more quickly, the queue may grow longer if the processing time on the router stays the same and no additional routers are brought online. Complicating an analysis is the fact that most processors do not simply process packets in a queue on a first-in-first-out basis, but follow some priority-based system to ensure that packets that need the highest service levels get processed first.

queuing theory

The analysis of queues and queuing is the branch of mathematics called **queuing theory**. Queuing theory defines ways for studying queuing, including questions such as: How often will the input rate exceed the processing rate? How long will the waiting lines (queues) grow assuming a certain arrival rate and processing time? How many servers are required to handle a certain input rate? How long will the delay be? For more detailed information, do a search for "queuing theory" on the Internet.

## 13-8  SPECIFIC WAN SYSTEMS

Communications carriers have developed and provide several high speed WAN services that they offer as products. These WAN products are generally used by larger organizations that have extensive networking requirements. All carriers do not offer all of these services, however, so the network designer must consult with the carriers to determine which products best meet their needs.

## X.25

X.25

Packet switching technology was first standardized by the ITU-T's recommendation of **X.25,** which defines the interface between a computer and a packet data network. Many public packet switching networks, especially in Europe where X.25 has been the most popular, use the X.25 standard; but it may also be used when an organization establishes a PDN.

The standard defines three layers of protocols

- packet layer
- link layer
- physical layer

that correspond to layers 3, 2, and 1 of the OSI model.

X.21

The flow of data is illustrated in Figure 13-6. User data are passed down to layer 3, the packet layer, where it has the packet header appended. This becomes the X.25 packet. The packet is passed down to the link layer, where the LAPB header and trailer are appended to make the LAPB frame. LAPB provides for the reliable transport of the packet across the link. The frame is then passed down to the physical layer for transmission through the network. The physical level of X.25 officially uses an electrical standard known as **X.21,** which defines the electrical signals on the circuit. When X.25 networks are implemented in the U.S., however, the RS-232-C electrical standard, which is more common in this country, is substituted.

The packet level provides a VC service. A DTE is allowed to provide up to 4,095 simultaneous VCs over a single physical link, which can use these circuits any way it pleases. A server, for example, might assign a separate VC to each application running on its processor. This multiplexing capability is an important part of X.25 capabilities.

X.25 has several formats and can use 3-, 7-, or 15-bit sequence numbers. Different packet types are used at various stages of the connection. Some are used when the VC is established, while others are used during normal data transmission. Two of the packet formats for 7-bit sequence numbers are shown in Figure 13-7. The first two bits of the flag field vary depending on the exact operation underway, but the last two bits are always 10 when 7-bit se-

FIGURE 13-6 User data has control information appended as it passes down through the X.25 layers.

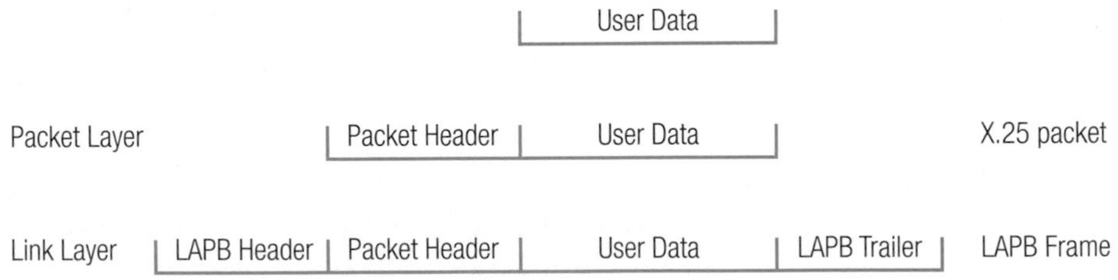


FIGURE 13-7 The formats of typical X.25 frames.

Control packet for virtual calls with 7-bit sequence numbers

| Fields | Flag | Address | Packet Type | Additional Information |
|---|---|---|---|---|
| Bits | 4 | 12 | 8 | Variable |

Data packet with 7-bit sequence numbers

| | Flag | Address | Send Sequence No. | Receive Sequence No. | User Data |
|---|---|---|---|---|---|
| Bits | 4 | 12 | 7 + 1 | 7 + 1 | Variable |

quence numbers are used. The 12-bit address is normally subdivided into a 4-bit group number and an 8-bit channel number. The use of the eighth bit in the 7-bit sequence number field varies. User data are broken into blocks of a maximum size defined by the particular implementation of X.25.

Flow and error control at the packet layer are virtually identical in format and procedure to that used for HDLC. A sliding window protocol is used, which provides better line utilization efficiency than a stop-and-wait protocol would yield. In addition to sequence numbers in the packets, X.25 provides a reset capability to reinitialize a VC and a restart capability to reinitialize all VCs. Both of these capabilities are used when serious errors occur on the physical circuit or network, and both cause packets in transit at the time of the reset or restart to be lost.

## Frame Relay

Packet switching and PDNs were developed in the 1960s and early 1970s when data transmission circuits were mostly analog and not as reliable as they are today. Therefore, packet switching technology has a large amount of error checking and control built in that often proves to be unnecessary today, especially with the use of digital circuits that have low error rates.

**frame relay**

**Frame relay** was developed to reduce the overhead of packet switching and provide more efficient data transmission, and it was designed to operate on multimegabit speed lines. There are two logical planes of operation: the **control plane**, which is involved in the establishment and termination of logical connections; and the **user plane**, which is responsible for the transfer of data. The control plane uses a separate logical channel for signaling, and is similar to the common channel signaling used for circuit switching services discussed earlier in the chapter.

**control plane**

**user plane**

The actual transfer of user information is done in the user plane using the LAPF protocol, which divides messages into variable length frames for transmission through the network. A frame consists of a 1-byte flag, an addressing field that is 2 bytes by default but which can be extended to 4 bytes; a variable-length data field (from 1 to 64,000 bytes); a 2 byte frame check sequence (cyclic redundancy check); and a 1 byte terminating flag byte as shown in Figure 13-8. Part of the address field serves the same function as the VC number in X.25. Frame relay hardware at each end of a connection builds and disassembles frames out of other kinds of data streams, such as asynchronous terminal input, LAN packets, and digitized voice signals, and sends them out serially on a frame relay network. The variable-length frames give the equipment great flexibility in dynamically allocating the bandwidth to multiple data streams and changing priorities as required by the applications.

Frame relay has approximately one quarter of the overhead of basic packet switching. Unlike packet switching, which requires an acknowledgement for every packet from every node through which it passes, frame relay frames keep track of the addresses of all of the nodes through which they travel and the final destination sends an acknowledgement back through the same path on the network by looking at the node addresses stored in the received frame.

Because the frame relay protocol has been streamlined to make it fast and efficient, it has less ability than some other protocols to deal with circuit congestion. Queuing theory shows that if traffic on a circuit gets too heavy,

**FIGURE 13-8** The frame format used by a frame relay system.

| Fields | Flag | Address | Data | FCS | Flag |
|--------|------|---------|------|-----|------|
| Bytes  | 1    | 2–4     | Variable | 2 | 1 |

committed information
rate (CIR)

port speed

the throughput drops quickly and dramatically, so it is in the best interest of all users to keep circuit congestion under control. Frame relay systems accomplish this control by applying the concepts of a **committed information rate (CIR).** A company that subscribes to frame relay service leases a circuit of a certain speed, usually called the **port speed,** to the carrier's office. The port speed is the maximum rate at which data can be transmitted. The customer contracts with the carrier for a certain CIR measured in bits per second, which is usually up to one-half of the port speed, and the price paid is determined by the CIR.

The basic mechanism for relieving congestion in a crowded frame relay network is to discard frames. In normal operation, the user can send data up to the port speed but if the network gets congested, the vendor may discard frames that exceed the CIR. For example, a frame relay user might acquire a circuit with a port speed of 256 Kbps and a CIR of 64 Kbps. When necessary, data can be sent at up to 256 Kbps, but anything over 64 Kbps is subject to being discarded if the network gets congested while the data are being sent. Any data sent at less than 64 Kbps is within the CIR and normally gets through, although it should be pointed out that there is no guarantee. If the network becomes extremely congested, even frames within the 64 Kbps CIR may be discarded. If the network is properly designed, this situation should be rare, however.

public frame relay
network

Communications carriers that offer data transmission services provide the majority of frame relay networks deployed today. These are referred to as **public frame relay networks,** and the switching equipment is located at the central offices of the carrier. Subscribers are charged based on their use of the network, but are relieved from administering and maintaining the frame relay network equipment and service. Some organizations are deploying **private frame relay networks,** for which all of the equipment is owned by the enterprise, and the network's operation, maintenance, and administration are also its responsibility.

private frame relay
network

## Asynchronous Transfer Mode (ATM)

Frame relay dramatically increases the throughput of packetized data transmissions; however, there can still be delays in the network that frame relay systems cannot prevent. Some data, such as real-time voice or video, are not very tolerant of delays. **Asynchronous transfer mode (ATM),** sometimes called **cell relay,** was developed to effectively eliminate the problem of delays. ATM is an evolution of frame relay and has been standardized by the ITU-T. It reverts to fixed-length packets of 53 bytes called **cells** that can be assembled and disassembled more quickly than variable-length frames, thus improving on the efficiency of frame relay. ATM is designed with circuits that operate at speeds from 25.6 Mbps to 622.08 Mbps. The use of T-3 circuits for ATM is common.

asynchronous transfer
mode (ATM)

cell relay

cell

The high speed circuits, fast switching speeds, low error rates, and fast processing of the fixed length cells combine to effectively eliminate delays in transmission and make ATM suitable for voice processing. A constant rate data channel can be guaranteed even though packet switching technology is being used. If a user needs to deliver synchronized video and sound, ATM is a technology that will meet the requirement. Digital voice, data, and video information can simultaneously travel over a single ATM network at high speeds, using varying amounts of bandwidth as needed.

ATM networks are typically designed to be able to handle many types of traffic simultaneously, such as voice, video, and real-time data. Although each data stream is handled as a stream of 53-byte cells, the way in which the flow of cells is prioritized and handled depends on the characteristics of the flow and the needs of the application. For example, voice or real-time video must be handled with almost no delay, whereas other types of data are delay tolerant.

To meet the transmission requirements of diverse applications, ATM has five service categories that are used by an end system to identify the type of service required from the ATM network. The categories are:

- real-time service
    - constant bit rate (CBR)
    - real-time variable bit rate (rt-VBR)
- non-real-time service
    - non-real-time variable bit rate (nrt-VBR)
    - available bit rate (ABR)
    - unspecified bit rate (UBR)

**constant bit rate (CBR) service**

**Constant bit rate (CBR) service** is used by applications that require a fixed and continuously available data rate, such as that which would be available on a leased or private circuit. Examples of CBR applications include telephone connections, videoconferencing, and others that involve people at both ends of the connection communicating in real time. Delays on these kinds of communications are annoying and often make the communication unproductive and frustrating to the participants.

**real-time variable bit rate (rt-VBR) service**

**Real-time variable bit rate (rt-VBR) service** is also used by applications that require minimal delays in transmissions. However, the distinction is that the transmission rates tend to be somewhat bursty, such as might be found with compressed video transmissions.

**non-real-time variable bit rate (nrt-VBR) service**

Applications that are candidates for **non-real-time variable bit rate (nrt-VBR) service** are those such as automobile or airline reservation systems and financial transaction systems. These applications have a requirement for fast response time but compared to voice applications, they can tolerate some delays—especially if they are infrequent. When employing this service, the user specifies the peak and average cell rates that are required and a measure of how bursty the traffic is. With this information, the network can allocate resources to provide relatively low delay and minimal cell loss.

**available bit rate (ABR) service**

After the available circuit capacity is allocated to one of the aforementioned three services, the remainder is available for the **available bit rate (ABR) service**. An application that uses ABR specifies the peak cell rate it will use and the minimum cell rate it requires. The network allocates resources to ensure that the ABR application receives at least its minimum cell rate. An example of an application that is a good candidate for ABR is a LAN-to-LAN connection. If the ATM circuit cannot immediately handle the traffic, it can be buffered in the LAN until circuit capacity is available.

**unspecified bit rate (UBR) service**

After ATM circuit capacity is allocated to all of the above services, there may still be some capacity available. This unused capacity is available for the **unspecified bit rate (UBR) service**, which uses the ATM circuit on an "as available" basis. UBR traffic is forwarded on a first-in-first-out basis, using capacity not consumed by other services, so both delays and cell losses are possible. This service is suitable for applications that can tolerate those delays and possible cell losses, which is typical of TCP-based traffic.

The basic architecture of ATM is shown in Figure 13-9. The ATM layer provides packet transfer capabilities and applies to all services that ATM

FIGURE 13-9   The architecture of ATM.

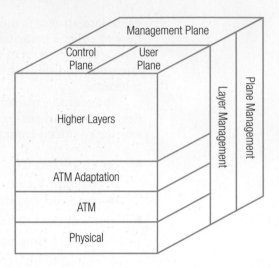

offers. The ATM adaptation layer is unique for each service. At the transmitting end, it maps higher layer information into ATM cells and performs the reverse function at the receiving end. It also handles transmission errors, segmentation and reassembly, and flow control for ATM transmissions.

Like frame relay, ATM also has several planes of operation. The control plane performs call and connection control. The user plane handles information transfer, including error control, once a connection is established. The management plane performs a management function that relates to the entire ATM system and provides coordination between all of the planes and layers. As you can imagine, in a system as complicated as ATM, there is considerably more overhead than with simpler transmission systems. However, high circuit speeds and efficient cell management still allow ATM to yield throughput rates far in excess of other systems.

**user-network interface (UNI)**

The format of ATM cells can be one of two types, which differ only by one field in the header, as shown in Figure 13-10. The **user-network interface (UNI)** format is used when applications put data into or remove it from the

Cell Format

| Field | Header | Data (Payload) |
|---|---|---|
| Bytes | 5 | 48 |

Header Format — User-Network Interface

| Field | Generic Flow Control | Virtual Path Identifier | Virtual Channel Identifier | Payload Type | C L P | Header Error Control |
|---|---|---|---|---|---|---|
| Bits | 4 | 8 | 16 | 3 | 1 | 8 |

Header Format — Network-Network Interface

| Field | Virtual Path Identifier | Virtual Channel Identifier | Payload Type | C L P | Header Error Control |
|---|---|---|---|---|---|
| Bits | 12 | 16 | 3 | 1 | 8 |

FIGURE 13-10   The cell and cell header formats for ATM.

network-network
interface (NNI)

network, and the **network-network interface (NNI)** format is used within the network. In the UNI format, the generic flow control field can be used by applications to alleviate short-term overload conditions in the network. The virtual path identifier field (VPI) and virtual channel identifier (VCI) fields together constitute the destination address of the cell. The payload type field indicates whether data or control information is being carried and also gives an indication as to whether the cell has encountered congestion on the circuit. The cell loss priority (CLP) bit indicates whether the cell is low priority and can be discarded if necessary or higher priority and should be discarded only if no other alternative is available.

The header error control byte is interesting. It is a polynomial-based check character, like a CRC, but the input to the calculation is only the remaining 32 bits in the header. Most check characters in protocols such as HDLC are calculated based on a much longer input string of bits, which provides excellent error detection. The fact that ATM's input is much shorter allows the check character to be used for some error correction as well as error detection. This is because there is enough redundancy in the check character to recover from certain error conditions.

ATM combines the strength of traditional packet switching (bandwidth efficiency) with those of circuit switching (high throughput, low delay, and transparency). The technology and capabilities of ATM networks are still evolving, and they merit close attention by organizations that have a need for high capacity circuits that have a wide variety of data flow types (e.g. voice, video, computer data). Because of their high capacity and flexibility, ATM circuits tend to be expensive, so the cost compared to the needs of the applications must be understood before the use of an ATM circuit can be justified. For the most current information about ATM, go to http://www.atmforum.com/ on the Internet.

## Synchronous Optical Network (SONET)

Synchronous Optical
Network (SONET)

**Synchronous Optical Network (SONET)** is a standard for transmitting data on optical fibers, and was originally created to allow easier connection between carriers that were using different vendor's products for their optical networks. SONET has become the *de facto* standard for carrying voice and data traffic over an optical network, and ANSI has written a standard for it. SONET provides for transmission at gigabits per second (Gbps), as shown in Figure 13-11. Europe uses a similar standard, as approved by the ITU-T, but it has different designations for the various circuit speeds.

**FIGURE 13-11**
Comparative data rates for the SONET and ITU-T optical fiber transmission standards.

| Synchronous Optical Network (SONET) | ITU-T Designation | Data Rate |
|---|---|---|
| OC-1 | | 51.840 Mbps |
| OC-3 | STM-1 | 155.250 Mbps |
| OC-9 | STM-3 | 466.560 Mbps |
| OC-12 | STM-4 | 622.080 Mbps |
| OC-18 | STM-6 | 933.120 Mbps |
| OC-24 | STM-8 | 1.244 Gbps |
| OC-36 | STM-12 | 1.866 Gbps |
| OC-48 | STM-16 | 2.488 Gbps |
| OC-192 | STM-64 | 9.953 Gbps |
| OC-255 | | 13.219 Gbps |

While the communications carriers originally developed SONET for their own use, it is now available to users who need the capacity it offers. For example, some organizations use SONET in their MANs to link locations in a metropolitan area. The carriers are still the primary users, however, because they have thousands of miles of optical fiber installed. Notice that the basic OC-1 data rate is slightly faster than the T-3 data rate. Telephone companies and other carriers are replacing their T-3 and T-4 services with SONET, especially between exchange offices. For more information about SONET, check the information on the Internet at http://www.sonet.com.

## Integrated Services Digital Network (ISDN)

**Integrated Services Digital Network (ISDN)**

The **Integrated Services Digital Network (ISDN)** is less of a network and more of a set of standards than the name implies. The ISDN standards were developed by the ITU-T as a vision for the direction that the world's public telecommunications system should take. They believed that ISDN would eventually replace leased and switched circuits as we knew them.

ISDN can best be visualized as digital channels of two types, as shown in Figure 13-12. One type, the "B" (bearer) channel, carries up to 64 Kbps of digital data. The other type, the "D" (delta) channel, carries 16 Kbps of data and is used for signaling. These two types of channels are packaged according to ISDN standards into two types of access services. The **basic rate interface (BRI)**, also known as 2B + D, provides two 64-Kbps B channels and one 16-Kbps D channel. The two B channels can be combined to yield a single channel operating at 128 Kbps. BRI is made available in homes and offices on standard twisted pair wiring.

**basic rate interface (BRI)**

**primary rate interface (PRI)**

The other type of access is known as **primary rate interface (PRI)**, or 23B + D. Primary rate access provides twenty-three 64-Kbps B channels for carrying data and one 64-Kbps D channel for signaling. The total capacity of twenty-four 64-Kbps channels happens to equal the carrying capacity of a T-1 circuit as it is defined in the U.S., Canada, and Japan. In Europe, primary access is defined as 30B + D, which matches the capacity of a European E-1 circuit.

The large bandwidth provided by ISDN circuits can be used for digitized voice and data. With basic access in the home, a person could be having a telephone conversation and simultaneously transmitting data at 64 Kbps from a PC. A business that has a primary ISDN access group could subdivide the

**FIGURE 13-12**   ISDN basic and primary access arrangements.

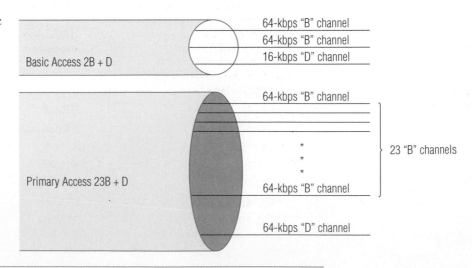

bandwidth in any way necessary to meet the needs of its application set. Half of the capacity, or 772 Kbps, might be used for television transmission while the other 772 Kbps is further subdivided to support twenty-four voice conversations at 16 Kbps and six 64 Kbps data channels. At another time, the bandwidth could be configured differently—all under the control of the customer. In fact, these configuration changes could be programmed into a computer so that the ISDN capacity is automatically reconfigured at certain times of the day. There could be a daytime configuration, a nighttime configuration, or any other combination to meet the business needs of the company.

**broadband ISDN (BISDN)**

**narrowband ISDN**

An upgrade to ISDN, called **broadband ISDN (BISDN),** has been defined but has not yet been widely implemented. To distinguish this new network and the new services it offers from the original concept of ISDN, that original concept is now being referred to as **narrowband ISDN.**

Broadband ISDN has three services:

- a FDX circuit operating at a speed of 155.52 Mbps
- a FDX circuit operating at 622.08 Mbps
- an asymmetrical circuit that contains two simplex channels, one of which operates at 155.52 Mbps and the other at 622.08 Mbps

The first two options would be used as very high speed data circuits, whereas the third option would typically be used where the flow of data in one direction is much greater than in the other.

BISDN circuits are actually transported from one node to another using ATM for transport. ATM is transparent, and the user of a BISDN circuit is not aware that ATM is operating in the background. Furthermore, BISDN is backward compatible, meaning that a standard narrowband ISDN BRI or PRI transmission can be handled transparently on a BISDN circuit.

The benefits of ISDN are as follows:

- It provides efficient multiplexed access to the public network.
- It has the capabilities to support integrated voice and data.
- It has a robust signaling channel, which is important for network management.
- It provides an open system that is internationally defined.

ISDN service has been implemented more slowly in the U.S. than in many other countries in the world, partly because the carriers have had difficulty agreeing on precise standards. The reasons behind this are twofold: 1) they have not actively marketed the service; and 2) costs have been high. There have also been frequent problems getting ISDN service to operate properly when it is first installed. In Japan, Australia, and a few other countries, however, ISDN has been used by businesses for data circuits for many years, and now ISDN is installed in many homes for little more than the cost of a regular analog telephone line.

## 13-9  SWITCHED MULTIMEGABIT DATA SERVICE (SMDS)

**Switched Multimegabit Data Service (SMDS)**

**Switched Multimegabit Data Service (SMDS)** is a high-speed switched digital service offered by some of the communications carriers. Because the user does not have a dedicated line between locations, SMDS is a connectionless service. Data to be transmitted via SMDS is broken down into 53-byte cells. Two SMDS speeds are available; either 1.544 Mbps (T-1 speed) or 44.736 Mbps (T-3 speed). The difference between SMDS and standard T-1 service is that a user must lease

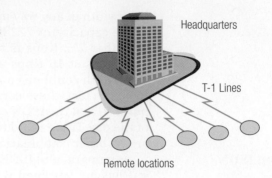

**FIGURE 13-13** The SMDS configuration is usually less expensive than the topology that only has T-1 circuits.

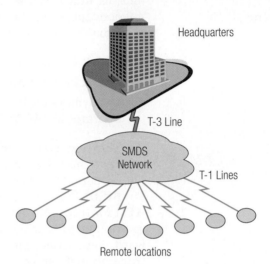

a point-to-point T-1 circuit, whereas with SMDS the user leases a T-1 circuit to the carrier's nearest office at both ends, and the carrier handles the transmission in between using normal, shared communication facilities. For example, if an organization wanted to connect each of its eight locations to headquarters at 1.544 Mbps, it could either lease eight T-1 lines, one from each location to headquarters, or it could lease a 1.544 T-1 line from each location to the nearest carrier's office where it would access the SMDS network. At headquarters, the organization might lease a 44.736 Mbps T-3 line from the carrier's office to its headquarters, as shown in Figure 13-13. Although a detailed cost analysis would have to be done for the particular locations involved, in most instances, configuration using the SMDS network would be less expensive.

## Virtual Private Networks (VPNs)

**virtual private network (VPN)**

A **virtual private network (VPN)**, which you studied in Chapter 12, allows a company that has multiple sites to enjoy the advantages that both public and private networks offer. The technology gives the company the appearance of having a private network but it uses public networks, including the Internet, to carry network traffic between the company's sites. The VPN, sometimes

**tunnel**

called a **tunnel**, acts as a direct, secure connection between locations. Most VPNs fall into one of two categories: site-to-site or remote access. VPNs are most often used to let remote workers access their companies' servers securely. VPN hardware and/or software restricts packets so they can only travel between company sites by coding or encrypting them so they are unintelligible, even if they are accidentally sent elsewhere.

A key attribute of VPNs is that they deliver secure communications. The way this is normally achieved is through a set of standardized protocols called

IP Security (IPsec)

transport mode

tunnel mode

**IP Security (IPsec),** which were developed by the Internet Engineering Task Force (IETF). IPsec's purpose is to support the secure exchange of packets at the IP layer of the TCP/IP protocol, and it has been most widely used to implement VPNs. IPsec supports two encryption modes: **transport mode** and **tunnel mode.** Transport mode encrypts only the data portion of each packet but leaves the header untouched. The more secure tunnel mode encrypts both the header and the data. On the receiving side, IPsec-compliant software decrypts each packet. IPsec will be discussed in more detail in Chapter 17—after you have studied encryption and digital certificates.

VPNs have been around for a long time, though we haven't always called them by that name. Companies have sent their private data over public packet networks, frame relay networks, and ATM networks for many years. What is different today is the use of the Internet to send private data; and of course, by comparison, the Internet is nearly free. Encrypted data sent through a VPN using the Internet is a very cost effective way for many organizations to achieve secure communications. Internet-based VPNs can save a company thousands of dollars in circuit charges, and the Internet is available everywhere. Furthermore, companies can build their own VPNs using readily available hardware and software.

## ■ SUMMARY

In this chapter, you have studied the ways in which WANs differ from other types of networks. You have also looked at the ways traffic is routed in a network and the impact that congestion has on network performance. While routing and congestion control are issues for all networks, they are especially important to WANs. You have also studied many of the technologies that communications carriers offer as products. With this information, you can see that there are many choices and technologies available for constructing WANs, and careful study and analysis must be done to select the right one.

Chapter 14 will introduce you to internetworking—connecting several networks together to form an internet. You will study TCP/IP, UDP, and some tools that can be used to test and debug internets.

## ■ REVIEW QUESTIONS

13-1. Explain the terms *circuit switching* and *packet switching*.

13-2. Explain why it is important for any routing technique to have alternate routes available to send messages.

13-3. Explain the function of a PAD.

13-4. Why is packet switching another form of multiplexing?

13-5. Why is it necessary to understand the ramifications of using a packet switching network when very fast response time is required in an interactive system?

13-6. What is a datagram?

13-7. Explain the term *virtual circuit.*

13-8. How can packets arrive out of sequence in a packet switching network?

13-9. What are the advantages and disadvantages of centralized routing? Of distributed dynamic routing?

13-10. What are the disadvantages of broadcast routing?

13-11. Describe the function of a router.

13-12. How does congestion occur in a network?

13-13. When packets need to be discarded, why may discarding the last packet(s) received be unfair?

13-14. Explain why e-mail traffic is said to be loss sensitive but delay insensitive.

13-15. Describe some places or situations when queuing would occur in a network.

13-16. Identify three tone signals used in the telephone system.

13-17. Describe how frame relay works.

13-18. What advantages does frame relay have over standard packet switching?

13-19. What differing assumptions about the transmission circuits does a frame relay network make, as contrasted with a packet switching network?

13-20. Why is ATM so efficient and fast?

13-21. Explain the difference between ATM's CBR and UBR services.

13-22. When might an organization want to consider using SONET services?

13-23. Distinguish between ISDN's BRI and PRI.

13-24. Explain when a VPN may be a useful choice for an organization that wishes to connect its sites with a WAN.

## TRUE OR FALSE

13-1. WANS are generally understood to be those networks that cover a large geographic area.

13-2. WANS are usually implemented with bus and ring topologies.

13-3. Organizations usually build their own WANs by laying cable and using contractors.

13-4. Network signaling can take the place of protocols on data networks.

13-5. Users must break their messages into packets before sending them through a packet data network.

13-6. A packet switching network does not establish an actual physical link between two nodes that wish to communicate.

13-7. All datagrams that constitute a message are handled as a unit as they flow through a packet network.

13-8. Datagram service does not guarantee that packets will be delivered.

13-9. VCs can be leased from communications carriers.

13-10. When centralized routing is employed, a central computer keeps a table of all the terminals on the network and the paths or routes to each.

13-11. Distributed routing places the responsibility for building and maintaining routing tables on some of the nodes in the network.

13-12. Adaptive routing is more flexible than static routing.

13-13. Routers are specialized computers that perform routing in a network.

13-14. Congestion occurs on a network only during the cold season.

13-15. Congestion control is the attempt to manage congestion by reducing the flow of new packets into the network or by routing packets around congested circuits or nodes.

13-16. Applications have differing needs for network service.

13-17. Queuing delay in a network is usually trivial and can largely be ignored.

13-18. X.25 is the ITU-T's recommended standard for frame relay service.

13-19. X.25 has flow and error control mechanisms.

13-20. Frame relay got its start with the bucket brigades in early fire departments.

13-21. Frame relay was developed to reduce the overhead of packet switching and to take advantage of multimegabit lines.

13-22. The basic mechanism for relieving congestion in a crowded frame relay network is to discard frames.

13-23. Some data, such as real time voice or video, is not very tolerant of network delays.

13-24. ATM uses fixed-length packets of 53 bytes called cells.

13-25. ATM networks are typically designed to be able to handle many types of traffic simultaneously, such as voice, video, and real time data.

13-26. Examples of ATM's UBR applications include telephone connections, videoconferencing, and others that involve people at both ends of the connection communicating in real time.

13-27. ATM's header error control byte can be used for some error correction as well as error detection.

13-28. ATM circuits tend to be expensive.

13-29. SONET is available only for communications carriers to use.

13-30. ISDN can best be visualized as digital channels of two types.

13-31. ISDN service has been implemented more slowly in the U.S. than in many other countries in the world.

13-32. SMDS is a high-speed switched analog telephone service.

13-33. VPNs provide good data security.

13-34. Data sent through a VPN is transmitted through a public network.

13-35. Unfortunately, the Internet cannot be used for VPNs.


## MULTIPLE CHOICE

13-1. Which of the following routing techniques are used in WANs?

    a. dynamic routing

    b. distributed routing

    c. static routing

    d. All of the above.

13-2. Delays in networks can come from _____.

    a. propagation

    b. switching

    c. queuing

    d. All of the above.

13-3. Which of the following was developed to overcome the overhead of packet switching and provide more efficient data transmission?

    a. X.25

    b. circuit switched systems

    c. frame relay

    d. RS-232

    e. X.21

**13-4.** Frame relay deals with circuit congestion by applying the concepts of
a _____.

    a. CIR

    b. PLL

    c. CBR

    d. out-of-band signaling

    e. SS7

**13-5.** In the context of ATM, a cell is _____.

    a. the geographic boundary of the network

    b. a 53-byte transmission unit

    c. the boundary of the area in which voice traffic can be handled

    d. the place where the designer is kept for specifying an overly complex network design

**13-6.** In ISDN, the service that provides two 64 Kbps B channels and one 16 Kbps D channel is called _____.

    a. PRI

    b. BISDN

    c. the D channel

    d. BRI

    e. None of the above.

**13-7.** VPNs _____.

    a. can send data through the Internet

    b. can handle traffic relatively securely

    c. can restrict outside packets from entering the VPN

    d. are usually quite cost effective

    e. All of the above.

## ■ PROBLEMS AND PROJECTS

**13-1.** What type of routing would be used in a public packet switching network? Why?

**13-2.** Think of an application where a PDN's datagram service could be used successfully, considering that the PDN does not guarantee the arrival of datagrams or their arrival sequence.

**13-3.** Talk to some companies in your area and find out if they are using frame relay or ATM services. Find out what applications require the use of such a high-speed network. Ask if there were any problems installing the service and getting it to work. Find out if the network is reliable on a day-to-day basis.

**13-4.** Visit a company in your area to discuss their use of VPNs. Are they confident in the security of the VPN? Is the VPN cost effective for their applications? What did they use to provide similar network service before implementing the VPN? What additional capabilities would they like to have that the VPN does not provide.

**C A S E   S T U D Y**

## ECKLES, FEINMAN, AND MACKENZIE—PART 4

The details for EF&M's leased line WAN were almost complete when Mr. Block received a call from the local telephone company's sales representative, Jennifer Schay, requesting an appointment to discuss a WAN offering that she felt might meet EF&M's needs. Mr. Block scheduled an appointment for the following week. At the meeting, Ms. Schay made a proposal for EF&M to install a public frame relay network instead of leasing individual lines. She explained that EF&M could get all of the benefits of having leased lines without having to be responsible for the equipment at the ends of the circuits. She stated that the circuit capacity to each location could be adjusted as message traffic grew or fell so that the service objectives of good throughput and response time at minimal cost could be maintained. She also stated that, because EF&M's network would use public circuits and equipment that were already installed, the cost should be less than that of a leased line network. However, she could not give exact figures because she did not know what assumptions Mr. Block had made when configuring the network he had been planning to install.

**QUESTIONS**

1. What additional information should Mr. Block be requesting from Ms. Schay to accurately compare her frame relay proposal to the leased line network he had been planning?

2. Mr. Block had also heard that it is possible for a company to install a private frame relay network. What would be the pros and cons, compared with the public frame relay network that Ms. Schay proposed?

3. What would be the major factors in Mr. Block's decision whether to propose the leased line network or the frame relay network to the managing partners?

# INTERNETWORKING

## ■ OUTLINE

Part Four examines the ways in which networks are connected to one another to form internets. TCP/IP, the protocol of internets, is explained in detail. The Internet and its history, evolution, and current usage are described. Many practical Internet tools and applications are introduced. Although you might have used some of them, you may learn new ways to realize their full potential.

Chapter 14 delves into the technology of internetworks and explains how networks are connected together. You will study both the TCP and IP protocols and understand their role in internets. You will examine several internetworking tools and look at the output of their operations.

Chapter 15 presents the Internet. You will explore the fascinating history and background of the Internet to aid your understanding of its current situation and environment. You will explore various ways of connecting to the Internet.

Chapter 16 discusses the World Wide Web and explains URLs, HTTP, and HTML. You will see an example of how to create a simple web page. You will learn the "how tos" and "whys" of various Internet and Web applications or tools, such as e-mail, Internet telephony, and instant messaging.

# INTERNETWORKING

## ◼ OUTLINE

## ◼ KEY TERMS

acknowledgment (ACK)

Address Resolution Protocol (ARP)

anycast

autoconfiguration

checksum

Classless Inter-Domain Routing (CIDR)

connection-oriented

datagram sockets

DHCP discover message

DNS servers

domain name system (DNS)

Dynamic Host Configuration Protocol (DHCP)

dynamic IP address

dynamic window sizing on congestion

end systems

error-checking

finger

finish segment (FIN segment)

flow control

full-duplex (FDX) transmission

hexadecimal

intermediate system

Internet

Internet Control Message
Protocol (ICMP)

Internet Corporation for
Assigned Names and
Numbers (ICANN)

Internet Message Access
Protocol, version 4
(IMAP4)

Internet Network
Information Center
(InterNIC)

Internet Protocol, new
generation (IPng)

Internet Protocol,
version 4 (IPv4)

Internet Protocol,
version 6 (IPv6)

internetwork/internet

IP address

IP multicast backbone
(Mbone)

logical bitwise AND
operation

multicast

multicasting

name server lookup
(nslookup)

octet

open systems

packets

ping

point-to-point

Post Office Protocol,
version 3 (POPv3)

request for comment
(RFC)

resolver

root servers

routing table

sequence numbering

Simple Mail Transfer
Protocol (SMTP)

slow start

socket

static IP address

stream sockets

stream transport

subnetwork (subnet)

subnet mask

subnetworks

supernetting

synchronization segment
(SYN segment)

three-way handshake

top level domain (TLD)

traceroute

Transmission Control
Protocol (TCP)

unicast

User Datagram Protocol
(UDP)

virtual network

whois

zero compression

## ■ OBJECTIVES

After you complete your study of this chapter, you should be able to:

- describe the RFC process and how it helps internetworking technology to evolve;
- explain the functions of the TCP/IP protocol layers;
- explain the functions of IP;
- explain the IPv4 and IPv6 addressing systems;
- describe the five classes of IP addresses;
- describe how Internet domain names get resolved;
- explain the problems of IPv4 that IPv6 solves;
- describe the functions of TCP; and
- describe the functions of UDP.

## 14-1    INTRODUCTION

Internet

Even people who know very little about networking know and love the Internet. The history and development of the Internet is "the fun stuff" of networking. Internetworking, however, refers to the connection of several diverse networks that run and are paid for on their own, retaining their own identity and requiring special mechanisms to communicate with each other. When the word **Internet** is capitalized, it refers to the globe-spanning network of networks that has put the entire world at our fingertips. The most exciting and intriguing part of the Internet is the World Wide Web. It is what most people think of when they refer to an internet. Chapter 15 discusses the Internet and its history, browsers, and the World Wide Web. Underlying all the excitement, however, is an even more fascinating and complex technology.

An internet must provide a link between networks, routing and delivering data between processes on computers of different networks while accommodating several variations among those networks. These include addressing schemes, maximum packet size, network access mechanisms, time-outs, error recovery, and other differences. The requirements of internetworking are met by the IP and other software in the perennial and versatile, phenomenal and flexible TCP/IP suite. Chapter 14 examines the principles of internetworking, introduces the hardware devices used, and describes internet architecture and the TCP/IP internetworking protocols, including the next generation IPv6.

One of the challenges when discussing internetworking and the Internet is to identify which of the technologies are long lasting and which are likely to disappear within a few years as newer, more capable technologies replace them. In the next three chapters we will discuss technologies that we believe will survive for several years, remembering that in the fast-paced communications world, four or five years is a long life for many products and capabilities.

## 14-2    PRINCIPLES OF INTERNETWORKING

internetwork/internet

An **internetwork** or **internet** carries the concept of networking one step further down the road to universal connectivity by joining multiple networks or types of network into one large, uniform communications system. An internet is the connection of two or more networks of any type. The most common implementation is the connection of several packet switching networks by using TCP/IP protocols and routers.

A single network often has inadequate resources to meet all its users' needs. Furthermore, networking technologies are designed to meet specific requirements—and one size or type does not fit all. Organizations, therefore, have often adopted different types of networks depending on the needs of their particular departments or locations. At a university, a LAN technology like Ethernet, discussed in Chapters 10 through 12, might be the best solution for connecting the offices in an administration building. A WAN technology like frame relay, which you studied in Chapter 13, may provide better connectivity for the statewide continuing education system. This diversity and free choice are desirable, but they also carry with them a problem. Because of incompatibilities in electrical specifications, network hardware, physical-addressing schemes, and packet formats, diverse networks cannot simply be plugged together. Each exists as an isolated island in the archipelago with no causeway to connect it with the others.

Internetworking solves the problem by connecting these heterogeneous network islands. The individual networks that are interconnected, which may

**subnetworks**

**end systems**

**intermediate system**

**virtual network**

maintain their own identity, are usually referred to as **subnetworks.** Each subnetwork supports the devices or computers, known as **end systems,** attached to it. Software on all the attached computers, along with routers, provide a causeway between islands and perform the relay and routing of messages necessary for universal service between them. The routers and bridges that form the communication path are referred to as **intermediate systems.** To the user, an internet of underlying physical networks and routers appears to be a larger network because its hardware and software create a **virtual network** system that appears as a single seamless entity, though no such uniform network exists. Figure 14-1 illustrates a simple internet.

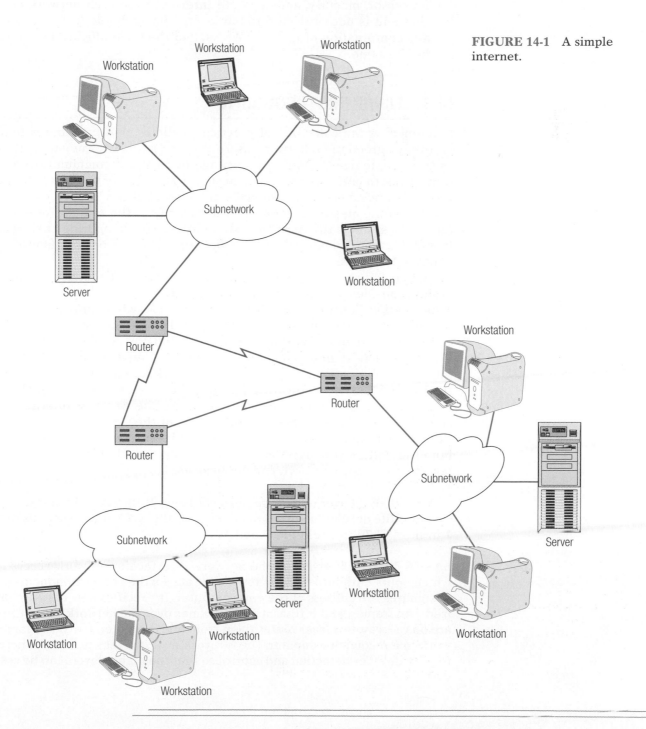

**FIGURE 14-1** A simple internet.

## 14-3   INTERNET HARDWARE

Two basic types of hardware that you studied in Chapter 10, and which differ mainly in the protocols employed, are used for connecting networks in internets.

- A bridge operates at level two of the OSI model and acts as a relay of frames between networks that use the same technology and protocol.

- A router connects two networks at level three of the OSI model and is able to send packets to similar or dissimilar networks. It is the basic hardware between incompatible networks. A router has a conventional processor, memory, and separate interfaces for each network connection and is not restricted to any particular technology. It can connect any combination of LANs or WANs, and the technologies don't need to be the same.

## 14-4   TCP/IP PROTOCOL SUITE

A protocol is the collection of practices, policies, and procedures that are mutually agreed upon between users so they are able to communicate. Just as two people need a common language or rules for communication when they speak to one another, so two hosts (in TCP/IP, any two computers from PCs to mainframe) need protocols or rules of behavior and conventions when sending messages to one another. TCP/IP is the protocol of **open systems;** i.e., systems that provide a standards-based computing environment. It makes communications possible between any two hosts, despite differences in hardware.

**open systems**

When I first encountered the acronym, TCP/IP, I thought it stood for, "think, consider, ponder, ignorant person." TCP/IP is actually an acronym for Transmission Control Protocol/Internet Protocol, which provides the "rules of the road" for internets and the Internet. The letters represent the names of its two most important protocols, but TCP/IP is in fact a suite of many. TCP/IP is more than its name implies. It is the universal language for computer communication through an internetwork and it is the glue that binds the Internet and its World Wide Web together. It is, above all, a stack of protocols without which one cannot function in the world of internetworked computers. Figure 14-2 shows a comparison of the OSI reference model and the TCP/IP protocol stack. The stack has five layers (though some people combine the bottom two layers making a four-layer stack: physical, network interface, internet, transport, and application.

**LAYER ONE**   Layer one is the physical layer. It includes the hardware (cable, satellite or other connection media, and the NIC). It corresponds to layer 1 in the OSI 7-layer reference model.

**LAYER TWO**   Layer two is the network interface or network access layer, which splits data into packets to be sent across the connection medium and designates the address of the end computer. It specifies how data are organized into frames, and it transmits the frames over the network. Once the data are on the way, this layer routes them from one computer across the same network to a receiving computer. The network access layer's primary function is to provide error detection and control so that the higher layers can be assured

FIGURE 14-2 A comparison of the layers of the OSI Reference Model and the TCP/IP protocol stack.

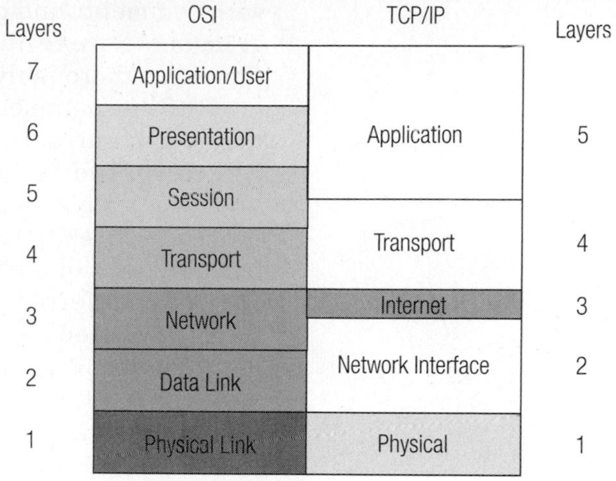

| Layers | OSI | TCP/IP | Layers |
|---|---|---|---|
| 7 | Application/User | Application | 5 |
| 6 | Presentation | | |
| 5 | Session | | |
| 4 | Transport | Transport | 4 |
| 3 | Network | Internet | 3 |
| 2 | Data Link | Network Interface | 2 |
| 1 | Physical Link | Physical | 1 |

of error-free transmission over the link. It is similar to the data link layer (2) of the OSI model.

**LAYER THREE**  Layer three is the Internet layer. Without it, data would never get to the right place. This is where IP and the IP address work. It receives the packets from the Network Interface layer and sends them, through one or more routers, to the correct address by the best route. There is no corresponding layer in the OSI model.

**LAYER FOUR**  Layer four is the transport layer which, like the fourth layer in the OSI model, routes data to its destination. It makes sure that packets have no errors and that they arrive in the correct order.

**LAYER FIVE**  Layer five is the application layer, which establishes and coordinates a connection between two computers and then converts files from one format to another so two computers that use different formats can speak the same language. Each protocol of layer five specifies how one particular application uses an internet. Finally, it does the work of e-mail, file transfer, remote log on, and browsing the World Wide Web. It corresponds to layers 6 and 7 in the OSI model. Both hosts and routers have the TCP/IP protocol software, although routers don't need some of the layers (especially layer 5).

## 14-5  REQUESTS FOR COMMENT (RFC)

request for comment (RFC)

Internetworking protocols and technology continue to evolve. One of the methods of that evolution is the **request for comment (RFC).** Two websites in particular are helpful for finding any RFC from number 1 ("Host Software" by S. Crocker, dated April 7, 1969) to the present. www.ietf.org/rfc.html is a searchable index, and www.rfc-editor.org is the actual RFC editor's page, which was maintained by Jon Postel for 30 years. For those who are interested to know more, http://www.postel.org/remembrances/ is an interesting tribute to the man and his work.

All of the protocols in the TCP/IP suite are defined by documents called RFCs. Whenever a person conceives a new idea or improved capability, he or she writes an RFC, which is then published on the Internet. The RFC is assigned a number by which it will always be known, and reviewers respond with comments and constructive criticism. The RFC is revised and after programmers have tested it, it becomes an official standard. In this way, TCP/IP remains a thoroughly democratic process.

RFCs form the body of literature concerning Internet protocols and standards. The current index for Technical Specifications (November 2001) is RFC 3000. The literature also includes many humorous or entertaining essays, especially those dated April 1 of any year. One essay, RFC 1607 ("A View From The 21st Century") tells the history and future of the Internet as seen from the eyes of a person working on Mars in 2023. It was written by Vinton Cerf, often referred to as "The Big Daddy of the Internet." From 1972 to 1976, Cerf researched networking and led the project at Stanford University that developed TCP under a DARPA research grant. The history of the Internet and TCP/IP are intertwined and are discussed in greater detail in Chapter 15. Another interesting read is RFC 2555 ("30 Years of RFCs") detailing the history of the RFC process and highlighting some of its milestones. For those who enjoy poetry, there is even a smattering of that among the technical and scientific data. RFC 968 is a poem by Vinton Cerf called "Twas the Night Before Start-up." The one by D.L. Covill, RFC 527 "Arpawocky," is derived from Lewis Carroll's "Jaberwocky." Techies and poets alike will love them.

## 14-6   INTERNET PROTOCOL (IP)

**Internet Protocol version 4 (IPv4)**

IP is responsible for the basic connectivity between networks, though it is not concerned whether data arrive without errors. That is handled by other protocols, such as TCP. The current version of IP is **Internet Protocol version 4, (IPv4)**. A newer version, called IPv6, is a bigger and more versatile "brother" that many Internet sites are starting to implement. It is discussed in a later section of this chapter.

### Classful IP Addressing

**IP address**

The **IP address** is the core of the IP. Every host on a TCP/IP network must have a unique address—similar to a telephone number or a street address—a place to send and receive data. Each IP address actually identifies not a specific computer, but a connection between a computer and a network. A router with multiple network connections, therefore, must be assigned an IP address for each connection.

Early on, when engineers were designing the protocol, they included in the packets themselves the address information they needed to reach their proper destinations. Thus, routers were able to make their own decisions about how to send individual packets over an internet. The IPv4 address is a 32-bit address divided into two sections: the network name (NET_ID) and the host name (HOST_ID). The NET_ID, which identifies every TCP/IP network connected within an internet, is used for high-level routing between networks in much the same way an area code is used in a telephone network or the country and city designate a geographical address. The HOST_ID indicates the specific host within a network and is often referred to as a node. For example, 192.16.227.101 is an address that identifies the network and the individual host on that network.

An IP number is written as four fields or bytes, eight bits each, separated by dots. It looks like this: `Field1.Field2.Field3.Field4`. A sample address, which is explained later, is `206.11.20.81`. Each field can be a number from 0 to 255. All hosts on the same network have the same network number, but each host/network interface on the same network has a unique host number.

FIGURE 14-3   The range
of decimal values in the
first eight bits of each
address class.

| Class | From Decimal Value | To Decimal Value |
|-------|--------------------|------------------|
| A | 0 | 126 |
| B | 128 | 191 |
| C | 192 | 223 |
| D | 224 | 239 |
| E | 240 | 255 |

The IP addressing scheme includes three primary classes of networks (A, B, C) that are used for host addresses and two special classes (D, E). The range of decimal values that designate the class to which an address belongs is listed in Figure 14-3. The only difference between them is the length of the NET_ID subfield. A class is recognized by the decimal value of the first 8 bits, called an **octet**. Notice that the decimal number 127 is not included in the chart in Figure 14-3. That is because it is used for internal testing on local machines.

octet

As you see, there are five different address classes. The first byte of the first octet, expressed in binary, determines the class of the address.

- Class A addresses start with 0.
- Class B addresses start with 10.
- Class C addresses start with 110.
- Class D addresses start with 1110.
- Class E addresses start with 1111.

**CLASS A**   Class A is intended for 126 enormous networks, each of which can address almost 17,000,000 hosts. The first field is always a number from 1–126 (none begin with 0). The Class A address, illustrated in Figure 14-4, has an 8-bit network prefix that includes the highest order bit, set to 0, and a 7-bit network number. The 8-bit prefix is followed by a 24-bit host number, totalling 32 bits (4 octets).

**CLASS B**   Class B is designed for 16,384 big networks, each of which can have up to 65,536 hosts. It is the size needed by some universities and larger companies. The first field of a Class B address is always a number between 128 and 191. It has been difficult to get a new Class B address for quite a while because the space has been in danger of being exhausted. The address, illustrated in Figure 14-4, has a 16-bit network prefix that includes the two highest order bits, set to 10, and a 14-bit network number. The 16-bit prefix is followed by a 16-bit host number.

FIGURE 14-4   Comparison
of Class A, B, and C
addresses.

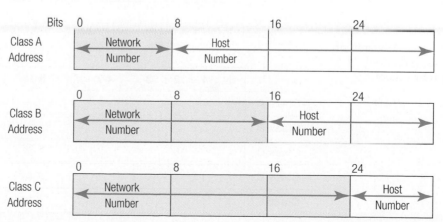

**CLASS C** Class C is meant for everyone else—the 2,097,152 small networks, each of which may have only 254 hosts (0 and 255 are reserved.) The first field of a Class C address is always a number between 192 and 223. Obviously, most networks are class C. The address, illustrated in Figure 14-4, has a 24-bit network prefix that includes the three highest order bits, set to 110, and a 21-bit network number. The 24-bit prefix is followed by an 8-bit host number.

Thus, our IP address 206.11.20.81 is a class C address. The network prefix (address) is 206.11.20 and the host number (address) is 81.

**multicasting**

**CLASS D** Class D is reserved for **multicasting,** a special way of transmitting information from a server to a set of several clients at the same time, for instance, audio and video conferencing or Internet radio and TV. The decimal value of the first byte in Class D ranges from 224 through 239. The leading four bits are set to 1110.

Multicasting works like this: days or weeks ahead, sponsoring organizations announce the class D network address that the server will use for transmission. There are many available channels. At the assigned date and time of the broadcast, one tunes or configures the client software for the proper class D address. Multicasting works just like ordinary radio or TV, except that it is on the Internet. Real-time applications require special purpose, multicast-aware routers so packets always arrive in proper order with none missing.

**IP multicast backbone (Mbone)**

These routers on the Internet form the **IP multicast backbone (Mbone).**

**CLASS E** Class E is reserved for future use. The decimal value of the first byte in Class E ranges from 240 through 255. The leading four bits are set to 1111.

Although the dotted decimal number is easier for humans to read, binary numbers are all that computers can read. Just as the decimal system is base 10, the binary system is base 2. The only possible values are 1 (on) or 0 (off). A byte is made up of 8 bits. Figure 14-5 shows the binary system of numbering and how values are shown.

The router determines the class to which an address belongs by the first four bits of the IP address. Figure 14-6 shows the division of the five classes, and the first four bits of the address indicate the class of an address.

**FIGURE 14-5** Binary system numbering.

In the decimal system, the number 206 requires 4 columns: the 100s, 10s, and 1s. In the binary system, 8 columns are needed: 128, 64, 32, 16, 8, 4, 2, and 1s.

| 128 | 64 | 32 | 16 | 8 | 4 | 2 | 1 |
|-----|-----|-----|-----|-----|-----|-----|-----|
| 1 | 1 | 0 | 0 | 1 | 1 | 1 | 0 |

**FIGURE 14-6** Division of five classes indicated by the first four bits of the address.

| | Bits | | | | | | | |
|---------|---|---|---|---|-----|------|-------|-------|
| | 0 | 1 | 2 | 3 | 4-7 | 8-15 | 16-23 | 24-31 |
| Class A | 0 | | | | | | | |
| Class B | 1 | 0 | | | | | | |
| Class C | 1 | 1 | 0 | | | | | |
| Class D | 1 | 1 | 1 | 0 | | | | |
| Class E | 1 | 1 | 1 | 1 | | | | |

## Subnetting and Subnet Masks

What happens if a Class C network has more than 254 nodes? Remember, a node can be a computer, a router, a printer, a managed hub, or another network device. What happens if an organization has an internet that includes one or more WANs and a number of locations that each have multiple LANs? Each of an organization's networks could acquire a separate IP number; however, the vast number of available IP numbers is rapidly diminishing and other solutions are needed.

**subnetwork (subnet)**

One option is to create a **subnetwork** or **subnet,** a separate part of an organization's network that is identifiable—such as a college library, the university relations department, or an offsite campus—and represents all the machines housed in one building or on the same LAN. Without subnets, an organization would require multiple connections to the Internet, one for each of its physically separate networks, an unnecessary use of the limited number of network addresses available. Internet routing tables outside the organization would need to know and manage routing that could be handled by routers within an organization more efficiently. Very common reasons for subnetting are the need to control network traffic and to help with issues of security.

**subnet mask**

By dividing the whole network into subnets, the entire organization can connect to an internet with a shared network address. All LANs on the site have the same network number and to the rest of the Internet it appears as if the site is one single network. This "deception" is accomplished by the **subnet mask,** a 32-bit number applied to the IP address that tells the router how to interpret the bits of the address. It is a screen of binary digits that identifies which bits are the network part of the address and which bits are the host (or node) part of the address. The 1s in the mask represent the network bits and the 0s represent the host bits. A "1" in the mask says, "Look at the bit in this position in the address." A "0" in the mask says, "Don't look at the bit in this position in the address." Using a mask saves a router's having to handle the entire 32-bit address because it looks only at the bits selected by the mask to determine the network address.

In effect, bits are borrowed from the host address section of the network address to be used as the subnet address so that each subnet has its own unique address. A computer is configured with both an IP address and an appropriate subnet mask. To separate the network address from the host address, the subnet mask is applied mathematically to the full 32-bit IP address in every packet. The subnet mask must be the same for each computer on the network. Figure 14-7 illustrates the default subnet mask for each class.

In the Class A subnet mask, for example, the 255 appears in the first group of eight bits. As you can see, this is converted in binary (0 = off, 1 = on) to 11111111, which means that all eight bits are "turned on" and mask out the first octet of the address. This tells a computer that the network information is contained within the first octet.

**FIGURE 14-7** Default subnet masks.

| | Dotted Decimal | Binary Representation |
|---|---|---|
| **Class A:** | 255.0.0.0 | 11111111.00000000.00000000.00000000 |
| **Class B:** | 255.255.0.0 | 11111111.11111111.00000000.00000000 |
| **Class C:** | 255.255.255.0 | 11111111.11111111.11111111.00000000 |

FIGURE 14-8  The logical AND operation applied to 2 bits and the results.

| First Bit | 1 | 1 | 0 | 0 |
|-----------|---|---|---|---|
| Second Bit | 1 | 0 | 1 | 0 |
| Result | 1 | 0 | 0 | 0 |

**logical bitwise AND operation**

When we say that the 32-bit number is mathematically applied to the IP address, we mean that a **logical bitwise AND operation** is performed between the IP address and the subnet mask to result in the network address. The logical AND operation compares two bits. If they are both 1, the result is 1. If not, the result is 0. Figure 14-8 illustrates the operation.

For example, using a hypothetical Class C IP address, 206.11.20.81, and applying the default Class C subnet mask, 255.255.255.0, results in the network number 206.11.20 and the host number 81, as illustrated in Figure 14-9.

Using subnetting, an organization can use some of the bits in the host part of the address to identify a specific subnet. The 32-bit IP address stays exactly the same, but the bits are interpreted differently. Effectively, the IP address then contains three parts: the network number, the subnet number, and the host address.

To illustrate, let us continue to look at a class C IP address: 206.11.20.81. First, we convert each of the eight-bit digits in the dotted-decimal address to binary numbers, because each decimal digit represents a string of binary digits. The IP address 206.11.20.81 converts to 11001110.00001011.00010100.01010001.

Because this is a Class C address, the first 24 bits are the network address, 206.11.20; and the next 8 are the original host address, 81. When a subnet mask is applied to this address, part of the host address is interpreted as a subnet address and the rest as the host address. Figure 14-10 illustrates what happens when a mask is applied to a Class C IP address.

If the subnet mask, 11111111.11111111.11111111.11100000 (255.255.255.224) were used, for example, it would tell the router to look at the first 27 bits and not to bother with the last 5 bits. Because bits 1–24 are always used for the network address, bits 25, 26, and 27 are interpreted as the subnet address. When

FIGURE 14-9  Default subnet mask applied to a Class C address.

| Class C IP address | 11001110 | 00001011 | 00010100 | 01010001 | 206.11.20.81 |
|--------------------|----------|----------|----------|----------|--------------|
| Default Class C Subnet Mask | 11111111 | 11111111 | 11111111 | 00000000 | 255.255.255.000 |
| Network Address | 11001110 | 00001011 | 00010100 | 00000000 | 206.11.20.000 |

Notice that three extra bits are added to the default Class C subnet mask.

FIGURE 14-10  A subnet mask applied to a Class C address.

| Class C IP Address | 11001110 | 00001011 | 00010100 | 01010001 | 206.11.20.81 |
|--------------------|----------|----------|----------|----------|--------------|
| Subnet Mask | **11111111** | **11111111** | **11111111** | **11100000** | 255.255.255.224 |
| Subnet Number | 11001110 | 00001011 | 00010100 | 010 | 2 |
| Host Address | 00000000 | 00000000 | 00000000 | 00010001 | 17 |

**FIGURE 14-11** Converting decimal numbers to binary.

A simple way for "non-mathematicians" to convert decimal numbers to binary is to use a scientific calculator. Instead of rushing out to purchase one, use the calculator in the Windows set of accessories and set it to scientific mode.

1. Make sure that the Dec (decimal) option is selected, and type in the first octet's decimal number (204).
2. Select Bin (binary).
3. Read the 8-bit binary number (11001100). It may be necessary to add a zero or more at the left to make up the eight positions.
4. Continue the same for each succeeding octet.

204.13.220.16          11001100.00001101.11011100.00010000

the router looks at those three bits in the address of the incoming packet, it sees binary 010 and interprets them as a subnet address of 2 and sends the packet to subnet 2. When the packet arrives at subnet 2, it is delivered to host 17 as indicated in the last 5 bits of the address (10001).

Thus, the router can move packets more quickly because it has to deal only with the three bits of the subnet address. When the packets arrive at the proper subnet, they are delivered to the designated host address. Subnetting allows for shorter routing tables and greater versatility in network addressing.

Appendix 3 contains more information about binary math. Figure 14-11 shows how to convert decimal numbers to binary numbers in a very simple way.

If your mind reels with the excitement of all these numbers and you would like to know more, you may find a number of Web resources, such as http://www.ralphb.net/IPSubnet/ or http://www.learntosubnet.com, that are available to teach you to do subnetting math. If you would rather not worry about the necessity for such extreme measures, brilliant engineers have been developing IPv6, which will be explained in greater detail after a little more information about converting these numbers to more friendly names.

## Classless Inter-Domain Routing (CIDR)

**Classless Inter-Domain Routing (CIDR)**

Another option for dealing with the decreasing number of addresses used by most IPv4 Internet sites is **Classless Inter-Domain Routing (CIDR)**. CIDR is very closely related to subnetting. Use of the original IPv4 system of classes resulted in the waste of many addresses. For example, a Class C network could include up to 254 hosts each, but might use only 104, thereby wasting the other 150 allowable addresses. Or a Class B network might need considerably more than 254 addresses, but far fewer than the 65,533 allocated. When CIDR was first developed, only 3 percent of the assigned addresses were being used, though the Internet was running out of unassigned addresses, especially in Class C.

Global backbone Internet routers were also reaching capacity. As the Internet exploded in size, so did the number of routes between networks. It has been estimated that a new network is connected to the Internet every thirty minutes. **Routing table** maximum size is about 60,000 entries, and if something weren't done, all Internet growth would cease.

**routing table**

The CIDR addressing scheme was developed so that each IP address could be restructured to include a network prefix of anywhere from 13 to 27 bits, rather than the generalized network prefix of 8, 16, or 24 bits prescribed by the IPv4 process. In this way, a block of addresses could be assigned to networks that have very few hosts as well as to those that have more than 500,000 hosts, and thus more efficiently meet an organization's specific needs. In a CIDR network address, a number after the original dotted-decimal address designates how many bits are used for the network prefix. For example, in the CIDR address 204.11.20.16/19, the /19 indicates that the first 19 bits of the 32-bit address are used to identify the network, and the remaining 13 identify the specific host.

**supernetting**

The grouping of several Class C networks into contiguous address blocks is called **supernetting.** Similar to the way phone numbers are grouped under an area code, according to the CIDR addressing scheme, a hierarchy is set up of a single high-level route entry that represents many lower-level entries in a routing table. Internet service providers (ISPs) are assigned large blocks of addresses, and they in turn reallocate portions of their address blocks to customers. Each time a customer logs on, the ISP assigns a temporary or **dynamic IP address.** According to the old Class A, B, and C addressing scheme, one applied for an address through the appropriate Internet registry (InterNIC) and received a **static IP address** that one owned even if the ISP changed.

**dynamic IP address**

**static IP address**

Three IP network addresses have been reserved for private networks to use for internal use, as described in RFC 1918. These addresses are 10.0.0.0 (default mask: 255.0.0.0), 172.16.0.0 (default mask: 255.240.0.0), and 192.168.0.0 (default mask: 255.255.0.0). If you are part of a private internal network, intranet, or home LAN, you may recognize one of these addresses. Routers on the Internet never forward packets coming from these addresses.

## 14-7   DOMAIN NAME SYSTEM (DNS)

**domain name system (DNS)**

Obviously, the IP address is a somewhat complicated string of numbers. In order to locate and communicate with a host on the network, one would have to type the entire string. Fortunately, we have the **Domain Name System (DNS)** to serve as a "mnemonic" device for making the addresses easier to remember. For example, the domain name "www.ulv.edu" is easier to remember than "206.16.118.1." A vital part of linking users to the Internet is providing the DNS service. The DNS stores copies of text addresses and the 32-bit IP addresses that are associated with them in a distributed database, which means that the information is not stored on any one server, but on many different servers around the world.

**top level domain (TLD)**

Internet hosts use a hierarchical naming structure comprising a **top level domain (TLD),** domain and subdomain (optional), and host name.

### Top Level Domains

The following is a list of the top level domains:

- **.com:** commercial organizations
- **.edu:** educational institutions, today usually limited to 4-year colleges and universities
- **.net:** network providers
- **.org:** nonprofit organizations
- **.int:** organizations established by international treaty
- **.gov:** US Federal Government agencies
- **.mil:** US military

Internet Corporation for Assigned Names and Numbers (ICANN)

In November of 2000, the first new set of TLDs since 1988 were approved by the **Internet Corporation for Assigned Names and Numbers (ICANN).**

- **.aero:** Sponsored by aviation industry
- **.biz:** businesses, unsponsored
- **.coop:** Business Cooperatives
- **.info:** general use
- **.museum:** museums
- **.name:** individuals
- **.pro:** professionals (lawyers, positions, and other professionals)

DNS is usually represented in a tree-like structure illustrated in Figure 14-12, and each level falls within the domain above it. The computer named "Ralph" is within the domain of students, which is in the domain of ulv, within the domain of .edu.

A domain name is best understood reading from left to right, with the generic top-level domains at the end of the name. The DNS is illustrated in Figure 14-13. In the host name, **"student.ulv.edu,"** for example, the TLD is **"edu,"** which refers to educational institutions. Today, **"edu"** is usually limited to 4-year colleges and universities. The domain is **"ulv"**, which refers to the University of La Verne, and **"student"** is the name of the host server.

## Resolving a Domain Name

Any person should be able to reach any IP address in the world by typing in its domain name. To ensure that a datagram, a term you encountered in Chapter 9, reaches its proper destination, the name must be translated into a numeric address so that other computers can read it. This translation process is known as "resolving the domain name," and it is the function of the DNS.

**FIGURE 14-12   A DNS tree.**

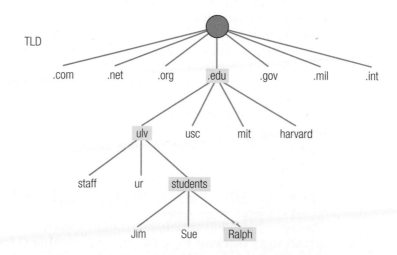

**FIGURE 14-13   The domain name system.**

| Computer Name | Company/organization | Top-Level Domain |
|---|---|---|
| student | ulv | edu |

**Internet Network Information Center (InterNIC)**

ICANN, created in 1998, is the nonprofit, private-sector corporation responsible for managing and coordinating the DNS to ensure universal resolvability. Historically, the **Internet Network Information Center (InterNIC)** had authority for registering all domain names, but when the registration business opened to competition in June 1999, the number of registrars grew rapidly until there are now over 100.

**root server**

Several special computers, called **root servers,** are distributed around the world and are coordinated by ICANN. The root servers contain the IP addresses of all the TLD registries, including country-specific registries like .fr (France) and .uk (United Kingdom) and global registries like .com and .net.

**DNS servers**

Thousands of computers, called **DNS servers,** are located strategically with organizational networks or ISPs across the entire Internet and regularly download and copy information from the root servers. If it were not for these DNS servers, the main root servers could not handle the billions of requests, and the system would bog down.

**resolver**

When a person types a domain name such as http://www.unitedcancer.org into a browser, special software called a **resolver** responds by querying the network's primary DNS server, which is specified on the local host when TCP/IP information is set up. If the local DNS server has the information in its cache, that is, if it can resolve the domain name with its IP address, it returns the information to the requesting host computer. Administrators set specific time parameters or a time-to-live (TTL) for the cache so that the information sent back to the browser is current. The TTL says how long a given record is valid before a DNS server should update the address information in its cache.

If the local DNS server is not able to supply the information from its database, it queries a server farther up the tree. If that server cannot supply the information, it will query the next higher level until an authoritative server is contacted from other DNS servers on the Internet. The authoritative server is one that can supply the information without requesting it from farther up. As soon as that happens, the information is returned to the primary DNS server, and the browser receives the information it needs to send the user to the proper URL. All of this querying happens very quickly so the delay is not usually very long. If the operation does time out, a second try often succeeds, because by then, the authoritative server will have had time to reply to the request and the local DNS server will have stored the information in its cache.

Without a globally unique address, the DNS system would be as unpredictable and unreliable as the telephone system would be if two people had the same telephone number. There must be a single authoritative name and number listing for hosts on the Internet, just as there is a listing of international telephone numbers. If you would like to read more about the DNS, there are several excellent websites: http://www.dns.net/dnsrd/ and http://www.howstuffworks.com/dns.htm.

## 14-8   INTERNET PROTOCOL, VERSION 6 (IPV6)

**Internet Protocol, version 6 (IPv6)**

**Internet Protocol, new generation (IPng)**

The newest version of IP is **Internet Protocol, version 6 (IPv6),** sometimes referred to as **Internet Protocol, new generation (IPng).** Because the Internet was growing so rapidly—doubling in size every year—engineers began to worry in the late 1980s that IPv4 would not be able to keep up with future growth. It had served a computer market that drove its growth, but many foresaw that future growth would come not only from that market, but also from others such as nomadic personal computing devices, networked entertainment, and device control (heating, cooling, and lighting equipment, motors, etc.). Because home appliances, cellular phones, and automobiles will be or are currently connected to the Internet and will need global addresses, even manufacturers of these products pay close attention to the need for a new generation of IP.

IPv4 provides over 4 billion addresses, yet many have predicted that we could run out of addresses by the year 2010, though subnetting and CIDR have somewhat reduced that threat. The shortage of IPv4 addresses, as well as technical limitations in deploying new protocols, became more apparent in the early 1990s, and the Internet Engineering Task Force (IETF) began an effort to solve the issues. Finally, in January of 1995, IPv6 was chosen as the next generation of Internet Protocol and its specifications were published in RFC 1752, "The Recommendation for the IP Next Generation Protocol." IPv6 solves many addressing problems and additional limitations, but it is meant to be an evolutionary step rather than a drastic step away from IPv4. The transition from one to the other must be gradual and won't be totally implemented for several years. The changes and special features of the new version are listed below:

## Addressing

IPv6 has a 128-bit address, four times longer than IPv4, but it provides an exponentially larger number of addresses. According to Robert M. Hinden, who has been active in the IETF since 1985 and is currently document editor for the IPng working group, "This is 4 billion times 4 billion times 4 billion ($2^{96}$) times the size of the IPv4 address space ($2^{32}$)." If that fact does not sound impressive, the sight of so many commas may! The number looks like this: 340,282,366,920,938,463,463,374,607,431,768,211,456. Another scientist, Christian Huitema, concluded that 128-bit IPv6 addresses could provide 1,564 addresses for each square meter of the surface of the Earth (about 32 addresses per square inch of dry land).

**hexadecimal**

The IPv6 address is eight groups of 16-bit numbers separated by colons, which is called "colon hexadecimal notation." Each number is written as four **hexadecimal** (base-16) digits. For more information about the hexadecimal numbering system, see Figure 14-14 and Appendix A.

A sample IPv6 (hexadecimal) address looks like the following:
FFCC:1350:6B35:FFFF:D488:AC63:6388:FFAD

When written in dotted decimal notation, it would become:
255.255.19.32.139.53.255.255.212.136.172.99.99.136.255.173

**zero compression**

It is easy to see that colon hexadecimal notation expresses an address in far fewer characters. Additionally, using **zero compression,** sequences of zeros may be replaced with two colons. Thus, the address, CCFF.0.0.0.0.0.0. FFCC becomes CCFF::FFCC. In addition to the improvement in addressing,

**FIGURE 14-14** The hexidecimal system.

Hexadecimal-base 16 from Greek "hex" meaning 6 and Latin "decem" meaning 10. The decimal numbers 1–15 are represented by the digits 0–9 and the alphabet figures A–F.

Examples:

    Binary (base 2) "11111111" = Decimal (base 10) "255"
                          = Hexadecimal (base 16) FF

    Binary "11001100" = Hexadecimal "204" = Hexadecimal "CC"

FIGURE 14-15   A comparison of the IPv4 and IPv6 header structures.

**IPv4 Header Structure**

| Bits | 4 | 8 | 16 | 24 | 32 |
|---|---|---|---|---|---|
| 32 bits | Version | IHL | Type of Service | Total Length | |
| 32 bits | Identification | | | Flags | Fragment Offset |
| 32 bits | Time to Live | | Protocol | Checksum | |
| 32 bits | Source IP Address | | | | |
| 32 bits | Destination IP address | | | | |
| 32 bits | Options & Padding | | | | |
| | Data | | | | |

**IPv6 Header Structure**

| Bits | 4 | 8 | 16 | 24 | 32 |
|---|---|---|---|---|---|
| 32 bits | Version | Priority | Flow Label | | |
| 32 bits | Payload Length | | | Next Header | Hop Limit |
| 128 bits | Source Address | | | | |
| 128 bits | Destination Address | | | | |

IPv6 introduces further advantages over IPv4. Figure 14-15 shows a comparison of the IPv4 and the IPv6 header structures. The most obvious difference is the expansion of the address space from 32 bits in IPv4 to 128 bits in IPv6. The fields of the IPv4 header are as follows:

■ **Version (4 bits)**—This group of 4 bits is always set to 0100 (4) to specify the version of IP that created the packet. IPv6 is always set to 0110 (6).

■ **Internet Header Length (4 bits)**—This group of bits is the length of the packet header in 32-bit words, and thus signifies where the data begin.

■ **Type of Service (8 bits)**—This group of bits gives transport-layer requests about handling the packet and details precedence, delay, throughput, and reliability specifications.

■ **Total Length (16 bits)**—This group of bits specifies the length of the whole IP packet in octets.

Because different network architectures allow different maximum frame sizes, the packets are sometimes divided into smaller units called fragments. The fragments must be reassembled after they reach their destination. The following three fields are used in fragmentation:

■ **Identification (16 bits)**—These bits make up is a sequence number that, along with the user protocol and source and destination addresses, identifies a datagram uniquely.

- **Flags (3 bits)**—These bits are control flags that allow or disallow fragmentation and reassembly of packets. If a "do not fragment" bit is set, the router discards the datagram and sends an error message to the sender. The sender can send smaller packets until it determines at what size fragmentation occurs.
    - Bit 0 is reserved and must be zero
    - Bit 1: do not fragment bit (0=may fragment and 1=don't fragment)
    - Bit 2: more fragments bit: (0=last fragment and 1=more fragments)
- **Fragment Offset (13 bits)**—These bits indicate where this fragment belongs in the original datagram.

The rest of the fields in the IPv4 header are as follows:

- **Time to Live (8 bits)**—This group of bits specifies the maximum time (in seconds) the datagram can remain in the Internet, preventing infinite looping. Each router that handles the packet decreases the time to live by one, so that by the time the field reaches 0, it is discarded by the router and an error message is sent to the sender.
- **Protocol (8 bits)**—These bits specify the next higher protocol used in the datagram's data section so the destination IP can deliver the data to the right entity at the end.
- **Checksum (16 bits)**—These bits are used to detect errors and are applied only to the packet header.
- **Source Address (32 bits)**—These bits contain the IP address of the sending site.
- **Destination Address (32 bits)**—This group of bits contains the IP address of the receiving site.
- **Options (variable)**—This field specifies special treatment for the packet requested by the sending user.
- **Padding (variable)**—Padding is used to ensure that the datagram header has a length of a multiple of 32 bits.

The fields of the IPv6 header are as follows:

- **Version (4 bits)**—This group of 4 bits is always set to 0110 (6) for IPv6.
- **Priority (4 bits)**—Priority identifies the desired delivery priority of the packets, divided into two categories: congestion-controlled traffic, which can be delayed if the network is busy, and noncongestion-controlled traffic like real-time audio and video, which cannot be delayed and should be discarded instead.
- **Flow Label (24 bits)**—Flow label is still experimental, but is used with the priority field. A flow is defined by IPv6 as a sequence of packets that need to go to a single destination and that require special handling by routers to get them there as quickly as possible, and together, so they arrive in order. The source labels all packets destined for the same destination with same flow label.
- **Payload Length (16 bits)**—This group of bits defines the length of the payload, or the rest of the IPv6 packet after the header.
- **Next Header (8 bits)**—Next header, the basic header, may be followed by options like an IPv4 header, and this field identifies which type of option

header follows the basic one or it designates a higher layer header like UDP or TCP.

- **Hop Limit (8 bits)**—Hop limit is the same as time-to-live in the IPv4 packet; this field specifies the remaining hops allowable for the packet.
- **Source Address (128 bits)**—The source address is the IP address of the originating site in colon hexadecimal notation.
- **Destination Address (128 bits)**—The destination address is the IP address of the receiving site in colon hexadecimal notation.

## Other Improvements in IPv6

To keep pace with the phenomenal growth of networking technology, IPv6 needed to provide several other technological improvements over IPv4. Chief enhancements include, but are not limited to:

- **Three types of addressing** provide greater flexibility and efficiency in routing:
  - **unicast** (one host to one other host along the shortest path)
  - **anycast** (one host to the nearest of multiple hosts that share a common address prefix) can update routing tables along the line
  - **multicast** (one host to multiple hosts that can be at many locations) is mandatory in IPv6

- **Autoconfiguration** or "stateless host autoconfiguration" allows a device to assign itself a unique IP address without needing the intervention of a server.

- **Flow labels** identify a sequence of packets that need to arrive in real-time for high quality communications and consistent throughput for streaming multimedia.

- **Increased security** is provided, as well as user authentication, data integrity, and encryption.

- **Simplified, but more flexible header structures** differentiate between headers that need to be examined by intermediate routers and those that need only be examined by end nodes.

- **Interoperability and compatibility** ease the transition from IPv4 to IPv6. IPv6 is backward compatible (it recognizes both version 4 and version 6), so the changeover from one to the other can be gradual.

- **Overall network performance** is improved or speeded up because options are specified in an extension to the header that is examined only at the destination.

### unicast
### anycast
### multicast
### autoconfiguration

## 14-9 TRANSMISSION CONTROL PROTOCOL (TCP)

**Transmission Control Protocol (TCP)**

**Transmission Control Protocol (TCP)** was developed in the 1970s as part of a research project on network interconnection by the Defense Advanced Research Projects Agency (DARPA), and it remains the most complete and widely accepted protocol available for networking. It, along with IP and the other family members in the protocol suite, is the protocol for internets and the Internet. It can communicate between hosts with completely diverse hardware, architectures, and OSs.

TCP was intended, according to Jon Postel, "for use as a highly reliable host-to-host protocol between hosts in packet-switched computer communications networks and in interconnected systems of such networks." TCP is connection-oriented and provides point-to-point, reliable FDX stream transport communications with reliable startup and delivery of all data before shutdown. Whoa! Let us examine these statements one at a time.

TCP provides direct communication from an application on one computer to an application on one other computer. This connection is called **point-to-point** or "end-to-end" because it exists between exactly two endpoints. It transmits a sequence of bytes between them, dividing the data stream into segments.

Furthermore, because the two computers are connected to networks that necessarily share media, data must be broken into chunks or **packets** that are manageable so no two hosts monopolize network resources. A **stream transport** of data means a continuous sequence of bytes is transmitted without notation of records or guarantee that a packet arrives in the same size pieces it was sent.

TCP works at the transport level of the layered architecture, corresponding to layers 4 and 5 of the OSI model, just above the basic IP. It assures that segments of information of variable lengths, packaged in datagram "envelopes," arrive at their proper destination correctly and in the proper order. This is important because IP does not guarantee delivery of packets. TCP receives requests or data from a user, stores it in a TCP segment, and gives it to IP, which routes it through an internetwork. The TCP on the receiving end gets the segment, responds to the information in it, extracts the data, and gives it to the user application. This basic transaction is illustrated in Figure 14-16.

The connection is a **full-duplex (FDX) connection,** which means that data can flow in either direction. It is reliable and **connection-oriented,** meaning that it goes through three distinct phases: connection establishment, information transfer, and connection release.

**point-to-point**

**packets**

**stream transport**

**full-duplex (FDX) connection**

**connection-oriented**

**FIGURE 14-16** TCP is a connection-oriented end-to-end service.

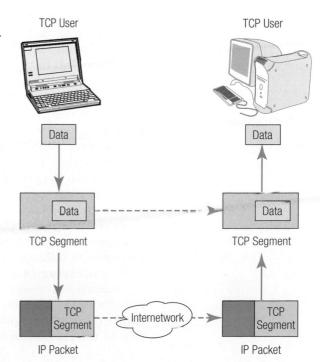

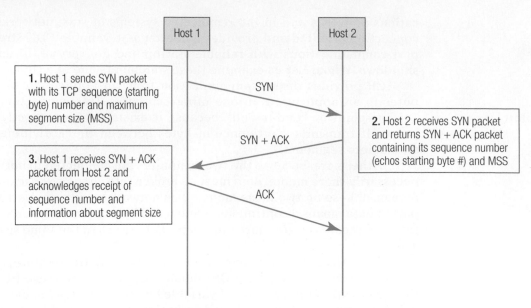

**FIGURE 14-17**    Opening handshake.

## Connection Establishment

First, TCP establishes a connection between two nodes that can be considered unreliable systems that intend to exchange data over a network that can also be considered unreliable. In establishing a connection, therefore, the two hosts go through a **three-way handshake,** illustrated in Figure 14-17. They say:

three-way handshake

> Computer 1: "Hi, I'm computer 1 and I want to send you something."
> Computer 2: "Okay, send away."
> Computer 1: "Okay, here it is, including packets."

## Information Transfer

When a packet arrives at its destination, TCP continues a dialogue to communicate about the data that are being transmitted and tells the network to resend any lost data. **Sequence numbering,** which assures that packets arrive in the proper order, and **error checking,** which assures that they arrive correctly, are two of the most important functions of TCP. Because data are broken up by the IP layer into separate packets to transmit, each packet is assigned a sequence number to make certain that all data are delivered in the proper order. The sender requires a positive **acknowledgment (ACK)** from the receiver within a specified time-out period. If an ACK is not received within that time interval, the data must be retransmitted. When the data are received at the other end, the sequence numbers are used to resequence the packets properly if they have been received out of order and to eliminate duplicates. Error checking is handled by appending a **checksum** (check character), which you encountered in Chapter 4, to each packet. It is examined at the receiving end and the damaged packets are discarded. If a packet is damaged, it must be resent. Figure 14-18 illustrates sender and receiver events.

sequence numbering

error checking

acknowledgement (ACK)

checksum

    The bytes are sent by way of the sliding window flow control protocol that you studied in Chapter 7. TCP flow control is different in that the sequence numbers refer to sequences of bytes rather than packets. Additionally, each side of the transmission (by using the segment's window field) can dynami-

**FIGURE 14-18** Sender and receiver events.

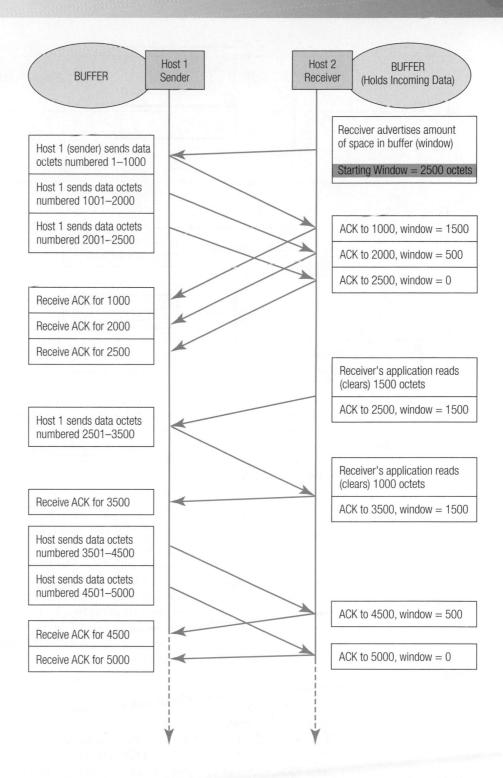

cally change the size of the other's sending window. **Flow control,** illustrated in Figure 14-19, governs the amount of data transmitted by the sender. Every packet has a sequence number so each can be acknowledged. A buffer holds data that is incoming and when the receiver sends an ACK to the sender, it includes a "window" indicating the range of acceptable sequence numbers beyond the last successful transmission, as you saw in Figure 14-18. The window indicates how many octets, starting with the acknowledgment number, the sender may transmit before it receives further permission. For example,

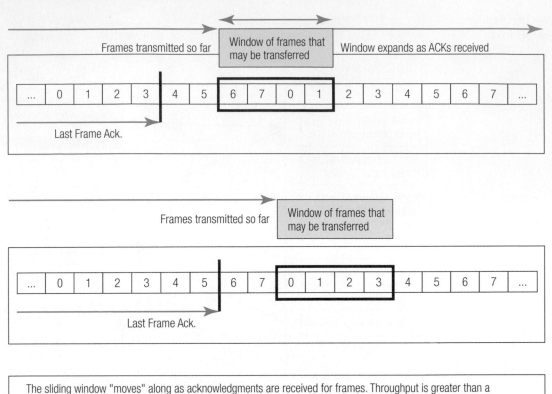

The sliding window "moves" along as acknowledgments are received for frames. Throughput is greater than a stop-and-go flow control since packets in the sliding window don't have to be acknowledged after each transmission before another is sent.

**FIGURE 14-19**    Flow control: sliding window.

acknowledging number 4 indicates that all octets up to but not including number 4 have been received, and the receiver indicates that it can now accept octets from numbers 4 through 7.

Sliding window protocol has two common implementations, as you learned in Chapter 7: Go-back-n Protocol and Selective Repeat Protocol. The difference is that Go-back-n requires that the frames be received in exactly the same order in which they are sent; Selective Repeat requires that the receiver hold on to frames that are out of order until they can be sent to a higher layer in the proper order. The receiver accepts only the frame it is supposed to receive next and discards the rest.

## TCP Congestion Control

In large networks, internets, and especially on the Internet, congestion (see Chapter 13 for more on congestion) can cause packet loss. If it receives multiple transmission requests, TCP assumes that packets have been dropped and that there is congestion on the circuit. TCP takes the initiative to help control the congestion by immediately adjusting its sending of data down to a single message that must be acknowledged. Gradually it increases the number of messages it sends before requiring an acknowledgement until the number eventually reaches a rate of half the receiver's window. At that time TCP slows down the rate of increase. By then, optimistically speaking, the congestion is eased.

A number of techniques intended to improve TCP congestion control have been implemented since 1981 when RFC 793 (see http://www.faqs.org/rfcs/rfc793.html) outlined the protocol specification and stated, "Be conservative in what you do, be liberal in what you accept from others." These techniques include retransmission timer management and window management.

Most efforts to estimate retransmission times involve different kinds of averaging—from simple averaging over a number of segments of observed round-trip to more involved algorithms used to calculate the current round trip delay. The purpose of all these techniques is to determine how fast the node can safely put new traffic back into the network without increasing the congestion.

**slow start**

**dynamic window sizing on congestion**

In current implementations of TCP, two send window management techniques are also used: **slow start** and **dynamic window sizing on congestion.** According to the slow start algorithm, the rate at which acknowledgments are returned by the other end determines the rate at which the sender introduces new packets into the network. The advertised window is flow control imposed by the receiver, based on the amount of buffer space available at the receiver.

In slow start, a congestion window, called "cwnd," is added to the sender's TCP. It is flow control imposed by the sender, based on the sender's assessment of the network's congestion. The beginning congestion window size is equal to one segment and is increased by one segment when an acknowledgment is received. At that point, the congestion window is increased from one to two segments. When each of them has been acknowledged, the congestion window is upped to four, and so on, exponentially increasing the size of the congestion window. When an intermediate router on an internet begins to discard packets, the sender knows that its capacity has been reached and the congestion window has grown too large. This increase is enough to let TCP feel out a connection's bandwidth and allow the network to accustom itself to the increased load.

Dynamic window sizing on congestion alters the size of the sliding window by setting the size of the window to half its current size when time-outs occur (indicating congestion). When acknowledgments are received, the congestion window size is increased by one segment. Eventually, the minimum of the receiver's advertised window and congestion window can be sent. This pattern of congestion window adjustment from greater to lesser continues as long as the connection is maintained.

## Connection Release

**synchronization segment (SYN segment)**

**finish segment (FIN segment)**

When all data are sent, TCP uses another three-way handshake to terminate the connection reliably. While the term **synchronization segment (SYN segment)** describes the opening handshake, the term **finish segment (FIN segment)** describes the messages in a closing handshake. The closing is illustrated in Figure 14-20.

## TCP Header

The TCP PDU is called a TCP segment and its header, illustrated in Figure 14-21, has a minimum length of 20 octets. The rest of the TCP segment contains user-supplied data of variable size.

The fields of the TCP header are as follows:

- **Source Port (16 bits)**—The source port specifies the application that sent the segment.
- **Destination Port (16 bits)**—The destination port tells to which application on the receiving computer the segment is being sent. This is not the IP address, but the port on the computer through which the application

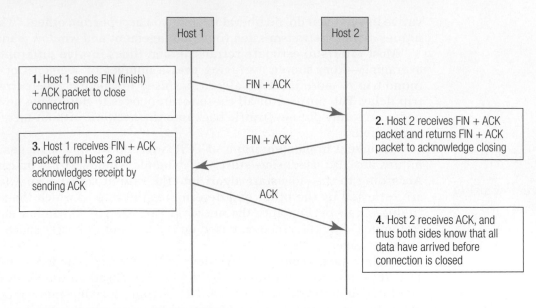

**FIGURE 14-20** A closing handshake.

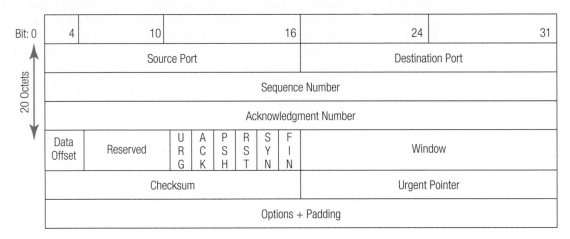

**FIGURE 14-21** A TCP header.

is running. For example, the destination port for FTP would be 21, one of the well-known ports assigned to commonly used applications.

- **Sequence Number (32 bits)**—The sequence number bits give the sequence number of the outgoing octets of data carried in the segment. Each byte sent by TCP is numbered, and the receiving application uses the sequence number to reorder the segments regardless of the order in which they arrive. It also uses this number to compute an ACK number.

- **Acknowledgment Number (32 bits)**—This group of bits specifies the next incoming byte sequence number the receiver expects, in effect saying, "I have received all bytes prior to the one I've specified."

- **Data Offset (4 bits)**—This group of bits specifies the size (a multiple of four bytes or the number of 32-bit words) of the header. This number allows the receiver to know where the data starts.

- **Reserved (6 bits)**—This group is not used and is reserved for future use.

- **Flags (6 bits)**—This group specifies when other fields contain meaningful data.

- **URG** indicates that the urgent pointer field is significant.

- **ACK** indicates that the acknowledgment field is significant (contains meaningful data).

- **PSH**—Push function allows an application to send the data earlier than usual; as an example, for smooth, quick display of incoming video screen data.

- **RST**—Reset the connection. When something abnormal happens, both sides end the connection to stop data flow and increase the buffer space.

- **SYN**—Synchronize the initial sequence numbers.

- **FIN**—Last TCP data segment, no more data coming from sender.

- **Window (16 bits)**—Contains the number of data bytes the sender can accept beyond those already acknowledged (specifies how much additional buffer space is available for incoming data) and corresponds roughly to the window size of the sliding window protocol.

- **Checksum (16 bits)**—This field includes a checksum for both the TCP segment header and the data, and is used for transport-layer error detection. The algorithm, which is not considered as strong as other error detection algorithms such as CRC, interprets the segment contents as a series of 16-bit numbers and sums them.

- **Urgent Pointer (16 bits)**—If the URG flag is set, the segment contains urgent data and the receiving TCP must deliver it to higher layers ASAP. The urgent pointer specifies the last octet in a sequence of urgent data so the receiver can distinguish urgent from nonurgent data.

- **Options & Padding (variable)**—Allows both sides of a connection to be aware of limitations, such as buffer size, that the other side has. One option allows them to agree on a 32-bit window field, rather than a 16-bit field (as when high bandwidth lines are used to transfer large files). Another option specifies the maximum segment size they will accept.

## 14-10  USER DATAGRAM PROTOCOL (UDP)

**User Datagram Protocol (UDP)**

**User Datagram Protocol (UDP),** which is illustrated in Figure 14-22, provides access for upper-layer applications to IP's connectionless features for delivery of packets, enabling a flow of data among computers. It does not provide sequence numbering or error checking. The packet is discarded if an error is detected, and no further action is taken. UDP is said to be "connectionless," because it does not require hand shaking or resending of data if there is an error. Basically, UDP adds a port-addressing capability to IP. The header includes the source port and destination port; the length field, including header and data; and the checksum. The checksum field in UDP is optional.

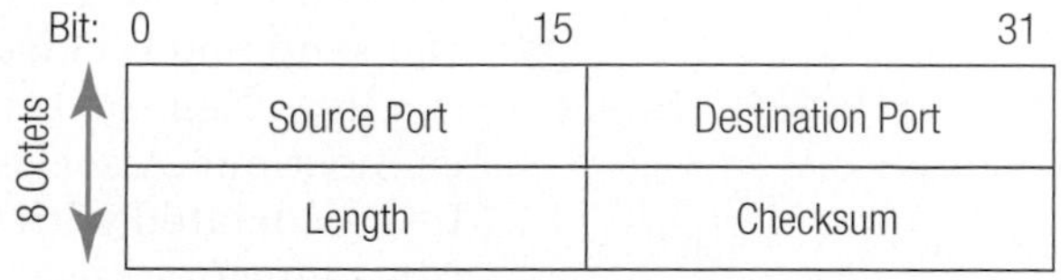

**FIGURE 14-22**  A UDP header.

Though it is less reliable than TCP, UDP is able to send large quantities of data over a network quickly and is therefore used for broadcasting. It permits an application to send a message at any time, to any destination. A sequence of messages can be sent quickly, each to a different destination. It is therefore commonly used with multimedia applications such as real-time video conferencing, streaming audio and video, and Internet telephony. All of these applications can tolerate a small fraction of packet loss, but UDP lacks any provision for congestion control. Packet overflow at routers could occur, creating serious problems. The features of error checking and sequence numbering, however, can also be added by applications that choose to use UDP. Many streaming applications today run over UDP, but they have built-in acknowledgment and retransmission to reduce packet loss. Not all TCP traffic is always allowed through all firewalls. UDP is often used as a way around that in video or audio streams like RealAudio.

Another application-layer protocol that uses UDP rather than TCP is DNS, which was discussed earlier in this chapter. The DNS application in a host constructs a DNS query message and passes the message to an application program interface called a **socket**. (You will read more about sockets in the next section.) Without performing any handshaking, UDP adds a header to the message and passes the segment to the network layer. At this layer, the UDP segment is enclosed in a datagram and sent to a name server. If a reply comes, it is sent to the inquiring host. If the reply does not come, the query is either sent to another name server or the application is told it cannot receive a reply (URL not found).

Because UDP does not allow the connection-related features of TCP, it is more robust at lower layers (internet and network) and does reduce the overhead of establishing and maintaining connections. This lower overhead is desirable in many instances, even at the transport level—for example, when sampling data must be collected periodically. Even if occasional data were lost in that case, the next sampling would compensate for the loss. UDP is used for routing information protocol (RIP) routing table updates because the updates are sent periodically, and lost packets are soon replaced by more current data. Figure 14-23 illustrates the relationship between the TCP/IP layers when using TCP or UDP as transport protocols.

**socket**

## 14-11    SOCKETS AND CLIENT-SERVER COMMUNICATION

The Universal Resource Locator (URL) is an important mechanism for accessing any site or resource on the Internet. Sometimes, however, you may need to write programs to communicate between a client computer and a server computer at a lower level. The terms "client" and "server" refer to the two processes that communicate with each other. One of the processes (the client) connects to the other process (the server) to make a request for information. The client needs to know the address of the server, but the server does not need to know the address or even the existence of the client before the connection is established. Once a connection is established, both sides can send and receive information.

In a client-server environment, each side constructs a socket to establish connections. A socket is one end of an interprocess communication channel. It is associated with a specific port number on the computer so the TCP layer can identify the application to which data are to be sent. Each of the two processes establishes its own socket by calling subroutines in the operating

FIGURE 14-23 The relationships between TCP/IP and UDP layers.

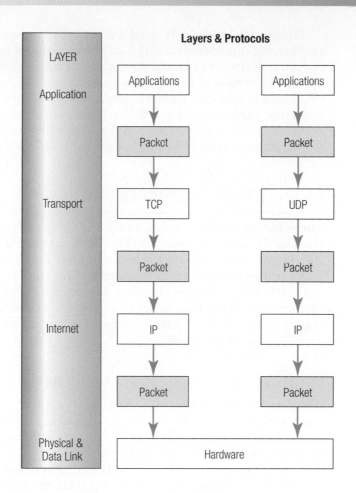

system software of the computer on which it is running. The establishment of the socket is a little different for the client and the server and is explained below.

The client:

1. creates a socket by calling the `socket ()` subroutine
2. connects the socket to the address of the server by calling the `connect ()` subroutine
3. sends and receives data using the `read ()` and `write ()` subroutines

The server:

1. creates a socket by calling the `socket ()` subroutine
2. binds the socket to an address using the `bind ()` subroutine (for a server socket on the Internet, an address consists of a port number on the host computer)
3. listens for connection requests using the `listen ()` subroutine
4. accepts a connection with the `accept ()` subroutine
5. sends and receives data using the `read ()` and `write ()` subroutines

At the end of a connection, both sides close the connection and the server continues to listen for other connections.

stream sockets

datagram sockets

There are two widely used socket types, **stream sockets** and **datagram sockets.** Stream sockets use the TCP protocol and treat communications as a continuous stream of characters, while datagram sockets use the UDP protocol and have to read entire messages at once.

If you would like to learn more about programming client-server interfaces and using sockets, the following websites offer excellent information:

http://java.sun.com/docs/books/tutorial/networking/sockets/index.html

http://www.javaworld.com/javaworld/jw-12-1996/jw-12-sockets.html

## 14-12　OTHER PROTOCOLS

There are many other protocols most of us use every day that are included in the TCP/IP suite, and we use them without seeing what is going on behind the scenes. Here are just a few of the ones that allow us to do such amazing tasks and enjoy such great communication with each other. Several of them are discussed in greater depth in Chapters 15 and 16. There are also excellent sources on the Web if you would like to examine any of them further. We simply mention them here to illustrate the variety and importance of the TCP/IP suite of protocols.

### Address Resolution Protocol (ARP)

Address Resolution
Protocol (ARP)

**Address Resolution Protocol (ARP)** is a protocol that maps an IP address to a computer's MAC address (burned into a chip on the NIC) that is recognized in the local network so packets can be transmitted. A table (ARP cache) correlates each MAC address and its corresponding IP address. The rules for correlating them and providing address conversion in both directions are provided by ARP. When a router on a LAN receives an incoming packet that is destined for a particular host, it requests the MAC address that matches the IP address from the ARP program. If it finds the address in the ARP cache, the packet can be sent to the machine (with the right packet length). Otherwise, ARP broadcasts a special request packet with the IP address to all hosts on the LAN, requesting that the one with that IP address respond with its MAC address. The IP address and the corresponding MAC address are then stored in the ARP cache (so another broadcast request for the same address can be avoided in the future), which sends the packet to the MAC address that replied. There is also a Reverse ARP (RARP) to enable host machines that don't know their IP address to request it from the router's ARP cache.

### Dynamic Host Configuration Protocol (DHCP)

Dynamic Host
Configuration Protocol
(DHCP)

**Dynamic Host Configuration Protocol (DHCP)** automatically assigns IP addresses and subnet masks and keeps track of them without a network administrator's having to configure the information about a computer in the database that a server uses. The use of DHCP has been called "plug-and-play networking," and has made home networking much easier for nontechnical people. Servers have permanent addresses assigned to them and maintain a pool of addresses from which a computer can lease an IP address. The computer advertises a request or **DHCP discover message**, which includes the name of the computer and its NIC address. Any available DHCP computer answers the request by offering an IP address, and the client computer grabs the first one offered and broadcasts its acceptance. The lease belongs to the computer for as long as the administrator has designated the length of the lease, though it can usually be extended.

DHCP discover message

## File Transfer Protocol (FTP) and Trivial File Transfer Protocol (TFTP)

File Transfer Protocol (FTP), discussed in Chapter 16, allows a user to transfer files (who would have thought!). It is an easy way for computers to exchange files on the Internet. FTP can operate both as a protocol (when used with applications) or as a program (when users employ it to perform tasks). It seamlessly allows the user to log into an FTP server to manipulate directories, type file contents, and to transfer files. Trivial File Transfer Protocol (TFTP) allows file transfer between users, but it is faster (though less reliable) than FTP because it uses UDP rather than TCP. It only transfers files and there is no security for authentication, so it is seldom used except when the user knows exactly where to find the files he wants and security is not important.

## HTTP and Secure Hypertext Transfer Protocol (HTTPS)

HTTP transfers HTML (both are discussed in Chapter 16) documents from servers on the World Wide Web to the browser. It is the protocol that Web browsers and Web servers use to talk to each other. HTTPS is a more secure version of HTTP and allows servers and browsers to sign, authenticate, and encrypt an HTTP network packet.

## Internet Control Message Protocol (ICMP)

**Internet Control Message Protocol (ICMP)**

**Internet Control Message Protocol (ICMP)** is an error-reporting or message control protocol between a host server and a gateway to the Internet and is usually sent in response to a datagram. It is a user of IP, though at the same level, and must be implemented along with it. The ICMP message is encapsulated with an IP header and is transmitted as a datagram in the customary way. ICMP messages typically report errors in the processing of datagrams, and are sent to provide feedback about the communications environment. For example, control messages include: "destination unreachable," when a datagram cannot reach its destination because the host is either down or does not exist; "echo request (ping)," to find out whether a certain destination is reachable; and "echo reply" as a response to such a request. A "source quench" is sent when a router does not have enough buffering capacity to forward a datagram, and "redirect" is used when the router can direct the host to send traffic on a shorter route.

## Post Office Protocol, v3 (POP3) and Internet Message Access Protocol, v4 (IMAP4)

**Post Office Protocol, version 3 (POP3)**

**Internet Message Access Protocol, version 4 (IMAP4)**

**Post Office Protocol, version 3 (POP3)**, and **Internet Message Access Protocol, version 4 (IMAP4)** allow users to move their email from the Internet Service Providers' servers onto their own, thus enabling one to retrieve e-mail from anywhere. They can be used with or without SMTP. IMAP4 provides more features than POP3, such as the ability to scan message headers and download only selected messages, and to create and manage folders.

## Simple Mail Transfer Protocol (SMTP)

**Simple Mail Transfer Protocol (SMTP)**

**Simple Mail Transfer Protocol (SMTP)** is the mail transfer protocol for the Internet that defines how messages move from one e-mail server to another. An e-mail message is created by a mail user agent, like Netscape Communicator's

Messenger or Eudora, and is sent from one computer or digital device to another. E-mail and its protocols are discussed in Chapter 16.

### Telnet

Telnet is a terminal emulation program that connects a remote computer to a server and allows the computer to act like it is on the network. It stands for "telephone network" because it usually occurs over such a network. It is covered in Chapter 16.

## 14-13    INTERNETWORKING TOOLS AND APPLICATIONS

Several tools and applications allow users to learn information about Internet hosts and domains. They can be accessed from the DOS prompt in Windows operating systems or through the Web addresses listed under each tool.

### Name Server Lookup (nslookup)

**name server lookup (nslookup)**

**Name server lookup (nslookup)** allows users to search the domain name databases to determine the host system's IP address from its domain name or the host's domain name from its IP address. Linux and some UNIX-based operating systems and later Windows systems include nslookup. In Windows XP, enter the command on the "Command prompt" screen. A sample of output from nslookup is shown in Figure 14-24. To access Nslookup from the Web, go to http://kloth.net/services/nslookup.php.

### Whois

**whois**

**Whois** is a TCP/IP application that searches DNS databases to find the name of network and system administrators, RFC authors, system and network points-of-contact, and other people registered in appropriate databases, as well as domains, networks, and hosts. Data illustrated in Figure 14-25 include the company and/or individual name, address, phone number,

**FIGURE 14-24**    Output from nslookup.

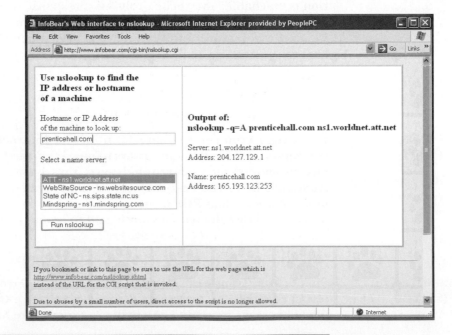

FIGURE 14-25 Output from whois (whois-data-from-Verisign).

```
Registrant:
Yahoo (YAHOO-DOM)
    701 First Avenue
    Sunnyvale, CA 94089
    US


Domain Name: YAHOO.COM

Administrative Contact, Technical Contact:
    Administration, Domain (DA16065)          domainadmin@YAHOO-INC.COM
    Yahoo! Inc.
    701 First Avenue
    Sunnyvale, CA 94089
    US
+1 408 731 3300 +1 408 731 3301
Record expires on 20-Jan-2010.
Record created on 18-Jan-1995.
Database last updated on 8-Oct-2002 01:40:01 EDT.

Domain servers in listed order:

NS1.YAHOO.COM                                 66.218.71.63
NS2.YAHOO.COM                                 209.132.1.28
NS3.YAHOO.COM                                 217.12.4.104
NS4.YAHOO.COM                                 63.250.206.138
NS5.YAHOO.COM                                 64.58.77.85
```

and electronic address of anyone who has registered a domain. Many websites contain Whois data. The original site created by InterNIC is www.internic.net/whois.html, which also gives a list of the many ICANN-accredited domain name registrars that are now taking domain name registrations for those who would like to own their own domain. ICANN has now opened up domain name registration to many other companies. You can try http://www.betterwhois.com/ to search all of them at the same time.

## Ping

Ping

**Ping** is one of the most widely available tools in the TCP/IP suite. It is frequently used by network administrators to determine the parts of the network that are operating properly and, if there is a problem, those that have failed. To check a connection from the MS-DOS window prompt, type `ping`, followed by a space, then the IP address of the device you wish to check. Then press Enter.

Mike Muss, who wrote the original program in 1983, said, "From my point of view, PING is *not* an acronym standing for Packet InterNet Grouper; it's a sonar analogy." Muss had done modeling of sonar and radar systems in college and, "inspired by the whole principle of echo location," he named the program after the "sound that a sonar makes." Ping allows the user to ascertain whether a remote host is active or inactive and to determine the round-trip delay in communicating with it. A sample output is shown in Figure 14-26. It uses ICMP echo packets to find out if a target machine is alive. The messages are sent, one per second until the program stops, and produce one line of output for each response received. This allows one to see the number of packets sent and received, the packet loss, and the elapsed time for each round trip.

Muss tells of an interesting use of his program by one network administrator. The man was having problems with an intermittent Ethernet and had linked ping to a vocoder program. A vocoder is a device that synthesizes

**FIGURE 14-26** Output from ping.

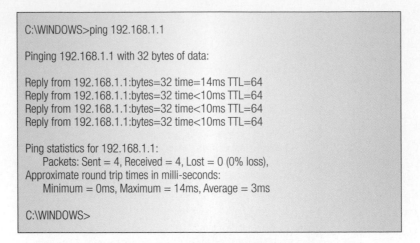

```
C:\WINDOWS>ping 192.168.1.1

Pinging 192.168.1.1 with 32 bytes of data:

Reply from 192.168.1.1:bytes=32 time=14ms TTL=64
Reply from 192.168.1.1:bytes=32 time<10ms TTL=64
Reply from 192.168.1.1:bytes=32 time<10ms TTL=64
Reply from 192.168.1.1:bytes=32 time<10ms TTL=64

Ping statistics for 192.168.1.1:
    Packets: Sent = 4, Received = 4, Lost = 0 (0% loss),
Approximate round trip times in milli-seconds:
    Minimum = 0ms, Maximum = 14ms, Average = 3ms

C:\WINDOWS>
```

**FIGURE 14-27** Output from traceroute.

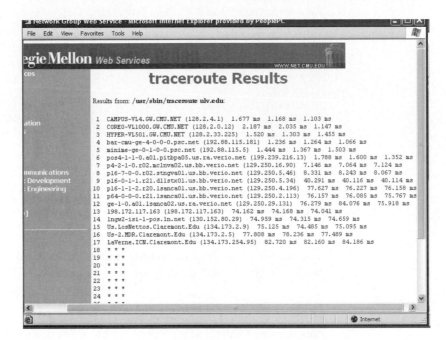

speech. He wired the vocoder's output into his stereo, turned up the volume, and allowed the computer to shout "ping, ping, ping" while he strolled through the building wiggling Ethernet cables. When the sound stopped, he had located the intermittent failure.

## Traceroute

Traceroute (tracert)

**Traceroute (tracert),** which also uses ICMP support, takes ping technology one step further. It allows users to learn the route that packets take from their local host to a remote host, tracing the intermediate routers along the path. A sample of its output is illustrated in Figure 14-27. Traceroute uses UDP. Traceroute is helpful for getting a picture of the Internet and for understanding where problems are in the Internet network.

Both ping and traceroute are available on many Windows-based operating systems. From an MS-DOS window in a Microsoft Windows system, type in `ping` or `tracert` and the name of the remote computer. The ping and traceroute capabilities are also widely accessible on websites that use the programs. One such website is http://www.net.cmu.edu/cgi-bin/netops.cgi. Type in the domain name, wait for the information, and if you don't succeed, try again.

## Finger

**Finger** may be used to find out who has logged in on another system or to find detailed information about the specific user. For security reasons, it is not widely used today.

The TCP/IP protocol suite includes many other protocols and applications. Two of the most basic and helpful are Telnet and FTP, which are discussed in Chapter 16. A growing body of information for each protocol or application exists in the RFCs. One of the strengths of TCP/IP is that it is independent of network model, transmission medium, specific vendors, OSs, or computer hardware. It runs on virtually everything. This versatility is one of its greatest assets and is the reason it is the most popular network protocol today. Though UNIX was the first to build TCP/IP into its system, most operating systems now come loaded with the software. TCP/IP continues to evolve from its government beginnings, and new capabilities are added to it regularly as the Internet becomes busier every day.

Today, TCP/IP is robust enough to support more growth than its early developers dreamed possible. It is versatile, independent, and constantly changing. The best part is that all the data moves around transparently without one's knowing what is happening. It works, and an Internet user does not need to worry about how it works

## ■ SUMMARY

An internetwork is two or more networks—LANs, MANs, and/or WANs—that are interconnected by routers and switches to pass traffic among the computers attached to any of the networks. Most internets use the TCP/IP protocols. Chapter 14 has examined the basic principles of internetworking, the protocols (TCP/IP) involved in Internet technology, and a few of the tools and applications of the protocols.

In Chapter 15, we discuss the global Internet and the World Wide Web, their history and development, and ways to connect to the Internet.

## ■ REVIEW QUESTIONS

14-1. What is an internetwork?

14-2. What is a subnetwork?

14-3. Compare and contrast a bridge and a router.

14-4. How does the RFC process help internetworking to evolve?

14-5. What is the purpose of the TCP/IP network access layer?

14-6. Layer _____ makes sure that packets have no errors and that they arrive in the correct order.

14-7. The two sections of the 32-bit IP address are the _____ and the _____.

14-8. The IP address designed for the largest networks is class _____.

14-9. How is multicasting used?

14-10. The IP address class that can handle the largest number of networks is _____.

14-11. What are two methods that are used to solve the problem of the diminishing number of available addresses in IPv4?

14-12. What is the purpose of the number after the slash in the CIDR addressing scheme?

14-13. What is the difference between a dynamic and a static IP address?

14-14. What is the purpose of DNS?

14-15. Explain how domain names are resolved.

14-16. What organization is responsible for managing and coordinating DNS to ensure universal resolvability?

14-17. What problems is IPv6 designed to solve?

14-18. How many bits make up an IPv6 address? How many are in an IPv4 address?

14-19. TCP works at the _____ level of the layered architecture.

14-20. Describe the three-way handshake.

14-21. Two of the most important functions of TCP are _____ and _____.

14-22. What problem does congestion cause on a network?

14-23. How does TCP control congestion on a network?

14-24. UDP is said to be connectionless because _____.

14-25. List several uses of UDP.

14-26. Two protocols that are commonly used in e-mail applications are _____ and _____.

14-27. What is the purpose of DHCP?

### TRUE/FALSE

14-1. An internet is several packet-switching networks connected by routers.

14-2. A bridge connects networks that use dissimilar technology and protocols.

14-3. A router can connect any combination of LANs and WANs.

14-4. TCP/IP makes it possible for two hosts to communicate, even if they have a difference in hardware.

14-5. TCP/IP is a combination of two important protocols.

14-6. IP works at layer 3 of the TCP/IP stack, while TCP works at layer 4.

14-7. RFC stands for "router function control."

14-8. Class A IP addresses are intended for only 126 networks.

14-9. The dotted decimal address 191.34.7.4 belongs to a host on a class C network.

14-10. Class D IP addresses are reserved for multicasting.

14-11. According to the CIDR addressing scheme in 204.11.20.16/19, the 19 means that the first 19 bits identify the host on a network.

14-12. A TCP/IPv4 header is 20 octets long.

### MULTIPLE CHOICE

14-1. What is the default subnet mask for a Class C network?

   a. 255.255.0.0
   b. 255.255.255.0

c. 255.0.0.0

d. 0.0.0.225

e. None of the above.

14-2. Which of the following binary numbers is the equivalent of the decimal number 206?

a. 11001110

b. 11001100

c. 11100110

d. 10110110

e. None of the above.

14-3. Which of the following decimal numbers is the equivalent of the binary number 11010011?

a. 197

b. 192

c. 211

d. 203

e. None of the above.

14-4. The dotted decimal IP address 192.228.17.57 is the equivalent of the following binary address:

a. 11010000101011100001000100111001

b. 10100000111001000000100100111101

c. 11000000111001100011000100110101

d. 11000000111001000001000100111001

e. None of the above.

14-5. What does the term "sliding window" relate to?

a. multiplexing

b. stop and wait

c. flow control

d. full duplex

e. None of the above.

14-6. How "big" is an IPv6 Internet address?

a. 32 bits

b. 32 bytes

c. 20 octets

d. 128 bits

e. 128 bytes

14-7. What is the main objective of the IPv6 proposal to the TCP/IP protocol suite?

a. reduce user response

b. update TCP/IP to remain compatible with new technology

c. allow for more Internet addresses

d. add a fiber optic specification to the TCP/IP suite

e. force the acceptance of the hexadecimal numbering system

14-8. What is the size, in bits, of the Net_ID field in a Class B Internet address?

    a. eight bits

    b. sixteen bits

    c. fourteen bits

    d. thirty-two bits

14-9. What does the "time-to-live" field (8 bits) do in an IP header?

    a. prevents infinite looping

    b. sets frame priority

    c. records the transmission time for tracert functions

    d. error checking

    e. frame sequence numbering

14-10. What is the address class for the following Internet address: 10111000100001100000010000011100?

    a. A

    b. B

    c. C

    d. D

    e. 1

## ■ PROBLEMS AND PROJECTS

14-1. Do some research in your organization to find out whether they have a DNS.

14-2. Look up the IP address of your school or employer.

14-3. Addresses beginning with 127 (01111111) are used for internal testing on a local computer. Ping 127.0.0.1 to test this—it should point you to your computer.

14-4. Convert this dotted decimal address to hexadecimal and binary: 206.147.3.12.

14-5. Go to http://www.net.cmu.edu/cgi-bin/netops.cgi and use the ping and traceroute facility to ping Prentice Hall. Try both from the DOS prompt.

# E PLURIBUS UNUM: INTERNETWORKING THE NETWORKS AT LORDSBURG UNIVERSITY

Lordsburg University was founded in the mid-nineteenth century as a small Normal School helping to prepare teachers in a people-centered, values-oriented, educational environment. The school grew over the years into a liberal arts college and finally began offering advanced degree programs at two locations off campus in the early 1970s, when it became a university.

In the 1980s, the university enthusiastically entered the computer age. During the early '90s, the installation of LANs—each with its own diverse technology—grew rapidly on campus. The individual networks grew up like boomtowns, however, and remained isolated islands. While most of the existing computers in the separate academic networks were Windows-based systems, certain ones such as the art, music, and communications departments used Macintosh computers. Separate LANs were installed for them so they could share graphics files and expensive printers. The administrative departments, also using Windows-based PCs, needed to share several databases and to coordinate the functions of admissions, the registrar, student accounts, and financial aid. The university relations office maintained a large database of donors and alumni and shared that information among the staff of fifteen employees. Most of the existing LANs were Ethernet, although there were a couple of token ring LANs, considered mavericks by the rest of the university community.

Senior management at the main campus determined that in order to maintain communication, improve speed and efficiency, and function as a unified whole, the university needed an ambitious, well-thought-out plan to internetwork these heterogeneous networks. They also wanted to connect to their two other campuses in towns 10 and 25 miles away. Through cooperation with a nearby, much larger university, they planned to connect to the Internet backbone at 1.5 Mbps. Upper management met with the director of information technology to work out a strategic plan to implement the changes as soon as possible. "Oh, by the way Mr. IT, keep the costs as low as possible. You are already over budget."

**QUESTIONS**

1. If you were the IT director, what would be your first step in trying to internetwork these diverse networks?

2. What kind of hardware and software would you need to add for interconnection of the LANs, the other campuses, and to access the Internet? What kind of topologies and standards would you use?

3. What difficulties do you foresee in trying to implement your new strategic plan? What would you do if the separate departments wanted to maintain their own autonomy and refused to meet the new university-wide standards?

4. Would you standardize the networks so that all LANs were the same technology, or would you allow diversity within the separate LANs? The MacIntosh computer users are dyed-in-the-wool Apple people who do not want to switch to PCs and Ethernet. Would they have to change?

# THE INTERNET

## ■ OUTLINE

## ■ KEY TERMS

ALOHAnet

asymmetric DSL (ADSL)

basic rate interface (BRI)

cable access

Computer Emergency
    Response Team
    (CERT)

dial-up networking
    (DUN)

digital subscriber line
    (DSL)

extranet

firewall

fixed wireless

in-band signaling

Integrated Services
    Digital Network
    (ISDN)

Interface Message
    Processors (IMPs)

Internet Architecture
    Board (IAB)

Internet backbone

Internet Engineering
    Steering Group (IESG)

Internet Engineering
    Task Force (IETF)

Internet Research Task
    Force (IRTF)

Internet service
    provider (ISP)

Internet Society (ISOC)

intranet

latency

line of sight (LOS)

| | | |
|---|---|---|
| Metropolitan Area Exchanges (MAEs) | Point-to-Point Protocol (PPP) | very-high-rate DSL (VDSL) |
| mobile wireless | primary rate interface (PRI) | virtual private network (VPN) |
| Network Access Points (NAPs) | satellite connection | WebTV |
| Network Address Translation (NAT) | Serial Line Internet Protocol (SLIP) | Wireless Application Protocol (WAP) |
| non-line of sight (NLOS) | symmetric DSL (SDSL) | World Wide Web Consortium (W3C) |
| out-of-band signaling | terminal adapter | |
| point of presence (POP) | Usenet | |

## ■ OBJECTIVES

After you complete your study of this chapter, you should be able to:

- ■ describe the birth of the Internet and its growth in the past 30 years;
- ■ explain the differences between the Internet and the World Wide Web;
- ■ describe the major groups that guide the growth and establish standards for the Internet;
- ■ explain the different types of Internet connection; and
- ■ describe network address translation and its purpose.

## 15-1   INTRODUCTION

As we stated in Chapter 14, even people who know very little about networking know and love the Internet—but why? Since the days when computers filled entire rooms, were housed behind glass walls, and were jealously guarded by technicians (mostly men) in white lab coats, people have sought to connect them. Humans are social beings, and even when engaged in intense research, they are rarely content to remain isolated from others. The need for connection is basic to our lives. That common desire for association is what drove the linking together of two computers and the interconnecting of sites when the first nodes of the ARPANET began their inexorable growth toward the globe-spanning Internet that we know and love today.

E-mail, as evidence of that drive to communicate, has been the "killer application" (Killer Ap) of internetworking since its earliest days. Researchers soon found that, despite the development of so many other new technologies, e-mail remained the application of the TCP/IP protocol suite that was used most often. Other forces have contributed to the emergence of the Internet and the World Wide Web during the past thirty years, as we shall see, but the primary spur to growth has always been communication and sharing of ideas. The problem of incompatibility has thwarted that goal to connect and communicate—as it does in all human relations!

This chapter describes the ways that visionaries and engineers were able to see beyond the problem to solve the obstacles of incompatibility and to build the phenomenal global connection that is the Internet and its World Wide Web. You will read the manifest benefits of determined commitment, the investment in research, and the development of telecommunications. You will also read the fascinating tale of many individuals who solved the big puzzle by fitting their individual pieces into the whole, thereby creating something far beyond their own small, though vital, contributions. The history of the Internet is the saga of scientists, engineers, military personnel, software developers, government, and businesses working together in a spirit of sharing and openness. The saga continues. How great it would be if all human efforts at connection and communication worked as well!

## 15-2   HISTORY OF THE INTERNET

Most college students have never lived in a world without PCs. They scarcely remember life before the Internet. It wasn't long ago, however, that neither PCs nor the Internet existed. Few communications inventions of the past have had such an impact on the world. The introductions of telegraph, telephone, radio, and television paved the way for the integration of telecommunications that we call the Internet.

### The 1950s

On October 4, 1957, the Soviet Union launched the first artificial satellite, Sputnik, and as a result they triggered the development of two important government agencies in the U.S. The Sputnik launch led directly to the creation of the National Aeronautics and Space Administration (NASA) in October of 1958, and ARPA in the same year. ARPA changed its name to DARPA in 1973. DARPA is the central research and development organization for the DoD. The ARPANET resulted from the research of this agency and eventually became the Internet of today.

### The 1960s

The 1960s was a decade of firsts. In 1962, a behavioral psychologist, J.C.R. Licklider of MIT and later the first director of DARPA's research program, wrote a paper envisioning an "intergalactic computer network" that would allow anyone to access data anywhere in the world from any computer.

Licklider did not foresee the number of computers that we now have, but his paper was prophetic in proposing the kind of "interactive computing" that PC users take for granted today. At that time, if a person worked with computers, he or she had to punch holes in cards and turn them over to someone else in the computer room to process. Licklider's vision was of what could happen in the future, but it took many people, countless technological advances, and several years to make his vision a reality. It is still a vision in process.

## SIDEBAR 15-1

J.C.R. Licklider
(Courtesy of M.I.T. Museum and Historical
Collections. Reprinted with permission.)

J. C. R. Licklider, who was called "Lick" by his friends, never achieved any great amount of fame or widespread recognition. He had a psychology background, not a computer science background, yet his visionary ideas inspired the actions of many shapers of the Internet and the World Wide Web.

Lick was born in 1915 and attended Washington University in St. Louis, where he received three bachelor's degrees in physics, math, and psychology. After working for several years at Harvard, he moved to MIT in 1950 and worked on a Cold War project called SAGE. It was his first experience with computers and it influenced his later thinking and writing about their exciting possibilities. Unlike most computers at that time, the SAGE computer worked in real time, giving results almost immediately after information was fed into the machine.

Licklider's work, "Man Computer Symbiosis," asserted that the goal in creating computers should be "to enable men and computers to cooperate in making decisions and controlling complex situations," that is, real-time interactive computing—a groundbreaking idea in 1960! In freeing the human mind by taking care of mundane tasks, a computer should augment human intellect.

He worked in two places that were very important to the development of what would become the Internet. Bolt, Beranek and Newman, Inc. (BBN) was the company that supplied the first computers that connected the ARPANET. Because of his influence, the architectural acoustics design firm changed its emphasis to computers and earned a reputation as a computer consultant firm. In 1962, Lick joined ARPA to find better uses for computers. He set up research contracts with leading computer research institutions and formed what he called the "Intergalactic Computer Network," a group that later created ARPANET. In a memo to the group in 1963, Lick proposed standardization among the different computer systems of the members, and the connection of the various computers—a network. Larry Roberts, one of its principal architects said of him, "Lick saw this vision in the early sixties. He didn't have a clue how to build it. He didn't have any idea how to make this happen. But he knew it was important, so he sat down with me and really convinced me that it was important and convinced me into making it happen."

In 1965, Licklider wrote *Libraries of the Future,* in which he described a plan to store and retrieve information electronically. He called it a "precognitive system," describing a desk that would be "primarily a display-and-control station in a telecommunication/telecomputation system—and its most vital part may be the cable ('umbilical cord') that connects it, via a wall socket, into the procognitive utility net." He saw the system connecting the user to, "everyday business, industrial, government, and professional information, and perhaps, also to news, entertainment, and education."[1] Sounds like the World Wide Web—in 1965! Unlike many after him, Lick often let others take credit for his ideas as long as they were accomplished. You may read J.C.R. Licklider's ideas and his papers at http://memex.org/liklider.pdf.

[1] Licklider, J. C. R. (1965) *Libraries of the Future.* Cambridge: The MIT Press, pp. 33, 34.

At the beginning of the decade at MIT, Leonard Kleinrock wrote a research paper entitled "Information Flow in Large Communication Nets," in which he discussed the concept of using packet switching, rather than the circuit switching of the telephone system, to send data.

## SIDEBAR 15-2

Leonard Kleinrock
(Courtesy of AP/Wide World Photos.
Reprinted with permission.)

Dr. Leonard Kleinrock, listed by the Los Angeles Times in 1999 as among the 50 people who most influenced business during the last century, is also known as the father of modern data networking. He admires the work of Dutch artist Mauritis Cornelis Escher, saying, "He used to dream of things that could never be built." Kleinrock himself seems to have lived his life dreaming about—and building—things that others thought could never be built.

As a child of six, while reading a Superman comic, he spied the plans for building his own crystal set, gathered the necessary ingredients, and put them together. He was amazed to hear music coming out of his creation and an engineer was born! He took night classes for 5 1/2 years at New York's City College to become the best student there, even while helping to support his family at his father's request.

A decade before the birth of the Internet, he created the basic principles of packet switching while a graduate student at MIT. His intention was to do something really important that "the rest of the pack wasn't doing," and the result was his research on packet-switching and queuing theory. Kleinrock earned his Ph.D. from MIT in 1963. Since then, he has served as a professor of computer science at the University of California, Los Angeles, and served as chair of the department from 1991–1995.

Although his ideas were ignored for several years, in honor of his pioneer work, his host computer at UCLA was chosen as the first node on the Internet in September of 1969. Kleinrock directed a staff of 40 graduate students in the transmission of the first message ever to pass over the Internet. Later, given the task of measuring and testing the network, he organized his staff into units to work on various projects. His influence on other Internet pioneers has been as important as his own significant contributions to networking. He has mentored some of the greatest names in networking, including people like Steve Crocker, Vinton Cerf, Bob Kahn, Ray Tomlinson, and many others.

In 2000, after taking an early retirement from teaching, Kleinrock founded Nomadix. It is a company designed to fulfill another of his dreams of things that could never be built—nomadic computing. It offers a complete range of products for companies that deploy wired and wireless Public Access Networks (PANs) so people can receive broadband Internet access at wide-ranging locations away from their offices. He sees the future "filled with broadband connectivity as widespread and invisible as electricity, and every room and perhaps human body will be designated as a "smart space." And why not? Who, in 1962, would have envisioned the spread of ubiquitous, accessible, easy-to-use networks as we know them today? Leonard Kleinrock, for one.

Later in the decade, Kleinrock played another major role at UCLA, but his early paper outlining packet-switching theory was one of the major puzzle pieces in the development of computer internetworking. Early in the 1960s, several other men concurrently developed the concept of networks that would send pieces of data in units: Paul Baran and others at Rand Corporation and Donald Davies and his colleagues at Britain's National Physical Laboratory. Davies was the first person to refer to the data units as "packets."

## SIDEBAR 15-3 °

Paul Baran
(Courtesy of Rand Corporation.)

Born in Poland in 1926, Paul Baran moved to the U.S. with his family two years later. He earned a degree in electrical engineering at Drexel University, married, and moved to Los Angeles. He worked for the Hughes Aircraft Company while taking night classes at UCLA. In 1959, Baran earned a master's degree in engineering and began to work in the computer science department of the Rand Corporation.

At that time, the Rand Corporation focused mostly on Cold War-related military problems, and Baran became interested in how to enable communication networks to survive a nuclear attack. To design a more robust communications network, he thought outside the box—use digital computers and introduce redundancy. His colleagues were skeptical. Later, Baran recalled, "Many of the things I thought possible would tend to sound like utter nonsense, or impractical, depending on the generosity of spirit in those brought up in an earlier world."[2]

He and Warren McCulloch, a well-known psychiatrist at MIT's Research Laboratory of Electronics, discussed the way the human brain does not rely on a single set of dedicated cells for a particular function. It is sometimes able to recover lost functions, therefore, by bypassing "downed" areas. Perhaps they could build a communication network that would function in a like manner.

Baran suggested a distributed network—a communication network that would allow several hundred major communications stations to talk with one another after an enemy attack. There would be no centralized switch. Each node would connect to several neighboring nodes and thus would have several possible routes to send data. If one were destroyed, another would be available.

Baran also suggested dividing messages into "message blocks" before sending them out separately across the network to be rejoined when they arrived at their destination. Donald Davies independently devised a very similar system in Britain at the same time, but called the individual pieces "packets." The name stuck. The nodes would use what he called "hot potato routing," a rapid store-and-forward scheme, and "dynamic routing" of continuously updated network information. When the ARPANET project began, Baran's distributed network and packet-switching schemes were adopted, and he became an informal consultant for them. His "impractical" practice of thinking outside the box benefited the entire world of computer networking.

[2] Hafner, Katie and Matthew Lyon. (1996) *Where Wizards Stay Up Late: The Origins of the Internet.* New York: Simon & Schuster, p. 55.

The first network experiment took place in 1965 when two computers, the Q-32 mainframe at System Development Corporation (SDC) in Santa Monica and the TX-2 computer at MIT's Lincoln Lab, shared data. It was the first WAN ever created. It allowed the computers to "talk" over a low-speed telephone line. Connection! Packet switching would improve on the experiment.

By the end of the decade, Lawrence G. Roberts at MIT and Robert Taylor at the Pentagon had established the first ARPANET plan to directly connect all the time-sharing computers over dial-up phone lines.

## SIDEBAR 15-4

Larry Roberts

Building on Licklider's ideas, Robert Taylor, director of ARPA's Information Processing Techniques Office, decided that ARPA should link the existing computers at ARPA-funded research institutions together, to share computing resources and results with everyone on the network. Taylor began looking for someone to manage the project and chose Larry Roberts, a shy man who was well respected because of his knowledge of computer science and who had good management skills and dedication.

In 1965, Roberts had worked on a smaller network computing project with Tom Marill, a psychologist who (because he had studied under Licklider) was interested in computers. They successfully linked Lincoln Lab's TX-2 computer in Massachusetts to the SDC Q-32 computer in Santa Monica.

Roberts was happy at Lincoln and did not want to leave, but Taylor eventually convinced ARPA's director, Charles Herzfeld, to persuade Roberts to take the position. Roberts said that Taylor got "Herzfeld to call up the head of Lincoln and say, 'Well, we have 51 percent of your money. Why don't you send Roberts down here as fast as you can?' And the head of Lincoln called me in and said, 'It'd probably be a nice thing for all of us if you'd consider this.'[3] Roberts was only 29 when he became manager and principal architect of the ARPANET.

In 1967, Roberts proposed his plan to connect all ARPA-sponsored computers directly over dial-up telephone lines, with host computers at each site handling networking functions. His plans did not meet with acceptance. A man named Wes Clark suggested that he leave the host computers alone and use small computers speaking the same language at each site to handle communications among them. The host computer would only have to communicate with its own small computer, which would act as a gateway to the network. Roberts adopted Clark's idea, and by the end of 1969, the first four nodes of ARPANET were connected.

Larry Roberts earned the nickname, "father of the ARPANET," by directing a team of engineers who created the network that would become the Internet. Once again, networking moved forward on the vision of a man willing to think in an entirely new way.

[3] Segaller, Stephen. (1998) *Nerds 2.0.1: A Brief History of the Internet.* New York: TV Books, p. 47.

One of the benefits of such a network was load sharing, an extension of time sharing, which would allow users to access an idle computer at a distant site if the local one was busy. Another benefit was data sharing, which allowed people in different parts of the country to share and exchange data with others interested in the same type of research. Not many people really considered communication as one of the major functions of the network, but Bob Taylor thought its primary use would be in allowing people to discover and to exploit common interests, even when they were separated geographically. Connection!

The proposal was to test a network of four nodes that would eventually build up to a dozen. The first four participants proposed were UCLA where Kleinrock taught, Stanford Research Institute (SRI), The University of California at Santa Barbara, and the University of Utah. Each site had one or more mainframe computers, but they were different computers that used different languages and OSs, and they were understood by exclusive groups of people. The problem was that they were incompatible and unable to communicate with each other. The proposal called for a minicomputer to be built for each site as an interface between the network and the mainframe nodes. Each minicomputer would use the same language and operating system. They would speak to their own mainframe and to one another, although the mainframes could speak only to their own local interface. Because their main function was to process messages from the network, the minicomputers or "packet switches" that correspond to today's routers were called **Interface Message Processors (IMPs).** The agency refined the overall structure and specifications for the network, then put out an RFQ in August of 1968 for the construction of the IMPs.

**Interface Message Processors (IMPs)**

In April of 1969, the Network Working Group (NWG), led by Steve Crocker, released RFC #1, "Host Software," which covered the Host-to-Host Protocol. Later, in RFC #1000, Crocker related, "Most of us were graduate students (in 1969) and we expected that a professional crew would show up eventually to take over the problems we were dealing with. We had accumulated a few notes . . . and we decided to put them together in a set of notes. The basic ground rules were that anyone could say anything and that nothing was official. And to emphasize the point, I labeled the notes 'Requests for Comments.' I never dreamed these notes would be distributed through the very medium we were discussing in these notes."

The relatively small company, BBN, was awarded a 1 million dollar contract for the IMPs. They used Honeywell DDP-516 minicomputers with 12 K memory and 50 Kbps lines provided by AT&T. The minicomputers had to be designed and built from scratch to very precise specifications. Nothing could be ordered from the Internet or delivered and set up by a local computer store as ours are today. Few people expected it, but the IMPs were delivered exactly on time nine months later—an appropriate time span for the "birth" of what would become the Internet. Though not an easy task in 1969, especially for a government project, they were delivered on schedule and on budget.

On October 1, 1969, the second IMP was installed at SRI and the first packets were sent from UCLA. Both sides were equipped with a pair of headphones and a speaker. Leonard Kleinrock relates the historic moment, "We now had two hosts who could talk to each other and all we wanted to do was have one of my graduate students log on to the machine from our host to the SRI host and all we had to do was type L O G and my guy Charlie typed in the L and he said, 'Did you get the L?' and the guy at the other end said, 'Got the L.' Charlie typed an O, 'I got the O.' Charlie typed the G. 'Get the G?' Crash – the SRI host went down. So the first message ever on the Internet was

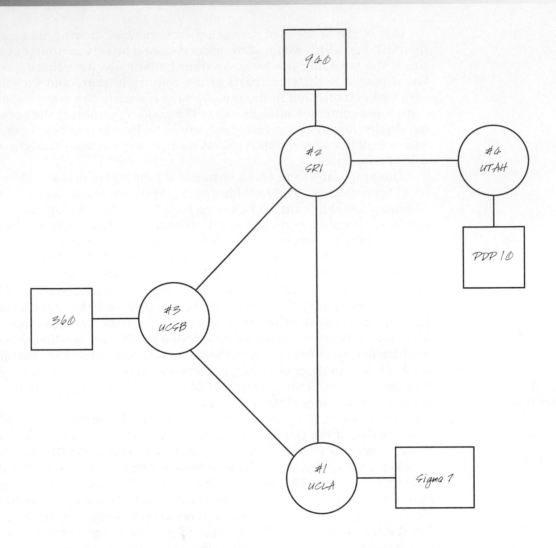

Node 1: University of California, Los Angeles (UCLA)          August 30--hooked up September 2, 1969
Node 2: Stanford Research Institute (SRI)                     October 1, 1969
Node 3: University of California, Santa Barbara (UCSB)        November 1, 1969
Node 4: University of Utah                                    December, 1969

**FIGURE 15-1**   The hand-sketched map of the first ARPANET nodes.

the word LO."[4] Later that day, the login was successful and the two computers communicated.

Even as early as July of 1969, Kleinrock anticipated the incredible growth of the network he had helped to create as he saw so many puzzle pieces falling into place. Networks were in their infancy. "But some day," when networks grew up, we would "see the spread of 'computer utilities,' which, like present electric and telephone utilities, will service individual homes and offices across the country," he prophesied. By the end of the decade, the four initial nodes were connected. The ARPANET was born. Figure 15-1 shows an original sketch map of the first four nodes on the ARPA network. It was drawn by an unknown ARPANET scientist in December, 1969. Mankind had taken another giant step that year, but this one had not yet been witnessed by the world.

[4] Segaller, Stephen. (1998), pp. 92–93.

30<sup>th</sup> Anniversary of the start of the Internet. (Used by permission of Robert de Violini, Stamp Exhibition of Southern California at www.sescal.org.)

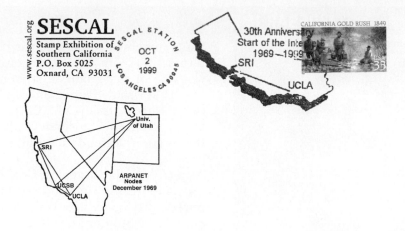

One of the byproducts of IMP technology was the creation of the first LANs. Although the ARPANET was designed to be a WAN, engineers found that, not only did the IMPs connect the widespread nodes, they also allowed multiple different mainframes at the same location to connect through their shared IMP. In technology, as in all of human life, progress occurs whenever incompatibility is overcome.

## The 1970s

The next decade brought many exciting developments in the history of the Internet. In 1970 Norm Abramson, a professor who moved from Stanford to the University of Hawaii to surf, began working on a radio-based system to connect the Hawaiian Islands together. He and his team of graduate students created a system that would later inspire a doctoral dissertation that would become Ethernet. Through their work, **ALOHAnet** became the very first wireless, packet-switched network. It was connected to ARPANET on the mainland in 1972.

ALOHAnet

Connections continued and new puzzle pieces fit into place. In 1974, BBN opened Telenet, the first public packet-data service, which was a commercial version of ARPANET.

ARPANET, established by the military branch of the government to share research and resources, was a communications network. As such, it had features that made people want to keep using it. In 1971, Ray Tomlinson of BBN developed e-mail to send messages across the distributed network. The ARPANET consisted of fifteen nodes at that time. Tomlinson also chose the @ sign as the "at" in an e-mail address. In 1973 an ARPA report showed that of all usage on the internetwork, three-fourths was e-mail. It was the largest network application for over a decade—until the World Wide Web. Queen Elizabeth II made early network history by sending e-mail on March 26, 1976. By the end of the 1970s, the ARPANET had expanded to over one hundred nodes.

The initial ARPANET host-to-host protocol was called Network Control Protocol (NCP). By 1973, however, many new networks within federal agencies, research establishments, and educational institutions had been created. Each had its own protocols, hardware, and software. Once again, the problem of incompatibility caused a major advance in networking technology. Bob Kahn at DARPA and Vinton Cerf at Stanford began research on protocols that would allow the incompatible collection of packet-switching networks to internetwork. They invented TCP/IP, which was discussed in Chapter 14.

## SIDEBAR 15-5

Vinton Cerf
(Courtesy of WorldCom/ Mark Harding, Photographer. Reprinted with permission.)

Robert Kahn
(Courtesy of www.livinginternet.com)

Many people have claimed the title of "father of the Internet," but Vint Cerf really earned the nickname. He was one of the graduate students at UCLA when the first IMP was delivered, and he is one of the coauthors (with Robert Kahn) of TCP/IP—the protocol that allowed ARPANET to connect all the networks together that is still the standard for all Internet communication.

As a child in Los Angeles, Cerf did very well in school, especially math. He also developed an interest in computers at a young age. He graduated with a degree in math from Stanford in 1965, but said later, "There was something amazingly enticing about programming. You created your own universe and you were master of it. The computer would do anything you programmed it to do. It was this unbelievable sandbox in which every grain of sand was under your control."[5]

After a stint at IBM, he enrolled at UCLA to pursue a Ph.D. in computer science, and became one of the senior members of Len Kleinrock's group of graduate students who ran the Network Measurement Center, an ARPA program set up in anticipation of building the ARPANET. The NWG, composed of students from the schools that were to be the first four nodes, met to discuss the network and its development problems. Vint described the group, "We were just rank amateurs, and we were expecting that some authority would finally come along and say, 'Here's how we are going to do it.' And nobody ever came along."[6] The group worked on several layered protocols, one of which was the host-to-host communication protocol, NCP.

While testing the new IMP at UCLA, Cerf met Robert Kahn, who had earned a Ph.D. from Princeton University in 1964. Kahn had worked for a while at AT&T Bell Laboratories, taught electrical engineering at MIT, and later worked at BBN. He helped build the IMP that was delivered to UCLA and the other three "first nodes." The two developed a good working relationship.

In 1972, Kahn demonstrated ARPANET connecting forty different computers at the International Computer Communication Conference. The network first became widely known to people from around the world at conference. Soon, other networks began to appear, each with its own way of doing things. Kahn and Cert realized that they needed some kind of gateway to allow all the independent networks that had sprung up to communicate,

[5] Hafner, Katie and M. Lyon. (1996), p. 139.

[6] Abbate, J. (1999). *Inventing the Internet.* Cambridge: MIT Press, p. 73.

but that seemed impossible because each had its own protocol and technology. They needed a standard that would allow them to link all the networks together so they could communicate, despite their differences.

Kahn's four goals for the TCP design were the following: 1) network connectivity, so any network could connect to another network through a gateway; 2) distribution, so there would be no central network administration or control; 3) error recovery, so lost packets would be retransmitted; and 4) black box design, so no internal changes would have to be made to a computer to connect it to the network.

In 1973, Vint Cerf and Robert Kahn presented a paper called "A Protocol for Packet Network Intercommunication," describing TCP. In 1978, it was split into two parts and TCP/IP was born—a new way of doing things for the network of networks that we now call the Internet.

PARC, which opened in 1970, was the single most important facility for the development of networking and the PC. It provided a free and open research atmosphere where scientists, engineers, and creative thinkers developed ideas and tools that were way ahead of their time. Another major development in the early seventies was the development of the first Ethernet network, based on the Ph.D. thesis by Robert Metcalfe.

His idea for networks stemmed from something he saw in ALOHAnet—a remedy for interruptions and collisions by random retransmission of packets. It was at PARC that Metcalfe and his colleagues developed Ethernet, based on his 1973 Ph.D. thesis. Figure 15-2 shows Metcalfe's original drawing of the "Ethernet." When PCs were publicly introduced in the next decade, there would be a way to network them. Connection!

**Usenet**

In 1979, Jim Ellis and Tom Truscott, computer science graduate students at Duke University, established the first **Usenet** (newsgroups). Steve Bellovin, a computer science graduate student at the University of North Carolina (UNC), wrote the first Netnews program to transfer files between two computers over a telephone modem connection. Since then, users all over the world have used these discussion groups to talk about thousands of different subjects.

**FIGURE 15-2**   Robert Metcalfe's original drawing of Ethernet.
(Used with permission of Dr. Robert M. Metcalfe.)

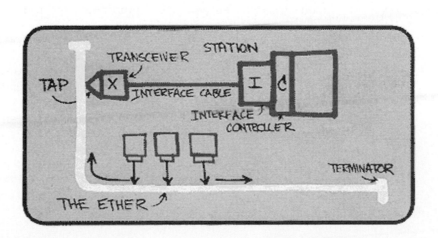

## SIDEBAR 15-6

Robert Metcalfe
(Used with permission.)

How many people have given up at the least sign of rejection? How many have withered when others laughed? How many of us have failed at something and decided we were no good and might as well not try any more? Fortunately, Bob Metcalfe did not react that way.

Metcalfe was born in 1946 in Brooklyn, NY. He earned degrees in electrical engineering and business management from MIT, and a master's degree in applied mathematics from Harvard. He began work on a Ph.D. in computer science there and worked at MIT, building the hardware that would link MIT to ARPANET.

In 1972, he was chosen to demonstrate the ARPANET to AT&T officials because of an informative booklet he had written for a conference. The system crashed during the demonstration, and Metcalfe recalled, "I looked up in pain and I caught them smiling, delighted that packet-switching was flaky. This I will never forget. It confirmed for them that circuit-switching technology was here to stay, and this packet-switching stuff was an unreliable toy that would never have much impact in the commercial world. It was clear to me they were tangled in the past."[7]

Laughter. Rejection. But, Metcalfe's reaction was not defeat. He said, "I saw that there are people who will connive against innovation. They're hostile to it. And that has shaped my behavior ever since."

The topic of Metcalfe's doctoral dissertation at Harvard was the ARPANET, about which he was so excited. Harvard flunked him because his dissertation was "not theoretical enough."

Failure. Metcalfe was angry, but he did not give up. He had accepted a job at PARC and he was told to come to PARC anyway and finish his doctoral work later.

Metcalfe had read a paper about the radio wave ALOHA network at the University of Hawaii. To handle collisions, Norm Abramson, the designer of ALOHAnet, had used a random access scheme. Whenever data needed to be sent, computers could transmit and then wait to receive confirmation of the packets' arrival at the destination. If a collision occurred, the sending computer would wait a very short, random period before retransmitting. Metcalfe knew how he could improve on the design, and it became the inspiration for his new dissertation.

He reworked the design, varying the random interval for retransmission and basing it on traffic load. The computer would wait longer periods before retransmitting if there were a lot of traffic. This would improve efficiency by limiting the number of repeat collisions. Metcalfe submitted his new dissertation and finally earned his Ph.D. At PARC, given the job of connecting the new Altos PCs, Metcalfe modified his technology even more, using cables and making several other adjustments to his version of ALOHAnet.

Metcalfe refused to give in to rejection, ridicule, or failure. Because of it, he succeeded. But more than that, he also introduced the world to the technology used by the majority of networked computers today: Ethernet.

[7] Hafner, Katie and M. Lyon. (1996), p. 139.

## The 1980s

The 1980s brought many significant changes to the world of computer technology and to the emerging Internet. By the end of the decade, largely because of the introduction of the PC, the number of connected hosts had gone from about 200 to almost 200,000.

In the 1970s, almost ten years before they appeared publicly, PCs were used on desktops at PARC and were connected by cable in a crude LAN. They were used only at Xerox PARC, however, and were not developed commercially for use outside the corporation. What is now called the first PC was really offered as a mail-order product by a man in New Mexico in 1975. Ed Roberts saw something that company management at Intel could not see in their microprocessor or "chip," which was mainly used in calculators and traffic lights. He built a kit computer based on Intel's 8080 chip. His Altair 8800, the first PC, was featured on the cover of *Popular Electronics*. It had no place to connect a monitor, keyboard or printer, no software, and little memory. It possessed only a front panel that had switches for programming—one bit at a time—but it was cheap ($495 assembled and $360 in kit form) and sometimes even faster than research lab machines.

An interesting side note is that the daughter of the *Popular Electronics* technical editor, Les Solomon, gave the computer its name. Solomon asked his daughter what the computer on Star Trek was called. She replied, "computer." She told him to name it "Altair" because that's where the Starship Enterprise was going that night.

The IBM PC arrived in 1981, which was a milestone for networking. It allowed American businesses to perceive the PC in a whole new way. Through networking and by allowing businesses to process information and share data, it became a business tool—not just a toy for hobbyists and engineers. The creation of IBM clones and the Apple MacIntosh (the first computer with built-in networking), in 1984 created more and more public demand. When there were enough computers to be networked, networking became commercially important. Novell Data Systems introduced Netware software in 1983. It allowed several PCs to talk to one another and share resources, thus creating LANs. More and more institutions—public and private—began building networks and connecting to one another and to ARPANET. In 1982, the DoD declared TCP/IP as the standard for connecting the various types of networks.

January 1, 1983 was set as transition day when all hosts on the ARPANET would convert simultaneously to TCP/IP from NCP. In the same year,

The Altair computer
(Courtesy of the Computer
History Museum. Reprinted
with permission.)

ARPANET split into ARPANET and MILNET. By 1986, the National Science Foundation's NSFNET was created to serve the entire higher education community in all disciplines, and use of the TCP/IP protocol became mandatory for the network. Thus, the definition of the Internet became "a connected set of networks, specifically those using TCP/IP." In order to identify the type of institution on the Internet, the DNS was created, introducing six large domains: edu, gov, mil, com, org, and net.

In 1989, a symposium was held at UCLA to celebrate the 20-year anniversary of ARPANET. The following year, that pioneer internet was formally decommissioned. One negative note at the end of the decade, the sending of the Morris worm through the Internet affected 6,000 of the 60,000 hosts online. As a result, the **Computer Emergency Response Team (CERT)** was created for facilitating response to computer security threats on the Internet.

**Computer Emergency Response Team (CERT)**

## The 1990s

The 1990s became the decade of Internet commercialization. Commercial services had begun to emerge with CompuServe and AOL by the end of the previous decade. In 1991, the NSFNET lifted commercial restrictions on the use of the Internet and opened the door for electronic commerce.

In 1991, the next great puzzle piece was snapped into place when Tim Berners-Lee, a British researcher at CERN in Switzerland, created a program to overcome the incompatibility of the networks on the Internet and make information accessible to all.

### SIDEBAR 15-7

Tim Berners-Lee
(Courtesy of CERN/ European Organization for Nuclear Research. Reprinted with permission.)

Tim Berners-Lee may have been named one of the 100 most influential people of the 20th century, and he may be called the "Father of the Web," but he is not like the many men who have profited from his World Wide Web. It is his creation, and yet he has always chosen the nonprofit road for himself and his invention. Even now, he heads the World Wide Web consortium (W3C), the body that seeks to get everybody to agree on openly published protocols rather than hindering each other—and everyone else—with their own proprietary systems and technology. Berners-Lee is concerned about the direction that the Web has taken because it is not at all what he intended. He has a higher vision of what it can be.

Berners-Lee is the son of mathematicians, whose parents were part of the team that programmed the world's first commercial stored-program computer, the Manchester University "Mark I." Born in 1955, Tim was raised in London by parents who taught him to think unconventionally—out of the box. While at Oxford, where he earned a degree in Physics in 1976, he built his own computer out of spare parts and a TV.

Berners-Lee has always remembered a discussion he had with his father when he was in high school. They were talking about how to make a computer intuitive, able to make connections like the brain does rather than in the rigid hierarchies and matrices as a computer does. The human brain can link all kinds of random data. Certain smells remind one of a specific time and place, and suddenly all kinds of other memories and bits of information flood in—and somehow connect. He says that the idea stayed with him, "that computers could become much more powerful if they could be programmed to link otherwise unconnected information."

In 1980, while working on a six-month software consulting job with CERN, the famous European Particle Physics Laboratory in Geneva, he began to build on his ideas to create his first web-like program, called Enquire. It was named after a Victorian book that he had seen as a child on his parent's bookshelf: *Enquire Within Upon Anything.* The purpose of the software was simply to link words in a document to other files on his computer and to help him remember the many names and bits of data he needed to remember but often forgot. Later, he began to ponder how he could link to information on other people's computers, without having to put all the information into huge databases. Rather, he thought, he could open his documents and his computer to anyone anywhere and allow them to link to his information. They could do the same. He envisioned the Web as a place where anything is potentially connected with anything else and is available to anyone.

Berners-Lee described the formulation of his inventions—HTML, HTTP, URLS, and the World Wide Web—not as a linear solving of one problem after another, but as the swirling together of many different thoughts, influences, and ideas from many different sources. He believes that countless, nameless people contributed to his creation, which evolved out of his growing realization that there was a power in arranging ideas in an unconstrained, weblike way.

His original idea was that people could create and share ideas more easily on the Web, not just access information or engage in entrepreneurial enterprise. He still works behind the scenes at W3C to ensure that we can all continue to share ideas with one another—openly and freely.

The World Wide Web program that he created consists of three major components:

1. The Universal Resource Locator (URL) is an address through which one can access any site located on the Internet. An example is http://www.prenticehall.com/. The first part of the URL indicates the protocol used, in this case, HTTP, but it could be FTP, NEWS, MAILTO, etc. WWW stands for World Wide Web. The next part of the string designates the host's name, and it could also include the folder or directory on the host and the name of a file or document. The last part of the URL address is the top level domain.

2. HTTP is the client/server protocol that allows text and graphics to be transmitted over TCP/IP so pages look the same no matter what kind of computer system a person uses.

3. HTML is the scripting language that is used for creating World Wide Web pages. It describes how graphics and text will appear when displayed on the screen.

The 1990s brought many other innovations to the Internet. In 1993, Mosaic (the first Internet browser that provided a graphical interface to search the Internet) was developed at the University of Illinois. The browser opened the Internet to people everywhere, providing a tool to navigate and a way to find things. Content providers were also able to provide websites that appealed to users visually, rather than straight text on a gray background. Netscape, a rewrite of Mosaic by its original programmers, followed soon thereafter. Finally, Microsoft's Internet Explorer became Netscape's strongest competitor.

The years between 1991 and 1994 truly transformed the Internet with the introduction of the World Wide Web, the browser, and the content shift from only government and educational research to commercial interests as well. Interconnected network providers began to route main U.S. backbone traffic and country domains continued to increase. In 1998, the rate of new computers being added to the Internet reached an average of one per second. New technologies continued to attract more and more users and by the year 2000, despite dire Y2K predictions, the Internet had grown to over 70 million attached computers.

## 15-3   DESCRIPTION OF THE INTERNET

Some say that growth of the Internet has slowed since the beginning of the new millennium, but Dr. Lawrence Roberts, one of its founding fathers, insists that traffic volumes still triple every year. In any case, the Net is now a user-friendly place where beginners who venture forth have just as much access as veterans who blazed the trail for all of us over thirty years ago. It places the world at one's fingertips and can deliver information—as well as garbage—in an instant. Figure 15-3 illustrates the growth in the number of hosts in the DNS, according to the Internet Domain Survey of the Internet Software Consortium. Today's Internet is truly, if not intergalactic, at least global—a network of networks that provide vast amounts of information as well as human connectivity, communication, and collaboration.

Who owns and runs the Internet? No one group runs the Internet, but thousands of organizations and networks cooperate to pass information among them, and each pays for and runs part of it. In the U.S., the government, through organizations such as the NSF, funds high-speed backbones like the Very High-Speed Backbone Network Services (vBNS). It links together supercomputer centers and provides high-speed infrastructure to education and research communities. Other large corporations and organizations provide backbones that connect sites nationally and globally. Large private companies sell access to high-capacity lines that connect to the backbones. Individual local networks of government agencies, universities, private companies, and ISPs connect at regional and local levels.

When ARPANET began, and even as it grew in the U.S. and around the world, it was easy to map the entire network. That task is now almost impossible, though many organizations continue to try. Many websites, such as www.caida.org/, www.peacockmaps.com, and others have stunning representations of the Internet today. One site, http://www.cybergeography.org/atlas/atlas.html, is a fascinating collection of "cybermaps" dating back to the very first ARPANET node.

Many groups also guide the growth of the Internet and establish standards for its use. The following is a partial list:

**Internet Society (ISOC)**

■   The **Internet Society (ISOC)** (www.isoc.org) is a private, nonprofit umbrella organization that is, in its own words, "an international group

FIGURE 15-3 Growth of the Internet. Internet domain survey, July, 2002. (Courtesy of the Internet Software Consortium @ www.isc.org.)

**Number of Hosts Advertised in the DNS**

| Date | Survey Host Count | Adjusted Host Count[†] | Replied To Ping[*] | |
|---|---|---|---|---|
| Jul 2002 | 162,128,493 | | - | |
| Jan 2002 | 147,344,723 | | - | |
| Jul 2001 | 125,888,197 | | | |
| Jan 2001 | 109,574,429 | | - | |
| Jul 2000 | 93,047,785 | | - | |
| Jan 2000 | 72,398,092 | | - | |
| Jul 1999 | 56,218,000 | | - | |
| Jan 1999 | 43,230,000 | | 8,426,000 | |
| Jul 1998 | 36,739,000 | | 6,529,000 | |
| Jan 1998 | 29,670,000 | | 5,331,640 | [First NEW Survey] |
| Jul 1997 | 19,540,000 | 26,053,000 | 4,314,410 | [Last OLD Survey] |
| Jan 1997 | 16,146,000 | 21,819,000 | 3,392,000 | |
| Jul 1996 | 12,881,000 | 16,729,000 | 2,569,000 | |
| Jan 1996 | 9,472,000 | 14,352,000 | 1,682,000 | |
| Jul 1995 | 6,642,000 | 8,200,000 | 1,149,000 | |
| Jan 1995 | 4,852,000 | 5,846,000 | 970,000 | |
| Jul 1994 | 3,212,000 | | 707,000 | |
| Jan 1994 | 2,217,000 | | 576,000 | |
| Jul 1993 | 1,776,000 | | 464,000 | |
| Jan 1993 | 1,313,000 | | | |

[*] estimated by pinging a sample of all hosts

[†]adjusted host count was computed by increasing the old survey host count by the percentage of domains that did not respond to the old survey method

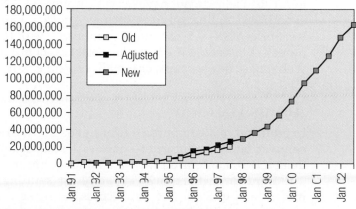

**Internet Domain Survey Host Count**

Source: Internet Software Consortium (www.isc.org)

dedicated to making the Internet work seamlessly around the world." It guides the direction and growth of the Internet and focuses on four pillars: standards, public policy, education and training, and membership. It also supports the following organizations:

**Internet Engineering Task Force (IETF)**

- **Internet Engineering Task Force (IETF)** (www.ietf.org) is "a large, open, international community of network designers, operators, vendors, and researchers concerned with the evolution of the Internet architecture and the smooth operation of the Internet."[8] Its working groups are organized by topic into several areas such as routing, transport, security, and others.

**Internet Architecture Board (IAB)**

- The **Internet Architecture Board (IAB)** (www.iab.org) is a technical advisory group of the ISOC and a committee of the IEFT. It is concerned with the architecture for the protocols and standards used by the Internet. It is also responsible for the editorial management of the RFC document series.

**Internet Research Task Force (IRTF)**

- **Internet Research Task Force (IRTF)** (www.irtf.org) states its mission, "To promote research of importance to the evolution of the future Internet by creating focused, long-term and small research groups working on topics related to Internet protocols, applications, architecture, and technology."[9]

**Internet Engineering Steering Group (IESG)**

- The **Internet Engineering Steering Group (IESG)** (www.ieft.org/iesg.html) is the executive committee of the IETF. It is concerned with Internet protocols and standards.

**World Wide Web Consortium (W3C)**

- **World Wide Web Consortium (W3C)** (www.w3.org), though not under the ISOC umbrella, is similar to the IETF. Its concerns are focused more narrowly on developing standards for the World Wide Web, and its members have commercial, academic, and research interests.

## 15-4 CONNECTING TO THE INTERNET

The point of networking is to connect—friends, kindred spirits, businesses, corporations, information and research centers, entertainment, and enrichment resources—with the whole world. Computers connect to the Internet in a variety and an ever-increasing number of ways. Many people have access through a university or business LAN that can connect directly to the Internet. Those who do not have access through a LAN connect through independent ISPs or online services such as America Online (AOL) or The Microsoft Network (MSN). This section examines some of the ways we—that is, our computers—connect to the Internet. To access content such as downloadable files, Web pages, newsgroups, or e-mail, several components are required.

### Access Hardware

In addition to a computer, a user needs hardware that establishes a physical connection to the Internet—hardware such as an analog modem, a cable modem, a DSL modem, an ISDN terminal adapter, a wireless modem, and NICs. The hardware's maximum capacity for sending and retrieving data determines how quickly one can access Internet content. The Internet's infrastructure, which includes the four components listed below, also affects speed of delivery. It provides content to a user's computer through these devices. All of these components work according to Internet protocols such as TCP/IP, FTP, HTTP, POP3, SMTP, HTML, and many others.

[8] From www.ieft.org.
[9] From www.irtf.org.

## Final-Mile Delivery Technology

Final-mile delivery technology determines how data are transmitted over the last connection between the ISP and a home or business. Technologies include dial-up access, ISDN, DSL, cable, Ethernet, wireless, and leased circuits. These are discussed in greater detail in the sections that follow. The technology you choose must work with your access hardware.

## The Final-Mile Delivery Channel

The final-mile transmission pipeline carries data between a modem or other hardware in a home or business and the ISP. It is here that bottlenecks in any Internet transmission usually occur. Channels include plain old telephone service (POTS) lines, television coaxial cables, fiber optic cables, mobile or fixed wireless airwaves, and direct broadcast satellites.

## Internet Service Provider (ISP)

**Internet service provider (ISP)**

An **Internet service provider (ISP)** is analogous to a phone company and the role it plays with the phone signal. The ISP charges a fee, usually monthly, to connect subscribers to its own Internet-connected servers, providing a gateway to the Internet. It can be a local, regional, national, or international provider. It can also provide e-mail, Usenet, Web space, and Web hosting servers. The connection of servers and computers in an ISP also forms a LAN.

## Backbones and Connections

**Internet backbone**

The Internet is actually a hierarchy of smaller networks connecting to larger ones, and each level of the hierarchy pays the next level for the bandwidth they use. Individuals connect to local ISPs, which connect to regional networks, which connect to national networks, which connect to the largest providers on the **Internet backbone,** a very high bandwidth network run by large companies and organizations. It connects to international networks through satellite links and underwater cables. Routers connect ISPs with dedicated T-1 or T-3 lines of speeds from 1.54 Mbps to 45 Mbps, to cables called backbones that have line speeds of 155 Mbps and higher. Backbones are the high-speed transmission channels, including fiber optic cables and satellites, that carry digital data from point to point and connect cities and major telecommunications centers. They have the capacity to handle massive amounts of data. Line speeds of the various types of backbone cable are shown in Figure 15-4.

**Network Access Points (NAPs)**

**Metropolitan Area Exchanges (MAEs)**

Traffic is exchanged at large hubs called **Network Access Points (NAPs),** which are classified as Tier 1 or Tier 2. The largest hubs on the Internet, Tier 1 NAPs, are huge connection points called **Metropolitan Area Exchanges (MAEs).** The major telecommunications operators connect their networks at a MAE. The two original MAEs were MAE West, located in San Francisco, and MAE East, located in Washington, D.C. There are now three MAEs in the U.S. MAE Central is located in Dallas, Texas. The NAP in Chicago has grown to the point that it may soon become a MAE. Each Internet packet goes as far up the network hierarchy as necessary to get to its destination and must travel along its own network as far as possible. Packets change networks at a NAP or a MAE. Figure 15-5 shows the major NAPs and MAEs in the U.S.

Thus, data travel from an individual user to the local ISP, to regional ISPs, to national ISPs, and sometimes to international access carriers, and then back again. It is interesting and helpful for network administrators to trace

**FIGURE 15-4** Backbone speeds.

| Line Speeds | Type of Line | Technical Names |
|---|---|---|
| 56 Kbps | Copper wire | 56 K or DSO |
| 1.544 Kbps | Copper wire | T-1 |
| 2.048 Kbps | Copper wire | E-1 (Europe only) |
| 45 Mbps | Copper wire | T-3 or DS-3 |
| 155 Mbps | Fiber optic | OC-3c or STM-1 in Europe |
| 620 Mbps | Fiber optic | OC-12c or STM-4 in Europe |
| 2.5 Gbps | Fiber optic | OC-48c or STM-16 in Europe |
| 10 Gbps | Fiber optic | OC-192c or STM-64 in Europe |

**FIGURE 15-5** Major NAPs and MAEs.

**Metropolitan Area Exchanges**
MAE West in San Francisco
MAE Central in Dallas
MAE East in Washington D.C.

**Network Access Points**
New York City
Houston
Los Angeles

The largest NAP, located in Chicago, has grown so much that it is on the verge of becoming the next U.S. MAE.

a packet's trip to and from their own network using traceroute, discussed in Chapter 14. Commercial software like VisualRoute (http://www.visualware.com/visualroute/index.html), a visual, fast, and integrated ping, whois, and traceroute program, automatically analyzes connectivity problems and displays a geographical map of the data's journey.

## 15-5 TYPES OF CONNECTION

Although most people connect to the Internet through dial-up service, many ISPs now provide faster connections. More and more people are beginning to use higher-speed devices. Experts expect the trend not only to continue, but also to accelerate in the future. Most home users have three or four broadband options from which to choose when they wish to connect to the Internet: ISDN, DSL, cable, fixed wireless, and satellite. Dedicated T-Carrier systems (T-1 and T-3 circuits) provide another choice, although the cost of setup and subscription fees are so high that most home users are content to leave such connections to large companies. Fractional T-1 service offers a lower cost (though still expensive) option than a full T-1 circuit because customers can use only the line capacity they need, but such service is not available in all areas.

Most of these broadband technologies have been discussed in earlier chapters; however, the emphasis here is on the way they provide Internet connection to home users.

### Dial-up Networking (DUN)

**dial-up networking (DUN)**

Most people still dial into an ISP by using simple telephone **dial-up networking (DUN)** and connecting through a modem. Modems usually connect at 56 Kbps, though older ones may do so at 28 Kbps or slower. The major advantage of DUN is that it uses existing copper analog telephone wires that are available almost everywhere, except in developing countries where other options are actually more feasible. Dial-up networking is usually less expensive than alternatives.

When a person dials into a number provided by the ISP, the modem translates the digital data into analog data that can travel over phone lines. It taps into a phone company switch, which translates it back to digital data and routes it to one of the modems at the ISP. If a modem is available, the connection is made. If not, it gives a busy signal and tries again. Many ISPs are not located close to the user's area. To eliminate long-distance charges and facilitate connections, they usually provide a locally maintained computer **point-of-presence (PoP)** with a dedicated line to the ISP, called a **point of presence (PoP)**. After the modems connect, they determine communication speed and other important information.

The terminal server at the ISP checks to verify the user name and password. Finally, a full Internet connection is made by using the dial-up protocols, which you first encountered in Chapter 7. They use either **Serial Line Internet Protocol (SLIP)** or (more often) the more reliable and versatile **Point-to-Point Protocol (PPP)** from the TCP/IP suite. SLIP was the first protocol for relaying IP packets over dial-up lines and does not include several of the features of PPP, which has largely supplanted it. PPP can share a line with other users and has error detection and authentication. It supports dynamic address assignment and link testing and can multiplex different protocols over a single link, which SLIP cannot.

A firewall provides security by filtering packets traveling between the Internet and the ISP. A screening router examines the header of every packet to check the identity of the senders and receivers as well as the protocol and type of Internet service being used. The router can keep certain types of packets from being sent or received and block traffic from suspicious users or destinations. Chapter 17 examines various network security options.

**Serial Line Internet Protocol (SLIP)**

**Point-to-Point Protocol (PPP)**

### Integrated Services Digital Networks (ISDNs)

**Integrated Services Digital Network (ISDN)**

**Integrated Services Digital Network (ISDN),** which was discussed in Chapter 13, is an alternative that is being replaced by much faster technologies. Recent surveys have indicated, however, that ISDN customers are the most satisfied group among those who use high-speed connections. Some people use it because of its reliability. When ISDN was first introduced, its transfer rate of 128 Kbps, achieved by connecting the two 64 Kbps B channels together, was considered fast because it more than doubled the speed of the fastest (56 Kbps) modems. Even their speed was unheard of in 1984. Its rate is now dwarfed by the speed of the three most popular types of connection.

**terminal adapter**

ISDN is delivered through a special type of local telephone line and uses a hardware device called a **terminal adapter,** which is sometimes called an ISDN modem. It enables users to send digital data over existing copper cable telephone wires. It manages different types of phone, fax, and computer data on the same telephone lines. There are different types of ISDN service, but the most common is called **basic rate interface (BRI).** With BRI, a telephone line is divided into three distinct channels for data. It has two 64 Kbps B channels and one 16 Kbps D channel, and is commonly referred to as 2B+D. The B channels can be used to send data simultaneously, so one can talk on the phone through one channel and "surf" the Internet over the other. The D channel sends the signaling information, routing the data sent by the B channels. This is called **in-band signaling.** If the phone company is not able to use the D channel, the routing information is sent over the B channels and must take 8 Kb in each channel to use for signaling information. Thus, each B channel can carry only 56 kilobits of data. This is referred to as **out-of-band signaling.** The ISDN BRI is illustrated in Figure 15-6.

**basic rate interface**

**in-band signaling**

**out-of-band signaling**

**primary rate interface**

The other type of ISDN is **primary rate interface (PRI),** usually reserved for very large companies that can pay a higher price for the much higher transmission speeds delivered from a combination of 23 B channels and a 64

FIGURE 15-6    ISDN BRI.

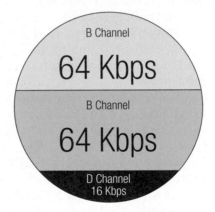

In-Band Signaling

Out-of-Band Signaling

Kbps D channel. If all the B channels are working together, speeds up to 1.47 Mbps can be obtained.

ISDN also allows two computers to communicate directly without going over the Internet. It is, therefore, often used by businesses that want to create highly secure private networks among several offices and for employees who telecommute. Some people and businesses like the ability to integrate Internet, voice, and fax services into one line from one provider. ISDN is used primarily in areas where the other types of service are unavailable, and it is more popular in other countries than it is in the U.S.

## Digital Subscriber Line (DSL)

digital subscriber line
(DSL)

**Digital subscriber line (DSL),** though often plagued by problems with provider installation and services, is growing in popularity because of its availability and relatively low initial investment for users. It and cable access, which is discussed in the following section, seem to be the main competitors for the "top-dog" position in high speed Internet access. Like ISDN, DSL allows users on a single phone line to talk on the telephone while using the Internet. However, DSL enables connection speeds from 1.5 Mbps to 55 Mbps, depending on the type of DSL technology used. Its transfer speeds can be the same as a T-1 line, but at less hassle and lower cost. To work properly, however, the user must be located within a few miles of the switching office. The faster the connection, the closer the office must be. It is for this reason that many rural areas cannot receive DSL service.

DSL also uses an interface device commonly called a DSL modem—one in the home and one at the telephone company office. It is not really a modem, however, because it sends and receives all data as digital data so there is no need for translation between analog and digital signals. It allows the simultaneous use of the same phone lines for both phone and data. The phone line is divided into three channels: one for talking on the telephone, one for sending data, and one for receiving data.

The difference between the types of DSL is the speed of upload and download. There are several different types of DSL in North America, although new kinds are still being developed. The types most frequently offered by an ISP are **asymmetric DSL (ADSL)** and **symmetric DSL (SDSL).** The newest development is **very-high-rate DSL (VDSL).**

asymmetric DSL (ADSL)

symmetric DSL (SDSL)

very-high-rate DSL
(VDSL)

- ADSL has more bandwidth for downloading and less for uploading. ADSL upstream data transfer rates are between 64 Kbps and 1.54 Mbps, and downstream rates are between 256 Kbps to 9 Mbps. Because most people download more frequently than they transfer data upstream, these asymmetric rates are desirable unless one runs a Web server. Home users usually connect using ADSL.

- SDSL has upload and download channels that are equal, with data transfer speeds that can reach up to 2.3 Mbps. If one is primarily downloading from the Internet, SDSL can waste bandwidth.

- VDSL is generally used in businesses and requires closer proximity to the phone company's answering DSL. Top speeds of about 52 Mbps can be achieved.

## Cable Access

Cable television systems were originally designed to carry signals in one direction—from the cable TV company to the subscriber. In recent years, many of the systems have been reengineered to carry signals in both directions so they can be used as high-speed communication circuits. One of the primary uses of such circuits is for broadband Internet access from the home.

The use of such broadband connections has increased drastically in the last few years because of the popularity of music and video on the Internet and the need to send bigger files faster. With downstream speeds up to 1.5 Mbps and upload rates up to about 300 Kbps, cable (like DSL) offers speeds equal to a T-1 line at a far lower cost. A splitter divides the coaxial TV cable coming into a home into two connections: one cable to the TV box and the other to the cable modem that attaches to an Ethernet network card inside the computer. Users are able to watch television while others use the computer because their signals travel simultaneously on different frequencies. Within the broadband spectrum on the coaxial cable, the computer signals travel on a 6 MHz channel.

**cable access**

The cable company divides each town or city into nodes, with about 500 homes in each node, to be located on a single LAN. The main drawback to **cable access** is that if many people on the same node try to access the Internet simultaneously, the access is slower—though never as slow as on an analog modem. All the nodes connect via a high-speed fiber optic line to a head-end cable that handles all the nodes in several nearby towns. The head-end receives television transmissions from satellites and has Internet access through high-speed links to the Internet. It then delivers television programming and Internet access to the cable customers. Because the head-end also has high-speed Internet servers and proxy servers that cache in their memory the most current versions of the more frequently accessed sites on the Internet, customers can get high-speed access to sites.

## Web TV

Every day, TV and the Internet continue to merge their technologies. The Internet has become more and more like television in its ability to play videos and music and even to broadcast live video feeds. Internet technology is also being used to develop more interactive television experiences.

**WebTV**

Another type of Internet connection that is gaining in popularity is a technology that enables one to browse the Web while watching television. A **WebTV** set-top box plugs into the television and accomplishes many tasks. It has normal connectors to the television and cable service and special connectors to a modem and phone line. The box has memory to run a Web browser along with other software and hardware and can accept a printer just as a computer does. Other peripherals could possibly be added in the future. Because television screens and computer monitors use different technologies to display on screen, the set-top box also converts the red-green-blue (RGB) of the Web to the National Television Standards Committee (NTSC) technology used by televisions.

**virtual private network (VPN)**

To access the Internet, the WebTV box connects to the WebTV network, which is actually a **virtual private network (VPN)** knit together by encryption technology. ISPs, working with WebTV across the country, provide access through local points of presence (PoP). Web servers on the VPN provide capabilities such as e-mail and other services. A series of proxy servers, run by the WebTV network, speed up access to Internet sites by caching frequently accessed Web pages and delivering them at a higher speed than would be possible if they were accessed directly from the Internet. WebTV uses its own proprietary Web browser designed for optimal display on a television set, though it adheres to the same HTML standards as other browsers. Users surf the Web through the use of a remote control device that enables them to scroll, move around the screen, and click objects as a mouse would do on a computer. They can browse the Web, watch television, or do both simultaneously.

## Wireless and Satellite Connections

While most users connect to the Internet through a standard 56 Kbps modem and dial-up service, the content and capabilities of the Internet today continue to outgrow these slower connections, causing more and more people to desire high-speed broadband connections. Although DSL and cable services offer the most popular means of broadband access, residents in rural or out-of-the-way areas cannot, and may never, connect to the Internet in either way. The problem is that they live too far from the central hub that connects to the Internet, and it is not economically feasible for phone companies or cable providers to upgrade their systems. The "last mile," or the distance from the central hub to an individual home, is the most expensive to cover. For such individuals and for those who would prefer fewer wires and cables, the newest technologies—wireless and satellite—offer the best possible alternatives. Though both are somewhat slower and involve certain problems that other methods of broadband connection do not, they may provide a solution for those who have no other way to connect over that "last mile."

**mobile wireless**

**MOBILE WIRELESS** **Mobile wireless** technologies include cellular phones, Personal Digital Assistants (PDA), palm computers and other mobile devices. Mobile wireless devices provide e-mail services, instant messaging, and access to Internet content through minibrowsers. They are able to connect to the Internet through modems on PCs and corresponding transfer software (e.g., ProxiWeb) on palm tops or by cellular technology using the **Wireless Application Protocol (WAP).** Their screens are small, however, and they usually cannot display anything but the simplest graphics. The bandwidth for current cellular phones is only about 9.6 Kbps. Web pages must be reformatted into Wireless Markup Language (WML) to be viewed properly. Mobile wireless technology is one of the fastest growing connection services today, however, and new possibilities open almost daily.

**Wireless Application Protocol**

**fixed wireless**

**FIXED WIRELESS** **Fixed wireless,** a term used to distinguish it from mobile wireless technologies, is the use of radio or microwaves to provide a link between two stationary points—an ISP or its hub and a user's computer. Fixed wireless operates at higher frequencies than mobile wireless technologies, thus providing greater bandwidth and better signals. The person who wishes to connect to the Internet does so through a modem or NIC that acts as a transceiver for radio signals. The transceiver is connected to an antenna located on or near the house. A request for a Web page is sent via radio waves to a large hub antenna. The hub forwards the request to the ISP through a series of connected antennae or through underground fiber optic cables that connect to the ISP. The request is sent to the Web server, then back through the same route.

Fixed wireless networks are not affected too often by bad weather because most wireless ISPs offer a service that works in the 2.5–2.7 GHz range rather than at higher ranges of the microwave spectrum, which can be affected by severe weather. As with cable service, radio waves are a shared resource, and the traffic can slow down connection speed if too many people try to access the Internet in one area. The major limitation of fixed wireless, however, is interference. Antennae must be located within direct **line of sight (LOS)** of each other, a limitation that restricts many users. Anything can

**line of sight (LOS)**

non-line of sight (NLOS)

obstruct the path—buildings, water towers, branches, and even leaves. Many customers have signed up for wireless service in the winter only to have their service disrupted when leaves grow out in the spring!

A new technology, called **non-line of sight (NLOS)** is being developed by several fixed wireless providers, however, and may solve even this problem. NLOS uses special antennae that compress radio waves that carry data into smaller, more precise beams that can penetrate objects that normally obstruct the path of radio waves. Fixed wireless is not available everywhere, but it is a developing technology, and limitations and unavailability issues are diligently being addressed.

**BLUETOOTH**    Any Bluetooth-enabled device can connect to the Internet through a home computer or Bluetooth-enabled modem by using the technology discussed in Chapter 10.

satellite connection

**SATELLITE CONNECTION**    **Satellite connection** works in the same way as other fixed wireless systems by converting digital signals to radio waves that communicate with the central hub. If a person has an unobstructed view of the sky over the equator, a satellite dish can deliver broadband access to his or her computer. Satellite access is currently the most costly broadband option, but some companies offer a one-way system that uses traditional dial-up connection for upload and high speed satellite connection for downloads. The biggest drawback of this type of connection, however, is its greater signal delay, called **latency**. Delay is caused because the receiving antenna isn't just a few miles away as in other fixed wireless systems, but 22,300 miles away in geostationary satellite orbit. Because it is available almost everywhere, satellite connection offers the greatest hope for those in rural areas or those who live in places that do not have an unobstructed path to the ISP's tower.

latency

Figure 15-7 shows the many paths that data take through the Internet and the many types of connections that are made on the way from a website to the end users.

## 15-6   INTRANETS AND EXTRANETS

intranet

The use of Web servers and browsers has been extended within organizations for private use. Many organizations build **intranets** with the same technology used on the Internet. The difference is that the access to intranets is limited to members of the organization or other authorized persons. Intranets typically use the same network that an organization uses for other purposes, including accessing the Internet. Usually a computer that has special software, a **firewall,** is installed between the Internet and the rest of the organization's network, as shown in Figure 15-8. The function of a firewall is to prevent unauthorized people from coming through the Internet into the organization's private network and accessing the intranet and private information. Intranets have proven to be very useful in many organizations as a communications tool for disseminating news and other information to employees for knowledge sharing, conducting internal discussions, bulletin boards—in general, anything the Internet is used for, but on a private, internal basis.

firewall

extranet

The term **extranet** is sometimes used when a group of people, such as customers or suppliers, is allowed to pass through the firewall and access authorized sections of the intranet. By allowing admittance to an extranet, companies can permit their regular customers to gain access to special information that is not available to the general public. Extranets provide the

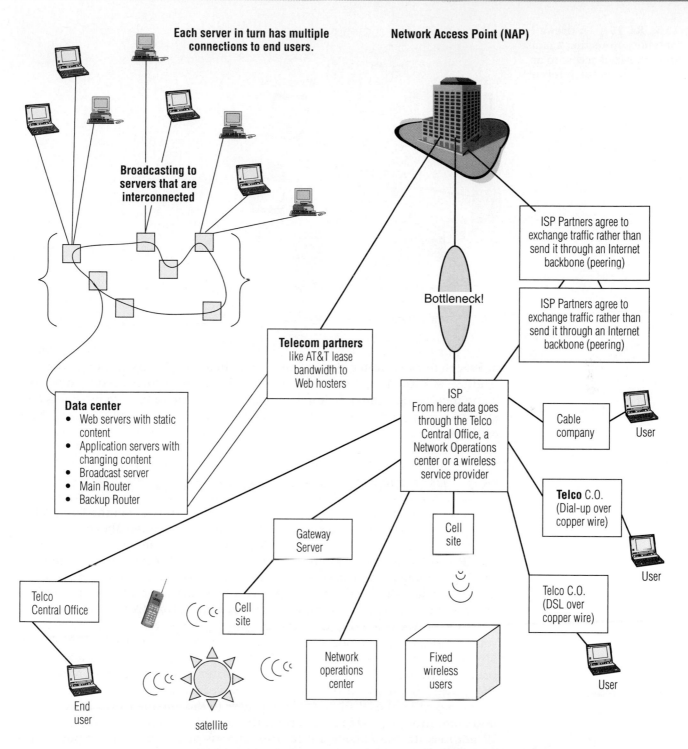

**Broadcasting to servers that are interconnected**

Each server in turn has multiple connections to end users.

**Network Access Point (NAP)**

**Data center**
- Web servers with static content
- Application servers with changing content
- Broadcast server
- Main Router
- Backup Router

**Telecom partners** like AT&T lease bandwidth to Web hosters

Bottleneck!

ISP Partners agree to exchange traffic rather than send it through an Internet backbone (peering)

ISP Partners agree to exchange traffic rather than send it through an Internet backbone (peering)

ISP From here data goes through the Telco Central Office, a Network Operations center or a wireless service provider

Cable company

User

**Telco** C.O. (Dial-up over copper wire)

User

Telco C.O. (DSL over copper wire)

User

Gateway Server

Cell site

Telco Central Office

Cell site

Network operations center

Fixed wireless users

End user

satellite

**FIGURE 15-7  Many ways to access the Internet.** Data flow through the Internet in an intricate mesh of converging and diverging paths. It is not the neat, organized system that is usually represented in network books. There are innumerable highways, roads, and pathways through which data must travel, and many entities share in the transportation of information through the system to its final destination. The figure above shows some of the players discussed in this chapter and the ways they interact to deliver data to end users.

**FIGURE 15-8**  A firewall provides protection against unauthorized access to an intranet from the Internet.

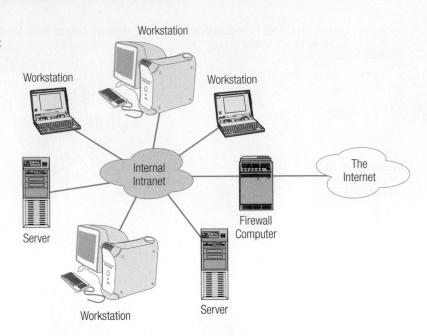

ability to treat certain groups of customers in a special way, although they introduce additional access requirements. Because security issues have become increasingly important in business and government, both intranets and extranets require passwords, login names, and other security measures that are above and beyond those required for normal websites.

## 15-7  NETWORK ADDRESS TRANSLATION (NAT)

**Network Address Translation (NAT)**

Increasing numbers of homes now connect to the Internet via the DSL, cable modem, fixed wireless, and satellite technologies discussed above. Normally, when a PC connects directly to a cable modem or DSL modem, the ISP gives the IP address to that computer. Although most ISPs connect only one computer per home to their service, users can share access and allow several computers to use a single IP address. This is accomplished through the use of an Internet standard called **Network Address Translation (NAT).** On the home network or LAN, the PC gets its IP address from the hub or router. The router's address is the one seen from the outside. The internal network usually has an arbitrary address like 10.0.0.0/8 or 192.168.0.0/16 because these prefixes will never be assigned on the Internet. The address assigned to the PC is a special, internal IP address used only inside the network. The IP address looks like the IP address of the router to the outside world. When a second computer accesses the Internet, the router gives it a different internal IP address. To the outside world, the address of the second computer also looks like the IP address of the router. Several computers can connect in the same way, and each will have a unique internal address, but the same external address. When a packet leaves the network, NAT translates the local address to a globally unique address. When it enters the domain, NAT translates the globally unique address to the local address. To the ISP and the outside world, the customer appears to have a single computer attached to the Internet. NAT not only allows several computers to share an ISP address, but it also shields one's true IP address from the Internet, thus providing an extra measure of security.

## ■ SUMMARY

The growth of the Internet from the first days of the ARPANET to the vast web of connected networks that we know today is an amazing story. This chapter has provided historical background and a description of the Internet, followed by a discussion of several of the different technologies that enable people to connect to the Internet.

Chapter 16 presents several Internet applications and tools that allow people to enjoy all of its rich resources and entertainment.

## ■ REVIEW QUESTIONS

15-1. Distinguish between an internet and the Internet.

15-2. Trace the history of the Internet from the earliest days of ARPANET to the present. What do you see as the major contributing factor to its growth, or can it be narrowed to one factor?

15-3. How did the early Internet or ARPANET differ from the modern Internet?

15-4. Where were the first four nodes on the ARPANET located?

15-5. What was the function of an IMP?

15-6. Why was the TCP/IP protocol developed?

15-7. What is Usenet?

15-8. What is the CERT and why was it first created?

15-9. What is the World Wide Web?

15-10. Who owns the Internet?

15-11. Describe the major groups that guide the growth and establish standards for the Internet.

15-12. Discuss the components that are required for accessing the Internet.

15-13. What is an ISP?

15-14. Explain the terms *Network Access Point (NAP)* and *Metropolitan Area Exchange (MAE)*.

15-15. List and briefly explain five types of connection with which an individual might access the Internet.

15-16. What is the difference between an intranet and an extranet? Explain how they relate to the Internet.

15-17. What is NAT and how does it work?

### TRUE/FALSE

15-1. ARPA was created as a result of the Sputnik launch in 1958.

15-2. J.C.R. Licklider was a computer technician who wrote about the "intergalactic computer network of the future" in 1962.

15-3. The first node of the ARPA network was set up at Stanford Research Institute.

15-4. Dr. Leonard Kleinrock is often called the father of modern data networking because of his research on packet-switching networks.

15-5. Lawrence Roberts developed the first plan for the ARPANET.

15-6. The first four nodes of the ARPANET were connected in 1969.

15-7. Norm Abramson, a professor who loved to surf, moved to Hawaii and created a radio-based system to connect the islands.

15-8. The first person to refer to data units as packets was Paul Baran.

15-9. E-mail was first developed in 1971 by Vint Cerf.

15-10. The first Ethernet network was based on the Ph.D. thesis of Bob Metcalfe.

15-11. The original NCP originally developed for the ARPANET was replaced by TCP.

15-12. The first PC, called Altair, was developed by Ed Roberts in 1975.

15-13. The IBM PC was the first computer with built-in networking.

15-14. The DoD declared TCP/IP as the standard for connecting networks in 1982.

15-15. CERT was created after the Morris worm infected 10 percent of on-line hosts in 1989.

15-16. Tim Berners-Lee announced the World Wide Web in 1991.

15-17. Internet Explorer was a rewrite of the original Internet browser, Mosaic.

15-18. The W3C was formed to develop standards for the Internet.

15-19. Final mile transmission refers to the last mile between a home and the ISP.

15-20. *MAE* stands for *Message Area Exchange.*

15-21. The largest hubs on the Internet are called NAPs.

15-22. Dial-up networking relies on two data link protocols: SLIP and PPP.

15-23. In-band signaling and out-of-band signaling are used to route data in ISDN service.

15-24. Digital subscriber line service offers connection speeds from 1.5 Mbps to 55 Mbps.

15-25. The main drawback to cable access is that if too many people try to use the line, the access becomes slower.

## MULTIPLE CHOICE

15-1. The "killer ap" of internetworking since its earliest days was _____.

    a. telnet

    b. e-mail

    c. FTP

    d. instant messaging

15-2. J.C.R. Licklider's contribution to internetworking was important because _____.

    a. he created the first RFC

    b. his ideas inspired later developments

    c. his inventions were the basis for Ethernet

    d. his money funded computer research

15-3. Packet switching was simultaneously devised by _____.

    a. Vint Cerf and Bob Kahn

    b. Steve Crocker and Paul Baran

c. Donald Davies and Paul Baran

d. Bob Kahn and Donald Davies

15-4. The hosts at the first four ARPANET sites were able to speak to each other because of the interface, called _____, at each site.

a. a node

b. a gnome

c. an imp

d. an ewt

15-5. E-mail and the @ sign were the invention of _____.

a. Steve Crocker

b. Jim Ellis

c. Tom Truscott

d. Ray Tomlinson

15-6. PARC was the single most important facility for the development of networking and the PC because _____.

a. they kept to strict deadlines and methods of research

b. they provided a free and open research atmosphere

c. they promoted the sale of inventions

d. they had PCs before anyone else

15-7. The World Wide Web program consisted of three major components: _____.

a. HTTP, URL, and HTML

b. FTP, URL, and HTTP

c. Mosaic, HTML, and URL

d. URL, FTP, and Mosaic

15-8. Bottlenecks in any Internet transmission usually occur _____.

a. at the ISP

b. at the modem

c. at the final mile transmission channel

d. at the NAP

15-9. The most common type of ISDN service is _____.

a. BRI

b. ADSL

c. SDSL

d. VDSL

15-10. An Internet standard that allows several computers to use a single IP address to share access and shields their IP address from the rest of the Internet is called _____.

a. FSK

b. NAT

c. LOS

d. WAP

## ■ PROBLEMS AND PROJECTS

15-1. Interview 10 different Internet users to find out:

    a. how much time they spend on the Internet each day;

    b. what form of Internet connection they have;

    c. what ISP they use;

    d. the cost of their Internet access;

    e. whether they use a home network to share Internet access with several users;

    f. what their favorite Internet site is;

    g. what they enjoy most about the Internet; and

    h. what they like least about the Internet.

15-2. Do some research on the Internet to determine several different methods of making payments online.

15-3. Conduct independent research on the following data transmission technologies in the context of providing Internet connectivity: ISDN, DSL, DUN, Cable, T-1, Fractional T-1, and satellite. Construct a chart showing: availability, data rates, setup and/or monthly service charges, equipment needed (other than a PC), and cost to buy or lease the needed equipment.

15-4. Research the different Internet access options in your area. Which do you think provides the best service at the most reasonable price? What are some of the aspects that need to be considered before making a choice of a provider?

15-5. Investigate the possibility of starting your own ISP. What steps would you need to take, and what would you need to learn to do so?

15-6. Many organizations have Internet access for employees. Research the ways in which the Internet is being used in companies today. What are some legitimate needs that it fulfills in business applications?

15-7. More and more organizations are restricting Internet access by their employees. Do you think such restriction is fair or necessary? Do you think employees really do abuse the use of the Internet at work? If so, what policies do you think should be implemented to prevent such abuse?

15-8. *Salon.com* magazine asked its readers to write computer error messages in haiku. Many other haiku messages about the Internet, computers, and networks have been circulated on the Internet and by e-mail. The haiku form is seventeen syllables—five in the first line, seven in the second, and five in the last. It describes one experience. Try your hand at writing a haiku about your own experience with the Internet or networking. An example from Salon's archives:

Stay the patient course

Of little worth is your ire

The network is down—*David Ansel*

C A S E   S T U D Y

## TO UNPLUG OR NOT TO UNPLUG: GOING WIRELESS ON CAMPUS

Excitement runs high in the university relations department at Blakeman College. The small northeastern college has just received one of the largest gifts ever donated to the institution from two affluent alumni. William M. Bridges and Samuel H. Ewor had been roommates during their undergraduate years in the early 1980s, and they shared a mutual fascination with networking. Each became wildly successful in e-commerce during the boom of the late 1990s, and each had the good sense to sell out before the new millennium brought financial ruin to many of their colleagues.

The only reservation the development directors had was that the donors make but one stipulation: the $750,000 in restricted funds must be used to implement a new wireless network throughout the entire campus, which covers roughly 100 acres. They want to make networking the exciting adventure it was for them by allowing students at their alma mater to enjoy wireless access through a campus-wide wireless network.

"Soon wireless technology will be built into everything—phones, tape recorders, consumer electronics, laptops—everything," said Mr. Bridges. "We want our students to be on the cutting edge, to have the freedom to experiment, to dream, to use wireless in all kinds of new applications." Dr. Ewor agreed, "Trying to imagine where we can go with this kind of technology is like trying to imagine what we could do with electricity even before it was invented." The men hint that further funds could be forthcoming *if* the network is implemented within the year, and *if* the students begin to use their freedom to dream up new infotech breakthroughs rather than new ways to cause trouble.

Schools all over the U.S.—and around the world—are installing wireless networks and turning students loose. The problem the university relations department faces is that they must convince the information technology department, who will deal with logistics of setting up a whole new infrastructure. Beyond that, the great security issues that a wireless network entails is a major concern. The vice president of the university must also convince the college's board of trustees on the wisdom of this move. The board is made up predominantly of over 60-year-old men and women who suffer from technophobia and cannot see the necessity for spending this windfall donation on *another* network when, "You can't even control what we have!"

The vice president of university relations, Ben Jerkens, calls a strategy meeting with the top directors of the department as well as the director of information technology and the network administrator to discuss and strategize the deployment that Bridges and Ewor propose.

**QUESTIONS**

1. A wireless network could change life on a campus profoundly—both in small and great ways. How do you think life would be altered socially, academically, and technologically? Do you think it would affect study habits, teaching techniques, and personal security?

2. What do you foresee as the possible objections that could be raised by the board of trustees? By the IT department?

3. What questions might the board and the IT department ask? How would you answer them if you were presenting the idea of a campus-wide wireless network?

# INTERNET APPLICATIONS

## ■ OUTLINE

## ■ KEY TERMS

anchor

Archie

body

Boolean operator

broadcast messages

browser

cache

cascading style sheets (CSS)

CGI application

channels

common gateway interface (CGI)

concept-based searching

control connection

controller

daemon

distribution list

e-mail server

encoder

Extensible Hypertext Markup Language (XHTML)

Extensible Markup Language (XML)

File Transfer Protocol (FTP)

gateway page

Gopher

graphics interchange format (gif)

H.323

header

hyperlink tag

Hypertext Markup Language (HTML)

Hypertext Transfer Protocol, Secure (HTTPS)

IMG tag

instant messaging (IM)

Internet radio

Internet relay chat (IRC)

interpreter

| | | |
|---|---|---|
| invisible Web | natural-language query | spider |
| joint photographic experts group (jpg) | network virtual terminal (NVT) | streaming audio |
| | | subject directory |
| listserv | newsgroup | tag |
| mailing list | newsreader | Telnet |
| Media Gateway Control Protocol (MGCP) | posting | terminal emulation |
| | search engine | thread |
| metafile | search tools | unmoderated newsgroup |
| metasearch engine | secure socket layer (SSL) | voice over IP (VoIP) |
| moderated newsgroup | Session Initiation Protocol (SIP) | well-known port number |
| Multipurpose Internet Mail Extensions (MIME) | | |

## ■ OBJECTIVES

After you complete your study of this chapter, you should be able to:

- ■ differentiate between the World Wide Web and the Internet;
- ■ discuss the three components that make up the World Wide Web;
- ■ create a simple Web page;
- ■ explain the way that mail works;
- ■ describe some of the most common Internet and Web applications;
- ■ explain how to download or upload a file using FTP;
- ■ explain the difference among the different types of search tools;
- ■ research a variety of topics on the Internet; and
- ■ know how to use some of the many Internet applications now available.

## 16-1   INTRODUCTION

Client-server computing became the buzzword in the computer-communications industry during the early 1990s. The Internet, largely based on the client-server model, also had its greatest surge of growth at that time. A client computer connects to the server computer through the network and requests information; then the server processes the request and delivers the resources to the client. As you learned in Chapter 15, there are many ways to access the Internet. Each time you do, you connect to a server and request the use of its resources—whether you access a World Wide Web server to request a Web page or handle incoming or outgoing e-mail through an e-mail server. This chapter discusses the applications we use, enabled by the client-server model of information delivery, to tap into the Internet's resources.

## 16-2   THE WORLD WIDE WEB

Many people, especially newcomers to the Internet, believe the terms "Internet" and "World Wide Web" are synonymous. Remember that the Internet is a hierarchy of smaller networks connecting to larger ones—a global network of networks. It is the countless number of computer hosts physically connected to each other by cables and wires and radio waves. In contrast, the World Wide Web is the whole universe of information attached to that network and accessible because of three major components discussed: the URL, an address through which one can access any site located on the Internet; HTTP, a client/server protocol that sets the rules for Web transmission; and HTML, the scripting language used for creating World Wide Web pages.

When Tim Berners-Lee proposed his new way of accessing data, he envisioned it as a web system of notes with links between them that would allow people to reference material from other notes or files. For that reason, his program is called the World Wide Web.

### Uniform Resource Locator (URL)

The uniform resource locator (URL) mentioned in Chapter 15 is the unique identifier for a Web page on the World Wide Web. Without a URL, it would be impossible for a computer to find and retrieve information on the Internet. It tells us several things including the type of transfer protocol used (HTTP, FTP, etc.) and the location or address of the page—the host computer, the directory, the file, and the file type of the document. The host computer part of the address is called the "domain name." The address http://www.ulv.edu/ur/index.shtml means: "Using the transfer protocol, *HTTP*, go to the World Wide Web host called *ulv.edu* (an institution of higher education), in a directory called *ur*, and retrieve the document with the filename *index.shtml*, which is a special type of html file explained later in this chapter. When an address does not contain a filename after the last slash mark, the Web server automatically delivers the default *index* file to the client. The URL could contain subdirectories after the *ur* directory: http://www.ulv.edu/ur/alumni/profiles/profiles.shtml or http://www.ulv.edu/ur/media/bgulv.shtml.

### Hypertext Transfer Protocol (HTTP)

Hypertext Transfer Protocol (HTTP) is the protocol from the TCP/IP protocol suite that defines how two computers will exchange text, sound, video, and graphics, as well as other multimedia components. It allows a file to contain links that you can select to transfer to other URLs or files. When you type *HTTP://* into your Web browser address field, you are telling your browser (the client) and the Web site server that you want to govern the transfer of files by the rules of HTTP. Then you type in the domain name and your browser sends a request, using HTTP code, to the IP address where the server is located on the Internet. At the Web server, an HTTP **daemon** program waits for requests, sends the requested file, and closes the connection. Programs that perform administrative tasks for the operating system are called daemons. They are processes that run in the background and perform various operations without human intervention. The name is derived from the daemons of Greek mythology, guardian spirits similar to the modern concept of a "guardian angel." E-mail handlers and print spoolers are typical daemon processes. Although daemon is a UNIX term, other operating systems provide support for daemons but sometimes call them by other names, such as system agents or services, in the Windows environment.

**daemon**

The connection does not have to be maintained for a long time, and after the request is delivered, the client does not stay connected to the server. For example, if you type http://www.ulv.edu/ into the browser window, the connection is made, the page is delivered, and the connection is closed. If an image needs to be displayed, the browser opens a new connection to the same server to obtain the image. One reason that a "hit" counter on a Web page does not always give an accurate record of the number of people who have visited the site is that each image on a page also counts as a "hit."

A committee for the IETF is developing other versions of HTTP to address certain concerns. That committee, including the original developer Berners-Lee, developed a new version called HTTP1.1, but it has not been used widely yet. It promises to send information faster and to decrease the amount of Internet traffic. You will recall that, according to HTTP, the connection between client and server is usually terminated after the Web page is sent. With HTTP1.1, the connection remains open so a browser can send several requests to a server without having to send a new one each time a page is accessed. In other words, one TCP connection, rather than several, would be required. HTTP1.1 also allows compression and decompression of HTML files, thus making the transmission speed faster.

**Hypertext Transfer Protocol, Secure (HTTPS)**

**Secure Socket Layer (SSL)**

Another form of HTTP, **Hypertext Transfer Protocol, Secure (HTTPS),** is especially important as people now fear identity theft and other types of fraud over the Internet. HTTPS is transmitted according to TCP and secured using **Secure Socket Layer (SSL),** an encryption protocol that uses a private key for access to the data. Sites are able to transmit confidential information such as credit card numbers using SSL. The beginning of the URL for these sites must be "https://" and the encryption and decryption work on both sides of the transaction. You can usually recognize a secure page or site by the small padlock icon in the lower corner of your browser.

## Hypertext Markup Language (HTML)

**Hypertext Markup Language (HTML)**

**Hypertext Markup Language (HTML)** is the primary language of the World Wide Web. The idea of hypertext and the indexing of information, however, has a much longer history than the code that was developed in 1991 by Berners-Lee. His HTML was based on an older code called Standard Generalized Markup Language (SGML), which grew out of an even older Generalized Markup Language (GML), created in 1969.

Originally, HTML simply linked text files to one another. Today, it enables Web developers to incorporate all kinds of multimedia files into their sites. It is not really a programming language like Java or C++, but a scripting language that gives guidelines for how to display text, images, and multimedia files. HTML links pages and other Internet resources together, and it is the ease with which it connects data instantaneously from several different sources on the Internet that is the true power behind the code. Without the unseen HTML code behind the displayed page to hold all its content in place, the Web itself would not exist. The use of HTML is discussed in greater detail in the section on creating and maintaining Web pages later in this chapter.

## 16-3  CLIENT-SERVER COMPUTING

Client-server computing takes place on the Internet according to the same basic sequence as on other networks:

1. Server application starts, waiting for client contact
2. Client specifies server location and requests communication

3. Client and server exchange messages

4. Client and server terminate communication after data are sent

On the Internet, client-server computing works in the following ways:

Web servers are always "on," waiting for clients to contact them. The user types in the location (URL) of an application on a particular Web server and requests communication. The user's browser software (client) issues a request (e.g., a specific Web page), which is broken into HTTP packets and sent across the Internet's TCP/IP communications infrastructure to the host computer (Web server).

Each request contains a URL corresponding to either a static document or a dynamic one. The software on the host server that houses the website makes it possible for the host to extract the actual request from the packets, locate a requested page, and return it to the client. A static Web document is a file that resides on the Web server and can be displayed rapidly because its contents do not change.

**common gateway interface (CGI)**

**CGI application**

Databases and other similar applications are accessed and controlled through a **common gateway interface (CGI).** Through a CGI, the Web server interacts with outside resources such as databases. It is the "gate" through which the HTTP server requests data. The script, called a **CGI application,** is written to perform a certain task such as searching a database. It is stored in a special directory (often named cgi-bin) on the Web server. When a user accesses a page, fills out a form, clicks a link to send the request, the CGI program connects to the database, requests the information, and formats it so the user can understand it. The format may be text, graphics, video, sound, or a list of URLs.

A CGI application allows the contents of a document to change each time the browser requests it. A dynamic Web page, which looks the same as a static page to the user's browser, is created whenever a request is made. For example, if you enter a message in a Web page's guest book, the page will contain your entry the next time you access it. Whenever you enter a keyword in a search engine form, it dynamically creates the viewable page, based on the keyword you entered. Amazon.com and other e-commerce sites create pages dynamically, based on a user's profile and click choices. Although the ISP maintains TCP/IP connection to the Internet after the exchange of information, the HTTP connection is closed when the Web page is transferred. For example, if you order something online, then try to return to a previous page, you may receive an error message because that particular connection has been closed. You may go to another page, but the page you accessed dynamically will have disappeared.

**well-known port number**

Server machines make their services available using numbered ports on the server, one for each service available to the Internet. Clients connect to services at specific IP addresses and on a specific port number. A **well-known port number** is the port number of the most well-known or often-used services that are available on the Internet. Some of the best known port numbers are:

| | |
|---|---|
| 21 | ftp |
| 23 | telnet |
| 25 | smtp |
| 37 | time |
| 42 | nameserver |
| 43 | nicname (Who is) |
| 70 | gopher |
| 79 | finger |
| 80 | WWW |
| 110 | POP3 |

## 16-4   BROWSERS AND BROWSING

browser

A **browser** is the interactive client program that requests information from Web servers throughout the Internet and displays the pages built with HTML. It allows a user to navigate the huge repository of information on the World Wide Web and then displays text, graphics, programs, and video applications on the computer's screen. When a user clicks on an item that has been highlighted or "linked" according to HTML format (for example, http://www.amazon.com), the browser accesses the designated Web page from the server on which it is housed and exhibits the new information on the screen. Browsers use a URL to determine which server to contact as well as which protocol to use. A browser consists of a **controller** that calls a client or set of clients to fetch the document from its remote server, and **interpreters** that display documents by translating the HTML into the appropriate on-screen output. When an item is received, it is stored in a special part of the disk memory, called a **cache,** to make future access faster and more efficient.

controller

interpreter

cache

The two most popular browsers today are Microsoft Internet Explorer and Netscape. Netscape incorporates many features of the original Mosaic browser developed at the University of Illinois in 1993. There are others, including Opera and Lynx, a text-only browser for UNIX shell users. Although online services like AOL originally had browsers of their own, most of them currently offer Netscape or Internet Explorer.

A Web browser can also support e-mail (indirectly through e-mail Web sites) and FTP, although they do not actually require a browser. Other specialized client programs, discussed later in this chapter, are more popular for e-mail and FTP.

## 16-5   CREATING WEB PAGES

### Hypertext Markup Language (HTML)

As was stated earlier, HTML is the primary language of the World Wide Web. It is not difficult to learn, even if you have never seen programming code of any kind. It is a simple scripting language that is popular among all levels of Web designers. HTML allows each browser to display contents differently because it gives the browser general guidelines for display rather than detailed formatting instructions. There are many good books, such as *Web Design in a Nutshell* by Jennifer Niederst, and there are several excellent websites, like http://www.hwg.org/, which will teach you the basics of HTML and take you far beyond the scope of what is presented here. We include a few simple instructions to get you started, if you have not yet created your own Web page.

header

body

Each HTML document is made up of two major portions: the **header** and the **body.** (An exception is when the document contains a frameset in place of the body, but that case is beyond the scope of this book.) The header, or "head," contains particular information about the document and the body holds the data. One thing that is important to remember is that a browser begins to act upon instructions as soon as they are received. This happens even as the document is downloading; therefore, the instructions must appear in proper order as the browser reads from top to bottom.

tag

An HTML document contains **tags,** which are commands that define the way text or layout should appear. The tags are enclosed within less-than (<) and greater-than (>) symbols, and most commands require an opening and an ending tag. The end tag places a backward slash (/) after the less-than sign to let the browser know when that particular command ends. It is not necessary to write all the tags in uppercase letters, but it is easier to distinguish them

**FIGURE 16-1**  Chart of common HTML tags.

| Beginning tag | Ending tag | How is it used? |
|---|---|---|
| <HTML> | </HTML> | Indicates to the browser the beginning and ending of an HTML-coded document |
| <HEAD> | </HEAD> | First part of an HTML document includes a title and commands that are not displayed |
| <TITLE> | </TITLE> | Document title that appears in the title bar of the browser. The title is also what is displayed on someone's bookmark list and what identifies your page to search engines |
| <BODY> | </BODY> | The largest part of the HTML document. It holds the content of your page that is displayed within the text area of your browser window |
| <A HREF> | </A> | The "anchor" that establishes hyperlinks |
| <IMG SRC> | Needs no ending tag | Inserts a picture on a Web page |
| <FONT> | </FONT> | Defines a font (size, type, color and other attributes) |
| <P> | Needs no ending tag | Inserts white space between lines of text (used to separate paragraphs) |
| <BR> | Needs no ending tag | Line break. Move to the next line |
| <H1> to <H6> | </H1> to </H6> | Six levels of headings, numbered 1 through 6 (1 being the largest) are used to define headline styles. They are typically displayed in larger and/or bolder fonts than normal body text |
| <I> | </I> | Formats text with italics |
| <B> | </B> | Formats text in bold |
| <HR> | Needs no ending tag | Horizontal rule |

from the actual content on your page if you do. Figure 16-1 illustrates some of the most common tags and their functions.

Although much of tag placement is up to the individual designer, all Web pages must include at least the following tags in exactly the same order:

<HTML>
<HEAD>
<TITLE>Choose your own title—thoughtfully!</TITLE>
</HEAD>
<BODY>
This is where your information goes
</BODY>
</HTML>

The first tag, <HTML>, tells the browser that this document is formatted in HTML code, and the end tag, </HTML>, which is placed at the very bottom of the document, lets the browser know that the coding ends there.

The second tag, <HEAD> </HEAD>, contains information about the document and serves as a kind of box to hold the other header tags, such as <META> and <TITLE>. Notice that the <TITLE> tag is required though <META>, which includes keywords or descriptions to aid search engines in locating your page on the Internet, is optional. The most commonly used element in the header is <TITLE>, which designates the title of the document that generally appears in the top bar of the browser window. Search engines rely on document titles heavily, so if you want your page to be found it is important to provide descriptive titles and avoid vague ones such as "Welcome" or "My first Web page." Another tag that appears in the header is <SCRIPT>. JavaScript and other scripts that provide dynamic action within the document (such as objects that change when the mouse is dragged over them, windows that pop up, or personalized pages that include a reader's name) can be placed in the header.

The fourth tag, <BODY> </BODY>, is the container that holds all the content that is displayed in the browser window. This is the main area, and any attributes within the body tag, such as font color or document background, apply to the entire page.

Beyond the basic structure, Web pages can become more and more complex with font and design attributes, but there are two elements that are very important, improve the appearance, and heighten viewer interest in them.

**hyperlink tag**

**anchor**

**Hyperlink tags,** called **anchors,** really make the Web what it is today by allowing readers to jump from document to document, idea to idea, and research in the nonlinear way humans think rather than in the sequential way they read a book. To include a link to another document or any text or image, enclose the link within the beginning <A HREF> and ending </A> anchor tags as illustrated below:

<A HREF="http://www.ulv.edu">University of La Verne</A>. The beginning tag also includes an equal sign (=) and the URL within quotation marks, while the closing tag indicates where the hyperlink ends on the page. The user simply clicks on the text she sees in the browser window and activates the hyperlink, which accesses the designated Web page.

**IMG tag**

**graphics interchange format (gif)**

**joint photographic experts group (jpg)**

**IMG tags** enable a designer to add a graphic, called a **graphics interchange format (gif)** or digitized photo, called a **joint photographic experts group (jpg)** to an HTML document. The code, which directs a user's browser to a picture of "my baby" is written like this: <IMG SRC="http://staff.ulv.edu/~schuhm/sampleweb/img/my_baby.jpg">. No end tag is needed. Figure 16-2a shows the code for a simple Web page and the way that it appears on the screen. Notice that a link can be anything between the anchor tags. In Figure 16-2a, text is used in the first link. However, a picture can also be used, as shown in Figure 16-2b, to link to another page or location on a page.

**cascading style sheet**

Today's Web environment is much more interactive and multimedia intensive, and HTML, being a simple language, cannot deliver all that designers want to be able to offer. It can embed other data such as multimedia, streaming video, audio, and other content within a page by referencing a file or plug-in that has its own instructions for executing more dynamic content, but the files must be written and saved in separate documents. Programmers also embed **cascading style sheets (CSS)** code within an HTML document, which brings formatting consistency on different browsers by separating content from formatting. It takes more time and effort to incorporate these capabilities into HTML documents, however, so several other markup languages have been proposed. Two of them are XML and XHTML. You can read more about them and HTML at the W3.org Web site: http://www.w3.org/MarkUp/.

**The Code**

```
1:  <!DOCTYPE HTML PUBLIC "-//W3C//DTD HTML 4.0 Transitional//EN">
2:
3:  <HTML>
4:  <HEAD>
5:  <TITLE>A Simple Sample Web Page</TITLE>
6:  </HEAD>
7:  <BODY>
8:  <DIV ALIGN="center">
9:  <H2>My Ultimate Driving Machine</H2>
10: <IMG SRC="img/my_baby.jpg" WIDTH="307" HEIGHT="135" BORDER="0" ALT="BMW">
11: <BR><BR><BR>
12: <P>
13: Here are two types of link:
14: <P>
15: 1. A text link: <BR>
16: <A HREF="http://www.amazon.com">Amazon.com</A>
17: <P>
18: 2. A graphic used as a link: <BR>
19: <A HREF="http://www.porsche.com/"><IMG SRC="img/porsche.jpg" WIDTH="269"
HEIGHT="134" BORDER="1" ALT="Porsche"></A>
20: </DIV>
21: </BODY>
22: </HTML>
```

**The Explanations**

| Lines | Explanation |
|---|---|
| 3-7, 21 & 22 | Basic HTML tags common to all web pages |
| 8 & 20 | Centers everything between these two tags |
| 9 <H2></H2> | A secondary heading—there are six levels of heading from the most important <H1></H1> to the least <H6></H6> |
| 10 | The image file in the directory called img for "my_baby", which is 307 pixels wide by 135 pixels high and has a border of 0 pixels. The ALT tag BMW is what one sees when the mouse is positioned over the picture |
| 11 <BR> | Three breaking lines. Notice the <BR> tag does not have an end tag |
| 12 <P> | A paragraph. Notice the </P> is optional |
| 16 | A text link to the URL for Amazon.com. Notice that it does not matter what text is placed between the beginning and ending tags. |
| 19 | A "hot" graphic used as a link. Notice the 1-pixel border around the jpg. The border could be 0, as in the BMW picture. |

**FIGURE 16-2a**   The HTML code for Figure 16-2b.

**FIGURE 16-2b** The simple Web page coded in Figure 16-2a.

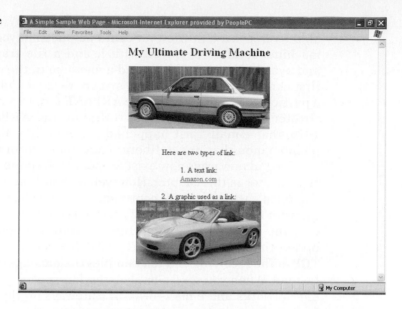

## Extensible Markup Language (XML)

**Extensible Markup Language (XML)**

**Extensible Markup Language (XML)** is another Web page formatting language that separates the content of a page from the presentation. It does not specify layout; it is not concerned with presentation. It is concerned with the organization of information on a page and helps you design text formats to structure your data. XML tags the different types of content and then uses other technologies, like style sheets, to determine how the content should look. This allows a developer to build the page content once and present it in many different ways to many different devices—computers, cell phones, and wireless Palm devices—without doing a lot of extra work. It can be customized to meet the specifications of each individual content developer, and when she redesigns one page, all the pages do not need to be rebuilt. Each time an opening tag occurs, it must have a corresponding end tag <X> </X>. Because the tags have no meaning assigned to them, tag names can be created as needed, making data easy to access.

**Extensible Hypertext Markup Language (XHTML)**

**Extensible Hypertext Markup Language (XHTML)** is a hybrid of XML and HTML and was approved by the World Wide Web Consortium and released in January 2000. It breaks the Web page design into separate "modules" so programmers can design and embed HTML-like multimedia tags for a variety of content into a single HTML document. A basic explanation and tutorials for both XML and XHTML, with links to more extensive information, can be found at http://www.htmlgoodies.com/. Another website, http://www.xml.com, is an excellent place to start for more detailed information.

## 16-6 INTERNET AND WEB APPLICATIONS

### Electronic Mail (E-mail)

Most people use the Internet to connect and communicate, so it isn't surprising that e-mail has remained the "Killer Ap" of internetworking since the beginning—1971. The first e-mail message was sent that year by Ray Tomlinson, an engineer at BBN, the company that had delivered the Interface Message Processors (IMPs) to ARPANET's four original nodes in 1969. He had been playing around with a program called SNDMSG, which he'd written for researchers and engineers at the company so they could leave messages for each other on their one computer. With the program, they were able to create a text file that could be put in anyone's mailbox on the same machine. Tomlinson played with it and a file transfer protocol, CYPNET, and eventually was able to send a message to the machine right next to the first computer. He chose the @ symbol to show that a particular user was *at* a particular remote host on the ARPANET. In two years, the application constituted 75 percent of all the traffic on the ARPANET. Tomlinson said in 1976, that e-mail "just happened . . . more like the discovery of a natural phenomenon than the deliberate development of a new technology."

Several new ways now exist for people to connect online, and they are discussed later in this chapter. However, with billions of messages traveling back and forth each day, e-mail continues to be the most popular application of the Internet for both business and personal communications. E-mail is also delivered the same way that other Internet data are sent. TCP on the sending end breaks the message into packets, IP delivers them to the proper location, and TCP at the receiving end reassembles the message on the mail server so it can be read. When you send e-mail on the Internet, it passes through many different networks and e-mail formats. Gateways on the Internet translate e-mail formats from one network to another so the message gets through.

E-mail is also based on client-server architecture. An e-mail client like Eudora, Microsoft Outlook, or Outlook Express allows you to look at your e-mail messages. Hotmail, Yahoo, and other free services use a client that appears in a Web page. AOL uses its own e-mail reader. Most e-mail clients allow a user to do several basic tasks. The e-mail clients display a list of message headers showing the sender, subject, time, date, and size of each e-mail message. By selecting a message header, you can read the e-mail, reply to it, forward it, or delete it. You can also create new messages and send them to the address of one or more recipients that are listed in your address book. Another capability, which was not available on early e-mail, allows you to add attachments of binary files like pictures, videos, sounds, and executable files. Because the Internet cannot directly handle binary files in e-mail, they must be encoded in schemes like **Multipurpose Internet Mail Extensions (MIME).**

**Multipurpose Internet Mail Extensions (MIME)**

MIME was originally developed by the IETF in 1992 (RFC 1521, replaced by RFCs 2045–2049) as an extension to SMTP. It extends the format of Internet mail to allow files, other than plain ASCII, to travel over the network. MIME uses base64 encoding, a standard algorithm for encoding and decoding non-ASCII data for attachment (any file in any format) to an e-mail message. For example, if you wish to send a binary file such as a PowerPoint presentation by e-mail, MIME encodes it into ASCII and sends it over the Internet, then converts it back to binary once it is received. The person receiving the attachment must be able to decode the file with the same encoding scheme. Fortunately, many e-mail clients now support MIME, and most e-mail software now decodes it automatically, allowing users to send and receive graphics, audio, and video files. Nearly all Web browsers also support various MIME types, allowing them to display or output files that are not in HTML format.

**e-mail server**

An **e-mail server** has a list of accounts, one for each person who can receive e-mail on the server. An account, or user name, can be any name: binny, pcascio, george, schmedlitz, ralph, etc. The server also has a text file for each account in its directory, such as binny.txt, pcascio.txt, george.txt, schmedlitz.text, or ralph.txt. When you, George, want to send a message such as, "Ralph, how are you doing on the software problem?" you type the message into the e-mail client, indicate that it should go to ralph@ulv.edu, and press the Send button. The e-mail client connects to the e-mail server, which is always running and waiting for clients to contact it, then passes the name of the recipient (Ralph), the sender (George), and the body of the message to the server. The server formats the information and adds it to the bottom of the ralph.txt file. The file entry looks something like this:

> From: george
>
> To: ralph
>
> Ralph, how are you doing on the software problem?

As other people send e-mail, the messages are added to the bottom of the text file in the order received. When Ralph wants to look at the e-mail, his client connects to the server. The server responds to requests by the client to: 1) send a copy of the ralph.txt file; 2) erase and reset the ralph.txt file; 3) save that file on Ralph's machine; 4) using "From:" as the separator, parse the file into different messages; and 5) show Ralph the list of message headers.

A typical e-mail server machine runs two different servers using two protocols you first met in Chapter 14. The SMTP server, listening on well-known port 25, handles outgoing mail. The POP3 server, listening on port 110, handles incoming mail. Figure 16-3 shows a simple e-mail server.

The e-mail client interacts with the SMTP server to handle the relay when you press the Send button. The SMTP server on your host may have conversations with other SMTP servers to actually deliver the e-mail. For example: My e-mail ID is schmedlitz and my account is on ulv.edu. I am using the stand-alone e-mail client, Eudora. The name of the mail server is mail.ulv.edu. I want to send e-mail to rhsnail@aol.com. The following hypothetical scenario and Figure 16-4 demonstrate the way it works:

1. I compose a message and click Send.
2. Eudora connects to the SMTP server at mail.ulv.edu using port 25 (the well-known port that handles outgoing mail).
3. Eudora communicates to the SMTP server the sender's address (schmedlitz@ulv.edu), the recipient's address (rhsnail@aol.com), and the body of the message, (Hi, Randy. Can you meet Thursday to discuss the new website? Best regards, Sam). The SMTP server breaks the recipient's address into two parts: rhsnail and AOL.com (the domain name). Because the recipient is at another domain, the SMTP needs to communicate with that domain.
4. The ulv.edu SMTP server communicates with a DNS server, asking for the IP address of the SMTP server for AOL.com. The DNS server returns one of the IP addresses for the SMTP operating at AOL.com.
5. ulv.edu's SMTP server connects using port 25 with the server at AOL.com and has the same text conversation that Eudora, my mail client, had with the SMTP server for ulv.edu, and gives the message to the AOL.com server.

**FIGURE 16-3**   A simple e-mail server.

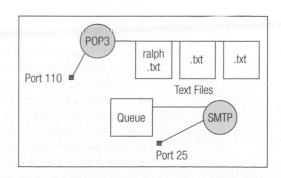

**FIGURE 16-4** Sending an e-mail message—SMTP servers at two different domains.

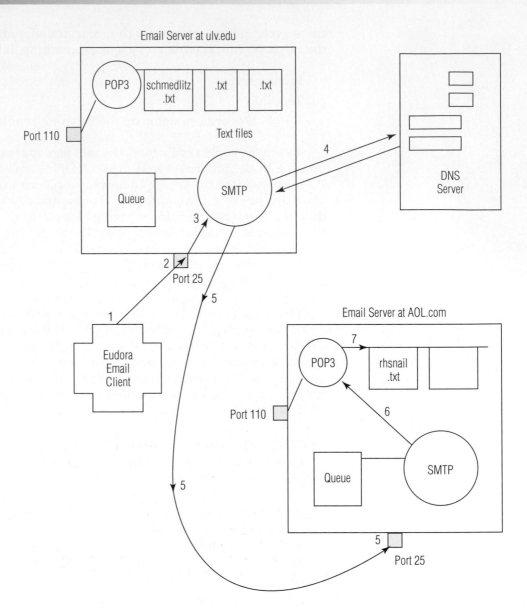

6. AOL.com's server recognizes that rhsnail's domain name is AOL.com and hands the message to its POP3 server (incoming).

7. The POP3 server puts the message in rhsnail's mailbox.

The preceding scenario assumes that all is well and the servers are able to connect with each other. If the server at ulv.edu is not able to connect with AOL.com's server, my message goes into a queue. A program called "sendmail" is used by most SMTP servers to send the mail (hence the name; programmers are very logical people!). Sendmail will keep trying to send the mail, notify you if there is a problem, and after a predetermined length of time (typically five days), most will give up and return the mail to the sender undelivered.

Internal routers decide whether the recipient is on the same network or outside the network. Had my mail been intended for pcascio on the same network, ulv.edu, the SMTP server would have handed the message to the POP3 server for ulv.edu. A series of text files, one for each e-mail account, is maintained by the POP3 server. The server appends the message to the bottom of pcasio's text file when it arrives. Pcasio's e-mail client, Eudora, connects to the POP3 server using port 110 when she logs in with her account name (pcascio) and password (can't tell you that!). The POP3 server, which acts as an interface between Eudora and the text file containing her messages, opens pcascio's text file and she can read her mail.

Many other aspects of the system become more complicated, but the basic e-mail procedure, like many discoveries or inventions that have changed our lives dramatically, is really very simple.

## Mailing Lists

**mailing list**

A **mailing list,** which is a type of broadcast e-mail, is a database of people interested in a particular topic. On some types of mailing lists, one person can send a single message, such as a newsletter, to every address on the database by means of a program, called a mail reflector, running on an Internet computer. On a different type of mailing list, called a **listserv** (the computer that sends the messages is a list server), if one person sends an e-mail, everyone on the list can read the message. There are mailing lists for every conceivable topic and anyone can communicate by subscribing to the list.

**listserv**

## Distribution Lists and Broadcast Messages

E-mail users often find that they need to send the same message to the same group of people regularly, such as those in their department or members of a project team. E-mail systems provide a capability called **distribution lists** for this purpose. Users can create a list of people to whom they want to send the same e-mail. They give this list a name and then use that name as the destination for a future e-mail. The e-mail software recognizes the name, looks up the distribution list, and sends the e-mail to all of the people on the list.

**distribution lists**

A similar capability, called **broadcast messages** allows the same e-mail to be sent to everyone on the network. This is sometimes used by system operators to send an informational message such as, "The system will be going down in five minutes for maintenance" to all users. The broadcast capability needs to be used with care, however, because it generates an e-mail for every user on the network and can cause a network slowdown if the number of users, and therefore messages, is large.

**broadcast messages**

## Usenet /Newsgroups

**newsgroup**

A **newsgroup** is a continuous public, electronic discussion forum that is open to people everywhere. It is like a giant bulletin board where anyone can leave a message about any subject, and it is organized into sections and subsections. Along with e-mail, newsgroups are one of the oldest methods of communication on the Internet. Since 1979 when the original Usenet began, millions of people have joined thousands of interest groups in ongoing online discussions. Usenet offered instant access to information and an online community long before most of the world knew about the Internet. Since the rise of the World Wide Web in the early 1990s, Usenet has faded in popularity. About half of Usenet users now come from outside the U.S., in countries where fast Internet access is not as readily available and the Web is not as widely used. Nevertheless, it is still a fascinating information and communication tool, and discussions are as wide-ranging and diverse as the whole fascinating world. Newsgroups are organized in a hierarchical structure, and they cover a wealth of different topics.

Physically, newsgroups are made up of computer files that contain individual contributions to the discussions currently in progress about topics that are agreed upon and arranged according to interest. Many long-time Usenet contributors resent the changes that have occurred over the years and the unmanageable growth that has resulted. The largest general category today is alt (alternate), a catch-all category for any conceivable topic. Though there are now thousands of interest groups in hundreds of categories, Usenet's original categories included:

1. comp (computers)
2. humanities (arts and culture)
3. misc (miscellaneous)
4. news (news and current events)
5. rec (recreational)
6. sci (science)
7. soc (social)
8. talk (general discussion)

The name of a newsgroup, going from left to right, provides the general to specific category information. For example, "rec.arts.poems" is a discussion group for people who are interested in posting or reading poetry in the arts section, which is part of the overall recreational category. A list of Usenet groups is available at http://www.usenet.org. Another good listing of countless groups is http://groups.google.com. Google has also archived the past twenty years of Usenet postings, with access to more than 700 million messages, dating back to 1981. This is a huge collection of Usenet articles, and the timeline of some of the especially memorable articles and threads is a fascinating first-hand historical account. There you may read Tim Berners-Lee's announcement dated 1991-08-06 13:37:40 PST: *WorldWideWeb—Executive Summary* or Linus Torvalds' post about his pet project: "a program for hackers by a hacker"—Linux. If that doesn't excite you, try Marc Andreessen's announcement of Netscape in 1994 or my favorite missed opportunity posted in 1994 by Jeff Bezos, entitled *Well-capitalized Seattle start-up seeks Unix developers:* "Familiarity with Web servers and HTML would be helpful but is not necessary"—Amazon.com. For everyone else there are the first mentions of Star Wars Episode 6, Madonna, Michael Jordan, Britney Spears, and—you go discover.

**moderated newsgroup**

**unmoderated newsgroup**

**thread**

**posting**

Newsgroups can be either moderated or unmoderated. In a **moderated newsgroup,** a human moderator or moderators read all the messages before they are posted and discards any that seem to be inappropriate for the group. An **unmoderated group,** the more common type, is one in which all messages are put directly onto the server. Each news server has special software that maintains a file for each newsgroup serviced by that server. To take part in an ongoing conversation, which is called a **thread,** users read messages and respond to them by entering a message into a newsgroup; this is called **posting.** As messages are posted, Usenet servers distribute them to other sites with Usenet servers that carry the newsgroup. Newsgroups are not maintained on one single server but are copied to hundreds of them all over the world. In contrast, forums and discussion boards or bulletin boards, though similar, are kept on a single server maintained by the originator of the forum.

Participating in a newsgroup involves a few simple steps:

**newsreader**

■    When you are ready to subscribe, you must know the name or IP address of your ISP's news server. Normally, your ISP provides you with the news server's connection information. If you do not have a **newsreader** program on your computer, there are many free, publicly accessible news servers such as http://www.newzbot.com/. NewsXpress, a Usenet newsreader for Windows, can also be downloaded from ftp.malch.com.

■ To access a newsgroup, you need reader software that lets you read and respond to messages. Using the Network News Transfer Protocol (NNTP), part of the TCP/IP suite, the newsreader client connects to the news server according to the configuration you have set up. You can subscribe to the groups that interest you so new messages in your group will automatically be delivered to you. You may also cancel your subscription if you are no longer interested.

■ Once the news server is set up, the newsreader shows you the whole list of newsgroups that your news server carries. Not every group is carried by every news server, but many administrators will add a group if there is demand for that particular category. You choose the groups in which you are interested and click "subscribe." Usually you can sort quickly through the list using search functions provided by most newsreaders.

■ When you access a newsgroup and establish a connection, the newsreader downloads all the new messages in the group to which you have subscribed. You may simply read the messages, choose to respond to any of the messages, or start a new thread of your own. Posting a message to the newsgroup is as easy as replying to an e-mail. Using NNTP, your newsreader sends the message to the news server, which saves your message by appending it to the end of the large text file for that newsgroup.

■ The news server sends the file with the updated information to one or more other news servers that compare the files they receive with their own and add any differences they find to their own text files. In this way, they avoid overwriting any new messages that come in during the update. The changes are copied to each news server until all are updated. Other subscribers are able to read your new message with all the others that have been posted. After a certain length of time, or when the text file reaches a certain length, the messages at the beginning of the file are put in an archive text file.

## Chat and Instant Messaging

One of the interesting archived messages on Usenet is the first mention among techies of IRC chat—in February of 1989. How many people connected to the Internet today have *not* participated in chatting or instant messaging? They are two of the most immediate ways to communicate with others over the Internet, and they also run on a client-server model. A "chat room" is actually software that allows a group of people to type messages that are seen by the rest of the group in real time.

**Internet Relay Chat (IRC)**

**INTERNET RELAY CHAT (IRC)** IRC is one of the most popular means of communication—the equivalent of CB radio—on the Internet. In 1988, Jarkko Oikarinen, tinkering around at the University of Oulu, Finland, sent out a new freeware application called **Internet Relay Chat (IRC)**. The first IRC server at tolsun.oulu.fi is still running. People who were identified by nicknames, called *handles,* could log onto the chat server using a client and talk to several people at once. The word "relay" became a part of the application's name because servers relayed the messages to other servers, allowing people to take part in a discussion carried over several IRC servers. Some websites use proprietary chat software that enables users to chat only while on the site. Proprietary software does not use the IRC protocol.

**channels**

Today, using IRC, people all over the world are able to hold real time conversations on thousands of different topics, called **channels.** As you type a message using IRC, everyone on that particular channel can read and respond to you, and you can simultaneously hold side conversations with individuals in that channel. The channels reside on servers all around the world. The IRC client on your computer communicates with a server that is part of a global IRC server network, connected in a spanning-tree fashion. That is, each server is connected to several others, but not all servers are connected to one another. Figure 16-5 illustrates the spanning tree of IRC. In order to chat, you need client software on your computer and a connection to an IRC server. When you connect to a server, you choose a particular channel to join, choose a username (handle) to identify yourself, and join in the discussion. Your message is sent from one server to another, always taking the shortest route through the network to its final destination.

Beyond the usual casual and often pointless conversations, chat rooms have practical applications as well. Using online "help desks" and live chat with customer representatives, many e-commerce sites have been able to personalize their service to increase visitor satisfaction, turn visitors into buyers, and actually earn revenue over the Internet! During the Gulf War in 1991, IRC gained international fame as updates from around the world came across the wire. Most IRC users gathered on a single channel to hear the reports. During the coup against Boris Yeltsin in September of 1993, IRC had similar uses when IRC "chatters" gave live reports from Moscow about the unstable situation. Recently IRC chat kept users up to date and kept relatives in touch during and after the September 11, 2001 tragedy.

**instant messaging**

**INSTANT MESSAGING (IM)**    IM is like a chat room for only two people at a time. The first **instant messaging (IM)** program to grab public attention was ICQ, which is shorthand for "I seek you." Created by three young friends in Israel, a country of only 6 million people, it became an Internet sensation overnight when it was released in November of 1996. By June of 1998, the number of users was twice as large as the entire population of the tiny country. Today, early user numbers are sometimes even auctioned on eBay because of the prestige associated with "owning" them! ICQ caught on so quickly because it allowed communication that was far more immediate than bulletin boards or even e-mail. Not long after ICQ was introduced, AOL introduced their AOL Instant Messenger (AIM), which soon became the leader in instant messaging (in fact, ICQ's parent company, Mirablis, was acquired by AOL in June 1998). It was followed by MSN Instant messenger and Yahoo! Messenger.

For communicating, instant messaging utilities use proprietary protocols, although AIM still allows nonmembers to communicate with AOL members. The IEFT is working on a standard protocol for instant messaging, but it is still in development. To send an instant message, you need to run the client software on your computer and connect to the Internet. The client opens a connection to the IM login server and checks your screen name and password, then sends them, the IP address, and the port number assigned to your IM client, along with your "buddy list," to the message server. The server checks to see if anyone on your list is online, makes a temporary file that has connection information for you and your buddies, and keeps you informed of their presence throughout the connection. When you send a message, the message is sent right to the client software on the other person's computer, and your communication is carried on directly between the two clients without the instant messaging server being involved. Because your client has the IP address and port number of the buddy's computer, you chat directly with each other. When you are finished "messaging" and you log off, your client

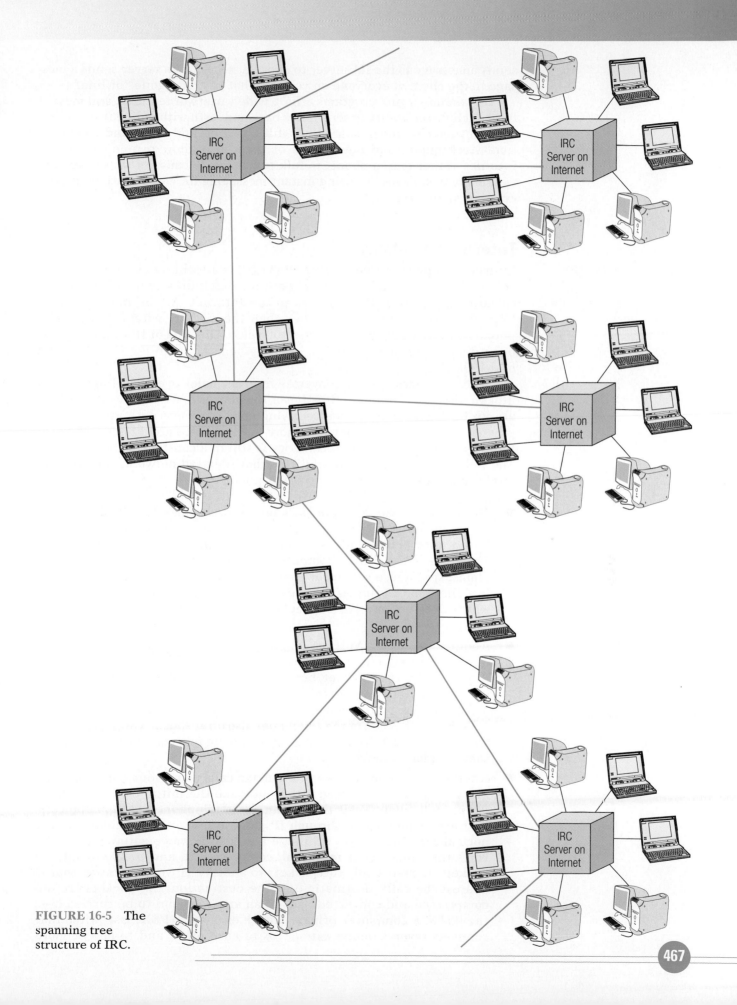

**FIGURE 16-5** The spanning tree structure of IRC.

sends a message to the IM server to end the session. The server sends a message to the client of everyone on your list that you have gone "offline."

Instant messaging programs offer a wide variety of features, and most of them include the ability to send notes back and forth with online friends; create a custom chat room; share links, files, sounds, and links; and view real-time stock quotes and news. Most of them also allow people to use the Internet, rather than a phone, to talk to friends. Because of these capabilities, many businesses are using instant messaging for collaboration on projects and virtual conferences.

## Internet Telephony

voice over IP (VoIP)

Internet telephony or **voice over IP (VoIP)** is a technology that transmits voice conversations over IP-based networks, including everything from local area and private IP networks to the Internet. As the name implies, VoIP uses packet switching rather than the circuit switching that telephone networks have used for over 100 years. The idea of IP telephony has been discussed since the 1970s, but only began to gain popularity in the mid-1990s.

Voice messages must be converted from an analog to a digital signal, then broken into small chunks and sent over the network, just as other IP packets are, to be reassembled at the receiving end. The voice data are also compressed to travel over the network more quickly. There are different forms of Internet telephony and the technology is still in a constant state of change. The following are three different ways that IP-based networks, private and public, allow people to communicate by phone.

- There are several software packages and schemes for helping you to make "phone calls" from your PC to another on the Internet by speaking into a microphone and listening through speakers and a sound card. These are referred to as computer to computer calls. You need a microphone, speakers, a sound card, and an Internet connection, preferably a fast one. Many of the instant messaging programs allow this type of call, which does not involve a telephone. The only cost is the normal ISP charge.

- Another way to use VoIP, calling a telephone from a computer, also requires a software client like Net2Phone or Dialpad. The software is downloadable from the Internet, but charges for PC-to-phone-calls range from two cents for domestic to much higher fees for international calls. Most of the services offer much lower rates than traditional long-distance calls, however. Some of the companies also offer special calling cards that allow users to call from a standard telephone to a computer running the same vendor software.

- Another technology allows you to make calls using your normal phone, but your voice is digitized after you make the initial call. When most people talk about VoIP, they mean these telephone-to-telephone calls that are accomplished through IP gateways. The call originates like a normal call, but it is sent through a special IP voice gateway that converts the voice signal to digital, compresses it, and breaks it into IP packets. It then sends the packets to another IP voice gateway that is nearest the call's destination. At the destination, the packets are uncompressed and converted back to an analog signal to be carried over the PSTN. A company's private branch exchange (PBX) is a switch that connects several phone extensions to each other and to one or more outside lines. It can be a digital PBX that converts each phone's analog signal to digital data before sending over an IP network. Thus, it too is a gateway because it connects devices on different types of networks so they can communicate.

The growth in bandwidth availability has increased the value of IP telephony, and VoIP has many advantages, including the following:

- The cost of calls on packet switched networks could be half that of those on traditional circuit switched networks because of the more efficient use of bandwidth. Fewer long distance trunks are needed between switches. It is more efficient because several packet switched calls can occupy the same bandwidth as one circuit switched call, and the connection time is minimized. For the duration of one call on a circuit switched network, the PSTN must dedicate an FDX 64 Kbps line. Because VoIP uses voice compression and the bandwidth is used only when data are transmitted, packet switched networks would require only about 14 Kbps.

- Calls are cheaper because they can bypass phone company fees. In businesses, mobile workers can call in over the Internet without paying higher cell phone or calling card prices. Because VoIP packets are sent to the gateway nearest the receiving end, users on a company's WAN can make a local call out of a long distance one. For instance, a caller in a company's office in New York could call a person in Seattle and route the call through a corporate gateway in Everett, Washington.

- VoIP also offers greater functionality through free add-on services and features such as call forwarding and caller ID. Voice mail can go directly into the same inbox where e-mail and faxes go, thus increasing efficiency. Conference calls and call forwarding can be set up easily and without extra fees.

- Voice and Internet access traffic can be carried over the same phone line simultaneously.

While VoIP has many advantages, there are also several disadvantages, including the following:

- Poor voice quality caused by latency has been the main disadvantage to VoIP. Several variables are responsible for end-to-end delay (latency): the amount of traffic on IP networks, packet size, and the number of routers and gateways that packets have to travel through. On the public Internet, there may be rapid fluctuations in the amount of traffic that would cause delays and cause a reduction in voice quality. The transport protocol used for VoIP systems is User Datagram Protocol. UDP is good because acknowledgments don't need to be made for lost packets; however, this can cause some fluctuation in voice quality if more than 1 percent packet loss occurs.

- The relative lack of security is another drawback to VoIP. The use of encryption could solve the problem but could potentially add more overhead and greater latency to packets because of the processing delay.

- A major disadvantage to VoIP has been the lack of standards among vendors, applications, and protocols. Several organizations, however, have worked together in establishing standards to encourage the growth of VoIP services. The problem is that each protocol has its own zealots who seek to promote it as the one true standard.

H.323

Media Gateway Control Protocol (MGCP)

Session Initiation Protocol (SIP)

The two major standards contenders are **H.323** from the ITU and **Media Gateway Control Protocol (MGCP)** from the IETF. Each of them relies on other protocols to complete its tasks. One other important protocol that was developed specifically for IP telephony is a more streamlined **Session Initiation Protocol (SIP)**. It is said to be more scalable, easier to implement, and faster than H.323. SIP connects devices with other devices using IP addresses in much the same way that HTTP uses the URL address to connect Web browsers to servers.

Great claims were made in the past that Internet telephony would do away with the need for traditional telephone service. Some even predicted it would happen by the year 2001. Despite all the promises, however, the Internet has neither replaced the telephone nor delivered no-cost service for long distance calls. While there are many advantages to VoIP, there are also many disadvantages. The good news is that new technologies are overcoming many of the problems and, while the transition is a more tedious process than once predicted, Internet telephoning has come a long way since its beginning in the mid-1990s. The PSTN and VoIP are likely to coexist for several years, but the competition is probably good for spurring developers to improve the reliability, QoS, and cost effectiveness of VoIP.

## Internet Radio

Internet radio

**Internet radio,** like many of the breakthroughs and discoveries in internetworking, appeared first on college campuses. Several schools began to offer Internet radio rebroadcasting in 1994. The University of North Carolina's WXYC, which has been broadcasting on traditional radio for 25 years, claims to be the first radio station to simulcast around the clock on the Internet. In 1995, using Real Audio technology, Radio HK in Los Angeles became the first commercial 24-hour radio station programmed only for the Internet. Since the late 1990s, traditional radio broadcasters have simulcast their programming on the Internet, but at the beginning of the 21$^{st}$ century, Internet radio has undergone a major revolution that promises to expand programming, connectivity, and the way it works. As wireless devices become more and more advanced, they will be able to feed Internet broadcasts to cell phones, PDAs, and car radios.

Unlike traditional radio stations, which are limited by the power of their transmitters and the available broadcast spectrum, Internet radio has no geographic limitations—it reaches around the globe. It can go far beyond audio to include links to documents, graphics, training, interactivity, and even message boards and chat rooms. Listeners can download audio files in WAV, MP3, AU, or other digitized formats from websites or FTP sites and store them on their computers. To play the files, they need an audio player, software with which most Web-savvy users are familiar. Often the files, which are large even when compressed, take a long time to download, and listening is possible only after the sound file has been downloaded completely.

streaming audio

metafile

Most people prefer listening to continuous broadcast **streaming audio** files, which require three components: player software on the user's computer, a dedicated server, and encoding software to convert audio into a streaming format. What actually happens is that the browser contacts the Web server, and the server returns a small text file (a **metafile**) with the URL of the requested sound file. The browser launches an audio player like RealPlayer or Windows Media Player and tells the streaming audio server to deliver the sound clips. The streaming server determines the speed at which the user is connected and adjusts the file size to the speed of the connection. A higher-speed connection provides better sound quality because it allows

**encoder**

more data to be sent at once. An **encoder** converts audio content into the streaming format. The sound clip is compressed and sent in IP packets using UDP, which does not keep resending packets if they are dropped or damaged as TCP does. Resending would constantly interrupt the broadcast. On the receiving end, packets are put into a buffer until it is full and then sent to the player to deliver sound, even while it continues to receive packets.

One intriguing Internet radio site is Live365 (http://www.live365.com), which offers thousands of stations that play every possible genre of music from all over the world. Listeners can set preferences and presets for any number of stations. They have created a community for broadcasters and listeners who interact through chat rooms and message boards. Live365 provides tools to help professional broadcasters and individuals alike to set up Internet radio stations and to stream their own audio content around the world. It provides them with bandwidth, software tools, and storage space on Live365 servers so that anyone can become a broadcaster. Broadcasters can choose live feed from their computers, stored feed from files that they have uploaded to the Live365 servers, or relayed broadcasts from other Internet sites. The site has paid all necessary royalties and fees and has secured licenses with the necessary recording performance groups. They also provide legal guidelines for broadcasters in keeping with the Digital Millennium Copyright Act of 1998.

In mid-2002, the site and others like it was hard-hit when court cases brought by recording artists demanded that even small campus or private radio stations pay royalties each time a song was played. Although the case lowered the price stations were required to pay, it was enough to knock many stations off the air and cause others to require small fees to be paid for access by individual listeners. The battle is on-going.

## 16-7 INTERNET TOOLS

The wealth of information and entertainment available and the ability to share resources on the Internet is sometimes overwhelming. Several useful tools help people tame the experience and make their time online more productive. In Chapter 14, you read about two of the most common and useful tools that are part of the TCP/IP suite of protocols: FTP and Telnet. Because of the vast amount of information available on the Internet, it sometimes feels impossible to find exactly what you are looking for. Search engines and other organizational aids can bring order to the chaos and make the information overload more manageable.

### File Transfer Protocol (FTP)

**File Transfer Protocol (FTP)**

**File Transfer Protocol (FTP)** gives people the ability to perform one of the most popular activities on the Internet: downloading and sharing files. Before networks, people had to rely on physical transfer of files by "sneakernet," so called because the main method of transferring files was by walking from one computer to another, often on feet shod in sneakers. Data were copied to a disk or magnetic tape and carried or shipped to another computer, then loaded into the machine. FTP, one of the oldest application protocols still used on the Internet, runs on a client/server model like many other Internet services. It allows users to connect to a remote computer that offers FTP service and download or, in some cases, upload files. The client application can be a program included in a Windows-based system, one of several commercial programs like CuteFTP or WS_FTP, or it can be the browser using FTP behind the scenes to download files. Because all computers connected to the Internet use TCP/IP, they can transfer files even when they are using different operating systems.

FTP transfer can be used interactively. The user runs an FTP client that establishes communication with a specific server to transport files. They can also be used for batch transfer, whereby a program like the MIME e-mail interface interacts with the FTP server, then informs the user if the communication has succeeded or failed, all the while hiding the FTP interface from the user.

It works like this. The client software on a user's computer contacts the FTP server from which he wants to download or upload files. A daemon runs on the FTP server and handles all transactions, such as asking for an account number or user name and the user's password. FTP prompts the user to enter a command, carries out the command, and then issues another prompt. The TCP connection to a remote machine that an FTP client uses to send **control connection** commands and receive responses is called a **control connection**. There are several different FTP commands, although many of them are no longer used. Some commands define how many files will be transferred, help maneuver around the program, or define what kind of compression should be used for files. The most common commands include:

- OPEN: to initiate a connection between the client and server so files can be exchanged
- DIR: to request a listing of the directories and their contents
- GET: to request that a file be transferred from the remote to the local host (downloaded)
- MGET: to request multiple files be downloaded
- CD: to change directories
- SEND: used to request that a file be transferred from the local to the remote host (uploaded)
- PUT: is the same as SEND
- MSEND: used to upload multiple files
- MPUT: is the same as MSEND
- CLOSE: used to end the transfer system

For each file transferred, the client and server establish a data connection, send one file, and close the connection. If more than one file is transferred, a new data connection is established for each transfer, and then closed. Although many data connections can be established and closed, the control connection remains open throughout the whole session. Figure 16-6 illustrates the way this works. The client establishes the control connection to the server and keeps it open; the server establishes the data connection, which closes automatically after each transfer. An end-of-file condition is used to inform the other side that the file transfer is complete. Because the command link stays open, the user can change directories or can download another file. After all transfers have been made, she logs off, and the command link closes, disconnecting from the FTP server.

FTP defines two different transfer modes to allow transfer of most types of files.

- ASCII: to send basic text files (with .txt extension)
- BINARY: to send nontext files (with extensions such as .exe, .zip, .jpg, .gif, and .tif)

FIGURE 16-6 Control and data connections used in FTP.

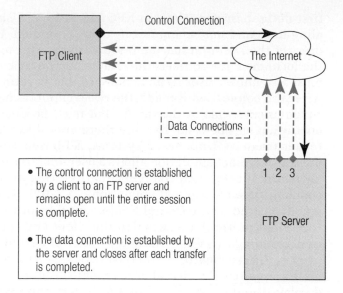

- The control connection is established by a client to an FTP server and remains open until the entire session is complete.

- The data connection is established by the server and closes after each transfer is completed.

Remember that to send a binary file, you must change to binary mode, or the file will not be usable. Most people have received files that look like gibberish because they were sent in the wrong mode. The FTP client application does not usually warn you to switch, although some commercial programs do so automatically.

On sites where a user has access permission to upload files as well as download them, for example on his own website, he must type a login and password. Many other sessions require login and password to download or upload files. For public FTP sites on the Internet, however, Anonymous FTP allows the download of a multitude of free files, programs, plugins, and documents. Early systems permitted visitors to use the password "guest" to transfer files, but most sites today require a user to access files by typing "anonymous" as the user name and his e-mail address as the password.

The commands are used with text-based FTP systems. FTP programs that have a more intuitive interface are available to simplify file transfer tasks. Most Web browsers render FTP sites as Web pages. Downloading files is simply a matter of clicking on links that lead to them. To upload files, however, an FTP client is still necessary. One of the most user-friendly programs, called CuteFTP, has a graphical interface that permits a person to enter such information as host and user names, passwords, and transfer modes. It lists the files on both computers and the rest is just "click," "drag," and "drop" to upload or download files. Although FTP was invented in 1985, and other tools have since been developed, it is still the most widely recognized and used method of transferring files.

**Archie**

**Gopher**

Two older tools from the TCP/IP suite, **Archie** and **Gopher,** are useful tools to search Anonymous FTP sites. Archie serves as an index, a virtual card catalog for anonymous FTP archives on the Internet. Gopher is helpful for searching the Internet when you don't have a browser. Are there still some of you out there? Gopher digs through the mountains of information on the Internet and displays the information, then starts the application you need to deliver it to you. Obviously, in these days of the World Wide Web and search engines, these tools are not as popular, but they are still useful.

## Telnet

**Telnet**

**Telnet,** a program that allows you to connect to other computers on the Internet, is the terminal-remote host protocol developed for ARPANET and

**terminal emulation**

first defined by Jon Postel in RFC 318 in 1972. Using Telnet is similar to dialing in to a remote computer by using a modem. You must know the IP address of the host that has the resources you want to use. The Telnet client on the local machine contacts the remote computer by using its IP address. You must also know a user ID and password that is valid for the remote computer. After the connection is made, the two computers negotiate the way they will communicate. One of the things that must be negotiated is which **terminal emulation** will be used. Because there are all kinds of computers on the Internet (such as Unix-based systems, NT-based computers, Macintosh, and others), terminal emulation allows a user's computer to emulate (imitate) the keyboard, display, and computer that the remote system expects. The most common type of terminal emulation is VT-100, which was a dumb terminal manufactured by the Digital Equipment Corporation many years ago.

**network virtual terminal (NVT)**

Telnet protocol assumes that the client and server are both **network virtual terminals (NVTs)**. Each NVT has a virtual keyboard and a virtual printer. The keyboard, as you type text, sends data from your NVT to the remote computer. The virtual printer, which is not really a printer, receives and displays the data on the computer screen. The text accumulates in a buffer on your computer as you type. When you give a command to send (by pressing Enter, for example), the data are sent, along with the host's and your own IP addresses, across the Internet. Sent at the same time are specific Telnet commands that the other NVT uses to determine how to respond to the transmitted data. The Telnet host receives and processes it and returns to your NVT printer (screen) the results of using the data or running the command on the remote computer.

To Telnet to a remote computer:

- Start the Telnet client application on your computer.
- With the username and password that have been determined in advance, log on to the remote computer.
- Type the commands that work on the operating system of the remote computer. Even if your computer uses a Windows operating system, you must use Linux commands to Telnet to a Linux system.
- Exit from the Telnet session.

On the Internet, there are public Telnet sites that publish their names and addresses so that you can access their files. It is also helpful to be able to Telnet into your own office computer in order to work from home. More and more companies allow people to telecommute rather than add to traffic congestion in big cities. Many organizations, however, do not allow Telnet capability because of the security threat it implies, so the capability is not automatically available on every computer connected to the Internet. Some organizations require that a user have a static, recognizable IP address rather than a dynamic one that changes periodically, so network administrators always know from whom the session is originating. The current trend is for companies to create VPNs connecting remote employees and telecommuters.

## Search Tools

**search tools**

The Internet and its World Wide Web are fascinating repositories of information. The millions of pages offer a mind-boggling range of topics from aardvarks to Zyzzyva (really!). The problem is, how do you find what you are looking for? Some of the most useful tools on the Internet, and without which Web travelers could become utterly lost, are **search tools.** Although there are

FIGURE 16-7 Examples of common Boolean operators.

| Searching . . . | Results in . . . |
|---|---|
| "and" | **Combustible and apricots** Documents with both words |
| "or" | **Combustible or apricots** Documents with either word; usually the greatest amount of matches |
| "not" (some use "and not") | **Combustible not apricots** Documents about combustible, but not about combustible apricots; a good way to limit the search |
| Quotation marks | **"Combustible apricots"** Documents about combustible apricots. Surprisingly, there were no results. |

many types of tools, and there are differences in the way they work, all perform three basic tasks:

- searching the Internet based on key words or phrases
- indexing the words and their locations (URLs)
- providing links to those URLs

**Boolean operator**

The procedure seems very simple: you go to one of the many search engine sites, click in the window, and type your topic of interest. A few seconds later, a list of choices is displayed on your screen. Effective searching, however, actually involves building a query and submitting it through the search engine. A query can be a single word, but to refine or extend the search requires the use of **Boolean operators,** shown in Figure 16-7. George Boole (1815–1864) was a mathematician and logistician who developed ways of expressing logical processes that use algebraic symbols (known as symbolic logic), which became the basis for computer database searches. The three most common Boolean operators are "and," "or," and "not." A good search engine's advanced search page will explain other helpful operators that can narrow the search even further. In addition, quotation marks around words cause them to be treated as a phrase that must be found exactly within the file.

**search engine**

"Search engine" has become a generic term, but the truth is a search engine is only one of several types of search tool on the Internet, including the following:

**spider**

1. A *search engine* is an indexed database of Web sites. When you perform a search, most search engines use special software robots called **spiders** to build lists of the words found on individual sites. Building the lists is referred to as Web Crawling. Actually, the spider doesn't crawl randomly around on the Web. You must register your site before the spider is deployed to index it, and you must ask each search engine to have its spider read your site individually. The better the information in the page's meta tag descriptions, key words, and page title, the higher its rank in the listings. When you visit a search engine, the spider-indexed pages are displayed. The pages in the database are always rather stale, but when you click on the links provided in a search engine's results, you get a current version of the page. This is why you often click on a search result and recieve a "file not found" message. This is also why it is important for a Web page developer to send a brand new page, that is, one that no one has ever linked to before, to various search engines requesting that the URL be included in the database.

Many types of pages and links are excluded from search engines, either because they are dynamically generated or are excluded by search engines according to policy. For example, many script pages contain "spider traps" that bog them down in infinite loops. Spiders are programmed to back off from them. Additionally, all sites that require a login or password are closed to spiders because only humans can type the required information. Many pages that contain primarily images or graphics are also closed, because there is no text or link for the spiders to "read." Some sites, however, do contain databases of images that can be searched. Three of the best search engines can be found at www.Google.com, www.AlltheWeb.com, and www.AltaVista.com. Several newcomers joined the list of search engines in 2002, but www.iLor.com added something new to ease the tedious search process. When a link is selected, a small box appears on the screen with options to, among other things, anchor to the search results while clicking through to others and avoid having to hit the back button repeatedly to return. Figure 16-8 shows a screenshot of Google, one of the most popular search engines on the Internet.

**metasearch engine**

2. A **metasearch engine** is a utility that searches several search engines and subject directories, compiling the results in a convenient display rather than searching each directory or index individually. A metasearch engine does not maintain its own database, but searches those of other search engines. www.Metacrawler.com, www.hotbot.com, www.ixquick.com, and www.surfwax.com are the URLs of several well known metasearch engines. Figure 16-9 shows an example of the metasearch engine called Metacrawler. One problem is that most of them do not include Google, one of the best search engines, and most do not allow searchers to refine their quests.

**subject directory**

3. Another type of search tool is a **subject directory** such as the commercial tools, Yahoo! and About.com, which are sometimes referred to as portals. Academic general subject directories like http://www.lii.org, http://infomine.ucr.edu, and http://www.academicinfo.net are also subject directories. Subject directories are built by human selection, rather than robot programs, and are organized into subject categories. They do not contain the full text of the Web pages they link to, but contain search

**FIGURE 16-8** Example of a search engine (google.com).

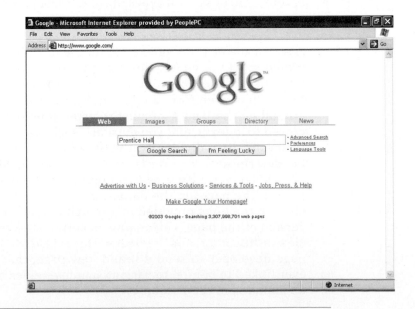

FIGURE 16-9 Example of a metasearch engine (Metacrawler).

titles, descriptions, and subject categories using broad or general terms. Subject directories are smaller than the databases of most search engines, though they vary greatly in size. Content is hand selected and evaluated carefully before it is added. There are a large variety of subject directories and each has unique content. One such directory is illustrated in Figure 16-10.

gateway page

4. Special subject directories, sometimes called **gateway pages,** contain lots of links to Web pages that have important resources on specific topics. An "expert" who has spent a lot of time searching the Web compiles the pages as guides to specific fields, subjects, or disciplines. There are commercial examples, but special subject directories are usually used for academic research. Yahoo!, as shown in Figure 16-11, is an example of a gateway or portal page.

invisible Web

5. The visible Web is what you find when you search subject directories and search engines. The **invisible Web** is all the rest of the thousands of databases on the Internet that cannot be located by search engines. It actually

## SIDEBAR 16-1   GOOGLE FUN

Most of us rely on search engines to get around on the Internet. What would we do without them to locate the elusive bits of information we require almost daily? An intriguing game, fit for the new millennium, has evolved from this habit.

Since January 2002, Googlewhacking has grown into quite a craze. The rules are simple: You type two unrelated words (which must be found in the dictionary at www.dictionary.com) into Google. Do not use quotation marks around your entry. The goal is to receive one, and only one, result from the search engine. If you are successful in your search, you can record your "pure whack" to The Whack Stack.

Read the rules, history, and the latest entries at www.googlewhack.com. Recent whacks in the Whack Stack include "unorthodox newsgirl," "apoplectic nogs", and "snowman trickledown." Can you top them? Remember that you must obtain only a single result.

**FIGURE 16-10** Example of a subject directory (infomine.ucr.edu).

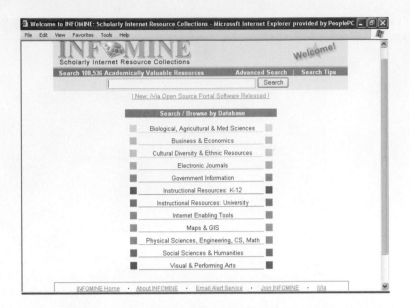

**FIGURE 16-11** Example of a commercial gateway (subject directory) (Yahoo!).

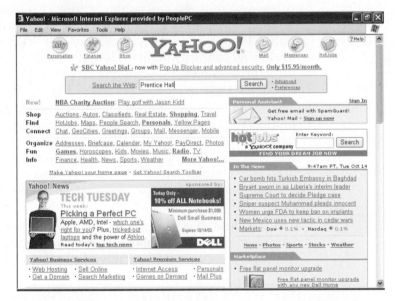

consists of two or three times as many pages as what can be found by search engines and subject directories. The best way to find these valuable searchable databases on the Web is by using the subject plus the word "database" in Google and other search engines or in the subject directory, Yahoo! For example, to find a database for Internet movies, type "Internet movies database." To find a database on carnivorous plants, type "carnivorous plants database." A valuable resource for the invisible Web is http://www.invisible-web.net, a companion to the book called *The Invisible Web: Finding Hidden Internet Resources Search Engines Can't See* by Chris Sherman and Gary Price. The book includes 1,000 databases the authors have identified that are available on the Internet, but not accessible by spiders. The Web site, shown in Figure 16-12, includes a directory that lists databases in several different categories, covering such addresses as a database website of the A&E TV Show *Biography* that contains over 25,000 biographies of famous people—all invisible to search engines.

6. Currently, researchers are studying many alternative ways to search. Boolean searches are literal inquiries in which the engine looks for exact

**FIGURE 16-12** The invisible web database.

**FIGURE 16-13** Example of a natural-language query site (ask.com).

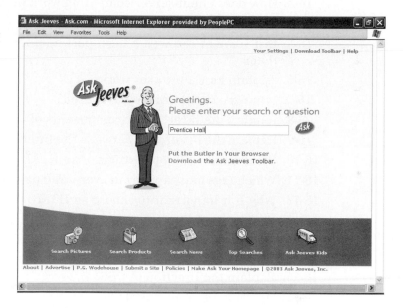

**concept-based searching**

words or phrases. One type of research concerns **concept-based searching,** which uses statistical analysis of pages that contain the words or phrases you search to find other pages that might interest you. Still other

**natural-language queries**

researchers have explored **natural-language queries** in which you type a question phrased exactly as you would ask the question of a real person. Figure 16-13 shows the most popular natural language site today: Ask Jeeves (http://www.ask.com).

## ■ SUMMARY

The Internet has changed our world dramatically, perhaps more than any other invention in the last 50 to 100 years. In a very short time, it has become an almost indispensable tool for governments, educational institutions, students, researchers, entrepreneurs, businesses, and corporations around the globe. It has changed the way we learn and the way we communicate. It has made our world smaller, yet in many ways much larger. It has brought us together and has driven us apart. The Internet has been used both for good and for evil, in the best of times and the worst of times. Chapter 16 has discussed some of the myriad uses for the Internet and World Wide Web. There are many more applications that are waiting to be discovered. The direction it takes in its future evolution is up to all of us because it belongs to no one, and yet to everyone.

One of the primary notions that the Internet has challenged is the meaning of personal privacy and, as a result, our feelings of individual and national security. Chapter 17 examines some of the security and privacy issues involved in all types of networks.

## ■ REVIEW QUESTIONS

16-1. What is the function of a URL?

16-2. What are the differences between HTTP and HTTPS?

16-3. How does client-server computing work on the Internet?

16-4. Explain the CGI and its function.

16-5. List some of the well known port numbers and the services that use them.

16-6. Explain how a browser works.

16-7. What is a cache and how is it used?

16-8. Explain the three major components of the World Wide Web.

16-9. Explain the difference between the Internet and the World Wide Web.

16-10. What are the major portions of an HTML document?

16-11. Which tags must appear in every Web page in exactly the same order?

16-12. Why is it important to choose an HTML document title carefully?

16-13. What is the function of an anchor in an HTML document?

16-14. What are two different types of graphics files that are used for Web pages?

16-15. Explain the function of CSS.

16-16. Describe the way e-mail works.

16-17. Explain the difference between the SMTP server and the POP3 server. On which ports do they listen?

16-18. Explain the differences between instant messaging and chatting.

16-19. What are the benefits and disadvantages of instant messaging and chatting?

16-20. Describe three ways that people are able to communicate over IP-based networks by phone.

16-21. Explain the advantages and disadvantages of VoIP.

16-22. How does Internet Radio differ from traditional radio stations?

16-23. Describe how FTP works.

16-24. Explain the difference between the two different transfer modes in FTP.

16-25. What is Telnet and how is it used?

16-26. Compare and contrast the various types of search tool on the World Wide Web. Give examples of each.

16-27. What is a Boolean operator and what is it used for?

## TRUE/FALSE

16-1. The Internet and the World Wide Web are different names for the same thing.

16-2. The URL tells what transfer protocol is used and gives the address of a Web page.

16-3. Programs that perform administrative tasks for the OS are called daemons.

16-4. HTTPS stands for hypertext transfer protocol server.

16-5. HTML is based on an older code called Standard Generalized Markup Language.

16-6. CGI is the standardized way the Web server interacts with outside resources like databases.

16-7. A well known port is the place on a computer where one plugs in the printer.

16-8. A cache is a special part of disk memory where items on Web pages are stored to make them load faster the next time the page is visited.

16-9. The two major portions of an HTML document are the title and the body.

16-10. Most images used on Web pages are either in .gif or .png format.

16-11. The HTML tag <meta></meta> includes key words and descriptions to aid search engines in locating pages on the Internet.

16-12. XML separates the content of a page from its presentation.

16-13. Two types of e-mail servers are SMTP and PPP3.

16-14. IRC chat uses a spanning-tree structure that connects each server to several, but not all, other servers.

16-15. The main disadvantage of VoIP has been latency, which causes poor voice quality.

16-16. Two standards for IP telephony are SLIP and MGCP.

16-17. Audio data are compressed and sent in IP packets over TCP to ensure that they arrive at their destination.

16-18. Besides the user's computer, streaming audio requires a dedicated server and encoding software to convert audio into a streaming format.

16-19. FTP is one of the oldest application protocols on the Internet.

16-20. Two different transfer modes for FTP are ASCII and binary.

16-21. Binary files are basic text files.

16-22. The most common type of terminal emulation for Telnet is VT-100.

16-23. When you use a search engine, software robots called "spiders" then crawl around the Web searching for your key words.

16-24. One problem with search engines is that they can't search dynamically generated pages or those that require a login.

16-25. Hotbot.com is an example of a search engine.

## MULTIPLE CHOICE

16-1. The thousands of databases on the Internet that cannot be located by search engines are collectively called _____.

a. subject directories

b. portals

c. invisible Web

d. gateway pages

16-2. When a URL does not contain a filename after the slash mark, the Web server automatically delivers the default file, which is most often called _____.

a. mypage.html

b. index.com

c. index.html

d. www.html

16-3. Daemon is a term first used by what operating system?

a. UNIX

b. LINUX

c. Windows

d. NetWare

16-4. Search engines rely heavily on what required HTML tag pair to locate pages?

a. <body><body>

b. <html></html>

c. <title></title>

d. <head></head>

16-5. The e-mail server that handles outgoing mail is:

a. POP3

b. SLIP

c. LDAP

d. SMTP

16-6. A database of people interested in a particular topic that receives broadcast e-mail is called a _____.

a. newsgroup

b. mailing list

c. Internet relay

d. spam base

16-7. The FTP transfer mode that allows one to send nontext files is _____.

a. ASCII

b. anonymous

c. binary

d. hexadecimal

16-8. A program on a website that maintains a database of Internet sites is called a _____.

a. subject directory

b. search engine

c. metasearch engine

d. invisible Web

16-9. Special directories that contain lots of links to websites that contain important resources on specific topics are also called _____.

 a. invisible Web

 b. metasearch engines

 c. natural language queries

 d. gateway pages ~

16-10. A search tool that is built by human selection rather than robot programs is called a(n) _____.

 a. invisible Web

 b. metasearch engine

 c. subject directory ~

 d. search engine

## ■ PROBLEMS AND PROJECTS

16-1. There are many tales on the Internet of personal meetings and even marriages that have resulted from chatting, instant messaging, and e-mail exchanges. Investigate the literature and report on two or three positive and negative experiences resulting from Internet meetings. Do you think it is possible to actually get to know a person through on-line correspondence?

16-2. Using one of the search engines described in this chapter, research IPv6. What are its advantages over Ipv4, and what are its disadvantages?

16-3. Use four different types of search tools to research artificial intelligence. What differences did you notice?

16-4. Go to an anonymous FTP site and download a document. What steps did you take to do so. How would you upload a file?

16-5. Create your own simple Web page using the instructions in this chapter or one of the helps suggested. Do not use an HTML editor like Front Page. Use Notepad and hard code it yourself. Include pictures and a few hyperlinks.

16-6. Check to see if your ISP provides Web page space as part of your contract. If so, post your Web page and launch yourself onto the World Wide Web.

16-7. Internet Radio has in the past few years been the subject of a lot of controversy. Use a search tool to investigate the controversy and the outcome of the debates between music providers and small, independent Internet stations. Decide where you stand on the issue based on your research.

16-8. Many people believe that the Internet began as a research and educational tool and has become too commercial. Is it possible to make a lot of money using the Internet? Can you think of an entrepreneurial scheme to make money (legitimately!) by using the Internet? Try developing a simple business plan to sell your idea to investors.

16-9. Investigate Internet2 on the Internet and report on your findings. Do you think the project is necessary and important? Give reasons for your answer.

16-10. The history of the Internet is fascinating to read and most people who lived during the early days of its development had no idea what was going on. New and exciting discoveries are still happening today, though most of us are completely unaware of them! Try to think outside the box and imagine where technology will take us in the next few decades. What unimagined wonders lie before us? Where are we going and how do we get there from here? *Wired* magazine contains such fodder for your imagination, as do many other technical magazines. Read about some of the possibilities, dream about how you will take the opportunities, and write about what you will achieve.

## HELEN'S SEARCH FOR ROOTS

Helen B. has always been curious about her family's history. She is part of the one and only family with her last name in the U.S. and for all she knows, in the world. She is intrigued by stories her father had told about his ancestors in Sweden whose past seems shrouded in mystery. All she knows is that the grandparents on both sides had immigrated from Sweden to the U.S. late in the 1800s. Helen's father told her that his grandfather had changed the family name to the one she has always known. One story her father had told her was that his own grandfather had been involved in an expedition to the North Pole in a hot air balloon. That is all she knows, but she wants to know more.

Because Helen is a mother of four young children, her life is very busy. She does not have the time or money to do extensive research outside her home. What she has is an insatiable desire to know more about her roots—and Internet access. She consulted Ancestry.com, which gave her a lot of information about relatives and ancestors in the U.S. She used the Ellis Island site, and searched its records as well as census records that were available online. Another site, http://www.Cyndislist.com, gave many links to genealogy-related sites. She wrote e-mail and letters to sleuth leads about her roots. What Helen needs, however, is more information about what had happened before the family came to the U.S. from Sweden.

To begin her search, Helen did what most people do when they want to find something on the Internet. She used a search engine. She typed in her family name at Google.com and hit *Search*. In .06 seconds, a list of 70 entries popped up. After eliminating those for each of her known relatives, she narrowed the list to Web sites concerning other people who have her own last name. Helen sent a message to the only one with an e-mail address listed on a Web page.

Within a few days, she received a reply. She was part of a larger family. The man told her that he was definitely related to her and there were only three families in Sweden with that name. She was related to them as well! The name she had found using the search engine happened to be her father's uncle's son. His grandfather had been involved in construction of instruments used in a hot air balloon expedition to the North Pole in the late 1890s! She also learned that the family name had indeed been changed. This information opened new doors of exploration into her family's history.

The newly found relatives have exchanged e-mail several times since then, and Helen is learning more about her family "on the other side of the pond." They also plan to exchange digital pictures of their other family members. She says, "Isn't it exciting? I don't think I would have found him without the Internet!"

**QUESTIONS**

1. Obviously, genealogists searched for roots many years before the advent of the Internet. How did they go about it? What do you think were the most effective methods of searching for one's roots? What problems might they have encountered?

2. In what ways have the Internet and the World Wide Web made life easier for people who want to search for their ancestors or do any kind of research? Do you think there are problems connected with online research?

3. Are there instances in which you think it would be easier to do more conventional researching? Do you think it is possible that a day will come when we don't need to consult libraries or hard copy documents for information?

4. Do a little research on the Internet about your own roots. What did you learn?

5. What advancements in research technology do you foresee in the next five years? Do you expect that your life will change because of these advancements? In what ways?

CASE STUDY

# NETWORK MANAGEMENT

■ OUTLINE

Part Five examines the considerations for designing, installing, and operating networks. You will learn why networks must be managed and don't just "run themselves," and why attention must be paid to network security, problem resolution, performance, and documentation.

Chapter 17 examines the vital topic of network security and explains many ways in which networks can be made more secure. You will cover encryption, digital signatures, and digital certificates in detail, and you will understand the importance of user IDs and strong passwords. You will investigate the threat of viruses and other network perils as well as steps that can be taken to minimize their impact.

Chapter 18 explains the network design and implementation process. You will learn that designing a new or changed network is a multiphase activity that requires user involvement along the way. You will study the various steps in the process, steps that are described and illustrated.

Chapter 19 describes the network management and network operations process. You will explore the reasons for managing a network and the standard management functions that are put into a network context. You will learn the practical issues of day-to-day operation of a network—including problem management, performance management, configuration management, and change management—and you will be given suggestions for performing each of these activities.

CHAPTER 17

# NETWORK SECURITY

## ■ OUTLINE

## ■ KEY TERMS

active security attacks

altering message contents

antivirus programs

application-level firewall

asymmetric key

bit-level encryption

Caesar cipher

call back

certificate authority (CA)

ciphertext

Data Encryption Standard (DES)

decryption

denial of service

digital certificate

digital signature

disaster

disaster recovery planning

eavesdropping

encryption

firewall

hacker

hash

hash function

hashing

infected

Internet Security Association and Key Management Protocol/Oakley (ISAKMP/Oakley)

| | | |
|---|---|---|
| key management | polyalphabetic cipher | signature |
| masquerading | Pretty Good Privacy (PGP) | strong password |
| message digest | | symmetric encryption techniques |
| monoalphabetic cipher | private key | |
| network security policy | proxy server | transposition cipher |
| packet filtering | public key | Triple DES |
| packet-level firewall | public key encryption (PKE) | user identification code (user ID) |
| passive security attacks | | |
| password | scrambler | virus |
| plaintext | secure socket layer (SSL) | worm |

## ■ OBJECTIVES

After you complete your study of this chapter, you should be able to:

- ■ explain why it is necessary to consider network security;
- ■ discuss management's responsibility for network security;
- ■ describe the key elements of a network security policy;
- ■ list and explain the types of security threats to a network;
- ■ explain the purpose, pros, and cons of encryption;
- ■ describe how symmetric and asymmetric key-based encryption systems work;
- ■ explain the uses and importance of digital signatures and certificates;
- ■ describe the various types of network access control that can be implemented;
- ■ discuss the need for disaster recovery planning; and
- ■ describe the elements of security for the home network.

## 17-1 INTRODUCTION

In previous chapters, you learned how network hardware and software systems operate and how applications use networks. This chapter describes network security and explains the types of security threats to a network and the various measures that can be implemented to increase a network's security.

Security is more than just preventing unauthorized access to and use of a network. It also includes being able to recover from security incidents that do occur and from potentially more serious outages caused by deliberate disruptive acts or natural disasters such as earthquakes, floods, or tornadoes.

## 17-2    WHY NETWORK SECURITY IS NEEDED

In just the last few years, the world has become a more dangerous place. When terrorist attacks, which have occurred all over the world, recently struck the U.S., our own level of awareness and concern about the threat of such events jumped several notches. Almost daily, we read about computer and network viruses—either about new attacks or the dangers of more potent viruses that are difficult to track and stop. We are strongly encouraged to install antivirus software if we own a computer. You may have experienced an attack on the Internet, during which you weren't able to access your favorite websites for several hours. Most corporations have experienced one or more outages because of viruses or denial of service attacks, although they are often loathe to report the attacks, sometimes out of embarrassment.

This increase in terrorist attacks on the general population, as well as on specific segments of our society's infrastructure, comes at a time when large and small organizations of all types are becoming increasingly dependent on networks to carry on their activities. Networks have become assets like computers, data, and information. Without these assets, most organizations find it impossible to conduct business. Communications with customers, suppliers, employees, and other organizations are handled primarily through networks. The loss of the network communications channel could effectively cripple an organization. No longer can a business be operated without having access to information and a reliable communication system. The network asset must be protected like other assets and surrounded with proper controls and the appropriate security. No wonder there is such a strong interest in the subjects of network and computer security. Organizational leaders and employees in all segments want to know what they can do to safeguard networks, their computers, and their livelihoods.

In the past, networks, when they existed, were mainly private. Therefore, they were fairly easy to control. With the rise of the Internet and its use for conducting business, parts of most organizations' networks are more open and vulnerable to unauthorized access, computer viruses, and attacks that are more aggressive than ever. The potential disruptions of application systems running on computer networks or the corruption of the underlying data are good reasons for organizations to take network security very seriously and to take action. Usually, the value of the data stored on networked computers far exceeds the cost of the networks themselves.

Notice that we did not say, "the chances of a network security problem are eliminated." It is virtually impossible to eliminate *all* network security problems. Solutions that work well today may not provide adequate protection tomorrow because technology continues to advance. Determined, creative, and unscrupulous people find ways to bypass or work around even the most stringent network security measures. We can minimize the risk of a major network security incident, however, by making it extremely difficult, expensive, or both to break through an organization's security defenses.

There is a wide body of literature, tools, and techniques oriented toward the protection of computers and their data from accidental or malicious misuse, theft, and destruction. In this chapter, we will focus on the tools and techniques necessary to protect data during its transmission through a network.

## 17-3 MANAGEMENT'S RESPONSIBILITY

In addition to the traditional responsibilities of designing and operating networks, the network management staff has a very important security responsibility. Not only does the network management staff have this responsibility, but senior management must lead the way by understanding the security issues and indicating to all employees that network security is important to the organization's well being. Without senior management sponsorship of security initiatives, the network management staff may not get the cooperation and support it requires from employees at all levels in the organization.

The fact that the information and tools needed to penetrate corporate networks are widely available has provided further impetus for a heightened concern about network security by companies throughout the world. For a company to adequately manage information security on the network, it must have the following:

- a network security policy that clearly defines the reasons why security is important to the company
- clearly defined roles and responsibilities to ensure that all aspects of security are performed
- a security implementation plan that describes the steps needed to implement the policy
- an effective implementation of appropriate security hardware and software
- a plan to deal with any security breaches that do occur
- a management review process to periodically ensure that the security policies and standards are adequate, effective, and are being enforced

**network security policy**

Each of these elements must be present. The **network security policy** is management's statement of the importance of and their commitment to network security. The policy needs to describe in general terms *what* will be done, but does not deal with *the way* the protection is to be achieved. Writing the policy is complex because, in reality, it is normally a part of a broader document: the organization's information security policy. The network security policy needs to clearly state management's position about the importance of network security and the items that are to be protected. Management must understand that there is no such thing as a perfectly secure network. Furthermore, network security is a constantly moving target because of advances in technology and the creativity of people who would like to break in to a network or its attached computers. Measures put in place to minimize security risks today will need to be upgraded in the future, and upgrades usually have a price attached, for which management will have to pay.

Simply writing the policy does not put the practices, procedures, or software in place to improve the security situation. That requires followthrough and communication with all employees so that they understand the emphasis and importance senior management in placing on security. Management, at all levels, needs to support the policy and periodically reinforce it with employees in various ways. IT and network staff may need to install additional hardware, software, and procedures to perform automated security checking.

Sometimes management appoints a network security officer who is responsible for seeing that the security policy and practices are carried out.

The security officer also investigates violations of the security policy and makes recommendations about additions to the security plan or changes that should be made. Most often, the security officer role is a part-time job for a member of the networking staff. However, it is important to ensure that the security responsibilities aren't short-changed by the press of other day-to-day work.

The management review process is a periodic check that the security program is operating properly. The initial step in the review process may be a security audit performed by the company's inside or outside auditors. The audit report serves as the basis for the management review.

## 17-4   TYPES OF THREATS

Security threats to a network can be divided into those that involve some sort of unauthorized access and all others. Once someone gains unauthorized access to the network, the range of things they can do is large. At the innocuous end of the scale, they may do nothing. Some people are just interested in the challenge of breaking through the security and have no interest in doing anything further. They may, however choose to monitor network traffic, called **eavesdropping,** for the purpose of learning something specific and perhaps disclosing it to others, or for the purpose of analyzing traffic patterns. Traffic analysis could lead to the observation, for example, that a flurry of traffic between two specific military bases occurs just before fighter jets are launched—and this pattern might be observed without even reading the content of the messages.  The above examples are all forms of **passive security attacks.** They are difficult to detect because the perpetrator does nothing overt but simply listens on the network.

The types of unauthorized access we usually think of, however, are the **active security attacks** whereby, after someone gains unauthorized access to the network, they take some overt action. Active attacks include **altering message contents, masquerading** as someone else, **denial of service,** and planting **viruses.**

- **Altering message contents** means changing the contents of a message, causing the message recipient to be misinformed or deceived. Examples include changing the value in a financial transaction, the name of a person authorized to conduct certain business, or a flight number.
- **Masquerading** is pretending to be someone else on the network, typically someone who had more privileges. A person might masquerade as a legitimate business on the Internet in order to obtain an unsuspecting purchaser's credit card number.
- **Denial of service** occurs when someone floods a site with messages faster than they can be handled, thereby degrading network performance. Other forms of denial of service include anything that prevents the normal use of communication facilities. For example, simply passing on e-mail chain letters can clog a network with unnecessary traffic and effectively deny service to legitimate users.
- **Planting viruses** can occur in many ways, but the most common are through an attachment to an e-mail or by downloading software containing a virus when a user logs on to an Internet website. Viruses range widely in their sophistication, destructiveness, and ease of eradication, but they are almost all troublesome.

eavesdropping

passive security attacks

active security attacks

altering message contents

masquerading

denial of service

viruses

Other types of security threats include:

- **Physical damage** to the network control center or any network facilities, such as circuits, switches, modems, servers, or data files.

- **Nonmalicious disruptions** caused by routine occurrences such as circuit failures, server failures, software bugs, and mistakes made by service or operations personnel. These kinds of disruptions need to be planned for as a part of normal network operation, and contingency plans should be put in place for the times these disruptions occur. These kinds of problems are usually not too serious unless they continue for long periods of time.

- **Disasters** caused by "acts of God" or acts of man, such as floods, fires, tornadoes, earthquakes, and bombings. These outages are severe and are usually of long duration. If contingency plans are not in place, disasters can literally put companies out of business.

## 17-5  ENCRYPTION

With so much information being transmitted by microwaves and satellites, it is virtually impossible to prevent the unauthorized reception of the signals. The problem is that neither the sender nor the receiver may be aware of the unauthorized reception until the unauthorized receiver has used the information for some illegal purpose, such as fraud. Furthermore, even signals sent on wired media are susceptible. The environment on WANs is different from LANS, or a computer room where data are transferred over cables that only run a short distance and are often heavily shielded. Data transmitted using WAN communications circuits travel relatively long distances on various media and are essentially unprotected. On both WAN and LAN circuits, it is relatively easy to find a place to tap cables, such as in out-of-the-way equipment rooms or in underground cable vaults.

To provide reasonable assurance that messages transmitted through a network remain confidential, they must be encrypted. For many years, encryption was rarely used except by the government, but it is widely used by companies and other organizations today because of the concern for data security and privacy. Financial institutions, for example, are big users of encryption techniques to conceal account numbers and amounts in the data they transmit. Encryption is of interest in both voice and data communications because sensitive information is communicated using both methods.

encryption

plaintext

ciphertext

symmetric encryption techniques

**Encryption** is the transformation of data into a meaningless form unreadable by anyone without a decryption key. Unencrypted information (often in readable form) is called **plaintext,** while encrypted data are called **ciphertext.** Modern encryption technology uses a mathematical algorithm and keys that are provided by the user. The encryption algorithm may be in the public domain, but the encrypted data can still be private because of the keys. Simple encryption techniques are described as **symmetric encryption techniques,** which means that the decrypting process is just the reverse of encrypting. A mathematical formula scrambles or encrypts the data using a key (usually a large number) that is provided by the user. To decrypt the data, the mathematical formula essentially processes the encrypted data in reverse, using the same key that was used to encrypt it. More complex encrypting techniques are asymmetric, meaning that the decryption process is different from the encryption process. We will look at both techniques in the paragraphs that follow.

## Monoalphabetic Ciphers

**monoalphabetic cipher**

A **monoalphabetic cipher** is a simple symmetric encryption scheme in which one plaintext character is replaced by another character. For example, the letter B may be substituted for an A, a C for a B, and so forth. This technique is very simple and very old, reportedly dating back to the days of Julius Caesar, hence it is sometimes called a **Caesar cipher.** As you can see, however, the technique is so simple that human analysts and computers can rapidly break this type of code. Therefore, while it is widely used, it is mainly found in children's games and other noncritical applications.

**Caesar cipher**

Some key attributes of a monoalphabetic cipher are that the same substitution character is always used for the corresponding plaintext character—a B for an A, C for a B. Any substitution character can be used. A # symbol could be substituted for an A, an ! symbol could be substituted for a B, but it is always the same, at least in a given message. It is convenient if there is a mathematical relationship between the original character and the substitution character because then computers can easily do the encrypting and decrypting. For example, as shown in Figure 17-1, using the ASCII code, if a binary 3 is added to the binary value of the letter A, it becomes the binary value for the letter D. So, the encryption algorithm might be to add a binary 3 to the binary value of the plaintext character yielding the encrypted substitution character. Figure 17-2 shows the plaintext and encrypted versions of a simple message using our "+3" encrypting algorithm.

Simple and easy to understand, isn't it? The problem is that it is too simple, because when all characters always have the same substitution character, one can look for the most frequently occurring letters in the encrypted message and make an educated guess that they are probably among the most often used characters such as *e, a, n,* and *t.* Also, a monoalphabetic cipher does nothing to conceal the original word lengths, so one can guess that encrypted words of one letter might be *a* or *I,* two-letter-encrypted words might be *or, is, an, it,* or *on,* and three-letter-encrypted words may be *and* or *the.* If you hadn't seen the plaintext for the message in Figure 17-2, it probably wouldn't take you too long to decode the message, and a suitably programmed computer could do it even faster.

The lesson to be learned is that a secure encryption system should mask the frequency with which letters occur and should conceal word lengths.

## Polyalphabetic Ciphers

**polyalphabetic cipher**

A **polyalphabetic cipher** solves one of the above problems by changing the letter frequencies. Like a monoalphabetic cipher, it substitutes each plaintext character with another, but not always the same one. A cipher is polyalphabetic if a given letter of the alphabet will not always be enciphered by the same ciphertext character.

FIGURE 17-1 Adding a binary 3 (011) to each ASCII character yields a new character.

| Letter | Binary Value | Add Binary 3 | Yields | |
|--------|--------------|--------------|--------|---|
| A | 1000001 | + 00000011 | 1000100 | D |
| B | 1000010 | + 00000011 | 1000101 | E |
| C | 1000011 | + 00000011 | 1000110 | F |
| D | 1000100 | + 00000011 | 1000111 | G |
| E | 1000101 | + 00000011 | 1001000 | H |
| F | 1000110 | + 00000011 | 1001001 | I |
| G | 1000111 | + 00000011 | 1001010 | J |
| H | 1001000 | + 00000011 | 1001011 | K |
| I | 1001001 | + 00000011 | 1001100 | L |
| J | 1001010 | + 00000011 | 1001101 | M |
| K | 1001011 | + 00000011 | 1001110 | N |
| L | 1001100 | + 00000011 | 1001111 | O |
| M | 1001101 | + 00000011 | 1010000 | P |
| N | 1001110 | + 00000011 | 1010001 | Q |
| O | 1001111 | + 00000011 | 1010010 | R |
| P | 1010000 | + 00000011 | 1010011 | S |
| Q | 1010001 | + 00000011 | 1010100 | T |
| R | 1010010 | + 00000011 | 1010101 | U |
| S | 1010011 | + 00000011 | 1010110 | V |
| T | 1010100 | + 00000011 | 1010111 | W |
| U | 1010101 | + 00000011 | 1011000 | X |
| V | 1010110 | + 00000011 | 1011001 | Y |
| W | 1010111 | + 00000011 | 1011010 | Z |
| X | 1011000 | + 00000011 | 1011011 | [ |
| Y | 1011001 | + 00000011 | 1011100 | \ |
| Z | 1011010 | + 00000011 | 1011101 | [ |
| [ | 1011011 | | | |
| \ | 1011100 | | | |
| ] | 1011101 | | | |

FIGURE 17-2 An encrypted message using the "+3" algorithm.

```
Plaintext:      SEND ONE DOZEN ROSES TO MY SWEETHEART IMMEDIATELY

Encrypted
Text:           VHQG RQH GR]HQ URVHV WR P\ VZHHWKHDUW LPPHGLDWHO\
```

An important example of polyalphabetic encryption is the Vigenère cipher developed in 1586 by the French diplomat Blaise de Vigenère. To encrypt by Vigenère cipher, you need a keyword and the Vigenère square shown in Figure 17-3. To encrypt a message, we write the keyword repeatedly over the text of the message. The letter of the keyword that is above a plaintext letter determines the row of the square that will be used to encrypt the plaintext character.

**FIGURE 17-3** A Vigenère square.

**Message letters**

| | A | B | C | D | E | F | G | H | I | J | K | L | M | N | O | P | Q | R | S | T | U | V | W | X | Y | Z |
|---|---|---|---|---|---|---|---|---|---|---|---|---|---|---|---|---|---|---|---|---|---|---|---|---|---|---|
| **A** | A | B | C | D | E | F | G | H | I | J | K | L | M | N | O | P | Q | R | S | T | U | V | W | X | Y | Z |
| **B** | B | C | D | E | F | G | H | I | J | K | L | M | N | O | P | Q | R | S | T | U | V | W | X | Y | Z | A |
| **C** | C | D | E | F | G | H | I | J | K | L | M | N | O | P | Q | R | S | T | U | V | W | X | Y | Z | A | B |
| **D** | D | E | F | G | H | I | J | K | L | M | N | O | P | Q | R | S | T | U | V | W | X | Y | Z | A | B | C |
| **E** | E | F | G | H | I | J | K | L | M | N | O | P | Q | R | S | T | U | V | W | X | Y | Z | A | B | C | D |
| **F** | F | G | H | I | J | K | L | M | N | O | P | Q | R | S | T | U | V | W | X | Y | Z | A | B | C | D | E |
| **G** | G | H | I | J | K | L | M | N | O | P | Q | R | S | T | U | V | W | X | Y | Z | A | B | C | D | E | F |
| **H** | H | I | J | K | L | M | N | O | P | Q | R | S | T | U | V | W | X | Y | Z | A | B | C | D | E | F | G |
| **I** | I | J | K | L | M | N | O | P | Q | R | S | T | U | V | W | X | Y | Z | A | B | C | D | E | F | G | H |
| **J** | J | K | L | M | N | O | P | Q | R | S | T | U | V | W | X | Y | Z | A | B | C | D | E | F | G | H | I |
| **K** | K | L | M | N | O | P | Q | R | S | T | U | V | W | X | Y | Z | A | B | C | D | E | F | G | H | I | J |
| **L** | L | M | N | O | P | Q | R | S | T | U | V | W | X | Y | Z | A | B | C | D | E | F | G | H | I | J | K |
| **M** | M | N | O | P | Q | R | S | T | U | V | W | X | Y | Z | A | B | C | D | E | F | G | H | I | J | K | L |
| **N** | N | O | P | Q | R | S | T | U | V | W | X | Y | Z | A | B | C | D | E | F | G | H | I | J | K | L | M |
| **O** | O | P | Q | R | S | T | U | V | W | X | Y | Z | A | B | C | D | E | F | G | H | I | J | K | L | M | N |
| **P** | P | Q | R | S | T | U | V | W | X | Y | Z | A | B | C | D | E | F | G | H | I | J | K | L | M | N | O |
| **Q** | Q | R | S | T | U | V | W | X | Y | Z | A | B | C | D | E | F | G | H | I | J | K | L | M | N | O | P |
| **R** | R | S | T | U | V | W | X | Y | Z | A | B | C | D | E | F | G | H | I | J | K | L | M | N | O | P | Q |
| **S** | S | T | U | V | W | X | Y | Z | A | B | C | D | E | F | G | H | I | J | K | L | M | N | O | P | Q | R |
| **T** | T | U | V | W | X | Y | Z | A | B | C | D | E | F | G | H | I | J | K | L | M | N | O | P | Q | R | S |
| **U** | U | V | W | X | Y | Z | A | B | C | D | E | F | G | H | I | J | K | L | M | N | O | P | Q | R | S | T |
| **V** | V | W | X | Y | Z | A | B | C | D | E | F | G | H | I | J | K | L | M | N | O | P | Q | R | S | T | U |
| **W** | W | X | Y | Z | A | B | C | D | E | F | G | H | I | J | K | L | M | N | O | P | Q | R | S | T | U | V |
| **X** | X | Y | Z | A | B | C | D | E | F | G | H | I | J | K | L | M | N | O | P | Q | R | S | T | U | V | W |
| **Y** | Y | Z | A | B | C | D | E | F | G | H | I | J | K | L | M | N | O | P | Q | R | S | T | U | V | W | X |
| **Z** | Z | A | B | C | D | E | F | G | H | I | J | K | L | M | N | O | P | Q | R | S | T | U | V | W | X | Y |

*Keyword letters* (vertical axis label)

Let's look at an example. Suppose the message we want to encrypt is "I love studying networking" and the keyword we have chosen is "youmustbecrazy." We make a table like this:

| **Keyword** | y | o | u | m | u | s | t | b | e | c | r | a | z | y | y | o | u | m | u | s | t | b | e |
|---|---|---|---|---|---|---|---|---|---|---|---|---|---|---|---|---|---|---|---|---|---|---|---|
| **Message** | i | l | o | v | e | s | t | u | d | y | i | n | g | n | e | t | w | o | r | k | i | n | g |

To encrypt the first *i*, we look in the *y*th row of the *i*th column of the Vigenère square to find *g*. To encrypt the next letter, *l*, we look in the *o*th row of the *l*th column to find *z*. The encrypted message is thus:

| g | z | i | h | y | k | m | v | h | a | z | n | f | l | c | h | q | a | l | c | b | o | k |
|---|---|---|---|---|---|---|---|---|---|---|---|---|---|---|---|---|---|---|---|---|---|---|

Certainly, the encrypted message, "g zihy kmvhaznf lchqalcbok," is more difficult to figure out than the previous example encrypted with a monoalphabetic cipher. But if you think about it for a moment, you will see that there are just 26 ways to encrypt a letter or a word. In a long message, common words such as *the, and, a, I,* and others may appear many times and an experienced cryptographer or computer trying to decrypt the message may spot patterns that provide important clues to the encryption technique used. Furthermore, while a long key, such as the one used above is better than a short key for encrypting the plaintext, even in this simple case, the key is more than half as long as the original text, and communicating it to the authorized receivers and storing it securely are separate problems that must be dealt with. Hence, while the polyalphabetic cipher is an improvement over the monoalphabetic cipher, it is clearly not strong enough in these days of powerful computerized decryption techniques.

## Transposition Ciphers

**transposition ciphers**

**Transposition ciphers** rearrange the letters in the plaintext message rather than substituting cipher characters for them. Typically, the text to be processed is filled into a table and the ciphertext is obtained by reading the table a different way. For example, if we wish to encode the message, "Company results are as expected," we might put the letters into a table as follows:

| c | o | m | p | a |
|---|---|---|---|---|
| n | y |   | r | e |
| s | u | l | t | s |
|   | a | r | e |   |
| a | s |   | e | x |
| p | e | c | t | e |
| d |   |   |   |   |

We would then transmit the characters by column instead of by row. We would send "cns apd oyuase m lr c prteet aes xe." Alternately, we could employ a secret number, such as 24351, that indicates that the columns will be transmitted in a different sequence. In that case, column 2 would be sent first, followed by column 4, and so forth. The resulting message would be: "oyuase prteet m lr c aes xe cns apd," a slight variation of the first encrypted version of the message.

Transposition ciphers are not very secure, however. The letter frequencies are maintained so that an unauthorized receiver might notice the high frequency of common letters, which would be a good indication that letter substitutions had not been used. If the receiver suspected that a transposition cipher had been used, she might try grouping the letters into matrices of various sizes, looking for words to emerge. A computer could try thousands of combinations and would break a simple transposition cipher very quickly.

Of course, a transposition cipher can be made more complex by, for example, putting the text into the table by diagonals or spirally. Furthermore, a double transposition could be performed in which the encrypted text is further transposed by putting it into a second table and transposing it again. Nonetheless, transposition encryption techniques are still not as secure as other techniques that will be discussed.

## Bit-Level Encryption

bit-level encryption

The next level of sophistication in encryption technology is **bit-level encryption.** This technique ignores the characters that make up the message to be transmitted and instead works with the individual bits that make up the characters. A key, which is also a string of bits, is applied to the bits of the plaintext to encrypt it. A common method is performed as follows.

The encryption key is determined as a certain number of bits, basically the more the better. Sixty-four and 128 bit keys are common. The plaintext message is divided into strings of bits that are the same length as the key. Each string of plaintext bits is encrypted by computing the exclusive OR (XOR) between it and the encryption key. The exclusive OR is a mathematical operation of Boolean algebra and can be described verbally as "Either A or B, but not both," meaning that if in a given position of the string either the plain text bit or the encryption key bit is a 1, the encrypted text bit is a 1. However, if both the plain text and encryption key bits are the same, either both 1s or both 0s, then the encrypted text bit is a 0. This is illustrated in Figure 17-4.

It turns out that the XOR operation is reversible. XORing the encryption key against the encrypted text will yield the original plaintext, as illustrated in Figure 17-5. Decrypting the text is not a reversal of the encryption operation but a repetition of it. The encryption and decryption keys are the same.

The longer the key, the greater the security of a bit-level encryption, but as with the other encryption systems you have studied so far, there is always the problem of communicating the key to the authorized receiver of the message in a secure way.

## The Data Encryption Standard (DES)

With powerful computers available to assist those who would try to receive and decrypt messages illicitly, none of the methods discussed so far is strong enough to stop a determined effort to break the code. What is needed is an approach that uses a complex series of steps to encrypt data while still keeping encryption keys short enough to be manageable.

Data Encryption Standard (DES)

One well-known encryption technique is the **Data Encryption Standard (DES),** which was developed by IBM in the early 1970s. The DES algorithm, in its original form, encrypts blocks of 64 bits using a 56-bit key that yields $2^{56}$, or more than 72 quadrillion possibilities! The algorithm uses a 19-step combination of substitutions and transpositions similar to the simpler encryption techniques you studied earlier. The output of each step is input to the next step, with the last step producing the encrypted 64-bit block to be

**FIGURE 17-4**  Bit-level encryption using the XOR operation. For simplicity, only a 16-bit substring of text and a 16-bit encryption key are used.

| | |
|---|---|
| Plaintext: | 1010111001100010 |
| Encryption key: | 1110010110000101 |
| Encrypted text: | 0100101111100111 |

**FIGURE 17-5**  Decryption is a *repetition* of the encryption process using another XOR operation.

| | |
|---|---|
| Encrypted text: | 0100101111100111 |
| Encryption key: | 1110010110000101 |
| Plaintext: | 1010111001100010 |

**decryption**

transmitted. At the receiving end, the reverse process, **decryption,** occurs, using the same steps in reverse and the same key. The entire DES process has been implemented in VLSI chips that can be designed into other hardware, making the encryption process very fast, despite its complexity.

Given the rapid increase in computing power that has occurred in recent years, the DES encryption standard is vulnerable to a brute force attack. A powerful computer could be built that would have a good chance of determining a DES key in three or four hours by trying all $2^{56}$ key possibilities. To solve the problem, a new version called **Triple DES** was developed. Triple DES doubles the length of the key to 112 bits. The block of plaintext is encrypted with the first 56 bits of the key. Then it is encrypted again with the second 56 bits, and finally a third time with the first 56 bits. The resulting encrypted text is much harder to decrypt and would require $2^{112}$ unique attempts instead of $2^{56}$ for standard DES.

**Triple DES**

Because the receiving end must know which key the transmitting end used, methods must be put in place to get the key from the transmitting end to the receiving end while protecting its confidentiality. This takes a combination of technical and management techniques, and in many situations, **key management** is a high-cost overhead to the encryption. For example, couriers may have to be employed to deliver the keys, which are stored on magnetic tape. The couriers have to be trusted, and the tapes with the keys may need to be stored in secure boxes. The possibility that the keys could be disclosed is high. There are other techniques and technologies that alleviate the situation by allowing keys to be transmitted electronically, by employing combinations of keys, or by having the receiver solve a series of puzzles to determine the key. However, key sharing still represents a weakness in this and any other symmetric encryption system.

**key management**

## Asymmetric Key Encryption

In 1976, an alternative encryption technique was developed at Stanford University. Messages are encrypted with one key that can be made public. The recipient uses a separate private key to decipher the text. This technique, called **public key encryption (PKE),** was implemented by a team at MIT and is now marketed by RSA Security, Inc. The company's website may be found at http://www.rsasecurity.com/.

**public key encryption (PKE)**

As the name suggests, this encryption technique uses an **asymmetric key.** That is, the key used for encryption and the key used for decryption are not the same. A user, we'll call her Tammy, picks her own set of keys, an encryption key, and a decryption key. Tammy publishes the encryption key so that everyone has access to it, and it is referred to as the **public key.** She keeps the decryption key secret, and it is commonly referred to as the **private key.** When someone (call him David) wants to send her a message, he uses Tammy's public key to encrypt the message. She can decrypt the message using her private key. Similarly if Kate, Jeannine, or Jennifer wants to send Tammy encrypted messages, they can use her public key, but only Tammy can decrypt the message with her private key. The asymmetric key technique solves the problem of transporting the key between the sender of the message and the recipient.

**asymmetric key**

**public key**

**private key**

The decryption key used with the asymmetric key technique is normally two very large prime numbers, and the encryption key is the product of the two. It turns out that if the prime numbers are sufficiently large, it is almost impossible to reverse the multiplication and deduce the original two numbers (the decryption key) if only the product (the encryption key) is known. In practical applications, the prime numbers chosen are very large—in the range of $10^{130}$ to $10^{310}$. Using the largest numbers, it has been estimated that the combined efforts of one hundred million PCs would take one thousand years to crack such a key!

The great advantage of asymmetric key encryption is that it solves the problem of key exchange. Tammy doesn't care who knows her public key because it is used only for encrypting messages. She still needs to keep her private key, the one used for decryption, secret, but she can safeguard its identity. Because it is relatively invulnerable, asymmetric key encryption has been widely implemented in products such as Netscape Navigator, Lotus Notes, and Internet Explorer, and it is in general use when data are encrypted on the Internet.

## Pretty Good Privacy (PGP)

**Pretty Good Privacy (PGP)**

**Pretty Good Privacy (PGP)** is an asymmetric encryption/decryption program for e-mail, computer data, and voice conversations. It was developed in 1991 by Phillip R. Zimmerman, who distributed the software on the Internet for no charge. PGP is such an effective encryption tool that Zimmerman was sued by the U.S. Government for putting it in the public domain and hence making it available to enemies of the U.S. After a public outcry the lawsuit was dropped, but it is still illegal to use PGP in some countries.

PGP has become one of the most common ways to protect data on the Internet because it is effective, easy to use, and still free. PGP is based on the asymmetric key method using private and public keys. To encrypt a message using PGP, you need the PGP encryption package, which is available at http://www.pgp.com/ and from a number of other sources. PGP can also add digital signatures (discussed in the next section of this chapter) to messages, thereby assuring the receiver that the message is authentic. There is a plethora of information about PGP on the Internet. Conduct a search in Google or another search engine and you will find many sources.

## Other Encryption Systems

While PGP was the first of a genre of products that made it relatively easy for anyone to encrypt their information, there is a host of other products available that provide the same or similar capability. One of the most widely available is Microsoft's Encrypting File System, which is built into the new technology file system (NTFS) of Windows 2000 and XP Professional. It is a form of PKE that provides a basic level of protection and is very easy to use. You right click on any file or folder you want to encrypt, select Properties/General/Advanced, and then click on the "Encrypt contents to secure data" check box and the file or folder is encrypted. WinZip 9.0 has 128- and 256-bit AES encryption for zipped files. ScramDisk provides 64- or 128-bit encryption and its successor product, DriveCrypt, offers 1,344-bit military strength encryption. There are other products, too, and one would do well to search the Internet for the latest information about available products before making a selection.

## Voice Scrambling

**scramblers**

In the voice world, we can identify a person we are talking to by the sound of his or her voice. In most situations, this provides adequate security, but for those cases where more security is required, voice encryption devices, commonly called **scramblers,** can be used. They make the voice transmission unintelligible to anyone who does not have a descrambler, effectively rendering wiretapping useless. Scramblers are used to some extent in government and the Department of Defense, but are not widely used in industry.

The decision to encrypt data (or scramble voice) must be made carefully. The cost of the encryption hardware or software can be determined easily. The time that it takes a computer to encrypt or decrypt the data if software is used can be calculated and a monetary value placed on it. One must also calculate the throughput delays that occur during the encryption/decryption process and determine whether they are significant. Finally, the administrative or management costs of managing the keys, keeping them secure, and changing them regularly must be considered.

## 17-6 DIGITAL SIGNATURES

**digital signature**

A **digital signature** is the network equivalent of signing a message and guaranteeing that the contents have not been changed. The receiver knows that the message could have come only from you, and you cannot deny that you sent it. Like a written signature, the purposes of a digital signature are to guarantee that the individual sending the message really is who he claims to be, that the message has arrived intact, and that the sender cannot dispute that he sent it. For a digital signal to be effective, someone else should not be able to imitate (forge) it, and it should be capable of being automatically time stamped. There are a number of encryption techniques that guarantee this level of security.

Digital signatures are especially important for electronic commerce and are a key component of most authentication systems. They can be used regardless of whether the document they are attached to is encrypted or not. To sign a message, the sender simply invokes a software routine that builds the signature using a private key known only to him. The recipient can decode the signature using the sender's public key and knows who sent the message because only the sender has the private key that performed the encryption. No one else could have created the encrypted message that was decrypted with that public key. In this way, the author of the message has been validated.

**hash function**

**hashing**

**message digest**

**hash**

To ensure that the contents of the message are not changed, digital signature software usually contains another routine. This routine, called a **hash function,** uses a mathematical process called **hashing** that crunches the data and calculates a unique value for the document called the **message digest** or the **hash.** The hash function works such that if anything in the document changes—a space is added, two characters are reversed, etc.—the calculated hash value will be different. Therefore, if the hash is calculated again at the receiving end of the transmission and the value is the same, the recipient knows that the message is exactly the same as the one that was sent.

Look at Figure 17-6 for an example. Assume that you were going to send a sales agreement to a real estate agent in another city. You want to give the agent the assurance that the document is really from you and that what he receives is exactly what you sent.

- you copy the contract into an e-mail note
- the hash function calculates the hash for the e-mail message (note that the original message still exists)
- the software then encrypts the hash using your private key—the encrypted hash is your digital signature and it is appended to the original message

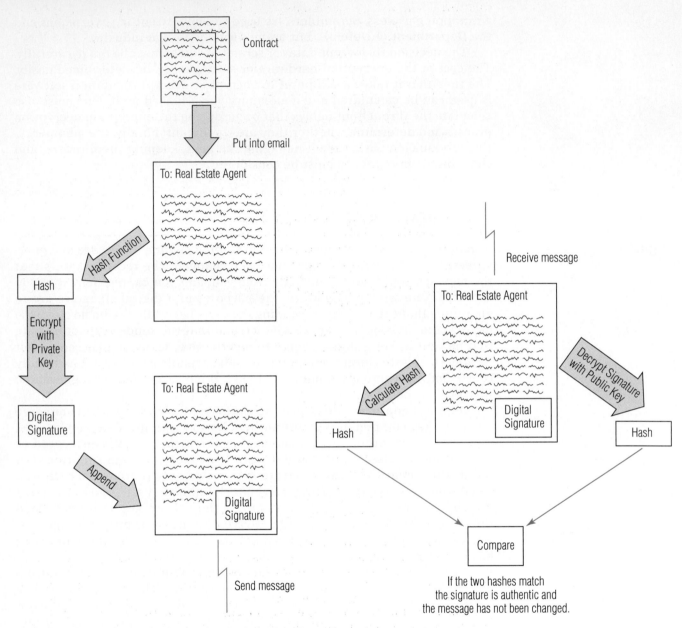

**FIGURE 17-6**    The digital signature process.

At the other end, the real estate agent receives the message:

- to make sure it is intact and from you, the agent's software calculates the hash of the received message
- it then decrypts the hash that was appended to your message using your public key
- if the hashes match, the received message is valid

Note that, in this example, the message itself was not encrypted when it was transmitted—only the digital signature was. The process works equally well if there is also a need to encrypt the entire message to protect its contents. The advantage of not encrypting the entire document, especially if it is long, is the savings in processing time at both ends of the transmission for the encryption and decryption process.

## 17-7  DIGITAL CERTIFICATES

**digital certificate**

A **digital certificate** is a password-protected, encrypted data file that identifies a transmitting entity and certifies that it is who it says it is. The certificate contains the name of the person or individual, a serial number, an expiration date, a copy of the certificate holder's public key (which serves to verify the digital signature of the sender when she encrypts it with her private key), and the digital signature of the holder so that the recipient can verify that the certificate is real. Using certificates and keys, the sender and receiver can authenticate each other, an important capability in many transactions, especially in a buy-sell relationship where the parties probably do not know each other and where money is being exchanged for goods or services. Without digital certificates, it would be possible, though perhaps difficult, for a person to substitute a private-public key pair and impersonate someone else for fraudulent purposes.

**certificate authorities (CA)**

A small number of companies, called **certificate authorities (CA)** issue digital certificates. The role of the CA is to guarantee that the organization or individual granted the certificate is who he claims to be. The certificate also guarantees that the holder's public key really belongs to him. A trustworthy CA will issue a certificate only after verifying the identity of the certificate's subject. The CA usually has an arrangement with a financial institution or credit card company, which provides it with information to confirm an individual's or organization's identity. Digital certificates can be kept in online registries so that users can look up other user's public keys.

A certificate is valid only for the period of time specified by the CA that issued it. The certificate contains information about its beginning and expiration dates. The CA can also revoke certificates it has issued, and it maintains a list of revoked certificates. This list is published by the CA so that anyone can check the validity of any certificate.

Using digital certificates can protect your security when dealing with personal or financial transactions on the Internet, because they bind the identity of the certificate holder to a pair of electronic keys. The certificate assures that the keys actually belong to the person or organization specified. Most Web browsers come with certificates installed for some CAs and other organizations. You can install and remove certificates for other organizations that you deal with. The advantage is that online transactions with those entities become automatic with all of the security checking done for you by the browser behind the scenes. In Internet Explorer, for example, you go to the Tools menu, click Internet Options, click the Content tab, and then click Certificates. You can, of course, use the help function to obtain a detailed explanation of the many options available.

If you need to obtain a certificate yourself because, for example, you publish software and you want the CA to certify to others that the software came from you, you would follow these steps:

1. Send a certification request containing your name, public key, and other information to a CA.
2. The CA creates a message from your request containing most of the data in the certificate, signs the message with its private key obtaining

a digital signature in the process, and returns the message and the signature to you. The two parts together form the certificate.

3. You send the certificate to a correspondent to convey trust in your public key.

4. The correspondent verifies the signature on the certificate using the CA's public key. If the CA's signature is verified, the correspondent knows that he can accept your public key as valid.

Anyone can verify at any time that the certificate was signed by the CA without access to any secret information. One only needs to get a copy of the CA's certificate in order to access its public key.

## 17-8   IP SECURITY (IPSEC)

IPsec was introduced in Chapter 13, so you know that it is a standardized set of protocols designed to support the secure exchange of packets at the IP layer. IPsec provides security for the transmission of sensitive information over unprotected networks such as the Internet. IPsec acts at the network layer, protecting and authenticating IP packets between IPsec-compliant devices.

**Internet Security Association and Key Management Protocol/Oakley (ISAKMP/Oakley)**

For IPsec to work, the sending and receiving devices must share a public key. This is accomplished through a protocol known as **Internet Security Association and Key Management Protocol/Oakley (ISAKMP/Oakley),** which allows the receiver to obtain a public key and authenticate the sender using digital certificates.

IPsec provides the following network security services:

- data confidentiality—The IPsec sending station can encrypt packets before transmitting them across a network.

- data integrity—The IPsec receiver can authenticate packets sent by the IPsec sender to ensure that the data has not been altered during transmission.

- data origin authentication—The IPsec receiver can authenticate the source of the IPsec packets sent. This service is dependent upon the data integrity service.

- Anti-replay—The IPsec receiver can detect and reject packets that have been received correctly but which are sent more than once (duplicated).

These services are all optional and may be used or not used according to local security policy.

IPsec provides secure tunnels between two peer nodes, such as two routers or servers. The user defines which packets should be sent through these secure tunnels and determines the parameters used to protect the packets. When IPsec sees the sensitive packets, it sets up the secure tunnel and sends the packet through the secure tunnel to the remote peer. Multiple IPsec tunnels can exist between two peers to secure different data streams, and each tunnel may have separate parameters. For example, data could be encrypted using the DES standard for one tunnel, and using the RSA algorithm for a second tunnel.

One common use of VPNs with IPsec is for a mobile user to establish a secure connection back to his office. For example, a salesman could establish an IPsec tunnel between his laptop and a corporate firewall to gain access to the corporate network from a hotel room in the evening. All of the traffic between the salesman and the firewall will be authenticated. The salesman could then establish an additional IPsec tunnel with a server on the corporate network, requesting data privacy services by having the data encrypted. All of this can be set up in the software so that the connections are established quite automatically—the salesman does not need to be a network guru to make it happen!

## 17-9   SECURE SOCKET LAYER (SSL)

One particular need for security that deserves special mention is that between a Web browser and a Web server on the Internet. When, for example, a home user wants to purchase an item from a website, the buyer may need to supply her credit card number. She wants assurance that the number will be secure while traveling through the Internet.

secure socket layer
(SSL)

Netscape developed **secure socket layer (SSL)** as a transport level technology for authentication between a Web browser and a Web server. SSL runs above the TCP layer and below the application layer and negotiates point-to-point security between a client and a server. It allows an SSL-enabled server to authenticate itself to an SSL-enabled client, allows the client to authenticate itself to the server, and allows both machines to establish an encrypted connection.

SSL server authentication allows a user to confirm the server's identity. An SSL-enabled client can use standard techniques of PKE to check that a server's certificate is valid and has been issued by a certificate authority listed in the client's list of trusted CAs. SSL client authentication allows a server to confirm a user's identity. Using the same techniques as those for server authentication, SSL-enabled server software can check that a client's certificate is valid. This confirmation might be important, for example, if the server is sending confidential financial information to a customer and wants to be sure of the recipient's identity.

The SSL protocol includes two subprotocols: the SSL Handshake Protocol and the SSL Record Protocol. The Record Protocol defines the format used to transmit data. The Handshake Protocol uses the record protocol to exchange a series of messages between the SSL-enabled client and server when they first establish a connection. In this way, they authenticate themselves to each other and establish which encryption technique they will use. Acceptable techniques include DES, Triple DES, RSA, and several others. Symmetric key encryption is much faster than PKE, but PKE provides better authentication techniques. Normally, the client and server identify the strongest encryption technique they have in common and use that for the SSL session. Once the handshaking is complete, the communication proceeds until either the client or the server terminates it.

Both Netscape Navigator and Internet Explorer support SSL, and many websites use the protocol when they need to obtain confidential information. By convention, Web pages that require an SSL connection start with https:// instead of http://. You can recognize the secure nature of the connection by the "s" or the little lock at the bottom of the Web browser's screen when a secure connection is enabled.

## 17-10 VIRUSES

No discussion of network security would be complete without at least a brief mention of computer viruses, which also includes **worms**. Actually, most viruses are more of a problem for the OSs of computers, but because most computers these days are attached to networks and because viruses are most often transported from place to place through a network, they become a network issue.

Initially, virus programs were written by **hackers**, people who write programs for enjoyment. Early viruses were clever programs that simply proved to the hacker that he could cause a certain action to occur, most likely with no harm intended. It didn't take long, however, for more malevolent people to use the clever virus programming for more harmful purposes, and the reputation of hackers went from neutral to negative. Even today, the term hacker usually conjures up thoughts of evil programmers, a reputation that is not entirely deserved. Some are and some aren't.

A virus is usually a set of computer instructions that attaches itself to a program in a computer. When the program executes, the virus causes it to do something that was not originally intended by the program's designers. Program files that have a virus attached are said to be **infected**. We tend to think that all viruses do harmful things, but that isn't necessarily so, although the fact that they have entered a computer without being invited can be considered harmful in itself. On the other hand, some viruses do obviously harmful things such as erasing files or even entire hard disks.

Rather than being located on a computer's disk, some viruses copy themselves into memory and become memory resident. They typically change one of the OS's internal tables that contain the addresses of service routines, which provide operating system services to user programs. When a user program requests the service, the virus program gets control, does its deed, and then branches to the service routine. Because this all happens very quickly, the user is none the wiser and has no idea that the virus program executed until the results of its execution become evident, sometimes much later.

Viruses spread much like their biological counterparts—by sharing. One of the most common ways viruses spread is through infected files attached to e-mail messages. When a recipient opens the infected e-mail attachment, the virus infects his computer. Some viruses even search the infected computer for addresses of other e-mail correspondents and automatically send infected e-mails to all of them. Once the e-mail is opened on another newly infected machine, the search begins again. In this way, the virus can propagate itself in just a few minutes to thousands of computers. Viruses can also spread when users download infected programs from a server or copy infected files from a diskette or other removable media. Because a virus that enters a server used by hundreds or thousands of people can spread very quickly, owners of servers and websites usually take strong measures to ensure that the files on their hardware are clean and virus free.

**Antivirus programs** work by looking for a sequence of computer instructions that is unique to the virus. This sequence, called the **signature**, is stored in a file that comes with the antivirus program along with the signatures of all other known viruses. When the antivirus program executes, it scans the disk of the computer it is searching, looking for any byte patterns that match the patterns in the signature file. When a match is found, a virus has normally been detected, and the user is usually notified with a message on the screen of the computer, asking or suggesting what action to take. Antivirus programs also know how to deactivate viruses, and the usual response of the user is to have the antivirus program perform the deactivation.

*worm*

*hacker*

*infected*

*antivirus program*

*signature*

As new viruses are written and their signatures are determined, companies that sell antivirus programs update their software and signature files and notify their customers that updates are available. Subscriptions are available and for a small fee the better vendors, such as Norton and McAfee, will automatically download updates to a subscriber's computer through the Internet.

Installing an antivirus program on every computer and keeping the signature file up-to-date is the best way the average person or organization can prevent virus attacks from causing serious damage. It is important to assume that viruses will enter your home or workplace computer, either through the network or by the sharing an infected file. Prevention, by having an up-to-date antivirus program in place and running, is the best way to deal with the threat.

## 17-11   NETWORK ACCESS CONTROL

Network access adds another dimension to the protection of data and information. Using networks, data can be accessed by people from anywhere in the world, and a new set of questions emerges:

- How do we know who is at the terminal?
- Once we know who is at the terminal, is the person authorized to access the data or information?
- What operations are the terminal user authorized to perform?
- Is it possible that the communications lines could be tapped?

There are three primary ways that someone can gain unauthorized access to an organization's network:

1. Accessing from another network such as the Internet
2. Dialing directly into the network
3. Using a workstation located on the organization's premises

Several types of people try to gain unauthorized access to corporate networks. The most infamous and widely publicized are dedicated professional hackers (the malevolent kind) who break into networks and computers with malicious intent, perhaps to destroy data, commit fraud, or—in the case of government networks—commit espionage. A second group, almost as well publicized, is made up of people who break in mainly to prove they can do it. If they are successful, they may do harm (such as destroying data) or they may simply leave messages that, in effect, say, "I was here." People in this category may also be hackers who are experts on network security, or they may be casual users who simply surf the Internet looking for networks or websites that are easy to break into, perhaps because the network or website managers have "left the door open," so to speak. An additional type of intruder is an employee who has legitimate access to an organization's network but who tries to access unauthorized information.

### User Identification and Passwords

**user identification code (user ID)**

Network access control techniques begin by ensuring that all legitimate users of a network have a unique **user identification code (user ID)** and

**password**

secret **password.** Users should be required to log in each time they use a workstation on the network by entering their identification code and password. Employees should be required to change passwords frequently—at least every 60 days—and should be required to create **strong passwords.**

**strong password**

Strong passwords have the following characteristics:

- are at least seven characters in length (the longer, the better)
- include upper and lower case letters, numerals, and symbols
- have at least one symbol character in the second through sixth position
- have at least four different characters
- look like a sequence of random letters and numbers

Also, they should not:

- contain any part of the user's user ID
- use any actual word or name in any language
- use numbers in place of similar letters
- reuse any portion of an old password
- use consecutive letters or numbers, like "abcdefg" or "234567"
- use adjacent keys on the keyboard, like "qwerty"

Software should automatically record the user identification and password, along with the date, time, and workstation ID in a central file on a computer so that a complete record is kept of all users of the system. When someone tries to log on and enters an incorrect password a predetermined number of times, his ability to log on should be disabled, recorded in a security log, and a security officer should be notified. Reactivation of the user identification code should be done only when it has been determined that the user really is authorized. Supervision usually is required to reauthorize the user, and a new password is issued.

**call back**

Dial-up data lines are especially vulnerable to unauthorized access. One security technique used with dial-up data circuits is **call back.** With a call back technique, the user dials the computer and identifies herself. The computer breaks the connection and then dials the user back at a predetermined number that it obtains from a table stored in memory. The disadvantage of this technique is that it does not work very well for salespeople or other people who are traveling and calling from various locations. The handshake technique requires a terminal with special hardware circuitry. The computer sends a special control sequence to the terminal and the terminal identifies itself to the computer. This technique ensures that only authorized terminals access the computer—it does not regulate the users of those terminals.

In addition to these techniques, it is important that network operations management monitor the use of dial-up computer ports for suspicious or unusual activity. Reading a printed log of all dial-in accesses or attempts is the way this is usually done. In particularly sensitive applications, such as the transmission of financial transactions or data about new product developments, encryption can be employed to scramble the data so that if unauthorized access to the computer or data is obtained, the data are still unreadable without further work to decrypt them.

**FIGURE 17-7** A firewall at the boundary of two networks.

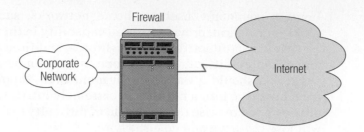

## Firewalls

firewall

A relatively effective technique for limiting unauthorized access to an organization's network from outside is to install a **firewall.** A firewall is a combination of hardware and software that enforces a boundary between two or more networks, for example, between a corporate network and the Internet to which it is connected, as shown in Figure 17-7. Without a firewall, anyone on one network could theoretically get into the other network and pick up or dump information. The primary purpose of the firewall, in this case, is to provide a single point of entry and exit from the corporate network by controlling access from one network to another. The firewall allows access to resources on the Internet from inside the organization and controlled access from the Internet to the internal network's computers and data. One company, whose employees all use PC workstations, allows all of its people to pass through the firewall and access an Internet website that is managed by another organization and that contains information about the employees' 401K retirement savings program.

While there are several ways to implement a firewall, traditionally it is implemented using a router, a server, or both in combination. A router running **packet-level firewall** software can examine all network traffic at the packet level, allowing or denying packet passage from one network to the other based on the source and destination addresses. This technique is called **packet filtering.** A server can act as an **application-level firewall** if it examines and controls data at the application level. The server looks at entire messages and does a more detailed analysis of the appropriateness before making a decision whether or not to let the traffic pass.

packet-level firewall

packet filtering

application-level firewall

proxy server

A **proxy server** is a form of application server that works differently. Proxy servers change the network addresses from one form to another so that users or computers on one network do not know the actual addresses of the nodes on the other network. Using the Internet example, computers or users on the Internet would think there is only one node on the corporate network, the proxy server. Internet users would not know that other nodes exist behind the proxy server nor the addresses of those nodes. Only the proxy server would have the table that translates between the real internal addresses of the workstations and computers and the fake addresses that are used on the Internet.

Firewalls normally log all of the activity so that information about network access and detail is available for later analysis, either because of a problem or for routine security audits. The firewall must also provide a method for a security administrator to configure and update its access control lists to establish and modify the rules for access according to the security policy.

Firewall hardware and software is available for use on home networks. Software products such as Zone Alarm and Black Ice are available in both free and "for pay" versions that can be downloaded from the Internet.

Routers commonly used on home networks, such as those provided by Linksys or Belkin, provide firewall capability in their hardware and software.

While user identification, passwords, and firewalls can be put in place to make it more difficult for someone to gain unauthorized access to the network, you should always bear in mind that stopping a determined hacker from breaking into a network is extremely difficult. Most security measures are designed to raise the threshold of difficulty to the point where the hacker will lose patience and go elsewhere.

## 17-12   PHYSICAL SECURITY

The primary emphasis of physical security is to prevent unauthorized access to the communications room, network operations center, or communications equipment, which could result in malicious vandalism or more subtle tapping of communications circuits. It may also be necessary or desirable to inspect the facilities of the common carrier through which the communications circuits pass. Physical security can be thought of as the lock and key part of security. The equipment rooms that house communications equipment should be kept locked. Terminals may be equipped with locks that deactivate the screen, a keyboard, or an on/off switch. In lieu of actual locks and keys, magnetically encoded cards that resemble credit cards can be used to activate terminals or to unlock doors. These cards could also serve as a personnel identification badge. PCs can employ screen savers that blank the screen after a predetermined period and require the entry of a password to allow the PC to resume normal operation.

Protecting laptop computers deserves special attention. Because they are so portable, laptops are prone to being left unattended and are easily stolen. If the owner has stored user IDs and passwords on the laptop, a practice that should be strongly discouraged, the thief may have easy access to a company's network. Laptop theft does not always occur out of the office, by the way. More laptops mysteriously disappear within company premises than is commonly believed. Companies frequently don't report laptops that are stolen "on premises," either because they believe it is an internal matter or because they are embarrassed to report the problem.

## 17-13   PERSONNEL SECURITY

Having employees who are motivated, security conscious, and well trained in the use of proper security tools is a very effective security technique that organizations should not overlook. Trained employees may not prevent a hacker from breaking into the corporate network, but the likelihood that an intrusion is discovered and reported quickly is greatly increased. Furthermore, having employees who routinely do not leave their PC workstations logged on and unattended and who protect their laptop computers when they are traveling reduces the possibility that a number of the simpler security breaches will occur.

Personnel security involves using one or more of the following techniques:

- screening or security checking of prospective new employees before they are hired
- identifying employees and vendor personnel through badges or identification cards

- reminding employees about their security responsibilities and the organization's concern for security through active security awareness programs
- ensuring that employees are properly trained in their job responsibilities
- ensuring that error prevention techniques are in place to detect accidental mistakes, such as keying an erroneous amount

Network management personnel should be charged with the responsibility to see that these measures are in place, and employees' security knowledge and awareness should be checked from time to time, perhaps as a part of a security audit.

Many network security breaches are caused simply because employees make honest mistakes, either because they are inadequately trained or because they are careless. When security breaches do occur, it is important to track down the root cause and identify what corrective action is necessary to ensure that that particular problem does not occur again. Network security people often learn something from such investigations; they often point out holes in the security system that had not previously been identified nor considered.

## 17-14   DISASTER RECOVERY PLANNING

As the network becomes a vital part of an organization's operation, plans must be made for recovery steps to be taken if a natural or other disaster destroys the network operations center or part of a network. Organizations that have centralized computing capability must also be concerned about disaster planning for the computer center. Furthermore, it has become evident in recent years that another type of disaster must be planned for—a disaster or other outage at a communication company or telephone company office that serves the organization. In May 1988, a large fire struck a telephone company CO in Hinsdale, Illinois, leaving more than 35,000 customers, including many businesses, without data or telephone communications service for more than a week. Some companies that were dependent on network service actually went out of business. Others were seriously inconvenienced. As another example, in August 1989, workers of NYNEX, a large New York Telephone Co., were on strike for several weeks. Customers were not able to get new communication facilities installed, and repair calls took far longer than normal. Clearly, situations like these will occur again in the future. Companies must protect themselves by having adequate plans for emergency communications service if disaster strikes their communications company. Management's responsibility is to ensure that the proper disaster recovery planning is done and that the network capabilities can be restored.

**disaster recovery planning**

**disaster**

**Disaster recovery planning** is a part of the planning for normal system outages. For our purposes, a **disaster** is defined as a long-term outage that cannot be quickly remedied. A fire, flood, hurricane, or earthquake may be the cause. No immediate repair is possible, and the network or a significant part of it is unusable. Figure 17-8 is a checklist for disaster recovery planning.

Again, planning is the key. Having backup servers at an alternate site and the ability to switch the communications lines to the alternate location is a viable alternative in many situations. In lieu of that, being able to quickly obtain new servers from the vendor may be possible. Most vendors state that they will "take the next computer off the manufacturing line" to replace a computer damaged in a disaster. Given the thousands of servers that are produced each

FIGURE 17-8   A checklist for disaster recovery planning.

> **Considerations for Disaster Recovery Planning**
>
> 1. What level of service should be maintained during a disaster?
> 2. How will the organization communicate internally?
> 3. Where will help desks and command centers be located?
> 4. Are policies and procedures in place to handle customer and other incoming calls in a professional manner and to provide timely information?
> 5. Are computers and their data sufficiently backed up?
> 6. What happens in the event of an evacuation?
> 7. What is the sequence for recovery? Which departments must be put back in operation first, second, etc.?
> 8. Are procedures in place for regular testing of the disaster recovery plan?

day, this sounds like it should guarantee quick delivery of replacement machines. However, in practice, getting a server with the right configuration, memory size, disk capacity, and other needed features can sometimes take weeks rather than days. One small ISP recently lost its e-mail server and was unable to get a replacement e-mail server from the manufacturer for over four weeks. The customers were without e-mail service for that time, and the fact that they weren't billed was not enough to keep them from moving to other service providers who could give reliable service.

Even if replacement servers can be obtained, it is of no use if a suitable facility cannot be found to house them. Of equal importance is the ability to switch the network to the new computer site, again something that may be relatively easy if it has been planned for ahead of time. Communication companies have developed techniques and facilities to allow networks to be switched to alternate sites, a capability that is demanded by companies that have put disaster recovery plans in place.

Sometimes it is possible to work out a mutual aid pact with another company. Both organizations agree to back each other up in case of a disaster. Companies that have computer centers that do a lot of batch processing are easier to back up with mutual aid pacts than are companies that mainly do online processing and have extensive networks. With proper planning, however, extra lines could be installed between the companies, providing at least some backup transmission capability. If the two companies are in close physical proximity, they must be concerned about a disaster that would hit both of them simultaneously. An earthquake or tornado could easily hit companies in a several-mile radius and effectively neutralize any mutual aid backup plans.

Whatever plan is developed for disaster recovery, it must be specific for different kinds of disasters. Corning Inc., located in Corning, New York, had a disaster plan detailing how the company would recover from a fire. However, in 1972, the town of Corning was hit by a massive flood, which literally put the Corning network and computer center under water. Although some of the procedures previously developed for fire were appropriate, many were totally useless or inappropriate for problems caused by water damage.

Disaster recovery plans must be tested. Rarely will all of the problems of a real disaster be covered when the plan is written. Although testing cannot fully simulate a real disaster, it does identify weaknesses in the plan. Tests of the disaster plan can be conducted in unique ways. One company's network manager worked with a computer vendor to develop a disaster test. Late one night, the vendor's service manager removed a critical but obscure part of the main server. When the operations staff could not bring the server up the next morning, they called the vendor for service. The vendor's technicians tried for several hours but were unable to diagnose the problem; therefore, they called for help from the national support center. In the meantime, the prolonged server outage caused the company to activate its disaster recovery plan. Because only the network manager, the company president, and the vendor service manager knew the real nature of the outage, the "test" was extremely realistic. It was allowed to run for over twenty-four hours before it was revealed to be a test. Although there was some grumbling, there was also a general consensus among the network users and management that much valuable information had been gained.

As a company becomes increasingly reliant on its network, it must constantly reassess how long it can afford to be without the network and the systems it supports. Getting the users involved in assessing the impact of an extended outage caused by a disaster is one way to build a case for management to support spending time and money on developing and maintaining disaster recovery procedures.

## 17-15   WIRELESS NETWORK SECURITY

Security for wireless networks deserves special attention because they are especially vulnerable to unauthorized access and because they are becoming increasingly more popular. Businesses and home users are quickly adopting wireless networks—and for good reason: they are cheap, convenient, easy to set up, and provide great mobility. However, the freedom from tangled cables comes with a price. A wireless network can broadcast far outside your home or office building. With an antenna and some widely available hacking software, anyone sitting nearby can passively scan all the data flowing in your network. Here are several things that the owner of any wireless network should do to protect his network.

- Adjust the signal strength on your wireless access point (AP). Some APs even let you adjust the signal direction. Place APs as far away from exterior walls and windows as possible, and then adjust the signal strength so that you can barely get connections near exterior walls. Even so, signals may leak outside.

- Use strong passwords to protect each AP. Many people never change the password that comes with the AP when they buy it. Hackers know this and check the default passwords for all of the AP brands when they first try to break into a wireless network.

- Use the 128-bit WEP security protocol if it is available on your AP. It really isn't difficult to crack, but it does provide another layer of protection that may discourage the casual hacker.

- Limit access rights to those who have a need to use the wireless network. Chances are, not everyone in the office needs wireless access.

- Authenticate users by installing a firewall that supports VPN connectivity. Require users to log on as if they were dialing in remotely.

- Limit the number of user addresses to just as many users as you actually have. Then, if someone isn't able to log on you'll know that an unauthorized user has made it through the security and is using one of the ports.

- Encrypt transmissions so that even if they are intercepted they will be nearly impossible to understand

These techniques will certainly improve the security of your wireless network, but they may not be enough. More sophisticated techniques are available from specialists, but they come at a high price. Furthermore, wireless network security is the subject of considerable ongoing research. The technology is improving constantly, so it is a good idea to regularly monitor the latest developments.

## 17-16  SECURITY FOR HOME NETWORKS

An increasing number of people have multiple computers in their homes and are installing networks to tie the machines together in order to share Internet access, data, printers, and other hardware. As long as the network stays strictly in the home, security concerns aren't too significant. Those that do exist are usually covered by the inherent capabilities of the OS software, such as Microsoft Windows XP. Windows XP allows a computer to have multiple users registered on one computer and for each user to have his own data files invisible to other users of the same machine. Mom, dad, and the kids can all set up the computer as though it were their own, even giving the home screen its own unique look if they desire.

Most home computer users connect their machines to the Internet however, and that is where the need for stronger security becomes more evident. If the computer connects to the Internet through a dial-up connection to an ISP for a few minutes each day to send and receive a few e-mails, a virus-scanning program that is regularly updated with the latest virus signatures may be all that is required. If, however, the machine is connected to the Internet for hours at a time and especially if it is connected full time, for example through a broadband service, a firewall program should be installed and should be set to warn the user when someone tries to access the computer from the network. Programs such as ZoneAlarm and Black Ice do a good job of protecting a network-attached PC and provide several levels of security, including making the computer invisible to people on the Internet who may be scanning to find unprotected machines.

It is possible to purchase more elaborate security equipment, such as routers with built-in firewall protection, that will provide yet stronger security. However, for most home networks, it is probably not necessary to go to that extent.

## ■  SUMMARY

This chapter has highlighted the need for network security and described the techniques that are most often employed to keep networks and the data on attached computers secure from outside attacks. Encryption techniques render a data stream unreadable to anyone who doesn't know the decryption algorithm and doesn't have the appropriate key. They also can provide a digital signature that allows a recipient to know who sent a message. Today's encryption techniques provide good privacy and security for most applications. Digital signatures and certificates confirm the identity of persons and ensure that documents have not been changed.

Viruses are a fact of life, but antivirus programs provide good protection if they are kept up-to-date and are used. Network access control techniques—user IDs and passwords—must be put in place as an absolute minimum on all networks. Physical security of the network circuits and control center are important, as are appropriate personnel security techniques for network staff members. Even most home networks need to have some security measures installed to deter hackers or others from mischievous or malicious actions.

In Chapter 18, you will learn about the steps that are required to design a network and implement it. Unique considerations for LANs, WANs, and internets are highlighted.

## ■ REVIEW QUESTIONS

17-1. Explain why network security is needed.

17-2. What is management's responsibility for network security?

17-3. What are the elements of a network security policy?

17-4. Identify five types of security threats to a network.

17-5. Explain why triple DES is an improvement over DES.

17-6. Explain the terms *asymmetric key, public key,* and *private key.*

17-7. Explain the advantages of an asymmetric key encryption system over a symmetric key system.

17-8. Explain why data encrypted using the asymmetric algorithm and a sufficiently large key is virtually invulnerable to unauthorized decryption.

17-9. What is a digital signature?

17-10. How are digital signatures implemented?

17-11. What is a digital certificate?

17-12. What is the function of a certificate authority?

17-13. What is PGP and how is it used?

17-14. How do viruses spread?

17-15. What is the best thing an organization or user can do to protect themselves against viruses?

17-16. Why is it important that network users have user IDs and passwords?

17-17. What are the characteristics of a good password?

17-18. Explain the purpose of a firewall.

17-19. Explain the term *physical security* as it relates to a network.

17-20. Identify four personnel security techniques.

17-21. Discuss the reasons that a company should have a disaster recovery plan for its network.

17-22. Identify five types of "disaster" that could disable a network.

17-23. Explain why it is necessary to test a disaster recovery plan.

17-24. Why are wireless networks especially prone to security violations?

17-25. List five things that can be done to minimize the security risks to a wireless network.

17-26. Describe several techniques that might be implemented to provide security in a home network.

### TRUE OR FALSE

17-1. Antivirus programs have reduced the overall risk of network security problems in the past few years.

17-2. It is virtually impossible to eliminate all possible network security problems.

17-3. Determined and creative people can ultimately find a way to bypass or work around even the most stringent network security measures.

17-4. Senior management in an organization does not have any responsibility for network security.

17-5. An example of a passive network security attack is eavesdropping.

17-6. Denial of service occurs when someone floods a site with messages faster than they can be handled.

17-7. Encryption prevents someone from eavesdropping on a network.

17-8. A secure encryption system should mask the frequency with which letters occur and should also mask the word lengths.

17-9. A polyalphabetic cipher changes letter frequencies.

17-10. The original DES is vulnerable to a brute force attack.

17-11. In many situations, managing the key is a high-cost overhead to the encryption system.

17-12. PKE uses three keys: the public key, the private key, and the user key.

17-13. A great advantage of asymmetric key encryption is that it solves the problem of key exchange.

17-14. PGP is of little value because the encryption system it uses is weak.

17-15. A digital signature is the network equivalent of signing a message and guaranteeing that the contents have not been changed.

17-16. To create a digital signature, the written signature is scanned and then digitized.

17-17. Hashing creates hash.

17-18. A digital certificate is a password-protected, encrypted data file that identifies a transmitting entity and certifies that they are who they say they are.

17-19. In order to grow, a certificate authority will normally issue a certificate to anyone without verifying who they are.

17-20. Once issued, a digital certificate is valid forever.

17-21. Computer viruses can be eliminated by inoculating a PC with an extra heavy dose of ions.

17-22. Program files that have a virus attached are said to be injected.

17-23. Computer viruses spread much like their biological counterpart—by sharing.

17-24. A relatively effective technique for limiting unauthorized access to an organization's network from outside networks to which it is connected is to install a firewall.

17-25. Firewalls normally log all of the activity so that information about network access and detail is available for later analysis.

17-26. The primary emphasis of physical security is to prevent unauthorized access to the communications room, network operations center, or communications equipment, which could result in malicious vandalism or more subtle tapping of communications circuits.

17-27. Having employees who are motivated, security conscious, and well trained in the use of proper security tools is an ineffective security technique.

17-28. Many network security breaches are caused simply because employees make honest mistakes.

17-29. Disaster recovery planning is best done after a disaster, when management is paying attention to the need.

17-30. Disaster recovery plans must be specific for different kinds of disasters.

17-31. Disaster recovery plans cannot be tested because it is impossible to invoke the disaster.

17-32. Wireless networks are invulnerable to security breaches because they transmit data at ultra high frequencies.

17-33. 128-bit WEP provides more than enough protection for wireless networks.

17-34. Home computers do not need security protection because no one outside the home is interested in the data stored on home computers.

## MULTIPLE CHOICE

17-1. Management's statement of the importance of and their commitment to network security is called the _____.
  a. network security strategy
  b. network security policy
  c. statement of network intent
  d. network performance standard
  e. network security standard

17-2. Examples of passive security attacks are _____.
  a. altering message contents
  b. masquerading
  c. denial of service
  d. All of the above.
  e. None of the above.

17-3. The encryption system that eliminates the problem of key exchange is _____.
  a. monoalphabetic cipher
  b. polyalphabetic cipher
  c. transposition cipher
  d. DES
  e. asymmetric key encryption

17-4. A digital signature _____.
  a. has no place in electronic commerce
  b. must be able to be imitated by someone else
  c. is the network equivalent of signing a message
  d. can be decoded by the receiver using the senders private key
  e. None of the above.

17-5. A digital certificate _____.
  a. is the same as a digital signature but can be framed
  b. is password protected
  c. never expires
  d. is issued by a signature authority (SA)
  e. uses the DES standard for encryption

17-6. PGP _____.

    a. was developed by the federal government

    b. is a CA that issues digital certificates

    c. uses a single key like DES

    d. is in the public domain –

    e. is difficult to find information about because it is such a strong system

17-7. One common method of network access control is _____.

    a. user IDs and passwords –

    b. encrypting the data

    c. locking the doors to the network operations area

    d. not linking the network to the Internet

    e. fire stops

17-8. A firewall _____.

    a. is usually a combination of hardware and software

    b. enforces a boundary between two or more networks

    c. normally logs all transactions that pass through it

    d. All of the above.

## ■ PROBLEMS AND PROJECTS

17-1. Develop a simple encryption technique to encrypt and decrypt alphanumeric data. Using your technique, encrypt the text of this problem. If you have computer programming experience, write a program to encrypt and decrypt data using the algorithm you developed. Compare the speed of your program to performing the encryption/decryption manually.

17-2. Make a list of things that might not be covered if a company had a disaster plan for a fire but the company was struck by a flood.

17-3. Visit a company in your area and discuss the network security measures that are in place. Write a short report describing why you think the measures are adequate or inadequate considering the company's business and the network security risks it faces.

17-4. Examine the Internet browser that you use at home or at work to see what capability it has for digital certificates and what digital certificates are already installed.

17-5. Do some research on the Internet to better understand PGP. Are different versions available? Is it really available for no charge? What limitations does the software package seem to have?

17-6. With a partner or in a team, download PGP from the Internet and set it up on your computers. Send encrypted messages to each other. **Note:** Completing this assignment will require you to do some research on PGP at the Internet site. Be sure you download the correct version of PGP for your computer.

## DISASTER RECOVERY

The terrorist attack on the World Trade Center in September of 2001 heightened many companies' awareness of the need to have a contingency plan in case disaster strikes. Individual companies in New York found that their own disaster recovery plans were stretched to the breaking point when they were suddenly uprooted from the offices in lower Manhattan. Before September 11, many companies relegated business continuity and disaster recovery planning to midlevel management or below. It was kind of a tab in the binder that had to be filled out but which often received scant attention.

Since September 11, many organizations have realized that there is no such thing as overplanning when it comes to preparing for the worst-case scenario. Senior management is giving a significant amount of attention to understanding what their business continuity and disaster recovery plans are and should be. Documentation of the much smaller World Trade Center bombing of 1993 shows that upwards of 50 percent of the businesses that were impacted were no longer in business three months after the event. It got down to the fact that they weren't prepared to handle the contingencies around something like that happening and the impact on their businesses. If they had to be evacuated from the trade center, they had no plans for where their staff would go. Or, if they had critical data stored on tape, disk, or even on paper, they no longer had access to it because they had to physically leave the building. While these types of things were critical to the survival of the business, many companies unfortunately had no plan to recover the assets that were necessary for the business to survive.

While it was mainly small and medium-sized companies that actually went out of business, large corporations that had significant operations in the World Trade Center also felt a major impact. Depending on the nature of the operation that was affected by the disaster and the amount of data and personnel backup that was available in other locations, large corporations may have felt anything from a minor disruption to a loss of business operating capability or loss of revenue.

While some companies had prepared contingency plans for expected catastrophes, such as hurricanes or floods, the events of September 11 are causing companies to start thinking about planning for the unthinkable. There truly is no such thing as overplanning for the worst-case scenario!

**QUESTIONS**

1. If your company had had its headquarters in the World Trade Center, what kind of disaster planning could have been done and what actions taken that would have been useful after the buildings collapsed on September 11, 2001? Would different planning have been necessary if it had been a sales office rather than the company headquarters?

2. Select the most likely disaster that could strike your school or workplace (e.g. flood, fire, hurricane, tornado, earthquake, bomb, hostage crisis) and write a plan that identifies what actions need to be taken ahead of time to lessen the impact of the disaster, and what actions would be taken at the time the disaster struck.

# NETWORK DESIGN AND IMPLEMENTATION

## ■ OUTLINE

## ■ KEY TERMS

network design

post-implementation audit

queuing

request for proposal (RFP)

statement of requirements

stress testing

workload generator

# ■ OBJECTIVES

After you complete your study of this chapter, you should be able to:

- ■ describe the process of designing a communications network;
- ■ discuss the phases of the network design process;
- ■ explain the importance of understanding the requirements for a network before beginning its design;
- ■ describe differences between the design of WANs, LANs, and internetworks.

## 18-1    INTRODUCTION

This chapter describes the process by which communication networks are designed and implemented. Proper design requires a detailed understanding of the ways in which the network will be used. Once the requirements are understood, the network designer can investigate alternative ways to design the network. While all communications networks have many similarities, there are some differences in the design techniques used for WANs, LANs, and internetworks. The designer must understand different communications technologies so that he can match them with the requirements to provide the optimal design at minimal cost. After the network is designed and the design is approved, the circuits, routers, cable, and other equipment are ordered and the network is implemented.

When done properly, network design and implementation is a structured process composed of several phases, each of which will be examined in this chapter. In most phases, several techniques are used to accomplish the work. After reading this chapter, you will have a good understanding of the network design and implementation process, as well as the specific tasks required.

## 18-2    THE NETWORK DESIGN AND IMPLEMENTATION PROCESS

network design

**Network design** is the process of understanding the requirements for a new communications network or changes to an existing network, investigating alternative ways for configuring the network, selecting the most appropriate choices to provide the required capability, and specifying (in detail) the parameters of the network so that the necessary equipment and software can be ordered and installed. Depending on the size of the network (or network change), the process may take anywhere from a few days to a few months to complete.

The work of designing and implementing a new network or a change to an existing network is normally viewed as a project and is broken into several phases of activity. These phases may be called by different names, and in some organizations some phases are bypassed or shortcuts are taken. Regardless, certain work must be performed. If shortcuts are taken in one step of the process, it is likely to lead to additional work or even rework later on—or worse, a new network that does not really meet the needs of the users or delivers less-than-expected levels of service or performance.

The phases of the process are:

1. develop the statement of requirements
2. investigate alternatives
3. network design
4. select equipment and vendors
5. prepare for implementation
6. implementation
7. cutover

Although this may seem like a large number of steps, on many network projects some of them can be completed very quickly, especially for smaller networks. For example, in a small organization, the manager who can approve the design and give the go-ahead to implement may actually be a part of the project team. Therefore, moving from the network design phase to selecting equipment can occur quickly without long delays waiting for management approval.

Throughout the process, it is important to document all aspects of the work, including the requirements, the alternatives considered, the alternative selected and why it was chosen, the estimated cost of implementing the network, and the expected timetable and results of the implementation.

## 18-3  REQUIREMENTS PHASE

**statement of requirements**

The design begins with a **statement of requirements.** Sometimes this is done formally, but just as often it begins with a discussion among users and the network staff about changing business conditions that will require new network capabilities or problems that exist with the current network. Perhaps a company is buying a competitor and there is a requirement to integrate the existing networks of the two companies. Maybe the business has grown and the existing network does not have enough capacity to handle the additional volume of orders and inventory transactions. Maybe the organization has downsized and the current network has more capacity than is needed to handle the e-mail traffic among the remaining employees, so a reduction in capacity is desirable to reduce costs. Perhaps a new technical capability, such as VoIP, has become practical and affordable and the organization could benefit by upgrading its existing network to take advantage of the capability. In recent years, there has been a strong desire by organizations to have the capability for prospective customers or users to access products and services using the World Wide Web. The ability to, for example, order products, register for classes, download software and documentation, and search for application information through the Internet has required many networks to be upgraded.

Whatever the motivation, the driving force behind the proposed network change should be documented in a form that is similar to the way other project proposals are documented within the organization. The network project will normally have to compete with other projects for funding, so having it documented the same way as the other projects will make it easier for management to compare the projects and decide whether to approve money or effort being spent.

The network staff may need to spend some time to ensure that they fully understand the requirements for the new or changed network. The requirements may include network coverage of new geographic areas, such as new company offices or operations in countries where the company has not previously done business. Maybe the requirement is to add wireless capability so that users can access the network from their laptop computers while attending meetings in conference rooms. Frequently, the requirements call for additional network capacity to handle a growth in network traffic, changing traffic patterns, or to provide better response time. Or it could be that the network reliability is not good enough, and something must be done to ensure that the network is available whenever people want to use it. In addition, the network staff needs to know the desired time schedule for expanding or upgrading the network and what, if any, constraints such as cost exist that might limit the choice of proposed solutions.

Once the requirements of the new or changed network are documented, the requirements document should be tested with various users throughout the organization to ensure that the problems with the existing network and the desired solutions are understood. Furthermore, some level of management approval must normally be obtained before work proceeds to the next phase. In some organizations the approval process is relatively formal, while in other organizations, particularly smaller ones, the approval may be given very informally. In any case, it is important that network designers obtain approval in a way that is consistent with internal procedures.

## 18-4  INVESTIGATING ALTERNATIVES

Once approval of the statement of requirements has been obtained, work can begin to discover and study alternative ways to meet the project's requirements. If it has not previously been established, this is the time when a project team should be formed to carry on the work. The team is best made up of a combination of specialists from the network department and users from parts of the company that will be affected by the change and who will benefit by its implementation. Sometimes a representative of management is also included on the team.

Given the wide choice of network products and services available today, there are usually several ways that the requirements for the new or upgraded network can be met. It is appropriate to examine at least several, if not all of them, to ensure that the best, most cost effective alternative is finally selected. Everyone tends to do work, including network design, based on personal experience and the way they did it the last time. Although experience is extremely useful in a field that is changing as rapidly as networking, it is important to continually assess options that may not have been available even months before. For example, the Internet frequently plays a part in network designs, either by the proposed use of its public facilities or by the establishment of a VPN that takes advantage of the Internet's ubiquity. A few years ago, these options weren't even available to be considered. The same is true of wireless and broadband network capability—today's options were yesterday's dreams. Vendors are producing a steady stream of new products and enhancements that need to be considered when designing a new network or upgrading an older one.

The project team should talk to a number of vendors and ask them to make proposals for meeting the new or expanded network's requirements. Depending on the geographic locations to be served, certain vendors or communications offerings may not be available. Obviously, if all of the locations are in major cities, more alternatives are likely to exist than if some of the organizations facilities are in small towns or rural areas.

Numerous questions need to be asked during this phase. Will one WAP serve the entire building under consideration or will multiples be needed? Is LAN cabling in place or will it need to be run? Should the Internet be used? Are packet switching facilities available in the locations? Can one vendor provide all of the equipment or services that will be needed or will multiple vendors be used? If multiple vendors are used, is their equipment compatible? What kind of user training will be required for the new capabilities being provided? It is important to put questions like these on the table and to get and understand the answers.

When alternatives are being investigated, costs must be considered. Often there are trade-offs between costs and service. In some cases, a technically viable alternative may have to be eliminated because its cost is prohibitively high. The cost information gathered while alternatives are being studied will be useful later for estimating the total cost of the network being planned, and it is certainly information that management will want to know before they make a commitment to go ahead with the project.

The objectives of this phase are to be sure that all relevant alternatives are considered and that inappropriate options are eliminated. Eliminating some alternatives helps to get the project focused on those that are truly the best choices and to select the one that should be recommended.

## 18-5   NETWORK DESIGN

After information about all of the alternatives has been gathered, the project team must analyze the information it has collected and begin to design the new or upgraded network. This is very difficult work! There are modeling and simulation tools available to help with the design process, but they require copious amounts of quantitative information about traffic patterns, response times, line turn around times, router and modem speeds, and so forth. Often, this information is not readily or precisely available, so it must be estimated. However, small differences in the values sometimes make huge differences in the predictions of the model or simulator. Nonetheless, the design must proceed.

If the locations of the network nodes have not been laid out on a map, that task should be done at this point. The map may be only a floor map of a building, as shown in Figure 18-1, or it could be a national or world map, shown in Figure 18-2, depending on the scope of the network. Many times, the relative locations of the network nodes suggest certain network topologies or configurations. Sometimes the topology of the network will be dictated by a preexisting network that is being enhanced or by the network of a vendor that is being used to carry traffic.

For WANS, knowledge of the expected traffic flows on the network is also an important piece of data at this point. This is because WAN circuit speeds are often much slower than LAN speeds, so capacity and responsiveness is a consideration. Estimates of how many e-mail messages and their length, how many inquiries to a database, the size of the response messages, and all other

**FIGURE 18-1** A wiring diagram of a small office building.

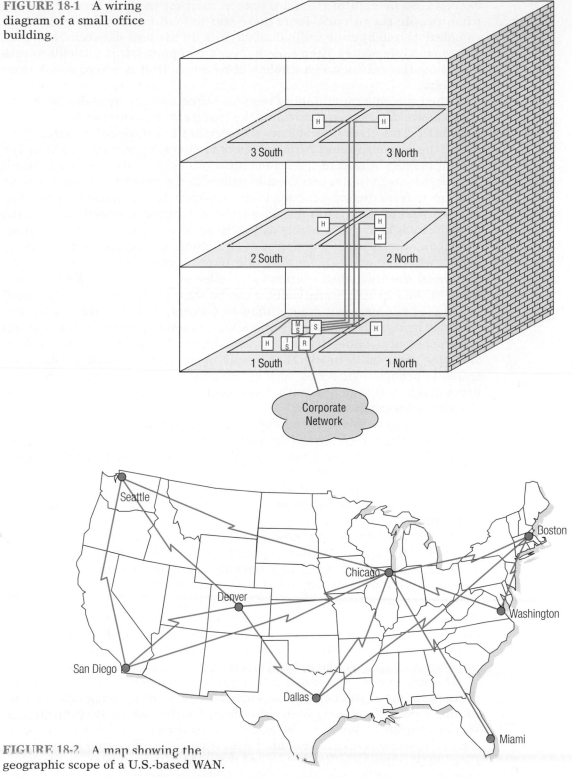

**FIGURE 18-2** A map showing the geographic scope of a U.S.-based WAN.

traffic that will flow on the circuits of the network are needed to determine if the speed of the circuits will be fast enough to meet the demand. Timing of the traffic flows is also important. If 1,000 e-mail messages are sent through a network each day, it makes a difference whether they are equally spread through the 24-hour period, all sent within normal business hours, or if, for example, 80 percent of them are sent in the first working hour of the day when people get to work. From these traffic load figures, it is possible to calculate throughput on individual circuits. In modern networks, however, where multiple routes often exist between two points, it is difficult to estimate how the network as a whole will respond. That is where simulations can help.

When the amount of data to be transmitted and the available hours are both known, designers can calculate the speed of the circuit required to carry the traffic. This gives the capacity requirement but does not necessarily indicate the responsiveness. Although there are many factors that make up the overall responsiveness of the communications system, the time to transmit the characters from the users' workstations to the servers and the response characters from the servers back to the workstations is, in most cases, a significant part of the overall response time. If a circuit is heavily loaded, the probability is high that **queuing** will occur somewhere in the network. Queuing occurs when a circuit or a piece of equipment is busy handling one piece of data when a request comes to handle another piece. (You've personally experienced queuing when waiting for a teller at a bank or to check in for a flight at the airport.) Statistically, it can be shown that if the use of a circuit or piece of equipment is greater than 40 percent, it is very likely that some traffic is being delayed because of queuing. Queuing in itself is not bad, but it is important to understand that it introduces variability into the transmission times on the network. That is why most response time numbers are stated in probabilistic terms, such as "90 percent of the transactions will be processed in less than 5 seconds, 95 percent in less than 10 seconds, and 100 percent in less than a minute."

Simulation tools are also useful for doing detailed analysis of the effects of queuing. Creating a simulation model of a network requires a detailed understanding of both the network and the simulation tool. Once the simulation model is created, it must be validated for the set of assumptions used in its creation. Only then can it be used to project the performance of the proposed network. Simulating networks is quite complicated but the results can be invaluable.

A simulation model can give answers to many "what if" questions, such as "What if the circuit speed is doubled?" "What if the transaction rate drops by 30 percent?" "What if I change the parameters in a router or increase the memory by 100 megabytes?" Furthermore, after the network is operational, a simulation model can help predict when the network will reach capacity by increasing the simulated number of transactions until response time degrades to unacceptable levels. A simulation model not only helps to make the most of the available resources but also confirms that changes planned for the network will have the desired effect.

If simulation is not used, it is still possible to estimate the performance characteristics of the network, though the effects of queuing and message routing may not be accurately accounted for. For example, projected response time to a user could be calculated by adding together the time for transmission of a certain amount of data from the workstation to the server, the processing time in the server, and the transmission time of the response back to the workstation. This simple calculation assumes no queuing or unusual routing of the messages takes place and gives a "best possible" response time. If this simple model shows that the "best possible" response time is inadequate, the network designer knows that the design must be improved so that the network will give satisfactory performance when it operates in the real world, which includes queuing and routing delays.

queuing

FIGURE 18-3 Response time at various line speeds.

| | 64,000 bps | 256,000 bps |
|---|---|---|
| Line speed | | |
| Line capacity | = 8,000 characters per second | = 32,000 characters per second |
| | (at 8 bits per character) | |
| If 100 million characters per day are to be sent, the total transmission time would be | 3.5 hours | .875 hour |
| 1,000 characters into computer | .125 sec | .03 sec |
| Computer processing time | .20 sec | .20 sec |
| 10,000 characters out to terminal | 1.25 sec | .30 sec |
| Total response time to user | 1.575 seconds | .53 second |

Let's look at an example. Suppose that a communication circuit must carry 100 million characters in an 8-hour business day while providing workstations with no longer than a 1-second response time. Because this is a simple example, we will assume that there is only one workstation on the circuit and that no queuing exists. We are also ignoring the overhead characters that a protocol would add to the transmission. As shown in Figure 18-3, a 64 Kbps circuit can transport 100 million characters in 3.5 hours, clearly meeting the capacity requirement. Suppose a typical transaction consists of 1,000 characters transmitted from the workstation to a server, followed by .2 second of computer processing time and 10,000 characters transmitted from the server back to the workstation. The figure shows that the 64 Kbps circuit yields a response time of 1.6 seconds and does not meet the response time requirement. A 256 Kbps circuit cuts the response time to .53 second and clearly meets the response time requirement. At the same time, it greatly exceeds the capacity requirement of the circuit because it can carry all of the day's traffic in only .9 hour. It may also be unaffordable! The network designer faced with these circumstances would probably want to consult with the user to determine whether the additional cost of the 256 Kbps circuit was justified for this application.

In the course of analyzing the data about network traffic and the configuration alternatives, it may be that more than one network configuration emerges as a possible candidate for the final design. In fact, it is a good idea to try to develop several alternative configurations. Each may have slightly different assumptions, use different equipment or vendors, and deliver different performance. It is virtually certain that there will also be cost differences between the alternatives.

## 18-6 SELECTION OF EQUIPMENT AND VENDORS

request for proposal (RFP)

Once the network has been designed, or when several viable alternative designs exist, the specific equipment, software, and vendors must be selected. This may be done on a relatively informal basis, in which the known or preferred vendors are contacted and asked for specifications and price quotes for specific pieces of equipment or services. Alternately, a more formal approach can be used in which the organization prepares a formal **request for proposal (RFP)** document and sends it to several vendors. The RFP document contains a detailed description of the requirements, including timing requirements and constraints, and asks the vendors to formally respond with a

**FIGURE 18-4** The items to be included in an RFP document.

| | |
|---|---|
| Introduction | A management overview of the company submitting the RFP and the problem or situation it wishes to have the vendor address |
| Table of contents | A detailed list of the contents of the RFP document |
| Description of the problem | A detailed description of the problem or situation that the vendor needs to address |
| Scope and requirements of the desired solution | A statement that frames the kind of response or solution the company expects to receive |
| Format, content, and due date of response | The information the vendor's response must contain, the format it needs to be in (e.g., electronic), and the date by which it must be submitted |
| Evaluation criteria | How the responses to the RFP will be evaluated |
| Estimated decision date | The estimated date the company will make a selection of which response, if any, it will accept |
| References | Several reference accounts for whom the vendor has performed similar work |

proposal by a certain date. Some RFPs give the vendors considerable latitude in preparing responses, and even ask for suggested solutions to specific design problems the project team has encountered. Other RFPs are more structured and present a detailed outline for the vendors' response. Figure 18-4 lists the type of information that should be included in an RFP. Similarly, Figure 18-5 outlines the type of information that would be included in a typical response from a vendor. The RFP is usually sent to several vendors so that the responses can be compared and alternative solutions can be considered.

When the RFP responses are returned, the network design team must evaluate them against the requirements presented to the vendors. Silly as it may seem, it is necessary to check to be sure that each vendor is proposing the type of products and services requested. Some vendors don't read RFPs very carefully! Vendor responses can be compared on the basis of the proposed solution, the price, the sales support provided, technical support offered, and product maintenance and repair service. Throughout this process, the project team may learn more about a vendor's true capabilities because in the response to the RFP, certain products or capabilities may be emphasized and others downplayed. A vendor's financial viability should be considered because there are always some vendors that are here today and gone tomorrow. It is not pleasant to get a network installed and three months later, when service is required, find that the vendor of certain critical equipment has gone out of business. Sometimes after analysis, pieces of one vendor's proposed solution are combined with parts of the proposal from another vendor to make a hybrid network that provides a unique combination of capabilities.

## Calculation of Costs

With one or more network configurations and actual cost information provided by the vendors in hand, the costs of the network designs or alternatives can be recalculated and compared. Just as there are technical trade-offs between different types of circuits, routers, modems, and other equipment, there is a cost/performance trade-off between vendor proposals. The objective of the cost analysis is to finalize configuration of the network that will

FIGURE 18-5 The typical kind of information included in a vendor's response to an RFP.

| | |
|---|---|
| **Introduction** | A brief introduction to the company |
| **Executive summary** | A brief summary of the proposed solution |
| **Table of contents** | A detailed list of the contents of the response to the RFP |
| **System design** | A full description of the proposed solution |
| **System features** | The capabilities of the proposed solution that uniquely solve the identified problems and/or distinguish this vendor and solution from the competition |
| **Growth capacity** | An explanation of the spare capacity built into the proposed solution and the additional capacity (add-on modules) that can be purchased later |
| **Installation and testing methods** | How the solution would be installed and tested |
| **Maintenance arrangements** | How maintenance support would be provided, and its cost |
| **Ongoing support** | What support the vendor will provide after the solution is installed and operational |
| **Installation schedule** | When the proposed solution can be installed or implemented |
| **Pricing and timing of payments** | The cost and when payments are to be made |
| **Warranty coverage** | What warranty protection the vendor offers |
| **Training and education** | How customer training will be conducted and the additional cost for training, if any |
| **Other recommendations** | Additional recommendations by the vendor that don't strictly fall within the scope of the RFP |

meet the capacity, functionality, performance, and other requirements at the lowest possible cost. The cost can than be compared with the benefits that the new or upgraded network will yield, and a decision can be made whether to move ahead to the implementation.

Network costs can be grouped into the following categories:

- circuit costs
- router and server costs
- other hardware costs
- software costs
- personnel costs

Calculating the cost of leased circuits is a complicated process that usually is left up to the communications carrier, although programs are available for companies that want to calculate the costs internally. The costs of routers, servers, modems, and other communications hardware can be obtained directly from the manufacturer or distributor of the equipment, or were included in the response to the RFP. The vendor usually quotes purchase prices because most companies buy (rather than lease) this type of equipment, but some vendors may also provide rental or lease options.

It is important to separate the costs of personnel who develop the network from the costs of those who will run and maintain it on an ongoing basis. The costs of the network analysts and designers are part of the project costs but are not part of the ongoing operational costs. Once the project is completed, the analysts and designers will move on to other projects. Costs for the personnel to operate and maintain the network may be based on actual salaries and benefits or on a standard amount the organization uses for personnel cost estimation.

Although it is relatively easy to identify the costs of a new or upgraded network, it is often more difficult to quantify the benefits. However, benefit estimates must be made in order to determine whether the new network is cost justified. Users and financial specialists in the organization can be very helpful in identifying the benefits that will accrue, and their help and advice should be solicited. Some of the types of benefits the users in a manufacturing company might identify include:

- improved customer service
- increased sales
- ability to sell a new product
- reduction of marketing expense
- reduction of inventory
- reduction of time needed to process routine work
- elimination of clerical personnel
- more accurate information because of an improved ability to share data
- improved employee morale

Obviously, some of these benefits are tangible and will increase revenue or save out-of-pocket expenses, whereas others are intangible, sometimes called soft benefits. As the list of benefits is identified, it should be quantified whenever possible.

Sometimes, the team may find that more information is required and they have to go back to vendors or others to gather more detail. There is often pressure to make a quick decision because the users want to get the new or upgraded network implemented quickly, but it is important that the team do whatever is necessary to ensure that a good decision is made. Normally, the team recommends one of the alternatives to a management group that has the authority to approve the project for funding and implementation. The recommendation needs to include the following elements:

- a brief restatement of the problem or business situation that the new or upgraded network will solve
- a brief management summary of the recommended solution
- a detailed description of the recommended solution, which may actually be presented to management in verbal form
- a statement of the planned implementation timing
- a statement of the estimated costs of implementing the project
- a statement of the estimated benefits that will accrue after the project is completed

Management people tend to think in financial terms, so the statement of estimated costs and benefits is very important. Normally, some of the costs and many of the benefits are truly estimates at this stage. If that is the case, it must be stated. The team needs to be prepared to answer questions about any aspect of the project, as some questions are usually raised when management and others in the organization review the project.

Sometimes management may not approve the team's recommended solution. Perhaps the cost is too high or the proposed benefits are too low. Perhaps during the study, business conditions have changed and the proposed design doesn't fit the changed conditions. Sometimes the project may be stopped at this point, but more frequently it leads to a recycling of the investigation—looking again at alternatives or identifying new ones. It is not uncommon for some recycling to occur, especially when projects are large or complex. The team should not be discouraged if they are asked to go back and consider other alternatives or otherwise modify their recommendation.

Once approval to proceed is obtained, the project team moves ahead to implement the project, normally as quickly as possible. Sometimes further design work is required, and in other cases the vendor or vendors whose proposal was selected simply need to be given the go-ahead.

## 18-7 PREPARATION FOR IMPLEMENTATION

Once approval to implement the network has been obtained, the project moves to the implementation stage. There is always a myriad of details, and if a project management tool such as Microsoft Project has not been used earlier in the project, it may be a good idea to begin using one now. Such software, which runs on a PC, is frequently the only practical way to keep track of all of the tasks and time dependencies. All of the design and implementation tasks must be built in to the project timetable and, depending on the size of the project, the team may find it beneficial to appoint one member to have the primary responsibility for keeping the project plan up-to-date and alerting other members of the team about timing issues or task dependencies.

Network projects can sometimes be implemented quickly, for example, if the project is relatively small and geographically limited in scope. Upgrading a LAN on one floor of an office building is an example of such a project. At other times, the project may take months to complete. Sometimes vendors have long lead times, for example, if new international circuits are to be installed, or the entire implementation may depend on the delivery of a key hardware component.

In any case, ordering equipment is normally one of the first actions taken after approval is given for the new or upgraded network. The two most important provisions in the equipment purchase order are equipment specifications and acceptance testing. The specifications define the products and services being purchased, and the acceptance test provides an objective basis for determining whether the equipment installation meets the buyer's expectations and is performing properly. Other important provisions of the purchase agreement should cover the vendor's warranty, maintenance arrangements, and the terms of the installation and cutover.

Other tasks that may need to be done after the equipment is ordered and before implementation depend on the nature of the network or upgrade, but may include installing communication wiring, such as CAT-5 cables; developing network policies, practices and procedures; writing standards; installing software; and some types of training. Obviously there will be different tasks for a new network than there are for one that is in place but being changed. Each of the tasks should be shown in a network implementation plan that may be produced by the project management software. Progress must be tracked against the plan to ensure that target dates for the network cutover to production usage will be met.

## 18-8    IMPLEMENTATION

Before equipment is delivered, preparations must be made for its installation. Physical planning is the process for determining where the equipment will be located, ensuring that adequate power and, if necessary, air conditioning are available, and seeing that any large pieces of equipment can be moved from the place where they are delivered, such as a shipping dock, to the place where they will be installed. Drawings may be required to show where all of the equipment will be placed, as well as how power and communication cables will be routed to it. Many vendors have specialists who can assist in the physical planning.

### Installation

The installation of communication cables such as CAT-5 wiring may be a significant item, depending on whether a network is being newly installed or upgraded. Cable installation is relatively easy and inexpensive if it is done during the construction of a building, or if the building has raised floors or suspended ceilings that can be used as cable passageways. However, if walls have to be opened so that cables can be installed, the process gets expensive quickly and can be time consuming. More often than not, the labor cost for installing cabling is significant while the cost of the cable itself is relatively small. Therefore, it is almost always a good idea to install cable with extra capacity (capable of handling higher speeds or more traffic) so that later, when the capacity is needed, additional cable does not have to be installed. The time for cable installation can also be a significant item and it must be included in the project plan.

One aspect of cable installation that is frequently overlooked or bypassed is labeling the cables. All networks have several cables and connectors interconnecting the pieces of equipment. On the day the equipment is installed, it is obvious what each cable is for and where it runs. However, a day, week, or month later, when there is a problem or a need to make a change, the purpose of the cables has been forgotten and tracing them can be difficult or impossible and time consuming. All cables should be labeled at both ends with a clear indication of what it connects to and/or its purpose. Neglecting this task will lead to extreme frustration at a later date!

Once the equipment arrives, it must be installed. Depending on the nature of the equipment and the terms of the purchase agreement, it may either be installed by the vendor or the organization's own communications staff. Most frequently, the initial installation is performed by the vendor, who also handles any required training at the same time. Personnel from the communications carrier install circuits. When pieces of equipment from different vendors are connected, it is important to ensure that the vendors work together and test the equipment while all are still on the premises. Then, if there is a problem, they can work together to solve it.

## Testing

After all of the equipment, circuits, software, and other components of the network have been installed, the entire network must be tested. Ideally, the testing should be broken into pieces so that subsets of the network are tested under a variety of conditions. Sometimes this is possible, but more frequently it isn't because many networks today are large and complex. It is important that every workstation on the network is verified to have connectivity and that it is able to send and receive messages and communicate with the appropriate servers. This type of test also exercises routers, modems, and circuits, and gives some assurance that they are also working properly.

If there is separate communications software used for managing the network, error tracking and reporting, or for other purposes, it must also be tested. Sometimes this testing can be conducted during normal working hours, but if the software testing would interfere with regular network operation, it may have to be done outside of normal business hours.

**stress testing**

Another type of testing that should be done is **stress testing.** Stress testing puts a heavy load of traffic on the network and gives a good indication of how the network will perform in real life. Certain program bugs show up only when a high volume of transactions is put through the software in a short period of time. Furthermore, the effects of queuing and the resultant degradation in performance will be seen first-hand rather than just being simulated.

**workload generator**

One way to stress test a network is by having many operators at workstations submit transactions and messages at higher-than-normal rates. A better way is by using a tool called a **workload generator,** a program that runs on one or more servers and generates transactions at predetermined rates. To the network, these transactions appear to come from workstations. Good workload generator programs allow the user to specify the type of transactions and the length of messages and responses to be generated, so that various transaction mixes can be simulated. The advantage of this approach is that, if properly set up, the program can simulate full network operation in a controlled way without requiring users to be involved.

The most important oversight of network testing plans is the failure to test the error handling capabilities of the individual components and the network as a whole. What happens if a certain router fails? How does the network react when a circuit goes down? What if the power to a key server fails? When a failed circuit is restored to service, do the modems and routers on that circuit automatically resume communications or must they be restarted manually? The acid test of error recovery capabilities is whether the individual recovery built into the components of the network will all work together when they are connected into the network system. To thoroughly test error recovery, errors must be introduced into the network during the testing phase by disconnecting circuits, powering off routers and modems, or injecting noise on a circuit with the appropriate test equipment.

## Training

Both the users of the communications network and the operational and maintenance staff may need to be trained to use and operate the new or upgraded network, particularly when significant new capabilities or technology are being introduced. On the other hand, if the network is simply being upgraded to add additional capacity, such as new or faster circuits or routers, training may be minimal.

The best way to train users is to select a small group of key users for initial training by the network design team. These key users get their early training and an opportunity to use the new or upgraded network, if possible. Then the early users train the majority using the experience they have gained. While there may be some classroom training to present background and overview material, the heart of the training is performed at the workstation, with users actually entering transactions and receiving responses. This also gives the users a feeling for how the network will perform so that they gain a sense of its characteristics and responsiveness.

Network operational and maintenance personnel will be trained by both the members of the project team and the vendors who install the equipment. Ideally, the operations staff will have been involved in the project since its inception and will already have at least a conceptual understanding of the network's design and new capabilities that are being added. The training then is a matter of getting hands-on experience with the commands and various real-life situations that can occur. Operations people can get good experience with the network while users are using it in a training mode. If the users do a good job of simulating real operation, the operations staff will get a good feeling for how the network will perform when it is finally put into production. Of course, not every error or unusual condition that will occur during real operation will occur during the training period.

## 18-9    CUTOVER

Finally, when all is ready, the new or upgraded network can be turned on or cutover to production usage. Frequently this is a major milestone for the organization, particularly if the project has been large or long running or if the new capabilities are especially notable to many people—employees, customers, suppliers, or others. Despite the thoroughness of the testing, there will almost certainly be some unanticipated startup problems. It is good practice to insist that technicians from the equipment vendors be on hand when the network or upgrade is first put into use, so that problems can be resolved as quickly as possible.

Cutovers of large new networks are frequently scheduled to occur on a weekend. There may be a substantial amount of last-minute work to be done, and the extra time afforded by the weekend allows the work to be completed and a final round of testing to be conducted before all users come back to work on Monday morning. If an organization works a five-day workweek, the cutover is sometimes scheduled for Thursday night. This gives one day of live network operation before the weekend, and then the weekend is available for correcting problems or adjusting to other unforeseen circumstances that become apparent on the first day of real operation.

With so many organizations using older networks or using the Internet for part of their networking activity, network upgrades are much more prevalent than full cutovers of totally new networks. When an existing network is being upgraded, the cutover activities, including the testing and training, may be much simpler than those indicated because only a subset of the full network needs to be tested. Furthermore, training may be minimal, especially if little or no increased functionality is being added. A faster connection from the organization's offices to the Internet requires no training because, typically, users' procedures don't change—they just enjoy the speed of the faster connection. Similarly, if a few workstations are added to a LAN, only the new workstations need to be checked out and the new users need to be trained. Procedures for network operational and maintenance personnel probably wouldn't change at all, except to make sure that they are aware of the new workstations and users. Many network upgrades are relatively transparent to existing users if they are smoothly implemented.

Soon after implementation, the project team must go back and ensure that all network documentation is updated as necessary to reflect the way that the project was actually implemented. Frequently there are differences between the way the network or upgrade was planned and the way it was actually implemented, and it is important that the documentation reflect the "as built" reality.

## 18-10    POST-IMPLEMENTATION AUDIT

post-implementation audit

While it is not normally considered a phase of network design and implementation, it is a good idea for an independent team from the organization to do a review a few months after the project is complete. Their purpose is to check the results of the network implementation to see if the claimed benefits are being received and to look for other problems that may have arisen because of the implementation. This check, sometimes called a **post-implementation audit,** can often identify small changes or adjustments which, if made, would significantly help the users or further improve the benefits that the new or upgraded network delivered. Few organizations actually take this step because their staff is too busy with other projects or the "next implementation," but finding time for this network checkup normally pays nice dividends in terms of ensuring that the network is operating as planned and that the organization really achieves the benefits that the new network or network upgrade was supposed to deliver.

## 18-11    CONSIDERATIONS FOR WAN DESIGN

WAN design varies from LAN design in several ways:

1. Geographic considerations for WANs are much broader than with LANs.
2. The network designers probably have to deal with one or more communication carriers.
3. Lead times to get circuits installed and tested may be measured in weeks or for international circuits, months, rather than a few days or even hours it would take to run a new cable for a LAN under the floor of an office building.
4. Traffic analysis is important because most WAN circuits are considerably slower than their LAN counterparts. WAN circuits can be severely impacted if users transmit many long files, even if the files are broken into blocks for transmission, as they should be.
5. Error rates on WAN circuits are typically much higher than on LANs, though the errors are typically masked by protocols and equipment with automatic retry and error recovery capabilities.

The implications for the designer mainly have to do with the number of vendors she may have to deal with and the amount of coordination required to ensure that all of the parts of the network are delivered and ready for implementation at the same time. There may also be differences in the service offerings of the carriers, meaning that the network design team needs to compare and evaluate alternative designs that are similar but different enough that trade-offs between the pros and cons of the various features need to be considered.

## 18-12 CONSIDERATIONS FOR LAN DESIGN

LANs operate at much higher transmission speeds than WANs, so the length of specific messages or raw throughput for a single message on a LAN is rarely a major consideration. However, LAN users routinely transfer files of information from servers to their workstation, and these files can be quite long compared to the messages of transaction processing or e-mail applications. Well-designed LAN software that is properly configured should allow the transmission of files without tying up the LAN excessively. The software should break the files into blocks and give other users a chance to use the network in between blocks of the file.

By way of contrast with WANs, LANS are installed in a relatively controlled environment, often inside a single building or at most a few buildings in close proximity to each other. Organizations normally design and install LANs with their own people or perhaps with the help of a consultant. Because LANs are normally smaller than WANs, the designs are often simpler and the design and implementation moves very quickly.

At the very low end is a LAN in a home. One family decided to install a LAN connecting their three computers on a Saturday morning and had the network up and running by mid-afternoon, after a phone call to their cable television supplier to subscribe to the "Internet Pipeline" service and a quick trip to the nearby computer store. The network consisted of a cable modem, a WAP router, NICs for two desktop PCs that were connected to the router by cable, and a PCMCIA wireless network card for a laptop computer that was located on another floor of the house and which made a wireless connection to the router. Two of the family's computers were running Windows 98, while the third computer was running Windows 95—so they weren't even using the latest versions of Windows, which does have improved networking capability. However, by following the instructions that came with the router and the NICs, the components of the network were connected, the software was installed on the computers, and one by one the computers came on line and were soon sharing the cable TV connection to the Internet.

LANs in organizations aren't usually planned, designed, and installed so quickly, but the projects don't have to be long and time consuming. One aspect that needs to be considered in any company is future growth. Rarely do LANs in businesses stay the same very long, and if the company is growing, the network will probably grow too. Ensuring that routers and servers have enough capacity for future growth is important to ensure smooth upgrading as new workstations are added. Similarly, while a 10-megabit Ethernet may seem fast enough at the beginning, it typically isn't long before users are asking for even higher speeds, so installing cabling that will handle 100-megabit or even gigabit Ethernets is prudent. It is much better to pay a little more for high capacity cable in the first place than to have to go back and tear out lower capacity cable and install the high capacity cable later.

The installation of the first LAN in an organization may mark the time when a specialist is hired to be in charge of the network and all of the computers. Ideally, the person would be brought in to participate in or lead the effort to plan and design the new network, but that may not always be possible. Having a person on the staff who focuses on computer and network support within the organization will pay dividends in terms of more effective computer and network use and increased productivity for other employees.

## 18-13  CONSIDERATIONS FOR INTERNETWORK DESIGN

Connecting one or more networks together implies a step up in the sophistication of the network designs and the staff to design, operate, and support the internetwork. Despite improvements in equipment performance and media capabilities, internetwork design is becoming more difficult rather than easier. The trend is toward increasingly complex environments involving multiple media, multiple protocols, and interconnection to networks outside a single organization's control.

Internetwork designers need to thoroughly understand the reason their organization is planning to build an internet and the requirements for it. Developing a model of the network is helpful. As is often the case in networking, the model might be envisioned as a series of layers that distinguishes, for example, between:

- high speed backbone services that carry traffic between networks
- networks that provide services to whole organizations, or large parts of an organization such as divisions
- subnetworks, such as departmental networks designed specifically to meet the needs of one group of users and perhaps supporting unique applications for them while providing them access to the entire internetwork

Once the requirements are known and a model is built, the designers must select the specific devices that fit their environment. The capabilities of internetwork devices such as bridges, switches, and routers, and the trade-offs between them must be thoroughly understood. Alternatives for backbone paths between networks must be evaluated and a technology must be selected. Decisions need to be made about alternative paths between networks, load balancing of the traffic between the paths, and overall internetworking reliability. There may also be decisions to be made about traffic prioritization to ensure that the most important traffic gets the first or best opportunity to use the network in case of overload or conflict.

All of this design work and decision making may need to be done working with designers from one or more organizations—people who represent the other networks that make up the internet that is being built. Frequent communication and coordination is mandatory, and having all parties agree on the model of the internetwork being built will go a long way toward ensuring compatible design goals and decisions.

## ■ SUMMARY

Designing and implementing a communications network is a multistep, iterative process. The degree to which an organization follows rigorous network analysis and design procedures will depend on the complexity of the network or network upgrade. Today, many networks are upgraded frequently and in small pieces, so the analysis and design can be done informally because the scope of the work and even the solution may be fairly obvious. Ultimately, management must determine the extent to which the work is formalized and documented.

Regardless of the size and complexity, a team studies the feasibility of the new or upgraded network and gathers more detail, so that members grasp the problems with the existing network and the requirements for the change. Then the team members, usually working with vendors that supply total or partial solutions to the problem, examine various alternatives for the new or upgraded network and prepare one or more designs. Each alternative is subjected to a cost analysis and one or more alternatives are presented to management for review and approval. After approval is given, equipment is ordered and plans are made for the implementation. Once the equipment is installed, it must be tested. Users and network operation and maintenance personnel must be trained. Finally, when all is ready, the new or upgraded network is cut over to production usage. Time should be allotted after cutover for cleanup activities such as upgrading documentation, and an audit of the network should be conducted several months later.

There are variations on the activities and unique aspects for WAN, LAN, and internetwork designs and implementation. These variations need to be taken into account by the design team as they plan for the new or upgraded network.

Chapter 19 presents the topics of network management and operation. Once a network is installed and running, it must be managed so that it will keep operating successfully. While the amount of time devoted to network management and operation varies with the size of the network, you'll learn why all organizations need to devote some time to this process.

## ■ REVIEW QUESTIONS

18-1. Why is it important to understand the requirements for a new network or network upgrade before design work begins?

18-2. Why is it important to have users involved in the network design activity?

18-3. Why is it important to investigate alternatives for a network design?

18-4. What should the design team do if management does not approve its recommendation for a new or upgraded network?

18-5. What is the network design *statement of requirements?*

18-6. Who should be included in the network design team?

18-7. What are the advantages and disadvantages of relying on one's previous experience when doing a network design?

18-8. Why might a network design alternative that is technically viable have to be eliminated from consideration?

18-9. What is the purpose of laying out the locations of the network nodes on a map?

18-10. Why is knowledge of expected traffic flows on a network important in the design process?

18-11. Explain the term *queuing.*

18-12. What is the importance of queuing in a network?

18-13. What are the benefits and difficulties of using a simulation model during the network design process?

18-14. What is an *RFP?*

18-15. Why is it important to calculate the costs of a proposed new or upgraded network?

18-16. List the categories of network costs.

18-17. Why is it important to separate the personnel costs of the network designers from the costs of the people who operate the network?

18-18. Why is it important to identify the benefits of a new or upgraded network?

18-19. List some of the benefits of an upgraded network that users in a manufacturing company might identify.

18-20. Why should project management software be used during network implementation?

18-21. Why is it important to have vendor service personnel on site during network testing and on the day of network cutover?

18-22. What is *stress testing?*

18-23. What is a *workload generator?*

18-24. Why is it important to test network error handling capability?

18-25. Describe some circumstances where a network is upgraded but users do not have to be trained.

18-26. If a network upgrade is well tested, why should any unexpected problems occur the day the upgrade is cutover to production usage?

18-27. What is a *post-implementation audit?*

18-28. Explain the importance of doing a post-implementation audit after a new network or network upgrade project is completed.

18-29. List some of the considerations that make WAN design different from LAN design.

18-30. List some of the things that make internetwork design more complicated than either WAN or LAN design.

**TRUE OR FALSE**

18-1. Depending on the size of the network (or network change), the network design process may take anywhere from ten to twelve months to complete.

18-2. The network design begins with an evaluation of alternatives.

18-3. The reasons for a new network or network change should be documented in a form that is similar to the way other project proposals are documented within the organization.

18-4. Because an organization's network requirements are so specific, there is usually one and only one way a network should be designed.

18-5. The Internet rarely plays a part in network designs.

18-6. When alternatives are being investigated, costs must be considered.

18-7. The simulation of networks is relatively simple and straightforward.

18-8. An RFP document contains a detailed description of the requirements, including timing requirements and constraints, and asks the vendors to formally respond with a proposal by a certain date.

18-9. Calculating the cost of leased circuits is a complicated process that usually is left up to the communications carrier.

18-10. It is important to separate the costs of personnel who develop the network from the costs of those who will run and maintain it on an ongoing basis.

18-11. Although it is relatively easy to identify the benefits of a new or up-graded network, it is often more difficult to quantify the costs.

18-12. Management people tend to think in financial terms so the statement of estimated costs and benefits is very important.

18-13. Network projects can sometimes be implemented quickly, for example, if the project is relatively small and geographically limited in scope.

18-14. Installing network cabling is usually a simple thing, so no money should be spent for additional capacity until it is needed.

18-15. The purpose of stress testing is to see how the network operations staff will react when the going gets rough.

18-16. A network workload generator is a manager who thinks up a lot of tasks for his staff to do when they would not otherwise be busy.

18-17. The most important oversight of network testing plans is the failure to test the error handling capabilities of the individual components and the network as a whole.

18-18. When an existing network is being upgraded, the cutover activities—including the testing and training—may be much simpler than when a totally new network is being installed.

18-19. The designer of a WAN may have to deal with more communication carriers than the designer of a LAN.

18-20. Internetwork design is more complicated than LAN design.

**MULTIPLE CHOICE**

18-1. Which of the following is not a phase of network design as described in the text?
   a. developing the statement of requirements
   b. investigating alternatives
   c. network design
   d. cost analysis
   e. implementation

18-2. Management approval is normally required _____.
   a. at the beginning of the project
   b. after the network is installed and they can see how it is operating
   c. at the end of most phases of the network design process
   d. every two weeks
   e. only under exceptional circumstances

18-3. When an RFP is returned from a vendor, the network team must _____.
   a. check the vendor's financial viability
   b. check to see that the vendor is proposing the type of products and services requested in the RFP
   c. evaluate the response against the requirements presented to the vendor
   d. compare the responses from the vendors that responded to the RFP
   e. All of the above.

18-4. Which of the following might be benefits of a new network in a manufacturing company?

   a. improved customer service

   b. addition of network operational personnel

   c. increase in marketing expense

   d. additional network cost

   e. None of the above.

18-5. Which of the following statements is true?

   a. Network cabling is often more expensive than the cost of the labor necessary to install it.

   b. It is best to install cabling with just enough capacity to meet today's requirements.

   c. Cabling does not need to be labeled because it can easily be traced.

   d. All of the above.

   e. None of the above.

18-6. Internetwork designers must _____.

   a. deal with multiple organizations

   b. consider the high speed backbone that will carry traffic between networks

   c. understand how routers, switches, and bridges work

   d. consider traffic prioritization issues

   e. All of the above.

## ■ PROBLEMS AND PROJECTS

18-1. Discuss the criteria that might be used for prioritizing the list of network upgrade projects that could be undertaken in an organization, assuming that there are not enough people to work on all of them at the same time.

18-2. Management normally understands the economic implications of a new or expanded network better than the technical aspects. How would you quantify the benefits of a new network that would provide e-mail capability to your company's thirty-five locations throughout the U.S.? What might be the benefits of tying your customers to the network and letting them use it to communicate more effectively?

18-3. A point-to-point circuit from Albuquerque to Charleston is being designed. The projected traffic on the circuit is 4 million characters during the business day, with 15 percent of the traffic occurring during the busy hour. If less than a 2-second response time is required, what speed circuit would you recommend be installed? Why?

18-4. If traffic on the circuit described in Problem 3 were expected to grow at 40 percent per year, compounded, how would that change your recommendation?

18-5. Identify some ways that access to the Internet could be used in a contemporary network design for a small manufacturing company.

18-6. List some of the benefits that the faculty in a small university would identify if the school's network were upgraded to include network

**CASE STUDY**

access in all of the dormitory rooms. What benefits would the school's administration identify? What benefits would the residents of the dormitories identify?

## THE PATENT DEPARTMENT'S LAN

The patent department in a large manufacturing company has some special applications that they want to implement using a LAN to connect the patent attorneys and other support staff in the department. One of the patent attorneys also happens to be very knowledgeable about computers and has implemented a network in his home that ties the family's five computers together, allowing them to share files and high-speed satellite-based access to the Internet. He has convinced the manager of the department that implementing a LAN among the twenty-five people in the department will be very easy and can be done in less than a week.

The manager of the department, having some political savvy, realized that it would be a good idea to talk to the company's IT department and get their blessing on the project. He and the "technical" patent attorney met with the IT manager and two of his technical specialists, but the meeting did not go well. The IT people strongly objected to the patent department installing its own network and insisted that it would be more difficult and time consuming than the technical patent attorney believed. However, the IT manager also said that his department had no plans, money, or time to install a network in the patent department within the next two years.

After much heated discussion, concessions were made on both sides. IT agreed that the patent department could go ahead with its network, providing they did some analysis to think about future requirements for the LAN after the first application was installed. They also requested that the patent department make a drawing of the proposed network and show what would be required to implement it, including a list of hardware and software, the timetable, costs and expected benefits—in other words, a simple network design. The manager of the patent department agreed that they would follow the corporate standards for networks that IT had written, including the requirement that all LANs use the Ethernet technology, and that he would entirely pay for the network out of his departmental budget. He also agreed that they would dedicate their technical patent attorney to the project full time until the network was implemented. IT agreed to provide a person to participate on the project team full time.

**QUESTIONS**

1. What other members should be added to the team for designing the patent department's LAN? Do they need to be full-time members or could they participate on a part-time basis?

2. What future requirements for the LAN do you think the patent department personnel will identify?

3. Assuming no other network exists in the department now, what are the elements of the costs that will be identified for the new network?

4. What benefits will the department realize from having the network?

5. How long do you think it will take to implement the network in the patent department? What assumptions did you make to reach your answer?

# CHAPTER 19

# NETWORK MANAGEMENT
# AND OPERATION

## ◼ OUTLINE

## ◼ KEY TERMS

agent

change coordination
  meeting

change management

Common Management
  Information Protocol
  (CMIP)

configuration control

controlling

directing

help desk

levels of support

management information
  base (MIB)

network management

network management
  systems

network operation

organizing

outsourcing

patch panel

performance
  management

planning

problem escalation

problem management

problem tracking
   meeting

protocol analyzer

remote monitoring
   (RMON)

service level agreement

Simple Network
   Management Protocol
   (SNMP)

staffing

trouble ticket

## ■ OBJECTIVES

After you complete your study of this chapter, you should be able to:

- explain why it is necessary to manage networks;
- describe the tasks that must be done to manage the network activity;
- describe the functions of the network operation group;
- describe how network problems are diagnosed and repaired;
- describe how network performance is monitored and measured;
- explain how the network configuration is documented and controlled;
- discuss the importance of having change management procedures; and
- describe how network management software operates.

## 19-1  INTRODUCTION

This chapter deals with the tasks required to manage and operate a communications network. It is not always obvious to the lay person that a network must be managed, but in this chapter you will learn why management attention is not only necessary but vital to the successful operation of a network. The operation of a communications network is a complex but interrelated set of activities, some oriented toward normal routine operations and others that are performed when problems occur. The various facets of network operation must work together cohesively to provide the user with consistent, reliable service.

## 19-2  DEFINITION AND SCOPE OF NETWORK MANAGEMENT AND NETWORK OPERATION

network management

network operation

**Network management** is the set of activities that direct the resources required to keep a network operating over the long term. **Network operation** is the set of activities required to keep a communications network operating on a short-term, day-to-day basis. Network management includes traditional management activities such as planning, budgeting, controlling, and supervising, whereas network operation is concerned with immediate matters such as keeping circuits running, handling error conditions that cannot automatically be corrected by the equipment or software, responding to users' problems and questions, and ensuring that the network is performing well. The proper view of the scope of both network management and network operation is the same view that the user has of the network. It is an all-encompassing view in which all of the elements that are required to deliver communications service to the user are equally important. If users think any of the elements are not functioning properly, the network is "down." If a server or one of the application programs running in it is not operating, the user cannot receive the service he or she expects, and the network operation group should be concerned about the problem and involved in getting that service restored. From the user's perspective, any time he or she wants to use a workstation on the network to perform any service or to run any application, all of the required network and computing hardware and software should be available.

Network users have become accustomed to this level of service because, in general, most of today's telecommunications infrastructure is quite reliable. ISPs, cable television networks, DSLs, dial-up connections—generally work reliably and are ready when people want to use them. The telephone network is another example of a network service that is known for reliability. For most of us, waiting for a dial tone when we lift the handset rarely occurs. We expect that when we want to make a telephone call, the network will be ready to serve our needs—and it is.

Unfortunately, some networks in businesses and other organizations do not operate at that same high level of reliability. In many companies, several network failures per day or erratic response times are considered normal or good enough. This is not to imply, however, that all networks must be as reliable as the telephone system. The service requirements (QoS) of the organization that owns the network must be defined and the network must be designed to meet those requirements. If 24-hour availability of the network is not required, it is a waste of money to design the network for 24-hour operation. If an outage or two each week is not critical (albeit inconvenient for the users), perhaps it is not worth spending money to provide service that is more reliable. The key concept is that each company must define the service level it expects from its communications network.

Network management and operations people have the challenging responsibility of ensuring that the defined requirements for availability and reliability are met. In most companies, the service requirement also includes requirements about consistently good response time and fast problem resolution. The network staff can meet these service objectives only if the scope of its responsibility is defined broadly.

In some companies, however, the network management group is viewed more narrowly as having the responsibility for lines and modems only. By limiting the scope, major pieces of the network may be left with no management. The proper scope of network management and operation responsibilities includes the following:

- user workstations
- modems
- communications lines
- routers
- multiplexers
- communications software
- any other components that are a part of delivering communication services to users

In addition, the network management personnel need to be familiar with the computers and applications software on the network. Admittedly, there is some potential overlap with the functions of the computer operations staff, and in each company the lines of responsibility between the two groups must be clearly defined. However, the network management people are in the best position to view the entire process of delivering information from the computer to the user and are, therefore, in the best position to communicate with the user and to see that problems are resolved.

The same network management staff may also be responsible for the proper operation of the voice network. Historically, different groups have handled the voice and data network operation in a company, but there is no organizational or technical reason why they shouldn't be brought together. There may be strong political reasons for not combining the two groups, but it is probably in the best interest of the organization to overcome these objections and move toward a single network management staff.

## 19-3  WHY IT IS IMPORTANT TO MANAGE THE NETWORK

One might ask why it is necessary or worthwhile to spend any time or effort managing the communications network. There are three primary reasons:

1. The network is an asset.
2. The network is a resource on which organizations become dependent.
3. Networks in many organizations are growing or changing rapidly.

The communications network, as well as computers and applications, are assets of the organization and are vital to its operation. Perhaps this can be most easily understood by thinking about the importance of the telephone and what would happen if it were not available. Similarly, organizations that have networks, computers, and workstations are finding that they are increasingly dependent on the reliable operation of that equipment in order to do business or fulfill their mission. This dependence is similar to the organization's need for good people, sufficient financial resources, reliable suppliers, and loyal customers. Each of these assets must be managed, and the communications network is no exception.

Viewing the network as an asset implies that its creative use can give the organization advantages. A company's network might be tied to the Internet to make it easy for customers to get product information and order products. Networks might be used to give production people instantaneous access to material requirements or to give service people access to a database containing solutions to customer problems. Network facilities also may be used to improve the productivity or effectiveness of the employees by making it easier for them to exchange information, schedule meetings, or gain approvals. Universities that offer courses that can be taken over the Internet offer a convenience to students that non-networked schools cannot match. Lack of imagination is the major factor limiting the creative use of communications networks.

Networks in many organizations are growing at a rate of 15 to 50 percent per year, compounded. The breadth of service being provided and the amount of money being spent on networks makes network management virtually mandatory. Without management, there would be chaos. In particular, network operation must ensure that the service provided to existing users of the network does not degrade as new users are added.

Furthermore, they must ensure that change (growth) is implemented in a controlled manner.

## 19-4   NETWORK MANAGEMENT IN SMALL ORGANIZATIONS

Even in small organizations, networks must be managed. Successful small companies may experience a lot of change and/or rapid growth, and in that environment, network management is especially important. Although small organizations cannot afford to have very many people working on network management tasks, at least one person must be given the overall responsibility for the network—even if it is only part of his job. Furthermore, someone must be responsible for the day-to-day operation of the network and workstations because, just as in large companies, the small organization may be dependent on the network for its day-to-day operation.

Many of the tasks described in the rest of this chapter may be handled quite informally in a small organization, but the basic framework and techniques that are discussed are just as relevant as in larger organizations. With a vast majority of employees now having experience with PCs, either at home or on the job, the situation can easily arise where "everyone is an expert" and has his or her own thoughts about the way the network should be run. That's another reason why it is especially important to be clear in a small organization about who has the responsibility and authority for network-related decisions. The network manager job can be exciting and rewarding, and can provide an opportunity for a relatively young person to be responsible for a significant activity. On the other hand, positions of this type are often stressful and demanding, and keep the incumbent hopping even beyond normal working hours.

## 19-5   THE FUNCTIONS OF NETWORK MANAGEMENT

The business objective of network management is to satisfy the organization's and user's service expectations by providing reliable network service with sufficient capacity, consistently good performance, and fast problem resolution over the long term. To achieve this, certain activities must be performed—activities that are the same as or similar to those performed in other departments of the organization. These activities are:

- Staffing
- Organizing
- Planning
- Directing
- Controlling

These functions are described in detail in all management textbooks, so what will be discussed here is only a brief summary of how the concepts are applied to network management.

### Staffing

staffing

**Staffing** is a management function that is particularly challenging for network managers because there is a high demand for (and a shortage of) people who know about networks. Colleges, universities, and technical schools all offer programs and degrees that focus on educating people for careers in networking, but the demand has outstripped the supply for many years. Other sources of people are communications carriers and the military, both of which provide excellent, albeit frequently very specialized, training to their people.

If the organization can afford to have more than one person on its networking staff, a mix of skills is required. It is highly desirable to have planning, conceptualizing, administrative, operational, problem solving, and technical skills, but seldom can all of these be found in one person. With only one or a few people on the networking staff, it is hard to maintain the right mix of skills. If the department is larger, the task is somewhat easier. Hiring people who have the right aptitudes and the ability and interest in continuing to learn is very important because the networking world is continually changing in both the technological and regulatory dimensions. Therefore, continual upgrading of one's knowledge is a necessity and the right kinds of employees will find this prospect exciting.

Outside consultants can be used on occasion to supplement the knowledge of the internal staff, particularly when very specialized expertise is required. However, if the expertise applies to a technology that is to become a part of the organization's network, the organization needs to develop some in-house knowledge of the subject.

**outsourcing**

Total **outsourcing** of the networking activity is another alternative for the organization to consider. Companies such as EDS, IBM, and others make a business of designing, implementing, and operating networks (and computer centers) for other organizations. When they are engaged, they normally take over all responsibility for staffing and all other parts of network planning and operation. Some organizations feel that outsourcing is an excellent idea because networking is not their mainstream activity. Other organizations feel that networking is too vital to outsource and they would rather retain total control inside.

## Organizing

**organizing**

**Organizing** is grouping people to accomplish the mission of the department. If the department consists of only one person, there isn't much organizing to do! Even if there are only a few people, the task of organizing is probably simple because the people have been hired for specific jobs and they presumably have the skills to do the job for which they were hired. As the size of the staff grows, organizing becomes more complex because people will have overlapping skills. There will be more possibilities for job rotations to vary experience, additional training for employee development, and even job movement to and from other parts of the organization.

One decision that management must make when organizing the network department is how much overlap there will be with other departments in the company. For example, as new equipment is required, will the network department purchase it on their own or will they use the resources of the organization's purchasing department? Similarly, what will be the division of responsibility between the networking department and the accounting department with regard to financial matters?

There are always many ways to organize people to carry out their responsibilities. The groupings of activities described in this book are typical of the way networking is being carried out in organizations, but they are not the only possibilities. Although each network group has certain basic activities to perform, there is always the flexibility to tailor the organization to the talents of the individuals in the group. An organization chart of a typical networking group is shown in Figure 19-1. The chart implies a department of at least five people. However, if fewer are available, certain work—such as network operation and technical support—could be done by one person.

**FIGURE 19-1** Typical telecommunications department organization.

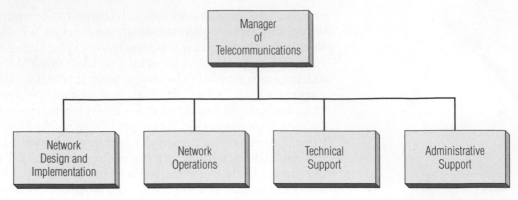

## Planning

planning

In any organization, **planning** is required, but it is especially necessary in a field like networking, where change occurs continually. Networking change comes in three dimensions.

- the organization's needs change
- technology changes
- the regulatory environment changes

Some organizations have very detailed, rigorous, and scheduled planning processes while others operate informally and put plans together only when required. Networking activities need to be consistent with the organization's culture but must also have enough forethought and rigor so that the organization doesn't get surprised in an unfortunate way.

Suppose, for example, that the organization's use of the network is growing and the network staff can see that the network will run out of capacity in two or three months. Suppose that it will take two months to get budgetary approval for additional network equipment, one month to get the equipment delivered, plus one month to get it installed. What we have is the making of a nasty surprise for the organization when the network runs out of capacity and there is no way to get it upgraded for several weeks. In some organizational cultures, heads may roll! Proper anticipation and planning will avoid such a crisis.

At a minimum, the network staff should make a one-year plan at the beginning of each year. Planning starts by gathering input from executive management about the strategies and directions of the organization. Network plans must be aligned with and supportive of the organization's goals, and the best way to understand those is to talk with executive management directly. User departments within the organization, such as the marketing department, should also be approached for input. They may have ideas about new capabilities or may be receiving comments or feedback from customers that can be translated into the need for new or upgraded network capability. For example, they may know that the major competitor is planning to allow customers to order products through the Internet, a capability that will provide a significant advantage in the marketplace.

The network staff itself can add technological input to the plan. Their knowledge of industry directions and new networking technologies that might successfully be applied within the organization is unique and valuable because new technology can sometimes be applied to give competitive advantage. There also needs to be operational input about capacity, reliability, and performance issues with the current network. This input may come both from the network operations staff, and by listening to the comments and feedback from user departments within the organization.

You can see that successfully gathering input for the network plan requires a lot of communication with people at all levels of the organization and (ideally) from customers outside the organization. Communication and information gathering takes some time if it is done properly, so it must be started well before the plan is due to be completed.

After the information is gathered, it must be analyzed and translated into specific requirements for new network capability or capacity and the approximate timing for their implementation. With the list of requirements and desired timing, the required resources can be estimated and measured, both in terms of the number of people and the amount of money it would take to implement the plans. Sometimes there are constraints that dictate that all of the items cannot be completed on the desired schedule. For example, the plans may suggest a list of desired network upgrades that would require four people working full time for six months to implement. If there are only twenty people in the company, it is unlikely that four of them will be assigned (or hired) just to work on networking projects—unless the company is in the networking business!

Normally, the leader of the network group, his manager, and perhaps other managers in the organization—up to and including executive management—meet to resolve the differences between what network upgrades have been requested and are desirable, and which can be afforded. The forum for this reconciliation takes many forms, depending on the size and culture of the organization. Ultimately, it does get resolved and the plan is approved.

Some larger organizations have a multilevel planning process during which they develop long-term plans, medium-term plans and short-term or project plans. Typical time horizons for these plans are five-years, three years and one year. In the networking business, projecting five-year and even three-year plans is difficult because of the rapid advances in technology; however, if the organization demands it, a best-effort attempt must be made. In that case, it is very important to state what assumptions are being made while putting the plan together. Typical assumptions that might be stated include:

- The number of students in the university is expected to stay stable over the five-year planning horizon.
- The number of patient rooms in the hospital is expected to increase by 5 percent next year and 20 percent three years from now.
- Sales in a company are expected to grow by 3 percent per year.
- The cost of long distance circuits used for data transmission is expected to drop by 1 percent per year.
- Salaries of network personnel are expected to increase by 4 percent per year, slightly higher than the salaries for other employees because of the heavy market demand for such individuals.

Input from others in the organization needs to be gathered to ensure that the assumptions are realistic.

When the plan is finally approved, it is important to remember that it is just that—a plan. It represents the best thoughts of those who prepared the plan at a given point in time. However, conditions change and it is important that the plan be updated when necessary to keep it realistic.

FIGURE 19-2 The mission statement of one company's network department.

---

**Mission of the Network Department**

The mission of this department is to provide the company with a communications network that will meet the needs of our customers and employees for interactive data and voice communications at an acceptable cost. The department is also responsible to ensure that the company has a staff that has sufficient expertise to operate the network in an efficient, cost-effective manner.

---

## Directing

directing

Management's responsibility for **directing** is to ensure that the mission and plans of the network organization are executed on a timely and accurate basis. This is best achieved by first specifying the overall mission for the department and then ensuring that it is understood by the members of the group. The network department of one company had the mission statement shown in Figure 19-2. Once the mission statement is written, it must be explained to members of the department and their questions must be answered. It is important that each person in the department understand the mission and their role to help achieve it. Management's role is to ensure that employees are motivated and have their own personal objectives that are aligned with and are supportive of the mission. Personal objectives are frequently written annually, soon after the overall plan for the department is established.

Other common techniques used in directing the department are requiring each staff member to write a monthly report and holding regular review meetings for all projects currently underway. In the operational area, a regular review of network performance statistics alerts management to potential problems and assures employees that good performance is important. The purpose of all of these techniques is to improve communication within the department and to allow individuals to gain recognition for the results they are achieving. If other people in the organization describe the network department with words such as *"results-oriented," "proactive,"* and *"service-oriented,"* it is a good indication that the department is successful in its work.

## Controlling

controlling

Unfortunately, the word **controlling** often has a negative connotation, but it simply means ensuring that the department is performing according to the plans it has made. Control activities are very important to any management process. Even the best-laid plans are subject to change, and part of management's responsibility is ensuring that those changes are made consciously and with a full understanding of the implications. In the network department, two major controls are financial controls and those applied to ensure that the QoS is being maintained.

FINANCIAL CONTROLS    Financial controls take several forms, but the most common form is the measurement of actual expenses against a budget. Budgets in most organizations are prepared annually, and expenses are usually summarized monthly. In some organizations, network expenses are charged back to the user departments each month, based on either a preestablished rate or on actual usage of the network. Actual usage is difficult to measure, however, so basing the chargeback on some preestablished rate is most common.

The types of expenses that a networking department incurs include:

- **salaries and wages**—the total amount of money, including overtime, paid to employees in the department
- **employee benefits**—the amount paid for medical, dental, life, disability, other insurance, retirement, savings, and other benefit programs, often calculated as a percentage of the salaries and wages amount
- **rental/lease**—the amount paid to vendors for the use of equipment or software that has not been purchased
- **maintenance**—the amount paid for the repair of equipment or software or for service contracts to cover future repairs
- **depreciation**—funds budgeted to cover the depreciation of expense for items that have been purchased and are depreciable assets
- **supplies**—the amount paid for items such as general office supplies, paper for printers, ink cartridges, and subscriptions to periodicals
- **education and training**—expenses for classes, general seminars, and other educational activities
- **travel**—the amount spent for the expense of taking a trip, such as airline tickets, hotels, and meals
- **utilities**—the amount paid for heating, air conditioning, and telephone
- **building/corporate overhead (sometimes called "burden")**—many organizations assess a flat fee to each department for the use of office space and other facilities. This is sometimes expressed as an overhead rate, which may be based on the number of square feet occupied, the number of people in the department, or the size of the rest of the budget.

A spreadsheet program is an invaluable tool to use for both budgeting and expense management. As equipment is added or other changes that affect the budget are made, they can be recorded in the spreadsheet as an aid to projecting actual expenses for the rest of the year and for preparing the following year's budget.

Periodically, it is necessary to check the total expenses and compare them to the budget to ensure that costs are under control. Normally, reports are provided each month by the accounting department in a format similar to the one shown in Figure 19-3. The left side of the report shows the actual expenditures for the current month, the budget for the month, and the variation from budget. The right side shows the same information on a year-to-date (YTD) basis. With this type of report and the appropriate detailed information to back it up, the networking manager and staff can keep close track of the money his department is spending and, if necessary, take appropriate steps to keep expenses in line with the budget.

**QUALITY OF SERVICE** Network departments should have service-level agreements for the services they provide. The service-level agreements should be developed with and agreed upon by the users of the network. Typical service-level agreements set a level of expectation regarding network availability and response time, and will be discussed in more detail later in this chapter, in the section on performance management. Responsibilities must be assigned, typically to the network operation group, for monitoring and reporting performance against the service-level agreement and for negotiating changes in the agreements to address users' changing requirements.

FIGURE 19-3 A monthly network department expense report.

| Telecommunications Expenses July 2004 | | | | | | |
|---|---|---|---|---|---|---|
| Current Month | | | | Year to Date | | |
| Detail Actual Expenses | Budget | Variance | Type of Expense | Detail Actual Expenses | Budget | Variance |
| 9,626.49 | 9,800 | 174 | Salaries and Wages | 66,841.99 | 67,400 | 558 |
| 2,695.42 | 2,744 | 49 | Benefits | 18,715.76 | 18,872 | 156 |
| 190.85 | 150 | −41 | Supplies | 1,632.00 | 1,050 | −582 |
| 5,219.38 | 5,700 | 481 | Maintenance | 36,266.32 | 39,900 | 3,634 |
| 1,119.21 | 300 | −819 | Outside Services | 1,119.21 | 2,100 | 981 |
| 575.76 | 700 | 124 | Travel | 3,885.64 | 4,900 | 1,014 |
| 382.19 | 360 | −22 | Telephone | 2,674.49 | 2,520 | −154 |
| 12,519.38 | 12,700 | 181 | Rental/Lease | 82,184.58 | 84,300 | 2,115 |
| 830.00 | 830 | 0 | Overhead | 5,810.00 | 5,810 | 0 |
| 3,019.00 | 2,600 | −419 | Depreciation | 20,874.00 | 19,130 | −1,744 |
| 36,177.68 | 35,884 | −292 | Total Expenses | 240,003.99 | 245,982 | 5,978 |
| | | −0.81% | Variance as a % of Budget | | | 2.43% |

## 19-6   NETWORK OPERATION AND THE NETWORK OPERATIONS GROUP

Network operation is made up of the following six activities:

1. day-to-day operations
2. problem management
3. performance measurement and tuning
4. configuration control
5. change management
6. management reporting

Each of these activities interrelates with the others. In large companies, a separate department might handle each of the activities, but in small organizations one person may perform all of the functions. You will study each activity separately as though it were done by a separate department, and will examine where interrelationships occur.

The network operations group is the heart of network management. It is most easily visualized as a group of people who reside in a place called the network operation center, where the network is run. The network operations group has many similarities to traditional computer mainframe or server operations groups. In some companies, the two groups are combined or report to the same supervisor. The network operations group is responsible for the management of the physical network resources; activation of components such as lines or routers, perhaps manually rerouting traffic when circuits fail; and execution of normal and problem-related procedures.

If the network does not operate 24 hours per day, 7 days per week, there may be a daily routine of starting and stopping the network. To start the network, communications software is loaded in all of the computers and routers that are software driven. Then, when necessary, commands are issued to instruct the software to activate the circuits. (In most cases, PCs start communicating automatically when the appropriate software is loaded.) At the end of the day, there may be a similar process for shutting down or deactivating the network. Individual terminals may be stopped as people leave work; circuits may be individually deactivated; and after the entire network is shut down, the communications software may be removed from host computers, freeing the memory for use by other programs.

To reiterate, the aforementioned procedures are relevant only in networks that do not operate 24 hours per day. More and more networks are left in an operational status all of the time, which makes daily network starting and stopping procedures irrelevant.

When the network is operating, the network operations staff is responsible for monitoring its behavior. Because communications circuits and terminals—especially on a WAN—exist in relatively uncontrolled environments, unusual conditions and problems are a certainty. Good telecommunications software provides regular status information for the network operations group. It identifies which components of the network are operating normally and which are having problems. Often, the status is in the form of a workstation's visual display that is updated every few seconds to give a current, real-time picture of the network's operation. Well-designed network monitoring hardware and software should quickly alert the network operations group when problems occur, so that appropriate actions can be taken. Problem identification and resolution are discussed extensively in the next section.

Another responsibility of the network operations group is to collect statistics about the network's performance and to watch developing trends that may affect performance. The statistics-gathering process should be a routine part of the operation, and software that automates and simplifies the task is available. When performance or other problems occur, additional information should be gathered. Although the first responsibility is to get the problem solved and get the network operation back to normal, the secondary responsibility is to gather data that can be analyzed later to prevent the problem from recurring. In networks where the performance data are gathered automatically by hardware and software, the network operations group must ensure that the data-gathering mechanisms are working properly.

The network operations staff normally has other responsibilities, such as problem management, configuration control, or change management—each of which will now be discussed in detail.

## 19-7  PROBLEM MANAGEMENT

problem management

help desk

**Problem management** is the process of expeditiously handling a problem from its initial recognition to a satisfactory resolution. One of the important subgroups of network operation is the **help desk**. The help desk is the single point of contact with users when problems occur. Ideally, a single telephone number is established and users are instructed to call the help desk whenever they have problems with any of their communications equipment.

The first responsibility of the help desk personnel is to log each problem that is reported. Information may be kept manually, but there is software available that allows entry of the problem into a database, where it can be tracked until the problem is resolved. A sample of a manual log sheet is shown in Figure 19-4. The types of information that are recorded include the date and time, the name of the user reporting the problem, the type of equipment that is being used (and its identification), and the symptoms of the

**FIGURE 19-4**  Help desk
log of each reported
problem.

| HELP DESK PROBLEM LOG | | | | | | |
|---|---|---|---|---|---|---|
| Date | Time | Name of Caller | Phone No. | Equipment Type | Symptoms | Resolution |
|  |  |  |  |  |  |  |
|  |  |  |  |  |  |  |
|  |  |  |  |  |  |  |
|  |  |  |  |  |  |  |
|  |  |  |  |  |  |  |
|  |  |  |  |  |  |  |
|  |  |  |  |  |  |  |
|  |  |  |  |  |  |  |
|  |  |  |  |  |  |  |
|  |  |  |  |  |  |  |
|  |  |  |  |  |  |  |
|  |  |  |  |  |  |  |
|  |  |  |  |  |  |  |

**FIGURE 19-4**  Help desk log of each reported problem.

problem being reported. The advantage of an automated problem logging system is that the information recorded in it can be made widely available to those who have a need for it, regardless of where they may be located. For example, technicians working in the field can connect to the system to look for problems in their area of responsibility and to update the status. Another advantage of an automated system is its ability to easily sort and report the problems in various sequences for later analysis.

In many cases, the help desk operator will be able to offer immediate assistance while the user is on the telephone. If, for example, a communications circuit or LAN with ten PCs on it has failed, it is likely that the help desk will receive several calls from users who have PCs on the circuit. After the first call, the help desk operator will be familiar with the problem and will be able to assure subsequent callers that action is being taken. Other types of problems, such as certain types of workstation errors, tend to be repetitive in nature. The help desk operator, on hearing the symptom, may be able to tell the user a particular sequence of keystrokes that will clear the problem or correct the error. Even in such simple cases, the problem should be logged. Later analysis may show that many users are having the same difficulty and that additional training or documentation is required.

Help desk operators should be provided with a script for at least a standard list of questions to ask all callers. Some of these questions should be designed to ensure that the proper data about the problem are gathered, such as "What is your name, employee number, and telephone number?" or "What type of workstation are you using?" Other questions are diagnostic in nature, such as, "Is the green light on your terminal lit?" or "Have you checked to be sure your computer is plugged in?" or "Are any other people sitting near you having a similar problem?" Some companies have developed flow charts or decision trees of questions that assist the help desk operator in diagnosing even relatively complex problems. The help desk person asks the user a series of questions, and the answers narrow the range of possible causes and determine which question will be asked next. Diagnostic tools such as these are simple forms of artificial intelligence and they are subject to automation.

**trouble ticket**     In large organizations, a **trouble ticket** is opened for each problem, often on a computer-based system that allows the trouble to be recorded in a database. In fact, the system that generates the trouble ticket may be the same system that contains the problem log. Everyone involved with resolving the problem works with the same "ticket" that is online, which gets updated in real time. Each person can be given the authority to view or update certain parts of the information. When the problem is resolved, the person who corrects it is usually the one who closes the trouble ticket and completes the form. The software may be programmed to automatically notify the help desk and the user. The ticket is then stored in the database where it can be referred to later, if necessary. An analysis of trouble tickets can identify trends. For example, a growing number of problems on a LAN may indicate a cabling or software problem that is the root cause of all the troubles. It is always desirable to find and fix the root cause of a series of related problems.

In addition to taking trouble calls, help desk operators in many organizations are also responsible for handling calls from people who have routine questions about the use of the network. Users may want to know, for example, if a certain location of the company is online and can be contacted through the network, how to operate an infrequently used capability of their workstation, or how to use a certain program. The organization must decide what types of routine questions the help desk operators will be trained to answer and then to provide guidance for the operators, telling them where to direct questions that they cannot answer or are not responsible for answering.

## Problem Resolution Levels

levels of support

One approach to problem tracking and resolution uses the notion of **levels of support.** The exact definition of the levels varies from organization to organization, but the idea is that the person who initially takes the telephone call about the problem has enough knowledge to be able to quickly resolve a high percentage—say 80 to 85 percent—of all the problems reported. Problems that cannot be resolved within a few minutes at this level, called level 1, are passed to level 2, which is made up of technicians who have a higher degree of skill, experience, or training. Level 2 personnel handle all of the problems remaining from level 1 and also those that must involve a vendor. Normally, it is expected that level 2 would solve 10 percent to 15 percent of the total problems that are reported.

All problems not solved at level 2 are passed to level 3, which is made up of communications technical support specialists or vendor specialists. Level 3 usually receives only about 5 percent of the problems—those that are extremely complex, difficult to identify, or difficult to solve. Problems that reach this level may require software modifications, hardware engineering changes, or other corrective actions that take a long time to put in place.

The advantage of the leveling approach to problem solving is that the person who has the lowest skill level and who is able to do so solves the problem, and highly skilled technical people are reserved to work on the most difficult problems.

## Escalation Procedures

Procedures need to be in place to escalate the status of a problem if it has not been resolved within a predetermined period of time. Certain problems are more critical than others and need more formal and rapid escalation. A single inoperative terminal may be escalated if it has not been repaired within 24 hours, whereas a router outage that brings down a large part of the network may be escalated immediately.

problem escalation

**Problem escalation** takes two forms. One type of escalation is to bring in additional technical resources to help solve the problem. The other type of

FIGURE 19-5   A problem escalation procedure.

**Technical:**

1. Level 1 (help desk) works on the problem for a maximum of 15 minutes. If problem is not resolved, pass it to level 2.

2. Level 2 (technician) works on the problem for up to 1 hour. If the problem is not resolved, notify the help desk supervisor and continue working on the problem.

3. If the problem is not resolved in 4 hours, get the appropriate level 3 (network specialist) involved. Level 2 retains "ownership" of the problem. It is level 2's responsibility to monitor the progress and to keep the user and the help desk supervisor informed about the status of the problem every 2 hours after level 3 gets involved.

**Managerial:**

1. The help desk supervisor is notified by level 2 if the problem has not been resolved in 1 hour.

2. If the problem is not resolved in 2 hours, the help desk supervisor notifies the supervisor of network operations.

3. If the problem is not resolved in 4 hours, the supervisor of network operations notifies the manager of telecommunications. The manager of telecommunications calls the manager in the user department to discuss the situation and decide on any extraordinary action to be taken.

4. If the problem is not resolved in 8 hours, the manager of telecommunications notifies the chief information officer (or equivalent) and discusses the actions taken to date, and the future plans to get the problem resolved. The discussion should also include the possibility of contacting vendor management if appropriate.

NOTE: These sample procedures do not account for actions to be taken if the problem continues after normal working hours. The actions to be taken depend on the nature of the problem and the criticality of telecommunications to the company.

escalation is to make users and management aware of the actions being taken to resolve the problem. Often, these escalations proceed at different rates. Figure 19-5 shows a sample of a generic escalation procedure. It is generic because it does not distinguish between types of problems that might be escalated at different rates. In many companies, problems are first ranked according to their severity. Severe problems are escalated very quickly, whereas problems that have limited impact or those that affect only one or a small group of users are escalated more slowly. The example in Figure 19-5 shows the differences between technical and management/user escalation.

From time to time, all open problems or trouble tickets need to be reviewed by network operation supervisors. Typically, this is done each day with an eye toward spotting unusual problems or those for which the normal problem escalation procedures may not be applicable. On an exception basis, supervisors can make decisions about the relative priorities of outstanding problems and whether to take extraordinary steps, such as accelerating the normal escalation procedures to resolve the problem.

**problem tracking meeting**

Another technique used by many organizations is a periodic **problem tracking meeting.** In this meeting, people from network operation, software support, vendor organizations, and perhaps computer operations and user groups review all outstanding problems. This type of meeting is an excellent communications vehicle and if the computer operations people are involved, it gives an opportunity to prioritize all of the unresolved problems that can affect people's use of the network, whether they are primarily computer- or network-related.

## Bypassing the Problem

If a problem is caused by a piece of equipment or a circuit failure, the ideal solution—from the user's point of view—is to bypass the problem, enable the user to keep working, and then diagnose and fix the problem later. A failing terminal or modem might be "fixed," from the user's perspective, by replacing it with a spare that is available for just such a purpose. The failed equipment can then be repaired or returned to the vendor for service. When it is repaired, it can either become a spare itself or be returned to the original user.

## Reconfiguration

patch panel

In the network control center where all of the circuits come together, spare equipment can be substituted by using hubs, switches, and **patch panels.** Depending on what equipment needs to be substituted, analog or digital switches can be used to switch a workstation to a different port on a hub, a circuit from a failing modem to a good one, or to bring a new server online. Sometimes, software switching may also be necessary to allow workstations to be addressed on the alternate ports, modems, or circuits. A patch panel is a piece of equipment on which each circuit or piece of equipment has one or more jacks. Using cords with plugs, the network technician can temporarily connect spare equipment into the circuits by inserting a plug into the appropriate jack on the patch panel.

Another technique for bypassing a failure is the use of dial-up lines as the backup for leased circuits. This technique is called "dial backup." Certain types of modems can handle both leased and switched connections and are designed to automatically make a dial-up connection if the leased circuit fails. The dial-up connection often operates at a slower speed, but for many applications, slower speed operation is preferable to being totally out of service.

## Problem Diagnosis and Repair

While solid failures are relatively easy to detect, intermittent failures can be difficult for even the most sophisticated hardware or software to spot and track. When a workstation, circuit, or router fails and stays out of service, hardware and software monitors can easily see the failure and can display information so that a technician can be dispatched to correct the problem. However, when a piece of hardware fails intermittently and randomly and then in a short time comes back online, the outage may be erased or ignored by the monitors before service personnel are notified to go check out the problem. Packets of data may have been lost, however, causing them to be retransmitted, thus adding to the network load. Because failures of this type tend to become worse over time as the hardware deteriorates, the frequency of the intermittent failures may increase, which causes a greater number of packets to be retransmitted. Retransmissions lower throughput and increase delay, causing overall network performance to be degraded.

Because it is not so easy and usually not economically attractive to have spare circuits or other expensive equipment available, the diagnosis and repair of many types of equipment problems are essential. On the one hand, routers and switches do not often fail, and because the diagnosis and repair require specialized equipment and training, they are almost always left to the vendor's maintenance people. On the other hand, because WAN circuits are more prone to failure, many companies find it desirable to have some testing equipment available to assist in diagnosing circuit problems.

Depending on whether an analog or digital circuit is to be tested, different types of equipment are required. Analog signals are analyzed with simple speakers, tone generators, butt sets, and conductive probes. The techniques and equipment are similar for all analog lines, whether they are used primarily for voice or for data. Digital circuits, or the digital sides of analog circuits, require the use of breakout boxes and oscilloscopes. Some modems are capable of running tests on the communications circuits to which they are attached. The types of problems this equipment can identify include frequency response, dB loss, and various types of distortion, problems that were described in Chapter 9.

The communications carrier that provides the circuit has extensive testing equipment, as well, and can normally be relied on to diagnose and resolve circuit problems. In many cases, however, additional information provided from tests at the user's end of the circuit greatly assists the vendor in problem resolution. Test data can pinpoint the exact location of the problem and help resolve it.

With a LAN, the wiring and cabling that comprise the circuits are usually privately owned, so either the company's network technicians or an organization that has been contracted to do the diagnosis and maintenance must do the analysis and problem determination work. LAN hubs, bridges, switches, and routers are often relatively "smart" and often have built-in diagnostic capability to help locate the source of trouble.

Most other modern communications equipment also has diagnostic capabilities. Modems usually have self-test routines that can be activated manually through the front panel or, under certain circumstances, that can be activated by the modem itself. Personal computers frequently have software-based diagnostic routines that the user can activate through a menu. One of the first questions the help desk should ask when a problem is reported is whether the appropriate equipment diagnostics have been run.

**protocol analyzer**

When all hardware appears to be working correctly, but communication is still impossible, it may be necessary to employ a device called a **protocol analyzer.** A protocol analyzer is an electronic instrument that can look at the actual bits or characters being transmitted on the circuit to determine whether the rules of the protocol are being followed correctly. Some protocol analyzers are designed to handle a specific protocol, such as IP or HDLC, whereas other equipment can examine and diagnose multiple protocols. When protocol analysis is performed, it is usually necessary to have software specialists involved because few hardware technicians are trained to understand the detailed characteristics and sequences of the protocols and data being transmitted.

A basic decision that companies must make is how much problem diagnosis and testing they will perform themselves and how much they will leave to vendors or other maintenance organizations. Often, the answer to the question is to use a combination of people, some from inside the company and others from the vendor. In that case, coordination of the work is important.

One reason why it is desirable to have appropriate diagnostic equipment and trained technicians on the staff of the user organization is that in today's multivendor networks, it is not always clear which vendor should be called when a problem occurs. For example, a WAN line from Colorado to California may have two local telephone companies, a long distance carrier, modem manufacturers, and workstation manufacturers involved. A LAN might have a router, switches, and workstations from different manufacturers. How does one determine the exact source of an error or the reason for an outage? Sometimes the user's technicians must perform tests on the network to determine exactly where the problem lies in order to know which vendor to call. Even if a specific vendor's equipment is clearly at fault, it may be possible to perform tests that further pinpoint the problem while the vendor's technician is on the way. This may greatly speed the process of repairing the failing component and may keep the cost of the technician's time to a minimum.

## 19-8   PERFORMANCE MANAGEMENT

performance
management

**Performance management** is the set of activities that measure the network performance and adjust it as necessary to meet users' requirements. The people responsible for network performance management use the statistical data gathered by the network operation staff. The data are analyzed and summarized, and the network performance is reported to management. This work also triggers performance adjustment activities or performance problem resolution, which is normally done by the communications technical staff. It also provides utilization data to network capacity planners. The location of the performance management responsibility within the organization depends on the size of the network department, the skill levels of the staff, and the preference of the network manager.

service level agreement

To determine whether the performance of a network is adequate as measured by its reliability and response time, preestablished performance objectives are required. Performance objectives may be established for the entire network or for a specified set of equipment or users in the form of a **service level agreement.** Service level agreements often involve stating that of the $x$ hours of the day or week when the user's terminal and applications should normally be available, the actual availability of those applications will be a certain percentage of $x$. It normally also contains a statement about the response time the user can expect at her workstation. A typical service level agreement might read like the following:

- The order entry application and customer service terminals will be operational from 7:00 a.m. to 8:00 p.m. EST each business day.

- The availability will be 98 percent, as measured at the user terminal. Downtime will not exceed 2 percent.

- Response time, measured from the time the user presses the Enter key until the response is received at the terminal will be less than one second 90 percent of the time and less than ten seconds 100 percent of the time.

This type of service level statement must be negotiated between the user and the network and computer operations people. The starting point should be to identify the user's requirements. The network and computer people may have an option to provide a better grade of service at an increased cost if the user is willing to pay for it, or conversely, less availability or slower response time if that is what the user can tolerate or is willing to pay for.

The other part of performance management is the actual tracking of the network's performance. Performance data about the network can be gathered by hardware, software, or a combination of the two. Recording the availability and responsiveness of the network is normally a software function, but it needs to be measured close to or in the user's workstation to ensure that it reflects what he is actually experiencing.

network management
systems

management
information base (MIB)

Several vendors offer a class of software known as **network management systems.** These systems are designed to help network operations people keep track of the status of a network and provide network performance data for later analysis. Most network management systems use a similar basic structure. Nodes such as workstations, servers, and other network devices run software that enables them to monitor and compile information about the state of the device in which they reside. This information is stored in a database called the **management information base (MIB),** where operators can examine it on a real-time or periodic basis. Summaries and statistical reports can be developed to show the entire network's performance, as well as highlight potential problem areas. The data can be compared to service level agreements to see if performance objectives are being met. The software can also send real-time alert messages to a central network management server when it recognizes problems. The central network management server receives the alerts and is programmed to react by taking appropriate actions, including operator notification, event logging, and automatic attempts at repair.

The central network management server can also proactively poll end stations to check the values of certain variables. Polling can be automatic or operator-initiated, and the software in the end station devices responds to the polls by accessing data stored in the MIB.

For voice networks, statistics are often gathered by the carrier that provides the circuits, as well as by PBXs and many smaller telephone systems. The carrier is usually willing to provide the collected statistics to the customer. Working together, the carrier and the customer can ensure that the network is properly configured for the actual traffic loads. In most PBX systems, statistics collection can be tailored to meet the particular requirements of the organization. Smaller telephone systems usually have less flexibility and provide a predefined set of standard statistics about each call, such as its duration, the extension number of the caller, and perhaps the outgoing circuit or trunk identification if one was used.

## Performance Reporting

In any type of performance measurement system, it is important to keep a history of performance statistics so that trends can be examined. One useful technique is to plot trend charts that show how certain network parameters, such as availability, response time, or circuit utilization, are changing over time. Some examples are shown in Figure 19-6. The trend charts should also show the standard or desired level of performance. Trend charts are particularly useful for watching parameters that change gradually over relatively long periods of time. While a gradual increase in response time might not be noticed for several weeks if the daily performance reports were the only information available, a trend chart would show the increase in response time more quickly.

Some of the parameters of the network that need to be tracked are:

- overall network availability and network availability: by segment, such as by circuit, geographic region, building, or even department
- response time: by hour of the day, by application, by circuit—measured from the user's point of view
- circuit utilization: by circuit and by time of day
- errors: by circuit, type of equipment, and software component
- routing: utilization of each circuit when multiple routes to the same destination are possible

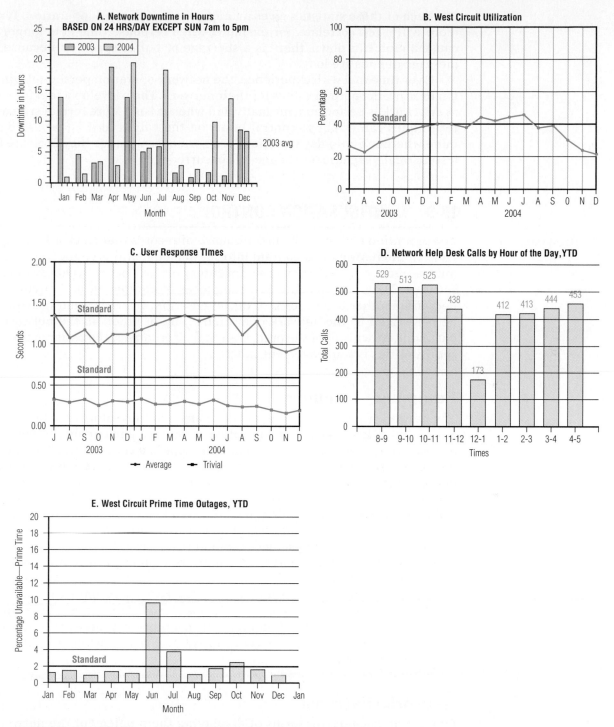

**FIGURE 19-6** These trend charts show several parameters of a network's operations. The standard level of performance is shown on many of the charts.

- buffer utilization: in the router, in controllers, and in the computer
- transaction mix: by time of day, over time
- queue lengths: in routers, in multiplexers, and in servers
- processing time: the time to process transaction messages in servers

Each of these statistics gives a unique view of network operation. Two or more will often correlate, for example, when response time gets longer because a circuit is down, there is a shortage of buffer space, or because the message queues are long.

Over time and with experience, the network operation personnel will begin to know the normal values for their network. They develop a feel for when the network is performing normally and when it isn't. More formal statistical techniques can establish control limits on the values so it is easy to determine whether day-to-day variations are normal or whether they indicate that a statistically significant change has occurred.

## 19-9    CONFIGURATION CONTROL

configuration control

**Configuration control** is the maintenance of records that track all the equipment in the network and contain information on how it is connected. One required record is an up-to-date inventory of all network hardware and software. Diagrams showing how the pieces of equipment and circuits connect are another useful form of documentation. Configuration control may be performed by the network operation group or others in the network department. As with all of the organizational alternatives, the assignment of responsibilities is a management function.

### Equipment Inventory

The network equipment inventory is like any other inventory system in that it is updated to keep track of the installed equipment and circuits, as well as all additions and deletions. If the inventory is kept in a computerized system, the data can easily be manipulated, sorted, or reported in different ways. Network operations personnel might want to see a report of all of the workstations of a certain model or may need to find the location of a server that has a certain serial number. Management might be interested in data about the total value of all the terminals or the total costs of all circuits. Such information is obtained easily from a properly designed, computerized inventory of network equipment. An example of a report from a network equipment inventory system is shown in Figure 19-7.

Software can be purchased to keep these types of inventory records, or a simple system may be developed in-house. As an alternative, the company may decide that its network equipment inventory will be kept in the company's property ledger, the accounting system that tracks all of the company's physical assets.

### Network Diagrams

One of the most useful forms of displaying the topology of the network is a map that shows all of the network locations and the circuits that connect them. Examples of this type of map for a WAN are shown in Figure 19-8. Such maps can be produced in many sizes. Wall size versions can be hung in the network control center. Versions of an 8 1/2″ × 11″ size can be put in notebooks or made into transparencies for use in presentations or at meetings.

Another level of detail, as shown in Figure 19-9, is a listing of each circuit and the devices attached to it. Charts of this type usually indicate the circuit number assigned by the carrier, as well as the names and/or network ad-

FIGURE 19-7 Inventory list of network equipment.

| Account 7045-336 Detail by Device Code Run Date 06/25/2004 | | | | | | |
|---|---|---|---|---|---|---|
| Device Type | Model | Serial | | Site Code | Account Billed | Vendor Charge |
| **COMMCTL** 8911 | A54 | 00951A | | CMD | 7045-336-4X3 | 5228 |
| **ROUTER** 2070 | 31A | 12506 | | CMD | 7045-336-4X3 | 1182 |
| 2070 | 31B | D0055 | | CMD | 7045-336-4X3 | 1182 |
| 2590 | 41C | D0056 | | MID | 7045-336-4X3 | 1182 |
| 2590 | 41C | D4528 | | MID | 7045-336-4X3 | 1182 |
| 2590 | 41C | D5477 | | CMD | 7045-336-4X3 | 1182 |
| **SWITCH** 611A | | G1843 | | CMD | 7045-336-4X3 | 36 |
| 690D | | W3090 | | CMD | 7045-336-4X3 | 36 |
| **PC** XL-500 | P-100 | P0319 | | MID | 7045-336-4X3 | 38 |
| XL-500 | P-100 | P7802 | | CMD | 7045-336-403 | 38 |
| XL-500 | P-100 | Q1611 | | CMD | 7045-336-403 | 38 |
| XL-650 | P-200 | T0173 | | CMD | 7045-336-4X3 | 38 |
| XL-650 | P-200 | T1157 | | MMS | 7045-336-4X3 | 38 |
| XL-950 | P-200 | AE958 | | CMD | 7045-336-403 | 38 |
| XL-950 | P-200 | VI904 | | MID | 7045-336-4X3 | 38 |
| XL-950 | P-200 | T4790 | | MID | 7045-336-4X3 | 38 |
| XL-950 | P-200 | B1140 | | MMS | 7045-336-4X3 | |
| **PRINTER** 2700 | A | 32255 | | CMD | 7045-336-4X3 | 822 |
| 2700 | A | 32305 | | CMD | 7045-336-4X3 | 822 |
| 2700 | B | 32431 | | CMD | 7045-336-4X3 | 822 |
| 9412 | 4112 | 40435 | | CMD | 7045-336-4X3 | 723 |
| 9412 | 4112 | 40560 | | MMS | 7045-336-4X3 | 723 |
| 8000 | 5 | 40938 | | CMD | 7045-336-4X3 | 416 |
| 8000 | 5 | 41039 | | CMD | 7045-336-4X3 | 416 |

dresses of the routers and workstations and other equipment. Equipment model numbers and serial numbers should also be included.

A third level of detail is the wiring diagram. The wiring diagram may be drawn for a single department, a floor of a building, an entire building, or some other grouping of equipment. One version is a type of map that shows the actual locations of the devices on the floor or in the building as well as the connections between them. Another type of wiring diagram has no bearing on the actual location of the equipment but shows in detail the order cable runs and types of wire, twisted-pair numbers, and pin numbers of each component in the network.

Drawings and diagrams of the network are most easily developed and maintained on a computer aided drafting (CAD) system that captures the drawing in a computer database and simplifies the maintenance. CAD software that has enough capacity to handle most networks is available for PCs, so most network departments can easily afford the tool.

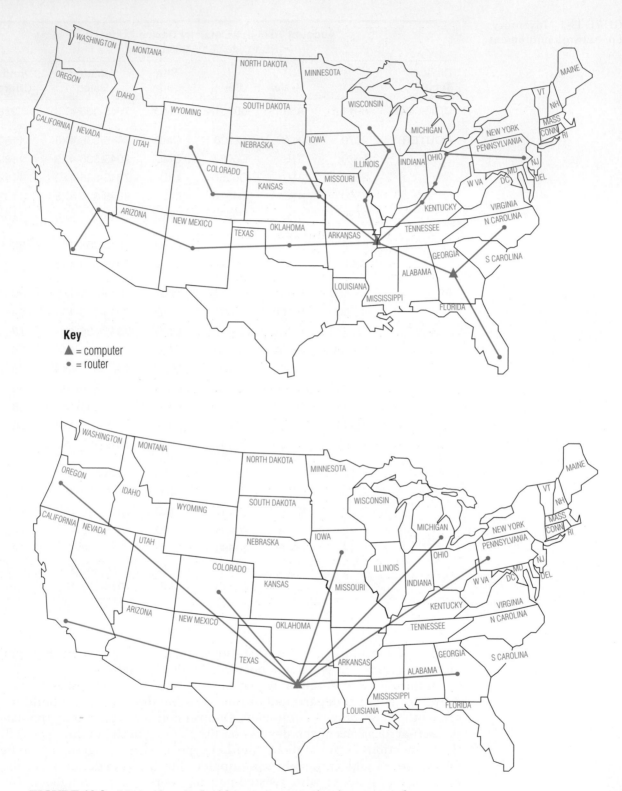

**FIGURE 19-8**    Maps of typical wide area communications networks.

FIGURE 19-9 Listing of circuits and attached routers.

| Circuit Name | Circuit Number | Router Type | Model No. | Serial No. | Network Address | Location |
|---|---|---|---|---|---|---|
| West | FDA3856B | 2520 | 4A | 135269 | 3E1C | Detroit |
| | | 2503 | 3 | 426578 | 3E9D | Chicago |
| | | 2503 | 2 | 890124 | 3E1A | Denver |
| | | 2501 | 2 | 182930 | 3E4F | San Fran. |
| South | FDA3472 | 2520 | 4A | 135269 | 3E1C | Detroit |
| | | 2503 | 3 | 42457 | 1A46 | Toledo |
| | | 2503 | 3 | 675645 | 1A3D | Memphis |
| | | 2502 | 2 | 276578 | 1A88 | Mobile |
| | | 2502 | 2 | 764190 | 1A6A | Miami |

## Other Documentation

Other network documentation includes:

- routine operating procedures
- problem escalation procedures
- the names and telephone numbers of a contact person at each location on the network
- vendor manuals for all hardware and software
- vendor contact names and telephone numbers for all hardware and software
- software listings for all network software
- disaster recovery plans

The network documentation should be backed up. Whether it is kept on-line in electronic form or printed, two duplicate copies should be kept, preferably one copy on site and one off site. Furthermore, a procedure to keep the backup copies up-to-date must be in place.

## 19-10   CHANGE MANAGEMENT

change management

**Change management** is an activity for monitoring all changes to the network and coordinating the activities of various groups in such a way that there is minimal impact on network operation and user service when changes are made. The change management activity is often called "change control." However, the word "control" tends to imply that many network changes are unnecessary and could be eliminated. Although many operations people would like to eliminate change to the network to preserve stability, it is hardly realistic to do so in a network environment. Change must be implemented in a planned, coordinated way. Most change management systems require that the person who is sponsoring the change fill out a "request for change" form, such as the one shown in Figure 19-10. A change may be the installation of a new terminal or other hardware, the addition of a segment to an Ethernet LAN, the reconfiguration of the circuit to support a new location, the recabling of a

FIGURE 19-10 A change request form that would be completed by the person requesting the change.

**Change Request Form**

Request
Date: _____                                         Request No. _____

Implementation
Date: _____    Requestor: _____

Type of change:    Addition _____    Modification _____    Replacement _____
                   Removal _____    Correction _____

Description of the change: _____
_____
_____
_____
_____

Assigned to: _____

Approvals:

Supvr. Network Operations: _____

Supvr. Technical Support: _____

_____

Implementation Data:

Date Change Made: _____

Comments: _____
_____
_____

FIGURE 19-11 A change coordination plan for a small network. Large networks would have a much more extensive list of changes.

| | Change Coordination Plan as of 10/25 | | | |
|---|---|---|---|---|
| Change # | Description | Planned Date | Responsibility | Date Completed |
| 1047 | Add Dallas to network | 10/27 | Vandewoe | |
| 1048 | Maintenance to NCP software | 10/29 | Morris | |
| 1049 | Add 5 VDTs in marketing | 11/15 | Vandewoe | |
| 1050 | Upgrade west circuit to 64 kbps | 11/28 | Aymer | |
| 1051 | Add router to administration's LAN. | 12/10 | Aymer | |
| 1052 | Update network management software. | 12/12 | Morris | |

floor in an office building, the installation of an updated version of network software, or any other activity that causes the network to operate differently. In most companies, all of the change request forms are sent to a single person, the change coordinator, who screens the requests to find obvious conflicts or other inconsistencies among the proposed changes. The change coordinator may also keep a master list of all planned changes, such as the one shown in Figure 19-11.

change coordination meeting

From time to time, the change coordinator should convene a **change coordination meeting** to be attended by representatives from network operations, software support, computer operations, vendors, users, and others who may be interested in or affected by the proposed changes. At the coordination meeting, the upcoming changes are reviewed and discussed. The plan, which shows when each change is scheduled to occur, the nature of the change, and the person responsible, is updated. Assuming no major obstacles are discovered, the plan is approved and the changes are implemented according to the plan, and all parties have full knowledge.

In larger organizations that have many network changes, the change coordination meeting is held weekly. In many networks, changes are implemented at night or on the weekend to avoid disrupting the network during normal business hours. Software changes, in particular, often require deactivating part of or even the entire network so that new software can be installed and tested, and usually the only time this can be done is at night, on the weekend, or at another time when network traffic is light.

When major changes to the network are anticipated, such as a complete reconfiguration of the circuits or the installation of a totally new service, the network operations people should participate with the network analysts and designers in the planning and design process. By participating in the development project, the operations people can stay in touch with coming events that will affect either the work they do or the procedures that are in place.

It is extremely important to keep the network documentation up-to-date as changes are made. Of course, if the documentation is kept online in a word processing or other system, the maintenance process is simplified. The proper way to keep network documentation up-to-date is to make it a part of the change management process so that it is done routinely at the time that changes are implemented. Although this statement may seem obvious, it is surprising how many organizations ignore the documentation or postpone updating it "until later when we're not so busy." This is tantamount to not doing it at all!

## 19-11  MANAGEMENT REPORTING

Management reporting of network operation activities and statistics is discussed here as a separate topic, although some management reporting is likely to be done by each group within the network department. Several different types of reporting need to be done for different levels of management. Generally, the higher the level of management, the more the data should be summarized and the more the reports should focus on the exceptions rather than routine detail. User management is primarily interested in data about network performance, particularly when it is compared to agreed-upon service levels. Network management is also concerned about the performance compared with service levels because their objectives are often based on providing the agreed-to service. They are also interested in basic operational statistics, such as the number of problems that were logged, the length of time it took to resolve problems, and the overall use of network facilities. Graphs normally are the most useful way to convey this type of information.

Different types of information are reported on different time schedules. In many networks, other than the smallest, a daily status review meeting is held to discuss the results of the previous day and any outstanding problems. This type of meeting is held most frequently early in the morning and is kept quite brief—normally 15 minutes or less. Some companies connect remote locations into these meetings, via audio or video teleconferencing, so that status information can be distributed widely and quickly.

Network performance and utilization statistics are sometimes calculated and distributed monthly, or they may be continuously available online. A useful variation of this approach, however, is to calculate performance numbers daily. If service levels are not being achieved, it is considered a problem and is handled through the problem tracking system. Because open problems are discussed at the daily status meeting, the performance problems get immediate attention.

Statistics in voice networks are similar to those in data networks. Telephone systems can generate statistics and measurements, such as trunk utilization and average call length. Much of the focus of telephone statistics is on long distance calling, which is frequently the most expensive part of a voice network. The number and duration of long-distance calls, evidence of call abuse, utilization of leased lines, and call queuing times, where appropriate, are all relevant to the efficient and effective operation of a voice communications network.

## 19-12   NETWORK MANAGEMENT FOR LANS

Managing the operation of a LAN would intuitively seem to be easier than managing a WAN, because the LAN covers a smaller geographic area and because the cabling is generally in a protected environment and is therefore less subject to transmission errors. It is true that when a LAN is first installed, it is often quite simple, in some cases being entirely the product of a single vendor who uses equipment and software designed to operate well together. However, as LANs grow, it is typical to add equipment and software from other vendors, such as inexpensive workstations, special purpose software, or new routers and switches. Furthermore, it often becomes desirable to link the LAN to other LANs, to MANs, or to WANs, in which case bridges, switches, routers, or gateways may need to be added. Although each of these additions may be small, the cumulative effect can be that the original small LAN grows into a complex piece of an extensive network. Add to this the fact that if the LAN is successful (and if it is growing, it probably is successful), the organization grows increasingly dependent on the LAN, so failures and outages are more likely to disrupt the company's business operation.

This growth in complexity and increasing dependence places a premium on good LAN management practices and efficient problem resolution techniques. The LAN administrator normally plays a critical part in both of these activities. Hence, the importance of his or her role is magnified.

The basic techniques of LAN management, which you studied in Chapter 12, are the same as for managing MANs or WANs, but many specialized tools are designed especially for LANs. One example is the NetWare management system, designed for Novell's LANs. The software allows a single workstation to manage an entire LAN, no matter how extensive or geographically dispersed it may be. Other LAN vendors have similar products.

It is fair to say that LAN management, as a part of the broader subject of network management, receives a great deal of attention from vendors and standards organizations because of the rapid growth of LANs and the growing reliance of organizations on all types of LANs.

## 19-13  NETWORK MANAGEMENT SOFTWARE

Managing a network of any size—other than the smallest, single-location LAN—requires assistance in the form of automation tools. Medium and large networks simply have too many hardware and software components for either an individual or a group of people to keep track of manually. When coupled with rapidly changing status conditions, monitoring and alerting activities are good candidates for automation. There are many analogies between a network's operation and the monitoring and control of a production line in a manufacturing plant.

What network management people want is the ability to select the best vendors for each of the network components and to be assured that all of the diverse pieces can be managed by a single network management system. Furthermore, if the network is really an internet made up of different networks that have diverse technologies, there is a need for a common network management protocol that can be used across all networks. This means that there is a need for certain hardware or software capabilities in workstations, bridges, routers, gateways, and servers to monitor and collect network performance information and to pass it to centralized network management software for analysis and action.

As was discussed earlier in the chapter, you can purchase network management system software to help network staff manage the network. In the diverse world of telecommunications, it may not surprise you to learn that two network management protocol standards have emerged, somewhat in competition with each other. The first is called the **Simple Network Management Protocol (SNMP)**. It is a *de facto* standard that originated in conjunction with the Internet to manage networks and devices using the TCP/IP protocol. The second is called **Common Management Information Protocol (CMIP),** and it was developed by the ISO. CMIP is newer than SNMP and is better in many ways; however, because there are many more SNMP devices currently installed than CMIP-based devices, it is not as widely used. CMIP monitors and tracks network usage for servers, routers, and other devices, much like SNMP does.

### Simple Network Management Protocol (SNMP)

An SNMP-managed network consists of three key components: managed devices, agents, and network management systems (NMSs). A managed device is a network node that contains an SNMP agent and resides on a managed network. Managed devices collect and store management information and make this information available to NMSs that use SNMP. Managed devices can be servers, routers, switches, bridges, hubs, computers, or printers. Information about the device is collected using another SNMP standard called **remote monitoring (RMON)**. RMON is a standard monitoring specification that defines a set of statistics and functions that can be exchanged between RMON compliant devices or software. Nine types of statistics are specified, and a vendor can select which of the nine types to implement, normally those most relevant to the device being monitored. An **agent** is a network management software module that resides in a managed device. An agent collects the information provided by RMON and translates it into a form compatible with SNMP. An NMS executes applications that monitor and control managed devices. NMSs provide the bulk of the processing and memory resources required for network management. One or more NMSs must exist on any managed network. The relationship between these components is shown in Figure 19-12.

**Simple Network Management Protocol (SNMP)**

**Common Management Information Protocol (CMIP)**

**remote monitoring (RMON)**

**agent**

**FIGURE 19-12** The structure of an SNMP managed network.

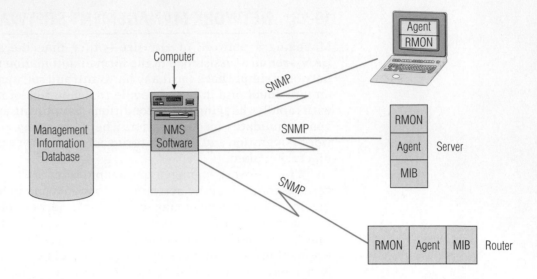

Hardware that uses SNMP—for example routers, gateways, and switches—collects information about itself and the circuits or other equipment connected to it and stores the information in the MIB. Some of the devices have their own MIB, but many of them store their information in a central MIB on a server. The network manager has a workstation that runs the network management application software that can access the MIB, analyze and process the data, and produce management information and reports. The network manager can also send commands or instructions to the devices and effectively manage and control the network. Although SNMP is a standard, many vendors have added their own extensions, so the MIB from one vendor's equipment may not be exactly compatible with the MIB from another. Hence, the user needs to be careful when selecting network management hardware or software from different vendors, both of which are supposed to be SNMP compliant.

Proprietary software packages that are designed to help the network's staff manage data networks are also widely available. They collect data from various sources, such as the hardware described earlier, and store the data in databases for analysis and action. These packages provide an array of status displays, commands, error analysis programs, performance measurements, capacity management, and reporting.

IBM's Netview network management products were originally programmed to assist in the management of IBM's SNA networks, but now there are several versions that can monitor and manage most kinds of WANs and LANs. Netview automates many network management tasks, including restarting devices that have been taken offline, perhaps because of temporary errors, sending alert messages when certain error threshold values are exceeded and reporting network performance statistics.

Novell's NetWare management system (NMS) was written to help manage Novell LANs. Each server on the network must have NMS software to gather statistics and monitor the status of the network and the devices attached to it. The network operator has a wide variety of commands at his or her disposal. These commands are used to gather the statistics, monitor the network in real time, issue commands, and generate reports. NMS modules are available to interface with devices that use the SNMP protocol and IBM's Netview.

There are also many software packages on the market to assist the network staff with activities, such as keeping equipment inventory, drawing network diagrams and maps, keeping track of changes, and charging costs to users. Software can run on mainframes, servers, or PCs, depending on the customer's requirement. Some vendors have integrated their software into modular packages so that the customer needs to buy only the pieces that are required. Most organizations should be able to find commercially available network management software that meets their needs.

## ■ SUMMARY

In this chapter, you have learned about the elements of managing and operating a communications network. Networks cannot simply be installed and left to operate. They must be managed to ensure that they continue to operate smoothly and reliably and that the organization is obtaining the maximum benefits from the network for the money invested in it. The functions of network management are the same as they are for the management of any department or group—staffing, organizing, planning, directing, and controlling. Network operation is made up of several elements, including problem management, performance management, configuration control, change management, and management reporting. Each of these elements relates with each of the others.

## ■ REVIEW QUESTIONS

19-1. Define *network management*.

19-2. Define *network operation*.

19-3. Why do network users expect a high level of service from a network?

19-4. List six elements that make up the scope of network operation.

19-5. List three reasons why it is important to manage a network.

19-6. How does network management in small organizations differ from what is done in large organizations?

19-7. What are the five activities of network management?

19-8. Why can it be challenging to properly staff a network department?

19-9. Explain the term *outsourcing*.

19-10. Why is planning necessary in the network department?

19-11. Why is it important to state the assumptions made when preparing a network plan?

19-12. List several techniques of *directing* the network department.

19-13. What is the most common type of financial control used by managers?

19-14. List the six activities that comprise network operation.

19-15. What is the function of the network help desk?

19-16. What is the first responsibility of the help desk personnel?

19-17. Explain the purpose of a trouble ticket.

19-18. In a star network, with a server at the center of the star, why should the network operations group be concerned with the reliability of the computer processing?

19-19. Explain the concept of problem escalation.

19-20. Describe the problem escalation process.

19-21. What is the purpose of having a problem tracking meeting?

19-22. Who should attend problem tracking meetings and change coordination meetings?

19-23. Is it possible to design a network that is totally redundant and does not need to be managed?

19-24. What are some ways to bypass problems in a network?

19-25. What is a service level agreement?

19-26. What are some network operation statistics that the network operations supervisor would be interested in seeing each day?

19-27. Some companies institute a moratorium on all network and computer changes at the end of each year. Why might such a moratorium be desirable?

19-28. What information should be kept in an inventory file of telecommunications equipment?

19-29. Why is the operational management of a LAN more or less complicated than managing a WAN?

19-30. What is the function of agent software in an SNMP-managed network?

19-31. List several techniques to ensure that when change is introduced into the network, it is implemented in a controlled, well-managed way.

## TRUE OR FALSE

19-1. Network management is the set of activities that direct the resources required to keep a network operating over the short term.

19-2. It may be acceptable in some organizations for a network to have an outage or two each week.

19-3. Network management and operations people have the responsibility of ensuring that the defined requirements for network availability and reliability are met.

19-4. The network management group is properly viewed as having the responsibility for lines and modems only.

19-5. Network management personnel need to be familiar with the computers and application software that use the network.

19-6. The communications network, as well as computers and applications, are assets of the organization.

19-7. Networks do not need to be managed in small organizations.

19-8. It is easy to staff a network management department with good people because it is an exciting career to work in and many people want to do it.

19-9. At a minimum, the network staff should make a one-year plan at the beginning of each year.

19-10. Network plans should be put together by the network staff without getting the confusing suggestions of others in the organization.

19-11. *Controlling* means ensuring that the department is performing according to the plans it has made.

19-12. The most common type of financial control is the measurement of actual expenses against a budget.

19-13. Network departments should have service level agreements for the services they provide.

19-14. When the network is operating properly, the network operations staff has little to do.

19-15. The primary function of the help desk is to train users and answer questions about their computer applications.

19-16. One type of problem escalation brings additional resources to bear to help solve a network problem.

19-17. Intermittent network problems are among the easiest to find and repair.

19-18. Most modern communications equipment has built-in diagnostic capabilities.

19-19. One reason why it is desirable to have appropriate diagnostic equipment and trained technicians on the staff of the user organization is that, in today's multivendor networks, it is not always clear which vendor should be called when a problem occurs.

19-20. To determine whether the performance of a network is adequate, preestablished performance objectives are required.

19-21. Network management systems are designed to operate a network, eliminating the need for a network operations staff.

19-22. In most networks, change occurs infrequently.

19-23. It is extremely important to keep the network documentation up-to-date as changes are made.

19-24. Generally, the higher the level of management, the more network detail should be shown and the less the reports should focus on the exceptions.

19-25. Managing LANs is unnecessary because of their simplistic nature.

19-26. Hardware that uses SNMP collects information about itself and the circuits or other equipment connected to it and stores the information in the MIB.

## MULTIPLE CHOICE

19-1. Finding qualified people to fill networking positions is a management function called _____.

   a. organizing

   b. controlling

   c. directing

   d. recruiting

   e. staffing

19-2. Asking another company to take over the design, implementation, and operation of a network is called _____.

   a. outplacing

   b. insourcing

   c. outsourcing

   d. botching

   e. retrenching

19-3. Grouping people to accomplish the mission of the department is called _____.

   a. teaming

   b. organizing

   c. training

   d. controlling

   e. directing

19-4. The process of expeditiously handling a problem from its initial recognition to a satisfactory resolution is called _____.

a. service leveling

b. problem resolution

c. problem diagnosis and repair

d. problem management –

e. reconfiguration

19-5. The set of activities that measure network performance and adjust it as necessary to meet users' requirements is called _____.

a. escalation

b. performance reporting

c. protocol analyzing

d. performance management –

e. service level reconciliation

19-6. The maintenance of records that track all the equipment in the network and how it is connected is called _____.

a. configuration control –

b. equipment inventory

c. circuit maintenance

d. network diagramming

e. implementation

19-7. The activity for monitoring all changes to the network and coordinating the activities of various groups in such a way that there is minimal impact on network operation and user service when changes are made is called _____.

a. service level management

b. change amelioration

c. controlling

d. change management –

e. None of the above.

19-8. SNMP is _____.

a. a protocol for high-speed data transmission on simple networks

b. a simple data transmission protocol for use on high-speed networks

– c. a network management protocol

d. an alternate name for the Common Management Information Protocol

e. IBM's protocol used in their network management software system

## ■ PROBLEMS AND PROJECTS

19-1. What factors should be considered when deciding whether to apply maintenance and patches to network software?

19-2. Write an appropriate service level agreement for an airline reservation system.

19-3. Most vendors keep a database of known technical problems with the hardware or software it sells. Do you think a vendor would ever let its customers have direct access to such a database? What would be the advantages and disadvantages of giving customers such access?

19-4. Make an appointment to visit the network staff at your school or place of work. Find out how its network management organization and procedures compare to those you studied in this chapter, but be sure to get answers to the following questions: How is the group organized? How difficult is it to recruit staff? What financial controls are in place? How do they track and report network problems? How do they manage changes to the network?

19-5. Write a mission statement for the proposed IT department described in the Case Study at the end of this chapter.

## THE HARMON COMPANY

The Harmon Company is a relatively small firm that manufacturers a number of automotive aftermarket accessories. The company has grown quite rapidly in the past fifteen years, as measured by sales, the number of employees, and its use of computers and networks. With regard to the latter, the CEO, Jack Michaelson, believes that it has reached a crisis point. Mr. Michaelson notes that the company now has LANs in all of its departments, each of which was set up individually by someone in the department when the group felt the need. Because they were set up at various times over the last eight years, the LANs and the PCs attached to them use different technologies and are, in many cases, incompatible with each other. It is impossible to communicate or share data company-wide by using the LANs because many of them are not interconnected. Failures are rampant and when problems occur, there tends to be a lot of finger pointing to try to blame someone else for the failure.

Trying to take a broad view of the situation, Mr. Michaelson also notes that the company's telephone system, which was set up and is managed by the Human Resources (HR) department, seems to be out of date compared to systems he has seen in other companies he has visited recently. Furthermore, no one in HR seems to have much interest in the phone system or improving it.

Mr. Michaelson feels that action needs to be taken to integrate the LANs and, ideally, to get to a common level of technology so that all PCs can communicate and share data. While the company has never had an IT department, he feels that it may be time to establish one and to identify a person who can take the leadership in this increasingly vital area.

**CASE STUDY**

**QUESTIONS**

1. How might Mr. Michaelson go about finding someone to lead a new IT department? What attributes should he look for in that individual? What kind of support will the IT leader require from Mr. Michaelson and other members of senior management?

2. What should be done to begin the process of straightening out the "LAN mess?" What benefits will the company see if it can get to a single LAN, or at least a few LANs that can be connected together. What objections do you think the departments will have to making changes to their LANs and perhaps their PCs? How can those objections be overcome?

3. What should be done about the management of the telephone system? Do you imagine that HR would object to changes? Would they be relieved to have someone else take it over? Can the telephone system be integrated with the LANs in any way?

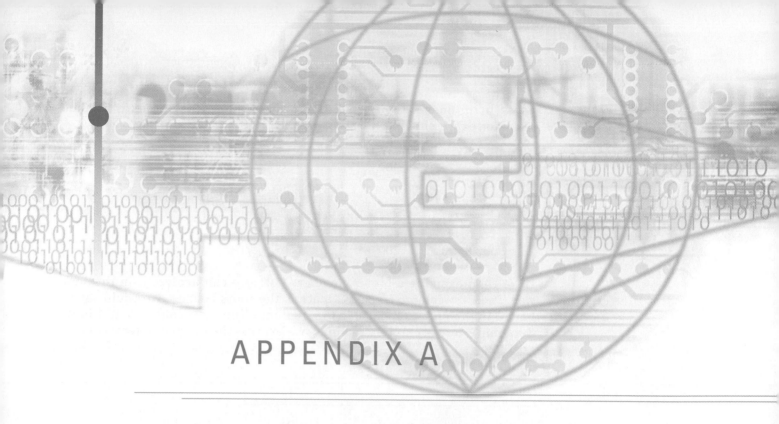

# APPENDIX A

## BINARY AND HEXADECIMAL NUMBERING

> There are 10 kinds of people in the world: those who understand binary, and those who don't.

### Binary

Most of us live in a decimal world. We think decimally. We add, subtract, multiply, and divide decimally. What's more, we've been doing so since we first did "take aways" by counting on our fingers and then had to unlearn it all when we encountered Miss Marony in math class! If you think about it, that is probably why we have a base-10 system—ten digits on our hands, ten digits in our number system. If we'd all been born with four fingers on each hand, we'd have to deal with an octal (base 8) world! Indeed, the older computer base system is "octal" or base eight. Kind of makes you wonder about those early computer programmers, doesn't it?

Eight bits do make a byte, but computers actually operate on a base-2 number system, known as the binary number system. The word "bit" is a shorthand way of saying binary digit. Of course, computers could be built to operate in base-10, but they would cost way more than any of us are willing to spend! A better way is for us to learn to speak their language. Remember that the decimal system uses the digits 0 1 2 3 4 5 6 7 8 9, whereas the binary system uses 0 1. How hard can it be—two digits as opposed to 10?

First let's examine a decimal number: 6,248. We immediately know that we are looking at six thousand, two hundred and forty-eight because the base-10 system is second nature to us now. Remember that each of those digits is simply a placeholder for the next higher power of ten. We could say we have 8 in the ones column, 4 in the tens, 2 in the hundreds, and six in the thousands; or expressing it in terms of powers of 10:

| 1000 | 100 | 10 | 1 |
|------|-----|-----|---|

$6 \times 10^3 +$      $2 \times 10^2 +$      $4 \times 10^1 +$      $8 \times 10^0$

$6000 +$      $200 +$      $40 +$      $8$      $= 6,248$

If we then examine a binary number: 1101, we can analyze it in the same way. The first column in base-2 math is the units column. We could say we have 1 in the units column, 0 in the 2 column, 1 in the 4 column, and 1 in the 8 column. More accurately, in binary we express the number in terms of powers of 2:

| 8 | 4 | 2 | 1 |
|---|---|---|---|

$1 \times 2^3 +$      $1 \times 2^2 +$      $0 \times 2^1 +$      $1 \times 2^0$

$8 +$      $4 +$      $0 +$      $1$      $= 13$

**REPRESENTING DATA**   Data are represented in the computer by a series of bits, usually arranged in 8-bit collections called bytes. 1 represents "on" and 0 represents "off." In binary, the left-end bit is called the most significant bit (MSB), and the right-end bit is called the least significant bit (LSB). Read from the most significant bit to the least significant bit. As illustrated below, a byte allows you to represent 256 values from 0 to 255. Don't you love it?

**MSB**                                                                    **LSB**

| $2^7$ | $2^6$ | $2^5$ | $2^4$ | $2^3$ | $2^2$ | $2^1$ | $2^0$ |
|-------|-------|-------|-------|-------|-------|-------|-------|
| Bit 7 | Bit 6 | Bit 5 | Bit 4 | Bit 3 | Bit 2 | Bit 1 | Bit 0 |
| 128 | 64 | 32 | 16 | 8 | 4 | 2 | 1 |

      0  = 00000000            95  = 01011111
      1  = 00000001            168 = 10101000
      2  = 00000010            192 = 11000000
     23 = 00010111            254 = 11111110
     57 = 00111001            255 = 11111111

So how do we represent letters or characters other than numbers in binary? Recall the ASCII code you first encountered in this text in Chapter 5. It is the most widely used code in computers and telecommunications networks today. Looking at the ASCII code chart in Figure 5-4, you can see the 127 standard code points. Creating a text document in a text editor like Notepad uses one byte of memory for each character, including spaces. Each character is represented by a number, expressed in binary numbers, to be transmitted from one computer on a network to another. Thirty-two (00100000) is the ASCII code for a space. For example, if you wanted to tell someone that you loved her, it would look like this:

| Letters | l | | l | o | v | e | | y | o | u |
|---|---|---|---|---|---|---|---|---|---|---|
| **Base-10** | 73 | 32 | 108 | 111 | 118 | 101 | 32 | 121 | 111 | 117 |
| Base-2 | 01001001 | 00100000 | 01101100 | 01101111 | 01110110 | 01100101 | 00100000 | 01111001 | 01101111 | 01110101 |

**BINARY MATH** You remember how to do decimal math, right? Binary math works the same way.

$$\begin{array}{r} 525 \\ +\ 499 \\ \hline 1024 \end{array} \qquad \begin{array}{r} 0110 \\ +1101 \\ \hline 10011 \end{array}$$

In the decimal addition, we start in the right column, the ones. We add 5 plus 9 and find that it is 14 so we put 4 in the ones column and carry the 10 into the next (tens) column. Adding 9 plus 2 plus 1 in the 10s column, we get 12 tens, so we leave 2 in the 10s column and carry 10 tens into the 100s column. There we add the 5, 4, and 1 (100s) and find that we have 10 hundreds. We leave 0 in the hundreds column and carry 10 hundreds into the thousands column. All of our words sound way more complicated than actually working the problem, because simple decimal math has become so automatic after all these years. Binary is the same, but less familiar.

In the binary problem, we have only 1s and 0s to work with. In the right (units) column, we add 0 plus 1 and get 1; in the second column, we add 1 plus 0 and get 1. So far, no problem. In the third column, however, we have 1 plus 1. We must zero out that column and carry the 1 to the fourth column. There we add our carried 1 to the 0 and 1. Again we must zero out the column and carry the 1 to the fifth column where we add it to a 0. One plus 0 is 1 so we can place a 1 in that column. Try another: 1101 plus 1010. Did you get 10111? I did. Let's do one more together. 1101 plus 1111. This is a little trickier. First column: 1 + 1 = 0 and carry 1, second column: 1 + 1 = 0 and carry 1, third column: 1 + 1 + 1 = 1 and carry 1, fourth column: 1 + 1 + 1 = 1 and carry 1, fifth column: 1 + 0 = 1. Notice that in the third and fourth columns we had to enter 1, not 0, and carry. Got it? Fun, isn't it?

**CONVERTING FROM BINARY TO DECIMAL** Suppose you want to convert base-2 numbers to base 10 so your decimal mind can comprehend them better, or decimal to binary so the computer can understand them better? No problem. Simply remember that each digit in binary represents a power of two.

| $2^7$ | $2^6$ | $2^5$ | $2^4$ | $2^3$ | $2^2$ | $2^1$ | $2^0$ |
|---|---|---|---|---|---|---|---|
| Bit 7 | Bit 6 | Bit 5 | Bit 4 | Bit 3 | Bit 2 | Bit 1 | Bit 0 |
| 128 | 64 | 32 | 16 | 8 | 4 | 2 | 1 |

For example: Convert 11001011 to the corresponding decimal number, using the list below to convert each binary digit to the power of two that it represents.

| Numbering | 7 | 6 | 5 | 4 | 3 | 2 | 1 | 0 |
|---|---|---|---|---|---|---|---|---|
| **Binary digits** | 1 | 1 | 0 | 0 | 1 | 0 | 1 | 1 |
| **Convert** | $1 \times 2^7$ | $1 \times 2^6$ | $0 \times 2^5$ | $0 \times 2^4$ | $1 \times 2^3$ | $0 \times 2^2$ | $1 \times 2^1$ | $1 \times 2^0$ |
| **Add** | 128 | 64 | 0 | 0 | 8 | 0 | 2 | 1 |

Answer: 11001011=203

Try another: Convert 01110110 to decimal. What was your answer?

| Binary digits | 0 | 1 | 1 | 1 | 0 | 1 | 1 | 0 |
|---|---|---|---|---|---|---|---|---|
| Convert | $1 \times 2^7$ | $1 \times 2^6$ | $0 \times 2^5$ | $0 \times 2^4$ | $1 \times 2^3$ | $0 \times 2^2$ | $1 \times 2^1$ | $1 \times 2^0$ |
| Add | 0 | 64 | 32 | 16 | 0 | 4 | 2 | 0 |

Answer: 118

**CONVERTING FROM DECIMAL TO BINARY**    Converting decimal to binary is easy, too, except that this time we are going to divide by 2 until we cannot divide any more. But wait, there's more. We must keep track of the remainders in each case. For example, convert the base-10 number 457 to binary. Leave a space on the paper so you can work from the bottom up. Divide 457 by 2. The answer is 228 with a remainder of 1. Write the remainder next to the answer. Now divide 228 by 2 and write the answer and remainder above and so on as illustrated below.

```
        1    r1
      2)3    r1
      2)7    r0
     2)14    r0
     2)28    r1
     2)57    r0
    2)114    r0
    2)228    r1
    2)457
```

What is the binary number? The remainders tell us. Begin with the answer to the last division problem and move to the right and down the remainders on the outside, writing the digits as you go. The result is the answer. In this case, the decimal number 457 converts to the binary number **111001001**. Try one more, and don't forget to work from the bottom up, and then include the first digit on top before you list the remainders. Convert 376 to a binary number. What is your answer?

```
        1    r0
      2)2    r1
      2)5    r1
     2)11    r1
     2)23    r1
     2)47    r0
     2)94    r0
    2)188    r0
    2)376
```

My answer is 376=**101111000**. If your answer is the same, you are ready for the hexadecimal (base-16) system. If not, practice a little more and you will have it. Your computer will appreciate you for understanding!

## Hexadecimal

If you become a computer programmer or computer engineer, you will work with hexadecimal math (base 16). IPv6 uses hexadecimal IP addresses and we will all have one some day, right? If you work on websites or with graphics programs, you may need to convert RGB (red, green, blue) color values to hexadecimal values for website background colors, etc. Even if you become an ice skater or a cake decorator, it's good to understand the hexadecimal system. You can always create figure Bs (11) on the ice instead of figure 8s or celebrate someone's 40th birthday with a nice hexadecimal number 28 on top of the cake (40 converts to 28 in base 16). They'll love you for it.

How do we make 16 digits out of only 10 single digits, 0–9? In hexadecimal math, each column stands for a multiple of 16 digits, 0–15. To represent the values of 10–15, we use letters: A is 10, B is 11, C is 12, D is 13, E is 14, and F is 15. Hexadecimal numbers look strange to our decimal-oriented eyes, but we need them and they are easy to convert to decimal numbers. The following comparison shows the numbers from 0 to 15 in decimal, binary, and hexadecimal.

| Decimal | Binary | Hexadecimal |
|---------|--------|-------------|
| 0 | 0 | 0 |
| 1 | 1 | 1 |
| 2 | 10 | 2 |
| 3 | 11 | 3 |
| 4 | 100 | 4 |
| 5 | 101 | 5 |
| 6 | 110 | 6 |
| 7 | 111 | 7 |
| 8 | 1000 | 8 |
| 9 | 1001 | 9 |
| 10 | 1010 | A |
| 11 | 1011 | B |
| 12 | 1100 | C |
| 13 | 1101 | D |
| 14 | 1110 | E |
| 15 | 1111 | F |

**CONVERTING FROM HEXADECIMAL TO DECIMAL** Converting from base 16 to base 10 is not difficult if we remember that each digit represents a power of 16. For example, to convert the hexadecimal number 239 to decimal, list the digits and, beginning at the right, number them starting at zero, as shown below. Then convert the numbers according to how many times the required power of 16 is needed. Finally, add the numbers together to get the corresponding hexadecimal number.

| Numbering | 2 | 1 | 0 |
|-----------|---|---|---|
| Hex. digits | 2 | 3 | 9 |
| Convert | $2 \times 16^2$ | $3 \times 16^1$ | $9 \times 16^0$ |
| Add | $2 \times 256 = 512$ | $3 \times 16 = 48$ | $9 \times 1 = 9$ |

Answer: 569

The expression can also be written, $569_{10}$, which means 569, base 10. So, $239_{16}$ = $569_{10}$. Now try one more for good measure. Convert $7B_{16}$ to decimal. Oh no!! Letters. That's all right. It works the same way. Observe:

| Numbering | 1 | 0 |
|---|---|---|
| Hex. digits | 7 | B |
| Convert | $7 \times 16^1$ | $11 \times 16^0$ |
| Add | $7 \times 16 = 112$ | $11 \times 1 = 11$ |

Answer: $7B_{16} = 123_{10}$

Wasn't that easy? The answer is $7B_{16} = 123_{10}$. Excellent. Now, let us go the other way.

**CONVERTING FROM DECIMAL TO HEXADECIMAL**   You remember the technique we used to convert from decimal to binary. NO? Go back and review. Yes? Carry on. Let us convert the decimal number 6,325 to its hexadecimal equivalent. Divide repeatedly by 16 this time, keeping track of your remainders as you go in the same way you did before. Remember to leave a space on the paper so you can work from the bottom up again. First, divide 6,325 by 16. The answer is 395 with a remainder of 5. Write the remainder next to the answer. Now divide 395 by 16 and write the answer and remainder above, and so on, as illustrated below.

$$
\begin{array}{ll}
\quad 1 & r8 \\
16\overline{)24} & r11 \\
16\overline{)395} & r5 \\
16\overline{)6325} &
\end{array}
$$

To write the answer in hexadecimal, start at the top answer and continue down the right side of the remainders. Remember to convert the 11 to its alphabetical equivalent hexadecimal digit.

The answer is $6,325_{10} = 18B5_{16}$.

Now convert 71,984 to hexadecimal notation. Remember to divide by 16, keeping track of your remainders as in the previous example. Begin by dividing 71,984 by 16. Follow the final answer to the right and down the remainders to write your solution in accurate hexadecimal notation.

$$
\begin{array}{ll}
\quad 1 & r1 \\
16\overline{)17} & r9 \\
16\overline{)281} & r3 \\
16\overline{)4499} & r0 \\
16\overline{)71984} &
\end{array}
$$

Answer: $71,984_{10} = 11930_{16}$. Couldn't you just keep working these all day?

If you really don't appreciate the challenge of the math, remember the little hint given in Chapter 14, Figure 14–11, for converting between decimal and binary using a scientific calculator or the one in the Windows accessories. It works as well to convert between decimal and hexadecimal.

**HEXADECIMAL VALUES IN COMPUTER GRAPHICS**   One last hint before we leave hexadecimal is for those of you who work on Web editing or use graphics programs like Adobe Photoshop. Although the newer versions of Photoshop allow you to choose between the RGB color values and hexadecimal values, it is helpful to know how to convert them yourself. In most graphics programs, the colors are expressed using their RGB values. For example, R:204, G:153, and B:255 is the RGB value string for a "pale dull violet" color. To translate those values to the hexadecimal value used on the Web, we convert the three individual RGB components to the corresponding base-16 values as we did above.

First, we divide 204 by 16: 12, r12 Next, we divide 153 by 16: 9 r9. Finally, we divide 255: 15 r15. This transfers to CC99FF, the hexadecimal value of RGB 204,153,255.

Now try one more before we turn you loose on the World Wide Web! What is the hexadecimal value of 51,102,255? Remember to divide each component by 16 and keep the remainder to arrive at the proper hexadecimal value. What color is the result?

The answer is 3366FF. If you would like to read more about the Webmaster's palette and colors on the Web, see http://www.visibone.com or http://www.webwhirlers.com/colors/colourandweb.asp. You may also find more information about binary math at http://www.math.grin.edu/~rebelsky/Courses/152/97F/Readings/student-binary.html.

If hexadecimal is more to your liking, this website will help you: http://www.pcnineoneone.com/howto/hex1.html.

## ■ PRACTICE PROBLEMS

A-1. Convert the following decimal numbers to binary:

a. 789

b. 352

c. 198

d. 999

e. IP address, 167.54.96.81. What class is it?

A-2. Convert the following binary numbers to decimal:

a. 11010001

b. 01110110

c. 00111011

d. 10110000

e. 11100011

A-3. Convert the following decimal numbers to hexadecimal:

a. 7,893

b. 34,962

c. 645

d. 29,831

e. RGB color 204,255,204

A-4. Convert the following hexadecimal numbers to decimal:

a. B76F

b. 98C4

c. 4C

d. 8,931

e. Hexadecimal color FF33CC to RGB color

A-5. Convert the following hexadecimal numbers to binary (hint: first convert to decimal, then to binary):

a. 7E

b. 37B

c. 130

d. 204

e. F3B6

## ANSWERS TO PRACTICE PROBLEMS

A-1. Convert the following decimal numbers to binary:

a. 789 = 1100010101

b. 352 = 101100000

c. 198 = 11000110

d. 999 = 1111100111

e. IP address, 167.54.96.81. What class is it?

10100111 00110110 01100000 01010001 is a Class B address

A-2. Convert the following binary numbers to decimal:

a. 11010001 = 209

b. 01110110 = 118

c. 00111011 = 59

d. 10110000 = 176

e. 11100011 = 227

A-3. Convert the following decimal numbers to hexadecimal:

a. 7,893 = 1ED5

b. 34,962 = 8892

c. 645 = 285

d. 29,831 = 7487

e. RGB color 204,255,204 = CCFFCC

A-4. Convert the following hexadecimal numbers to decimal:

a. B76F = 46,959

b. 98C4 = 39,108

c. 4C = 76

d. 8,931 = 35,121

e. Hexadecimal color FF33CC to RGB color = 255,51,204

A-5. Convert the following hexadecimal numbers to binary (hint: first convert to decimal, then to binary):

a. 7E = 1111110

b. 37B = 1101111011

c. 130 = 100110000

d. 204 = 1000000100

e. F3B6 = 1111001110110110

# APPENDIX B

## INTERNET URLS REFERENCED IN THE TEXT*

### Chapter 2

*http://www.sita.aero/*
*http://www.ivans.com/*

### Chapter 3

*http://www.iso.ch/*
*http://www.itu.ch*
*http://www.ietf.org*
*http://www.ansi.org*
*http://www.eia.org*
*http://www.ieee.org*
*http://www.nist.gov*
*http://www.neca.org*
*http://www.ecma.ch*
*http://www.etsi.org*
*http://www.itu.int/home*
*http://www.itu.int/ITU-T/*
*http://www.cisco.com/univercd/cc/td/doc/product/iaabu/centri4/user/scf4ap1.htm*
*http://www.ibm.com/*

### Chapter 5

*http://www.unicode.org*

* Internet URLs sometimes change or become inactive, so it is possible that you may find a URL that no longer works. If so, please use your web-search skills to locate the Website you were seeking.

## Chapter 6

*http://www.v92.com/*
*http://www.cablemodem.net*
*http://www.catv.org/*
*http://www.cablemodemhelp.com/*

## Chapter 9

*http://www.2wire.com/*
*http://www.dslforum.com/*

## Chapter 10

*http://www.howstuffworks.com/lan-switch.htm*
*http://www.warriorsofthe.net/*

## Chapter 11

*http://www.cisco.com/warp/public/cc/techno/media/lan/gig/tech/gigbt_tc.htm*
*http://www.nwfusion.com/research/ge.html*
*http://www.10gea.org/GEA1000BASET1197_rev-wp.pdf*
*http://www.10gea.org/*
*http://www.hiperlan2.com*
*http://www.80211planet.com*
*http://www.boingo.com*
*http://opennodes.org*
*http://www.warchalking.org*
*http://www.idc.com*
*http://www.fibrechannel.org/*

## Chapter 12

*http://www.novell.com/ products/netware/*
*http://www.microsoft.com/windows/default.mspx*
*http://www.hp.com/country/us/eng/prodserv/software.html*
*http://www.sun.com/learnabout/solaris/*
*http://www.novell.com*
*http://www.bell-labs.com/history/unix/*
*http://www.linux.com/*
*http://www.redhat.com*
*http://www.linux-mandrake.com*
*http://www.Dmoz.org*
*http://lugww.counter.li.org/*
*http://www.ssc.com/8080/glue/groups/*
*http://www.vpnlabs.com*
*http://www.homenethelp.com*

## Chapter 13

*http://www.atmforum.com/*
*http://www.sonet.com*

## Chapter 14

*http://www.ietf.org/rfc.html*
*http://www.rfc-editor.org*
*http://www.postel.org/remembrances/*
*http://www.ralphb.net/IPSubnet/*
*http://www.learntosubnet.com*
*http://www.dns.net/dnsrd/*
*http://www.howstuffworks.com/dns.htm*
*http://www.faqs.org/rfcs/rfc793.html*
*http://java.sun.com/docs/books/tutorial/networking/sockets/index.html*
*http://www.javaworld.com/javaworld/jw-12-1996/jw-12-sockets.html*
*http://kloth.net/services/nslookup.php*
*http://www.internic.net/whois.html*
*http://www.betterwhois.com/*
*http://www.net.cmu.edu/cgi-bin/netops.cgi*

## Chapter 15

*http://memex.org/liklider.pdf.*
*http://www.caida.org/*
*http://www.peacockmaps.com*
*http://www.cybergeography.org/atlas/atlas.html*
*http://www.isoc.org*
*http://www.ieft.org*
*http://www.iab.org*
*http://www.irtf.org*
*http://www.ieft.org/iesg.html*
*http://www.w3.org*
*http://www.visualware.com/visualroute/index.html*

## Chapter 16

*http://www.amazon.com*
*http://www.hwg.org/*
*http://www.w3.org/MarkUp/*
*http://www.htmlgoodies.com/*
*http://www.xml.com*
*http://www.usenet.org*
*http://groups.google.com*
*http://www.newzbot.com/*

*ftp.malch.com*

*http://www.live365.com*

*http://www.Google.com*

*http://www.AlltheWeb.com*

*http://www.AltaVista.com*

*http://www.iLor.com*

*http://www.Metacrawler.com*

*http://www.hotbot.com*

*http://www.ixquick.com*

*http://www.surfwax.com*

*http://www.googlewhack.com/*

*http://www.lii.org*

*http://infomine.ucr.edu*

*http://www.academicinfo.net*

*http://www.invisible-web.net*

*http://www.ask.com*

*http://www.Cyndislist.com*

## Chapter 17

*http://www.rsasecurity.com/*

*http://www.pgp.com/*

## Appendix A

*http://www.visibone.com*

*http://www.webwhirlers.com/colors/colourandweb.asp*

*http://www.math.grin.edu/~rebelsky/Courses/152/97F/Readings/student-binary.html*

*http://www.pcnineoneone.com/howto/hex1.html*

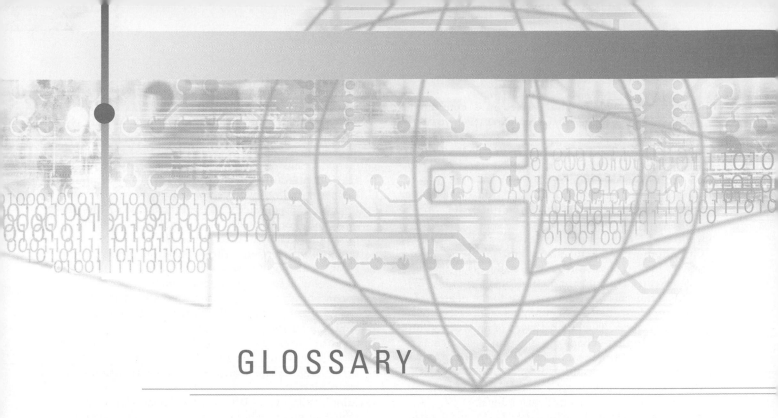

# GLOSSARY

**access point**   In a typical WLAN, the transceiver that connects to a wired LAN using standard cabling.

**acknowledgement (ACK) character**   A transmission control character transmitted by a receiving station as an affirmative response to the sending station.

**active hub**   A hub that serves as a repeater to boost the signal strength, thereby allowing longer cable runs out to individual workstations or servers.

**active security attacks**   A security attack in which the attacker takes overt action, such as altering message contents, masquerading as someone else, denying service, or planting viruses.

**ad hoc**   A mode in wireless transmission whereby the wireless devices can communicate directly with each other without the use of an AP.

**adaptive differential pulse code modulation (ADPCM)**   A variation of PCM, in which only the difference in signal samples is coded.

**adaptive equalizer**   An equalizer circuit that adjusts itself to the exact parameters of the incoming waveform, based on the known characteristics of a standard training signal.

**adaptive Huffman coding**   A type of character compression in which the text is continuously scanned to ensure that the fewest bits are assigned to the characters that appear most frequently.

**adaptive routing**   *See* dynamic routing.

**address resolution protocol (ARP)**   A TCP/IP protocol that maps a dynamic IP address to the physical or hardware address on a LAN.

**Advanced Encryption Standard (AES)**   The current, robust, government-approved encryption method that also replaces WEP and RC4 (the algorithm upon which WEP is based).

**agent**   A network management software module that resides in a managed device.

**algorithm**   A set of mathematical rules.

**AlohaNET**   The first wireless packet-switched network, developed in Hawaii and connected to ARPANET on the mainland in 1972.

**alphanumeric characters**   Pertaining to a character set that contains letters, digits, and usually other characters, such as punctuation marks.

**altering message contents**   Changing the contents of a message, causing the message recipient to be misinformed or deceived.

**American National Standards Institute (ANSI)**   An organization formed for the purpose of establishing voluntary industry standards.

**American Standard Code for Information Interchange (ASCII)**   The standard code, using a coded character set that consists of 7-bit characters, used for information interchange among computer systems, data communication systems, and associated equipment.

**amplitude**   The size or magnitude of a voltage or current's analog waveform.

**amplitude modulation (AM)**   (1) Modulation in which the amplitude of an alternating current is the characteristic varied. (2) The variation of a carrier signal's strength (amplitude) as a function of an information signal.

**analog**   Pertaining to data in the form of continuously variable physical quantities.

**analog circuit**   A communication circuit on which information transmitted can take any value between the limits defined by the channel.

**analog data**   Data with continuous values. *See* analog.

**analog signal** A signal that varies in a continuous manner. Examples are voice and music. *Contrast with* a digital signal.

**analog-to-digital (A/D) converter** A device that senses an analog signal and converts it to a proportional representation in digital form.

**analog transmission** A transmission technique whereby signals are sent on a circuit in analog form.

**anchors** Hyperlink tags.

**antivirus programs** Programs that search for viruses on computers and neutralize them.

**anycast** In IPv6, one of three types of addressing that provides greater flexibility and efficiency in routing. Anycast is a transmission from one host to the nearest of a number of hosts that share a common address prefix.

**application layer** The highest layer of an architecture and the one that carries out a useful task such as e-mail or an electronic spreadsheet.

**application-level firewall** A device, typically a router, that examines and controls the transfer of data between networks at the application level.

**application program interface (API)** A mechanism for application programs to send data to and receive data from a LAN.

**application server** On a LAN, a computer that provides processing capacity for applications that are shared by many people.

**Archie** An index or virtual card catalog for anonymous FTP archives on the Internet (primarily used pre-WWW).

**architecture** A plan or direction that is oriented toward the needs of the user. It describes "what" will be built but does not tell "how."

**asymmetric digital subscriber line (ADSL)** A digital transmission technology that delivers high-speed signals over twisted pair telephone wires. Speeds vary, and are normally slower upstream than downstream, but are in the range of 64 Kbps to 1.54 Mbps upstream and 256 Kbps to 9 Mbps downstream.

**asymmetric key encryption** An encryption technique in which the key used for encryption and the key used for decryption are not the same.

**asynchronous balanced mode (ABM)** An operating mode of HDLC used with combined stations; that is, either node may initiate a transmission on the circuit without receiving permission from the other.

**asynchronous response mode (ARM)** An operating mode of HDLC used when there is a primary station and one or more secondary stations. In this mode, the secondary stations may initiate the transmission of data or control without permission from the primary stations, but cannot send commands.

**asynchronous transfer mode (ATM)** A packet switching technique that uses fixed length packets called cells and is designed to operate on very high-speed, error-free circuits. ATM effectively eliminates any delay in delivering packets, making it suitable for voice or video transmissions.

**asynchronous transmission (asynch)** (1) Transmission in which the time of the start of each character or block of characters is arbitrary. (2) Transmission in which each information character is individually synchronized, usually by the use of start elements and stop elements.

**attached resource computer network (ARCNET)** A LAN architecture that was developed by Datapoint Corporation in the 1970s.

**attenuation** A decrease in the magnitude of the current, voltage, or power of a signal during its transmission. It is normally expressed in decibels.

**attenuation distortion** The deformation of an analog signal, which occurs when the signal does not attenuate evenly across its frequency range.

**autoconfiguration** The feature that allows a device to assign itself a unique IP address without the intervention of a server.

**automatic repeat request (ARQ)** An error correction technique. When the receiving DTE detects an error, it signals the transmitting DTE to resend the transmission.

**available bit rate (ABR) service** A service of ATM, which provides whatever capacity is left after the available circuit capacity is allocated to the CBR, rt-VBR, and nrt-VBR services.

**backbone network** The main, high speed network in a particular network system.

**background noise** *See* white noise.

**balun** An acronym that stands for balanced-unbalanced; also the name of a device that connects two different types of wire or cable. The balun is a small transformer that converts the physical characteristics of one wire type to another, e.g., from coaxial cable to twisted pair wire.

**bandwidth** The difference, expressed in Hertz, between the two limiting frequencies of a band.

**baseband** A form of modulation in which signals are pulsed directly on the transmission medium. In LANs, baseband also implies the digital transmission of data.

**baseband transmission** A transmission technique whereby the signal is transmitted in digital form, using the entire bandwidth of a circuit. Typically used in LANs.

**basic rate interface (BRI)** A type of ISDN service whereby a telephone line is divided into three distinct channels for data: two 64 Kbps B channels and one 16 Kbps data D channel.

**baud** A unit of signaling speed equal to the number of discrete conditions or signal events per second. If the duration of a signal event is 20 milliseconds, the modulation rate is 1 second/20 milliseconds = 50 baud.

**Baudot code** A code for the transmission of data in which 5 equal length bits represent one character.

**binary** When only two values or states are possible for a given condition such as "on" or "off," 1 or 0.

**binary digit** (1) In binary notation, either the digit 0 or 1. (2) Synonym for bit.

**Binary Synchronous Communications (BISYNC, BSC)** A protocol that uses a standardized set of control characters and control character sequences for synchronous transmission of binary-coded data.

**biphase coding** *See* differential Manchester coding.

**bipolar, nonreturn-to-zero (BPNRZ)** A signaling method whereby the voltage is constant during a bit time. Most commonly, a negative voltage represents one binary value and a positive voltage is used to represent the other. *Contrast with* bipolar, return-to-zero.

**bipolar, return-to-zero** Signals that have the 1 bits represented by a positive voltage and the 0 bits represented by a negative voltage. Between pulses, the voltage always returns to zero. *Contrast with* bipolar, nonreturn-to-zero.

**bit** Synonym for binary digit.

**bit-level encryption** An encryption technique that manipulates the individual bits of a message rather than working with characters.

**bit-oriented protocol** A protocol that uses bits, singly or in combination, to control the communications.

**bits per second (bps)** The basic unit of speed on a data communications circuit.

**bit stuffing** (1) The occasional insertion of a dummy bit in a bit stream. (2) In HDLC, a 0 bit inserted after all strings of five consecutive 1 bits in the header and data portion of the message. At the receiving end, the extra 0 bit is removed by the hardware.

**bit synchronization** A method of ensuring that a communications circuit is sampled at the appropriate time to determine the presence or absence of a bit.

**block** (1) A group of bits or characters transmitted as a unit. An encoding procedure is usually applied to the block for error control purposes. (2) A set of things such as words, characters, digits, or records handled as a unit.

**block check character (BCC)** In longitudinal redundancy checking and cyclic redundancy checking, a character that is transmitted by the sender after each message block and is compared with a BCC computed by the receiver to determine if the transmission was error free.

**Bluetooth** A wireless standard that is used to emit signals over a relatively short range. It was originally designed to connect short-range devices such as PCs, cordless telephones, PDAs, printers, headsets, and eventually home appliances through the use of a microchip transceiver embedded in each device.

**body** The major portion of an HTML document that holds the data or information displayed on a website.

**Boolean operators** Words that tell search engines which keywords you want your results to include or exclude, and whether your keywords need to appear close to each other.

**bridge** A device that allows data to be sent from one network to another so terminals on both networks can communicate as though a single network existed.

**British Naval Connector (BNC)** A bayonet locking connector used on slim coaxial cables such as those typically used for Ethernet.

**broadband** (1) A communications channel that has a bandwidth greater than a voice-grade channel and is capable of higher speed data transmission. (2) In the context of a LAN, a multichannel analog circuit that uses coaxial cable as the medium. A common use of the term is as it applies to a broadband cable system which, because of its multichannel capability, might be carrying a LAN on one channel, a television signal on another channel, and voice signals on a third channel. (3) In the context of a WAN, it means a high-speed circuit that has a transmission speed of 256 Kbps or greater, though the exact speed isn't precise.

**broadband ISDN (BISDN)** A high-speed ISDN service that provides FDX data transmission at either 155.52 or 622.08 Mbps.

**broadband transmission** (1) In LANs, an analog transmission on a high capacity cable with FDM. (2) An analog communications channel that has a capacity greater than a voice-grade channel and is therefore capable of higher speed data transmission.

**broadcast address** In HDLC, when a broadcast address is used in a frame, the frame is accepted by all secondary stations with which the primary station has established communication.

**broadcast message** A mechanism that allows the same e-mail to be sent to everyone on the network.

**broadcast routing** A simple routing technique, normally used only on CSMA/CD LANs, in which all packets are sent to all stations on the network.

**brouter** A device that provides the functions of a bridge and a router.

**browser** The interactive client program that requests information from Web servers throughout the Internet and displays the pages built with HTML.

**bus** A high-speed circuit of limited distance generally implemented within a single building. In a LAN, a physical facility from which data are transferred to all destinations, but from which only addressed destinations may read in accordance with appropriate conventions or protocols.

**bus network** A network in which the nodes are connected to a high-speed medium—the bus—which is of limited length. Bus networks are normally LANs.

**byte-count–oriented protocol** A protocol that uses a special character to mark the beginning of the header, followed by a count field that indicates how many characters are in the data portion of the message.

**cable access** Access to a network using cable television systems that have been reengineered to carry signals in both directions—from cable company to user and from user to cable company—so they can be used for high-speed communications circuits. Broadband cable Internet access offers downstream speeds up to 1.5 Mbps and upload rates up to about 300 Kbps.

**cable modem** A modem that links a DTE to a television system cable.

**cable TV (CATV) circuits** Communication circuits that are implemented on CATV systems that use technology to partition a part of the cable not being used to carry TV signals.

**cabling plan**   A document that describes how the wiring and/or cabling will be installed.

**cache**   In the context of the World Wide Web, a special part of the disk memory that stores pieces of information, thus making future access to websites faster and more efficient.

**Caesar cipher**   *See* monoalphabetic cipher.

**call accept packet**   In a packet switching system, a special control packet that signals that the setup phase for a call has been completed and a route through the network has been established.

**call back**   A security technique used with dialup lines. After a user calls and identifies herself, the computer breaks the connection and calls the user back at a predetermined telephone number.

**call back unit**   A hardware device that performs the call back function.

**call request packet**   In a packet switching system, a special control packet that asks for a connection to be established.

**call setup time**   The time taken to connect a switched circuit. The time between the end of dialing and the moment of answering by the receiving equipment.

**carrier extension bits**   Bits added to the end of a MAC frame to increase the amount of time a signal stays active before another device can transmit. This lets the frame travel longer and prevents the occurrence of too many collisions in the faster Gigabit Ethernet.

**carrier sense multiple access with collision avoidance (CSMA/CA)**   A communications protocol used on LANs in which a station listens to the circuit before transmitting in an attempt to avoid collisions.

**carrier sense multiple access with collision detection (CSMA/CD)**   A communications protocol frequently used on LANs in which stations, on detecting a collision of data caused by multiple simultaneous transmissions, wait a random period of time before transmitting.

**carrier wave**   An analog signal that contains no information.

**cascading style sheets (CSS)**   Code embedded within an HTML document that brings formatting consistency on different browsers.

**category 1 through category 7 cable**   Types of twisted pair cabling used for data transmission, the characteristics of which have been defined by the EIA.

**cell**   A fixed-length packet in an ATM system.

**cell relay**   *See* ATM.

**central office**   The place where communications carriers terminate customer lines and locate equipment that interconnects them.

**centralized mode**   Communication between an AP and the mobile terminal on a HiperLAN2 (similar to infrastructure mode on Wi-Fi).

**centralized routing**   A routing system in which the path through the network is determined by a single piece of hardware or software.

**certificate authority (CA)**   A trusted third party organization that issues digital certificates used to create digital signatures and public/private key pairs.

**CGI application**   A script (usually written in the PERL programming language) on a Web server that performs actions like searching or processing forms when the user clicks on certain buttons or links.

**change coordination meeting**   A meeting held to ensure that changes to a system are properly approved and communicated to all interested parties.

**change management**   The application of management principles to ensure that changes to a system are properly authorized and controlled to minimize the negative impact on the system's users.

**channel**   (1) A path of communication, either electrical or electromagnetic, between two or more points. *See* circuit and line. (2) The part of a communications system that connects the message source with the message sink. (3) A one-way communications path, such as a television channel.

**channels**   In IRC, different topics about which people chat.

**character assignment**   The unique groups of bits assigned to represent the various characters in a code.

**character compression**   A type of data compression in which characters are represented by a shortened number of bits, depending on the frequency with which the character is used.

**character-oriented protocol**   A communications protocol that uses special characters to indicate the beginning and end of messages.

**character stripping**   A data compression technique in which leading and trailing control characters are removed from a message before it is sent through a communications system.

**character synchronization**   A technique for ensuring that the proper sets of bits on a communications line are grouped to form characters.

**check character**   A character that is calculated by applying a predetermined mathematical function to the bits in a message to calculate a unique character called the check character.

**choke packet**   A control packet sent on a network, that requests that sending nodes slow the rate at which they are sending packets to the network or to stop sending altogether.

**ciphertext**   Encrypted data.

**circuit**   The path over which two-way communication takes place.

**circuit speed**   The number of bits that a circuit can carry per unit of time, typically 1 second. Circuit speed is normally measured in bits per second.

**circuit switching**   The temporary establishment of a connection between two pieces of equipment, which permits the exclusive use until the connection is released. The connection is set up on demand and discontinued when the transmission is complete. An example is a dial-up telephone connection.

**cladding**   The glass or plastic that surrounds the core of an optical fiber and acts as a mirror to the core.

**classless interdomain routing (CIDR)**  A protocol that allows Class C IP addresses to be assigned in numerous neighboring blocks. More than one block of network addresses are linked together in a "supernet."

**clear request packet**  In a packet switching system, a special control packet that signals that a call is complete and the route through the network can be torn down.

**client**  In a client-server network, the user or using computer that takes advantage of the facilities or services of server computers.

**client-server**  A type of processing in which certain computers, called servers, provide standardized capabilities such as printing, database management, or communications to other computers that are called clients.

**coaxial cable**  Cable consisting of one conductor, usually a small copper wire or tube, within and insulated from another conductor of larger diameter, usually copper braid or copper tubing.

**code**  A predetermined set of symbols that have specific meanings.

**code efficiency**  A measure of how few bits are used to convey the meaning of a character accurately.

**code point**  The number of possible combinations or characters in a coding system.

**codec**  A device that converts analog signals (typically voice signals) to digital signals (or vice versa).

**collision**  A condition that occurs when two or more terminals are trying to transmit a message at the same time, thereby causing both messages to be garbled and unintelligible at the receiving end.

**committed information rate (CIR)**  The contracted transmission speed on a frame relay circuit. Data sent within the CIR are highly likely to get through the network unless extremely severe network congestion occurs. Data sent above the CIR are subject to being discarded if the network gets congested.

**common channel interoffice signaling (CCIS) system**  A system for sending signals between telephone network COs.

**Common Gateway Interface (CGI)**  A standard for interfacing applications with information servers, such as HTTP or web servers.

**Common Management Information Protocol (CMIP)**  An ISO standard protocol for exchanging network management commands and information among devices attached to a network.

**communication**  1. A process that allows information to pass between a sender and one or more receivers. 2. The transfer of meaningful information from one location to a second location. 3. The art of expressing ideas, especially in speech and writing. 4. The science of transmitting information, especially in symbols.

**communications line**  Deprecated term for transmission line or transmission circuit.

**communications network**  A collection of communications circuits and other equipment that is managed as a single entity.

**communications server**  A server on a LAN that provides connection to other computers or networks.

**communications standards**  The rules that are established to ensure compatibility among similar communications services or several types of communications equipment.

**compaction**  *See* data compression.

**Computer Emergency Response Team (CERT)**  An organization created in 1989 as a result of the Morris worm, which infected a large part of the Internet. Its purpose is to facilitate responses to computer security threats on the Internet.

**concentrator**  A device that combines the signals from several slow-speed circuits onto a high-speed circuit.

**concept-based searching**  A type of searching tool that uses statistical analysis of pages that contain the words or phrases you search for to find other pages that might interest you.

**conditioned line**  A communications circuit on which the specifications for amplitude and distortion have been tightened. Signals traveling on conditioned circuits are less likely to encounter errors than on unconditioned circuits.

**conducted media**  Any medium where the signal flows through a physical entity such as a twisted pair wire, coaxial cable, or optical fiber.

**configuration control**  The maintenance of records that track all the equipment in a network and the way it is connected.

**congestion**  A network condition that occurs when traffic arrives at a node or arrives for transmission on a circuit faster than the node or circuit can handle it.

**congestion control**  Techniques used to attempt to manage the congestion on a network by reducing the flow of new packets into the network or by routing packets around the congested circuits or nodes.

**connectionless**  A type of transmission that allows an application to send a message to any destination at any time.

**connectionless routing**  The type of routing that occurs when no VC has been established. Each packet of a transmission is sent independently, and all may travel to the destination on different routes.

**connection-oriented**  A transmission through a network using a VC or a real circuit between the sender and the receiver. It goes through three distinct phases: connection establishment, information transfer, and connection release. The connection must be established before data are transmitted.

**connection-oriented routing**  The type of routing that occurs when a VC is built between the sending and receiving nodes. During the call establishment phase, all nodes along the path determine how they will route packets for the transmission.

**constant bit rate (CBR) service**  A service of ATM, which provides a fixed and continuously available data rate such as the rate that would be available on a leased or private circuit.

**contention**  A condition that occurs when several devices (PCs, workstations, etc.) are vying for access to a circuit and only one of them can get it at one time. Some method is usually established for selecting the winner and accommodating the losers.

**continuous ARQ** An error correction technique in which data blocks are sent continuously until the transmitter receives a signal from the receiver to resend one or more blocks that have been received in error.

**control characters** A character whose occurrence in a particular context initiates, modifies, or stops a control operation. A control character may have a graphic representation in some circumstances.

**control connection** The TCP connection that an FTP client uses to send commands and receive responses from a remote machine.

**controller** A component of the browser that calls a client or set of clients to fetch the document from its remote server.

**controlling** Ensuring that an organization is performing according to the plans it has made.

**control plane** The part of a frame relay system concerned with the establishment and termination of logical connections.

**copper distributed data interface (CDDI)** FDDI implemented over twisted-pair copper wire, supporting distances of 100 meters and data rates of 100 Mbps.

**core** The glass or plastic center conductor of an optical fiber that provides transmission carrying capability.

**crosstalk** The unwanted energy transferred from one circuit, called the *disturbing circuit,* to another circuit, called the *disturbed circuit.*

**current loop** An interface between a DTE and a circuit that indicates 1 and 0 bits by the presence or absence of an electrical current.

**cut-through switch** A switch that looks at an incoming packet's address and immediately sends it out to the destination LAN segment.

**cycle** A complete wave of an analog signal. The frequency is the number of cycles that are completed in one second.

**cyclic redundancy check (CRC)** An error checking technique in which the check character is generated by a cyclic algorithm. (2) A system of error checking performed at both the sending and receiving ends after a block character has been computed.

**daemon** Programs that perform administrative tasks for the OS.

**dark fiber** An optical fiber that has no accompanying electronics and light source, such as an LED or laser, which put light into the fiber to make it usable.

**database server** A server on a LAN that provides storage for database data, allowing a user to download only the information needed by his application.

**data circuit** Associated transmit and receive channels that provide a means of two-way data communications.

**data circuit-terminating equipment (DCE)** The equipment installed at the user's premises. Provides all the functions required to establish, maintain, and terminate a connection and the signal conversion and coding between the DTE and the line.

**data compression** The process of eliminating redundant bits or characters from a data stream before it is transmitted or stored.

**data encryption standard (DES)** An encryption algorithm designed to encrypt and decrypt data using a 64-bit key.

**datagram** In packet switching, a self-contained packet that is independent of other packets and can potentially traverse the network at high speeds. It does not require an acknowledgement and carries information sufficient for routing from the originating node to the destination node without relying on earlier exchanges between the nodes and the network. Neither the delivery nor the arrival order of datagram packets is guaranteed.

**datagram socket** Sockets that use the UDP protocol and have to read entire messages at once.

**data link** (1) The physical means of connecting one location to another to transmit and receive data. (2) The interconnecting data circuit between two or more pieces of equipment operating in accordance with a link protocol. It does not include the data source and data sink.

**Data Link Control Protocol (DLCP)** The rules governing the operation of a data link. *See* protocol.

**Data Link Protocol** *See* data link control protocol (DLCP).

**data service unit/channel service unit (DSU/CSU)** An interface device that ensures that the digital signal entering a communications line is properly shaped into square pulses and is precisely timed. The DSU portion of the device acts as a digital transmitter/receiver. The CSU portion provides circuitry to protect a communication carrier's network from excessive voltage coming from a customer's transmission equipment. *See also* digital transmitter/receiver.

**data terminal equipment (DTE)** The part of a data station that serves as a data source, data sink, or both, and provides for the data communications control function according to the protocols.

**decibel (dB)** (1) A unit that expresses the ratio of two power levels on a logarithmic scale. (2) A unit for measuring relative power. The number of decibels is 10 times the logarithm (base 10) of the ratio of the measured power levels. If the measured levels are voltages (across the same or equal resistance), the number of decibels is 20 times the log of the ratio.

**decryption** Converting encrypted data into plaintext. *Contrast with* encryption.

**delta modulation** A technique of digitizing an analog signal by comparing the values of two successive samples and assigning a 1 bit if the second sample has a greater value and a 0 bit if the second sample has a lesser value.

**demodulation** The process of retrieving intelligence (data) from a modulated carrier wave. *Reverse of* modulation.

**denial of service** Flooding a network or node with messages faster than they can be handled, thereby degrading network performance and preventing others from obtaining network service.

**detector** Circuitry that separates a received signal into its component parts, typically the carrier signal and the modulation signal.

**deterministic** The performance of the circuit using a network is said to be deterministic when it is possible to calculate the maximum amount of time it takes for any end station to be able to transmit.

**device control characters** A control character used for the control of ancillary devices associated with a computer or communication system, for example, for switching such devices on or off.

**dialback unit** *See* call back unit.

**dial-up networking (DUN)** The method for connecting to a network via a 56 Kbps (or slower) modem, through a simple telephone dial-up connection.

**dibits** A group of two bits. In four-phase modulation, each dibit is encoded as one of four unique carrier phase shifts. The four possible states for the dibit are 00, 01, 10, and 11. *Contrast with* quadbit *and* tribit.

**differential Manchester coding** A digital signaling technique in which a 0 is represented by the presence of a transition at the beginning of the bit period and a 1 is represented by an absence of a transition at the beginning of the bit period. A mid-bit transition also exists to provide clocking.

**differential phase shift keying (DPSK)** A modulation technique in which the relative changes of a carrier signal's phase are coded according to the data to be transmitted.

**digital** Pertaining to data in the form of discrete values or digits. The use of a binary code to represent data.

**digital certificate** A password-protected, encrypted data file that contains the name and other data that serve to identify the transmitting entity and certifies that it is who it says it is.

**digital circuit** A circuit expressly designed to carry the pulses of digital signals.

**digital data** Discrete data such as text or integers. *Contrast with* analog data.

**Digital Data Communications Message Protocol (DD-CMP)** A byte-count–oriented protocol developed by Digital Equipment Corporation.

**digital satellite service (DSS)** *See* direct broadcast satellite.

**digital signal** A discrete or discontinuous signal, the various states of which are pulses that are discrete intervals apart. *Contrast with* analog signal.

**digital signature** The network equivalent of signing a message and guaranteeing that the contents have not been changed.

**digital subscriber line (DSL)** The generic name for a technology developed to enable telephone companies to deliver digitized signals to subscribers at about 1.5 Mbps over existing twisted pair copper telephone wire. *See also* asymmetric digital sub-scriber line (DSL), symmetric digital subscriber line (SDSL), *and* very high-rate digital subscriber line (VHRDSL).

**digital transmission** A transmission technique whereby signals are sent on a circuit in digital form (pulses).

**digital-to-analog (D/A) converter** A device that converts a digital signal to an analog signal.

**digital transmitter/receiver** A device that takes digital pulses from a DTE and converts them, as necessary, for transmission on a digital circuit. At the receiving end, the reverse function is performed.

**digitized** To express or represent data that is not discrete data in digital form. For example, to obtain a digital representation of the magnitude of a physical quantity from an analog representation of that magnitude.

**digitizing distortion** *See* quantizing noise.

**direct broadcast satellite (DBS)** A satellite that has the primary purpose of sending signals directly to small antennas in homes or businesses. Because the receiving antennas are small, the satellite normally has a relatively high-powered transmitter.

**directing** Management's actions, taken to ensure that the mission and plans of the network organization are executed on a timely and accurate basis.

**direct mode** In HiperLAN2, communication between two or more mobile terminals (peer-to-peer) for ad hoc networking.

**direct sequence** A spread spectrum transmission technique in which bits from the original signal are combined with bits generated by a pseudorandom bit stream generator using Boolean math. The receiver, using the same pseudorandom bit stream, can reverse the Boolean math process and recover the original bits.

**disaster** A long-term outage of a network or computer center that cannot be quickly remedied.

**disaster recovery planning** The planning and preparation undertaken in anticipation of a severe, long-term outage of a network or computer center.

**disk server** A server on a LAN that provides simulated disks (disk storage area) to other computers.

**dispersion** The difference in the arrival time between signals that travel straight through the core of an optical fiber and those that reflect off the cladding and therefore travel a slightly longer path.

**distributed routing** A technique of routing messages in which some or all of the nodes maintain tables that show how messages should be directed to destinations.

**distribution cable** A subgrouping of individual telephone lines as they approach a CO.

**distribution list** A capability that allows a user to create a list of people to whom they want to send the same e-mail, and then send a duplicated message to the same group of people regularly.

**diverse network technologies** The ability of a network to support several types of communications and networking technologies.

**domain name system (DNS)** The commonly accepted way of identifying hosts on a network. Domain name servers maintain a database of numeric IP addresses and their corresponding domain names, and resolve them to locate the proper remote computers.

**domain name system (DNS) servers** Thousands of computers, located strategically by organizational networks or ISPs across the entire Internet, that regularly download and copy information from the root servers.

**double byte character set (DBCS)** A coding system developed by IBM that has $2^{16}$ code points that can be used to represent over 65,000 characters.

**downlink** The rebroadcast of a radio signal from a satellite back to Earth.

**dropouts** A momentary loss in signal, usually due to the effect of noise or system malfunction. In cellular telephone systems, dropout sometimes occurs when the signal is being transferred between cells.

**drop wire** The telephone wire running from a residence or business to a telephone pole, or its underground equivalent.

**duplex** *See* full duplex.

**dynamic host control protocol (DHCP)** The protocol that automatically assigns IP addresses and subnet masks and keeps track of them without a network administrator's having to configure the information about your computer in the database that the server uses.

**dynamic IP address** A temporary IP address issued by an ISP each time a user logs on.

**dynamic routing** A technique of routing packets in which the path of the packets may change based on network or traffic conditions.

**dynamic window sizing on congestion** A window management technique that alters the size of the sliding window by setting the size of the window to half its current size when timeouts occur (indicating congestion). The congestion window size is increased by one segment when an acknowledgment is received, and eventually the minimum of the receiver's advertised window and congestion window can be sent.

**E-1 circuit** The European designation for a digital circuit that is similar to a T-1 circuit. An E-1 circuit has a capacity of 2.048 Mbps.

**eavesdropping** Monitoring network traffic for the purpose of learning something specific and perhaps disclosing it to others, or for the purpose of analyzing traffic patterns.

**echo** The reversal of a signal, bouncing it back to the sender, caused by an electrical wave bouncing back from an intermediate point or the distant end of a circuit.

**echo checking** A technique for determining the correctness of a transmission. The received data are returned to the source for comparison with the original transmission.

**echo suppressors** A device that permits transmission in only one direction at a time, thus eliminating the problems caused by echo.

**electromagnetic interference (EMI)** The radiation of electrical and magnetic fields, which causes interference in signal transmission or reception in electronic equipment.

**e-mail server** A server that formats and handles incoming and outgoing electronic messages.

**encapsulation** Carrying frames from one layer or protocol as data within the frame of another layer or protocol.

**encoder** In the context of streaming audio, a procedure that converts audio content into streaming format.

**encryption** The transformation of data into a meaningless form unreadable by anyone without a decryption key.

**end office** A local telephone company CO designed to serve consumers or businesses.

**end of text (ETX) character** A control character that marks the end of a message's text.

**end system** The devices or host computers attached to a subnetwork.

**envelope delay distortion** An electrical phenomenon that occurs when not all frequencies propagate down a communications circuit at exactly the same speed.

**equalizer circuitry** Any combination of devices, such as coils, capacitors, or resistors, inserted into a transmission line or amplifier circuit to improve its frequency response. On data communications circuits, equalizer circuitry is typically installed in modems.

**error-checking** The process of checking a packet that is being transmitted over a network and determining whether the package or the data content within the package has been damaged.

**error correction** The process of correcting any errors detected during a transmission.

**error detection** The techniques employed to ensure that transmission and other errors are identified.

**escape (ESC) character** A code extension character used to indicate that the following character or group of characters is to be interpreted in a nonstandard way.

**escape mechanism** A method of assigning an alternate meaning to characters in a coding system. *See* escape character (ESC).

**Extended ASCII** An 8-bit version of the ASCII code in which the eighth bit is either an extra data bit or a parity bit.

**Extended Binary Coded Decimal Interchange Code (EBCDIC)** A coding system consisting of 256 characters, each represented by 8 bits.

**Extensible Hypertext Markup Language (XHTML)** A hybrid of XML and HTML approved by the W3C and released in January of 2000.

**Extensible Markup Language (XML)** A Web page formatting language that separates the content of a page from the presentation. XML tags the different types of content and then uses other technologies, like style sheets, to determine how the content should look.

**extranet** An Internet-like network sometimes provided to allow a group of people, such as customers or suppliers, to pass through the firewall and access authorized sections of the intranet.

**fast select polling**  A polling technique in which a station that does not have traffic to send does not need to return a character to the polling station.

**fat client**  An application designed so that almost all of the processing is done on a client computer and little is done on the server.

**feeder cable**  A grouping of several distribution cables as they approach a CO.

**fiber distributed data interface (FDDI)**  A standard for transmitting data on an optical fiber.

**fibre channel**  A set of communication standards developed by ANSI that allows storage devices in a SAN environment to be connected via a high-speed interconnection.

**fibre channel switch**  A switch that connects devices on a SAN and performs the same functions as a switch on an Ethernet network.

**file server**  A server on a LAN that provides storage for data files.

**File Transfer Protocol (FTP)**  An application layer protocol designed to efficiently transfer files between two computers on TCP/IP networks.

**finger**  A network tool that may be used to find out who has logged in on another system or to find detailed information about the specific user. For security reasons, it is not widely used.

**finish segment (FIN segment)**  The message in the TCP three-way handshake that closes the connection, ensuring that it is terminated reliably.

**firewall**  A combination of hardware and software that enforces a boundary between two or more networks. In the context of the Internet, a computer that has special software installed between the Internet and a private network for the purpose of preventing unauthorized access to the private network.

**fixed equalizer**  Electronic circuitry that shapes the transmitted wave by using the assumption that the communications line has an average set of parameters.

**fixed wireless**  The use of radio or microwaves to provide a link between two stationary points—an ISP or its hub and a user's computer. It operates at higher frequencies than mobile wireless technologies, thus providing greater bandwidth and better signals.

**flag character**  (1) In the HDLC-based protocols, the initial and final octets of a frame that have the specific bit configuration of 01111110. A single flag may be used to denote the end of one frame and the start of another. (2) A bit sequence that signals the occurrence of some condition, such as the end of a word.

**flow control**  A mechanism that governs the amount of data transmitted by the sender. The ability of the receiving end of the transmission to limit the amount or rate of data sent by the transmitting end.

**format effector characters**  A character that controls the positioning of information on a terminal screen or paper.

**forward channel**  The primary-transmission channel in a communications circuit. *Contrast with* reverse channel.

**forward error correction (FEC)**  A technique of transmitting extra bits or characters with blocks of data so that transmission errors can be corrected at the receiving end.

**four-wire circuit**  A path in which four wires, two for each direction of the transmission, are presented to the station equipment. Leased circuits are normally four-wire circuits.

**fractional T-1**  The subdivision or multiplexing of T-1 circuits to provide circuit speeds that are a fraction of the T-1's capacity.

**fragment free switching**  A switch that sends the packet out to the destination determined by the MAC address after storing only the first 64 bytes, because that is where most errors occur.

**fragmentation**  The process of breaking a message frame or segment into smaller pieces to fit the requirements of a given physical network. The reverse process is called *reassembly.*

**frame**  In HDLC, the sequence of contiguous bits bracketed by and including the opening and closing flag sequences. The vehicle for every command, response, and all information that is transmitted.

**frame bursting**  Allows a node to transmit several small frames consecutively without relinquishing control between frames for collision detection, thus eliminating the need for the overhead that carrier extension bits add.

**frame relay**  A low-overhead packet switching technique designed to operate on high-speed circuits in which each packet keeps track of the nodes it has passed through.

**free space optics (FSO)**  The use of laser beams to send data between locations that are within line of sight (LOS) of each other.

**frequency**  An attribute of analog signals that describes the rate at which the current alternates. Frequency is measured in Hertz.

**frequency division multiplexing (FDM)**  A technique of putting several analog signals on a circuit by shifting the frequencies of the signals to different ranges so that they do not interfere with one another.

**frequency hopping**  A spread spectrum transmission technique in which the signal is broadcast over a seemingly random series of radio frequencies, hopping from frequency to frequency at split second intervals.

**frequency modulation (FM)**  Modulation in which the frequency of an alternating current is the characteristic varied.

**frequency shift keying (FSK)**  Frequency modulation of a carrier by a signal that varies between a fixed number of discrete values.

**full-duplex (FDX) transmission**  Data transmission on a circuit in both directions simultaneously.

**gateway**  A connection between two networks that use different protocols. The gateway translates the protocols to allow terminals on the two networks to communicate.

**gateway pages**   Special subject directories that contain many links to Web pages with important resources on specific topics. An "expert" who has spent a lot of time searching the Web compiles the pages as guides to specific fields, subjects, or disciplines.

**Gaussian noise**   *See* white noise.

**geosynchronous orbit**   A satellite orbit that exactly matches the rotation speed of Earth. Thus, from Earth, the satellite appears to be stationary.

**gigahertz (GHz)**   One billion Hertz.

**go-back-n**   A type of flow control in which the sending station, on receipt of a NAK, resends the damaged or out of sequence frame and all frames after it.

**Gopher**   A helpful tool used for searching the Internet when one doesn't have a browser (primarily used pre-WWW).

**Government Open Systems Interconnection Protocol (GOSIP)**   A U.S. government specified subset of the OSI model that defines what parts of the OSI model the government will follow and, therefore, what products it will buy.

**graphic characters**   A character that can be displayed on a terminal screen or printed on paper.

**graphics interchange format (GIF)**   A format used to encode graphic images into bits so the computer can read them and display the picture on the screen. It is one of the two types of image file used on Web pages.

**group address**   In HDLC, when a group address is used in a frame, the frame is accepted by stations that are members of a predefined group.

**guard band**   *See* guard channel.

**guard channel**   The space between the primary signal and the edge of an analog channel.

**guided media**   *See* conducted media.


**H.323**   A protocol for VoIP from the ITU. It is one of several proposed standards.

**hacker**   People who write programs for enjoyment.

**half duplex (HDX) transmission**   Data transmission on a circuit in either direction but in only one direction at a time.

**handle**   An online nickname, especially in chat rooms.

**handshaking**   The process that occurs when two devices, such as two modems, exchange a set of predetermined signals for the process of negotiating transmission parameters, such as the speed they will transmit.

**hash**   A unique value for a document's digital signature created by the hash function.

**hash function**   When calculating a digital signature, a mathematical process (called hashing) that crunches the data in a document and calculates a unique value for the document called the message digest or the hash.

**hashing**   The mathematical algorithm for calculating the hash for a document's digital signature.

**head end**   The originating point of a signal in cable TV systems.

**header**   (1) The part of a data message that contains information about the message, such as its destination, a sequence number, and perhaps a date or time. (2) An important part of a HTML document that contains particular information about the document.

**help desk**   A subgroup of network operations that acts as the single point of contact with users.

**Hertz (Hz)**   The unit of frequency equal to one cycle per second.

**hexadecimal**   A base-16 number system, often used to specify addresses in computer memory.

**hierarchical network**   A network that has a tree structure. The top node in the structure is called the root node.

**High Level Data Link Control (HDLC) Protocol**   A bit-oriented DLCP that exercises control of data links by the use of a specified series of bits rather than by the control characters. HDLC is a protocol standardized by ISO.

**hiperLAN2**   A competing wireless technology to 802.11a and 801.11g. It was developed by the ESTI and operates in the 5 GHz frequency band with a transmission rate of 54 Mbps.

**home page**   The top or first page in a hierarchy of Web pages on a website.

**hub**   A device that serves as a connection point for all of the wires or cables on a LAN. Some hubs have intelligence and can perform error detection.

**hub polling**   A type of polling in which each station polls the next station in succession on the communication line. The last station on the line polls the first station.

**Huffman coding**   A type of character compression.

**hybrid network**   A network made up of several network topologies.

**hyperlink**   Underlined links that allow readers to jump from document to document, idea to idea, researching on the Web in the nonlinear way humans think.

**Hypertext Markup Language (HTML)**   A formatting tool used to format pages for the WWW.

**Hypertext Transfer Protocol (HTTP)**   The protocol used to carry WWW traffic between a computer using a Web browser and the WWW server being accessed.

**Hypertext Transfer Protocol, Secure (HTTPS)**   Server software that allows secure transactions to take place on the WWW.


**IMG tags**   Image tags that enable a designer to add a graphic or a digitized photo to an HTML document.

**impulse noise**   A sudden spike on a communications circuit when the received amplitude goes beyond a certain level, caused by transient electrical impulses, such as lightning, switching equipment, or a motor starting.

**in-band signaling**   In ISDN networks, when the D channel sends the signaling information, routing the data sent by the B channels.

**industry standard architecture (ISA)**   An older 8-bit or 16-bit local bus that transfers data between a CPU of a computer and its peripheral devices (like the NIC).

**infected** Program files that have a virus attached are said to be infected.

**information bits** In data communications, those bits that are generated by the data source and that are not used for error control by the data transmission system.

**information frame** In HDLC, information frames contain the data field that holds the information being transmitted across the network.

**infrared (IR)** Light waves below the visible spectrum. Infrared light can be used for limited distance, line-of-sight, or near line-of-sight transmission.

**infrastructure mode** A mode in wireless transmission in which communication of the hosts to a wired LAN takes place through APs or base stations.

**instant messaging (IM)** Real-time chatting between two people.

**Institute of Electrical and Electronics Engineers (IEEE)** The world's largest technical professional society. Responsible for many telecommunications and computing standards, as well as the 802 standards used in LANs. It focuses on advancing the development and sharing of electrical and information technology specifications worldwide.

**Integrated Services Digital Network (ISDN)** An evolving set of standards for a digital public telephone network.

**intelligent hub** A hub that can detect errors and provide assistance to a technician when attempting to locate a failing component.

**Interface Message Processors (IMPs)** A minicomputer built for each original ARPANET site and used as an interface between the network and the mainframe nodes. Each minicomputer used the same language and operating system. They spoke to their own mainframe and to one another, although the mainframes could speak only to their own local interface. Their main function was to process messages from the network.

**intermediate system** In the context of an internet, subnetworks that provide a communication path and provide the necessary relaying and routing of messages.

**International Organization for Standardization (ISO)** An organization established to promote the development of standards to facilitate the international exchange of goods and services and to develop mutual cooperation in areas of intellectual, scientific, technological, and economic activity.

**International Telecommunications Union (ITU)** The specialized telecommunications agency of the UN, established to provide standardized communications procedures and practices, including frequency allocation and radio regulation, on a worldwide basis.

**International Telecommunications Union-Telecommunications Standardization Sector (ITU-T)** The part of the ITU that deals with global telecommunications standards.

**International Telegraph Alphabet 5** The ITU-T's name for the ASCII code.

**internet** *See* internetwork.

**Internet** A TCP/IP-based, interconnected set of government, research, education, commercial, and private networks.

**Internet Activities Board (IAB)** A technical advisory group of the Internet Society. It is concerned with the architecture for the protocols and standards used by the Internet. It is also responsible for the editorial management of the RFC document series.

**Internet backbone** A very high bandwidth network run by large companies and organizations that connects national and international networks.

**internet connection sharing (ICS)** A service found on Windows 98 and later operating systems that allows a single internet—or other network connection—to be shared with a small network.

**Internet Control Message Protocol (ICMP)** An error-reporting or message control protocol between a host server and a gateway to the Internet, usually sent in response to a datagram.

**Internet Corporation for Assigned Names and Numbers (ICANN)** The nonprofit organization that has authority to administer the issuing of IP addresses and to authorize top level domains.

**Internet Engineering Steering Group (IESG)** The executive committee of the IETF, concerned with Internet protocols and standards.

**Internet Engineering Task Force (IETF)** A large, open international community of network designers, operators, vendors, and researchers concerned with the evolution of the Internet architecture and the smooth operation of the Internet.

**Internet Message Access Protocol, v4 (IMAP4)** A newer Internet e-mail standard that makes management of e-mail safer and easier. It allows users to scan message headers and download only selected messages, and to create and manage folders.

**Internet Network Information Center (InterNIC)** The group that had the authority for registering all domain names until 1999. Currently it is one of several registrars authorized to register domain names. It also promotes the discussion of Internet services and new tools and technologies for the Internet community.

**Internet Protocol, version 4 (Ipv4)** Version 4 of a part of the TCP/IP stack of protocols that is used in gateways to connect networks at layer 3 of the OSI model. Internet protocol describes software for tracking the Internet address of nodes, routing outgoing messages, and recognizing messages coming into the network.

**Internet Protocol, version 6 (IPv6)** A newer version of IP that provides 128 bits and offers billions more IP addresses than currently available with IPv4.

**Internet radio** A radio station that sets up a Web server attached to the Internet to broadcast its programming. Most stations can be heard using either RealPlayer or Windows Media Player.

**Internet relay chat (IRC)** Technology that allows groups of people to take part in live text communication on various subjects over the Internet. It uses special software and ASCII commands.

**Internet Research Task Force (IRTF)**  An organization that promotes research of importance to the evolution of the Internet.

**Internet Security Association and Key Management Protocol/Oakley (ISAKMP/Oakley)**  A protocol used by IPsec. Allows sending and receiving devices to share a public key.

**Internet service providers (ISP)**  A business that charges a fee, usually monthly, to connect subscribers to its own Internet-connected servers, providing a gateway to the Internet.

**Internet small computer system interface (iSCSI)**  A technology that allows data to travel to and from storage devices over an IP network—like the Internet.

**Internet Society (ISOC)**  A private, nonprofit umbrella organization that guides the direction and growth of the Internet and focuses on four pillars: standards, public policy, education and training, and membership.

**internetwork**  An interconnected set of networks.

**internetwork packet exchange (IPX)**  Novell NetWare's transport (layer 3 and layer 4) protocols.

**internetworking**  The interconnection of networks.

**interpreter**  A component of a browser. Displays documents by translating the HTML into the appropriate onscreen output.

**intranet**  A private network, modeled after the Internet and WWW, on which browsers and servers are used to provide access to information of use to a particular audience. Many organizations have implemented intranets as a way to disseminate information to employees.

**inverse concentrator**  A device that takes a high-speed data stream and breaks it apart for transmission over several slower speed circuits.

**invisible Web**  All the rest of the thousands of databases on the Internet that cannot be located by search engines.

**IP address**  A unique address of every host on a TCP/IP network as a place to send and receive data.

**IP Security (IPsec)**  A set of standardized protocols developed by the IETF for the purpose of supporting the secure exchange of packets at the IP layer of the TCP/IP protocol.

**isochronous transmission**  A data transmission process in which there is always an integral number of unit intervals between any two significant instants.

**joint photographic experts group (jpg)**  One of two types of image file used on Web pages. The jpg standard reduces the size of bitmapped images by a compression algorithm that compromises the absolute quality of the image's resolution and color fidelity, though its quality is high enough for display of photos on the computer screen.

**KERMIT**  An asynchronous protocol that normally uses 1,000-byte blocks and a 3-byte CRC. The block size can, however, be adjusted dynamically during the transmission, based on line conditions.

**key management**  The policies and procedures associated with ensuring that private encryption keys are kept confidential, and that keys are accessible only by those who have a legitimate need for them.

**kilohertz (KHz)**  One thousand Hertz.

**LAN emulation (LANE)**  A technology that imitates Token Ring and Ethernet LANs on an ATM backbone.

**laser**  A device that transmits an extremely narrow beam of energy in the visible light spectrum.

**latency**  Signal delay, waiting, or time delay.

**layer**  A collection of related functions that comprise one level of a hierarchy of functions. Each layer specifies its own functions and assumes that lower level functions are provided.

**leased circuit**  A circuit that is owned by a communications carrier but leased from them by another organization for full-time, exclusive use.

**level**  The amplitude of a signal.

**levels of support**  A concept related to a support organization that suggests that the minimum skills necessary to solve a problem should be used. *See also* problem escalation.

**light emitting diode (LED)**  A semiconductor chip that gives off visible or infrared light when activated.

**line**  (1) On a terminal, one or more characters entered before a return to the first display or printing position. (2) A string of characters accepted by the system as a single block of input from a terminal; for example, all characters entered before a carriage return or all characters before a terminal user presses the ENTER key. (3) *See* circuit.

**line of sight (LOS)**  A wireless transmission in which the path from the transmitter to the receiver must be a straight line and must be clear of obstructions.

**line turnaround**  A process of half-duplex transmission in which one modem stops transmitting and becomes the receiver and the receiving modem becomes the transmitter.

**link**  A segment of a circuit between two points.

**Link Access Procedure, Balanced (LAPB)**  A subset of the HDLC protocol that operates in FDX, point-to-point mode. It is most commonly used between an X.25 DTE and a packet switching network.

**Link Access Procedure, D-Channel (LAPD)**  A subset of the HDLC protocol. Provides data link control on an ISDN D channel in AMB mode. LAPD always uses a 16-bit address, 7-bit sequence numbers, and a 16-bit CRC.

**Link Access Procedure for Frame-Mode Bearer Services (LAPF)**  A data link protocol for frame relay networks. LAPF is made up of a control protocol, which is similar to HDLC, and a core protocol, which is a subset of the control protocol. The control protocol uses 16- to 32-bit addresses, 7-bit sequence numbers, and a 16-bit CRC. The core protocol has no control field, which means there is no mechanism for error control, hence streamlining the operation of the network.

**Linux**  A full-featured, powerful, open source OS based on Unix. Linux was created originally by Linus Torvalds and it is free and freely available on the Internet. Supports a wide range of software.

**listserv**  A different type of mailing list that enables everyone on the list to read a message sent by one person.

**local area network (LAN)**  A high-speed (2 Mbps and up) network that covers a relatively small geographical area, usually within a building or several buildings in close proximity to one another.

**local loop**  A channel connecting a subscriber's equipment to the line-terminating equipment in a CO.

**logical bitwise AND operation**  In subnetting, an operation performed between the IP address and the subnet mask to result in the network address. It compares two bits. If they are both 1, the result is 1. If not, the result is 0.

**logical link control (LLC)**  The DLCP defined by the IEEE for use on LANs.

**logical topology**  The way that data flow from workstation to workstation.

**longitudinal redundancy checking (LRC)**  A parity check performed on a group of binary digits in a longitudinal direction for each track.

**low Earth orbit (LEO)**  Satellite orbits between 300 and 1,000 miles above Earth.

**low-speed circuit**  A circuit that is typically designed for telegraph or teletypewriter usage at speeds from 45 to 600 bps and that cannot handle voice transmission. Used by the public telex network.

**mailing list**  A type of broadcast e-mail that is a database of people interested in a particular topic. It allows one person to send a single message to every address on the list.

**management information base (MIB)**  The database in which the SNMP protocol stores information about the operation of a network.

**Manchester coding**  A digital signaling technique in which there is a transition in the middle of each bit time. A 1 is encoded with a low level during the first half of the bit time and a high level during the second half. A 0 is encoded with a high level during the first half of the bit time and a low level during the second half.

**mark**  In asynchronous transmission, the mark signal is the normal no-traffic line condition in which a steady signal is transmitted. The mark signal is also the signal for a 1 bit.

**masquerading**  Pretending to be someone else on the network, typically someone who has more privileges.

**Mbone**  The multicast backbone is made up of special purpose, multicast-aware routers that always allow packets to arrive in proper order. It is a multicast channel is used for public and private audio and video broadcasts on the Internet.

**Media Gateway Control Protocol (MGCP)**  A protocol for VoIP from the IETF. One of several proposed standards.

**medium**  Any material or substance that can be used for the propagation of signals, usually in the form of modulated radio, light, or acoustic waves, from one point to another. Examples are optical fiber, cable, wire, water, and air. Free space is also a medium for electromagnetic waves.

**medium access control (MAC)**  A technique for determining which of several stations on a LAN can use the network.

**medium Earth orbit (MEO)**  Satellite orbits approximately 6,000 miles above the Earth.

**megahertz (MHz)**  One million Hertz.

**mesh network**  A network in which some or all of the nodes are connected to each other. In a fully interconnected mesh, each node is connected to every other node.

**message digest**  *See* hash.

**metafile**  A small text file with the URL of the sound file you want to play used for continuous broadcast streaming audio files.

**meta-search engine**  A utility that searches several search engines and subject directories, compiling the results in a convenient display rather than searching each directory or index individually.

**metropolitan area exchange (MAE)**  Huge connection points and the largest hubs on the Internet. They are Tier 1 NAPs.

**metropolitan area network (MAN)**  A network that spans an area ranging from a few buildings to 30 or 40 miles or so, though the distances are not precise. MANs normally operate at high speed.

**microwave radio**  Radio transmissions in the 4 to 28 GHz range. Microwave radio transmissions require that the transmitting and receiving antennas be within sight of each other.

**MIME**  An encoding scheme that allows binary and files other than plain ASCII to travel over the network.

**MNP5**  A compression algorithm that is a combination of Huffman coding and run length coding.

**mobile terminal**  A user's device that connects to an access point in HiperLAN2.

**mobile wireless**  Wireless service technologies that include cellular phones, PDAs, palm computers, and other mobile devices.

**modem**  A device that modulates and demodulates signals transmitted over data communication lines. One of the functions of a modem is to enable digital data to be transmitted over analog transmission facilities.

**modem eliminator**  *See* null modem.

**moderated newsgroup**  A newsgroup in which a human moderator reads all the messages before they are posted and discards any that seem to be inappropriate for the group.

**modulation**  The process by which some characteristic of one wave is varied in accordance with another wave or signal. This technique is used in modems to make DTE signals compatible with communications facilities.

**modulator**  A device that modulates a signal.

**monoalphabetic cipher** A simple symmetric encryption scheme in which one character in the plaintext is replaced by another character.

**multicast** In IPv6, one of three types of addressing that provides greater flexibility and efficiency in routing. Multicast is transmission from one host to multiple hosts that can be at many locations.

**multicasting** A special way of transmitting information from a server to a set of several clients at the same time; for instance, audio and video conferencing or Internet radio and TV. Except that it is used on the Internet, it works just like ordinary radio or TV.

**multidrop circuit** *See* multipoint circuit.

**multimode** A type of optical fiber that has a core that is approximately 50 microns (.050 millimeter) in diameter.

**multiplexing** (1) In data transmission, a function that permits two or more data sources to share a common transmission medium, such that each data source has its own channel. (2) The division of a transmission facility into two or more channels, either by splitting the frequency band transmitted by the channel into narrower bands (frequency division multiplexing) or by allotting this common channel to several different information channels one at a time (TDM).

**multipoint circuit** A circuit that has several nodes connected to it.

**multipoint operation** The operation of a protocol on a multipoint circuit.

**multistation access unit (MAU)** A wiring hub in a token ring LAN.

**name server lookup (nslookup)** An Internet tool that allows users to search the domain name databases to determine the host system's IP address from its domain name (or vice versa).

**narrowband ISDN** An alternate name for the original ISDN service. *See* integrated services digital network (ISDN).

**natural-language queries** A type of searching tool with which you type a question phrased exactly as you would ask the question of a real person.

**NetBIOS** A layer of software, originally developed by IBM, that allows applications programs to communicate within a LAN.

**network** (1) An interconnected system of computers, terminals, and other hardware established for the purpose of exchanging information or services. (2) An interrelated group of objects connected together in some way.

**network access layer** The layer of the architecture responsible for the physical transmission through the network, including correcting errors within individual packets, frames, or other segments of a message.

**network access point (NAP)** Large hubs, classified as Tier 1 or Tier 2, on the Internet backbone where traffic is exchanged.

**network address translation (NAT)** An Internet standard that allows a LAN to use one set of IP addresses for internal traffic and another set of IP addresses for external traffic.

**network architecture** A set of design principles used as the basis for the design and implementation of a communications network.

**network attached storage (NAS)** A device or group of devices that reside on a LAN and are dedicated to storage.

**network design** The process of understanding the requirements for a new communications network or changes to an existing network, investigating alternative ways for configuring the network, selecting the most appropriate alternative to provide the required capability, and specifying (in detail) the parameters of the network so that the necessary equipment and software can be ordered and installed.

**network interface card (NIC)** A simple digital transmitter/receiver that provides the electrical interface to a network. A NIC is often implemented as a plug-in circuit card for a PC.

**network management** The set of activities that direct the resources required to keep a network operating over the long term.

**network management systems** Computer software systems designed to assist network operations people to keep track of the status of a network and provide network performance data for later analysis.

**network-network interface** The ATM cell format used within an ATM network.

**network operating system (NOS)** The software that controls a LAN's operation.

**network operation** The set of activities required to keep a communications network operating on a short term, day-to-day basis.

**network security policy** Management's statement of the importance of and their commitment to network security.

**network topology** The configuration of a communications network; the way the circuits are connected together.

**network virtual terminal (NVT)** A DTE that differs from the receiving device in data rates, protocols, codes, and formats, but is still able to use the same network. It is able to do so because of a type of network processing that converts each device's data into a network standard format and then into the format of the other device.

**newsgroup** A continuous, public, electronic discussion forum that is open to people everywhere.

**newsreader** Software used to read and post articles on newsgroups.

**node** A point of connection into a network, such as a computer or terminal, or a point such as a router or a switch at which one or more transmission lines (circuits) interconnect. The term *node* derives from graph theory in which a node is a junction point of links, areas, or edges.

**non-acknowledgement (NAK) character** A control character sent by the receiving node to indicate that a transmission was not received correctly.

**nondeterministic** The performance of the circuit using a network is said to be nondeterministic when delays become unpredictable as the number of terminals or the amount of traffic grows.

**noninformation bits** In data communications, those bits that are used for error control or other purposes. The bits do not directly convey the meaning of the message.

**non-line of sight (NLOS)** The situation that exists when the antennae of a transmitter and receiver are not visible to one another.

**non-realtime variable bit rate (nrt-VBR) service** A service of ATM used by applications that have a requirement for fast response time, but, compared to voice applications, can tolerate some delays—especially if they are infrequent.

**normal response mode (NRM)** An operating mode of HDLC used when there is a primary station and one or more secondary stations on a circuit. The primary station polls the secondary stations, which may send data only in response to a poll.

**null modem** A device that eliminates the need for a modem when transmission distances are very short. A null modem is typically a cable that connects the transmit pin on one device to the receive pin on another device, and vice versa.

**octet** Eight bits of data, also called a byte.

**open nodes** Free public access where users can connect to a wireless network.

**open system** (1) A system in which the input data enter the computer directly from the point of origin or in which output data are transmitted directly to where they are used. (2) Systems that provide a standards-based computing environment.

**open systems interconnection (OSI) reference model** A telecommunications architecture proposed by the ISO. The OSI model is the standard reference point by which data communications networks are measured.

**optical fiber** A communications medium made of very thin, high purity glass or plastic fiber that conducts light waves.

**organizing** The management function of grouping people to accomplish the mission of the organization.

**orthogonal frequency division multiplexing (OFDM)** A next-generation modulation technique used in 802.11a standard wireless networking. It handles the higher data rates that are required for multimedia applications.

**out-of-band signaling** In ISDN networks, when routing information is sent over the B channels and must take 8 Kb in each channel to use for signaling information, thus allowing each B channel to carry 56 kilobits of data.

**outsourcing** The transfer of some of the activities of an organization to another organization, usually for the purpose of obtaining specialized services at a lower cost.

**packet** A sequence of binary digits (including data and control signals) that is sent through the network as a composite whole. The data, control signals, and possibly error control information are arranged in a specific format.

**packet assembly/disassembly (PAD)** The process of dividing a message into packets at the transmitting end and reassembling the message from the packets at the receiving end.

**packet data network (PDN)** A network that uses packet switching techniques for transmitting data.

**packet filtering** The process performed by a packet-level firewall of examining and controlling the transfer of data between networks at the packet level, allowing or denying packet passage from one network to the other based on the source and destination addresses.

**packet-level firewall** A device, typically a router, that examines and controls the transfer of data between networks at the packet level allowing or denying packet passage from one network to the other, based on the source and destination addresses.

**packet network** *See* packet data network.

**packet switching** The technique of sending packets through a network, sometimes by diverse routes.

**packet switching network** *See* packet data network.

**packetizing** The process of dividing a message into packets.

**parallel mode** *See* parallel transmission.

**parallel transmission** The simultaneous transmission of bits over a cable or circuit. *Contrast with* serial transmission.

**parity bit** A binary digit appended to a group of binary digits to make the sum of all the digits either always odd (odd parity) or always even (even parity).

**parity checking** An error checking technique that uses a parity bit for each character of data.

**passive hub** A device that acts as a pathway allowing data to flow from one device on a segment to another. It simply resends a signal without regenerating it.

**passive security attacks** Security attacks in which the attacker monitors or analyzes network traffic but does not attempt to insert new messages or disrupt existing traffic.

**password** A combination of letters, digits, and special characters that a person creates to uniquely identify themselves to a computer or network. Passwords should always be kept secret.

**patch cable** A short cable, with connectors at each end, that is used to connect two devices.

**patch panels** A device that allows a circuit or piece of equipment to be temporarily connected to other equipment or circuits.

**peer-to-peer** A LAN in which every node has equal access to the network and does not need to wait for permission from a control node to transmit or receive data at any time.

**performance management** The application of management principles to ensure that the performance of a system meets the required parameters.

**Peripheral Component Interconnect (PCI)** A high-speed (32-bit or 64-bit) local bus inside a PC or MAC that transfers data between a CPU of a computer and its peripheral devices–like the NIC.

**permanent virtual circuit (PVC)** In packet switching networks, a full-time connection between two nodes.

**personal computer memory card interface adaptor (PCMCIA)** The adapter on a laptop computer. The side of the card that fits into the PCMCIA slot has a row of 68 holes that fit the 68 pins inside the slot.

**phase** An attribute of an analog signal that describes its relative position, measured in degrees.

**phase amplitude modulation (PAM)** Modulation in which both the amplitude and the phase angle of a carrier are varied.

**phase jitter** An unwanted change in the phase of a signal.

**phase modulation (PM)** Modulation in which the phase angle of a carrier is the characteristic varied.

**phase shift** The offset of an analog signal from its previous location, as measured in degrees.

**phase shift keying (PSK)** *See* phase modulation.

**phone-line network** A type of network that uses existing phone lines as the medium to connect computers.

**physical topology** The way in which the wires actually connect computers.

**piconet** A connection of from two to eight Bluetooth devices.

**ping** A network tool (or TCP/IP protocol function) that tests whether a computer can communicate with a remote computer by sending a message and receiving a response.

**plaintext** Unencrypted data.

**planning** The function of identifying the actions necessary to achieve the objectives of an organization.

**Point of Presence (PoP)** A locally maintained computer with a dedicated line to the ISP, which may not be within a user's local area. It eliminates long-distance charges and facilitates connections.

**point-to-point circuit** A circuit connecting two nodes. *Contrast with* multipoint circuit.

**point-to-point operation** (1) The operation of a protocol on a point-to-point circuit. (2) Direct communication from an application on one computer to an application on one other computer.

**Point-to-Point Protocol (PPP)** An asynchronous protocol that includes capabilities for line testing, authentication, data compression, and error correction. It is primarily used by PCs to dial into a TCP/IP-based network, though it may be used on leased lines as well. It is more reliable and versatile than the SLIP protocol, which it has largely replaced.

**polling** (1) The process in which stations are invited, one at a time, to transmit. (2) Interrogation of devices for purposes such as to avoid contention, to determine operational status, or to determine readiness to send or receive data.

**polling list** A list that specifies the sequence in which stations are to be polled.

**polyalphabetic cipher** An encryption technique in which one plaintext character is substituted for another—but not always the same one.

**polynomial error checking** An error checking technique in which the bits of a block of data are processed by a mathematical algorithm using a polynomial function to calculate the block check character.

**port speed** On a frame relay circuit, the maximum transmission speed of the circuit between the customer and the frame relay carrier.

**post implementation audit** A review of a network or system shortly after it has been implemented for the purpose of identifying changes or adjustments that need to made.

**posting** Beginning a conversation or responding to comments by others by entering a message into a newsgroup.

**Post Office Protocol, v3 (POPv3)** The protocol used to retrieve mail from an e-mail server. It is independent of the transport mechanism so e-mail can be accessed from anywhere over the Internet.

**power line networks** A type of network that uses existing electrical wires as the medium to connect computers.

**Pretty Good Privacy (PGP)** An asymmetric encryption/decryption program for e-mail, computer data, and voice conversations.

**primary rate interface (PRI)** An ISDN service that provides twenty-three 64 Kbps B channels and one 64 Kbps D channel.

**print server** A server on a LAN and provides the hardware and software to drive one or more printers.

**private branch exchange (PBX)** A private telephone exchange connected to the public telephone network on the user's premises.

**private circuit** A communication circuit that is owned by a company other than a communications carrier.

**private frame relay network** Frame relay service established by an organization for its exclusive use.

**private key** In an asymmetric encryption system, the key that is kept secret and is never distributed.

**private network** A network built by a company for its exclusive use, which uses circuits available from a variety of sources.

**private voice network** A network built by an organization for its exclusive use and for the primary purpose of carrying its voice traffic.

**problem escalation** The process of bringing a problem to the attention of higher levels of management and/or bringing in more highly trained technical resources to work on solving the problem.

**problem management** The process of expeditiously handling a problem from its initial recognition to a satisfactory resolution.

**problem tracking meeting** A periodic meeting to discuss the status of all open problems that have not yet been resolved.

**propagation delay** The time necessary for a signal to travel from one point to another.

**protocol**   The set of rules governing the operation of functional units of a communication system that must be followed if communication is to be achieved.

**protocol analyzer**   An electronic instrument that can look at the actual bits or characters being transmitted on the circuit to determine whether the rules of the protocol are being followed correctly.

**protocol converter**   Hardware or software that converts a data transmission from one protocol to another.

**protocol data unit (PDU)**   A unit of a protocol consisting of the payload and protocol-specific control information.

**protocol stack**   A collection of software modules that, in combination, enable a protocol to work. It is called a stack because the modules are often viewed as being on top of each other, like the layers in an architecture.

**proxy server**   A device that changes the network addresses from one form to another so that users or computers on one network do not know the actual addresses of the nodes on the other network.

**public frame relay network**   Frame relay service offered by a communications company for public use.

**public key**   In an asymmetric encryption system, the key that is revealed (made public) to anyone who may want to use it.

**public key encryption**   An encryption technique in which messages are encrypted with one key that can be made public and are decrypted with a separate private key.

**public network**   A network established and operated by a communications company or telecommunications administration for the specific purpose of providing network service to the public.

**public switched telephone network (PSTN)**   A network that provides circuits switched between many customers for the primary purpose of carrying voice traffic.

**public telephone network**   *See* public switched telephone network.

**pulse code modulation (PCM)**   A process in which a signal is sampled, and the magnitude of each sample—with respect to a fixed reference—is quantized and converted to a digital signal.

**punchdown block**   A particular type of terminating block on which the connection is made by pushing (punching) the wire between two prongs with a special tool.

**quadbits**   A group of four bits. In 16-phase modulation, each possible quadbit is encoded as one of 16 unique carrier phase shifts. *Contrast with* dibit *and* tribit.

**quadrature amplitude modulation (QAM)**   A combination of PM and AM. Used to achieve high data rates while maintaining relatively low signaling rates.

**quality of service (QoS)**   (1) Measures of the performance of a network as seen by its users. (2) A measure or standard of the level of service provided by a carrier. In HiperLAN2 technology, a user can have several connections established, each assigned a specific QoS to prioritize traffic for different types of applications and levels of users.

**quantization**   The subdivision of the range of values of a variable into a finite number of nonoverlapping and not necessarily equal subranges or intervals—each of which is represented by an assigned value within the subrange. For example, a person's age is quantized for most purposes with a quantum of 1 year.

**quantizing noise**   The error introduced when an analog signal is digitized.

**queue**   A line or list formed by items in a system waiting for service.

**queuing**   The process of placing items that cannot be immediately handled into a queue to await service.

**queuing delay**   Delays in a network attributed to packets waiting in queues for service.

**queuing theory**   The branch of mathematics dedicated to the study of queues and queuing.

**radiated media**   Any medium that propagates the signal through the air or space, such as radio, infrared, or microwave.

**radio frequency (RF)**   Any frequency within the electromagnetic spectrum with wavelengths between the audio and the light range. The frequencies associated with radio and radar wave propagation are normally between approximately 10 KHz and 30 GHz.

**radio teletype (RTTY)**   Teletypewriter service in which signals are sent by radio waves.

**real-time variable bit rate (rt-VBR) service**   A service of ATM used by applications that require minimal delays in the transmissions; however, the distinction is that the transmission rates tend to be somewhat bursty, such as might be found with compressed video transmissions.

**reassembly**   The process by which a frame or message is put back together after being fragmented. *See* fragmentation.

**redundant array of inexpensive (or independent) disks (RAID)**   Several disk drives in a single housing that are treated as if they were one drive. Data are written redundantly on two or more disks so that if one disk fails, the data can be recovered.

**remote monitoring (RMON)**   A standard monitoring specification that defines a set of statistics and functions that can be exchanged between RMON-compliant devices or software.

**repeater**   A device that performs digital signal regeneration together with ancillary functions. Its function is to retime and retransmit the received signal impulses restored to their original shape and strength. A repeater moves all received packets or frames between LAN segments.

**request for comment (RFC)**   The process for creating a new standard on the Internet. New standards are proposed and discussed online until a consensus is reached and the standard is adopted and given a number, such as RFC 793, the standard for TCP.

**request for proposal (RFP)**   A letter or document sent to vendors asking them to show how a (network) problem or situation can be addressed. Normally, the vendor's response to the RFP proposes a solution and quotes estimated prices.

**resolver**   Special software that queries the network's primary DNS server, which is specified on the local host when TCP/IP information is set up in order to supply the proper IP address when a user types in a specific URL.

**reverse channel**   A means of simultaneous communications from the receiver to the transmitter over HDX data transmission systems. The reverse channel is generally used only for the transmission of control information and operates at a much slower speed than the forward channel. *Contrast with* forward channel.

**ring network**   A network in which each node is attached to two adjacent nodes.

**RJ-11**   A 6-pin connector commonly wired for four conductors and used in the telephone industry for connecting telephones to wall jacks.

**RJ-45**   An 8-pin connector commonly used for data transmission over standard UTP telephone wire.

**roaming**   The capability for wireless network users to move freely, without disruption, to their LAN communication. When the coverage area is blanketed with overlapping coverage cells, the wireless networking hardware can shift automatically to the AP that has the best signal.

**roll-call polling**   The most common implementation of a polling system, in which one station on a line is designated as the master and the others are slaves.

**root node**   The top node in a hierarchical network topology.

**root servers**   Special computers that are distributed around the world and are coordinated by ICANN and contain the IP addresses of all the TLD registries.

**router**   A piece of hardware or software whose primary function is to direct messages toward their destination, often from one network to another.

**routing**   The process of determining the path for a message through a network or internetwork.

**routing algorithm**   The logic that routers use to determine how to forward data.

**routing table**   In a router or some other internetworking device, a table that keeps track of routes to particular network destinations.

**RS-232-C**   A specification for the physical, mechanical, and electrical interface between DTE and DCE. *See also* V.24.

**RS-232-D**   A 1987 revision and update to the RS-232-C specification making it exactly compatible with the V.24 standard.

**RS-336**   A specification for the physical, mechanical, and electrical interface between DTE and DCE. This specification, unlike the RS-449 specification, contains a provision for the automatic dialing of calls under modem control.

**RS-449**   A specification for the physical, mechanical, and electrical interface between DTE and DCE. This specification was designed to overcome some of the problems with the RS-232-C interface specification.

**run length encoding**   A type of compression in which the input text is scanned for repeating characters which, when found, are reduced to shorter character strings.

**satellite connection**   An Internet connection service that works in the same way as other fixed wireless systems by converting digital signals to radio waves that communicate with the central hub by way of satellite.

**SC connector**   A connector used for optical fiber cable. The male connector pushes into a female connector with a friction fit.

**scatternet**   A network created when a device from one piconet (a connection of 2-8 Bluetooth devices) is also a member of another piconet.

**scrambler**   A device that encrypts voice communication by making it unintelligible to anyone who does not have a descrambler. Scrambling effectively renders wiretapping useless.

**search engine**   A program on a website that maintains a database of Internet sites. When you perform a search, the engine uses special software robots to build lists of the words found on websites.

**search tools**   Internet Tools that do three things: 1) search the Internet based on key words or phrases, 2) index the words and their locations (URLs), and 3) provide links to those URLs.

**secure socket layer (SSL)**   A transport level technology for authentication between a Web browser and a Web server.

**segment**   The single shared medium or one continuous electronic portion of a network that has been separated because of distance or traffic. Segments are connected to other segments by bridges or switches. The term is normally used only with LANs.

**segmentation**   *See* fragmentation.

**selective repeat**   A type of flow control in which the sending station, on receipt of a NAK, resends only the damaged or out of sequence frame.

**sequence numbering**   Assigning numbers to each packet, assuring that they arrive in the proper order.

**sequenced packet exchange (SPX)**   Novell's enhanced set of commands that are implemented on top of IPX and provide more functions, like guaranteed delivery of packets.

**Serial Line Interface Protocol (SLIP)**   A protocol for carrying IP over dial-up or leased lines. SLIP contains little negotiation capability and does not support error detection or correction. SLIP has largely been replaced by PPP.

**serial mode**   *See* serial transmission.

**serial transmission**   The sequential transmission of bits over a cable or circuit. The bits may be transmitted with or without interruption, provided that they are not transmitted simultaneously. *Contrast with* parallel transmission.

**server**   A computer that has software that provides service to other devices on the LAN. Typical servers are file servers, print servers, and communications servers.

**service generality** The ability for a network to support a wide variety of applications.

**service level agreement (SLA)** A set of performance objectives reached by consensus between the user and the provider of the service.

**serving CO** A telephone subscriber's local CO.

**session initiation protocol (SIP)** A protocol for VoIP that connects devices with other devices using IP addresses in much the same way that HTTP uses the URL address to connect Web browsers to servers.

**shielded twisted pair (STP)** Twisted pair wires surrounded by a metallic shield.

**shielding** A metallic sheath that surrounds the conductor in a cable.

**signaling** To communicate or indicate by signals.

**signaling rate** The number of times per second that a signal changes. Signaling rate is measured in baud.

**Signaling System No. 7 (SS7)** A signaling system used among telephone company COs to set up calls, indicate their status, and tear down the calls when they are completed.

**signal processor** Electronic circuitry that is designed to manipulate a digital signal.

**signals** A variation of a physical quantity used to convey data.

**signature** The unique bit pattern created by a virus's instructions.

**Simple Mail Transfer Protocol (SMTP)** The TCP/IP protocol that governs server-to-server transmissions and receptions of e-mail.

**Simple Network Management Protocol (SNMP)** A protocol that originated on the Internet for exchanging network management commands and information among devices attached to a network.

**simplex transmission** Transmission on a communications line in one direction only. Transmission in the other direction is not allowed.

**sine wave** The waveform of a single-frequency analog signal of a constant amplitude and phase.

**single mode** A type of optical fiber that has a glass or plastic core approximately 5 microns (.005 millimeter) in diameter.

**sink** The receiving station in a communications system.

**site license** An agreement, usually for software, that allows its use by an unlimited number of people at the site. The term *site* may be defined in different ways, according to the terms of the agreement.

**sliding window flow control** A flow control technique in which several blocks of data can be sent by the transmitting station before it receives an acknowledgement from the receiver.

**slot time** The minimum amount of time a NIC has to transmit a frame.

**slow start** A window management technique in which the rate at which acknowledgments are returned by the receiving end determines the rate at which the sender introduces new packets into the network.

**sneakernet** The method of transferring files by walking from one computer to another, often on feet shod in sneakers.

**socket** An application program interface that allows communication between a user's application program and TCP/IP. The socket number joins the IP address of the sender or receiver and the port numbers for the service being used.

**software metering** Software that keeps track of the number of simultaneous users of another piece of software installed on a server. The usual purpose of software metering is to prevent more people from simultaneously using the software than have been paid for in the software license agreement.

**source** The transmitting station in a communications system.

**space** In asynchronous transmission, the space signal is the signal for a zero bit.

**spiders** Special software programs that automatically build lists of the words found on websites.

**spooling** A technique of queuing input or output between slow-speed and high-speed computer hardware. Print spooling is most common. Output from several computers is queued (spooled) to a disk until a printer is free.

**spread spectrum transmission** A radio transmission technique in which the frequency of the transmission is changed periodically and usually randomly.

**staffing** The management function of ensuring that enough trained people are available to perform the tasks to meet an organization's objectives.

**star network** A network in which all circuits radiate from a central node, such as a cluster of servers or a host computer.

**start bit** In a start/stop system, a signal preceding a character or block that prepares the receiving device for the reception of the code elements.

**start of header (SOH) character** A transmission control character used as the first character of a message heading.

**start of text (STX) character** A transmission control character that precedes text and that may be used to terminate the message header.

**start/stop transmission** Asynchronous transmission in which a group of bits is preceded by a start bit that prepares the receiving mechanism for the reception and registration of a character and is followed by at least 1 stop bit that enables the receiving mechanism to come to an idle condition, pending the reception of the next character.

**statement of requirements** A description of the need for a new or changed network used by network designers.

**static IP address** A permanent IP address that a user always has; it remains the same.

**static routing** A routing technique in which the route or routes between two nodes on the network are fixed and can be changed only when the network is taken down and software tables are modified.

**statistical time division multiplexing (STDM)** The technique of combining signals from several sources without reserving specific time slots for each source but assigning time only when a source has data to send.

**ST connector** A connector used for optical fiber cable. The male connector is inserted into the female connector and twisted clockwise to lock it into place.

**stop and wait ARQ** An error checking technique in which each block of data in a transmission must be acknowledged before the next block can be sent.

**stop-and-wait flow control** A flow control technique in which each block of data must be acknowledged before the next block can be sent.

**stop bit** In a start/stop system, a signal following a character or block that indicates the end of the character or block.

**storage area network (SAN)** A dedicated network of storage-related devices such as tape drives, hard drives, and disk arrays that is physically removed from, but still connected to, the main network.

**store-and-forward switch** A switch that brings each incoming packet into memory and examines the destination segment. If it is busy, the switch holds the packet until the segment is free and then sends it out.

**stream socket** Sockets that use the TCP protocol and treat communications as a continuous stream of characters.

**stream transport** A continuous sequence of packets is transmitted over the Internet and, as in the case of audio or video, it starts playing on the screen before the entire file is downloaded to your computer.

**stress testing** Placing a heavy load on a network or system to see if it performs properly.

**strong password** Passwords that are difficult for someone else to figure out because they are at least seven characters long and contain a combination of uppercase and lowercase characters, numerals, and symbols.

**subject directory** Topical directories that are typically built by human selection rather than robot programs and are organized into subject categories.

**subnet** *See* subnetwork.

**subnet mask** A 32-bit number applied to the IP address. Tells the router how to interpret the bits of the address. It is a screen of binary digits that identify which bits are the network part of the address and which bits are the host part of the address.

**subnetwork** (1) In the OSI reference model, layers 1, 2, and 3 together constitute the subnetwork. (2) A portion of a network. (3) In the context of the Internet, one of the interconnected networks that also continues to operate on its own and maintain its own identity.

**subvoice-grade circuit** A circuit of bandwidth narrower than that of voice-grade circuits. Such circuits are usually subchannels of a voice-grade line.

**supernetting** The linking of several IP network address blocks into a "supernet."

**supervisory frame** In HDLC, supervisory frames are used to send a NAK when a frame is received incorrectly or when it indicates status.

**survivability** An attribute of a network that means that messages will get through no matter what happens, including war.

**switch** (1) In the context of a LAN, a device that connects two or more LAN segments together and allows all of the connections to operate simultaneously. (2) In the context of the telephone system, a device in a CO that makes the connection for telephone calls. (3) A PBX is sometimes referred to as a switch.

**switched multimegabit data service (SMDS)** A high-speed switched digital service offered by some communications carriers. Two speeds are available, either 1.544 Mbps (T-1 speed) or 44.736 Mbps (T-3 speed).

**switched virtual circuit (SVC)** In packet switching networks, a temporary connection between two nodes, established only for the duration of a session.

**switching delay** Delays in a network caused by devices such as switches, routers, and bridges.

**switching hub** A special type of hub that reads the address of the destination for each packet and forwards it to the proper port.

**switching office** A communications company office that contains switching equipment.

**symmetric digital subscriber line (SDSL)** One of the DSL family of services that provides equal speed channels in both directions. SDSL is capable of speeds up to 2.3 Mbps in each direction and is targeted at business customers. *See also* digital subscriber line (DSL).

**symmetric encryption techniques** An encryption technique in which the decrypting process is just the reverse of encrypting.

**synchronization character (SYN)** A character that is inserted in a data stream from time to time by the transmitting station to ensure that the receiver is maintaining character synchronization and properly grouping the bits into characters. The synchronization characters are removed by the receiver and do not remain in the received message.

**synchronization segment (SYN segment)** The message in the TCP three-way handshake that creates the connection, ensuring that it is established reliably.

**Synchronous Data Link Control (SDLC) Protocol** A bit-oriented DLCP developed by IBM. SDLC is a proper subset of HDLC.

**synchronous optical network (SONET)** A standard for data transmission on optical fibers.

**synchronous transmission** (1) Data transmission in which the time of occurrence of each signal representing a bit is related to a fixed time frame. (2) Data transmission in which the sending and receiving devices are operating continuously at the same frequency and are maintained by means of a correction in a desired phase relationship.

**Systems Network Architecture (SNA)** A seven-layer communications architecture developed by IBM to serve as the basis for future telecommunications products.

**T-1, T-2, T-3, and T-4 circuits** The designations for the members of the T-carrier transmission circuit family.

**tags** Commands that define the way text or layout should appear in an HTML document.

**T-carrier system** A family of high-speed, digital transmission systems designated according to their transmission capacity.

**telecommunications** Communication by electrical or electromagnetic means, usually (but not necessarily) over a distance.

**Teletype** Trademark of AT&T, referring to a series of teleprinter equipment.

**teletypewriter (TTY)** A slow-speed terminal with a keyboard for input and paper for receiving printed output.

**teletypewriter exchange service(TWX)** Teletypewriter-based messaging service provided by Western Union for use within the U.S. Similar to the international telex service.

**telex** An international messaging service that uses teleprinters to produce a hard copy of the messages.

**Telnet** A capability of the Internet that allows a person or computer to log on to another computer on the Internet.

**Temporal Key Integrity Protocol (TKIP)** A strong encryption process that includes frequent updating of the encryption key.

**terminal adapter** A hardware device, which is sometimes called an ISDN modem, used to deliver ISDN through a special type of local telephone line.

**terminal emulation** An application that allows a PC to mimic or emulate the operation of a dumb terminal for communication on a network, typically to a mainframe computer. The VT-100 terminal is one type that is frequently emulated.

**terminating block** A connector for communications wiring typically installed where wire enters a building. The terminating block often serves as a demarcation point (demarc) between the responsibility of the communications carrier and the owner of the building.

**text** The part of a data message containing the subject matter of interest to the user.

**thin client** An application designed so that little or no processing is done on the client computer; most processing is done on the server.

**third party copying** Serverless backup that allows a disk storage device to copy data directly to a backup device across the high-speed links of the SAN without any intervention from a server.

**thread** An ongoing conversation that continues over an extended period.

**three-way handshake** The process whereby two protocol entities synchronize during the establishment of a connection.

**time division duplex (TDD)** HiperLAN2 slotted structure whereby traffic is transmitted in a 2 ms MAC frame that contains user data for both uplink and downlink directions in addition to the protocol control information.

**time division multiplexing (TDM)** The technique of dividing a circuit's capacity into time slots, each of which is used by a different data signal.

**token** A particular sequence of bits in a token-oriented protocol. The terminal that has the token has the right to use the communications circuit.

**token passing** A technique for line control in which a particular sequence of bits, called a token, is passed from node to node. The node that has the token at any point in time is allowed to transmit.

**token passing protocol** A communications protocol that defines the way in which each device on a token-based LAN receives and passes the privilege, by the use of a token, to transmit over the single channel on the LAN.

**toll office** A CO at which toll circuits terminate. There is usually one toll office in a city, but large cities may have several COs where toll circuits terminate.

**tone signaling** Signaling performed by sending tones on a circuit.

**top level domain** The highest level in the hierarchal domain name system (for example, .com or .edu). The next level down refers to organizations and the next lower level to specific hosts.

**topology** The way in which a network's circuits are configured.

**traceroute** A network tool that allows users to learn the route that packets take from their local host to a remote host, tracing the intermediate routers along the path through the Internet.

**trailer** The part of a data message that follows the text.

**transmission control characters** Characters that cause certain control operations to be performed when they are encountered. Among such operations are addressing, polling, message delimiting, transmission error checking, and carriage return.

**transmission control protocol (TCP)** A set of transmission rules for interconnecting communications networks. A connection-oriented protocol that provides point-to-point, reliable, FDX stream transport communication with reliable startup and delivery of all data before shutdown.

**Transmission Control Protocol/Internet Protocol (TCP/IP)** A set of transmission rules for interconnecting communication networks. TCP/IP is the heart of the Internet and is heavily supported by the U.S. government. *See also* transmission control protocol (TCP).

**transmission efficiency** The ratio of information bits to total bits transmitted.

**transparent mode** A mode of the Binary Synchronous Communications protocol in which data, including normally restricted data link control characters, are transmitted only as specific bit patterns. Control characters that are intended to be effective are preceded by a DLE character.

**transport layer** The layer of an architecture that is responsible for sending or receiving an entire message through the network, including requesting retransmission if parts of the message are not received correctly.

**transport mode**   An IPsec operating mode that encrypts only the data portion of each packet but leaves the header untouched. *See also* tunnel mode.

**transposition cipher**   An encryption technique in which the letters in the plaintext message are rearranged rather than having cipher characters substituted for them.

**trellis code modulation (TCM)**   A specialized form of quadrature amplitude modulation that codes the data so that many bit combinations are invalid. TCM is used for high-speed data communication.

**tribits**   A group of 3 bits. In eight-phase modulation, each tribit is encoded as 1 of 8 unique carrier phase shifts. *Contrast with* dibit *and* quadbit.

**triple DES**   An enhancement of the standard DES encryption technique, which doubles the encryption key length to 112 bytes and encrypts the data three times.

**trouble ticket**   A formal document that describes an outstanding problem (with a network) that is yet to be resolved.

**trunk**   A telephone circuit between two COs or switching devices.

**tunnel**   A technique to provide a secure temporary path through the Internet or other IP-based network.

**tunneling**   A process used to form a secure private network. It basically places one packet inside another to send it over a public network.

**tunnel mode**   An IPsec operating mode that encrypts both the header and the data of each packet. Tunnel mode is more secure than transport mode. *See also* transport mode.

**twisted pair**   A pair of wires insulated with a plastic coating and twisted together. Used as a medium for telecommunications circuits.

**two-wire circuit**   A circuit formed by two conductors that are insulated from each other. It is possible to use the two conductors as a simplex, HDX, or FDX path.

**unguided media**   *See* radiated media.

**unicast**   In IPv6, one of three types of addressing that provides greater flexibility and efficiency in routing. Unicast is transmission from one device to one other device. In other words, a point-to-point communication.

**Unicode**   A standardized coding system that has $2^{16}$ code points allowing over 65,000 characters. However, an extension mechanism is also provided that allows over 1 million additional characters that can be used to represent all the characters of all languages.

**uniform resource locator (URL)**   The address that is used to specify a server and page on the World Wide Web.

**unipolar**   A digital signaling technique in which a 1 bit is represented by a positive voltage and a 0 bit is represented by no voltage.

**Unix**   A powerful multitasking, multiuser computer OS.

**unmoderated newsgroup**   A newsgroup in which all messages are put directly onto the server without any human intervention.

**unnumbered frame**   In HDLC, unnumbered frames establish how the protocol will proceed according to the setting of the five-bit M fields.

**unshielded twisted pair (UTP)**   *See* twisted pair.

**unspecified bit rate (UBR) service**   A service of ATM that provides service with whatever capacity is left after the available circuit capacity is allocated to all other services.

**uplink**   The radio signal beamed up to a satellite.

**USENET**   Newsgroups that were first created in 1979 among a group of computer systems as discussion groups (similar to bulletin boards). Newsgroups now transfer discussions about a wide range of topics via the Internet.

**User Datagram Protocol (UDP)**   The protocol in the TCP/IP suite that allows the exchange of datagrams without acknowledgment or guaranteed delivery by accessing the connectionless features of IP. *See also* datagram.

**user identification code (user id)**   A unique, usually meaningful code assigned to the user of a computer or network.

**user plane**   The part of a frame relay system concerned with the transfer of data.

**user-network interface**   The ATM cell format used when applications put data into or remove it from the network.

**V. standards**   Standards that define the connection of digital equipment (terminals and computers) to the public telephone network's analog lines.

**V.24**   An ITU standard for the physical, mechanical, and electrical interface between DTE and DCE.

**V.32**   An ITU-T standard for transmitting data at 9,600 bps, FDX, on a switched circuit.

**V.32bis**   An ITU-T standard for transmitting data at 14,400 bps, FDX, on a switched circuit.

**V.33**   An ITU-T standard for transmitting data at up to 14,400 bps, FDX, on 4-wire leased circuits.

**V.34**   An ITU-T standard for transmitting data at 28,800 bps, FDX, on a switched circuit. V.34 assumes that most of the transmission will occur on a relatively error free digital circuit.

**V.34bis**   An ITU-T standard for transmitting data at 33,600 bps, FDX, on a switched circuit. V.34bis assumes that most of the transmission will occur on a relatively error free digital circuit.

**V.42**   An ITU-T standard for error detection and error correction.

**V.42bis**   An ITU-T standard that specifies how modems will compress data before transmitting.

**V.44**   An ITU-T standard that specifies how modems will compress data before transmitting. V.44 compression is approximately 25 percent more effective than V.42bis.

**V.90**   An ITU-T standard for transmitting data at 56,000 bps, FDX, on a switched circuit. V.90 assumes that at least one end of the communications line has a pure digital connection to the telephone network. V.90 transmission is asymmetric in that the 56 Kbps data rate is only achieved on the half of the transmission from the all-digital end of the connection. Transmissions from the analog end follow the V.34bis standard and occur at a maximum of 33.6 Kbps.

**V.92** An ITU-T standard for transmitting data at 56,000 bps, FDX, on a switched circuit. V.92 is an enhancement to V.90 and includes faster startup times, a faster upload speed of 48 Kbps, a method to signal that another call is waiting to use the circuit, and a technique for taking a telephone call while staying connected to the Internet.

**value-added network (VAN)** A public data network that contains intelligence that provides enhanced communications services.

**vertical redundancy checking (VRC)** *See* parity checking.

**very-high-bit-rate digital subscriber line (VDSL)** One of the DSL family of services that transmits data in both directions at speeds of 51 to 55 Mbps over short twisted pair telephone lines of up to 1,000 feet, and as low as 13 Mbps at 4,000 feet. Some versions of this technology are asymmetric, like ADSL, and have an upstream channel of 1.6 to 2.3 Mbps. *See also* digital subscriber line *and* asymmetric digital subscriber line.

**very small aperture terminal (VSAT)** A satellite system using the Ku band of microwave frequencies, which require small receiving antennas.

**virtual channel identifier (VCI)** In an ATM header, the 16-bit field that identifies the VC (within a virtual path) that the data will travel from sending device to receiving device.

**virtual circuit (VC)** A temporary connection built between the sender and the receiver of a transmission (e.g. for a telephone call).

**virtual network** As contrasted with a leased or private networks, a virtual network appears to the customer as though it is dedicated for her exclusive use, but in reality it uses the PSTN to provide service.

**virtual path identifier (VPI)** In an ATM header, the 8-bit field that identifies the virtual path over which data will flow from the transmitting to the receiving device.

**virtual private network (VPN)** A technique for encapsulating data transmitted through public networks, such as the Internet, that achieves the appearance of a private network with data security.

**virus** A software program capable of replicating itself and usually capable of causing harm to a network or a computer.

**voice grade circuit** A circuit suitable for transmission of speech, digital or analog data, or facsimile with a frequency range of about 300 Hz to 3,300 Hz. Voice grade circuits can transmit data at speeds up to 56,000 Kbps.

**voice network** A network designed for the purpose of carrying voice signals. With the use of modems, voice networks may also be used to carry data.

**voice over IP (VoIP)** A technology that takes voice conversations and converts them to data packets, then sends them out over an IP packet-switched network such as the Internet.

**war chalking** Symbols marked on sidewalks to alert other people to the location of free wireless Internet access. The symbols are based on the chalk drawings that hoboes used during the Great Depression in the 1930s to mark the location of free food or lodging.

**war driving** Roaming with a laptop computer, a wireless NIC, and appropriate software (and sometimes a high gain antenna) to search for open wireless networks.

**wavelength division multiplexing (WDM)** A technique used when transmitting data through optical fibers in which many light beams of different wavelengths are transmitted along a single fiber simultaneously without interfering with one another. Each light beam can carry many individually modulated data streams, allowing very high data rates to be achieved.

**Web browser** Software written to provide access to the WWW and other parts of the Internet. The most famous browsers are Netscape and Microsoft's Internet Explorer.

**Web server** A server on a network that, among other things, stores data in pages that are formatted with HTML.

**WebTV** A technology that enables one to browse the Web while watching television using a set-top box that plugs into the television. It has normal connectors to the television and cable service and special connectors to a modem and phone line.

**well-known port number** Numbers that are 16-bit values from 0 to 1,023 assigned by the IANA for the most well-known services available on the Internet. The port number helps the Internet transport protocols to distinguish among the many connections to a single host that take place at the same time.

**white noise** The phenomena in all electrical circuitry, resulting from the movement of electrons. *Also known as* Gaussian noise *or* background noise.

**whois** An Internet tool that searches DNS databases to find the name of network and system administrators, RFC authors, system and network points-of-contact, and other people registered in appropriate databases, as well as domains, networks, and hosts.

**wide area network (WAN)** A network that covers a large geographic area, requires the crossing of public rights-of-way, and usually uses circuits provided by one or more communication carriers.

**wide band circuit** An analog circuit designed to carry data at speeds greater than voice-grade circuits.

**Wi-Fi protected access (WPA)** A security specification certified in May, 2003, that replaces the older security protocol, WEP. It is a subset of what will become the 802.11i standard and offers better security and stability. It uses a new key every time a data packet is sent over the air. *See also* Wired Equivalent Protocol (WEP).

**Wired Equivalent Protocol (WEP)** The original encryption technology for wireless networks, based on either 40-bit or 128-bit encryption and a single, static key.

**wireless**  The transmission of signals using radiated media.

**Wireless Application Protocol (WAP)**  Protocol that allows wireless mobile devices to connect to the Internet and the WWW using a special minibrowser for tiny screens.

**wireless network**  A network that uses any unguided media, such as radio waves or infrared waves.

**workgroup**  A peer-to-peer network.

**workload generator**  Computer software that generates transactions or other work for a network or computer for testing purposes.

**World Wide Web Consortium (W3C)**  Similar to the IETF, this organization focuses on developing standards for the World Wide Web. Its members have commercial as well as academic and research interests.

**worm**  A program that replicates itself repeatedly, potentially "worming" its way through an entire network.

**X. standards**  Standards that define the connection of digital equipment (terminals and computers) to digital lines.

**X.21**  A specification for the physical, mechanical, and electrical interface between DTE and a digital public telephone network.

**X.21bis**  A specification for the physical, mechanical, and electrical interface between DTE and an analog public telephone network. X.21bis is virtually identical to the RS-232-C and V.24 interface specifications.

**X.25**  A standard for data transmission using a packet switching network that encompasses the first three layers of the OSI reference model.

**XMODEM-1K Protocol**  A version of the XMODEM protocol that improves on the error handling capability and transmission efficiency.

**XMODEM-CRC Protocol**  A version of the XMODEM protocol that improves on the error handling capability.

**XMODEM Protocol**  An asynchronous protocol developed for use between personal computers, especially for transfers of data and files between them.

**YMODEM-G Protocol**  A variant of the YMODEM protocol. Expects the software to provide error correction and recovery.

**YMODEM Protocol**  An asynchronous protocol developed for use between personal computers, especially for transfers of data between them.

**zero compression**  In a hexadecimal IPv6 address, sequences of zeros may be replaced with two colons to compress the address. For example, CCFF.0.0.0.0.0.FFCC becomes CCFF::FFCC.

**ZMODEM Protocol**  An asynchronous protocol that uses a four-byte cyclic redundancy character and adjusts its block size depending on line conditions.

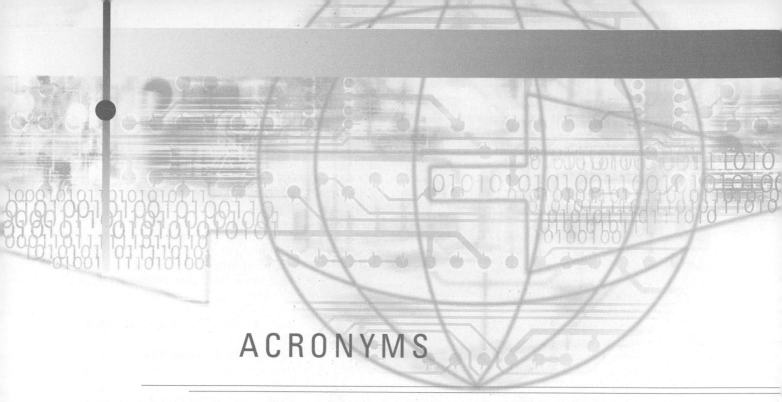

# ACRONYMS

| | | | | |
|---|---|---|---|---|
| A/D | analog-to-digital, 123–124* | | AT&T | American Telephone & Telegraph, 13, 15, 55 |
| AARP | AppleTalk Address Resolution Protocol, 300 | | ATM | asynchronous transfer mode, 181, 301, 364–367 |
| ABM | asynchronous balanced mode, 176 | | ATM | automatic teller machine, 6 |
| ACK | acknowledgement, 398 | | ATP | AppleTalk Transaction Protocol, 300 |
| ACK0 | acknowledgement, 170, 171 | | BBN | Bolt, Baranek, and Newman, Inc., 419, 423, 459 |
| ACK1 | acknowledgement, 171 | | | |
| ADDR | address of receiver, 174 | | BCC | block check character, 164, 237 |
| ADPCM | adaptive differential pulse code modulation, 124 | | BISYNC | Binary Synchronous Communications (BSC) Protocol, 169, 170–173 |
| ADSL | asymmetric digital subscriber line, 221–223, 439 | | BNA | Burroughs Network Architecture, 64 |
| | | | BNC | British Naval Connector, 195 |
| ADSP | AppleTalk Data Stream Protocol, 300 | | bps | bits per second, 119 |
| AES | Advanced Encryption Standard, 305 | | BRI | basic rate interface, 368, 438 |
| AFP | AppleTalk Filing Protocol, 300 | | BSC | Binary Synchronous Communications Protocol, 169, 170–173, |
| AIM | AOL Instant Messenger, 466 | | | |
| ALOHAnet | Wireless network in Hawaii, 425, 427 | | BSS | basic service set, 302 |
| AM | amplitude modulation, 117 | | CA | certificate authority, 503 |
| ANSI | American National Standards Institute, 54, 95, 259 | | CAD | computer aided drafting, 565 |
| | | | CAT 1 | category 1 cable, 190 |
| AOL | America Online, 434, 450, 455 | | CAT 2 | category 2 cable, 191 |
| AP | access point, 279 | | CAT 3 | category 3 cable, 191 |
| API | application program interface, 326 | | CAT 4 | category 4 cable, 191 |
| ARCNET | Attached Resource Computer Network, 289, 299 | | CAT 5 | category 5 cable, 191 |
| | | | CAT 6 | category 6 cable, 191 |
| ARM | asynchronous response mode, 177 | | CAT 7 | category 7 cable, 191 |
| ARP | Address Resolution Protocol, 406 | | CATV | cable TV, 139 |
| ARPA | Advanced Research Projects Agency, 61, 353, 418, 419 | | CCMP | Counter with Cipher Block Chaining Message Authentication Protocol, 305 |
| ARPANET | Advanced Research Projects Agency NETwork, 61, 422, 424–425, 428, 430 | | CDDI | copper distributed data interface, 295 |
| | | | CERN | physics lab in Geneva, 430 |
| ARQ | automatic repeat request, 238 | | CERT | Computer Emergency Response Team, 430 |
| ASCII | American Standard Code for Information Interchange, 95–96 | | CGI | common gateway interface, 454 |

*Refers to page numbers in the book.

# INDEX